Default Worksheet SmartIcons Toolbar

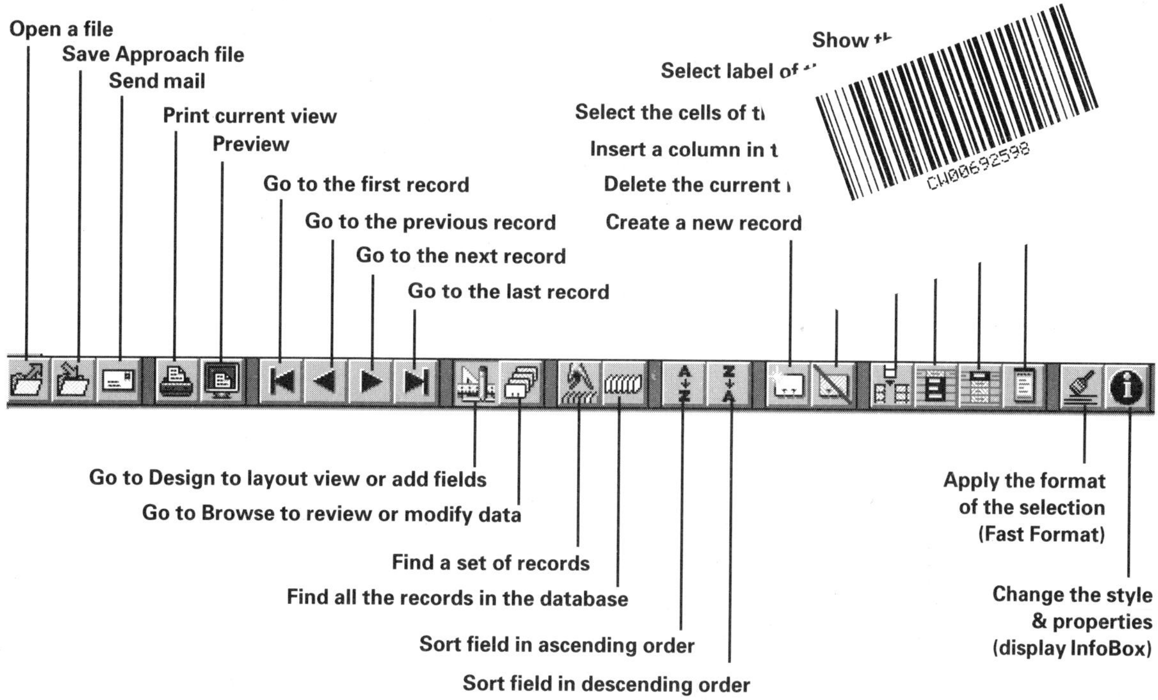

Open a file
Save Approach file
Send mail
Print current view
Preview
Go to the first record
Go to the previous record
Go to the next record
Go to the last record
Show th
Select label of t
Select the cells of t
Insert a column in t
Delete the current
Create a new record

Go to Design to layout view or add fields
Go to Browse to review or modify data
Find a set of records
Find all the records in the database
Sort field in ascending order
Sort field in descending order
Apply the format of the selection (Fast Format)
Change the style & properties (display InfoBox)

Default Text SmartIcons Toolbar

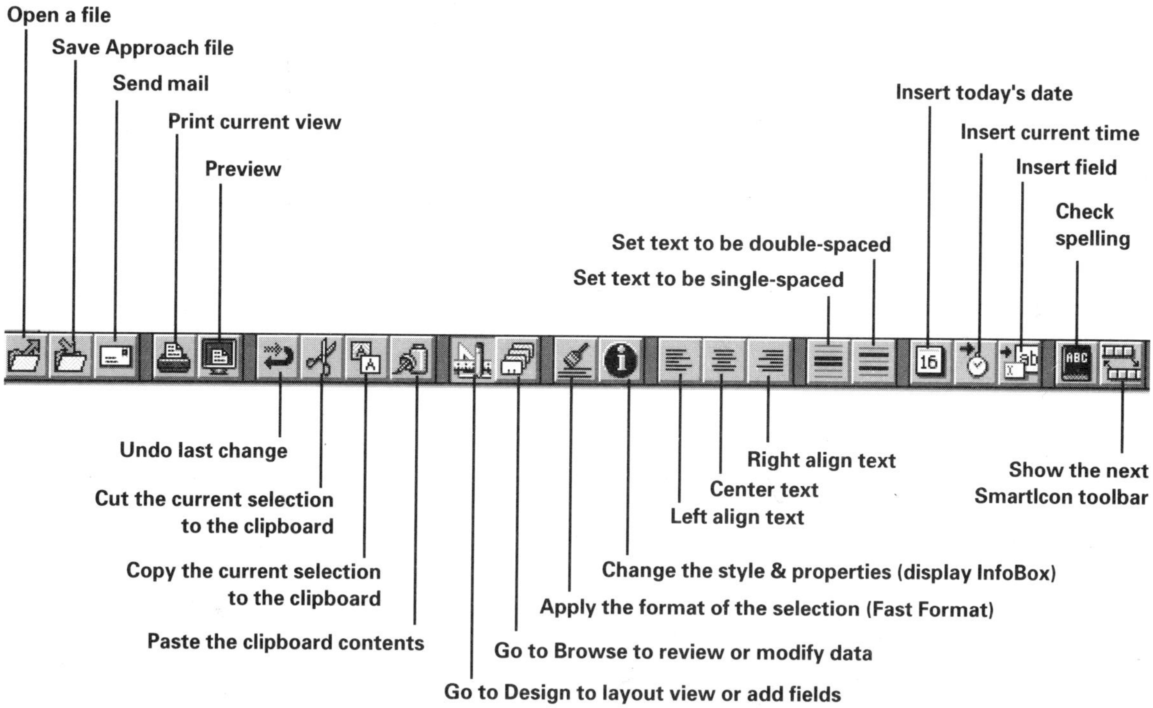

Open a file
Save Approach file
Send mail
Print current view
Preview
Set text to be double-spaced
Set text to be single-spaced
Insert today's date
Insert current time
Insert field
Check spelling

Undo last change
Cut the current selection to the clipboard
Copy the current selection to the clipboard
Paste the clipboard contents
Go to Design to layout view or add fields
Go to Browse to review or modify data
Apply the format of the selection (Fast Format)
Change the style & properties (display InfoBox)
Left align text
Center text
Right align text
Show the next SmartIcon toolbar

The Official Guides to Lotus® Software

SYBEX, in conjunction with Lotus Publishing, is pleased to present the most authoritative line of books about Lotus Software you can find. The line is called *Lotus Books* and they are the ONLY guides officially endorsed by Lotus Development Corporation, the world's third largest software developer.

No matter how many features you know about a particular software package or how creative you become in using your applications, there is always something more you can learn to make your work easier and faster. That's where *Lotus Books* tutorials and references can help.

Lotus Books offer you a wealth of advantages you can't get anywhere else. First of all, *Lotus Books* tutorials and references, thanks to the reputation of SYBEX and Lotus Publishing, feature the most respected and knowledgeable authors in the computer industry. Secondly, *Lotus Books* titles, as the only official books about Lotus software, are unmatched in their accuracy and insider expertise. Finally, there are books in the *Lotus Books* family for Lotus software users of nearly every level of skill. Whether you're a beginner, an expert, or somewhere in between, you'll be able to find useful, timely and relevant information that will make your time on the computer more productive and enjoyable.

Lotus Books tutorials and references cover the full range of Lotus software applications. There are books about cc:Mail, Lotus 1-2-3, SmartSuite, Approach and much more. You'll find *Lotus Books* wherever computer books are sold. Ask for them by name and soon you'll know the joy of learning about Lotus software from the Lotus software experts.

CompuServe®

SYBEX
Shortcuts to
Understanding

Mastering Approach® 3 for Windows™

James E. Powell

San Francisco ▲ Paris ▼ Düsseldorf ▲ Soest

ACQUISITIONS EDITOR: Joanne Cuthbertson

PRODUCT MANAGER: Richard Mills

DEVELOPMENTAL EDITOR: David Peal

EDITOR: Nancy Svoboda

PROJECT EDITOR: Kristen Vanberg-Wolff

TECHNICAL EDITOR: Tanya Strub

BOOK DESIGNER: Suzanne Albertson

PRODUCTION ARTISTS: Nadja Lazansky and Dan Schiff

SCREEN GRAPHICS MANAGER: Aldo X. Bermudez

PAGE LAYOUT/DESKTOP SPECIALIST: Stephanie Hollier

PRODUCTION ASSISTANT: Dave Nash

INDEXER: Nancy Guenther

COVER DESIGNER: Joanna Kim Gladden

Library of Congress Card Number: 94-68435

ISBN: 0-7821-1306-0

Manufactured in the United States of America

To Helen K. Patz
Thank you for your warm smile and your blazing red pencil.

Acknowledgments

This book has gone through several iterations, trying to find just the right mix of step-by-step instructions with the practical "why's" of working with each Approach feature. I'd like to thank David Peal for his persistence is getting the project off the ground and for suggesting the mix of information that became *Mastering Approach.* A special word of thanks to Kris Vanberg-Wolff for seeing this project through, Nancy Svoboda's rigorous questioning (to make things better), and Tanya Strub's eagle eye that helped ensure its accuracy and usefulness.

At Lotus Approach, a big tip of the hat to Jaleh Bisharat and Paul Santinelli. Their unending enthusiasm, suggestions, assistance, and guidance, as well as their exceptional cooperation, made working with Approach during its beta cycles a pleasure.

Finally I would like to thank Babette Rossmehyer, Vivien Worthington-Symthe, and Deloris Bork for their constant encouragement.

James E. Powell
Seattle, Washington
October 1994

Contents at a Glance

Table of Contents

▸▸ Foreword

Welcome to *Mastering Approach,* a guide to the latest version of Lotus Approach, the award-winning end-user database. You'll find this book a valuable addition to Lotus Approach's documentation. James E. Powell has been a Lotus Approach enthusiast since the original product's introduction. His clear explanations of database concepts will ensure that you leave this book with a thorough understanding of how to develop a database ideally suited to your professional or personal needs.

Lotus Approach succeeds because it makes relational database power easily available to computer users. Computer users today need access to the most important asset their company has—its data. They don't need to become expert programmers in order to find information, generate reports, perform crosstabs, write form labels, or generate mailing labels. With Lotus Approach, users can organize, manipulate, and analyze data from many different sources without having to learn an arcane programming language.

Released in July of 1994, the latest version of Lotus Approach offers over 200 new features. Powerclick reporting makes generating reports fast and easy. InfoBox offers one-stop shopping for all your formatting needs. Over 50 database templates enable you to quickly build your database using the professionally designed format. Lotus Approach Assistants with SmartMasters help you quickly build forms, reports, mailing labels, worksheets, crosstabs, and charts; and Lotus Approach's unique notetab interface allows you to flexibly advance or backtrack to those sections of the Assistant you desire.

With Lotus Approach, a marketing manager can create and track a mailing; a sales manager can customize his or her sales reports, form letters, and mailing labels; and a customer service manager can create a support system without wasting time on arduous programming. A more sophisticated IS professional can now quickly create custom applications and attractive, polished forms, mailings, reports, and systems, as well as use the relational power of Lotus Approach to marry information from many data sources. Whether you are a consultant who makes your living from application development, a corporate manager who wants to manipulate the valuable data stored at your company, or a business owner who wants to manage home-office data, analyze information, and track results, Lotus Approach is a powerful tool that will increase your personal productivity.

We are very proud of our new version, and I sincerely hope that you enjoy the tremendous productivity Lotus Approach will add to your work life. This book will also prove an invaluable tool in helping you understand the underlying database concepts in order to maximize your investment in the product.

Kevin Hardey
Founder and General Manager of Approach
Lotus Development Corporation

▸▸ Introduction

Welcome to *Mastering Approach 3 for Windows*. Approach is a unique software tool for storing and retrieving information. *Mastering Approach 3 for Windows* is a guided tour of this new and powerful database management system.

▸▸ Who Should Read This Book?

This book is designed for users familiar with Microsoft Windows, whether that be Windows 3.0, Windows 3.1, Windows NT, or Windows for Workgroups. If you aren't familiar with Windows, you may wish to review your Windows User's Guide, which explains the basics you'll need to know to work in the Windows environment.

If you're just getting acquainted with Approach, or have been using Approach for a year or more, this book can help you get the most out of your database work. If you are not familiar with databases—and studies show that only 20 percent of computer users know what a database is or does—you will find that Chapters 2 and 3 explain the basic database concepts.

You may already be familiar with database concepts or programs—perhaps you've already worked with a database program in DOS such as Alpha Four, dBASE, or Q&A. If so, we still suggest reading Chapters 2 and 3, as Approach handles database files and report and form files quite differently from most programs.

If you've been working with Approach, you'll find that this book serves as a refresher or reference for the features you use every day or as an introduction to features you haven't yet explored. As you become more proficient with Approach, you can explore new topics, such as using Approach as a front-end for external databases. *Mastering Approach 3 for Windows* includes information about the fundamental as well as the advanced features of this database management program.

While this book deals with version 3.0 features, you can also use many of the features from earlier versions of Approach. Approach 2.0 and Approach 2.1 use many of the same drawing tools and forms, let you create mailing labels and form letters, and present data in both Browse and Preview environments. Features new to Approach 3.0 include worksheets, charting, and the InfoBox.

This book assumes that you understand basic DOS terms such as drive, directory, and file, know how to work with floppy drives and hard disks, and can manage files (copy, delete, or move files).

▸▸ How This Book Is Organized

Mastering Approach 3 for Windows is arranged in three parts. In Part One, we look at the basics of Approach: how to set up a database; create forms, charts, and reports; enter, change, and delete data; organize data; create form letters and mailing labels; and print everything you create.

Part Two looks at more complex techniques within Approach. These features are not needed for everyday use, but they add considerably to your efficient use of Approach.

In Part Three, we'll build a contact manager application using all the features in Approach. We'll create several databases, join them, create forms, reports, macros, special toolbars, menus, and worksheets, and tie everything together.

▶ Part One: The Basics

Chapter 1 introduces you to the basics of Approach—what it can do for you. You learn the difference between Approach files and database files and discover the advantages of this unique design.

Chapter 2 provides a closer look at Approach. It provides an overview of the types of screens you'll see in Approach, including the various environments, such as Browse, Design, and Preview, that Approach uses to help you work with your data.

Chapter 3 explains what a database is, what a database can do for you, and illustrates the types of databases you may already be familiar with. In addition, it provides an overview of how a relational database differs from a nonrelational, or *flatfile*, database. You'll see the four steps you'll need to follow to create your own database, and how to use Approach's new templates to get you up and running in very little time.

Chapter 4 helps you understand how to work with databases that already exist. You may find you need to work with existing databases, such as a customer list from a service bureau or a list of clients from a coworker. You can also use Approach to work with spreadsheet files, and you'll learn how in Chapter 4.

Chapter 5 shows you how to modify your database. Your data needs may change, and Approach can change right along with those needs. In this chapter, you will learn how to add and remove fields, set field options, control validation options so that data entry errors are minimized, and you'll see briefly the power of formulas.

Chapter 6 shows you how to join multiple databases. When you combine the data in two or more databases, you can enjoy the incredible power of a relational database management system. In Chapter 6, you'll learn why you may want to use multiple databases and how to create a *join* between them.

Chapter 7 takes you step-by-step through the process of creating your first view, called a form. After databases have been created, you need to enter the actual data into database records. Chapter 7 shows you how to create a new form, change the fields on a form, and work in the Design environment to set field and form options. You'll learn how to align, copy, and modify fields on a form.

Chapter 8 gives you a close-up view of the many different types of fields you can place on a form. Everything from basic text fields to radio buttons, check boxes, and graphic images can be placed on a form, and Chapter 8 explains how.

Chapter 9 shows you how to enter new data, edit existing data, and delete data you no longer want or need using the forms you created in Chapter 7. You'll also learn how to navigate through the database, moving between records or moving to the beginning or end of a database, as well as moving between fields on a data entry form.

Chapter 10 discusses a new feature in version 3.0: worksheets and crosstabs. Worksheets resemble spreadsheet-like tables that can list multiple records on one screen. Crosstabs perform sophisticated analysis, showing you, in a spreadsheet view, average sales by region by product, for example.

Chapter 11 looks at how to build reports—everything from a simple columnar list of customers to sophisticated reports that sort and report data by groups, such as region, part, employee, or date.

Chapter 12 shows you how to find data within your database. Approach lets you find one or more records in a database (called a *found set*), and you can perform operations on this subset of data as though it were the entire database. In addition, Chapter 12 gives you the tricks you'll need to find duplicate or unique values, delete matching records, and find records using complex criteria. Chapter 12 also looks at how to sort data so your data appears in the order you wish, such as alphabetically by customer last name.

Chapter 13 takes reporting a step further. In this chapter, you'll learn how to merge fields with existing text to produce form letters and how to produce mailing labels to use with these letters.

Chapter 14 shows you how to get graphical—with charts. Approach includes a powerful charting capability in version 3.0, and Chapter 14 shows you how to create, modify, annotate, and print these charts.

Chapter 15 looks at how to print individual records, groups of records, reports, forms, mailing labels, and just about anything else.

▶ Part Two: More Advanced Techniques

Part Two takes a look at more advanced topics—topics you won't need to use every day but that pack a lot of punch when you learn what they can do.

Chapter 16 introduces the concept of a macro. Macros are used in many DOS and Windows applications to perform repetitive tasks. In Approach, macros are at the heart of developing applications, and Chapter 16 shows you how to create simple macros and build the foundation for a sophisticated application.

Chapter 17 explores custom queries, particularly those using multiple tables. The chapter also demonstrates how to use such queries to update multiple records in your database quickly and easily.

Chapter 18 shows you how to customize Approach. Not only can you control the SmartIcons toolbar, as you can in other Lotus applications, but you can set special menu options and database preferences.

Chapter 19 takes a look at formulas—the power behind performing calculations and manipulating your data. Formulas are available from a variety of locations with Approach, from field definition to report definition. Chapter 19 explains how to take advantage of formulas throughout Approach.

Chapter 20 details how to work with other applications and file formats. You'll learn how to import and export data, as well as how to import data in "foreign" formats. Although Approach understands the file formats of a variety of database applications, it can also use data from nondatabase programs, including Lotus Notes and Lotus 1-2-3. You'll also learn how to share information using OLE and electronic mail.

▶ Part Three: Building an Application

Part Three puts all the pieces together to show you how to build a practical, real-world application. You'll learn how to build a program that helps you manage your contacts—names, addresses, and appointments, as well as those miscellaneous "to-do's." The application used in the final part of *Mastering Approach 3 for Windows* combines many of the features and functions explained in previous chapters: fields, forms, reports, macros, calculated fields, sorts and queries, and export capabilities.

▸▸ Special Features of This Book

Throughout *Mastering Approach 3 for Windows,* you'll find tips and tricks that will help you accomplish your work more quickly. Besides the Guided Tour in Chapter 2, you'll find several examples of databases and applications created using Approach that explain the concepts of the chapter and hopefully stimulate your creativity.

Learning by example is often the most effective technique, and *Mastering Approach 3 for Windows* is full of real-world examples that show you the "how's" and the "why's" of database, form, and report design. Furthermore, the examples show you how to take Approach to the limit, giving you tips and suggestions for more interesting forms and reports beyond what you'll find in the Approach documentation.

Special notes throughout each chapter provide suggestions for designing work more effectively. By designing a database or form correctly the first time, you'll find you not only eliminate problems in the future but reduce the errors that arise when you change your basic designs. *Mastering Approach 3 for Windows* helps you do things right the first time. If you're new to databases, Part III explains a number of the design and development considerations you should keep in mind before working with *any* electronic database.

Where appropriate, cross references to related information are provided throughout the book.

▸▸ Conventions

As with most Windows applications, you can usually accomplish tasks using either the keyboard or the mouse. *Mastering Approach 3 for Windows* uses the following conventions in its illustrations, examples, and instructions:

- ↑, ↓, →, ← refer to the up, down, right, and left arrow key respectively. These are often referred to as the arrow keys when it may be possible to press more than one key to navigate to a particular location. On newer keyboards, these are separate keys. On older keyboards, these keys are found only on the numeric keypad, and can be used if the Num Lock mode is off.

- The Page Up key on your keyboard is written as PgUp. Likewise, the Page Down key is written as PgDn.
- Shortcuts that use a combination of keys are indicated with the plus (+) sign. For example, to force Approach to display all records, you can press and hold the Ctrl key and press the A key, then release both keys. This is written as Ctrl+A.
- Menu instructions use a right-pointing arrow. Thus, instructions to select the File menu, then select the Open option are written as File ➤ Open.
- Text you should type is clearly indicated, usually following the words "type" or "enter." For example, "Enter **6/1/94** in the date due field" means you should type the characters 6/1/94 (including the slashes) in the field specified.
- *Italic text* indicates a special condition or exception to the rule, or notes information of particular interest. Italic text is used to highlight circumstances that are unusual or of special interest.
- You can select a button by clicking on it or by pressing Alt and the underlined letter shown on the button. For example, the Add button may contain the text Add, indicating that you can use the keyboard shortcut Alt+A instead of clicking on the button. When there are two such options, instructions ask you to "Select Add" without specifying whether you should use the mouse or the keyboard.

Please note that the directions in this book refer to the left and right mouse buttons. This assumes you have not reversed the function of these buttons using the Windows Control Panel.

The Basics

PART ONE

CHAPTER 1

Approach, Its Features and Advantages

▸▸ FAST TRACK

In this chapter, we'll give you an overview of Approach's features and focus on some of the benefits of using Approach as your database. Because it is a relational database management system, Approach can manage just about any data you can think of—everything from maintaining simple lists to consolidating all of your data. In addition, Approach lets you:

- Create data entry forms for entering, changing, or deleting data
- Find existing data or sets of data (a mailing list of all of your customers in California, for example)
- Display charts for quick visual interpretation of your information
- Produce reports, charts, mailing labels, and form letters

With Approach, you can work with data in a variety of file formats. You can create your own databases or work with data that already exists in another file format, such as a customer database created by a coworker or a Lotus Notes database. Databases you create can also be used by others.

This chapter is of special interest for users new to databases. We'll demystify database terminology—you'll learn that databases are much simpler than you thought, and you'll gain the understanding necessary to create your own database.

What Is a Database?

Whether you know it or not, you've been working with databases most of your life. Let's look at how databases are used.

Databases You Already Know

In its simplest terms, a database is an organized collection of data about a related subject. For example, the telephone company keeps a database of its customers and it keeps a separate database of its employees. These databases are kept separate because they serve different purposes. The customer database allows all of us to use the telephone directory. The employee database allows the telephone company to pay its employees so that we can all use the telephone system.

Data within a database can be retrieved in many ways. For example, you access the telephone company's customer database in the form of a telephone book or directory. When you call the operator to find a telephone number, he or she is accessing the customer database, but is using a computer terminal to do so.

There are dozens of other database examples. For instance, the public library's database contains the names of titles and authors of works in its collections. The public library's database is available to you as a card catalog, or a computerized catalog available in many libraries. Your appointment calendar is another example. An appointment calendar contains several pieces of data: the name of the person you are meeting with, the location of the meeting, and the meeting's purpose.

Data Is Not Information

While a database contains data about your company's customers (such as first and last name, telephone number, billing address, payment history, and so on), a key benefit of using a database is that you can organize or rearrange data so that it becomes *information*. Databases store data—hence their name—but data is *not* the same as information.

Data refers to the bits and pieces of knowledge or facts stored within a database. My last name, the location of a meeting, or the city I live in are all examples of data that can be found in a database. These facts are important, but by themselves don't help me better understand much about the *collection* of data in a database. For example, it is vital that in a name-and-address database you store accurate data—my last name should not be misspelled, for example. But by itself, my last name cannot be used to solve a business problem. My last name must be used in conjunction with other data to determine a course of action. For example, a local hotel may know that I live in Seattle and attended a recent meeting in its conference room. Coupling this data with my last name, the hotel manager could decide to send me promotional materials concerning an upcoming event.

What you really want from your database is *information*—data that's put to use to answer a question. For example, each card in my Rolodex has a customer's name and address. Each card contains data about a single customer. I can turn that data into information by analyzing it: Perhaps I've noticed an increase in the number of orders shipped to California. How many of my clients live in California? If many of them do, perhaps I should open a field office there. My Rolodex database contains data (each customer's state), but I need information to make a business decision (how many of them are in California?). Using - Approach, I can turn data into information.

Here's another example: if you can answer the question, "What is the average age of my customers?", you'll have the *information* necessary to better understand your market and make better decisions about advertising. Computerized databases, such as Approach, play a key role in helping you quickly and easily turn data into information: They assist you in gaining the knowledge and understanding necessary to answer questions. You can spot trends (yearly sales are increasing in the Eastern region but declining in the Western region) or understand relationships (customers who buy refrigerators are more likely to buy a service contract than those who buy washing machines).

►► Records, Fields, and Approach

As we've said, a database is a collection of data organized about a subject, such as a customer, client, book, student, appointment, product, or order. A database contains a record for each subject. For example, each record in your customer database contains data about a single customer. Each record might contain the name of the company, its address, billing information such as credit limit and discount levels allowed, and so on. The pieces of data within a record are called *fields*. Figure 1.1 shows a customer database. Figure 1.2 shows the same data in another way, a worksheet view.

The customer database we've created to illustrate records and fields in Approach contains two records: one for Acme Construction and

FIGURE 1.1

A customer database

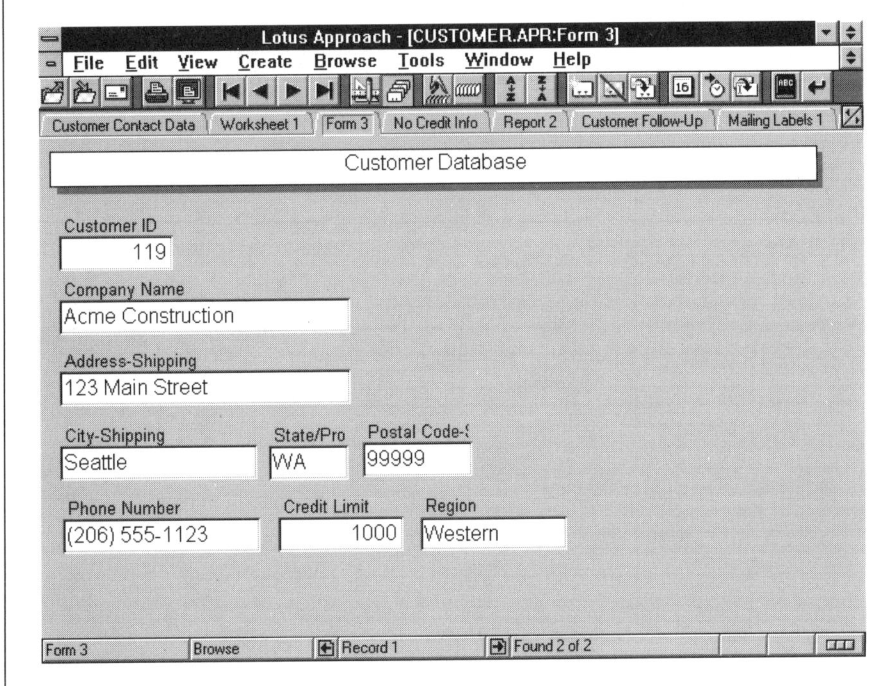

another for Bay Lumber. Each record contains the same set of fields (for example, there's a field for the company name and another for the company's credit limit), but the values within the fields (i.e., the data entered) are different. For example, the customer record containing data about Acme Construction contains the value $1,000 in the credit limit field. The record in the customer database for Bay Lumber contains the same field (credit limit), but the value in that field is $2,000.

A customer database exists as a physical file, either on your hard disk or on the hard disk of a computer on your network. You can create this file using Approach. Approach can also work with database files created in other database programs, such as Paradox or dBASE, or even a spreadsheet program such as Excel. Approach lets you store the file using a variety of file *formats.* File formats are a standardized way of defining how the data is stored on your hard disk. The name given to a file describes the physical organization of the data in the file. Your database file may be named CUSTOMER.DBF (if it is stored using the dBASE file format from dBASE) or CUSTOMER.DB (if it is stored using the Paradox file format). The extension—the letters that follow

FIGURE 1.2 ►

The same customer database shown in another way, a worksheet view

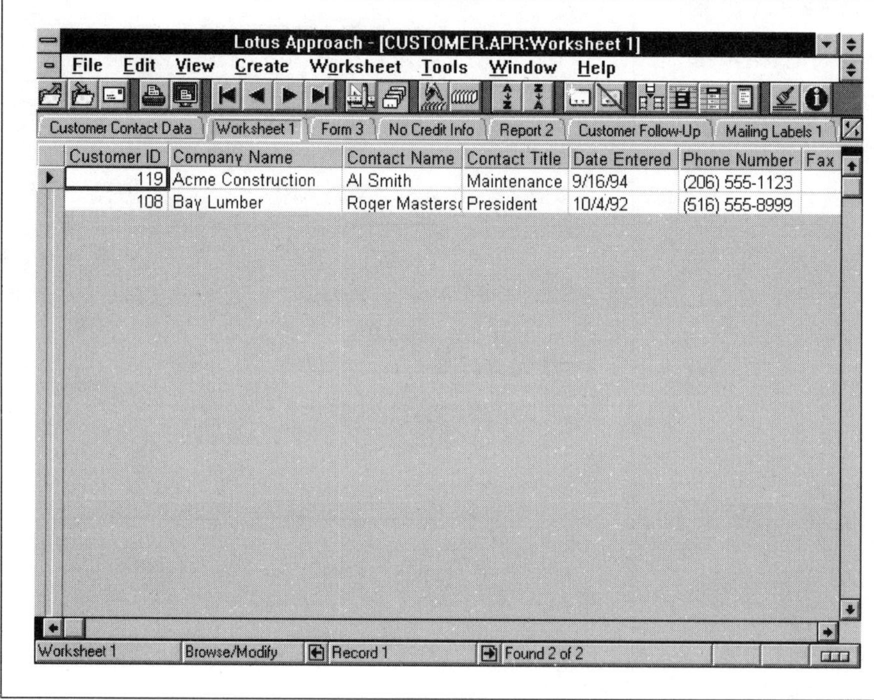

the period—indicates in which program's format the file was created. (More on this later.) This standard makes it possible for different programs to recognize and use the same data file.

►► What You Can Do with Approach

With Approach, you can create a database from scratch or use a database created by another application.

Approach is shipped by the manufacturer with several database templates predefined. When you start Approach for the first time, you'll see the Welcome screen, which lists several database templates (see Figure 1.3). You can use these templates as a starting point for your own database, or you can define each field yourself using Approach's Field Definition feature, shown in Figure 1.4. In fact, you can do both and save time if the template is almost—but not quite—what you want.

FIGURE 1.3

The Welcome screen

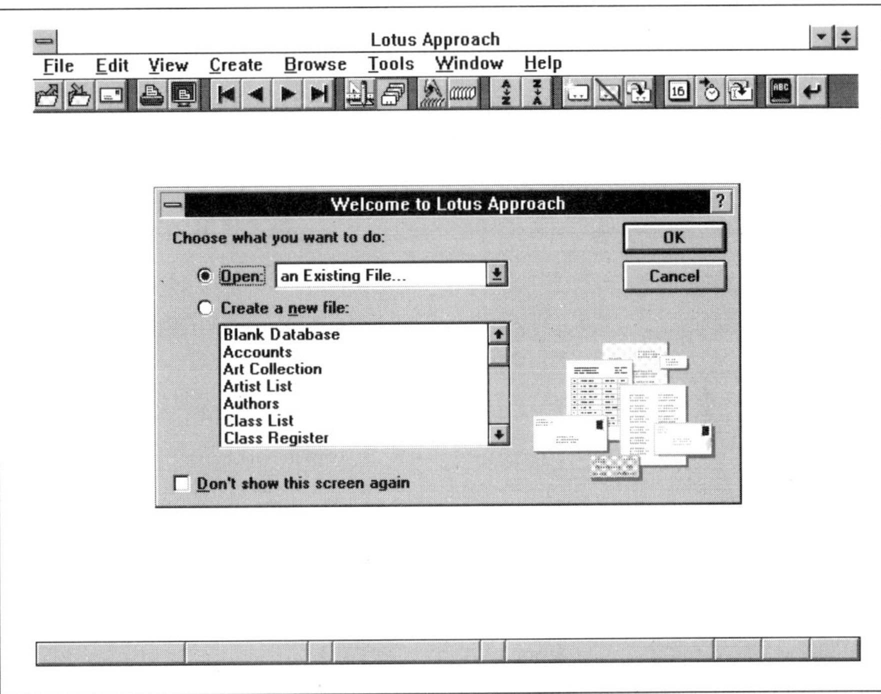

FIGURE 1.4

The Data Definition dialog box

Field Definition

Database: CUSTOMER View fields by: Custom Order OK Cancel 23 fields Insert Delete Print Options >>

Field Name	Data Type	Size	Formula / Options
Customer ID	Numeric	5.0	
Company Name	Text	30	
Contact Name	Text	30	
Contact Title	Text	30	
Customer Type	Text	20	
Date Entered	Date	Fixed	

Default Value | Validation

Nothing
Previous record
Creation date Modification date
Creation time Modification time
Data:
Serial number starting at: 1
Incremented by: 1
Creation formula Modification formula
Formula...

With Approach you can use the template to create a database, then make any modifications, such as change a field name.

No matter how the file is created (whether using Approach or another program), Approach enables you to:

- Add a new record to the database (data about a new customer named Clement Supply, for example)
- Modify existing records (change the credit limit for Bay Lumber)
- Delete a record (if Acme Construction goes out of business, you may no longer want to keep the data in your database)
- Compare sales by region or state
- Print a report showing the company name and credit limit of each customer
- Display a bar chart showing the average credit limit for customers in the Western region
- Print mailing labels to place on post cards announcing a special sale

Approach has all the power you need to run your daily business. It can read your database and print a form letter for every record (that is, one form letter per company) when your company moves and you want to notify your customers of your new address. You can use it for your personal needs too: You could, for example, keep a list of friends and family, then generate mailing labels for Christmas cards. You'll see how to create mailing labels and form letters in Chapter 13.

▸ Use Forms to Add, Change, Delete, or View Data

You're already familiar with filling out forms: job applications, supply requisitions, and credit applications. A form consists of distinct areas where you fill in the required data—your name, the current date, your annual salary, and so on. By completing the form, you are filling out "fields" of data for a large database (the company's job applicant database, orders database, or credit history database).

Forms in Approach let you arrange data and organize information on screen, in any way you like, to make reviewing and entering data easier.

You can even use graphical elements such as check boxes and pull-down lists to speed up data entry.

Using the form on screen, you begin compiling new information by entering data into fields. A form shows a single record at a time. You can include all or just some of the fields from your database in a form. In an existing database, you can use forms to add or display records and change or delete data in any (or all) of the fields.

Figure 1.5 shows a data entry form that lets you work with a customer's name and address, but does not provide access to the credit information. Figure 1.6 shows another data entry form that includes other fields from the same database, such as the credit limit. Both forms can be stored in the same Approach file, which consists of one or more databases, as well as the forms, mailing labels, and reports that use these databases.

Forms can also format your data. For example, while a database field may contain the date 12/30/94, you can display or enter this value on a form as Friday, December 30, 1994, Dec 30 94, or 30 Dec 94.

FIGURE 1.5

A Data Entry form

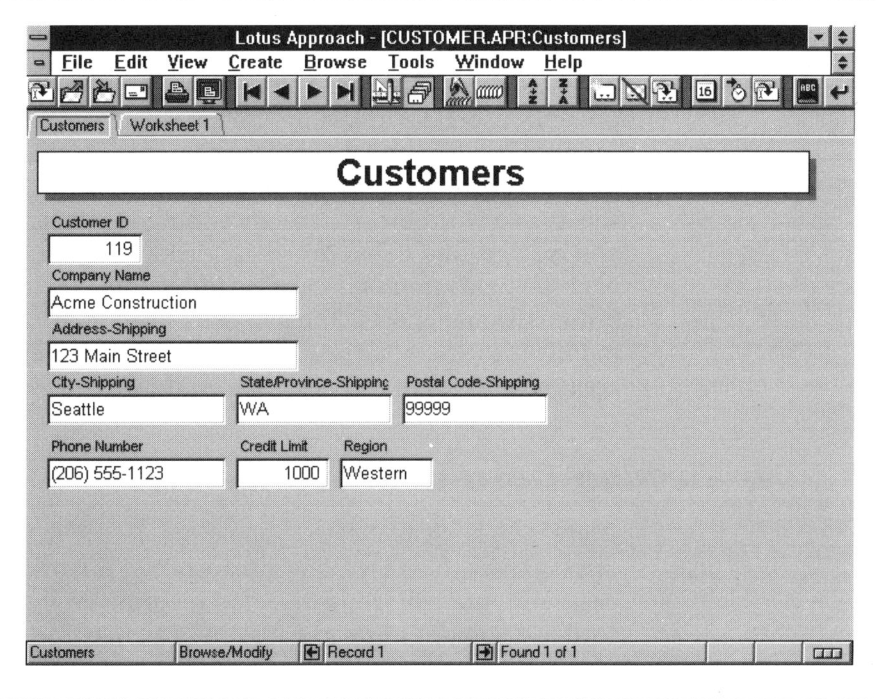

FIGURE 1.6

Another Data Entry form for the same database

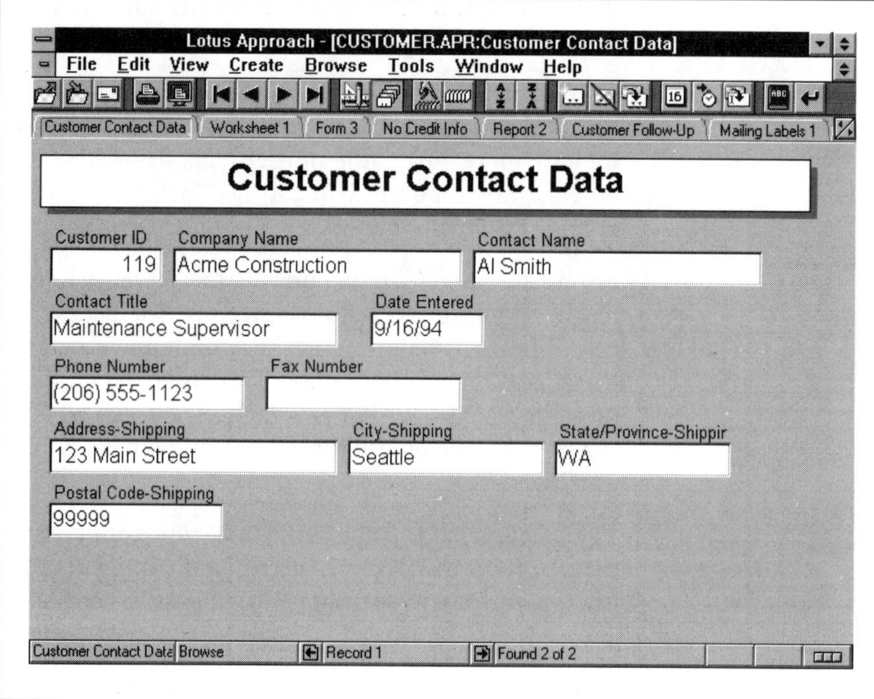

As you'll see in Chapter 7, building these forms is simple, thanks to Approach's use of form layouts called SmartMasters. SmartMasters are a series of predefined layouts that you can select in order to add impact to your forms and reports. SmartMasters are like predefined style sheets in a word processor—they include elements such as font size and background color. You can quickly create a default form that displays all fields from a database, add colors and styles, and even add 3-dimensional effects. You can use this quickly created form as is, or modify it to suit your needs. SmartMasters relieve the tedium of creating a data entry form from scratch.

▸ Viewing Data with Worksheets

Worksheets, such as the one shown previously in Figure 1.2, are familiar display tools that resemble spreadsheets. A worksheet shows your database contents (all or just selected records) as a gigantic list. Each record is displayed in a separate row. Each column represents a field.

Worksheets arrange data uniformly and can display more than one record at a time. You can rearrange the columns in any order you like, or show only selected columns. You can also change the column and row height, change the font color and style (italic, bold) based on a field's contents (negative values can be shown in red, for example). You can even sort the data by any column(s) (so you can view a list of customers by company name or zip code).

▶ Print Reports for Data Summaries or Analysis

Reports display data in your database using criteria you define. Suppose that each customer in the customer database is assigned to a regional office, where sales agents in that office are responsible for taking the customers' orders and ensuring that products are delivered on time. Figure 1.7 shows a report that includes a subtotal of the customer credit limit by region and a grand total for all regions. Reports in Approach can perform calculations (such as subtotals, totals, and averages)

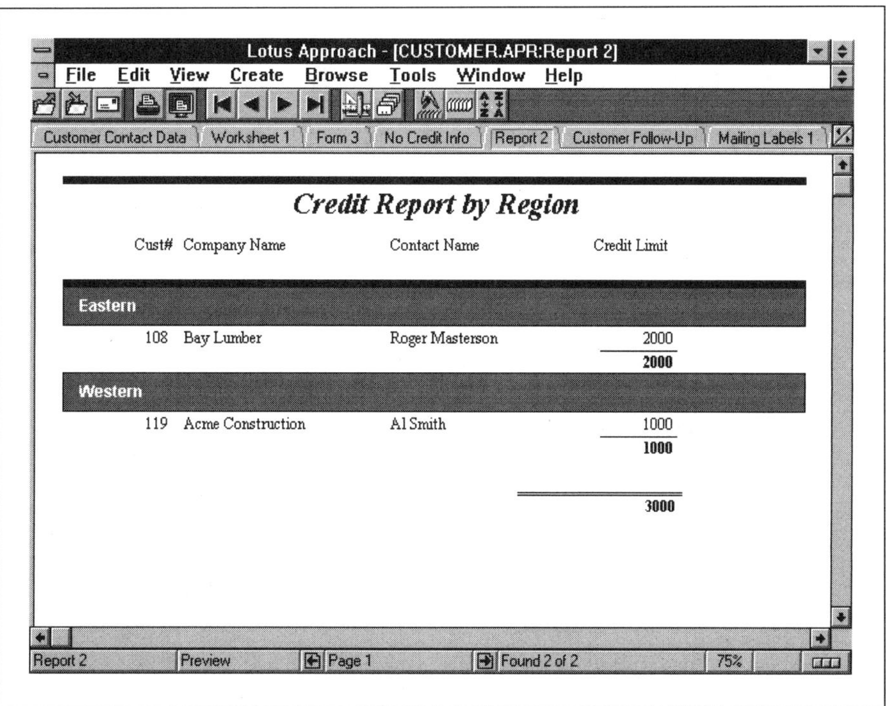

FIGURE 1.7 ▶

A report can summarize information and create subtotals and totals for quick analysis.

on fields that contain numbers, sort your data (alphabetically by customer name, for example), group your data (show a sales agent's orders by region, for example), and provide powerful perspective on your data using crosstabs. Reports are typically used to print information for others, serve as a printed, permanent record of data (as a paper backup, too), and summarize and sort data.

You can also view the reports on your screen. Reports can include data from all records or just some of your records, such as records for customers with credit limits below $1,000.

▸ Customize Communication with Approach

If you need to notify customers in your database about a change of address or an upcoming sale, or need to send out monthly statements, Approach can merge text (such as "We are pleased to announce we have raised your credit limit to...") with customer data from your database (the new credit limit in the customer record). Assuming you store the name and address as fields within your database as well, you can prepare a customized form letter to any or all customers in your database. Figure 1.8 shows such a form letter.

▸ Simplify Mailing with Approach

How do you send those form letters? If you need mailing labels, Approach can create them for you. Approach uses a layout similar to a form—you place the field on the label where you want it to appear, and depending on the type of labels you are using, Approach can print several labels on a page. Approach supports the standard mailing label layouts for Avery-brand labels. Figure 1.9 shows sample mailing labels in Approach.

▸ Gain Perspective, Chart Your Data

Charts help you analyze information visually. Charts do for data what reports can't—they give you an overall impression of your data. For example, you can more readily see information trends or abnormalities (unusual conditions) looking at a chart, rather than looking at a report. Approach supports the standard chart types (bar, line, pie, area) in a variety of styles (2D and 3D, for example). You can use a variety of

FIGURE 1.8

A form letter lets you merge fields from your database with predefined text and generate "customized" letters.

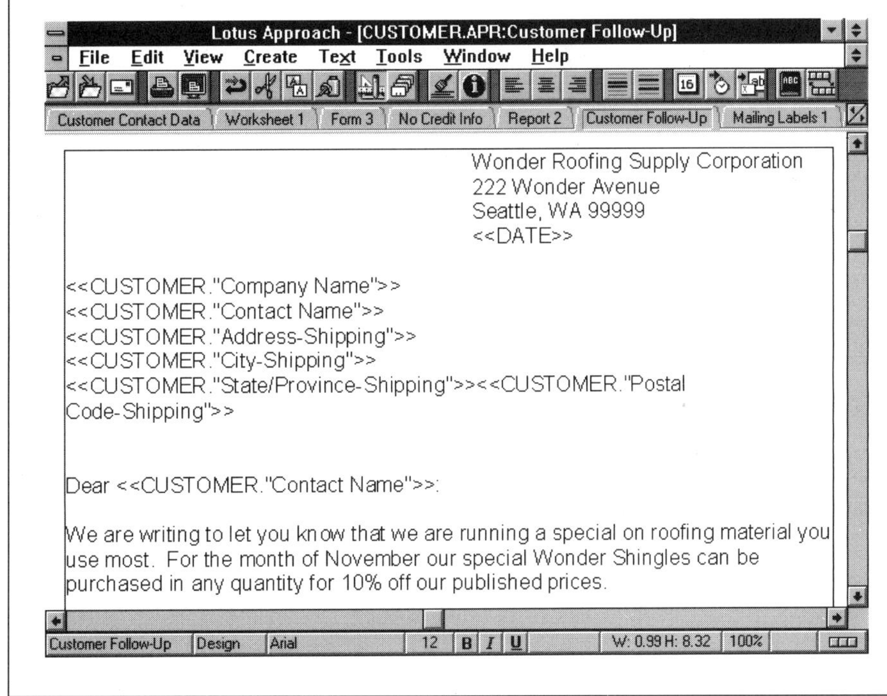

chart settings to provide just the right look to your data, then incorporate the chart in another application to create, for example, a word processed document. Figure 1.10 shows a pie chart illustrating the percentage of the total credit that is assigned to customers by region. As you can see, the outstanding credit is greater in the Eastern region.

Charts help you spot which sales agent is not meeting his or her goals or is lagging when compared to the average sales of all agents, or which sales region has consistently increased its sales month after month.

►► Database Files and Approach Files

Approach uses two kinds of files: one or more database files and an Approach file. The database files contain—you guessed it—your data. They can be created using Approach or a variety of formats, such as dBASE, Paradox, or a spreadsheet program. The Approach file contains the forms, reports, worksheets, mailing labels, and charts you

FIGURE 1.9 ▶

Mailing labels can be quickly generated from name and address fields stored in an Approach database.

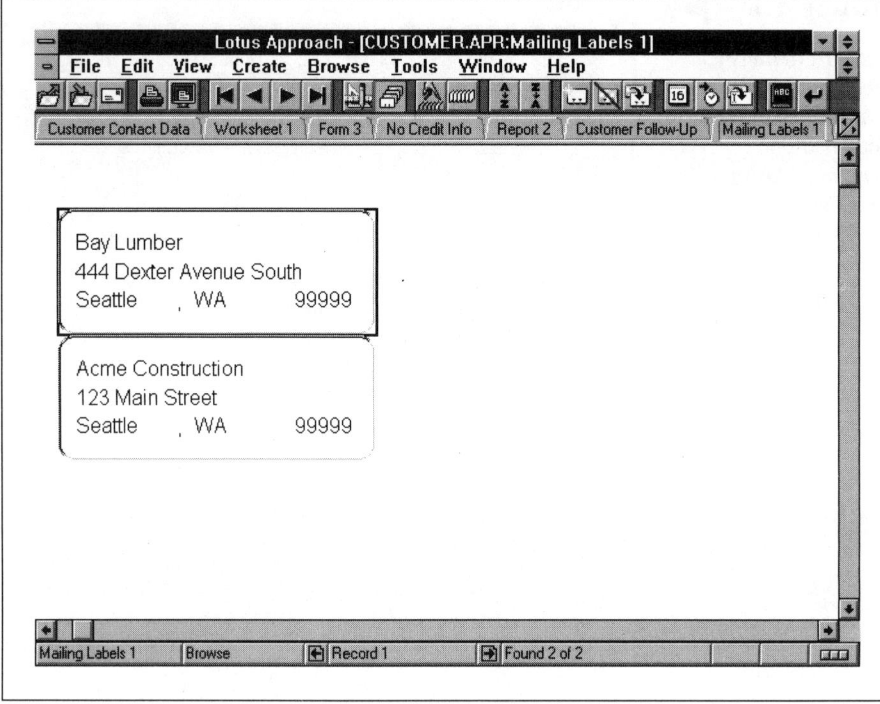

have been reading about in this chapter. The Approach file usually has the same file name as the main database you're working with, except it ends with an .APR extension. Thus, if you are working with a database named CUSTOMER.DBF, Approach will create a file named CUSTOMER.APR.

▸▸ **NOTE**

Approach is sometimes called a "front end" to your data because you do not actually work with the *database file(s)* directly, but rather with the forms, reports, mailing labels, and charts that *access* the actual data.

Approach accesses your database file in conjunction with its Approach file to organize your data and provide *information*. For example, when you work with the customer database, Approach uses the CUS-

FIGURE 1.10

Charts help you spot trends, unusual conditions, or problems quickly.

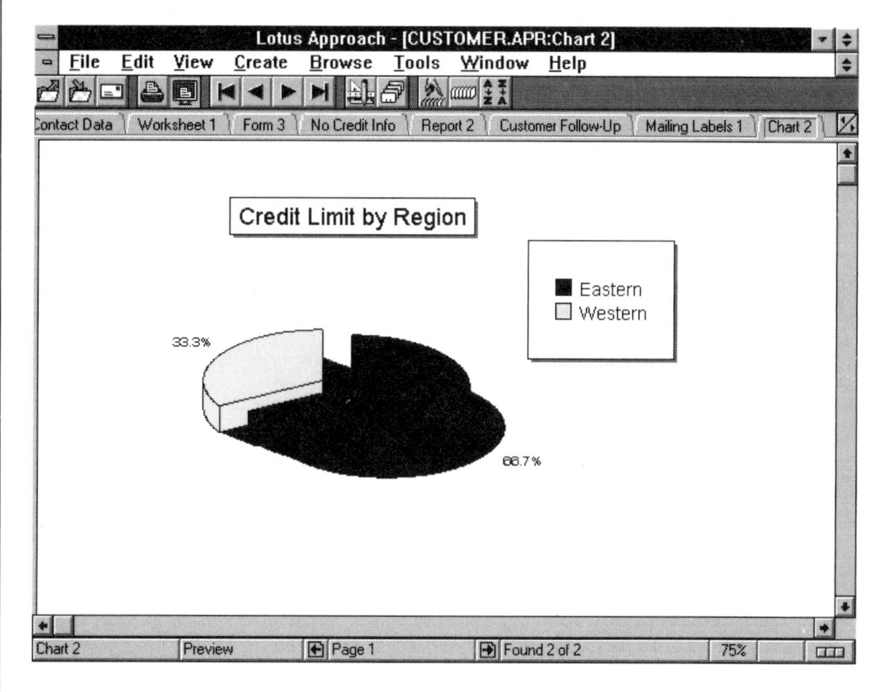

TOMER.DBF (your database file) and the CUSTOMER.APR file to organize the data into the forms and reports you've defined. That is, the .APR file "knows" the source of the data (your .DBF file) and the layout or views you've defined and puts your data together with your layout. In essence, the .APR file contains the instructions for which fields from the database appear on a form, how data in a report will be sorted, which records are selected for mailing labels, and so on.

Because of its unique design, Approach can provide you with more than one view of the same database. For example, we could use the Approach file SALES.APR and the data file CUSTOMER.DBF to organize the customer database for use by the sales department in a sales presentation.

Approach also helps you work with data stored in more than one database file. For example, you may have data about your customers stored in a customer database and data about their orders in an orders database, both of which are stored using dBASE format. Because Approach can electronically "join" the data in the two databases (you'll learn more about that in Chapter 6), you can retrieve information about any orders your customers have placed. Think of an Approach file as a window into your database. It contains the reports, labels, and crosstabs you've defined for the data, and knows where this data is stored (the names and locations of the databases).

►► The Advantages of Approach's Design

Working with database files and Approach files may seem confusing at first, but it actually offers many advantages. For example, because you keep your data separate from the forms and reports that work with the data, you can share your database(s) with other users. You can also work directly with *their* data, as long as the data is in a format Approach can understand (such as dBASE or Paradox). For example, you can buy a mailing list stored in dBASE or Paradox file format and be confident you can use the data in Approach, even though the data might not have been created in Approach.

In fact, you can read and write to dozens of formats, including FoxPro, Oracle SQL, IBM's DB2, and Microsoft/Sybase SQL Server. Through Microsoft's Open Database Connectivity specification (called ODBC for short), you can access databases in other formats, providing you have an ODBC driver for that format.

►► Summary and a Look Ahead

As you've seen in this chapter, databases let you store data about a topic, such as customers or orders, in records. Databases provide powerful analytical tools for spotting trends. Approach can handle vast amounts of information about your business or personal life, create mailing labels, data entry forms, and more.

You'll get a hands-on look at some of the power of Approach in the next chapter.

▶ ▶ CHAPTER 2

Working with Approach

▸▸ FAST TRACK

To use the Design environment 37

for creating or modifying data entry forms, reports, mailing labels, and other Approach views, select the Design icon from the toolbar, choose View ➤ Design, press Ctrl+D, or click on the second box from the left in the Status bar and select Design.

To use the Browse environment 42

for viewing data from database records, select the Browse icon from the toolbar, choose View ➤ Browse, press Ctrl+B, or click on the second box from the left in the Status bar and select Browse.

To use the Find environment 46

to search for records, select the Find icon from the toolbar (it appears as a hand walking across a set of cards), choose Browse ➤ Find, press Ctrl+F, or click on the second box from the left in the Status bar and select Find.

To use the Preview environment 49

for examining output before it is sent to the printer, select the Preview icon from the toolbar, choose File ➤ Preview, press Ctrl+Shift+B, or click on the second box from the left in the Status bar and select Preview.

To get help 59

select the Help menu option within the work area, press F1, or click on the question mark (?) icon in the upper-right corner of many dialog boxes.

►► As you've seen in Chapter 1, Approach offers some powerful features for storing and retrieving data. Now we'll take a guided tour through Approach. We'll do a little bit of everything, from creating a new database and entering data to displaying the data in a spreadsheet-like worksheet and generating a report. You'll learn all about the Approach program, from the screens to the "environments" you'll use to edit forms, create reports, and browse through your data. In addition, we'll show you many of the unique features of version 3.

For practice, we'll create a database and store data about products made by a typical manufacturing company. We'll also enter some sample data, display it in a worksheet, print an inventory report, and see how easy it is to create a chart.

►► Getting Started

For purposes of this guided tour, we are assuming you have already installed Approach on your computer. The installation process creates the Approach program group. To start Approach, double-click on the Approach icon within this program group in the Window's Program Manager.

You can also start Approach by typing its complete file name using Program Manager's File Run commands. With Program Manager displayed, select File ➤ Run. Enter the complete file name (including path) in the Command Line text box: C:\APPROACH\APPROACH.EXE. (See Figure 2.1).

FIGURE 2.1 

Starting Approach using the File ➤ Run commands

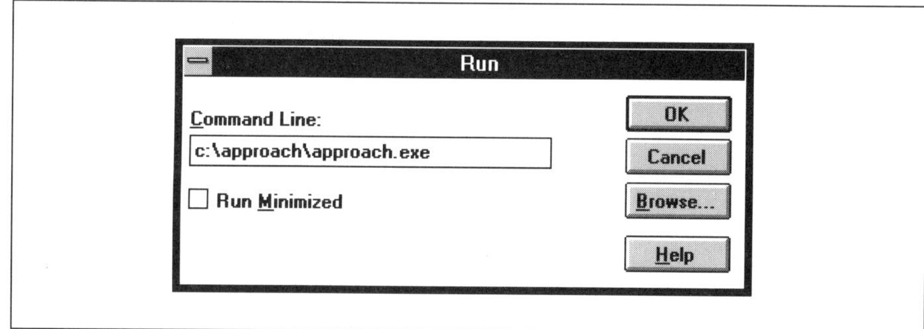

▶▶ The Approach Welcome Screen

When Approach runs for the first time, it displays the Welcome screen, shown in Figure 2.2. From this screen, you can choose to create a new database or open an existing one.

FIGURE 2.2 

The Approach Welcome screen

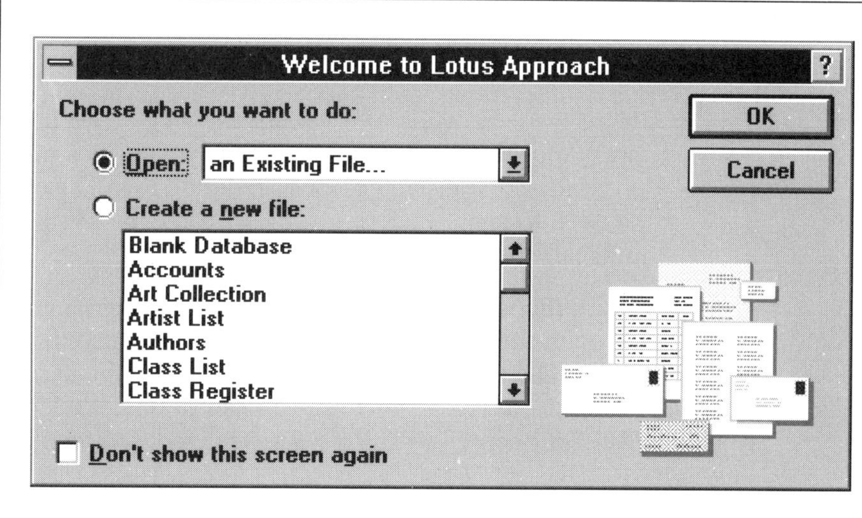

If the Welcome screen does not appear, don't panic. Either someone has already used Approach and selected Cancel at the Welcome screen, or the Approach preferences have been set to skip this screen.

If Cancel was selected from the Welcome screen during a previous session, there is no menu or keyboard shortcut that will return you to the Welcome screen during your current session. You must exit Approach and start the program again to display the Welcome screen.

If the Approach preferences have been set to skip this screen, you must change the preferences. To do so, *you must be working with a database.* That is, you must have an Approach file open. If you see only a blank screen, you're not working with a database. Select File ➤ Open and choose any Approach file on your system, such as one of the sample databases stored in the C:\APPROACH\SAMPLES subdirectory. (You won't change the file—you just need to have a file open, for some strange reason!) Select Tools ➤ Preferences to access the appropriate screen for changing the setup. Be sure the Display tab is in front, and check the Welcome dialog check box so that an X appears. Select OK. Exit Approach (select File ➤ Exit) and restart Approach.

►► TIP

If you prefer to work with the menus and do not want to see the Welcome screen when you begin Approach, check the Don't show this screen again check box.

Now, from the Welcome screen, let's begin. We'll use one of the shortcuts Approach provides—using a template as a model to quickly create a database. Approach comes predefined with a set of fields you're likely to need to keep track of products. You can start with this model, then make changes.

From the Welcome screen, select the Create a new file option. Scroll through the list and highlight Products by clicking on it once (this also selects the Create a new file option above the list), then click on the OK button. (As a shortcut, you can double-click on Products.) The Welcome screen with Products selected is shown in Figure 2.3.

Approach opens the New dialog box, shown in Figure 2.4, and prompts you to enter a database file name and a drive and directory location. Select the drive and directory first. If you installed Approach on

FIGURE 2.3

The Welcome screen with the Products template highlighted

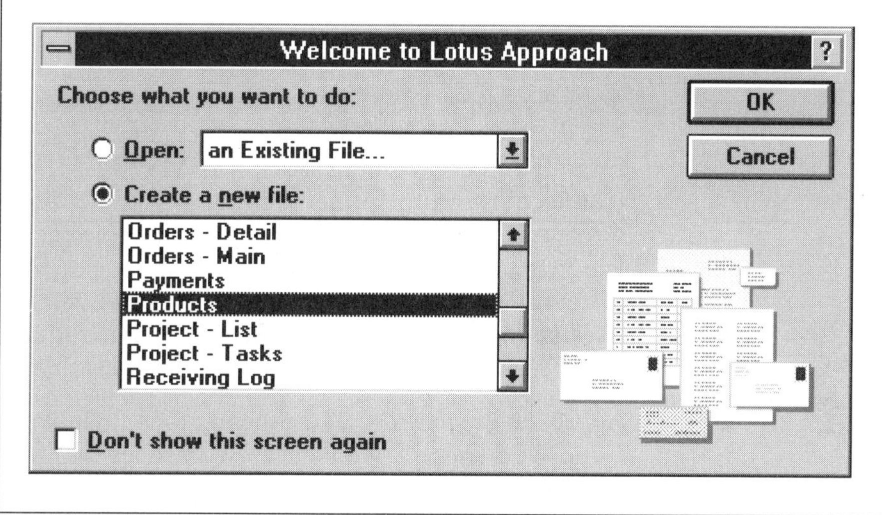

your C drive and accepted the defaults at installation, Approach suggests you create your file in the C:\APPROACH directory. If you want to save the file in a different directory, do so now. Separate directories can help keep your work better organized. You can keep "test" databases separate from your "real" work, for example.

FIGURE 2.4 

The New dialog box

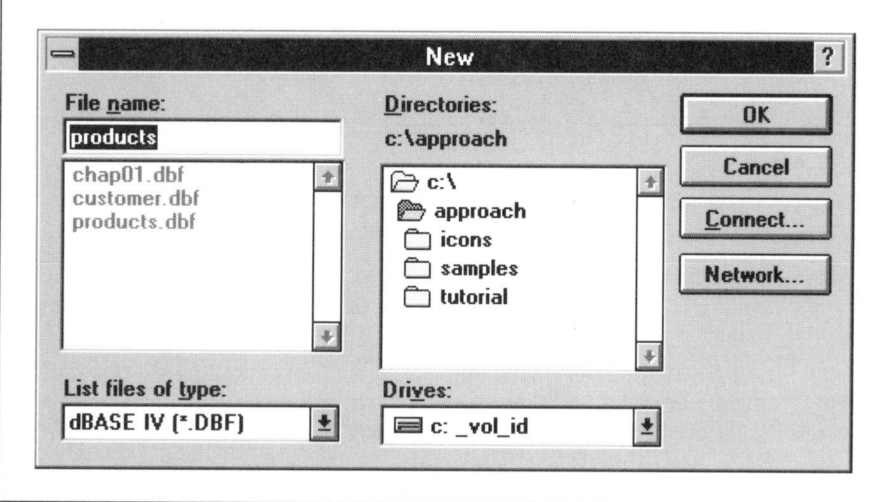

To create a subdirectory, switch to the Windows File Manager. Create a subdirectory, such as \MASTER, in the APPROACH subdirectory. Now you can save your files in this directory and keep them separate from the Approach program files. If you are working on a network, select the Network button to find the network location for storing your files. (If you are working with an IBM DB2-MDI Server, select the Connect button to connect to that system.) When you have selected a directory, enter a file name. By default, Approach suggests the name Products, the same name as the template. The file type should show dBASE IV (*.DBF), meaning that the data will be stored in the industry-standard file format for dBASE IV. The full name of our database will therefore be PRODUCTS.DBF. This is fine, so select OK.

Approach creates a screen showing tabs (just like a file folder) for Form 1 and Worksheet 1. We'll get to Worksheet 1 a little later in this chapter. Right now you should be looking at a form like the one shown in Figure 2.5.

FIGURE 2.5

The Form 1 screen

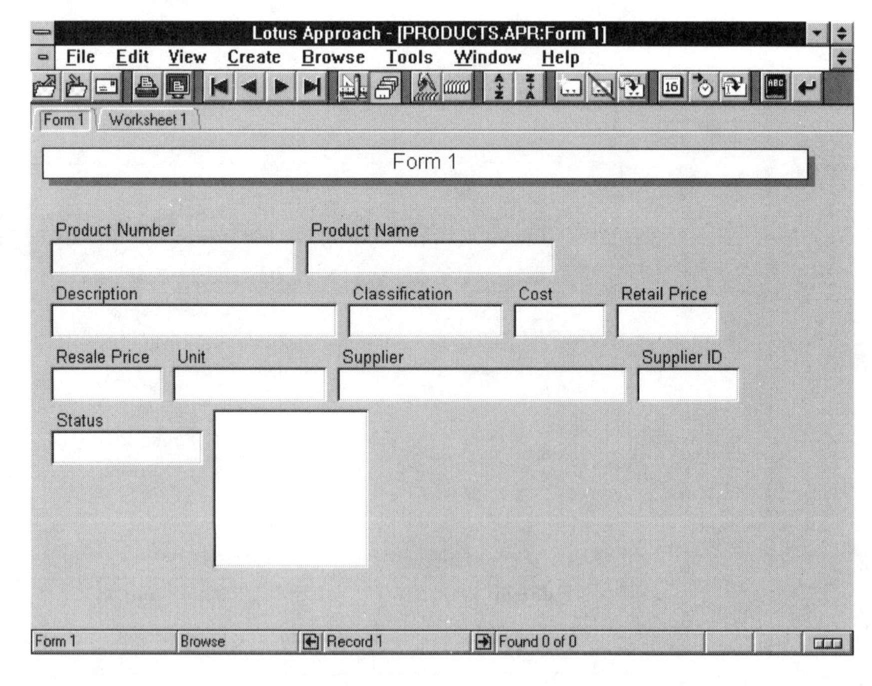

As you can see, in the center of the screen, called the *work area*, Approach displays the view (Form 1) you've selected. Approach also displays the tools, or *elements*, you need or request along the top and bottom of the screen. Let's take a few minutes to become familiar with these elements and the Approach work area.

►► The Approach Work Area

The Approach application window, also known as the Approach screen or work area, contains several elements, as shown in Figure 2.6. Each element is used to display information or perform a specific task. When you work in Approach, these elements change to meet your needs and may differ depending on the *environment* in which you are working. Later in the chapter we will take you step by step through Approach's four environments. For now, think of environments as modes of operation.

FIGURE 2.6 ►

The Approach work area

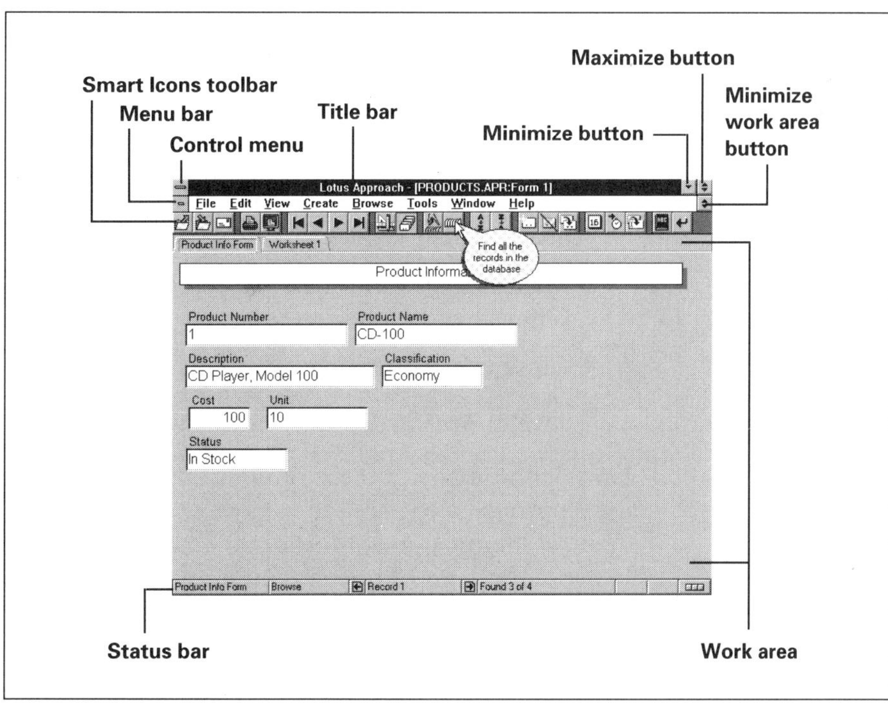

Before we begin a detailed introduction to the various elements, let's also quickly review fields, records, and views. As you learned in Chapter 1, fields contain pieces of information of a common type (text or numeric, for example). Records are a group of fields about a given subject (one of your customers or a supplier, for example). Views are the forms, reports, worksheets, charts, and mailing labels Approach uses to organize the data.

Now, let's learn more about the Approach work area, beginning with the top-left corner of your screen.

▶ Control Menu

The upper-left corner of the screen contains a small box that displays a minus sign. This is the Control box. Click on the box or press Alt+Spacebar now to reveal the Control menu. The Control menu gives you these choices:

- Restore changes the window to full-screen size.
- Move lets you reposition a window that is not full-screen size.
- Size lets you change the dimensions of a window that is not full-screen size.
- Minimize removes the Approach screen and displays the application as an icon. To return to full-screen mode, you must click on this minimized icon from within Windows. You can also click on the minimize button (to the right of the Title bar) to shrink Approach to an icon.
- Maximize fills the entire screen with the Approach work area, if it is not already full screen.
- Close exits Approach.
- Switch To lets you move to another Windows application.

Don't choose any of these options now. Instead, click anywhere else in the Approach work area to remove the Control menu. The Control menu is identical in all four of the Approach environments: Design, Browse, Find, and Preview. You'll learn about these environments in the section "Approach Environments" later in this chapter.

▶ Title Bar

The Title bar is located at the top of the work area and ordinarily displays the name of the program. However, if an Approach file is open, you will see the name of the file in the Title bar. Figure 2.5 (earlier in this chapter) shows the current Approach file name PRODUCTS.APR in the Title bar.

▶ Menu Bar

The Menu bar is located just below the Title bar. To select a menu from the Menu bar, press Alt, then the underlined letter in the option you want. For example, press Alt, then F to select the File menu, or press Alt+F. When Approach displays a list of options, don't choose any of them at this time. Instead, click anywhere in the Approach work area to remove the menu, or select another Main Menu option (such as Window or Help).

Notice that when you select a Menu option, the Title bar changes to display information about the purpose of the Menu option. For example, when you select File ➤ New, the Title bar changes to read "Create a new database and Approach file."

The Menu bar is identical in all four Approach environments.

▶ Maximize Button

The Maximize button is in the upper-right corner of the Approach window. Click on this button to toggle between displaying the Approach window in the entire screen area of your monitor and displaying the Window with smaller dimensions.

▶ Minimize Button

The Minimize button is located below the Maximize button. When you click on this button, Windows removes the Approach window from the screen and displays an icon in Windows.

▸▸ **TIP**

You can also toggle between display sizes by double-clicking anywhere in the Title bar.

▸ Minimize Work Area Button

Just under the Control Menu Minimize button is the Minimize Work Area button. This button changes the size of the Approach work area *within the Approach application window*. When you click on the Minimize Work Area button, Approach reduces the current work area to an icon within the Approach screen. Your work area now has two buttons: Minimize (reduces to an icon) and Maximize (restores to full size). Double-clicking on an icon returns the work area to its previous size.

▸ The SmartIcons Toolbar

When you click on an icon in a toolbar, Approach will perform the task associated with the icon. If you are unsure of the meaning of an icon, leave the mouse pointed to the icon and do not move it. After a few seconds, Approach displays a short message in a yellow balloon, as shown in Figure 2.6 (earlier in this chapter).

Icons are provided for the most common tasks in Approach. For example, the default Browse toolbar contains icons that let you open a file, save an existing file, move to the next or previous record, switch to the Design environment, and sort data. Figure 2.7 shows the Standard toolbar for the Browse environment.

There are one or more default sets of icons for each of the four Approach environments. You can also create your own and switch between toolbars defined for the environment you're working in. For now we'll just work with the standard SmartIcons toolbars.

▸ The Status Bar

The Status bar is displayed along the bottom of the work area. It provides information about the work area, and changes depending on the task you're performing. (If the Status bar is not displayed at the bottom of your screen, select View ➤ Show Status Bar.) For example, if you are

FIGURE 2.7

The Browse environment's standard SmartIcons toolbar

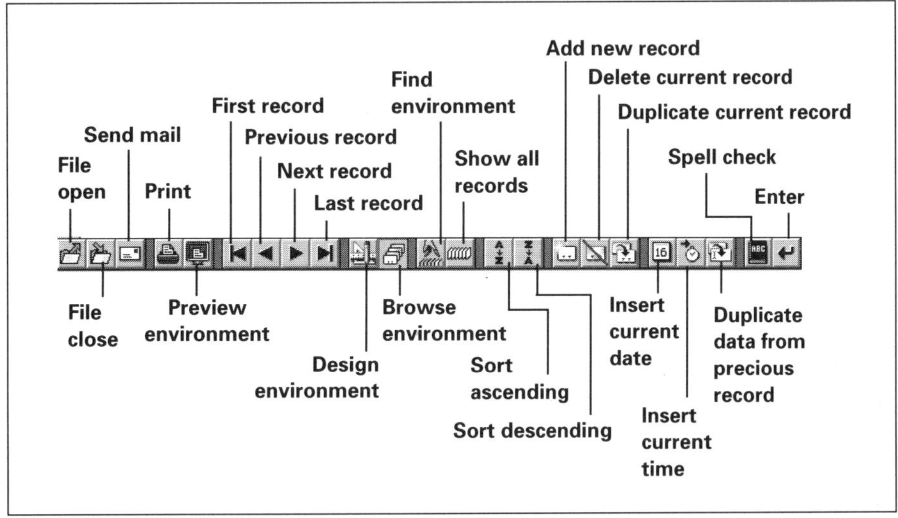

viewing data, the Status bar will show you the record number and total number of records you're working with. If you are changing the design of a data entry form, the Status bar will display the height and width of any object on the form or the position of the mouse. If you select an object on a form, such as a text field, the Status bar also displays buttons to let you change the font and font properties of the selected field.

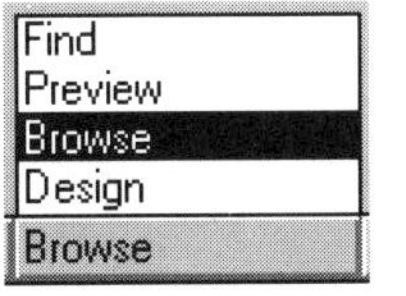

Some areas of the Status bar act as menus. For example, if you click the first box in the Status bar, you can change the active view. If you click on the second box in the Status bar, you can switch between environments. For instance, if you are in the Design environment, you can click on the second box in the Status bar (which reads "Design"). A list of the available environments will appear. Select Browse to switch to the Browse environment.

The Status bar is explained in greater detail when we discuss its use in creating and modifying forms and when navigating through the database. Those topics are covered in Chapters 7, 8, and 9.

▶ The Tabbed Work Areas

Approach displays tabs (just like a file folder) in the upper-left of the screen to indicate the name of the form you are using (see Figure 2.6 earlier in this chapter). If the tabs are not displayed, click on the View Tabs button in the SmartIcons toolbar or select View ➤ Show View

Tabs. When the tabs are displayed, the View tabs button in the toolbar has a gray slash through it. Click the icon to remove the Tabs. Click again on the icon to redisplay the tabs. Note that the View Tabs button is not part of the default toolbar, but may have been added to the toolbar by you or another user working with Approach.

To see Tabs whenever you open Approach, set the default as follows:

1. Select Tools ➤ Preferences. Approach displays the Preferences dialog box shown in Figure 2.8.
2. Select the Display tab.
3. Check the View tabs box (it should contain an X after you've selected it).
4. Select Save Default, then select OK.

Now let's move on to environments.

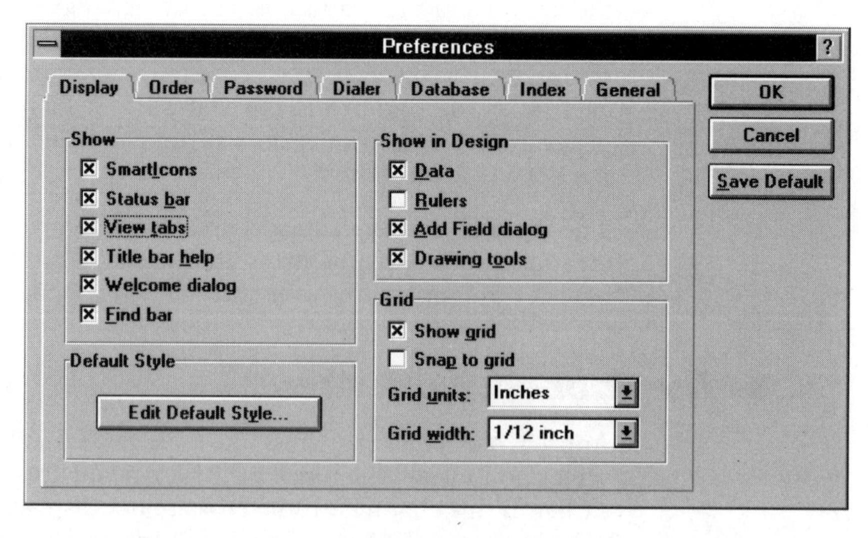

FIGURE 2.8 ▶

The Preferences dialog box

▶▶ Approach Environments

Approach has four environments, which you can think of as modes of operation. The environments are:

- Design, for creating or modifying data entry forms, reports, mailing labels, and other Approach views
- Browse, for viewing data from database records
- Find, for searching for records
- Preview, for examining output before it is sent to the printer

We'll step through each environment in this chapter beginning with the Design environment.

At this point, you should have created a \MASTER subdirectory and a database called Products.DBF (see previous section "The Welcome Screen"). Your screen should look like Figure 2.5, shown earlier in this chapter.

▶ The Design Environment

In the Design environment you're working with the layout of a form or report, selecting and positioning fields on a form, for example, or designing a report or worksheet. You are not working with the actual data, but you can see the data to help you plan your layout. Recall that your database consists of records (one per product), and each product record is made up of fields (such as Product Number, Product Name, Cost, and so on).

Right now we aren't going to modify the actual structure of the database and get rid of fields we don't want. That's pretty complicated, and our purpose here is to see what Approach can do, not get into all the nitty gritty details. You'll get into the details in Chapter 5.

Instead, we'll change the form to remove fields that we don't want or need. The fields for supplier data (Supplier and Supplier ID), for example, aren't needed, so we'll remove them from the form. These fields will remain in the database however, so we can put them back in the form later if we wish.

To begin, look at the Status bar at the bottom of the screen. (If the Status bar is not displayed, select View ➤ Show Status Bar.) The second box from the left should say "Browse," meaning you are in the Browse environment (Figure 2.5). We want to switch to the Design environment. To do so, use any of these methods:

- Select the Design icon from the toolbar.
- Select View ➤ Design.
- Press Ctrl+D.
- Click on the second box from the left in the Status bar and select Design.

Your screen should look like Figure 2.9. (If the Add Field box is missing, you can display it by selecting Form ➤ Add Field.)

In Design you can view the field names or actual data from the first record(s) in your database, but you cannot modify the data in these records.

Changing the Form in the Design Environment

Notice that when you changed environments, the menu, toolbar, and Status bar changed. Approach has added a floating toolbar containing drawing tools such as an arrow, the letters ABC, rectangles, circles, and other graphic elements. You'll learn more about these tools in Chapter 7.

For practice, try removing the fields containing supplier data. Click once on the white area under the heading Supplier. Approach changes the cursor to a hand and places four boxes, called *handles*, at the corners of the Supplier field. Press Delete and Approach removes the field from the form. Likewise select the Supplier ID field and press Delete. There's a large white box to the right of the Status field. Click on it and delete it, too.

Remember that these fields remain defined in the Approach database. They just aren't being displayed on the form. This option is useful if

FIGURE 2.9

The Form in the Design environment

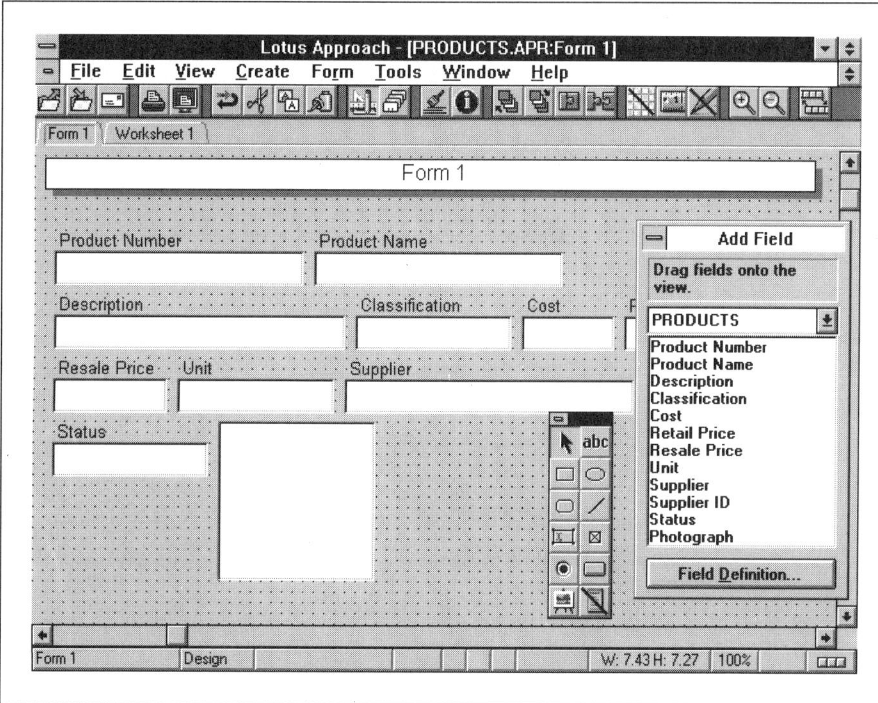

there is sensitive data, such as pricing information, that you don't want to make available to every user. In an employee form, for example, you might want to display a person's name and address but not display the annual salary amount. You can create a different form that displays this information to a special group of users.

To keep things simple, let's get rid of the Retail Price and the Resale Price fields. We'll only concern ourselves with the cost of each product. Select the Retail Price field and press Delete. Do the same with the Resale Price field. Your screen should now look like Figure 2.10.

The Design environment does more than just let us delete fields. We can also move a field. Click on the Cost field. Approach places the four handles at the corners of the field and changes the cursor into a hand. Now press and hold the left mouse button and drag the field to the left of the Unit field. When the Cost field is positioned where you want it, release the mouse. If the field isn't quite right, click and drag it until it's aligned properly. Your screen should look like Figure 2.11.

FIGURE 2.10

The Products data entry form with several fields removed

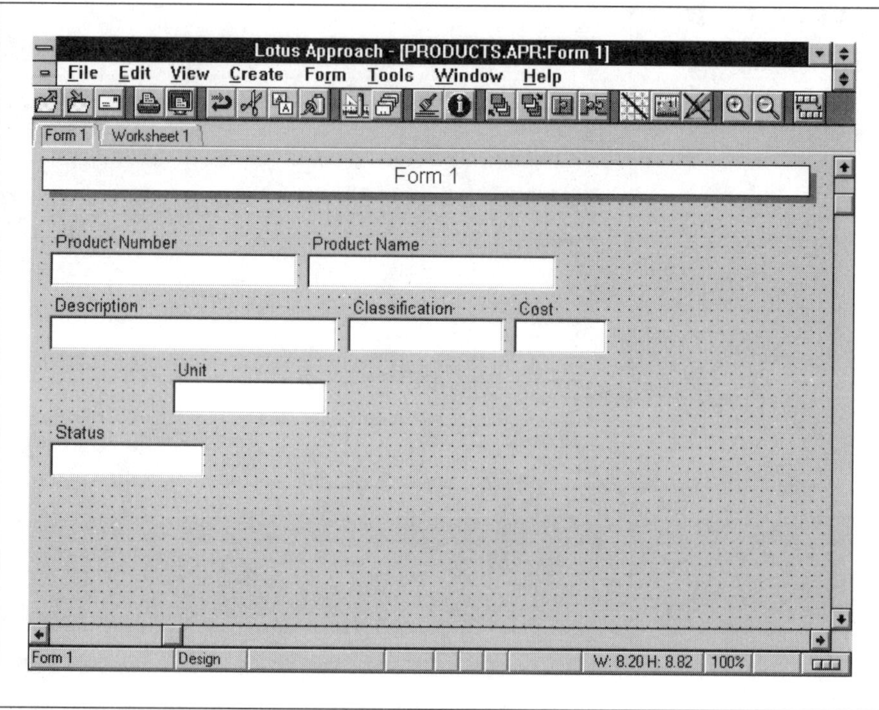

▸▸ **TIP**

You can also select multiple objects and align them by using the Object ➤ Align command. Approach displays a dialog box that allows you to select several alignment options.

Notice that Approach supplies small dots to help you align fields vertically and horizontally. If these dots, called *grids,* are not displayed on your screen, select View ➤ Show Grid to turn the grid on.

Let's make one more change before leaving the Design environment. Click on the box marked Form 1 at the top of the form to select it, then double-click on the box to edit the contents of the box. Approach displays a blue border around the box and places a flashing vertical

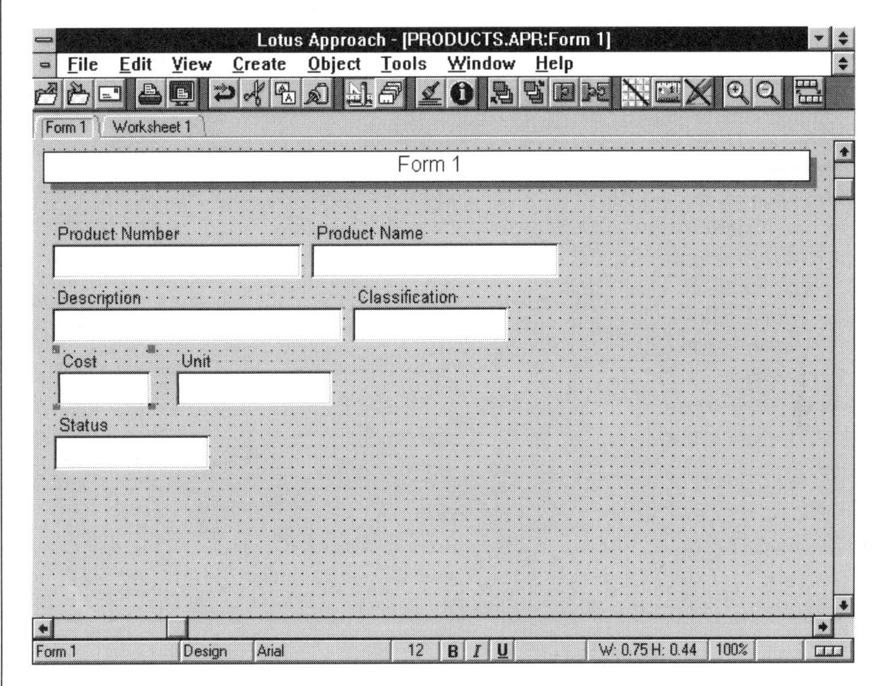

FIGURE 2.11 *The revised Form 1 view*

cursor, called the Insertion Point, near the Form 1 text. (Where the Insertion Point appears depends on where the mouse pointer is when you clicked on the text.) To select all the text, triple-click the mouse, then press Delete to clear all the text. Otherwise, press the Backspace or Delete keys until all of the text is erased. Type **Product Information**. As you do so, Approach centers your text within the box. Click anywhere outside the box to deselect it.

To give the tab for this form a meaningful name (what does Form 1 mean, anyway?), double-click on the words Form 1 in the tab itself. Approach expands the width of the tab and places an Insertion Point inside a text box. Unlike the heading we just changed, Approach has selected the entire text already. Therefore, we don't need to press the Backspace key to replace the text—we just start typing the new title. Type **Product Info Form**, then click anywhere outside of the tab.

The form should now look like Figure 2.12.

FIGURE 2.12 ▶

The Product Information Form with a new tab heading (Product Info Form) and new form heading. If you double-click on any object, the InfoBox (shown in the bottom-right corner) appears. We'll use the InfoBox regularly when creating views within Approach. You'll learn more about the InfoBox in Chapter 7.

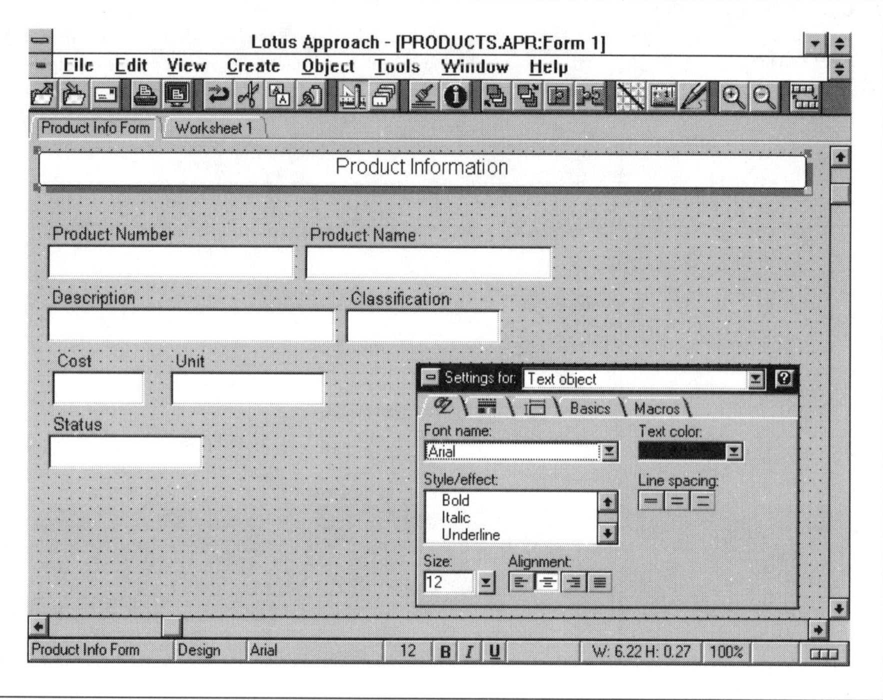

▶▶ **TIP**

If you wish to stop at any point in our tour, select File ➤ Save Approach File and enter the name PRODUCTS.APR if it is not already displayed in the file name box. This matches the name of the database file (PRODUCTS.DBF) and is the standard used by Approach for naming Approach files. To begin where you left off, select Open an Existing File from the Welcome screen, or select File ➤ Open, then choose PRODUCTS.

▶ *The Browse Environment*

Now it's time to actually enter product information into the database. You can do that in the Browse environment. Contrary to what its name implies, the Browse environment lets you do more than just *look* at your data. You can add new records, update or delete existing ones, find or sort your records, and print them.

The Browse environment is shown in Figure 2.13.

FIGURE 2.13

The Browse environment

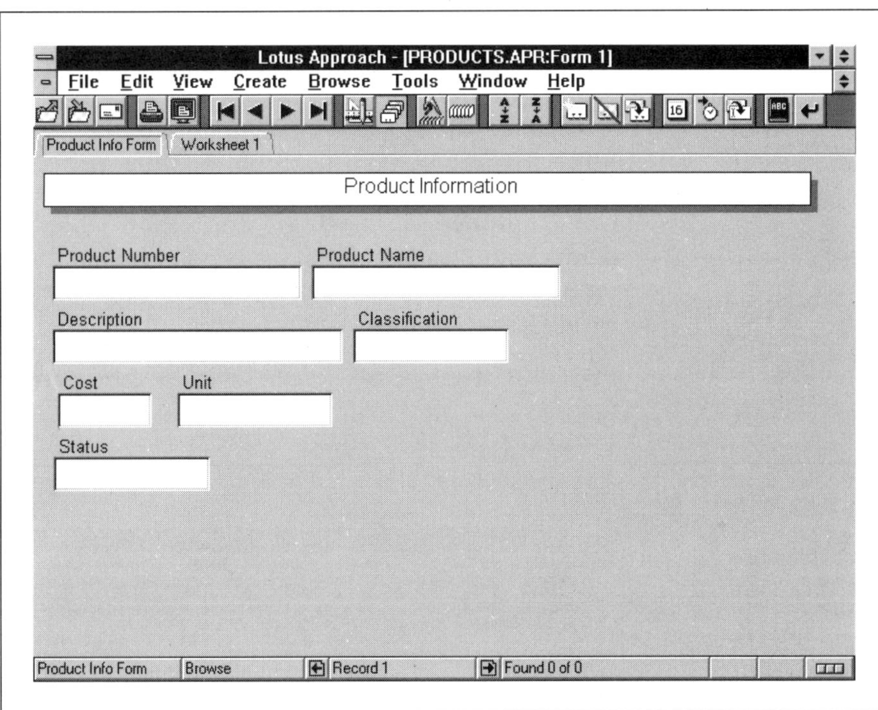

To switch to the Browse environment, use any of these methods:

- Select the Browse icon from the toolbar.
- Select View ➤ Browse.
- Press Ctrl+B.
- Click on the second box from the left in the Status bar and select Browse.

Let's explore the Browse environment by adding data about four products: CD-100, CD-200, CD-500, and CD-900. Click in the Product Number field and enter **1**. As soon as you move the Insertion Point into a field, the Status bar changes to Browse/Modify, indicating that you can view or modify (add, change, or delete) the data. Press the Tab key to move to the Product Name field, or click anywhere in the Product Name field. Enter **CD-100**. Press the Tab key to move to the Description field, and enter **CD Player, Model 100**.

In the same fashion, move to the Classification field and enter **Economy**—this is our economy model. Move to the Cost field and enter **100**. You can also enter 100.00, but the field is defined to only keep whole numbers, so the ".00" won't show when you move to another field. (You'll learn how to display numeric fields as currency in Chapter 8.) In the Unit field, enter **10**, and in the Status field enter **In Stock**, since we have 10 in stock.

Figure 2.14 shows the screen with the data entered in the appropriate fields.

FIGURE 2.14

A complete new record for product CD-100

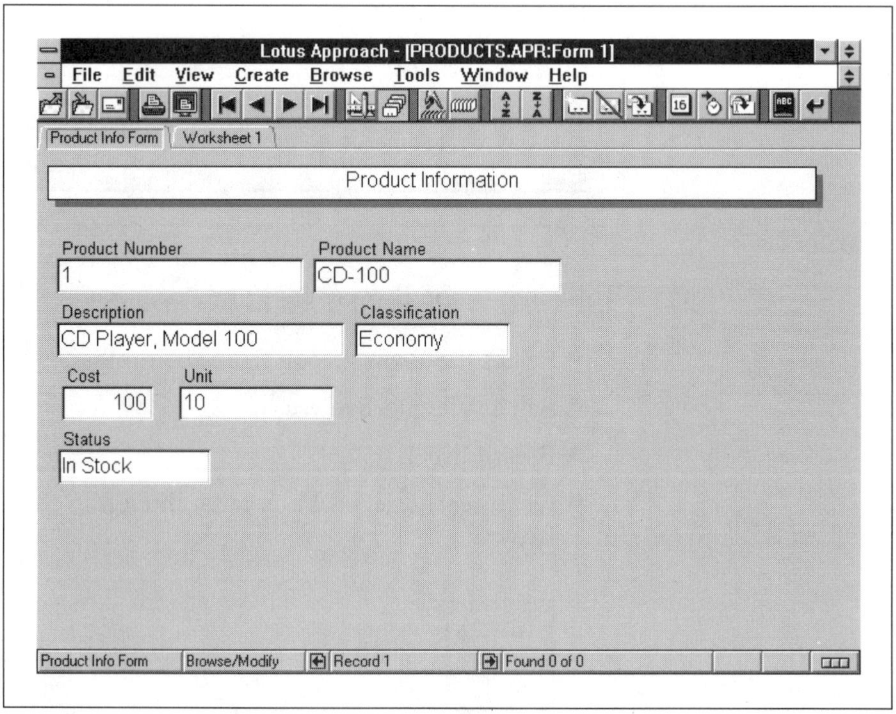

To add the next record, select Browse ➤ New Record, or press Ctrl+N. Enter the values for the fields in the second record as follows:

Field	**Value**
Product Number	**2**
Product Name	**CD-200**
Description	**CD Player with remote control**
Classification	**Intermediate**
Cost	**129**
Unit	**20**
Status	**In Stock**

To add the third record, select Browse ➤ New Record, or press Ctrl+N. Enter the following values for the fields:

Field	**Value**
Product Number	**5**
Product Name	**CD-500**
Description	**CD Player, Holds 5 CDs**
Classification	**Intermediate**
Cost	**159**
Unit	**25**
Status	**In Stock**

To add the last record, select Browse ➤ New Record, or press Ctrl+N. Enter the following values for the fields:

Field	**Value**
Product Number	**9**
Product Name	**CD-900**
Description	**Programmable CD Player**
Classification	**Advanced**
Cost	**229**

Field	Value
Unit	**10**
Status	**Back Order**

To move between records, use the VCR-like buttons in the toolbar. In the set of four buttons, the first goes to the first record in our database, the second goes to the previous record, while the third takes you to the next record and the fourth button takes you to the last record. As you move through the database, the Status bar shows you the record number currently displayed: Record 1 for the first record, Record 3 for the third record, and so on.

▸ The Find Environment

In the Find environment, you fill in an empty form to search for one or more records that meet your criteria. Figure 2.15 shows Approach in the Find environment using a search request to look for information

FIGURE 2.15 ▸

The Find environment

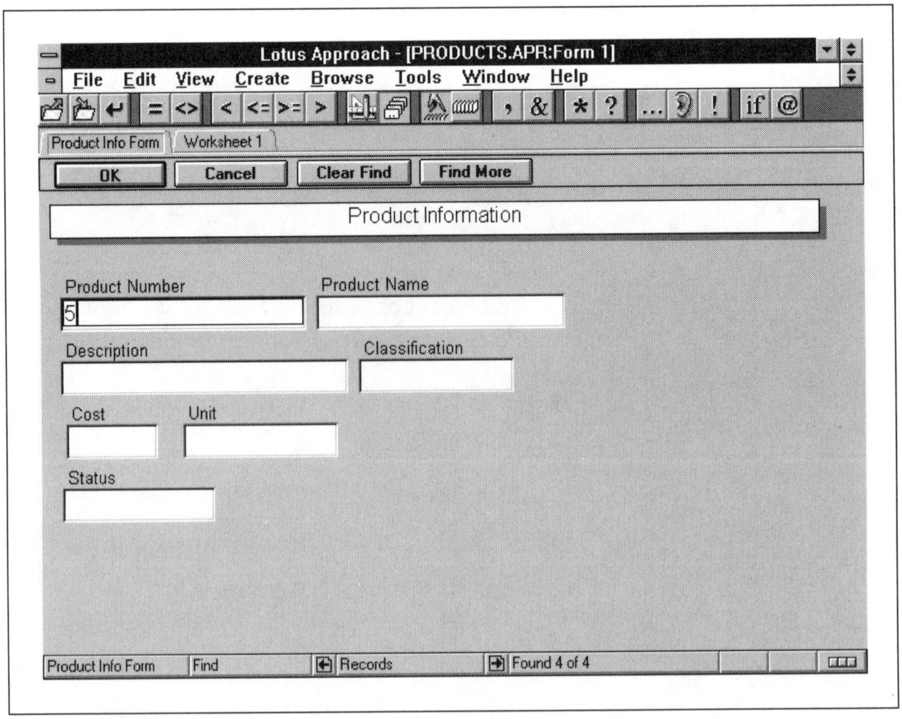

about product number 5. When you have entered the Find request, Approach will perform the search and return a set of records that matches the criteria you specified. This set of records is called the *found set*. We'll perform two search requests in the Find environment.

To switch to the Find environment, use any of these methods:

- Select the Find icon from the toolbar (it appears as a hand walking across a set of cards).
- Select Browse ➤ Find.
- Press Ctrl+F.
- Click on the second box from the left in the Status bar and select Find.

Notice that Approach continues to use the Product Information form we've been using all along, but it erases all values from the fields so you can enter your search criteria. (It also adds the four VCR-like buttons to the top of the form.) Approach makes it easy to find and display records by using a familiar form, the one you have just been using.

To find the record containing information about product number 5, click in the Product Number field and type **5**. Select the OK button at the top of the form. Approach returns the record that matches the criteria we specified—the record contains the value *5* in the Product Number field—and Approach displays it in the Browse environment.

Let's find the set of records that contains products that are in stock. Remember that three of the four products are in stock (only product 9 is back ordered). To perform this additional search, choose any of these methods:

- Select the Find icon from the toolbar.
- Select Browse ➤ Find.
- Press Ctrl+F.

- Click on the second box from the left in the Status bar and select Find.

Now enter **In Stock** in the Status field, and click the OK button. The search is case insensitive. Approach will find the three records if you enter *In stock*, *in stock*, or *in Stock*. However, you must have a space between "in" and "stock." Otherwise Approach will not find the matching records, since *instock* and *in stock* are considered different values.

When you switch to the Find environment, Approach replaces the toolbar with the one shown in Figure 2.16. Don't panic! Those buttons are useful for creating and refining more complex searches. They let us cancel the search, clear the criteria from the last search, or enter more criteria in order to specify more conditions. Our search is quite straightforward, so we don't need to use them, however. We'll explore the Find toolbar and buttons in Chapter 12.

This time, the Status bar shows you that Approach found three of four records matching the criteria, as shown in Figure 2.16.

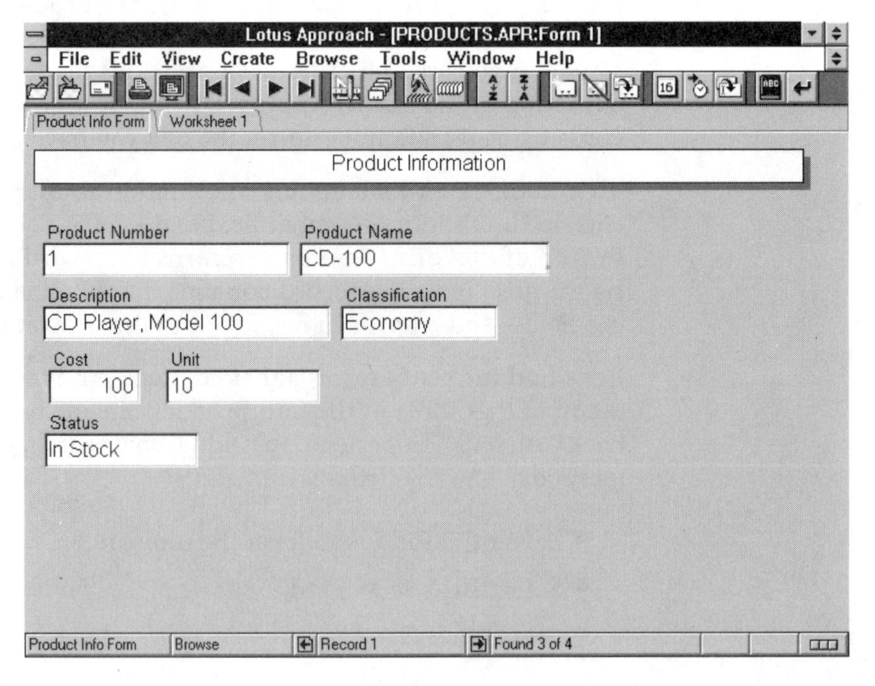

FIGURE 2.16 ►

Approach finds that three records in the database contain data about products in stock.

Found 3 of 4

You are now working with the *found set*, because three records were found with the value *In Stock* in the Status field. Use the VCR-like buttons in the toolbar to move among these record. The fourth record is still in your database—you haven't lost the data. However, the out-of-stock part did not match your criteria, so it's not shown.

To redisplay the entire database, select the Show All icon from the toolbar, select Browse ➤ Show All, or press Ctrl+A. The process of showing all records is sometimes called removing a filter in other database programs, since the found set is really a set of records that passes through a "filter."

There are plenty of other ways to find data, from the simple to the complex. Finding records is discussed further in Chapter 12.

▶ The Preview Environment

In the Preview environment you can display on your screen what the printed output will look like before Approach actually sends it to your printer. For example, you might like to look at the information shown in the current form before you actually create the paper output to make sure everything is laid out the way you want it. Thus, you can use the Preview environment to prevent wasting paper on incorrect output.

The Preview environment is shown in Figure 2.17.

It's time to switch to the Preview environment to see how the currently displayed record will look when you print it. To switch to the Preview environment, use any of these methods:

- Select the Preview icon from the toolbar.
- Select File ➤ Preview.
- Press Ctrl+Shift+B.

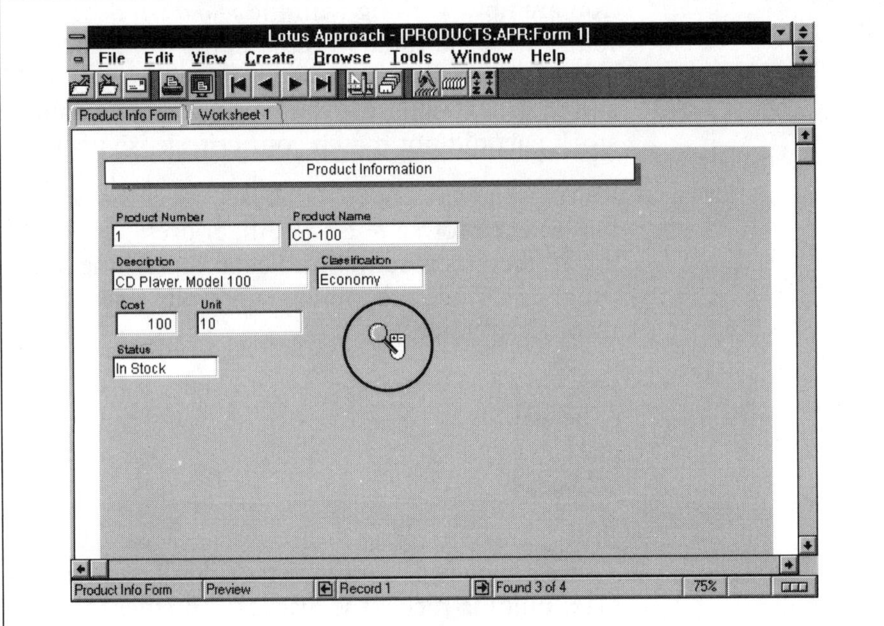

FIGURE 2.17

The Preview environment

- Click on the second box from the left in the Status bar and select Preview.

Now that you're in the Preview environment, the cursor changes to a picture of a mouse with a magnifying glass, indicating that you can change the size of your screen display. Click the left button on your mouse to zoom in or the right button to zoom out and get a "big picture" of what your output will look like when printed. The Status bar shows the zoom percentage in a box at the right of the bar. You can also click on this box to display a menu of the available zoom percentages and select the percentage you want.

To print the form, select File ➤ Print, select Ctrl+P, or click on the Print icon from the SmartIcons toolbar.

Approach displays the Print dialog box, shown in Figure 2.18. Select Current form to print the record that is currently displayed on your screen, then select OK. If you need to change the printer settings, click on Setup, or change any of the options shown in the Print dialog box. This dialog box is similar to those found in other Windows applications.

FIGURE 2.18 ▶

The Print dialog box

▶▶ Working with Data in Worksheets

If you haven't switched to the Worksheet view Approach created by default, do so now: Click on the Worksheet 1 tab or click in the first box in the Status bar and select Worksheet 1.

A *worksheet*, shown in Figure 2.19, displays the data from your database in tabular format. It looks remarkably like a spreadsheet such as one you might create using Quattro Pro, Microsoft Excel, or Lotus 1-2-3.

FIGURE 2.19

The mouse turns into a field name pointing to a wastebasket when you remove a field from a worksheet.

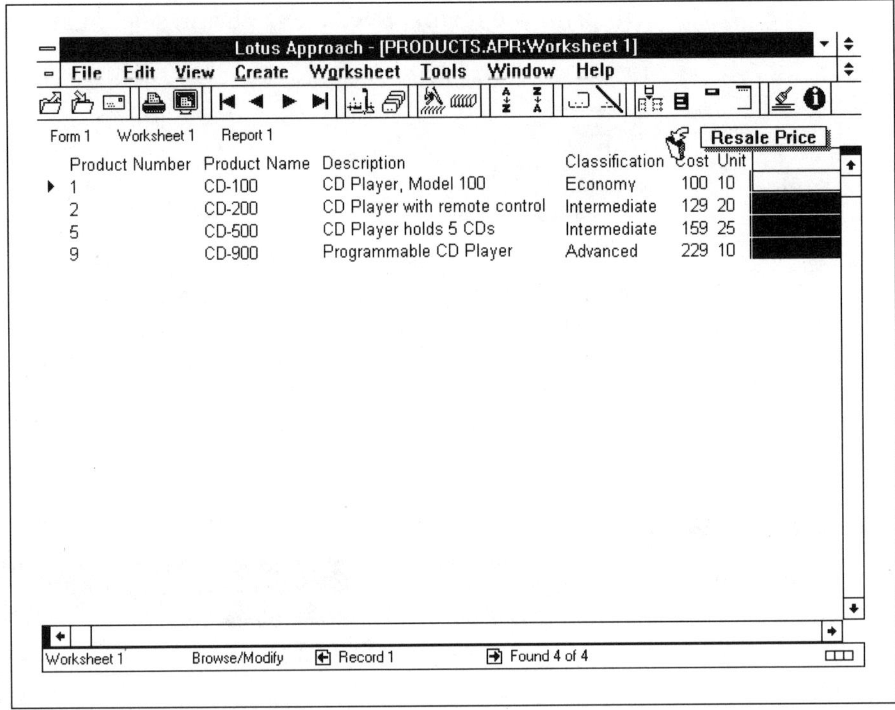

In a worksheet, data is displayed one record per row and one field per column. You'll learn more about worksheets in Chapter 10.

As with the default form (Form 1), Approach creates this Worksheet view with all fields displayed. Use the scroll (arrow) buttons at the bottom of the screen to get to fields that are beyond the current screen range.

Since we don't need several of the fields, let's remove some to make the display easier to work with. Click on the column heading Retail Price (a heading is the name of a column). The entire column will be selected (highlighted). Now drag the column heading up and to the left (to the right of the Worksheet 1 tab). The mouse changes to a hand, and the words "Retail Price" appear in a box pointing to a waste can as shown in Figure 2.19. When you see this waste can, release the mouse and Retail Price is trashed (that is, removed from the worksheet). Perform the same steps to remove the Resale Price column.

▶▶ NOTE

When you delete a field from a form, you are removing the data from the view but not from the database itself. Just as removing a field from a form does not delete the data from the database, removing a column from a worksheet changes the appearance of the worksheet but does not delete the data from the database.

Let's remove two adjacent columns in one step. Click on the Supplier heading, then hold the Shift key down and click on the Supplier ID heading. You can use the mouse: Click and hold the mouse over the Supplier heading and drag the mouse over the Supplier ID heading. (Unfortunately there is no way to select nonadjacent columns.) Approach highlights both columns. Drag either heading toward the top of the screen until you see a box that contains both field names and points to a trash can. Release the mouse to delete the columns. You can also remove the column named Photograph.

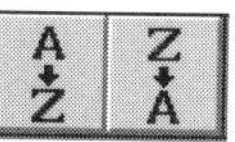

Now click on the Unit column heading. Click on the A-Z icon in the SmartIcons toolbar. This indicates that we want to sort the column from smallest value to the largest. When you click on the icon, Approach resorts the data and displays it as shown in Figure 2.20. The record containing the smallest value in the Unit field is in the top row. The record containing the next larger value is displayed in the second row, and so on.

Select the same column heading and click the Z-A icon. This resorts the data so that the largest value is listed first. Using this feature, we can, for example, see which product may be overstocked in inventory—the item listed at the top of this worksheet. (If you switch to the Preview environment, you'll find that you can also sort data there, too!)

We can also sort on more than one field at a time. For example, we can sort on Classification, and within Classification by Product Name or Product Description. Sorting options are more fully explained in Chapter 12.

As in most spreadsheet programs, you can resize the column widths by placing the cursor at the column border to the right of the field,

FIGURE 2.20

Data is re-sorted when you select a column and the Sort Ascending icon from the SmartIcons toolbar.

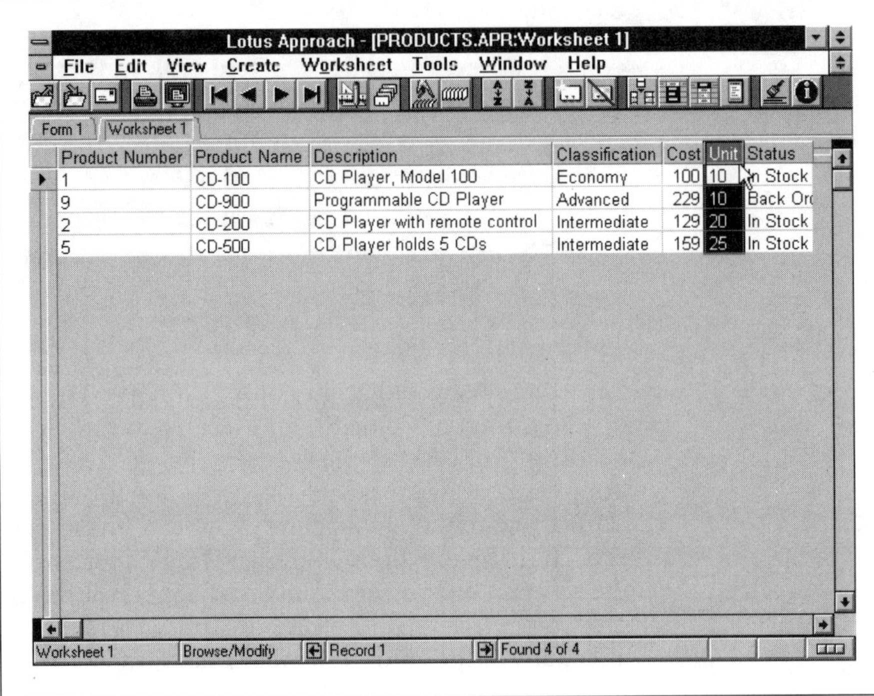

pressing and holding the mouse as you drag the two-headed arrow to the left or right to change the width. Likewise, you can change row height or rearrange the columns. You'll learn more about working with worksheets in Chapter 10.

The advantage of a worksheet is that it displays several records at once, making comparisons between two records easier. A Worksheet view is a good choice when you want to maintain a simple list of information, such as a part number and part description. In addition, worksheets aren't just for displaying data. You can also add, change, and delete records using a worksheet, but you'll learn about that in Chapter 10.

►► Creating a Report

To conclude our guided tour of Approach, let's create a simple list report. We'll do a calculation to show you how easy it is to create a report that lists the total number of products our typical manufacturing company makes. Yes, we know there are only four records, so we must have four products! However, if this were a larger database, we might need to generate a list of products with a subtotal by Classification, for example.

To help you create new views, Approach provides a set of Assistants that step you through the process of creating the view. There are Assistants for forms, reports, mailing labels, form letters, worksheets, crosstabs, and charts. We did not use the Assistants for forms and worksheets since Approach created a basic form and worksheet for us. However, Approach does not create a default report, so we'll create a report now.

To create a new report, select the Menu option Create. From the pull-down list of options, select Report, the view we want to create. Approach opens the Report Assistant, shown in Figure 2.21.

We'll create a *columnar report* that uses a *grand summary*. In a columnar report, each field appears in a column. The grand summary, or more commonly, the grand total, will calculate the number of parts on the list. Select Columnar with Grand Summary in the *SmartMasters* layout box. SmartMasters are predefined layouts that resemble style sheets in word processors. SmartMasters are a collection of properties, such as the font that will be used on a report, the placement of a title, and the background color of the view. For now, select the Default Style in the

FIGURE 2.21

The Report Assistant

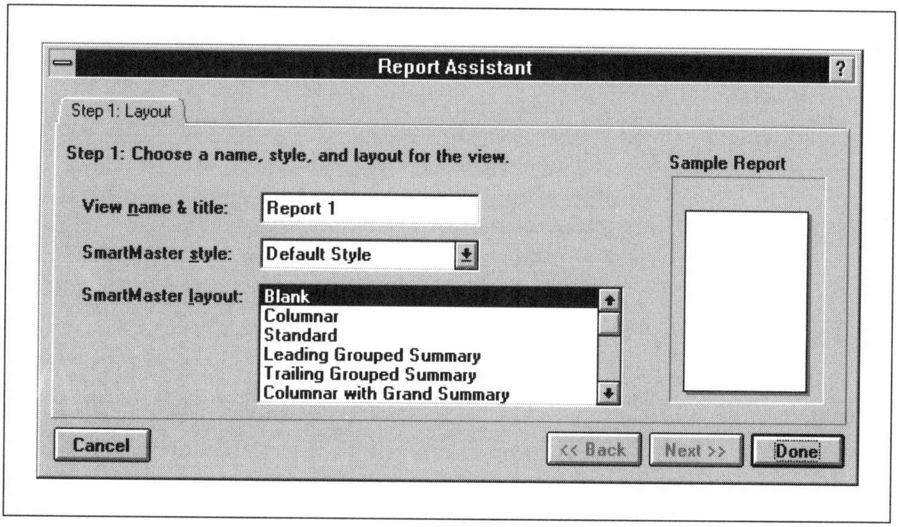

SmartMasters style pull-down list. (As you continue to work with Approach, you can explore the variety of formats available in SmartMasters.) Enter the name of the report in the View name & title text box. This will appear at the top of your report. Select the Next button (which is dimmed—unselected—until you make a choice). Your work area will display tabs (as described in the "Tabbed Work Area" section earlier in this chapter). You can jump between the three steps by clicking on any of the tabs in any order, but Approach will not create the report until options on all tabs have been selected.

Approach's Report Assistant asks us to identify the fields in the report. To keep this report simple, click on the Product Number field, then select the Add button. This adds the field from the Database fields list to the "Fields to place on view" list. We'll use a shortcut to add the Product Name to the report: Double-click on the Product Name field. If you add a field in error, select it from the "Fields to place on view" list and choose the Remove button, or double-click on the field name from the "Fields to place on view" list.

Click the Next button, or click on the Step 3 tab to move to the last step.

To calculate the number of records on the report, check the Calculate box. Sum is currently displayed, but we don't want to calculate a total. Instead, click on the down-pointing arrow and use the scroll box or up and down arrows in the scroll bar until Count is displayed. Count will count the records in our database based on the field we've selected. Click on Count.

We must also select the field. The file name to the right of "of field" identifies the current database. If we are using more than one database in Approach (a situation we discuss at length in Chapter 3), we would have to select from the databases available. In this example we have only defined one database, so there is no choice to make. Although it doesn't matter which field we count (because we are doing no calculations, simply counting), we have to choose one field or the Report Assistant won't create the report. Click on Product Number. Click on Done.

The Report Assistant goes to work, creating the report and displaying it in the Design environment. The report is shown in Figure 2.22. Notice that the report shows all your actual records, and it includes the total number of records (4). You can always tell what environment you

FIGURE 2.22

The new report in the Design environment

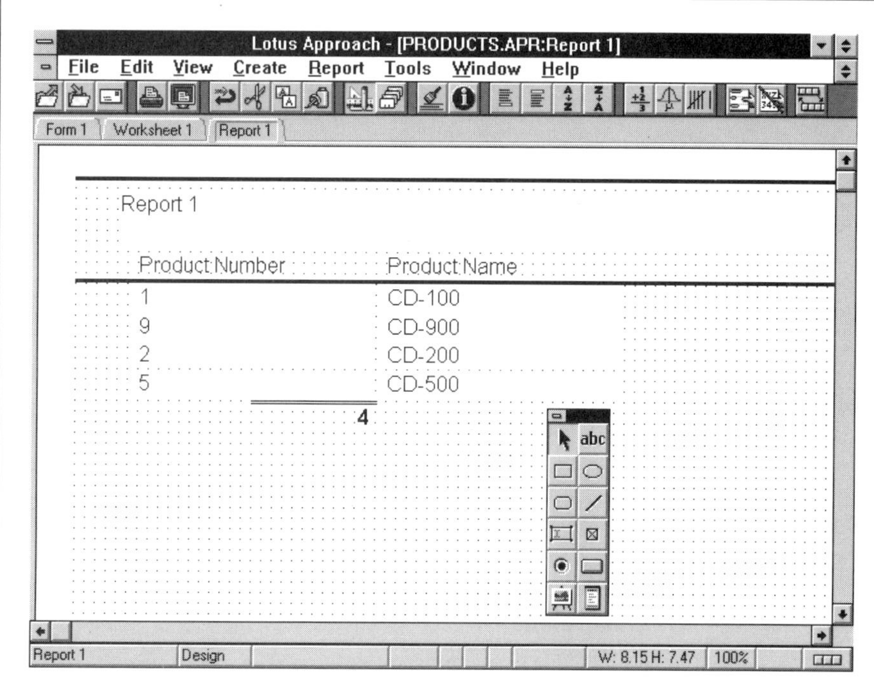

are in by looking at the second box in the Status bar. Incidentally, the current environment applies to all views. For example, if a report is in the Design environment, selecting any other form, worksheet, or report will also display it in the Design environment.

To see the result of the report with all database records in the Browse environment, click on the Browse icon in the SmartIcons toolbar, select View ➤ Browse, press Ctrl+B, or choose Browse from the second box in the Status bar. Approach then displays the report in the Browse environment, as shown in Figure 2.23.

The report has the less-than-meaningful name "Report 1." To change the name, double-click on it while in the Design environment. Approach will display a Text Editing box. Enter the new title, then click anywhere outside the box.

Here's a unique feature of Approach. Even though you are looking at a report of the data, you can actually edit your data from within the report. This is a handy way of making corrections when you spot errors. For example, if you notice that the stock on hand for product number

FIGURE 2.23

The new report in the Browse environment

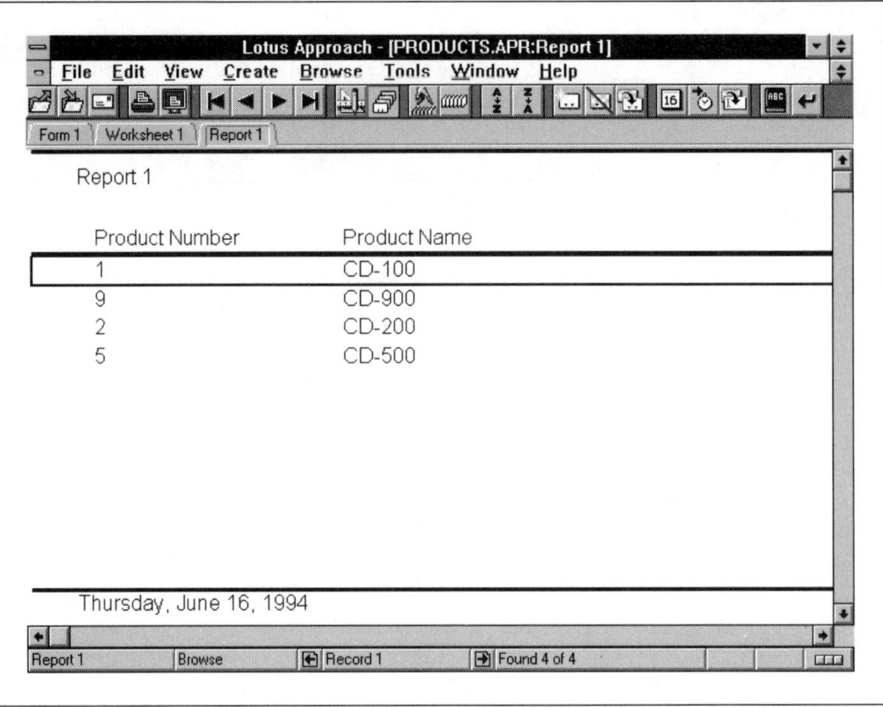

1 is wrong, you can click on the Unit field. Approach displays an Insertion Point cursor and you can press the Backspace key to erase the current value and enter the new value. This saves considerable time over moving to another form, finding the same record, and making the correction.

Notice that the report includes a line and the calculated number of records (4) only when you are in Design environment, shown in Figure 2.22 earlier in this chapter (and the Preview environment, which we haven't used yet, but which is useful when we're getting ready to print a form, as you'll learn in Chapter 15). When you are in the Browse environment, Approach displays only the records but no calculated fields.

▶▶ Getting Help

You can get help in several ways at any time within Approach:

- Select the Help menu option within the work area.
- Press F1.
- Click on the question mark (?) icon in the upper-right corner of many dialog boxes (see Figure 2.24).

The Approach Help System works exactly like help systems in other Windows applications. Consult your Windows User's Guide for an explanation of how to get help on particular topics, jump between topics, and close the Help System. You may wish to experiment with the Help System now. When you exit Help, you will be right back where you were before summoning help.

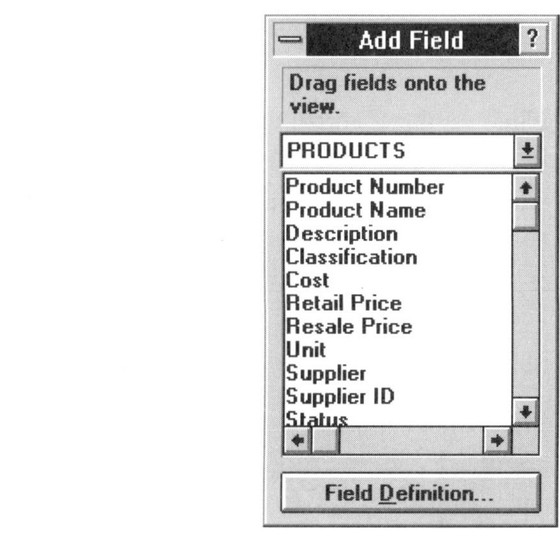

FIGURE 2.24 ▶

When you use dialog boxes, such as the Add Field dialog box shown here, Approach places a question mark (?) icon in the upper-right corner. Click on the icon to get context-sensitive help.

►► Save Your Work!

Before you leave Approach, be sure to save your work. Although the database records are automatically saved, Approach does *not* save the Approach file—the file that contains your form, worksheet, and report.

Select File ➤ Save Approach File and enter the name PRODUCTS. It is a good practice to save your .APR file every time you create or change the design of a view. You can click on the Save Approach file icon on the toolbar. You can open the Approach file when you start Approach again from the Welcome screen by selecting Open an existing file and selecting PRODUCTS, or from the main menu by selecting File ➤ Open and selecting PRODUCTS (be sure the file type is Approach; that is, it has an .APR extension).

►► Exiting Approach

To leave Approach and return to Windows, choose any of these methods:

- Click on the Control menu in the upper-left corner of the Approach window and select Close.
- Click on the Exit Approach icon in the SmartIcon toolbar; this icon is not part of the default toolbar, but may have been added by another Approach user.
- Press Alt+F4.
- Select File ➤ Exit.

If you've made any changes since the last time you saved your work, Approach will ask if you want to save them. Select Yes to save your work and No to exit Approach without saving your work.

►► Summary and a Look Ahead

In this chapter you've seen firsthand what Approach can do. You've created a new database, modified an existing form, displayed and sorted the data in a worksheet, and created a new report from scratch.

In Chapter 3 you'll learn how to create your own databases from scratch. You'll also learn how to modify the databases you create using templates.

▶ ▶ CHAPTER 3

Creating New Databases

▸▸ FAST TRACK

▶ *To set the field length* 83

enter the maximum number of characters for the field. Some field types, such as date, are predefined and cannot be changed.

▶ *To correct a mistake in your database definition* 89

delete a field by clicking in the gray box to the left of the Field Name, or by clicking in any entry in the table's row for the field you want to delete, then select the Delete button. To insert a field, click on any entry in the row of the field where you want the new field inserted and select the Insert button. The field where you've placed the cursor is moved down one row and a new, blank row is displayed.

▶ *To print a copy of your database definition* 89

select the Print button. Approach displays the Print dialog box. Select OK.

▶ *To save your database definition* 89

select File ➤ Save Approach File, press Ctrl+S, or click on the Save Approach File icon in the SmartIcons toolbar. If this is the first time you have saved your work, Approach displays the Save Approach File dialog box and asks for the drive, directory, file name, and database file format, and lets you set a password. Otherwise, Approach saves your work in the currently open Approach file.

▶▶ ***Y**ou* can use Approach to create databases for storing just about any data you can think of. You can start from scratch, or you can use a new feature introduced in version 3 called *templates*. Templates are model databases designed to include a majority of the fields you might want in a database. There are templates for creating customer lists, a household inventory, and employee lists, for example.

To get you started, we'll show you some tips on planning a new database, including how to decide on the types and number of fields. Then you'll learn how to cut down on the drudgery of creating a database by using Approach's templates. You'll also learn the four steps to creating a database from scratch: how to define database fields for each database, create a database file, specify field type, and specify field options. Finally, you'll learn how to save your changes so you can use your database in creating data entry forms, reports, cross tabulations (*crosstabs*), worksheets, mailing labels, mail merge letters, and charts.

Before jumping into the "hows" of creating or modifying existing databases, it's a good idea to take a step back and understand the components of a database.

▶▶ Parts of a Database

As you know, a database is made up of records, and a record is made up of fields. A database that stores attendance data about a company's truck drivers contains one *record* for each driver. Each record contains a trucker's name and address, his or her license number, the date he or she began working for the company, and so on. These individual pieces of data are stored in fields.

In this section you'll learn more about records and fields and see how Approach uses them to help you build and manage your data.

▶ Records

A database consists of *records*. A telephone company's database contains a record for each customer. For example, data about me (my name, address, and telephone number) comprises a database record, and information about my neighbor is stored in a different record.

You can think of a record as a collection of data related to or concerning a single thing. In an employee database, that "thing" is an employee. The employee database contains one record for each employee. The data from each employee is stored in a different record. The record containing data about me in the employee database is different from the data about any other employee, although many records may share some of the same values. For example, all employees may live in Seattle or Detroit, but no two records in the database contain information about me—there's only one record per employee.

▶ Fields

Records are made up of *fields*. Each field contains a single piece of data. In the telephone company's database record about me, there are several fields. One field contains my first name, another contains my last name, another contains my address, another contains the date service began, and a fifth contains my telephone number.

Each record in the database of a library contains data about a particular book. A record probably contains a field for the title of the book, its author, and its classification (either F for fiction or NF for nonfiction), and perhaps a Dewey Decimal System number if it is nonfiction.

Each field in a database record is characterized by its field name (first name, address, telephone number, and so on) and its field type (numeric, text, date, and others). We'll explain more about field types later in this chapter. You can assign fields a maximum length. For example, the Firstname field may have a length of 15, since you have determined that the first names of your customers never exceed 15 characters.

▶ Also Known As Rows and Columns

Sometimes you may hear the terms rows and columns used to describe records and fields (respectively). Approach can display records in a spreadsheet-like table, called a *Worksheet view*. Figure 3.1 shows such a view. The database consists of records, one per row, about a book (the title, author, date published, and so on). There is one record (row) for each book.

A column is equivalent to a field. One column contains the book's title, for example. Notice that the data in a column is always of the same data type. For example, the Author field is always alphanumeric (it may contain letters and numbers); entries in the Date Published field (column) are always dates.

Many computer users keep lists of data within a spreadsheet program and thus have built a database without even knowing it! The "2" in Lotus 1-2-3, a popular spreadsheet program, refers to its ability to serve as a database, although there are limits to the number of records

FIGURE 3.1 

Data in a database can be displayed in a spreadsheet-like table called a Worksheet view.

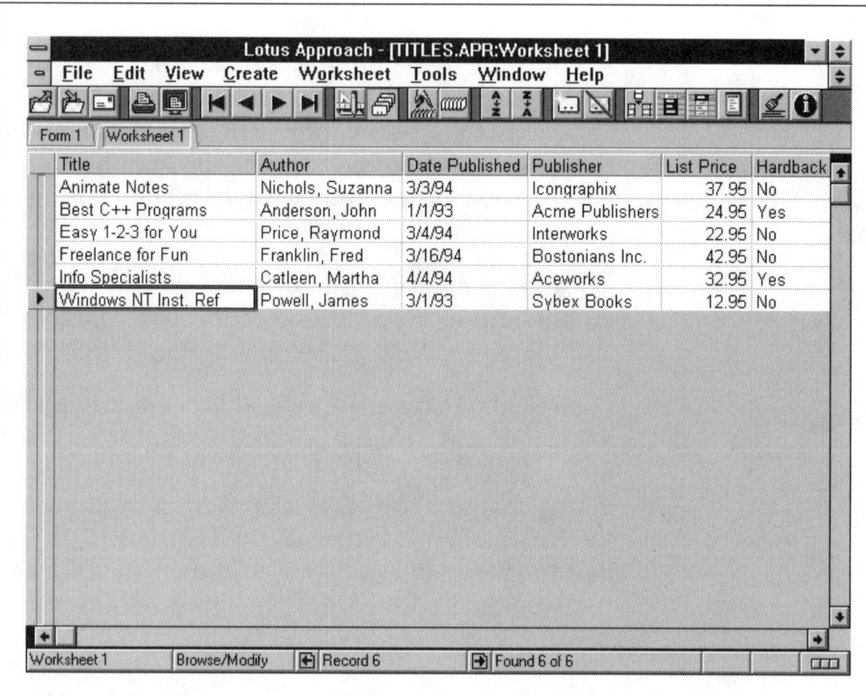

a spreadsheet can store (usually fewer than 10,000). A spreadsheet is useful as a small database, but pales when compared to Approach's ability to store and manage two *billion* records when using a Paradox database file type. If you typically use a spreadsheet to store your data, you may find that after you create a database in Approach you'll be happy working with Approach's Worksheet view.

►► Creating a New Database

There are two ways to create a new database: Use an Approach template or do all the work yourself. You make your choice at the Welcome screen. A partial list of templates and the Welcome screen are shown in Figure 3.2.

Templates serve as skeletons or outlines of the database you'll create. Templates contain field names and type, and specify field lengths for a "typical" database. If you use the templates provided in the Welcome screen, Approach copies the field definitions for you into a new database—one that you can name as you wish. For example, you can use the Authors template to create a database that stores data about writers, including fields for the first and last name, birthdate, and birthplace of each author. You'll save the actual database under a name you specify. Approach suggests the name AUTHORS, but you can just as

FIGURE 3.2 ►

The Welcome screen includes a list of database templates.

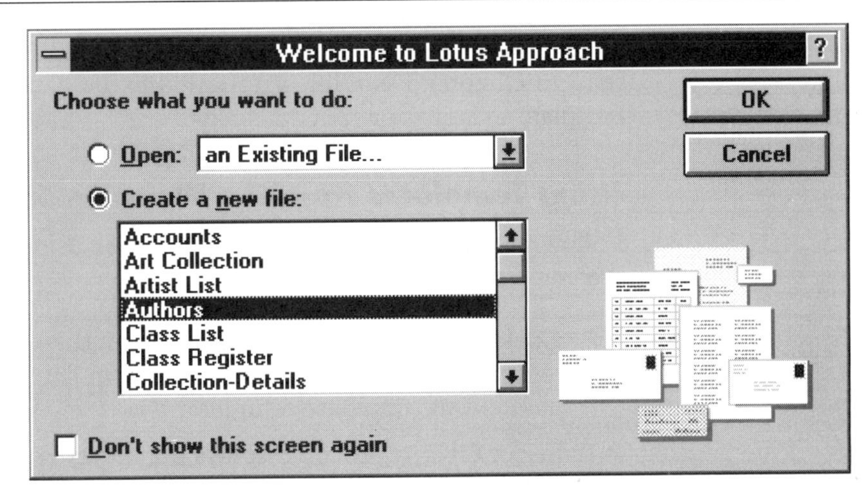

easily call your database WRITERS. If you need to create another database (to keep track of magazine editors, for example), you can once again use the Authors template, this time saving the database with a file name EDITORS.

Templates provide a quick way to create a new database. You don't have to accept everything the template creates, however. You can edit the layout of your new database by changing a field name, adding a field, or modifying the length of a numeric field. For instance, the Company Name field created from the Contacts-Names (Contact Name and Address) database template is only 30 characters long. However, if any of your contacts works for a company named Acme Widget Technology Corporation of America (which contains 45 characters, including spaces), you can either abbreviate the company name or expand the field length to 45, which will affect that field's length in all of the records in your database.

Alternatively, you may choose to create a database from scratch. To do so, you'll need to set up each field, give it a name, specify the type of data it can contain (a date, a number, or text, for example), specify a field length, and, if you wish, set up special conditions (such as requiring that a date field contain a value greater than or equal to the current system date). Fortunately, Approach makes this an easy process. All the steps are described here.

► Using a Template to Create a New Database

You have two options for beginning your new database using a template: Start at the Welcome screen or start with the Approach menu system. In Chapter 5 you'll learn to modify the database created from the template to suit your specific needs.

Using Templates from the Welcome Screen

Follow these steps to create a new database using a template from the Welcome dialog box (Figure 3.2):

1. Click on the Create a new file button, then select the database template you want from the pull-down list, or just click on the name of the database template.
2. Select OK. Approach displays the New dialog box, shown in Figure 3.3.

FIGURE 3.3

The New dialog box

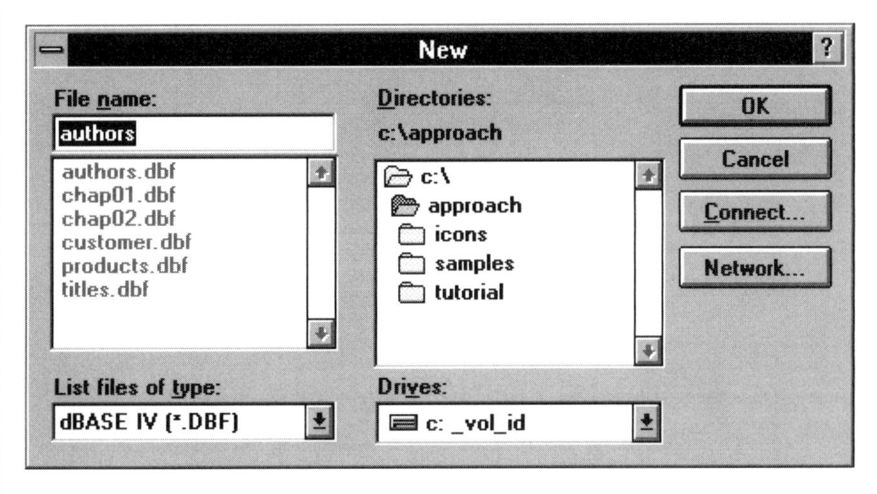

3. Select the destination drive and directory and the database file type (the file format that will be used to store the data). Then enter a name in the File name text box.
4. Select OK. Approach displays a default work area with two views defined—a Form view and a Worksheet view. A default work area for the Authors template for the Data Entry view, named Form 1, is shown in Figure 3.4.
5. Select File ➤ Save to save your database.

Using the File Menu to Create a New Database

Use these steps to create a new database from a template using the Approach menu system:

1. Select File ➤ New or click on the New File icon in the SmartIcons toolbar.

2. Approach displays the New dialog box, shown in Figure 3.3. Select the destination drive and directory and the database file. Then enter a name in the File name text box.

FIGURE 3.4

The default work area for a data entry form created using the Authors template

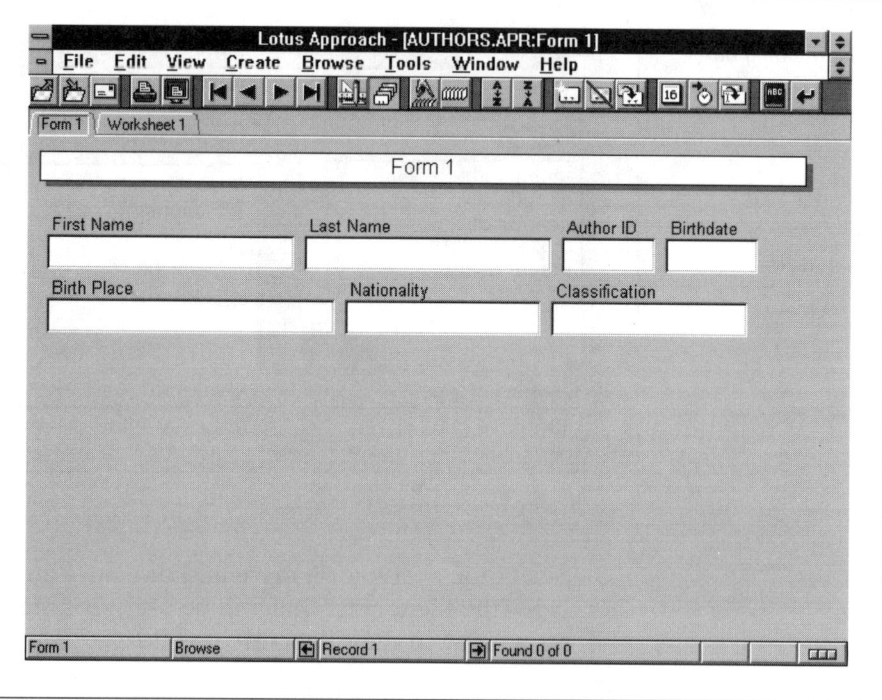

3. Select OK. Approach displays the Creating New Database dialog box, shown in Figure 3.5.
4. Select the template you want from the Template pull-down list. Approach displays a message that all current fields will be replaced. Click on Yes. Approach fills in the Field Name, Data Type, and Size columns.
5. If you have selected the wrong template, you may select another template, which will replace all entries in the table. You can also make individual changes to the fields in the list. When you are done, select OK.

►► **TIP**

The New File icon is not part of the standard SmartIcons toolbar but can be added. See Chapter 18 to learn how to modify toolbars.

FIGURE 3.5

The Creating New Database dialog box

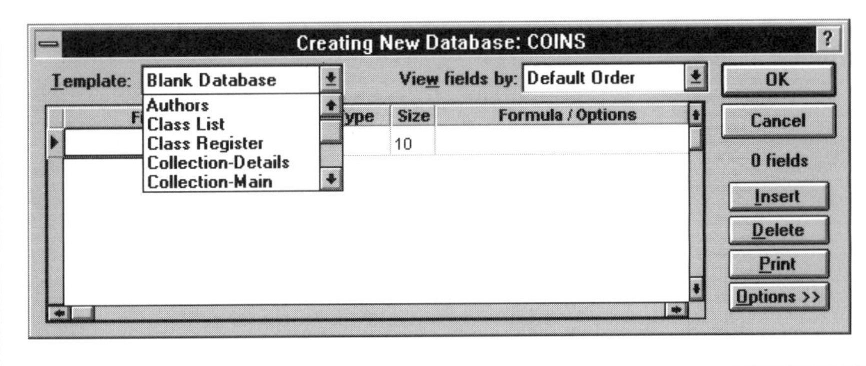

►► Four Steps to Creating a Database from Scratch

Although templates can save a lot of time, they are unsuitable for many database designs. For example, there is no template suitable for tracking the complex requirements of a hospital, the medical trials of a pharmaceutical company, or the location of cargo or equipment for a trucking company. For these and other specialized databases, you must create the database by defining each of the fields you'll need. Creating a database from scratch is a four-step process:

1. Create the database by defining the file: Specify the drive, directory, and database name, as well as the file format you want Approach to use to store the data.
2. Specify each field to be included in the database.
3. Specify a data type for each field.
4. Depending on the data type, you may need to specify the field's maximum size.

You may choose to specify special options, such as validation rules, which allow you to verify data entry, and default values, which allow you to enter data from a predefined list of values. These options are discussed in Chapter 5.

▸▸ Step One: Defining the Database File

The first step in creating a database is to tell Approach the name of the new file, where it will be stored, and the file type (file format) Approach should use to physically store the data on your hard drive.

To define a new database file from scratch (that is, without using a template):

1. Select Create a new file from the Welcome screen, then choose Blank Database. Alternatively, you may select File ➤ New from the Approach menu or click on the New File icon from the Smart-Icons toolbar.

▸▸ **NOTE**

The Welcome screen might not appear when you start Approach. If you selected Cancel from the Welcome screen during this session, there is no menu or keyboard shortcut to return you to it during the current session. You must exit Approach and start the program again. However, if you set the option in Approach to suppress displaying the Welcome screen, you must also open an existing database (any database will do), then select Tools ➤ Preferences. Be sure the Display tab is in front, and check the Welcome dialog check box so that an X appears. Select OK, then exit Approach and start the program again. Approach will then display the Welcome screen.

2. Approach displays the New dialog box, shown in Figure 3.3 earlier in this chapter. Select the drive, directory, and database file format you want to use. Then enter a new database file name in the File Name text box. Select OK.

3. Approach displays the Creating New Database dialog box (Figure 3.5) and displays the name of your database in the Title bar.

Instructions for filling in the database field table appear in the section "Let's Define Some Fields in Approach" later in this chapter.

▶ The "Creating New Database" Dialog Box

Use the Creating New Database dialog box, shown in Figure 3.6, to create a new database. The box contains a table with columns for defining each field's name, data type, and size (optional with some field types). You can also specify validation rules and default values for each field.

You can add new fields, insert a field between any two fields, delete a field, and print the database definition using this dialog box. When you change the database later (for example, to add a field), you'll use the Field Definition dialog box, shown in Figure 3.7, which is nearly identical to the Creating New Database dialog box. The only differences are

FIGURE 3.6 ▶

Fields filled in when creating a brand new database using the Creating New Database dialog box for a coin collection

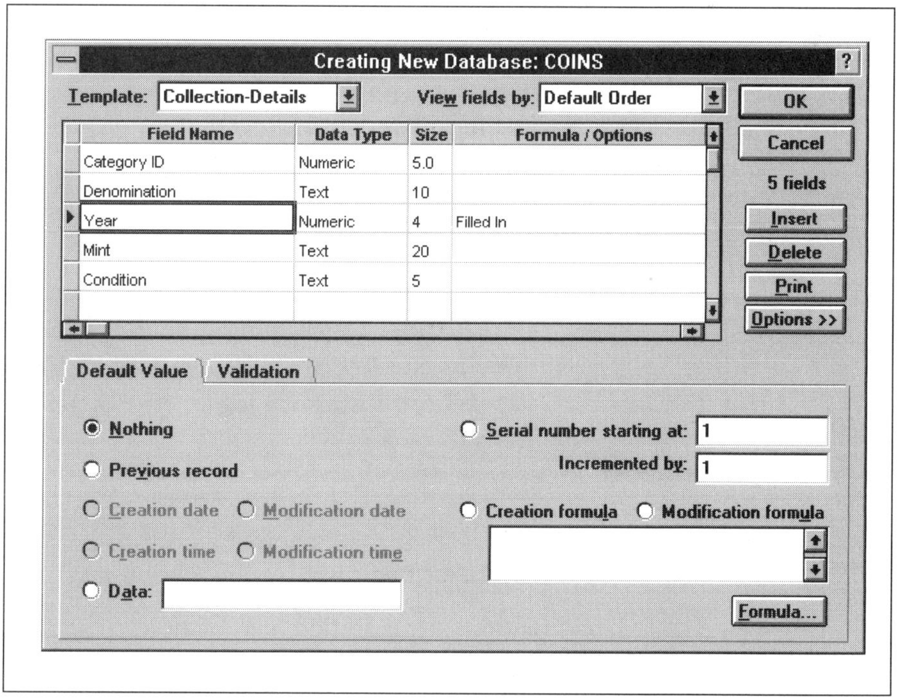

FIGURE 3.7 ▶

After you have created a database, you can modify the fields and field properties using the Field Definition dialog. You can learn more about modifying existing databases in Chapter 5.

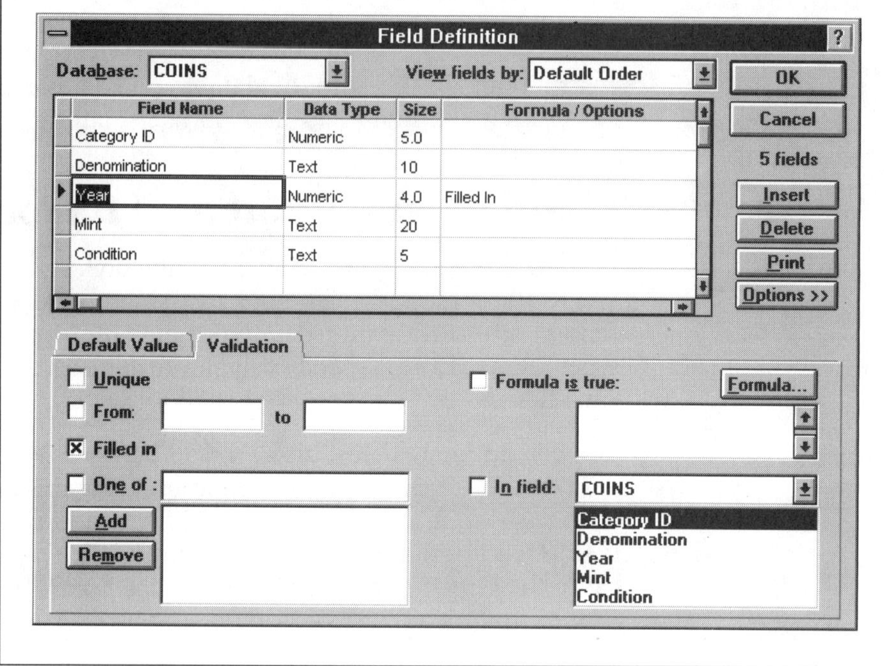

that the Field Definition dialog box has a different Title bar and its Database pull-down list shows only the databases that are part of the Approach file you are working with. You'll learn more about modifying existing databases in Chapter 5.

▸▸ **NOTE**

The order in which fields are defined is the order in which these fields will be displayed for all other tasks, such as the list of fields available for reports, mailing labels, and database joins. This order is called the default order.

Both Figures 3.6 and 3.7 show the options portion of the dialog boxes. These options will be discussed in Chapter 5.

The directions detailed here can be used to add, change, or delete fields when you create a new database or modify an existing one.

For each field, you must enter the field name and the field type, *at a minimum.* There are dozens of options you can add, which will be explained later. Some field types also require you to specify a field length.

To fill in the table, click in any of the cells of the table and enter the appropriate values. You'll learn more about filling in the table in the section "Let's Define Some Fields in Approach" later in this chapter.

►► Step Two: Naming the Fields

Each field within a database must have a unique field name. However, if your Approach file includes more than one database, the same field name may be used within each database. It is common to use the same field name in different databases that relate to each other. For example, if a PARTS database and an ORDERS database are part of the same Approach file, and each contains a field for the part number, it is common to have a field named Partnum in both the PARTS database and in the ORDERS database. In this way, an order containing a part number can reference the description for the part in the PARTS database. This association of two databases on the basis of a common field is called *joining* and is explained in Chapter 6.

In general, field names should describe the data stored within the field. For example, if you store a customer's first name in the Firstname field and the customer's last name in the Lastname field, you will know what each field contains. If you name the same fields Field1 and Field2, it will be more difficult (if not impossible) to quickly recall which field contains the customer's last name and which contains the first name.

When naming fields, keep these suggestions in mind:

- Avoid using special symbols, such as [and ~, since some file formats do not allow them.
- Instead of using a space in a field name, use the underscore (_), since some file formats do not allow spaces within a field name; for example, name a field Last_Name, not Last Name.
- Do not include a hyphen (-) in a field name, since including such fields in a calculation can be confusing—the hyphen in the name may be confused with the subtraction sign (–).

- Use numbers when needed, such as to indicate several fields that contain related information: AddressLine1, AddressLine2.

Some naming restrictions are imposed by the database format you select. For example, if you select the dBASE IV format (the default in Approach), field names must be 10 characters or less (7 characters for time and PicturePlus fields, which you will learn about in the next section). If you select Paradox, field names can be as long as 25 characters.

▸▸ Step Three: Defining the Field Data Types

The single piece of data in a field must belong to a specific data type. For example, a field may contain primarily letters and numbers, such as your name, your address, or the city you live in. You store this data in a text field. Likewise, another field might contain your annual salary or the amount of rainfall for a city; such information is stored in a numeric field. A numeric field also might be used in the library's database to keep track of the number of times a book has been checked out. Books that are not checked out frequently can be sold or discarded.

In addition to naming each field in a database, you must specify the type of data it contains. For example, you must tell Approach if the Birthdate field contains a number, a date, or text. You can probably guess that the Birthdate field contains a date, but Approach cannot. You must explicitly tell Approach the type of data the field will hold.

Data types help Approach *validate* the data, making sure that the data entered in a field is of the right type. For example, if you define a date field, you will not be able to enter text within that field. Furthermore, Approach makes sure that only valid entries are allowed. For example, Approach will not allow you to enter April 40, 1995 into a *date* field, although this would be allowed if you defined the field as a *text* field.

Field types are also used by Approach to reformat data for display. For instance, you can define the Hiredate field as a date type, then enter 11/1/94. Because Approach knows that the data entered must be a date, it can display the data in a variety of ways, such as November 1, 1994, 1 November 94, and so on. If Approach didn't know that the contents of the Hiredate field must be a date, it wouldn't be able to display the data in different formats. Although Approach can display the data in different formats, it stores the actual data in a standard format in the database file. Thus, the database contains 11/1/94, but Approach translates this data into November 1, 1994 if you so desire. (You'll learn how to do this in Chapter 8, which discusses format strings. A format string "MMMM", "DD", "YYYY" is used in this example.)

In some cases, Approach uses the data type to calculate how much space is required to store the data for that field. For example, date data types are always the same length in the file, and memo fields, which can be quite long, are stored in a separate physical file.

The data type is also required because Approach needs this information to export your data to another format. For example, suppose a coworker asks you to create a Paradox file containing the first name, last name, and birthdate of employees in your company, and you have already stored that data using the dBASE file format. To properly create a file that can be recognized by Paradox, Approach must know the field types of the data. In almost all cases, other database programs have the same requirement: They need to know the field name, its type, and its length (as you'll see in the section "Step Four: Selecting Field Lengths" later in this chapter).

▶ Field Types

The field types Approach supports are described in the following sections, listed alphabetically.

Boolean

Boolean fields contain only one of two values: Yes or No. You can also think of Boolean fields as containing the values true or false, or 0 or 1. However, by default, Boolean field values are displayed as Yes and No in Approach.

Boolean fields are useful for tracking a state of being in meeting or not meeting a particular condition or criterion. For example, in a real estate database that contains one record per home for sale, a Boolean field can be used to store whether the house has been sold. A Boolean field named Sold may contain Yes or No and would tell you if a house had been sold.

In a payroll database, you can use a Boolean field to store the type of employee: hourly or salaried. A Boolean field named Hourly can contain Yes (the employee is paid an hourly wage) or No (the employee is paid a fixed amount every pay period).

Calculated

A calculated field contains the result of a mathematical operation that uses other fields or constant values (such as 90%). You might use a calculated field to see how much an employee's annual salary would be if you gave him or her a 5% raise. The amount of the raise, a calculated field, can be computed by multiplying the value in the Salary field by a constant (0.05). Similarly, a calculated field can contain the sales tax amount for an order. If the database contains a field called Orderamt, you can create a calculated field, Taxamount, which can be calculated by multiplying the Orderamt field by a fixed percentage (a constant), such as 8.2%.

You can also define a calculated field to be the result of arithmetic performed on two fields within a record. For example, if an order record contains a Quantity field and a Price field, you can compute the total cost for that item by multiplying Quantity by Price and storing the result in a calculated field called Cost.

Calculated fields have a unique advantage: If a value in any of the fields used in the calculation changes, the value in the calculated field automatically changes. For example, if the customer calls to change the number of parts ordered, you will change the Quantity field. Approach will automatically recalculate the value in the Cost field by multiplying the value in the Price field by the new value in the Quantity field.

▶▶ **WARNING**

Calculated fields are limited in an important way: You cannot sort a database by calculated field. You can sort (rearrange) a database by the value in a text field, allowing you to list records for the value contained in a Lastname field, for example. You cannot, however, list records in a report in order by calculated field.

When you create a calculated field, Approach will ask you to define the formula. Formulas are explained in greater detail in Chapter 19. You must enter a valid formula before Approach will let you move to another field.

Date

A date field contains—you guessed it—a date. Date fields are particularly useful for storing information about events: the hire date of an employee, a couple's anniversary date, the date an invoice is due, the date of the last payment, or the date a patient was admitted to the hospital.

Although the way Approach stores the date in the database file is consistent, you can display the date in a variety of special ways, such as 9/23/93 or September 23, 1993.

You can also perform arithmetic on dates. For example, a record for a hospital patient can contain two dates: the date the patient was admitted to the hospital and the date the patient was discharged. You can use a simple formula to calculate the number of days the patient was in the hospital by subtracting the date admitted from the date discharged, then adding one to the result. Formulas are discussed at greater length in Chapter 19.

Memo

Think of a memo field as a very long text field. A memo field is often used to contain free-form notes about an employee, hospital patient, invoice, experiment, order, customer, or whatever the record is about. When you place a memo field on a data entry form, the memo field looks like a large text area, similar to a miniature word processor. Memos store whatever text you enter. The format you select applies to all text within the memo field—you can't select a word within the memo field and change it to boldface, for example.

A memo field can contain virtually unlimited text (up to 5,000 characters if you use the dBASE III+ format, and 64,000 characters if you use the dBASE IV or FoxPro 2.1 file formats). Use a memo field when you have a variable amount of text data, such as comments, notes, driving directions—anything with a length that can vary by record. Long memos cannot be accessed by dBASE III+ or IV. See the Approach User's Guide for specific limitations.

Numeric

Numeric fields keep track of numbers, such as hourly wage, price, credit limit, quantity, or account numbers. Numeric fields can contain negative or positive values: A Temp (temperature) field can contain the low temperature of a city for a particular day, for example, whether it's 10 below zero (–10) or 80 degrees above zero (80).

Numeric fields can be integers (whole numbers) or can contain fractional parts. When you define a numeric field, you must tell Approach how many digits the number will have, including how many digits in the number appear to the right of the decimal. Numeric fields can be used to store currency amounts ($4.95) and may contain only fractional parts (0.125).

You must define a field as numeric if you will use it in a calculation (subtotal or total on a report, or as a field in a formula for a calculated field, for example).

Although numeric fields can contain currency values (such as $4.95), Approach stores only the 4.95 portion of the value. By using formatting characters, you can display the value with the dollar sign. You'll learn about formatting in Chapter 8.

PicturePlus

A PicturePlus field can contain just about anything—a sound file, a graphic image, a complete word processed document, or a portion of a spreadsheet. You can fill a PicturePlus field using Copy and Paste (copying from another application, pasting that data in the PicturePlus field) or using the Paste Special command to insert an object using its file name. You can Crop (cut down) and Resize PicturePlus fields, but you cannot perform operations on these fields. For example, you cannot search for text contained within an object placed in a PicturePlus field. PicturePlus fields in dBASE and Paradox files cannot be viewed using dBASE or Paradox 3.5.

Text

Text fields are the most common field types in an Approach database. Alphanumeric characters (letters, numbers, and special symbols such as $#@&*) can be stored in a text field. You can create text fields up to 254 characters long. If you have text longer than 254 characters, use the memo field type.

Examples of text fields include customer name, address, job title; part number, part description, vehicle make and model; or book title.

The term "text" field is somewhat misleading. Text need not consist of only letters. An address, such as 123 Main Street, is text, even though it contains a numeric portion within it. You cannot perform any math on the numeric portion of a text field, however.

Time

Time fields contain time, maintained to the hundredth of a second. As with dates, you can perform arithmetic on two time fields to calculate the elapsed time of an event.

Variable

Variable fields are used to hold temporary values and are most often found in macros. Variables can also be used in formulas or when searching for records. Variable fields use a temporary storage area, so that although you define them as part of the database, they are actually not part of the physical database file that you save. Instead, variables defined in your database become available (and are automatically initialized) when you open the Approach file. A variable field can, however, be printed on a report or displayed on a form.

Variables are an advanced feature and are described in greater detail in Chapter 16, which discusses macros.

▸▸ Step Four: Setting Field Lengths

In addition to selecting the field type for each field, you may also have to specify the field's length. If in the Creating New Database or Field Definition dialog box the Size column says *Fixed*, you cannot change it—the size is predetermined by Approach. Otherwise, you can specify how many characters or numbers the field can contain. The field length tells Approach how long the largest entry will be, and is used to determine how much disk space must be used to store a field's value. A record with a City field defined as 10 characters long will take less hard disk space than a record with a City field defined as 15 characters long.

▶▶ **WARNING**

After you have defined the fields for a database record, you can change the name of a field, its type, or the field length. The length of a field can usually be increased without affecting your data, unless, of course, the field is already at its maximum length. However, if you choose to decrease the length of a field, you run the risk of losing data that must be shortened to meet the new length. You'll learn how to change the length of a field in the next section.

Field lengths are subject to the maximum field length supported by the database format you're using. For example, if you want Approach to create a database using the dBASE IV file format, which is the default Approach suggests, a text field can be up to 254 characters long. If you select the Paradox file format instead, a text field can contain up to 255 characters.

▶▶ **TIP**

When deciding on a field length, determine the length of the longest value you need to store. If most entries in the field will be short, and only one or two entries will contain long values, determine if the longer values can be abbreviated in order to use a smaller field length.

In some database formats, you don't even have to specify the field length for most fields. For example, if you select the Paradox file format, you need only specify the field length for a text field. Furthermore, some field types don't have a length: A Boolean field can contain only a Yes or No value, so Approach automatically knows how long the field must be.

▶▶ **WARNING**

Field length can be tricky for numeric fields. You can specify a length for a numeric field, but then Approach lets you enter a numeric value of *any length* in the field. When the cursor leaves the field, Approach reformats the value and truncates any extra digits. For example, if the Cost field (a numeric field) is specified as having three digits to the left of the decimal and two digits to the right and you try to enter 1234.567, Approach will beep when you type the "4" because that is the fourth digit in a field that can only contain three digits to the left of the decimal. However, you can enter the "567" portion without a warning beep from Approach. When you leave the field, Approach will truncate the value .567 to .56. (If you need to round the number, you'll need to use the *Round* function, described in Chapter 19.)

▶▶ Let's Define Some Fields in Approach

You can reorder the fields within a database after the database has been created, but it may take much more time to rearrange larger databases, so add the fields to your database in logical order, such as last name, first name, address, city, state, zip, rather than alphabetically. Fields can be added later as you work with the database; they are typically added to the *end* of the database.

Approach lets you select the display order of fields in a database, which does not affect the physical structure of the database—just choose the order you want from the View fields by pull-down list in either the Create New Database or Field Definition dialog box. Approach will also let you drag fields in the table to create a new field order. Click on the gray box to the left of the field name and drag the field to the desired position. (Such a change to the database structure may affect other

Approach files, however, and possibly the disposition of a coworker who uses the same database files [such as a dBASE file] and expects the original field order.)

While you are still working in the Creating New Database dialog box, shown in Figure 3.6 earlier in this chapter (or using the Field Definition dialog box if you are modifying an existing database, shown in Figure 3.7), follow these steps to define database fields for a new database:

1. Click on a cell in the Field Name column and enter the name of the field.

▸▸ **NOTE**

Limitations on field names vary by the database file format used when creating the file. Field names are limited by the type of database file format used. dBASE and FoxPro field names can be 32 characters long. However, long field names will be truncated to 10 characters when the database is used by an application other than Approach, such as dBASE or Excel. Paradox field names can be up to 25 characters long for text, numeric, and date fields, and up to 18 characters long for time, memo, Boolean, and PicturePlus fields. Appendices B, C, and D of the Approach User's Guide provide specific limitations for field names depending on the database file format used.

2. Press Tab to move to the Data Type column. To display the available field types, press Alt+↓, or press ↑ or ↓ to cycle through the choices. As a shortcut, type the first letter of the field type you want, such as N for numeric, T for Text, or T again for Time.
3. If a field type's length, or size, can be defined, an entry area will appear to the right of the Data Type column. If this Size box contains the word "Fixed," proceed to step 5.
4. Press the Tab key. Enter the maximum field length. If the field is a numeric field and the file format is dBASE or FoxPro, enter the number of digits to the left of the decimal point (to a maximum of 19), a decimal point, and the number of digits to the right of the

decimal point (to a maximum of 15). Note, however, that the total number of digits cannot exceed 19. Thus, if you use a size of 5.3 to indicate five digits to the left of the decimal and three digits to the right of the decimal, the total number of digits (5+3) is less than 19, so the size is acceptable. Ten digits to the left and ten digits to the right of the decimal would be more than 19 and would be unacceptable. If you specify too few digits to the right of the decimal point, field input will be truncated. For example, if you enter 123.456 in a numeric field defined with a length of 2 digits to the right of the decimal, the entry will be truncated to 123.45 and stored in the database using this shortened value.

5. Formulas and options appear in the fourth column in this table if they have been defined. Formulas and options are described in Chapter 5. Click on the Field Name cell in the next row to continue.
6. Repeat steps 1 through 4 until all fields are defined. If you made a mistake, correct it before proceeding (see "Making Corrections to Your Database Definition" later in this chapter).
7. Select OK. Approach creates the database and displays two default views—a data entry form and a Worksheet view.

Figure 3.8 shows a completed Field Definition dialog box with several fields defined. Note that for numeric fields the length is represented as a decimal value. For example, 7.2 means there are seven digits to the left of the decimal stored in the field value and up to 2 digits to the right of the decimal.

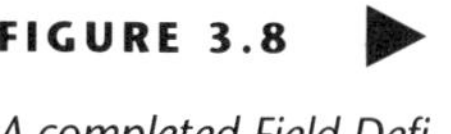
FIGURE 3.8

A completed Field Definition dialog box

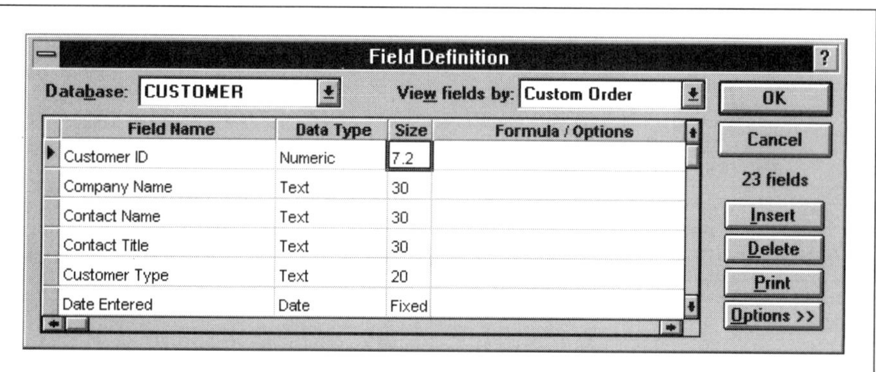

▶▶ **NOTE**

If you are using a Paradox file format, Approach displays the Choose Key Field dialog box (see Figure 3.9) after Step 7. The dialog box prompts you to define the *key*. A key must contain a unique value, such as a part number or social security number, and can be made up of one or more fields. Select the field(s) whose values will be unique, select Add Key Field, and then select OK.

FIGURE 3.9 

The Choose Key Field dialog box is used when you create databases in the Paradox file format.

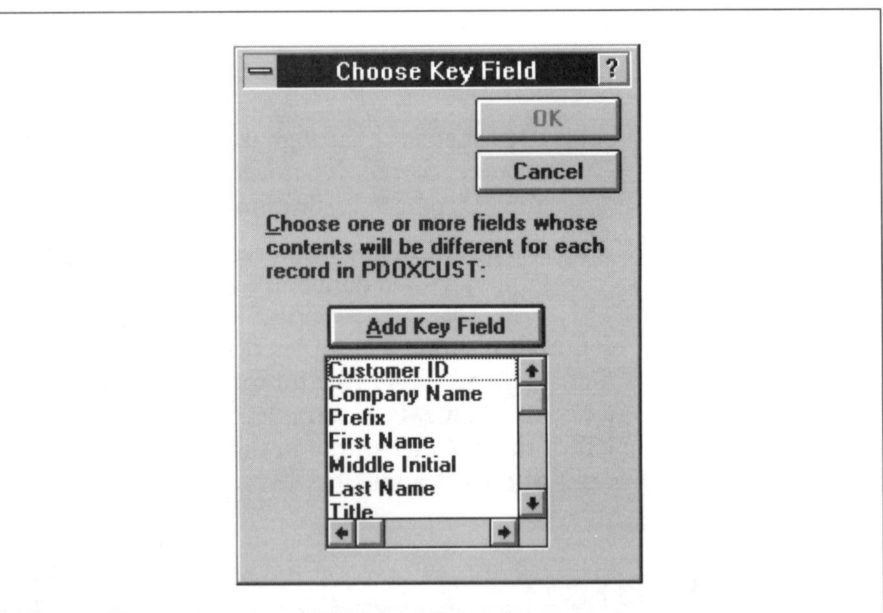

▶▶ **NOTE**

You can print your database definition by selecting the Print button at any time. This option provides a printed report of all the fields and the options you've selected for each field.

►► Making Corrections to Your Database Definition

If you make a mistake while you are creating a new database (or modifying an existing one), you can correct your errors before you save your work.

To delete a field in either the Create New Database or Field Definition dialog box, click in the gray box to the left of the Field Name or in any entry in the table's row for the field you want to delete, then select the Delete button.

To insert a field, click on any entry in the row of the field where you want the new field inserted and select the Insert button. The field where you've placed the cursor is moved down one row and a new, blank row is displayed. You can then redefine your fields using your corrections.

►► Printing Your Database Definition

To create a printed copy of your database definition from the Creating New Database dialog box (when creating a new database) or the Field Definition dialog box (when modifying an existing database), select the Print button. Approach displays the Print dialog box. Select OK.

►► Save Your Changes

While Approach will automatically save changes to the data in your database, it does *not* automatically save the Approach file you are working with. To avoid losing your work, you should save the Approach file frequently. (A good rule of thumb is to save the file after every 10 changes, or every 15 minutes, whichever occurs first.)

To save your Approach file, select File ➤ Save Approach File, press Ctrl+S, or click on the Save Approach File icon in the SmartIcons toolbar. If this is the first time you have saved your work, Approach displays the Save Approach File dialog box; and asks for the drive, directory, file name, and database file format; *and lets you set a password. Otherwise, Approach saves your work in the currently open Approach file. The Save Approach File dialog box is shown in Figure 3.10.*

FIGURE 3.10 ►

The Save Approach File dialog box

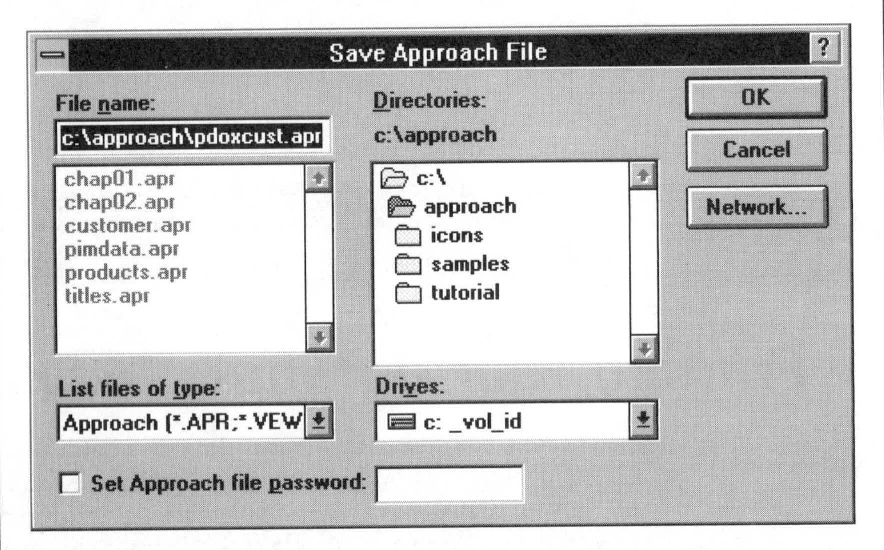

►► Summary and a Look Ahead

In this chapter you've learned about templates, the Approach shortcut for creating new databases based on a skeleton of fields and field types. You also learned about the four steps to creating a database:

1. Specify the drive, directory, database name, and the file format you want for the data file.
2. Specify each field to be included in the database.

3. Specify a data type for each field.
4. Specify a field length, if needed.

You also learned about the variety of field types available in Approach.

In subsequent chapters, you'll learn how to work with data in files that were created using a program other than Approach. For example, a coworker or service bureau may give you important census data in a dBASE file. You want to read this file and work with the data it contains even though the file wasn't created using Approach. Chapter 4 shows you how easy it is to do this.

Whether you create the file from scratch or use Approach to read the data stored in a non-Approach database, Approach offers some powerful features that ensure the data you enter is in a correct format—or at least a reasonable one. Chapter 5 shows you how to modify the design of a database, no matter what its source.

As your needs change, your database will need to keep pace with your new requirements. Approach lets you modify your database design by adding or removing fields, changing their field type, and adding formulas to perform calculations for you automatically. You'll learn about these features in Chapter 5.

▶ ▶ CHAPTER 4

Working with Existing Files

▸▸ FAST TRACK

▸ ***To open an existing Approach file using the Welcome screen*** **99**

choose any of the last five Approach files you used by pressing ↓ until the file name is displayed, then select OK, or press Alt+↓ to display the drop-down list, then select the file. If the file is not in the list of the most recently used files, select the Open option named "an Existing File..." and select OK, then choose the drive and directory that contains the Approach file you wish to open—be sure the "List files of type" option shows Approach. (If you want to use the Approach file in read-only mode, check the Read-only box.) Select the file name from the file list, or enter it's name (with or without the .APR file extension). If the database requires a password, Approach will ask you for it. Approach opens the Approach file and displays the form, report, crosstab, or other view that was active when you last used the file.

▸ ***To open a database created by another program, such as dBASE or Paradox*** **104**

use the Welcome screen and select Open and choose the "an Existing File..." option. Click OK. Choose the drive and directory that contains the database file you wish to open. Be sure the "List files of type" option displays the file type for the database you wish to open. If you want to open the database in read-only mode, check the Read-only box. Select a database file, then select OK. (If you selected a Paradox database, Approach needs to find a key field within that database.)

▶ *To create a database and an Approach file from spreadsheet data* 114

use the Welcome screen to select the file, or choose File Open and enter the spreadsheet file name (be sure the "List files of type" option displays the file type for the spreadsheet you wish to open, such as Excel or 1-2-3). Select OK. To select a named-range from a 1-2-3 spreadsheet, including a single sheet, select the sheet name or named range, from the Select Range dialog box. Check the "First row contains field names" check box if you want Approach to use the text in the first row of the spreadsheet or spreadsheet range as the field names. Select OK. In the Convert To dialog box, select the drive and directory for the database file. Select the database file type from the "List files of type" drop-down list. Enter a file name for the database file in the File Name box, then choose OK.

▶ *To save an Approach file* 117

select File ➤ Save Approach, press Ctrl+S, or click on the Save Approach File icon in the SmartIcons toolbar. Approach displays the Save Approach File dialog box, if you are saving the Approach file for the very first time. Enter the drive, directory, and file name in the appropriate text boxes. To set a password for the file, check the Set Approach file password box and enter the password in the text box to the right. If you set a password, you will have to enter this password when you open the file. Select OK.

►► **R*ecall*** that Approach uses two (or more) files when working with your data. The actual data is stored in one or more database files, and information about the forms, reports, and other views is stored in a separate Approach file. In Chapter 2, you created a database in dBASE IV file format and then created a matching Approach file (with the .APR extension) to save the form, worksheet, and report that organized and presented the dBASE file data.

Because data can be stored in a variety of formats—from dBASE and Paradox to Excel spreadsheets—this chapter focuses on how Approach can work with existing databases from other sources. For example, you may need to use Approach and a dBASE or Paradox file that was not created in Approach to generate a report. With Approach, it's quite simple to do, and you'll learn how to do it in this chapter.

If you intend to create and use databases only from within Approach, you can safely skip this chapter. Then, when you need to use data from another source, you can come back and learn how easy it is to use Approach and "foreign" file formats.

►► *Create a New Approach File from an Existing Database*

You can create new Approach files by opening existing database and Approach files, renaming those files, and saving them. It's that simple. Approach can even use files created in other file formats.

Approach can read and write to a variety of database file formats, including dBASE III+ and dBASE IV, Paradox 3.5 and 4.0, FoxPro 2.1, Oracle SQL, Microsoft/Sybase SQL Server, IBM DB2, Access, and

Lotus Notes. You must have the appropriate ODBC driver installed if you are using an ODBC data source.

NOTE

ODBC, which stands for Open Database Connectivity, is a standard facility within Windows to access data from other file formats. ODBC is explained in greater detail in the Approach User's Guide.

The Approach file contains both the views and the names of the database files used with the views. For example, the Approach files contain the instructions for how forms and reports are to be displayed and the names of the databases that supply the data presented in the forms or reports. An Approach file can contain up to 255 such database names, although a much smaller number is typical for most Approach files. Although you do not have to save the Approach file associated with any database file you use, it is usually a smart idea to do so, especially if you'll use the database file again—even if the file will contain different records. If you don't save the Approach file, you will need to redefine the views (forms, reports, and so on) you need to organize your data. You can view information such as the date and time of your last revision using the File ➤ Approach File Info command.

The database files used by views in the Approach file are always related to each other in some way, and are thus said to be *joined*. Joining multiple databases is more fully explained in Chapter 6.

Approach Files and Databases Act as a Team

Databases and Approach files work as a team. At least one Approach (.APR) file and one database file exist as a pair: When you open an existing Approach file, the program automatically looks for the associated database file(s). When you open an existing database for which there is no corresponding Approach file, Approach will create one.

If you create a new database in Approach, Approach creates a matching .APR file with the same name you gave the database, except for the .APR extension. You saw this in Chapter 2: You created the PRODUCTS.DBF file and when you saved your form and worksheet, Approach suggested the name PRODUCTS.APR.

When you ask Approach to "open a file," it defaults to the Approach file, not the database file, even when you are opening a foreign database for the first time. However, you can tell Approach to open the database file instead of the Approach file, although this is less frequently done. You generally work with the Approach file because it is your tool for organizing and viewing the data in the database.

The various situations in which you'll use files in Approach are described throughout this chapter. The following list summarizes what Approach can do if you initiate a specific file command.

When You Do This	Approach Does This
Specify the name of the Approach file	Approach opens the file and looks for the databases. If they are not found, Approach returns an error message.
Specify the name of a database, text, or spreadsheet file	If you tell Approach to open an existing database file (whether it was saved in a standard database file format or another file format, such as text or spreadsheet) and the Approach file exists, the .APR file is opened automatically. Otherwise, Approach creates a corresponding Approach file using the same file name as the database you're opening, with the file extension .APR. It will also create a default form and worksheet.
Ask Approach to create a new file	Approach creates both the database file and the Approach file. You can specify the format for the database file, such as dBASE, FoxPro, or Oracle SQL.

▶▶ How to Open an Existing Approach File

It's easy! Your Approach file contains definitions of the views as well as the list of databases used by these views. When you want to work with an existing database and an associated Approach file exists, the program will ask you for the name of the .APR (Approach) file. Approach then searches the contents of this file to find the names of the databases that are used in the views (reports, forms, crosstabs, mailing labels, and so on) and opens each view as well as each database.

When you install Approach and run it for the first time, the program displays the Welcome dialog box shown in Figure 4.1. You can open an existing database using this dialog box or, if it is not displayed, using the Approach menu system.

FIGURE 4.1 ▶

The Welcome screen

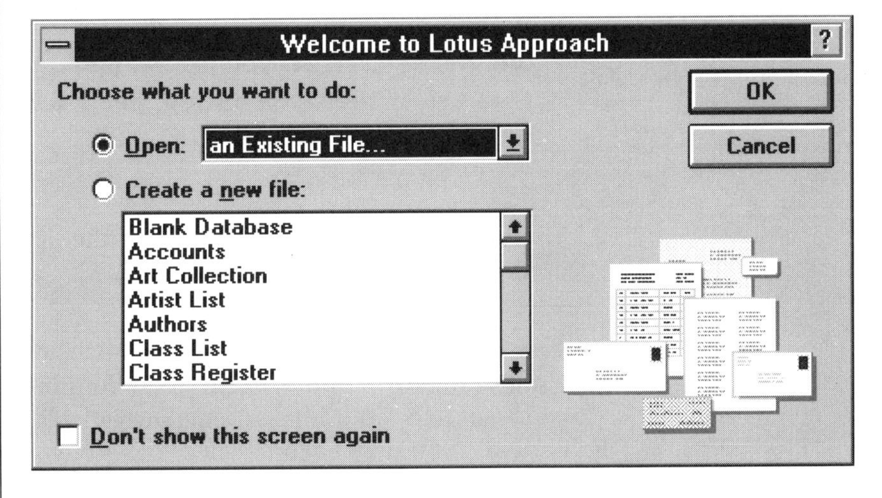

▶ Using the Welcome Screen

Use these steps to open an Approach file from the Welcome screen:

1. If you want to open an Approach file that was one of the last five Approach files you worked with, use any of the following options to select the file. Otherwise skip to step 2.
   - Press ↓ until the file name is displayed and select OK.
   - Press Alt+↓ or click the right pointing arrrow to the right of the "Open" drop-down list. To display the drop-down list; select the file by highlighting it with the mouse, pressing ↓ until it is highlighted, or entering its file number (from 1 to 5); then press Enter or click on OK.

   Now skip to Step 7.

▶▶ TIP

If you know the number of the database (typically, it will be number 1 if you are reopening the last open file), select the Open option, press Tab, and enter the file number (1 through 5).

2. To open an existing file that is not in the list of the most recently used files, be sure the Open option reads "an Existing File" and select OK.
3. Approach displays the Open dialog box shown in Figure 4.2. Choose the drive and directory that contains the Approach file you wish to open if it is not currently displayed. If your file is on a network, you may need to select the Network option and connect to the network that contains your file before you select the drive and/or directory.
4. Be sure the "List files of type" option shows Approach (.APR). This is the default.
5. If you want to use the Approach file in read-only mode, check the Read-only box. Read-only mode is useful when you want to display a database in a form or run a report but want to ensure that you don't accidentally change the form or report layout, delete a

FIGURE 4.2

The Open dialog box

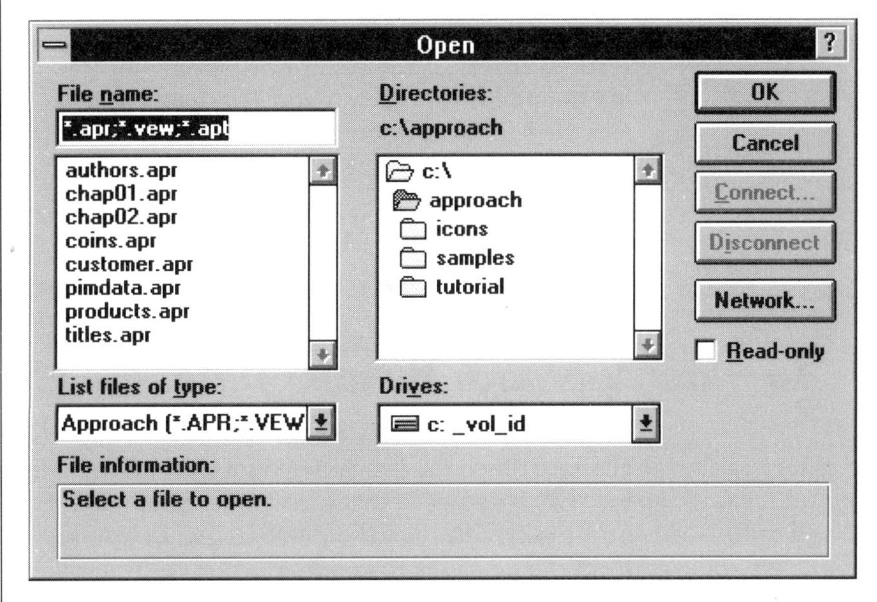

view, or add a new view. This option is in effect until you reopen the file, either during this session or when you use Approach at a later time.

6. Select the file name from the file list, or enter its name (with or without the .APR file extension). If you are opening a file from a previous version of Approach or use Lotus Notes, your file may have the extension .VEW or .APT instead. (The .VEW file is created by previous versions of Approach, while an .APT file is created when you attach an .APR file to Lotus Notes.) Select OK.
7. If the database requires a password, Approach will ask you for it. If you do not enter the correct password, Approach will not open the file. For more information about passwords, see Chapter 18.
8. Approach opens the Approach file and displays the form, report, crosstab, or other view that was active when you last used the file.

▶ Using the File Menu

If the Welcome screen is not displayed, you can open an existing file using the main Approach menu. To open the file, select File ➤ Open, select the File Open icon from the SmartIcons toolbar, or press Ctrl+O. Proceed from Step 4 above.

If the Approach file you want to open is one of the last five you have worked with, select the File menu and choose the number (1 through 5) shown in the pull-down list associated with the file you want.

▶ How Approach Handles Database Changes

Sometimes the database connected to the Approach file will have changed since the last time you used it. For example, you may be working with a database that a coworker produced. He or she has control over the structure of the database, while you are only reading the data from the database to generate a report. Your coworker, however, may need to change a field, delete a field, or even rename a field to suit his or her new requirements. Sometimes your coworker will add a field. If any of these changes are made, when you open the database again Approach will compare what it knows about the database and the field used on its forms with the database it finds. If there is a discrepancy, Approach will open the Field Mapping dialog box automatically (select Yes in the alert box displayed to continue), which is shown in Figure 4.3. When what Approach knows about the database(s) and what the database(s) actually looks like are out of sync, Approach uses the Field Mapping feature to rectify the discrepancy.

The Field Mapping dialog box lets you select a field in an Approach file and associate it with a field in your database. Arrows between a field in your Approach file and a field in the database indicate that the field has been mapped.

Use these steps to map fields in an Approach file to those in your database(s):

1. Click in the center column between the unmapped fields. An arrow will be displayed to indicate that the fields have been mapped. If you mapped a field by mistake, click on the arrow to unmap it.

FIGURE 4.3 

The Field Mapping dialog box

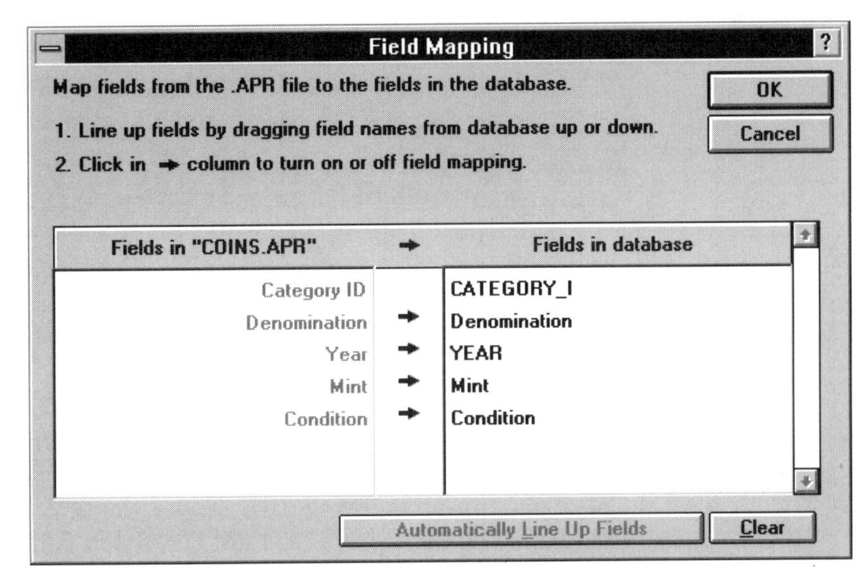

2. The names in "Fields in database" may be different from those in original database (for example, the field has been renamed or deleted and another field added in its place). If the field you want to map is out of order in "Fields in database," click on that field name and drag it to the new location.
3. Repeat Step 2 until all fields you want to use on the views are properly mapped.
4. Select OK.

NOTE

Not all fields must be mapped. However, if any of the unmapped fields appear on a view, such as a form or report, the field will be empty, since it no longer points to a valid database field. Use the Design environment to place fields from your database on a form. See Chapter 7 for details.

▶▶ TIP

To remove all mappings and start over, select the Clear button in the Field Mapping dialog box. To quickly map fields with the same field names, select the Automatically Line Up Fields button. This button is only available if none of the fields has been mapped.

▸▸ Opening a Database Directly

Approach can open an existing database file created by another application, such as dBASE, Paradox, Access, or FoxPro. For example, you may be given a dBASE file to work with—a coworker has compiled a list of part numbers using dBASE and wants you to run a report from the data. The dBASE file was not created in Approach or used in Approach before, so there is no corresponding Approach file to be opened. In this circumstance, you can open the database file and Approach will automatically create an Approach file and two default views.

- Form 1 contains a field on a data entry form for each field in the database.
- Worksheet 1 is a spreadsheet-like table for the database, one column per field and one row per record.

This is quite different from importing a database, which many competing database programs require you to do. When you import a database, you actually create a *copy* of the database, then make your changes to the copy of the database. When you want to give the file back to a coworker, you have to save your file into another file format, a process called exporting a file.

Approach, in contrast, lets you work with the original database file in its current format. No intermediate copy is needed.

Follow these steps to open a database and use it in Approach for the first time:

1. From the Welcome screen, select Open and choose the "an Existing File" option. Click OK. If the Welcome screen is not displayed, select File ➤ Open, click on the File Open icon in the

SmartIcons toolbar, or press Ctrl+O from the main menu. Approach displays the File Open dialog box shown in Figure 4.2 earlier in this chapter.

2. Choose the drive and directory that contains the database file you wish to open, if it is not currently displayed. If your file is on a network, you may need to select the Network option and connect to the network that contains your file before you select the drive and/or directory. (The Connect and Disconnect buttons may appear if you are connected to an IBM DB2-MDI server.)
3. Be sure the "List files of type" option displays the file type for the database you wish to open. By default the option is Approach, which is incorrect in this situation. Frequently used choices include dBASE, Paradox, Access, and Excel.
4. If you want to open the database in read-only mode, check the Read-only box. Read-only mode is useful if you want to browse the data but not change it, or use the database in a report without fear of changing or accidentally deleting records. Read-only mode also keeps the database available to others on your network while you view data or print a report. Since you are not asking the o perating system to allow you to write to the database, you won't be consuming computer resources or causing file contention problems.
5. Select a database file, then select OK. If you selected a Paradox database, Approach needs to find a key field within that database. If it cannot find a key field, it opens the Choose Key Field dialog box shown in Figure 4.4. Select the field or fields that provide a unique value for each record, then select OK. Typically the unique identifier is a numeric field and is among the first fields defined in the database.
6. Approach will create two default views, Form 1 and Worksheet 1. However, Approach does not save these views in an Approach file until you explicitly tell it to do so (see the section "Saving Files" later in this chapter).

FIGURE 4.4 ▶

You must choose the key field for a Paradox table if Approach cannot find it when you open an existing Paradox table.

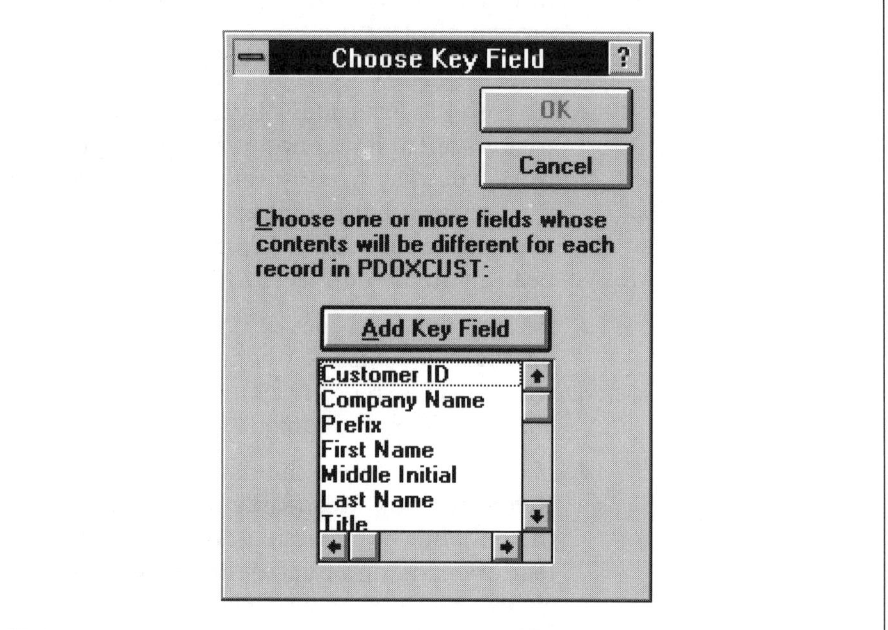

▸▸ Opening a Lotus 1-2-3 Spreadsheet File Directly

You can open a named range in a Lotus 1-2-3 spreadsheet and use Approach to modify the data. When you make changes, Approach saves your work in the original spreadsheet file, not in a new database. In this way, Approach acts as a front-end to data stored in your 1-2-3 spreadsheet. Approach supplies the database power directly to the spreadsheet data without making a copy of your spreadsheet or converting it to a separate database. This is useful if you wish to continue using a spreadsheet to store lists, such as part numbers or customer names and addresses, in columnar form.

Follow these steps to use Approach to work with data in a named range in a Lotus 1-2-3 spreadsheet:

1. From the Welcome screen, select Open and choose the "an Existing File" option. Click OK. If the Welcome screen is not displayed, select File ➤ Open, click on the File Open icon in the

SmartIcons toolbar, or press Ctrl+O from the main menu. Approach displays the File Open dialog box.

2. Choose the drive and directory that contains the spreadsheet file you wish to open, if it is not currently displayed. If your file is on a network, you may need to select the Network option and connect to the network before you select the drive and/or directory.
3. Be sure the "List files of type" option displays Lotus 1-2-3 (*.WK*) as the file type.
4. The Directories list displays the spreadsheet files. Select the spreadsheet file you want.
5. The File Name list displays the named ranges of the selected spreadsheet. Select the named range you want.
6. Select OK.
7. Approach displays the Convert To dialog box, suggesting you convert the data to a database using the dBASE IV file format. It uses the same file name as your spreadsheet in the same drive and directory as your spreadsheet. Change the file name, drive and directory, and file type, if necessary. Select OK.

►► Opening a Non-Database File Containing Database Data

Many applications can store database data in a format that is not directly usable by Approach, but these programs can export their data into a standard format that Approach can use. For example, a name-and-address manager may store a customer name and address in a proprietary format but can create a comma-delimited file. In such text files, each field value is separated by a comma, and each record is separated by a carriage return (similar to pressing the Enter key in a word processing document to begin a new paragraph).

Other applications use file formats that are not exclusively used for database information. For example, both Lotus 1-2-3 and Microsoft Excel can store data in rows and columns in a file format that Approach can read and understand.

Approach can turn these files into database files and create the associated Approach files using just a few steps.

▸▸ **NOTE**

When you open an existing database file and make changes, you are changing the data in the database file itself. However, when you open a non-database file and create a new database in Approach, you are no longer working with the original data, *but a copy of that data.* When you open a spreadsheet file or a text file, for example, and Approach converts the data into a .DBF file (dBASE), you are then working with the copy, not the original spreadsheet data. When you import data, you are adding or merging data to your existing Approach file (if it exists) or creating a new file (if it does not). Importing data into an existing file is described in greater detail in Chapter 20.

▸ Creating a Database from a Fixed-Length Text File

Unlike delimited files, which use a special character to separate fields, a fixed-length text file always places fields at the same position within each record. Thus, in a fixed-length text file, a company name and address file looks like this:

Company	Address1	Address2	City
Acme Construction	123 Main Street	Suite 800	Seattle
Bay Lumber	458 Mill Place		Redmond

Spaces are used to "fill out" any entry that is not long enough. In this example, suppose the data in the Company field is never more than 30 characters long. If the value for the Company name contains fewer than 30 characters, the rest of the field is "padded" with spaces so the entire name always takes exactly 30 characters. In the case of Acme Construction, we'll have 17 characters of text (including the space between Acme and Construction) and 13 spaces at the end of the name.

Note that Bay Lumber has a single address only, so the Address2 field will contain only spaces.

There is no need for special characters, such as quotation marks, around entries that contain special characters, since Approach looks for fields to begin in exactly the same location in every record.

Follow these steps to create a database and Approach file from a fixed-length text file:

1. From the Welcome screen, select Open and choose the "an Existing File" option. Click OK. If the Welcome screen is not displayed, select File ➤ Open, click on the File Open icon in the SmartIcons toolbar, or press Ctrl+O from the main menu. Approach displays the File Open dialog box.
2. Choose the drive and directory that contains the text file you wish to open, if it is not currently displayed. If your file is on a network, you may need to select the Network option and connect to the network before you select the drive and/or directory.
3. Select Text - Fixed Length in the "List files of type" pull-down list. Select the file you want to open and click on OK. Approach opens the Fixed Length Text File Setup dialog box, shown in Figure 4.5.

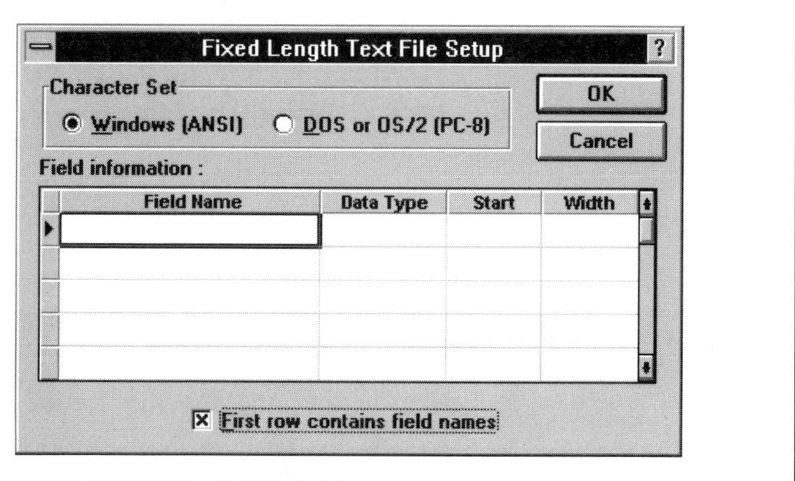

FIGURE 4.5 ▶

The Fixed Length Text File Setup dialog box

4. Select the character set. The Windows option uses the standard ANSI character set, while DOS/OS2 uses a different character set, called PC-8. Consult the person who created the text file to see which character set was used, or select one, experiment with it, and examine the results. You can always begin this process from step 1 and overwrite a previous database.
5. Check the "First row contains field names" box if you want Approach to use the text in the first row of the text file when naming fields in the database. Otherwise, if the first row of your data does not contain field names, you must enter them manually; enter the first field name in the Field Name list.
6. Press Tab or click on the first entry in the Data Type column and select a data type from the pull-down list. This data type must match the type of data in the field (for example, a numeric data type would be selected for fields containing values such as 123, 756, or 910). Enter the starting position of each field (usually 1 for the first field) and the width. Approach automatically enters the next starting position in the next row. You can override this starting position, however, if you wish to skip positions in your text file. See the Note.

►► NOTE

You do not have to account for all positions in a record. For example, if you only wish to extract the first name and last name of a customer in a text file, you can enter these fields and their corresponding starting position and width. All other characters for each record will be ignored.

7. Enter the rest of the field names (if your field names are not part of the first record), and enter the remaining field types and widths. A sample is shown in Figure 4.6.
8. Select OK. Approach displays the Convert To dialog box, shown in Figure 4.7.
9. Select the drive and directory for the database file.
10. Select the file format from the "List files of type" pull-down list.

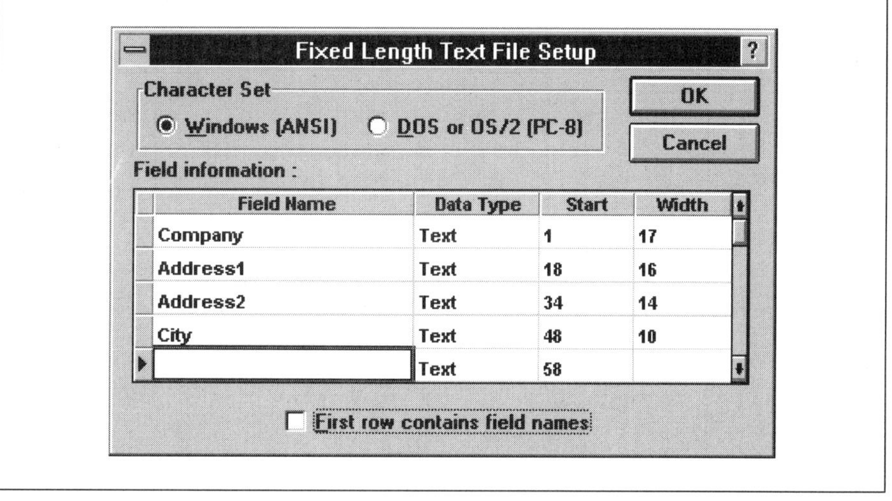

FIGURE 4.6

The Fixed Length Text File Setup dialog box with several fields defined

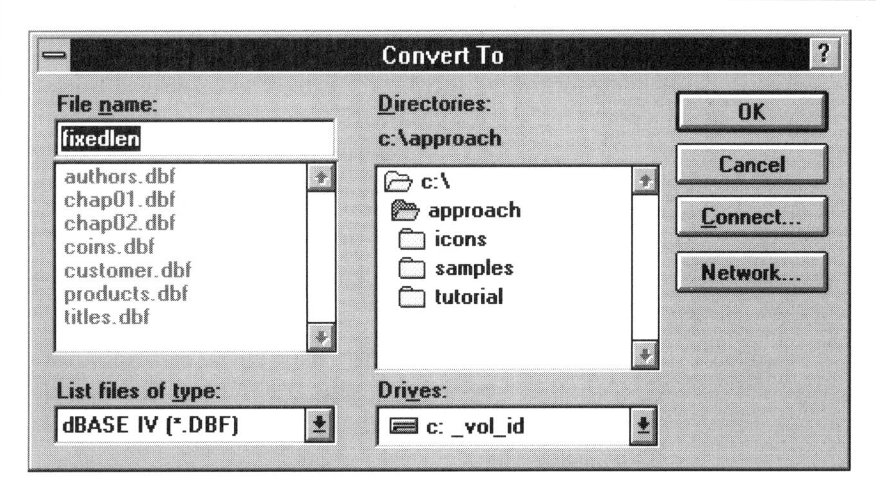

FIGURE 4.7

The Convert To dialog box

11. Enter a file name for the database file in the File Name box.
12. Select OK. Approach creates two default views, Form 1 and Worksheet 1. However, Approach does not save these views in an Approach file until you explicitly tell it to do so (see the section "Saving Files" later in this chapter).

▶ Creating a Database from a Delimited Text File

Approach can open data files that use delimited text. In such a file, each field value is separated by a comma, tab, or other character, and each record is separated by a carriage return (a new line). For example, when data is stored in an application in *comma-delimited* form, the data might look like this:

```
Company,Address1,Address2,City,State,Zip,Credit
Acme Construction,123 Main Street,Suite 800,Seat-
tle,WA,98199,1000
Bay Lumber,458 Mill Place,Tacoma,WA,98999,2000
```

Note that Bay Lumber has a single address only, so the two commas are placed together without any space between them to indicate that the field is empty (missing). If the field contents includes a comma, then the file puts the entire entry in quotation marks. For example:

```
LastName,FirstName,City,State,Zip
"Powell, Jr.",Robert,Seattle,WA,98199
```

Tab-delimited format is similar to other delimited text formats. Instead of separating fields with a comma, as in a comma-delimited format, the tab-delimited format uses the tab character to separate fields.

Each new line in a delimited text file represents a new database record. Thus, in the first example, there are three records (the first record contains the field names); the second example contains two records (it, too, uses the first record for field names).

When Approach reads this text data, it must know (so you must tell it) if the first record contains the field names. While field names are typically part of any database file, such as a dBASE file, this is not the case in a text file.

Use these steps to create a database and Approach file from a delimited text file:

1. From the Welcome screen, select Open and choose the "an Existing File" option. Click OK. If the Welcome screen is not displayed, select File ➤ Open, click on the File Open icon in the SmartIcons toolbar, or press Ctrl+O from the main menu. Approach displays the File Open dialog box.

2. Choose the drive and directory that contains the text file you wish to open if it is not currently displayed. Select the file you want to open. If your file is on a network, you may need to select the Network option and connect to the network before you select the drive and/or directory.
3. Select Text - Delimited in the "List files of type" pull-down list. Approach opens the Text File Options dialog box shown in Figure 4.8.
4. Select the character used to separate fields, such as a comma or tab. If a different character is used, select Other and enter the character in the text box following this option.
5. Select the character set. The Windows option uses the standard ANSI character set, while DOS/OS2 uses a different character set, called PC-8.

FIGURE 4.8

The Text File Options dialog box

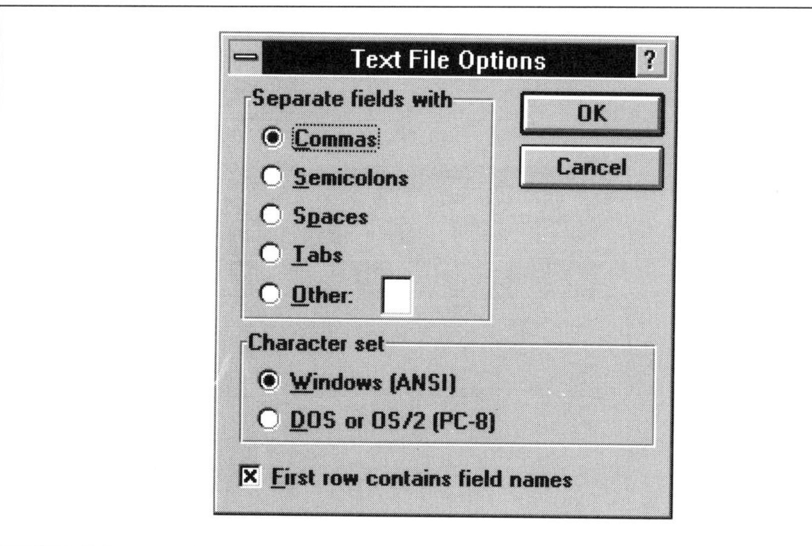

6. Check the "First row contains field names" box if you want Approach to use the text in the first row of the delimited text file when naming fields in the database.
7. Select OK. Approach displays the Convert To dialog box, shown in Figure 4.7 earlier in this chapter.
8. Select the drive and directory for the database file.

9. Select the file format from the "List files of type" pull-down list.
10. Enter a file name for the database file in the File Name box.
11. Select OK. Approach creates two default views, Form 1 and Worksheet 1. However, Approach does not save these views in an Approach file until you explicitly tell it to do so (see the section "Saving Files" later in this chapter).

▶ Creating a Database from a Spreadsheet File

A spreadsheet can store records in rows and fields in columns. For example, Figure 4.9 shows a portion of an Excel spreadsheet that Approach can understand and use as though it were a database, or convert the data into a database. Although the data is stored in columns named A, B, C, and so on, typically spreadsheet files use a field name in the first row of the data.

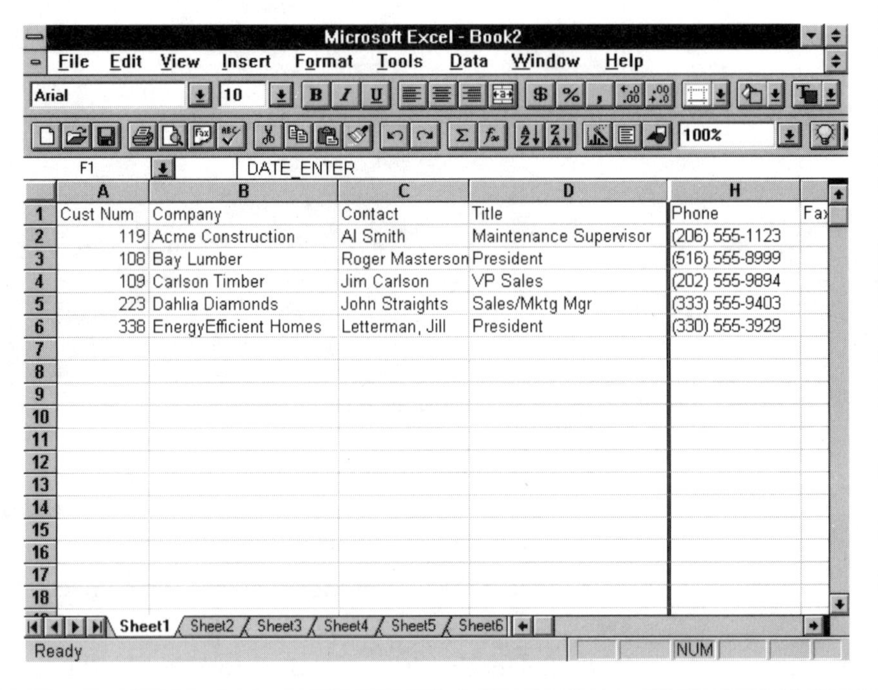

FIGURE 4.9 ▶

A spreadsheet file can be used to store data in a list. This list can be used by Approach as if it were a database.

You can use data in the entire spreadsheet or use data in a specific range (a block of rows and columns).

Use these steps to create a database and an Approach file from spreadsheet data:

1. From the Welcome screen, select Open and choose the "an Existing" File option. Click OK. If the Welcome screen is not displayed, select File ➤ Open, click on the File Open icon in the SmartIcons toolbar, or press Ctrl+O from the main menu. Approach displays the File Open dialog box.
2. Choose the drive and directory that contains the spreadsheet file you wish to open, if it is not currently displayed. If your file is on a network, you may need to select the Network option and connect to the network before you select the drive and/or directory.
3. Be sure the "List files of type" option displays the file type for the spreadsheet (such as Excel or 1-2-3) you wish to open. (By default the option is Approach, which is incorrect for this situation.)
4. Enter the name of the spreadsheet and select OK.
5. To select a named range from a 1-2-3 spreadsheet, including a single sheet, select the sheet name or named range from the Select Range dialog box, shown in Figure 4.10. Worksheet page names are in mixed case, while ranges are in ALL UPPERCASE.
6. Check the "First row contains field names" box if you want Approach to use the text in the first row of the spreadsheet or spreadsheet range as the field names.

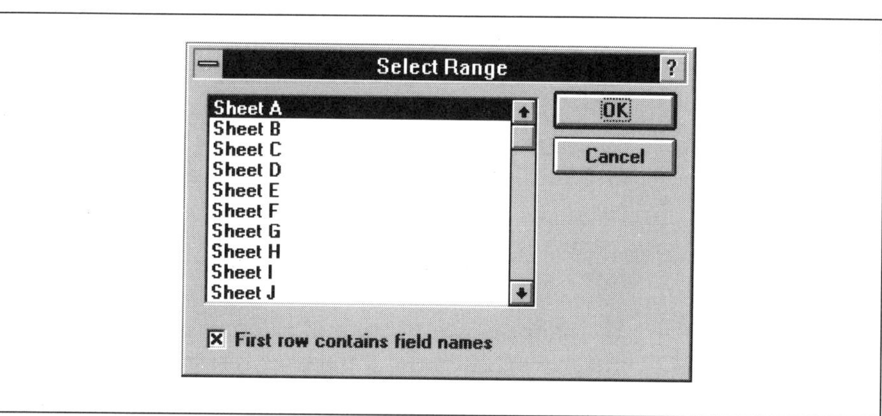

FIGURE 4.10

The Select Range dialog box

7. Select OK. Approach displays the Convert To dialog box, shown in Figure 4.7 earlier in this chapter.
8. Select the drive and directory for the database file. Select the database file type from the "List files of type" pull-down list. Enter a file name for the database file in the File Name box.
9. Select OK. Approach creates two default views, Form 1 and Worksheet 1. However, Approach does not save these views in an Approach file until you explicitly tell it to do so (see the section "Saving Files" later in this chapter).

▸▸ Creating a New Database

Approach also lets you create a brand new database, either by specifying each field or by using a template from the Welcome screen as a model. Using a template is by far the easier technique. With the template option, Approach creates a database using the name you supply, creating the fields and default forms for the database from the template. You can then modify the database structure: You can add or delete fields, change their length, and so on. With a template, Approach does the majority of the "dirty work" for you.

Instructions for creating a new database are fully described in Chapter 3.

▸▸ Saving Files

Although Approach will save your data when you add, change, or delete a record in your database file, it does not automatically save changes to your Approach file. As mentioned in many of the previous examples, Approach will create a new Approach file when you open a database or text file, but it does not automatically save the Approach file. You'll also want to save your Approach file if you change any of the views it contains. For example, if you add a report or modify a data entry form, save the Approach file so that you have these changes for future use.

You may also want to make a copy of the Approach file (for back-up purposes), copy the databases referred to in the Approach file, or copy all files.

▶ Saving an Approach File

Use these steps to save an Approach file for the first time or after you have made changes to the file:

1. Select File ➤ Save Approach, press Ctrl+S, or click on the Save Approach File icon in the SmartIcons toolbar. Approach displays the Save Approach File dialog box, shown in Figure 4.11, if you are saving the Approach file for the very first time.

FIGURE 4.11 ▶

The Save Approach File dialog box

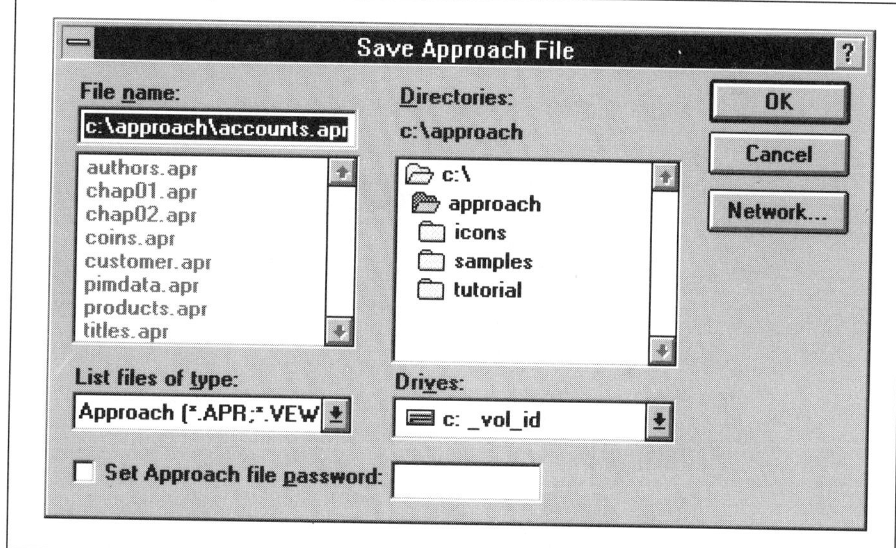

2. Enter the drive, directory, and file name in the appropriate text boxes.
3. To set a password for the file, check the "Set Approach file password" box and enter the password in the text box to the right. If you set a password, you will have to enter this password when you open the file.
4. Select OK.

After you save the Approach file for the first time, selecting the File ➤ Save Approach File option (or any of its shortcuts) saves the file without displaying the Save Approach File dialog box. Your data will be saved to the Approach file currently in use.

▸▸ Saving an Approach File and Databases Using Different Names

You can save a copy of the current Approach file using a different name. This is helpful if you want to experiment with an Approach file but want to leave the original intact.

Follow these steps to save an Approach file using a different name:

1. Select File ➤ Save As. The Save Approach File As dialog box, shown in Figure 4.12, appears.

FIGURE 4.12

The Save Approach File As dialog box

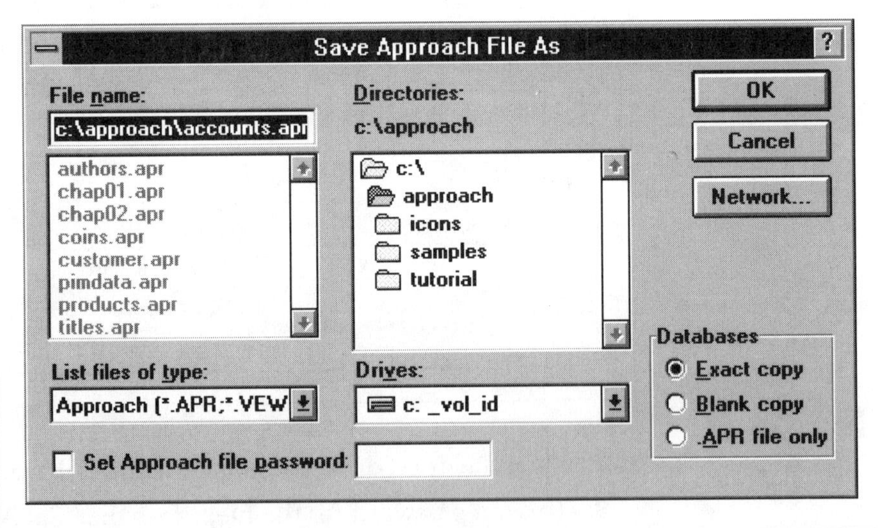

2. Select the new location (if desired) and enter the new file name for the Approach file. If you wish to set a password, check the "Set Approach file password" box and enter the password.
3. If you want to only copy the Approach file, but not the associated databases, choose the ".APR file only" box. Click OK and you are done. Otherwise, proceed to step 4.

4. To save a copy of every database in the current file, select the Exact Copy box. This will copy the database layout and all data records for each database. (Multiple databases can be part of a single Approach database, a topic discussed at greater length in Chapter 6.) Approach prompts you for the new name of each database, one database at a time.
5. If you want to copy the format of the database (a list of fields and field types) without copying the data records themselves, check the Blank copy option. See the Tip.

TIP

The Blank Copy database option is extremely useful if you have an Approach file set up for contact names and addresses for vendors and want to set up an identical system for customers. You'll want to copy the forms and reports created for vendors, possibly changing the report and form headings (replacing the word Vendor with Customer in report or form headings, for instance), but everything else will probably remain the same, or nearly so. You'll want new, empty databases to store the names and addresses of customers. The Blank Copy option creates new databases by defining each field and field type (for example, name is a text field of 20 characters, state is a text field that is 2 characters long, and so on). This option does not copy the data so the databases are empty, have a new name, and are ready for your input. As a result, you'll have a new customer database with all the field names and validation criteria that you defined for contacts in a brand new file ready for you to use.

6. Select OK.
7. Approach displays the Save Database As dialog box, shown in Figure 4.13, for each database in the Approach file. Enter the new location and/or name and select OK for each dialog box.

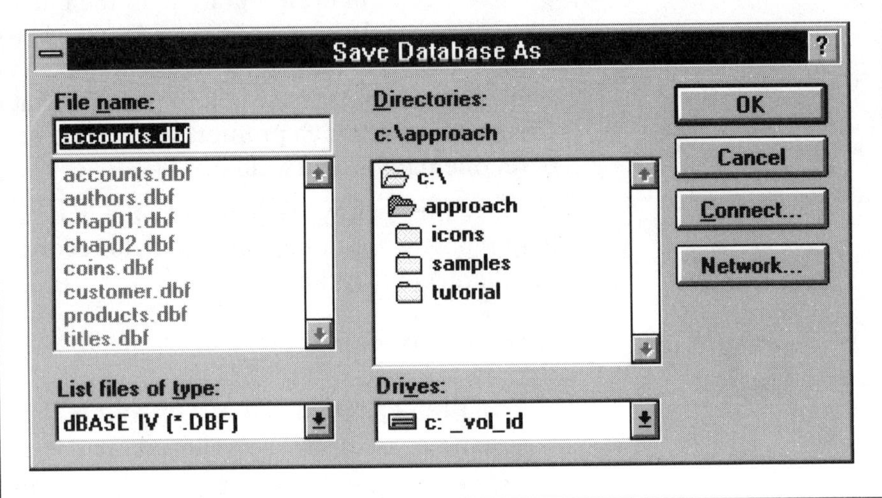

FIGURE 4.13 ►

The Save Database As dialog box

►► Closing an Approach File

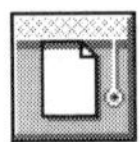

When you are finished using a file, close it by selecting File ➤ Close or click on the File Close icon in the SmartIcons toolbar. The File Close icon is not part of the default SmartIcons toolbar, but may be included if you or another user has modified the toolbar.

You can also minimize the file if you wish to reopen it to the same form you are currently working on. While closing and then reopening the Approach file returns you to the current form, minimizing a form saves you time, since you don't have to use the open/close steps. To minimize the form, select the small icon to the left of the File menu (it contains a minus sign) and select Minimize. Please note that this icon is located just beneath the Control menu icon, which is identical in appearance. You want to click on the bottom icon of this pair, the File menu icon for the current Approach form. See Figure 4.14.

►► Deleting an Approach File

You can delete an Approach file or one or more of the databases it contains. If you delete a database, all related files (including the separate file that stores memo fields) are deleted.

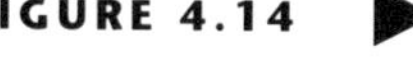

FIGURE 4.14

The Control file menu

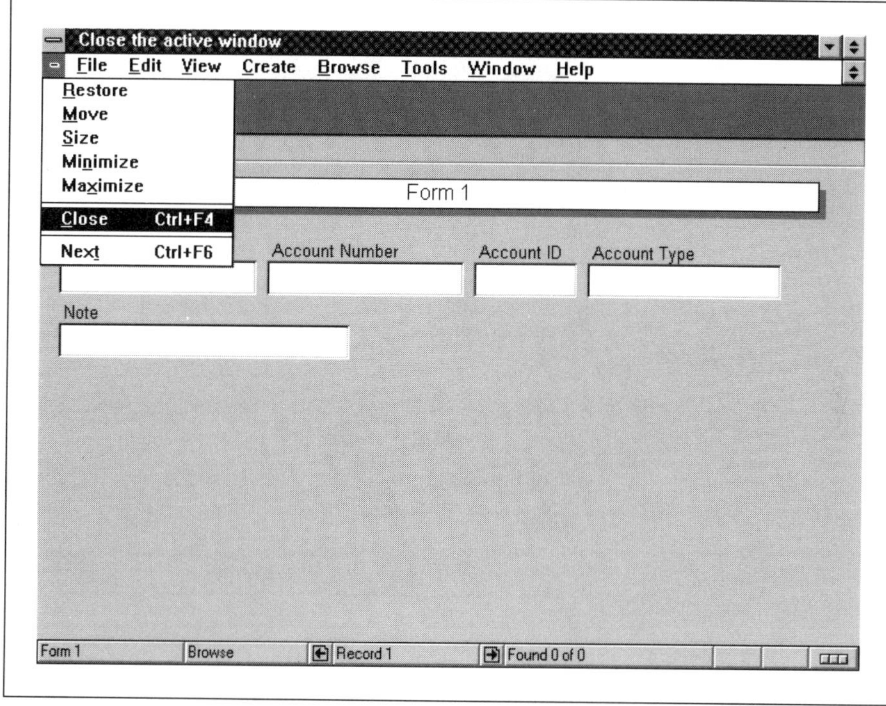

Use these steps to delete a file:

1. Select File ➤ Delete File. Approach displays the Delete File dialog box, shown in Figure 4.15.
2. If you want to delete a database file, select the appropriate file type from the “List files of type” pull-down list. Otherwise select the Approach file you want to delete and select OK.
3. Approach provides a warning message asking if you want to delete a file. Select Yes.
4. If you selected an Approach file in step 2, you will see one dialog box for each database file it contains. Select Yes to delete the file or No to keep it.

FIGURE 4.15

The Delete File dialog box

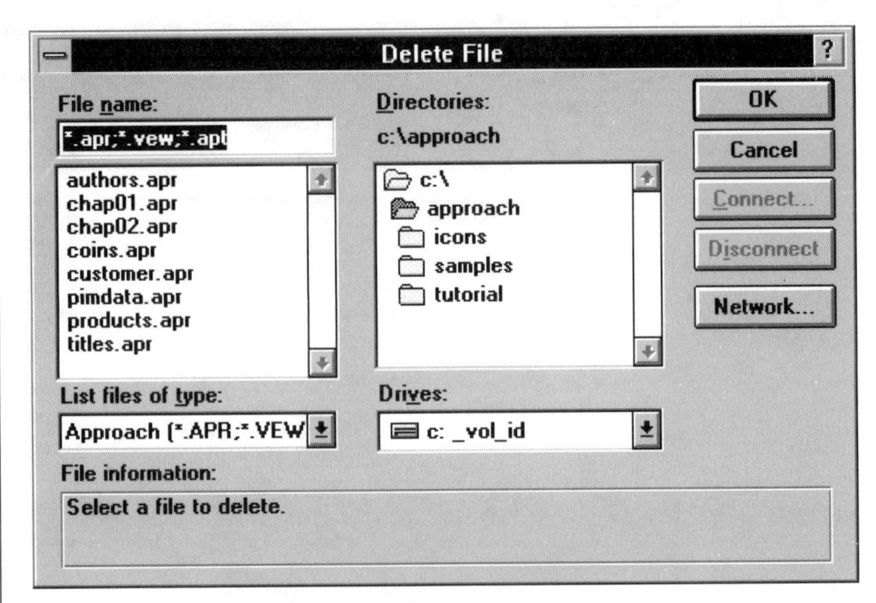

▸▸ Summary and a Look Ahead

In this chapter you've seen how to work with a variety of existing files. While most of your work will be done by opening existing Approach files, modifying them, and saving them, you may also want to use data stored in other locations (such as on your network) in formats you did not create yourself. For example, you may wish to use a parts list stored in a an Excel spreadsheet, a Paradox database, or a comma-delimited text file. Approach can handle this data by working with it directly (in the case of spreadsheet or database data) or by converting it to a database (for text data).

In Chapter 3 you learned how to set up a new database. Chapter 4 showed you how to work with data in formats other than Approach. Chapter 5 will show you how to manipulate data after it can be opened by Approach. For example, you'll learn how to modify the layout of a database, add new fields, remove existing ones, and create validation options (so the data you enter is correct).

▶ ▶ CHAPTER 5

Modifying Your Databases

▸▸ FAST TRACK

▸ *To change a field definition in an existing database* **128**

open the Approach file containing the database you want to change. Switch to the Design environment, then choose Create ➤ Field Definition. Select the database you want to modify from the Database drop-down list. Move to the cell in the table you want to change. Then type a new field name in the Field Name box. Select a new field type from the Data Type drop-down list or enter the first letter of the new field type, or enter a new field length (for some field type) in the Size column for each field you want to change. When you're done, select OK.

▸ *To remove a field* **131**

open the Approach file that contains the database you want to change, switch to the Design environment, and select Create ➤ Field Definition. Select the database you want to modify from the Database drop-down list. Double-click in the box to the left of the Field Name of the field you want to remove. Approach highlights the row containing the field you selected and places an arrow in the box. Select the Delete button. Click OK to confirm your delete request.

▸ *To add a field to an existing database* **132**

open the Approach File that contains the database you want to change, switch to the Design environment, and select Create ➤ Field Definition. Select the database you want to modify from the Database drop-down list. If desired, select the display order of the fields using the "View fields by" drop-down list. To add a field to the end of the database, select the Default Order option for the "View fields by" list, then click in the last row (first blank row) and enter the field name, data type, and size. Otherwise, to add a field within the middle of the field list, click in the cell row where you want the new field to be placed and click on the Insert button. The field in the existing row will be moved to the next row. Enter the field name, data type, and size for each desired new field. Select OK when done.

To set validation options 143

for a Boolean, date, numeric, text, or time field, click on the Validation tab of the Field Definition dialog box.

To define a default value with a creation or modification formula 150

select the field to contain the result of the calculation, then select Creation formula to define a formula Approach will use to fill the field for a new record. Select Modification formula to define a formula used to fill the field for new records and whenever a change is made to an existing record. Enter the formula directly in the text box below the formula options on the Default Value tab or select the Formula button in the bottom-right of the dialog box and build the formula using the Formula dialog box. If the formula is valid, the checkered flag icon is displayed in black and white without an X through it, and the "OK" button is enabled. Select OK when your formula is correct, or select Cancel to abandon your formula.

▸▸ **Although** Approach makes it easy to create a database from scratch or use a database created by another application, what do you do when your needs change? Fortunately, with Approach you're never "stuck" with a database design. In this chapter you'll learn how to change the structure of any database so that as your business needs change your database can keep pace with your new requirements.

For example, you may find that you need to keep track of a special code to separate business customers from your "preferred" customers. With Approach it's easy to add a field (perhaps a Boolean field) to differentiate the two classes of customers. Likewise, you may find that as you expand to international markets you'll need to expand the length of a first name, last name, or company name field. Approach makes this easy, too.

In this chapter you'll learn how to modify a field in an existing database, including removing and adding fields. You'll also learn about the abundance of field options that help you minimize data entry and reduce the possibility of data entry error. You'll also get a brief glimpse of how to use formulas to shorten your work.

▸▸ Changing a Field Definition in an Existing Database

You've seen in Chapters 3 and 4 how to build a new database or use Approach to read the data from an existing database. In Chapter 3 you learned how to change a field definition *before* the database was created, but in Chapter 4 we assumed that the database structure was not changeable. Further, up to this point we have also discussed database design without any concern for whether the database we created contained data records.

Approach is a very flexible program. You can change a database field definition for databases you create or those that you read, even after you have entered records into the database. The safest way to modify a field format is before data has been entered. However, Approach has been designed to let you change a field when you realize, for example, that a field has been defined with a field length that is too long, and is thus wasting disk space.

While you can modify the structure of an existing database using Approach, there are some limitations and situations you should know about:

- If you decrease the length of a field, data that is too long for the new field length will be truncated and permanently lost.
- Increasing the length of a numeric field is safe, as is increasing the number of positions to the right of the decimal point. If the field length is decreased, values are truncated, *not rounded.*
- If you change the field type, some data may not be converted. While changing from a numeric field to a text field is permitted, converting from a text field to a numeric field will result in a loss of data if the text field contains any *non-numeric* characters. However, Approach will display a warning before completing the conversion. Any other field type changes are extremely risky.

▶▶ **TIP**

If Approach cannot perform the conversion on your data, it displays a warning message.

▶▶ **WARNING**

It is *strongly* recommended that you back up your entire database and Approach file before changing any field definitions.

Use these steps to change a field definition:

1. Open the Approach File containing the database you want to change: Select File ➤ Open, select the File Open icon in the SmartIcons toolbar, or press Ctrl+O, then enter or choose the file name, and select OK.
2. Switch to the Design environment: Select View ➤ Design, press Ctrl+D, click on the second slot on the Status bar and select Design, or choose the Design icon from the SmartIcons toolbar.
3. Select Create ➤ Field Definition. The Field Definition dialog box appears, as shown in Figure 5.1.

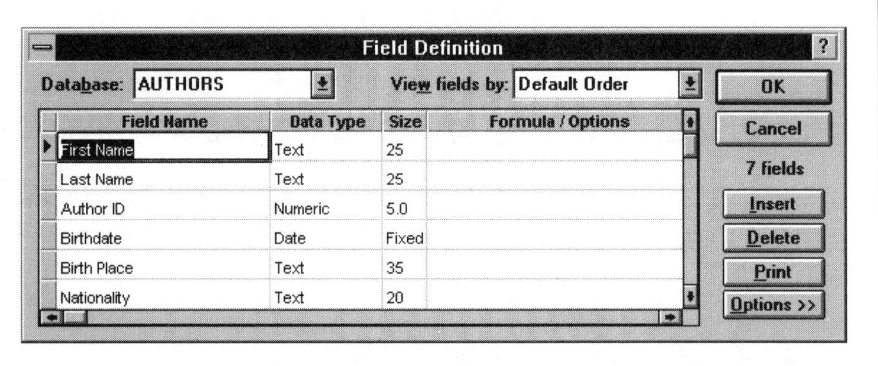

FIGURE 5.1 ▶ *The Field Definition dialog box*

4. Select the database you want to modify from the Database pull-down list. If desired, select the display order of the fields using the "View fields by" pull-down list.
5. Move to the cell in the table you want to change.
6. Use the following steps to change the field:
   - Type a new field name in the Field Name box.
   - Select a new field type from the Data type pull-down list or enter the first letter of the new field types (to change the field to a Time field, press T twice).
   - Enter a new field length (for some field types) in the Size column.

7. Repeat steps 4 through 6 until all fields have been changed.
8. Select OK.

▶▶ NOTE

If you change the name of a field, the new name change ripples throughout the Approach file, including all occurrences in calculations and macros.

▶▶ Removing Fields

You can delete a field that is no longer needed from any database. Use the following steps to remove a field:

1. Open the Approach file that contains the database you want to change: Select File ➤ Open, select the File Open icon in the SmartIcons toolbar, or press Ctrl+O, then enter or choose the file name, and select OK.
2. Switch to the Design environment: Select View ➤ Design, press Ctrl+D, click on the second slot on the Status bar and select Design, or choose the Design icon from the SmartIcons toolbar.
3. Select Create ➤ Field Definition. The Field Definition dialog box will appear.
4. Select the database you want to modify from the Database pull-down list. If desired, select the display order of the fields using the "View fields by" pull-down list.
5. Double-click in the box to the left of the Field Name of the field you want to remove. Approach highlights the row containing the field you selected and places an arrow in the box.
6. Select the Delete button.
7. Approach displays a message asking for confirmation. Click OK to delete the field.
8. Repeat Steps 4 through 7 until all fields you want to remove have been selected. Although you can highlight multiple fields, Approach deletes only one field at a time.

►► Adding Fields

In addition to changing fields and deleting them, you can add new fields, just as if you were creating the field as part of a new database. New fields are typically added to the end of the field list. However, you can enter a new field anywhere in the list. Remember that adding a field to any location other than at the end of the field list (using the Default Order display option) may affect other users that access your database file(s).

Use these steps to insert a field into a new or existing database:

1. If you are creating a new database, you are working in the Creating New Database dialog box, so proceed to Step 5. If you are working with an existing database, open the Approach File that contains the database you want to change: Select File ➤ Open, select the File Open icon in the SmartIcons toolbar, or press Ctrl+O, then enter or choose the file name and select OK.
2. Switch to the Design environment: Select View ➤ Design, press Ctrl+D, click on the second slot on the Status bar and select Design, or choose the Design icon from the SmartIcons toolbar.
3. Select Create ➤ Field Definition. The Field Definition dialog box will appear.
4. Select the database you want to modify from the Database pull-down list. If desired, select the display order of the fields using the "View fields by" pull-down list.
5. To add a field to the end of the database (the preferred, safest method), select the Default Order option for the "View fields by" list, then click in the last row (first blank row) and enter the field name, data type, and size. Proceed to Step 8.
6. To add a field within the middle of the field list, click in the cell row where you want the new field to be placed and click on the Insert button. The field in the existing row will be moved to the next row. Figure 5.2 shows the insertion of the Birth Time field. Compare this figure to Figure 5.1 (earlier in this chapter), which shows the database before the field was added.
7. Enter the field name, data type, and size. Notice that the "View fields by" box now shows Custom Order.

FIGURE 5.2

The Field Definition dialog box after adding the Birth Time field

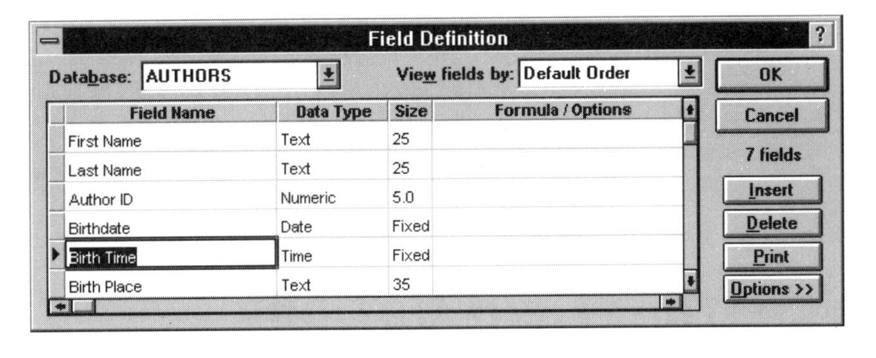

8. Repeat Steps 4 through 6 until all desired fields have been added.
9. Select OK to make the changes to the database.

NOTE

The "View fields by" option includes Custom Order (shows the fields in the physical order they are stored in the database file), Field Name (alphabetically by field name), Data Type (alphabetically by data type, then alphabetically by field name within data type), or Custom Order (the order in which you rearrange the fields, either by dragging and dropping fields or by inserting fields between existing fields). The choices you make for displaying the fields do not change the physical order of the fields in the database file itself.

When you add a new field to a database that already contains records, each record is modified to include the new field. However, the new field is blank—it contains no value. You can create a macro to fill the field with a default value. Macros are discussed in Chapter 16.

New fields are not automatically added to forms, reports, or other views. You must change these views manually, as discussed in Chapter 8.

►► **NOTE**

You can also rearrange fields in a field list. Simply double-click on the gray box to the left of the field name. The mouse arrow changes to a hand. Drag and drop the field to the desired location.

►► Setting Field Options

As their name implies, field options are optional—that is, you can set them if you wish, but these settings are not necessary. These options control behavior when a field appears on a form. For example, you can use the serialization option to specify that Approach automatically fill in incremental numeric values for each new record. This option is particularly useful in ensuring that each invoice record entered into the database contains a unique value and that no value is skipped. Figure 5.3 shows the field options portion of the Field Definition screen. By

FIGURE 5.3 ►

Approach uses Default Value options in the Field Definition screen to serialize the customer number field for all new records.

checking the "Serial number starting at" option, Approach will automatically fill in the next available number when a new record is created, as shown in Figure 5.4.

FIGURE 5.4

The data entry form will automatically fill in the next available serial number (beginning with 1000, which you set in the Field Definition option section) for new records.

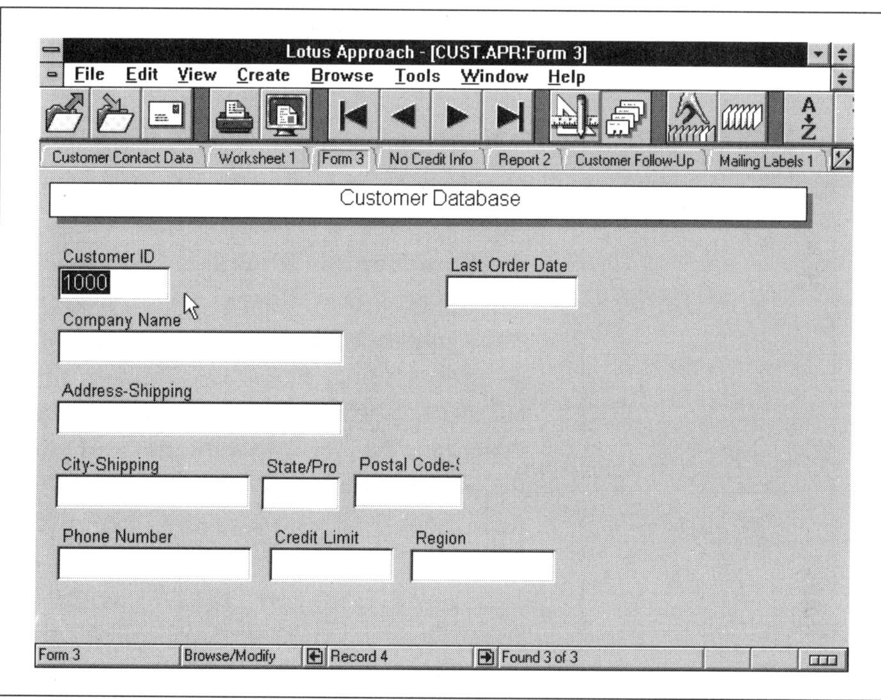

Other options let you restrict a field value to a particular range. For example, you can instruct Approach not to accept a date value that is less than the current system date. Field options also include filling in default values (current date or time, for example) and restricting entry of data to unique values.

You set a field option using either the Field Definition dialog box (for viewing and changing fields in an existing database) or the Creating Database dialog box (for creating fields in a new database). Both were described earlier in this chapter and operate identically. For this discussion, we'll use illustrations from the Field Definition dialog box.

The dialog box can display the field name, data type, size, and formula and options selected. When you select the Options button (in the bottom-right corner of the screen), Approach displays an expanded dialog box with tabs, as shown in Figure 5.3 earlier in this chapter. The tabs segregate the two types of options you can set. You can remove the Default Value and Validation tabs and return to the original dialog box by selecting the Options button again.

▸▸ **WARNING**

Since options are defined for the database used by the Approach file, it is possible that a record in the database field may contain a value outside the range you specify. How? Recall that a database may be used by more than one Approach file. Suppose, for example, the CUSTOMER database is part of a CUST Approach file (used for customer name and address maintenance by the Customer Service department) and part of the BILLING Approach file (used by the Accounts Receivable department to send invoices to customers). If a date field for the CUSTOMER database is restricted to dates between 1/1/90 and 12/31/99 when you open the database from the CUST Approach file, but there is no such restriction defined in the BILLING Approach file, it is possible for the Accounts Receivable employee to change a value to 1/1/85. When you display the record using the CUST Approach file, you'll likely notice that the 1/1/85 date value is outside your specified range (1/1/90 to 12/31/99). However, when you attempt to move to another record, Approach will again validate each field using your date range specification. Approach notes the problem and displays the out-of-range value in a dialog box, as shown in Figure 5.5. You cannot move to the next record until the date has been corrected.

FIGURE 5.5

Approach displays a warning message when a field contains an invalid value.

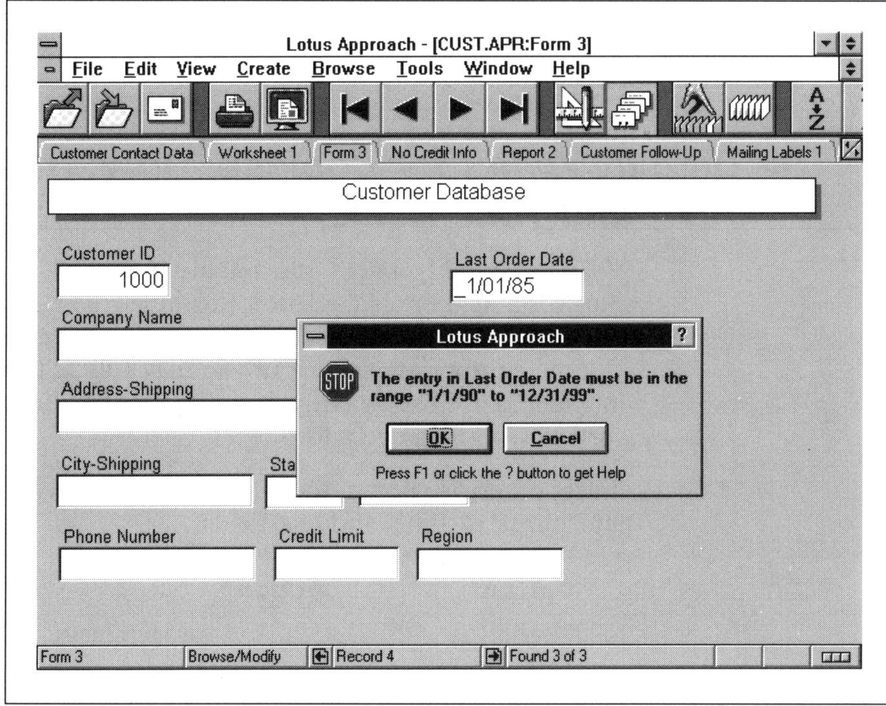

NOTE

Calculated, memo, PicturePlus, and variable fields are the exception. Options for these field types are explained in greater detail later in this chapter.

Approach dims (turns to light gray) the options that cannot be set for the data type you have selected. As you select different fields, Approach automatically adjusts the options in the tabbed sections to reflect your selection.

The field options you set here are used whenever you open the Approach file. For example, if you specify that a date field must be between 1/1/90 and 12/31/99, Approach will ensure that this condition is met everywhere: on any form, when editing data shown in any report, and in any worksheet.

▶ *Default Values for Boolean, Date, Numeric, Text, and Time Fields*

When you modify a field, the default options let you specify the initial value for a field or a calculation (formula) to be performed. If a value other than Nothing is selected, Approach will automatically fill the field with the appropriate value, but you may still edit the field if the field is not created as Display Only. (See Chapters 7 and 8 to learn about working with fields on a form.)

Unless otherwise noted, the following options work for all Boolean, date, numeric, time, and text fields:

Option	Action
Nothing	None; Approach leaves the field blank.
Previous record	Fills the field with the value from the last new or modified record.
Creation date	Fills in the current (system) date when the record is added; valid for text and date fields only.
Modification date	Fills in the current (system) date when the record is modified; valid for text and date fields only.
Creation time	Fills in the current (system) time when the record is added; valid for text and time fields only.
Modification time	Fills in the current (system) time when the record is modified; valid for text and time fields only.

Option	Action
Data	Enters the value typed into the text box to the right.
Serial number starting at	Places the value displayed in the text box to the right when a record is added; if your database currently has records and you wish to change the next serial number, enter the new value here.
Incremented by	Approach uses this value and adds it to the value in the Serial number field to determine the value for the field in the next new record. The value can be positive or negative.
Creation formula	Uses the value specified in the formula box below for all new records; formulas are discussed in the section "Using Formulas" later in this chapter.
Modification formula	Uses the value specified in the formula box below when a record is changed; formulas are discussed in the section "Using Formulas" later in this chapter.

NOTE

The serial number field is valuable for new records, but it cannot reserialize existing records. To renumber all existing database records, you must use a macro. See Chapter 16 for a description of a reserialization macro to perform this task.

▸ Options for Calculated Fields

The two tabs displayed for a calculated field let you define a formula to be displayed in a field or displayed on a form (as a subtotal or total, for example). You cannot edit the field size for a calculated field. Figure 5.6 shows the Define Formula options.

FIGURE 5.6 ▸

The Define Formulas options for a calculated field

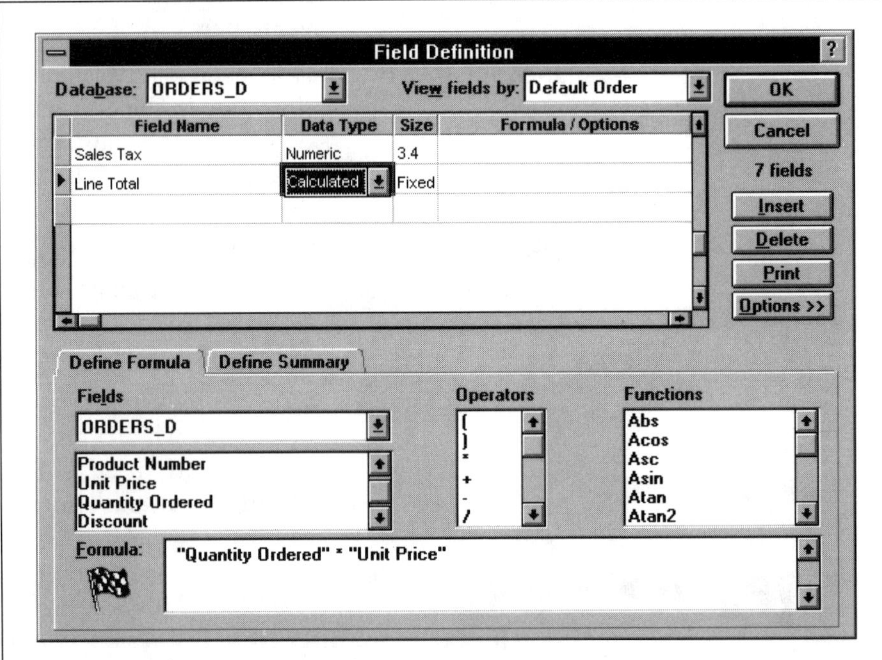

The Define Summary dialog box, shown in Figure 5.7, is used to define the formula for the field when it is used in summary calculations, such as on reports and forms. Formulas are described later in this chapter and at greater length in Chapter 19. Summary field definitions are described more fully in Chapter 11.

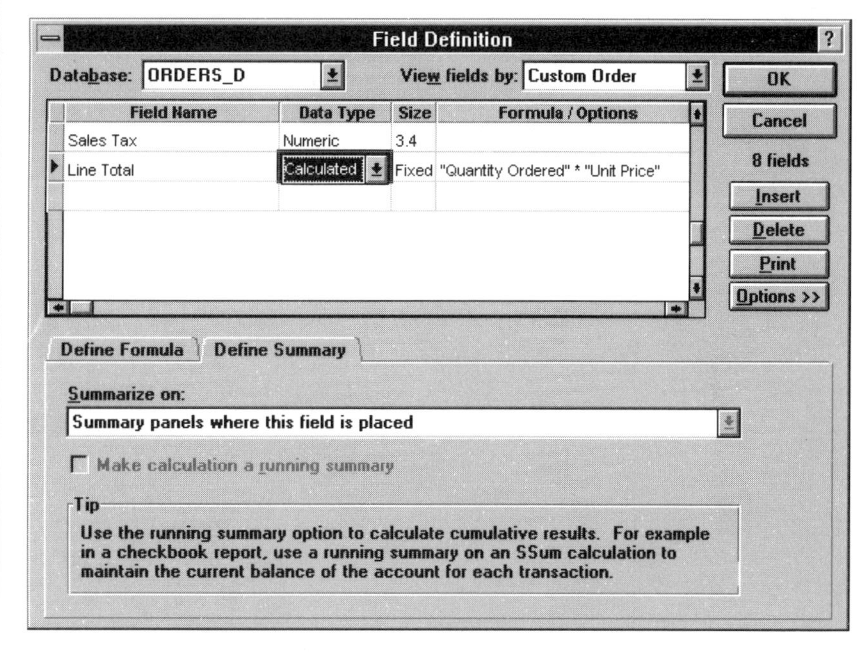

FIGURE 5.7

The Define Summary options for a calculated field

Options for Memo Fields

There are no options for memo fields. Memo fields are used to store free form text, such as notes about a customer or a description of a part in your inventory.

Options for PicturePlus Fields

PicturePlus fields are used to store data and documents that do not fit in the other categories. For example, you can store a graphic image of a part (hence the name "Picture") or a word processing document (hence the "Plus" part of PicturePlus) within a PicturePlus field. Approach can use OLE to place the object within the PicturePlus field.

Figure 5.8 shows the PicturePlus field options.

The PicturePlus option allows you to permit OLE objects to be placed within a field, and you can specify the default OLE object. These objects are defined using the Windows Registration database, which is

FIGURE 5.8

The PicturePlus field options

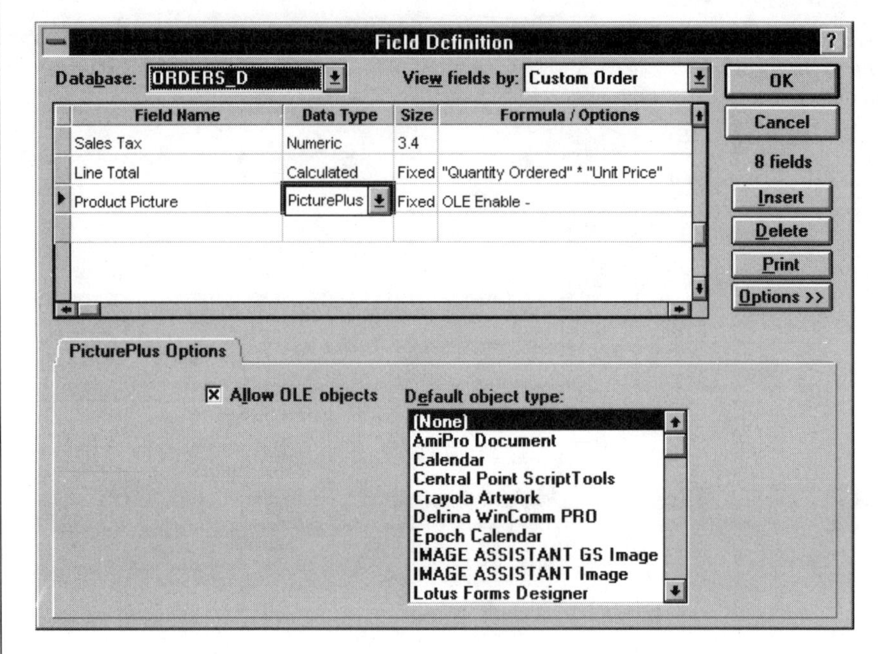

usually updated when you install or upgrade an application. Consult your Windows User's Guide for further details.

The Default object type is associated with an application. When you select a default, Approach will launch that application whenever you double-click or press the spacebar on an empty PicturePlus field.

▸ Options for Variable Fields

Variable fields are most commonly used in macros. In Approach you can specify the field type for the variable field. The default value you specify is set only when you open the Approach file. Figure 5.9 shows the Variable options.

FIGURE 5.9 ▶

The Variable options

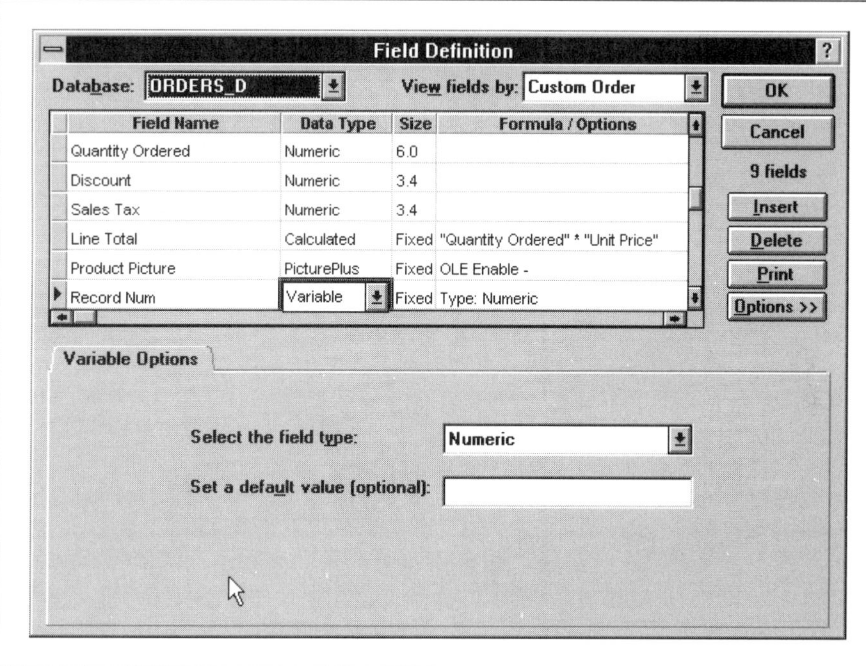

▶▶ Validation Options

When you enter a value in a Boolean, date, numeric, text, or time field, Approach can check your entry and make sure it conforms to restrictions you specify. For example, you may require that a field, such as Customer Last Name or Customer Account Number, be filled in whenever you add or change a Customer record. Just as the Default Value options apply to all views within an Approach file, validation rules will be checked no matter where you add or change data: in a data entry form, on a worksheet, or in a report. The Validation tab of the Field Definition dialog box is shown in Figure 5.10.

Approach performs some validation automatically. For example, when you specify a numeric field type, Approach does not let you enter "ABC" in the field. Likewise, you must enter a valid date in a date field—Approach will not permit an entry of 4/35/44 in a date field

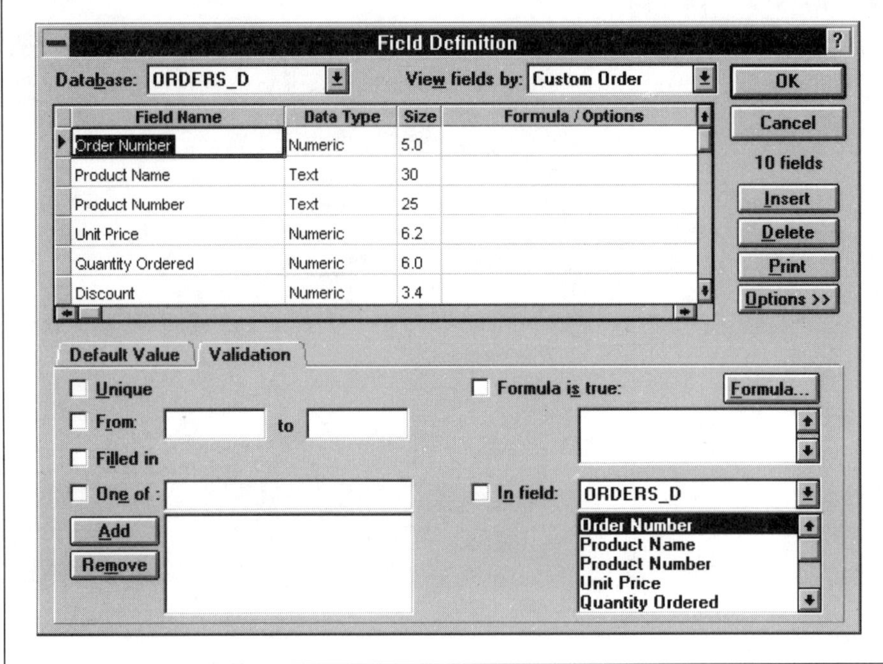

FIGURE 5.10

Validation options let you control which values Approach accepts for a field.

since there are only 30 days in April. Approach also allows you to specify other options. The following list shows validation options you can specify in addition to the automatic validation rules. More than one validation option can be selected for a field. For example, you can specify that a field value be unique and be filled in. To turn on an option, be sure the box to the left of the option is checked (contains an X).

Option	Meaning
Unique	The value entered in this field must be unique among all other records. The unique option is commonly used for key values, such as a customer number, which is necessary to identify a specific record.

From	For numeric, text, date, and time fields, you can enter the minimum and maximum values a field may contain (the "from" and "to" values). For numeric values, for example, you may enter **10** in the "from" value and **12** in the "to" value. With this setting, Approach will permit you to enter only 10, 11, or 12 in the field. To specify only a lower bound, enter a high value in the "to" box, such as 99999999 for numeric fields or ZZZZZZZZZZ for text fields.
Filled in	Approach requires that a value be entered in the field.
One of	The value entered in the field must be among those in the list shown. See the section "The One of Option" later in this chapter.
Formula is true	Approach evaluates the formula displayed in the box. If the formula evaluates to True, the field is valid. Otherwise Approach displays an error message. To create or edit the formula, select the Formula button. Formulas are discussed in the section "Using Formulas" later in this chapter.
In field	Approach will check all values in any field of another database that is part of the current Approach file. The field contents must match exactly.

▶ The One of Option

The *One of* option allows you to verify that the value you enter into the database is one of a predetermined list of values. Follow these steps to add values to the One of option:

1. Be sure the One of option is checked.
2. Enter the value you want to add in the text box to the right.

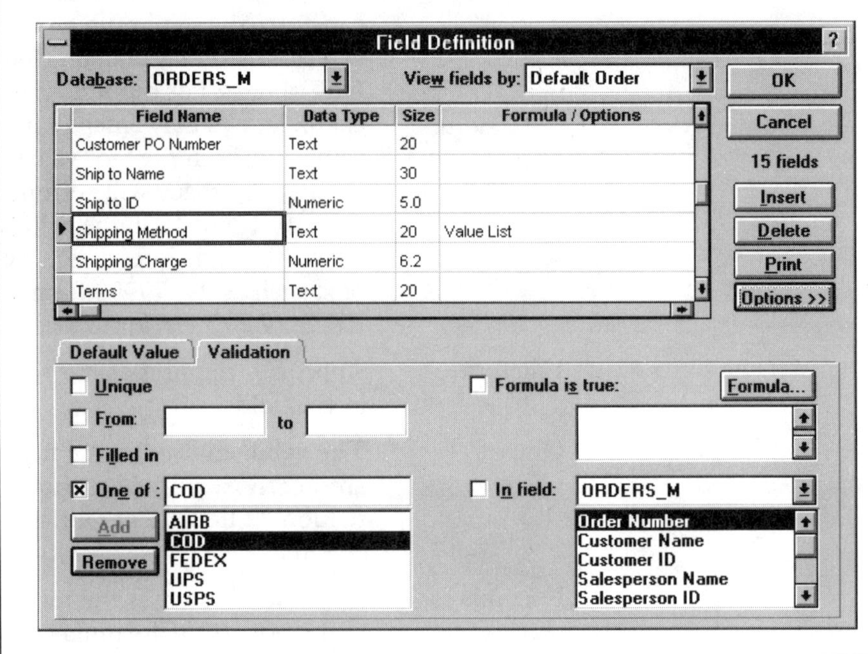

FIGURE 5.11 ▸

The One of option can be used to permit entry of only specified values. Shown here is the definition of the values for the Shipping Method field.

3. Select Add. Approach adds the item to the list. The item is added in ascending order (numerically or alphabetically according to the field type).
4. Repeat steps 2 and 3 until all values have been added. To insert a value in the list, enter the new value and select Add.
5. To remove an item from the list, highlight it and select Remove.

Figure 5.11 shows a One of option defined with five valid values. When you enter a value in the Shipping Method field in a form (shown in Figure 5.12), you must enter either AIRB, COD, FEDEX, UPS, or USPS.

FIGURE 5.12

The One of option in use on a data entry form. When you move to the Shipping Method field, only one of the five values can be entered.

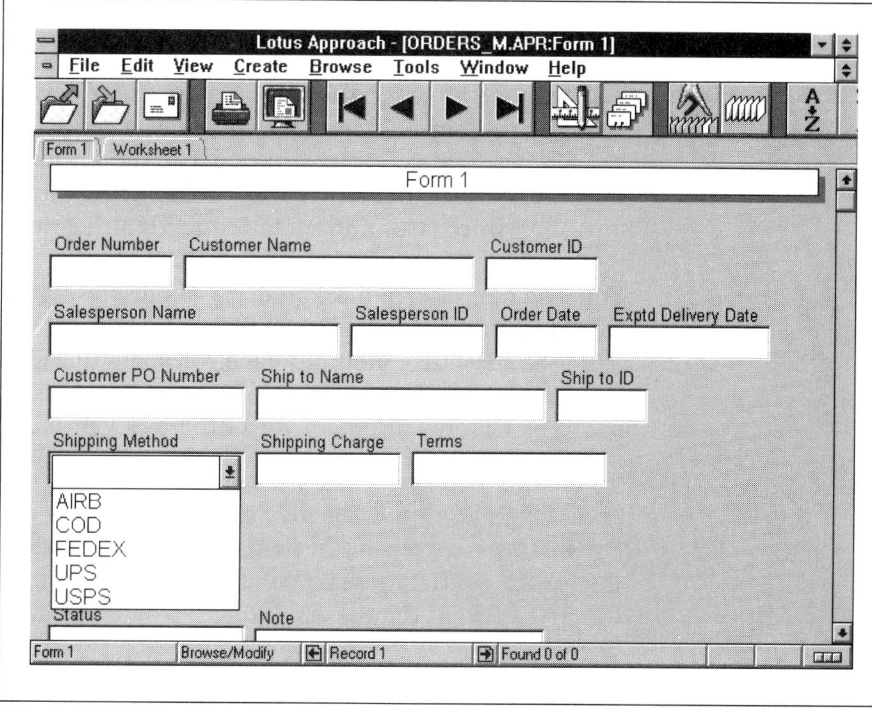

TIP

Values in the "One of" field are stored in alphabetic or numeric order. When you add this field to a form, you can tell Approach to display the permissible values in a pull-down list. It is easier for you to select values from a list when they are in order. You cannot rearrange values in the list (to put the most-used option first, for example) nor can you remove a value and add it in at a new location.

The In Field Option

The *In field* option is used to be sure the value entered exists in another field (in the same or different database). This option is a quick way to perform a validation by "looking up" a value in another table. The In field option only checks to make sure the value exists—it does not use the value in a calculation or add it to the database you're checking.

Use this option when the value entered in a field must exactly match a value in another field in the same or another database within the Approach file. For example, you may use the Orders_M database (Orders Main, one of the default templates included with Approach) to enter customer purchases and include the identification number of the salesperson taking the order. We'll call this field the Salesperson ID field. You also keep a separate database of all salespeople (you'll learn about working with multiple databases in Chapter 6); this database, named SALESPER.DBF, includes each salesperson's identification number (in a field named SalesID), his or her name, the store where employed, the salesperson's hire date, and other relevant information.

To ensure that when you are working with new or existing orders you enter a valid Salesperson ID (one that matches a record in the SALESPER database), set the In field option of the Salesperson ID field in the ORDERS_M database to be one of the values in the SalesID field of the SALESPER database.

Figure 5.13 shows the In field option set for the Salesperson ID field. When you enter a value in the Salesperson ID field on any Approach view (a data entry form or worksheet, for example), the value you enter must be found in the SalesID field of a record in the SALESPER database. In fact, to prevent errors, Approach will change the Salesperson ID field automatically to a drop-down list so you can select the value. (You can override this choice, of course. You'll learn more about placing fields on forms and how to enter data in your database in Chapters 7, 8, and 9.)

If the value does not match, Approach will display an error message, as shown in Figure 5.14. Approach's error message may appear somewhat cryptic in that it does not tell you why the entry does not match. Unfortunately, there is no way to override this message and make it more meaningful—to tell you that Approach could not find the value "7" in the SalesID field in any record in the SALESPER database, for example.

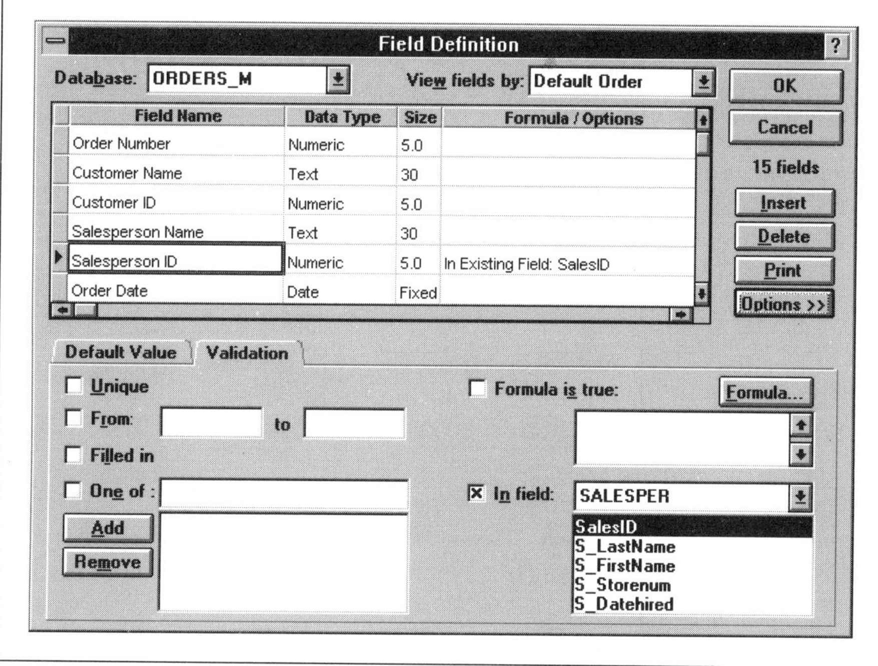

FIGURE 5.13

Using the In field validation options for the Salesperson ID field, any value entered in the field must match the same value in the SalesID field of the SALESPER database.

▸▸ Using Formulas

Formulas can be used in several places within Approach. You can:

- Define a calculated field that contains the result of a formula; you can display calculated fields in views, such as data entry forms, but you can never change the value of a calculated field.
- Specify the default value for a field based on the value in other fields; this technique saves data entry time. When this field appears on a form, Approach will fill in the calculated value, but you can always override it by typing in a new value.
- Define an if/then formula that must be "true" before a field is valid and the record can be added; these formulas are called validation formulas.

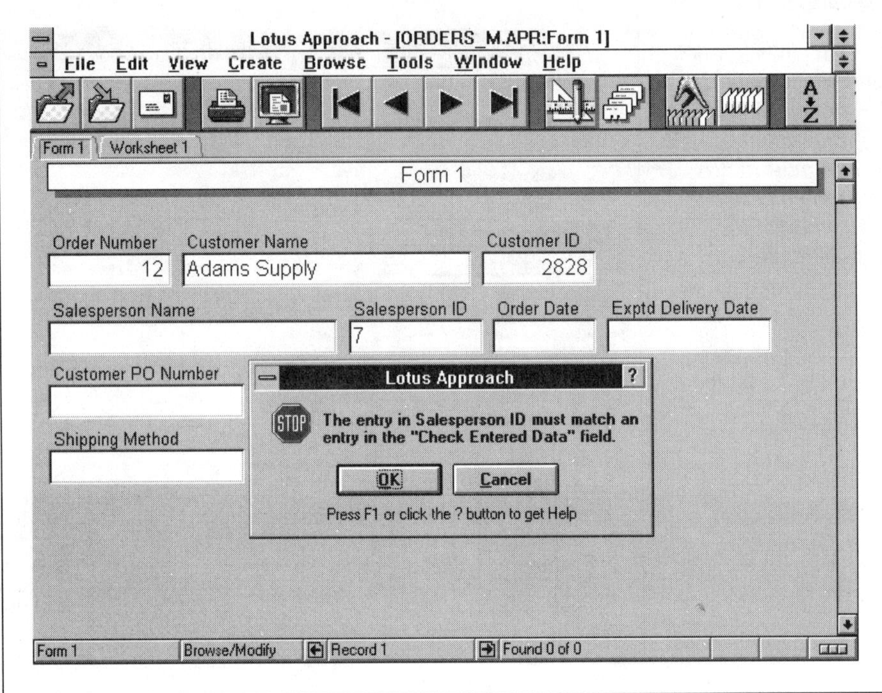

FIGURE 5.14 *The Orders form rejects a salesperson identification number if that number cannot be found in the SALESPER database.*

In any of these cases, you must define the calculation Approach performs to fill in the field value. Approach performs the calculation and updates the calculated value whenever the value of a field in the formula changes.

▸ Defining Formulas for Calculated Fields

You can define a calculated field to automatically compute the value based on two or more fields within a database. For example, suppose your database contains numeric fields named “Unit Price” and “Quantity Ordered,” and a calculated field named “Line Total.” You define Line Total to be the result of multiplying Unit Price times Quantity Ordered using the formula “Unit Price” * “Quantity Ordered.” You can select the fields by choosing them (clicking on them) from the Fields list. As you choose a field, operator, or function, the value is placed in the Formula box. If the formula is valid, the checkered flag is black. If the formula is not valid, such as

```
"Unit Price" *
```

then the flag contains a red X through it, the symbol for "not." The valid formula is shown in Figure 5.15.

FIGURE 5.15

Entering a formula for a calculated field

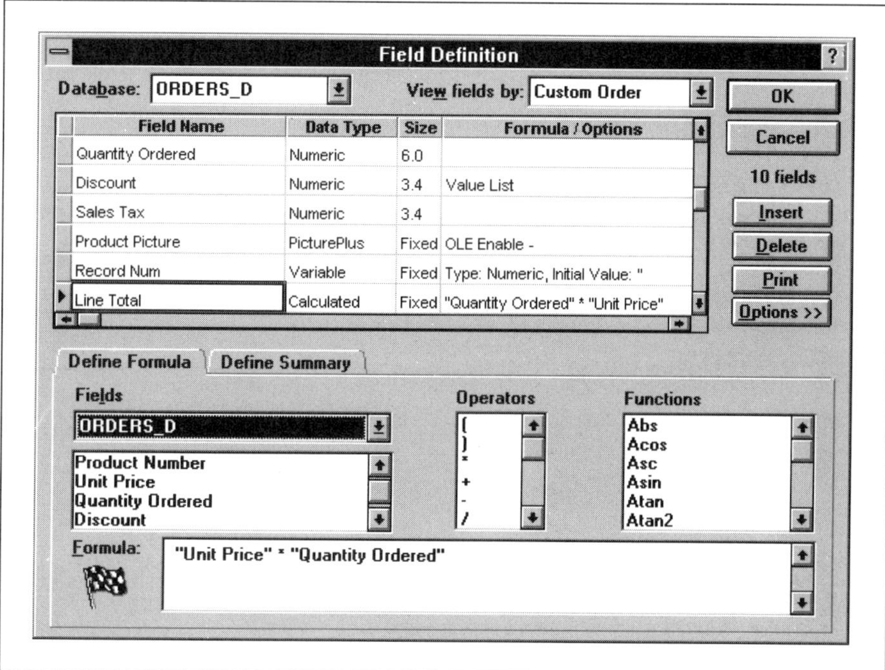

Field names are enclosed in quotes when the name contains more than one word. If the field had been named Price rather than Unit Price, the formula would read

```
Price * "Quantity Ordered"
```

If you are working with joined databases (two or more databases used in the same Approach file, which you'll learn about in Chapter 6), the database name and a period precede the field name. For example, if there were several databases included in the Approach file, the formula would read

```
ORDERS_PRICES."Unit Price" * ORDERS_AMTS."Quantity
Ordered"
```

Notice that the database name is always in all UPPERCASE letters, while the name of the field uses upper and lower case letters just as it appears in the Field Definition list.

When price, quantity, and calculated fields are displayed on a view and you change either the price of the item or the quantity ordered, Approach automatically calculates the new Line Total field. If you change both price and quantity fields, Approach will perform the calculation twice (once each time a field is changed). Figure 5.16 illustrates this example.

FIGURE 5.16

Approach can calculate the value of a field by applying a formula you define. Here the calculated field computes the product of price times quantity.

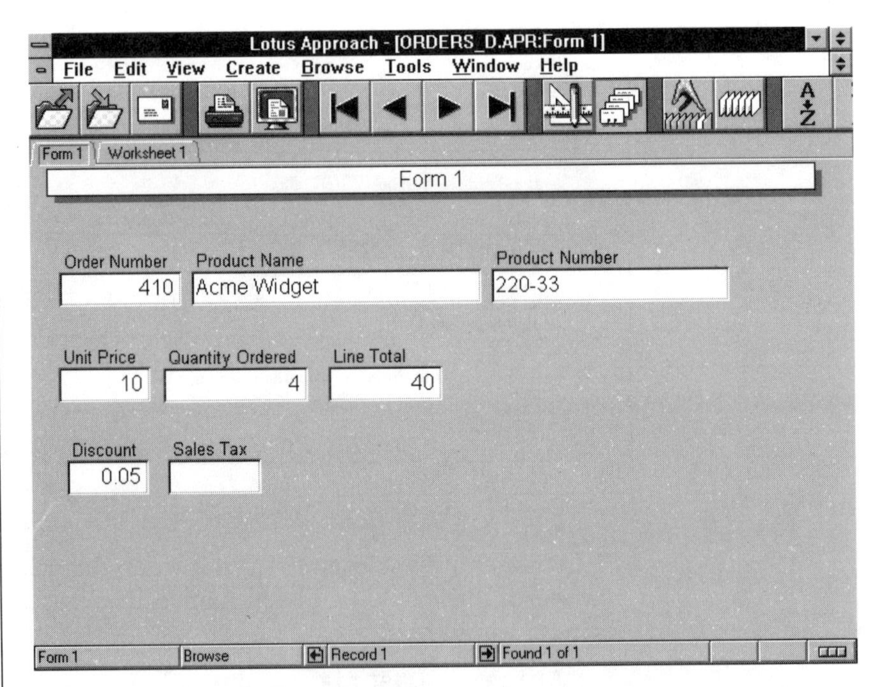

TIP

You can set the initial value of a Boolean field to 0 or 1, not "true" or "false," using a formula in Approach. For example, in the Field Definition dialog box, click on the Default Value tab of a Boolean field we'll call LargeQty, choose Creation formula, and enter IF(Quantity > 10). If the value in the Quantity field of the same record contains a value greater than 10, then LargeQty will contain 1 (true). Otherwise the LargeQty field will contain 0 (false).

Approach can also calculate subtotals and totals using what it calls *summary formulas*. Summary formulas are used in reports and in *repeating panels* (areas in which many records are displayed, such as a list of orders for a customer) on data entry forms. Summary formulas are described in Chapter 11.

▶ Setting Default Values with Formulas

You can save time entering values in a field by using a formula to compute the default value. For example, suppose you want to follow-up with a customer 30 days after the current date. First, you would create a field named Next Contact in the CUSTOMER database. Then you would enter a formula that gets the current system date and adds 30 days to it. To enter the formula, select the Next Contact field in the Field Definition dialog box and choose the Options button to open the Field Definition dialog box. The Default Value tab is already selected, as shown in Figure 5.17.

Select Creation formula and click on the Formula button. The Formula dialog box opens, as shown in Figure 5.18. (This dialog box closely resembles the Define Formula tab shown in Figure 5.15 earlier in this chapter.) From the Functions list, double-click Today. This tells Approach to start with today's date. Double-click the plus symbol (+) in the Operators list, then type in the **30**. This tells Approach you want a field value that is 30 days beyond the current date. When you select OK, your formula is placed in the formula box of the Default Value tab.

FIGURE 5.17

The Field Definition dialog box for the Next Contact field

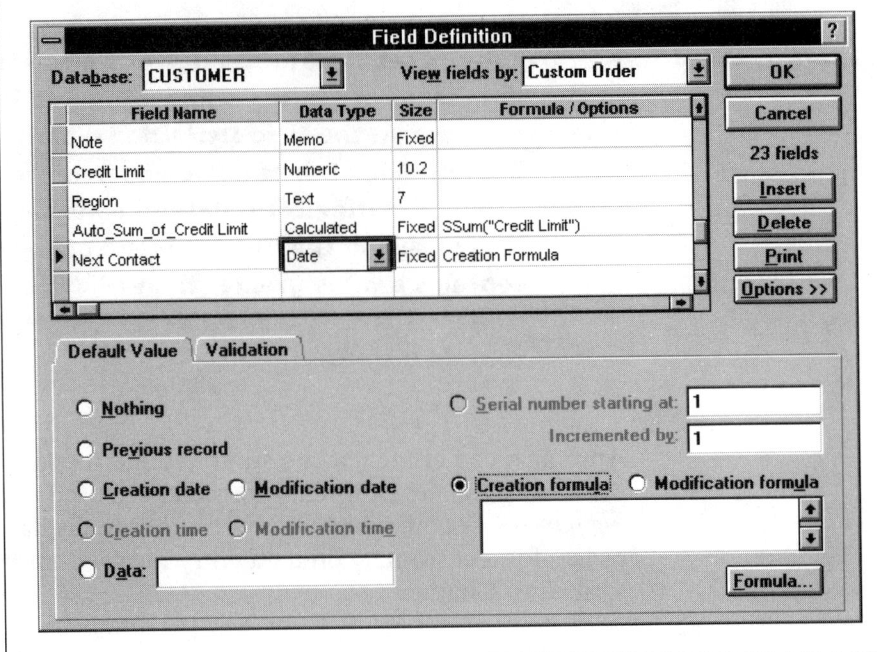

You can enter a formula directly in the Creation formula and Modification formula areas of the Default Value tab, or use the mouse to click your way to building formulas by selecting the Formula button. The Formula dialog box is typical of the options provided for creating formulas, providing selection lists to reduce errors and relieve you of memorizing the spelling of some functions.

When defining or modifying formulas, you can double-click on any field name, operator, or function and Approach will add them at the position of the I-beam within the Formula text box. You can also position the I-beam cursor within the Formula box directly and enter one or more characters as needed.

When you select a function, Approach will add parentheses at the end of the function name. You may have to enter other values or field

FIGURE 5.18 

The Formula dialog box

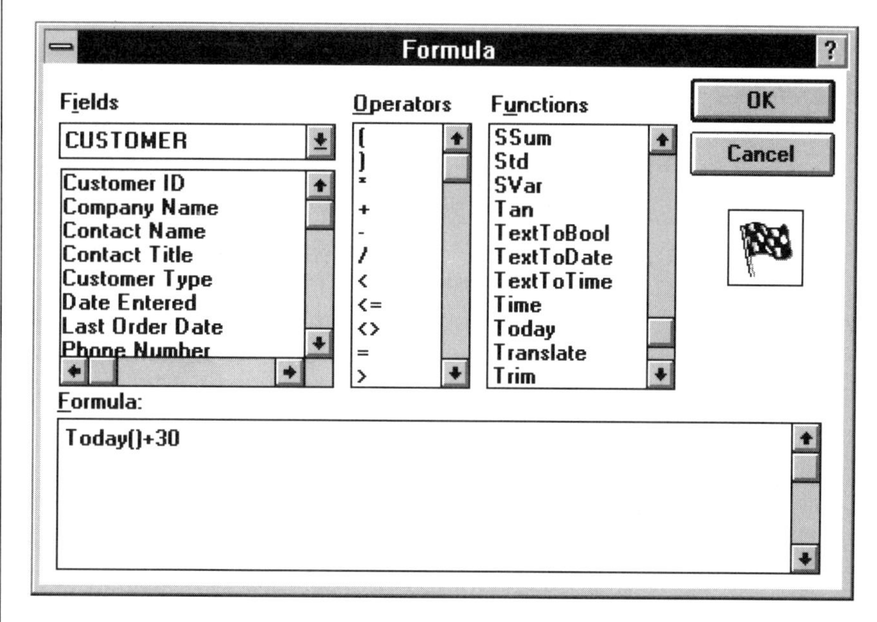

names between these parentheses, since some functions require data (called parameters) while others, such as Today( ), do not.

If your formula is incorrect, the checkered flag icon is grayed out and has a red X through it. If the formula is valid, the checkered flag icon is displayed in black and white and without the X.

Notice, too, that Approach lets you create a Creation formula and a Modification formula (see bottom-right of the Default Value tab shown in Figure 5.17 earlier in this chapter). As you might expect, Approach uses the Creation formula when you are entering a new record, and the Modification formula when you are changing data in an existing record.

▸▸ **NOTE**

Two caveats about formula are in order. Formulas are used for the field even if the cursor is not in the field for which the formula is defined. For example, Approach will fill in the Next Contact date (today's date plus 30 days) even if you never move the cursor to the next contact date field. Second, you can always override a formula for a default value. For example, if the next contact date falls on a holiday, you can move to the field and enter a value manually. The value you enter overrides the formula.

Reviewing the Steps

You can define a Creation Formula by opening the Field Definition dialog box (for existing databases) or using the Creating New Database dialog box when you define a new database. Be sure to select the Options button so the full dialog box is displayed.

Use these steps to define a default value with a Creation or Modification formula:

1. Select the field to contain the result of the calculation.
2. Select Creation formula to define a formula Approach will use to fill the field in a new record. Select Modification formula to define a formula used to fill the field whenever a change is made to an existing record. (If you don't create a Creation formula, Approach copies your Modification formula as the Creation formula automatically.)
3. You can enter the formula directly in the text box below the formula options on the Default Value tab. If the formula is incorrect, Approach displays a warning message until the formula is valid. If you wish to enter the formula using the Formula dialog box, proceed to Step 4.
4. Select the Formula button in the bottom-right of the dialog box (Figure 5.17). Approach displays the Formula dialog box.

5. Build the formula by highlighting the fields, operators, and functions as appropriate. Approach will display your formula as you build it and verify that it is valid.
6. If the formula is valid, the checkered flag icon is displayed in black and white and without an X through it, and the OK button is enabled. Select OK when your formula is correct, or select Cancel to abandon your formula.

Functions and detailed formula instructions are provided in Chapter 19.

FIGURE 5.19

Using a formula for validating field values

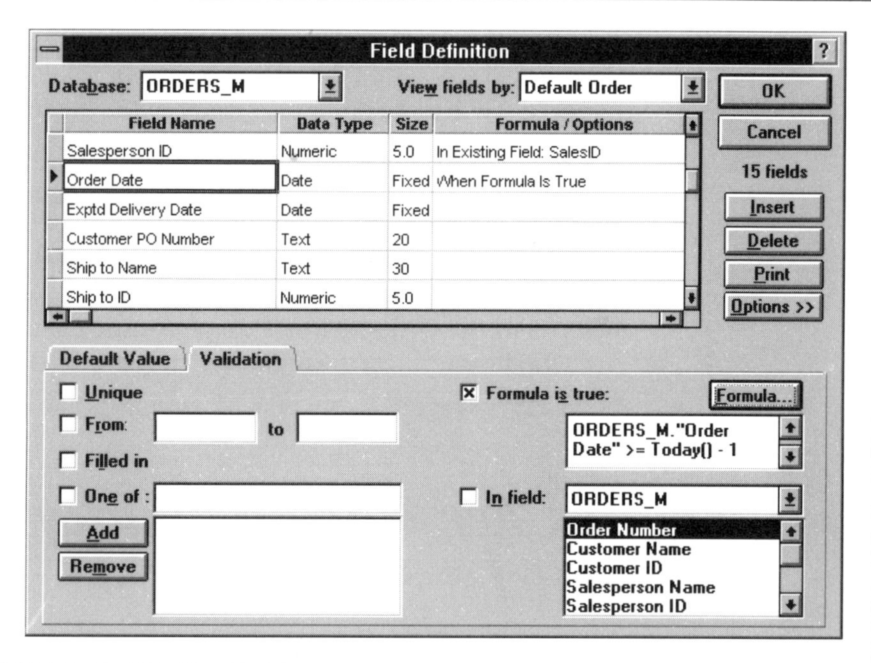

▶ Defining a Validation Formula

The third place you can use a formula is in data entry. Approach lets you ensure that an entry in a field is correct using the results of a formula. From the Validation tab of the Field Definition screen, shown in Figure 5.19, you can enter a formula directly or select the Formula button to display the Formula dialog box.

When you change a field value (in a data entry form, worksheet, or report, for example) used in a formula, Approach evaluates the formula using the new value. If the formula is true when the new value is used, the field value is valid and Approach will add or modify the record. Otherwise, Approach displays a warning message.

Validation formulas are slightly different from Creation or Modification formulas and formulas for calculated fields because Validation formulas must evaluate to True or False. Thus, validation formulas use comparisons. For example, suppose you want to ensure that the date you enter in the Order Date is never earlier than yesterday's date. That is, when you enter an order, the date of the order will be yesterday (you didn't finish up all of yesterday's orders before leaving work, for example), today, or any day in the future (the customer wants to place the order with an effective date of next week, for example). Thus, your validation formula must check to see that the order date is not for any date before yesterday.

In the Formula box you can enter ORDERS_M."Order Date" >= Today( ) – 1, or click on the Formula button and use the Formula dialog box to build the formula. This formula says that the order date field of the ORDERS_M database must be greater than or equal to the current date minus one. Thus, if today's date is 7/1/95 and you enter 6/30/95 in the Order Date field, the formula is true. If you enter 6/30/94, however, the formula does not evaluate to true, and the entry is rejected.

▸▸ Formulas Are Not Just Fancy Arithmetic!

Don't confuse using formulas with performing arithmetic. Using formulas, you can define the initial value of a field as the result of a calculation, even if the data type is not numeric. For example, suppose you have a customer name that is split into two fields: FIRST and LAST. FIRST contains the customer's first name, and LAST contains—you guessed it—the customer's last name. You can create a FULLNAME field that consists of the customer's first and last names by defining the formula as COMBINE(FIRST,' ',LAST), which combines (concatenates) the text in the FIRST field, a space, and the text in the LAST field. You create a space by typing a single quotation mark, pressing the spacebar once, and typing another single quotation mark. Notice also the commas separating each field from the next. If the FIRST field contains *Jim* and the LAST field contains *Powell*, the formula returns the result *Jim Powell* (notice the space between first and last names). Figure 5.20 shows the field formula to combine two fields and a space. When you enter the values in the FIRST and LAST name fields on a form, Approach displays the full name in the customer name field. You can combine only text strings, but Approach offers you several functions to convert other data types, such as dates and numbers, to text. See Chapter 19 for details.

FIGURE 5.20

You can define a formula to work with text fields as well as numeric fields.

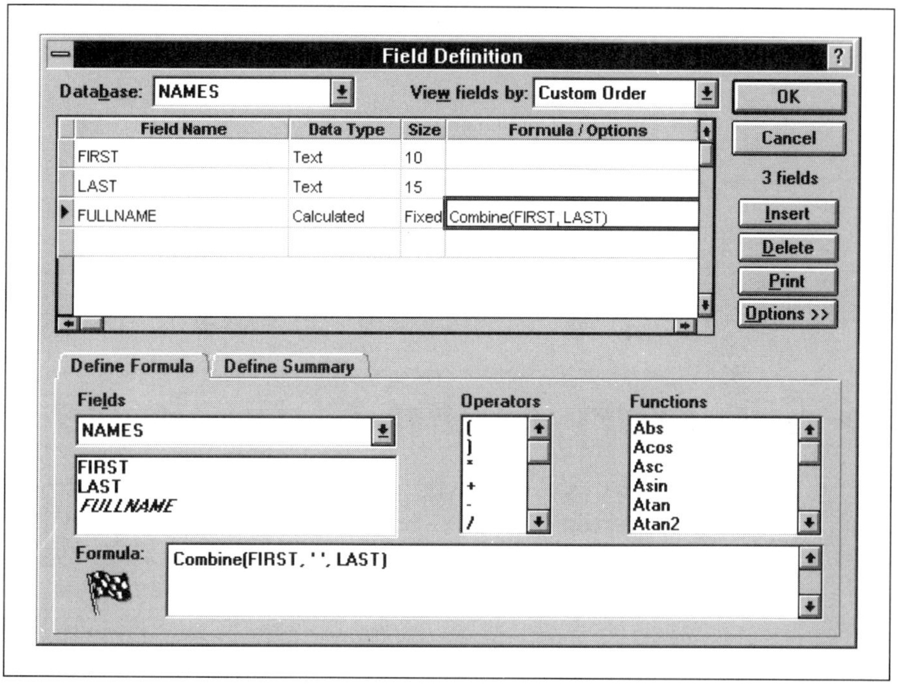

Notice that while the last name has been entered in Figure 5.21, the FULLNAME field does not contain the entire name as expected. Why? Because the formula in the FULLNAME field is only updated when the value in the LAST name field changes. Since the cursor is still in the LAST name field, that field hasn't "officially" changed. When you move the cursor to any other field, however, Approach recognizes that you have moved away from the LAST name field, and the FULLNAME field is updated, as expected, and as shown in Figure 5.22.

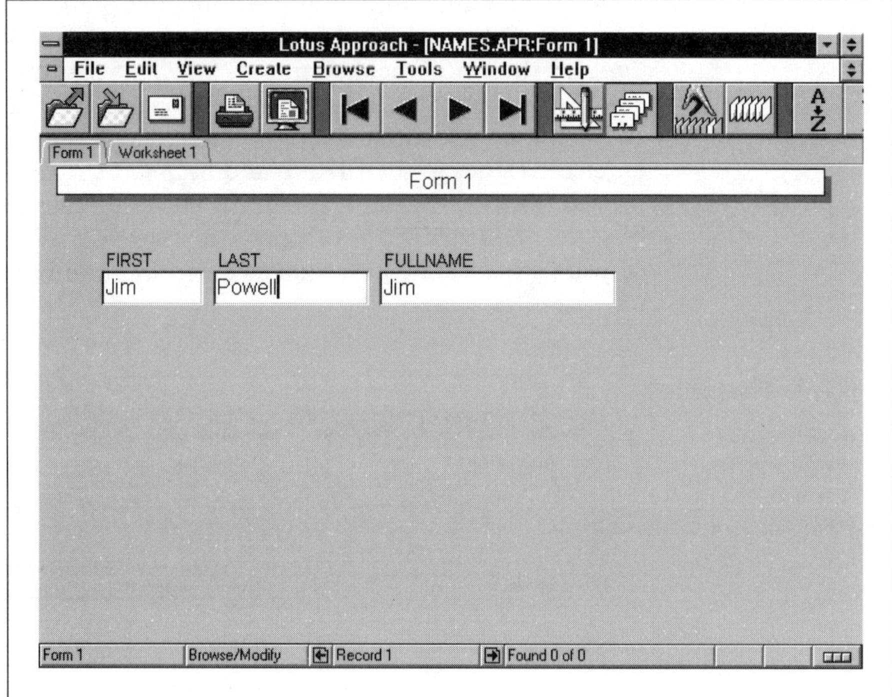

FIGURE 5.21 *You can place the FIRST, LAST, and FULLNAME fields on the same form. When the FIRST or LAST name is changed, the FULLNAME field is updated to reflect the change. Here the cursor is still in the LAST name field, so the LAST name field hasn't "officially" been changed.*

▸▸ Summary and a Look Ahead

In this chapter you've learned how to change the definition of an existing database. You've seen how you can add or delete fields. You've also seen how you can set default values for a variety of field types, including Boolean, date, numeric, text, and time fields. Approach's validation option and formulas let you specify further conditions on data in fields, and let you limit entries to a predefined set of values.

FIGURE 5.22

When you move the cursor out of the LAST name field, the FULL-NAME field is updated according to the formula.

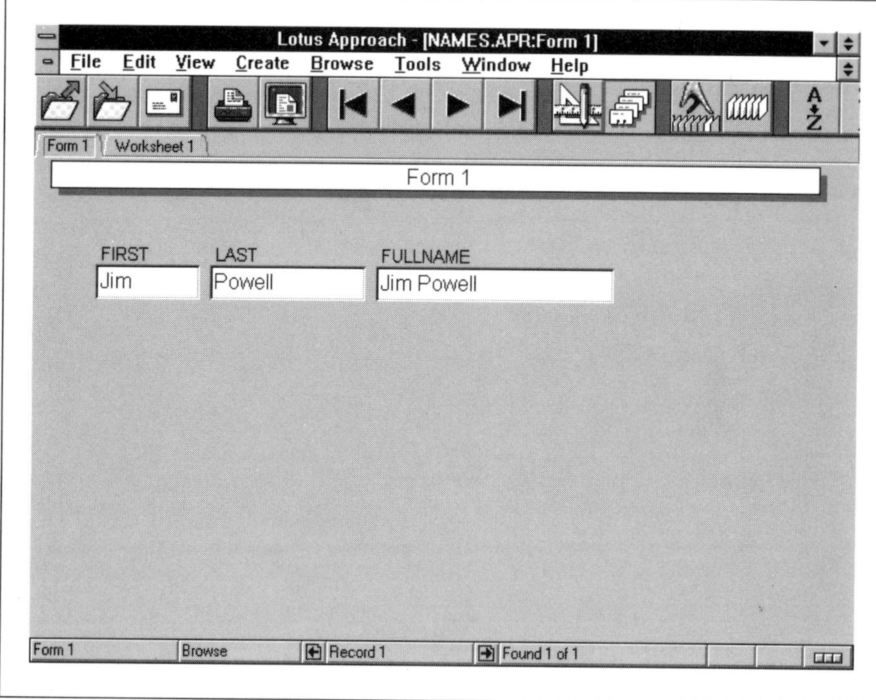

So far we've been working with single databases. In Chapter 6 you'll see how to take several databases you've created, using the techniques in Chapters 3, 4, and 5, and combine them into a larger application. The process of relating two or more databases is called *joining*. Joins reduce unnecessary repetition in your data and give you some powerful look-up and validation features for your forms and reports.

▶ ▶ CHAPTER 6

Working with Multiple Databases

▸▸ FAST TRACK

▶ To remove a join 186

select Create ➤ Join. Click on the line joining the two fields, then choose UnJoin. If there is any database in the Join dialog box that no longer contains a joining line, select the database (click on the list of fields) and choose Close. The database is removed from the dialog box. Select OK.

▶ To serialize new records in a database 189

select File ➤ Open. Enter the name of the Approach file that contains the primary database. Select OK, then choose Create ➤ Field Definition. Select the field you want to serialize. The field should have a field type of numeric. Click on Options and select the "Serial number starting at" option on the Default Value tab. To begin the next new record with a particular number, enter the number in the "Serial number starting at" text box. To increment this field by a value other than 1, enter the value in the "Incremented by" text box. Select OK to leave the Field Definition dialog box.

▸▸ **When** you want to maintain a simple list of things, such as the items in your coin collection, a list of employee names and telephone numbers, or the statistics of your favorite sports team, a single Approach database is all you need. Chapters 3, 4, and 5 explained how to set up a single database. There are times, however, when the data you need for a report, for example, is kept in two or more databases. This chapter explains when two databases are better than one and the differences between single-database applications, such as list keepers, and multiple-database applications.

We'll also explain why you may wish to take advantage of Approach's ability to add, update, delete, and report on data from more than one database simultaneously. You'll learn how to set up multiple databases and tell Approach you want to use them together.

The technique of maintaining data in more than one database and telling Approach how the databases are related (called *joining*) is a feature that distinguishes low-end from high-end database managers. Because so many of the features in Approach allow you to use fields from more than one database, it's important to understand when you should use multiple databases and how joins work before you create views such as data entry forms, worksheets, or reports.

Using multiple databases is also one of the least understood features of Approach, especially for beginners. Therefore, we'll use several examples to illustrate the differences between single-and multiple-database applications.

▸▸ When to Use a Single Database

If you use Approach to keep a list of items, a single database is all you may ever need. In a list, you are keeping track of unique elements. For example, if you own a hardware store, you can track your inventory using a single database. A single database can store the part number, a brief description, the quantity on hand, and perhaps the retail selling price.

Likewise, Approach's single databases can track your stock portfolio. The values in this database could consist of the stock symbol, the company name, the number of shares you own, how much you paid, and the current market value, for example. You can also include a calculated field to compute your gains or losses. If your portfolio is small (say, less than 30 stocks), this single database is certainly adequate.

We've just illustrated two important points for using a single database. If the elements in your database are unique (they have a unique part number, for example), or your data is relatively limited (fewer than 30 items, for example), you may manage your data quite simply using a single database.

▸▸ When to Use Multiple Databases

Now let's look at a different scenario. Suppose you manage a group of sales people who sell dental supplies to over 1,000 dental offices in your region. You need to track the orders each customer places. Besides keeping the name, address, and telephone number of each customer, you want to keep information about each order. To keep this example simple, let's say you want to store the date of the order and its total value, and since you have to write up each order on a pre-numbered form, you'll want to store the order number in your database as well. Thus, your database contains the following fields:

- Customer name
- Customer telephone number
- Customer address
- Customer city
- Customer state
- Customer zip
- Order date

- Amount of order
- Order number

Let's look at what happens when you keep the information in a *flatfile,* or a single database, containing the fields we've just listed. Every time you receive an order, you need to enter data into a new record. Figure 6.1 shows an example of the screen of an application you might create. Notice that you must enter the customer's name (Dr. Johnson's Dental Clinic), address, and telephone number, the date of the order, the total value of the order, and the order number for each new order.

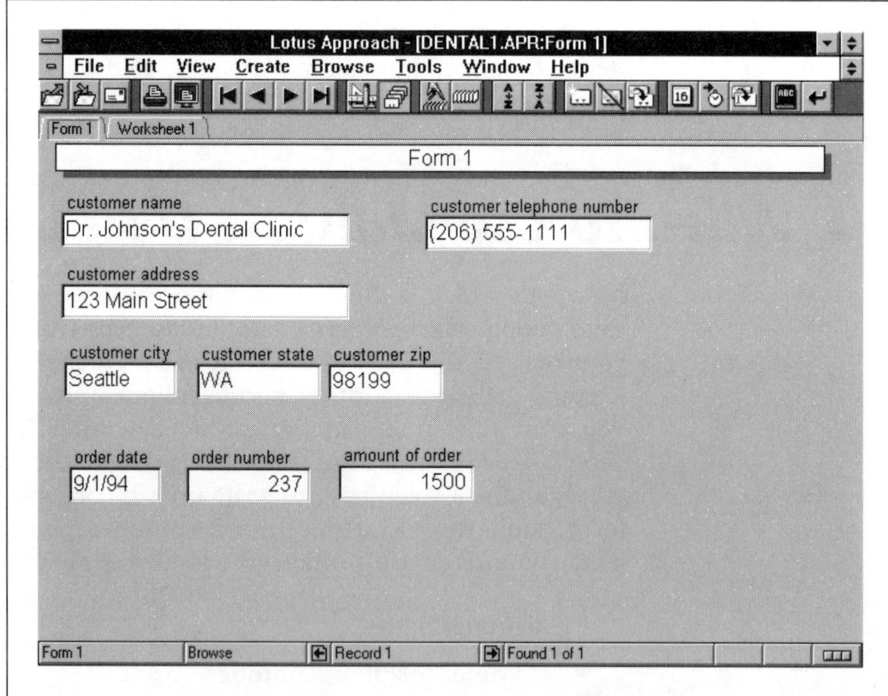

FIGURE 6.1 ▶

The Dental Clinic data entry screen

The next week Dr. Johnson's office calls and places another order. Once again you add a record to your Approach database, entering all the same data: the customer's name, address, and telephone number; the date of the order; the total value of the order; and the order number. While the order information has changed (you're recording data for a different date and order number, and the total value is probably different), it's unlikely that the customer's name, address, and telephone number have changed. Thus, while you're entering new values for the order, you're entering the same old values for the customer. This redundant customer information may cause problems, as we'll soon see.

As you have probably guessed, when Dr. Johnson's office calls to place its third order in a month, you will once again have to enter the customer's name, address, and telephone number. In fact, you'll have to do this for each new order—over and over and over again. This is certainly inefficient.

Using a flatfile to record this information has another problem. Suppose Dr. Johnson's Dental Clinic moves to a new location. We'll assume that not only does the address change but so does the telephone number. You'll certainly want to keep the most up-to-date information in your database, so you'll want to edit all the previously entered order records and change the address and telephone number. Otherwise, if you look up a previously entered order you'll be looking at the old address and telephone number. If Dr. Johnson placed only two or three orders, it wouldn't be too much work to change the address and telephone number in the database records associated with those orders. If Dr. Johnson's office placed orders once a week during the past year, you'll have to update 52 records. That's much more work.

When Dr. Johnson decides to move her office, another potential problem crops up. While you may be an excellent typist, the odds are you will make at least one mistake when you update the 52 records with her new address. This introduces the possibility that of the 52 records, 51 of them will list her address as 123 Main Street and one will list it as 132 Main Street. This obvious inconsistency in the database records leads to problems: Which address is correct?, for example.

In addition to wasting data entry time, flatfile databases waste considerable disk space. If Dr. Johnson's office has placed 52 orders over the past year, we have 52 records that contain the same information. That is, our hard disk contains 52 records that repeat her address and telephone number. With a flatfile (single) database, we are stuck with those 52 records that repeat the customer name, address, and telephone number. All that data takes up hard disk space, and since it's all the same, that amounts to a lot of wasted space. It would be much more beneficial if we could save the "repeated" information in one place.

►► Using Multiple Databases

Instead of using a single (flatfile) database to store customer orders, you can use two databases. In the first you'll keep just one record for each customer's name, address, and telephone number. In the second you can store the details about each order: the order date, the value of the order, and the order number. Figure 6.2 illustrates this design.

FIGURE 6.2 

A multiple database solution for orders

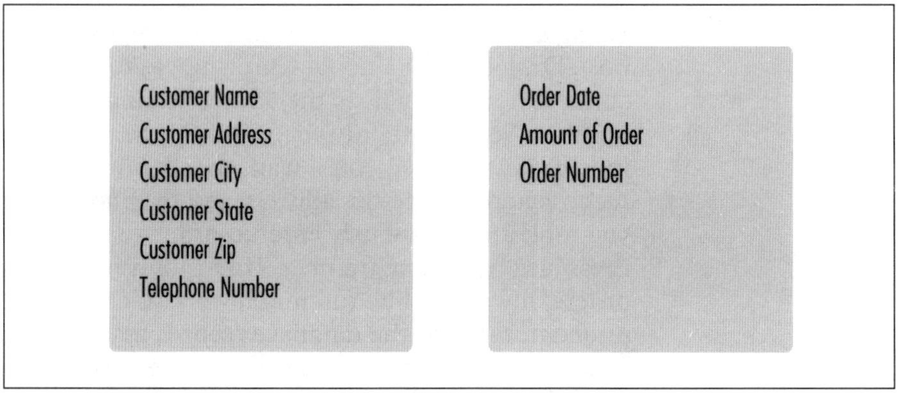

Customer Name
Customer Address
Customer City
Customer State
Customer Zip
Telephone Number

Order Date
Amount of Order
Order Number

In the CUSTOMER database you'll have these fields:

- Customer Name
- Customer Address
- Customer City
- Customer State
- Customer Zip
- Telephone Number

In the ORDERS database you'll have these fields:

- Order Date
- Amount of Order
- Order Number

That's almost all there is to it. You've separated the repeating information about a customer into a separate database. You'll need only one record in the CUSTOMER database for each customer, so that Dr. Johnson's clinic occupies only one record, not 52. Likewise, each record in the ORDERS database contains only information that is relevant to the order itself.

This design isn't complete, however. If you look at any order record in the ORDERS database, you'll only learn about the order itself, but there's no information about which customer actually placed the order. Therefore, what's missing from this design is a way to tie the two databases together, so you'll know which customer placed each order. (As it stands now, there is nothing in the ORDERS database that tells you which customer placed an order.) You must somehow connect the customer information with the correct record (or records) in the ORDERS database. This process of defining such a connection is called *joining*, since we are joining together two databases.

You join two databases by using a field that is common to both databases. That is, you select an existing field in each database, or add a field, that represents the same information. In this example, we'll add a customer number field to each database. The CUSTOMER database now contains the following fields:

- Customer Number
- Customer Name
- Customer Address
- Customer City
- Customer State
- Customer Zip
- Telephone Number

The ORDERS database now contains these fields:

- Customer Number
- Order Date
- Amount of Order
- Order Number

The new design is shown in Figure 6.3.

FIGURE 6.3 ►

The new database design, using two databases

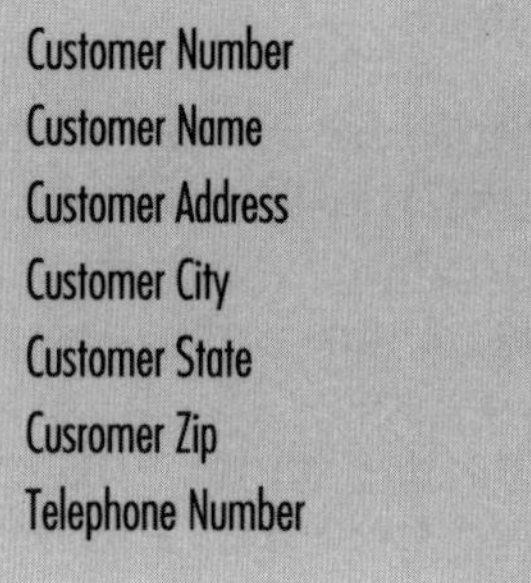

Each customer will be assigned a unique number. When the customer (dentist) places an order, the order record in the ORDERS database must include the same value in the Customer Number field as that used in the CUSTOMER database for that customer.

We'll assign Dr. Johnson's Dental Clinic customer number 100. Figure 6.4 shows an example of a data entry form for the CUSTOMER database. When we add a new customer, we assign the customer a new Customer number. For existing customers, we can look for the record by name (Dr. Johnson) or by customer number (100).

Similarly, when we enter a new order, we must enter the customer number (100) in the Customer Number field in the ORDERS data entry screen, as shown in Figure 6.5.

When Dr. Johnson calls again to place another order, we'll add a new record in the ORDERS database, using her customer number (100) in the new order record. By entering the customer number, we're telling Approach that the order is for Dr. Johnson's Dental Clinic without having to enter Dr. Johnson's name, address, and telephone number again. Approach will be able to find this information by looking for customer number 100 in the CUSTOMER database.

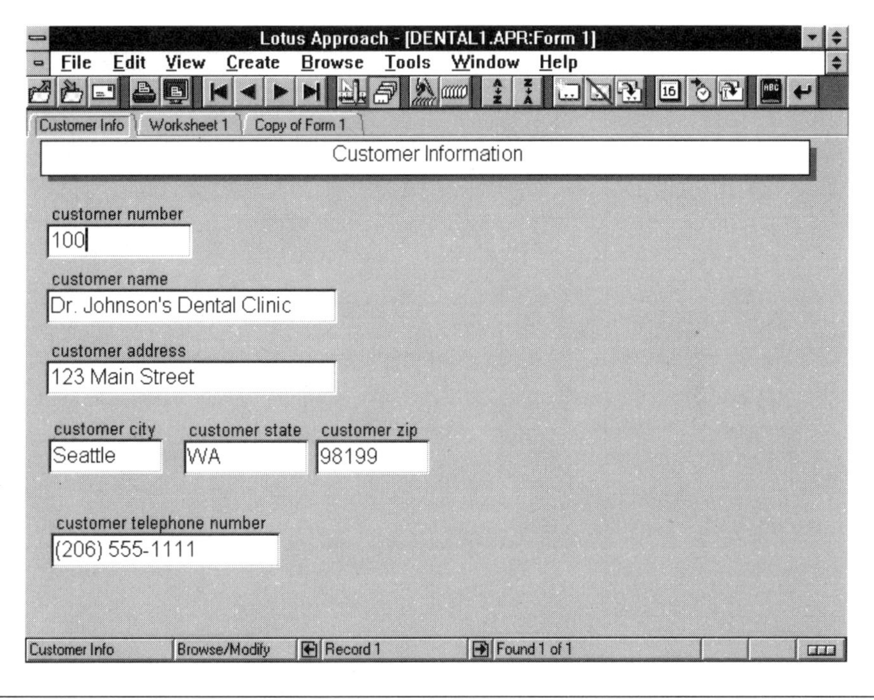

FIGURE 6.4

A data entry form for the CUSTOMER database

By using this common field, called the *join field*, and telling Approach that this field is common to both databases, we join the data from two databases to get the complete data (order data and customer data) about each order. For example, by joining the two databases using the common field called Customer Number, we can find Dr. Johnson's record in the CUSTOMER database, look at her customer number (100), and ask Approach to find all the orders that contain the same value (that is, 100) in the Customer Number field of the ORDERS database. Figure 6.6 illustrates this search screen. When you select the OK button, Approach returns the form with the customer data fields filled out—the same screen shown in Figure 6.4 earlier in this chapter. You'll learn how to perform a search in Chapter 12.

There is some redundancy in using the common field, of course. We've had to make the CUSTOMER database slightly larger to accommodate a Customer Number field, and *each* order stored in the *ORDERS* database must now contain a Customer Number field in each order record. However, when you compare this extra storage space requirement with our previous design, which stored the customer name *and*

FIGURE 6.5

A data entry form for the ORDERS database

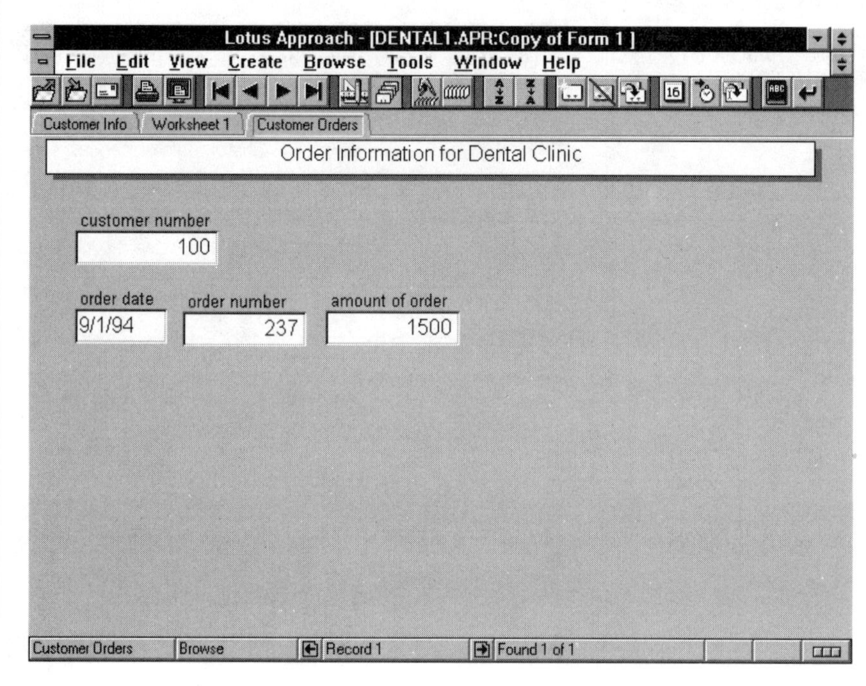

the address *and* the telephone number in each record, the savings in disk space (and data entry time) is clear.

Besides saving space, we've eliminated the two problems posed by the flatfile solution. For example, since we enter the address data into only one record of the CUSTOMER database:

- We have significantly reduced the possibility of human error during repetitive data entry. We can still make an error—there's nothing to stop us from transposing the digits in the address during data entry. However, if we do discover there's an error, we change only the one record (the single record in the CUSTOMER database)—and we won't have to search all of the records in the ORDERS database to make sure we haven't made a similar mistake in another record.
- We can easily change an address when, for example, Dr. Johnson decides to move her office. Again we enter the new address in only one record: the customer's record in the CUSTOMER database.

FIGURE 6.6

Searching for customer 100

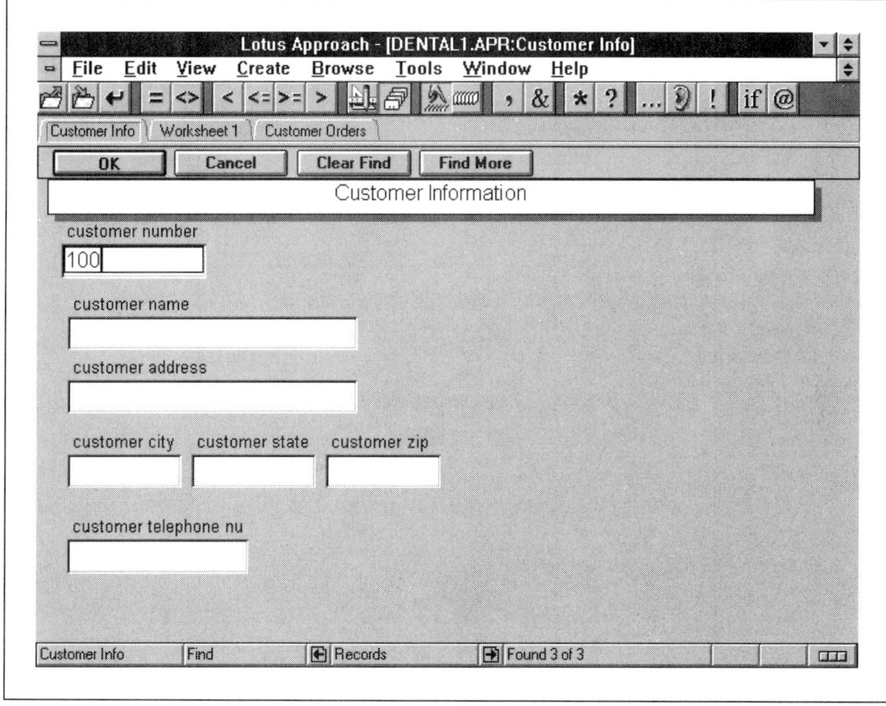

We don't have to enter the new address in each record of the ORDERS database, which saves us considerable time since Dr. Johnson's office places orders frequently.

►► How to Select the Join Field

Choosing a join field isn't as difficult as you may think. In some cases, the choice *actually* jumps out at you. For example, you're likely familiar with join fields in multiple databases without even knowing it. Your employer probably uses multiple databases to keep track of your payroll checks. The EMPLOYEE database keeps your name and address, an employee number (often it's your Social Security number), your job title, and the amount you earn per hour. A second database keeps track of the date of each paycheck, the check number, and the amount of the check. The records in the EMPLOYEE database and the records in the PAYCHECK database are "tied together" using a common field—your employee number. The EMPLOYEE database already keeps the employee number, so all you have to do is add that number to the PAYCHECK database, which stores one record for each paycheck you've received. By adding the employee number to the PAYCHECK database, you can now find the employee and the job title associated with any paycheck. Figure 6.7 shows this relationship.

FIGURE 6.7 

A payroll system uses an employee number to maintain the connection between records in the EMPLOYEE database and records in the PAYCHECK database.

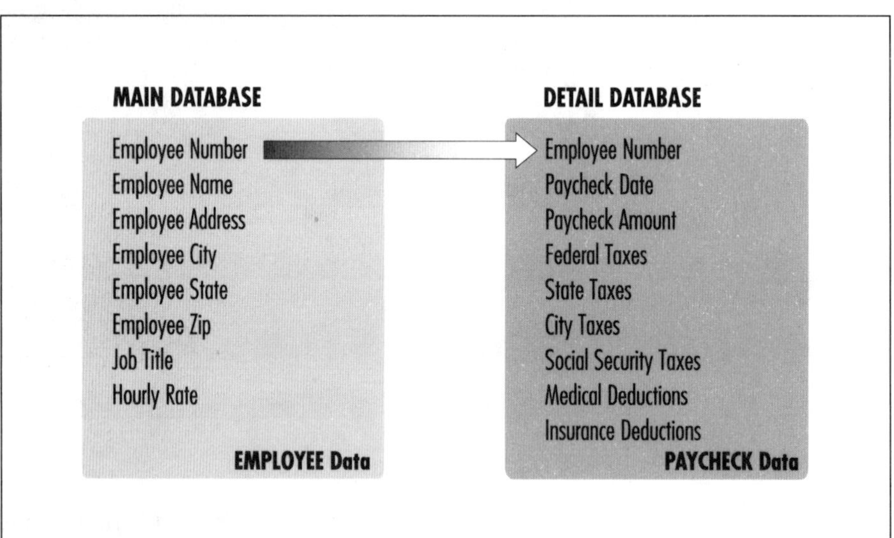

If you get a promotion and your job title changes, your employer will change the data in the Job Title field of the EMPLOYEE database, but your employee number does not change. Thus, the records in the PAYCHECK database don't have to be changed when your job title changes.

Whenever two or more databases are used on a form or a report, one database must be designated as the primary, or *main*, database. This is the database that contains a unique value in the join field. For example, when tracking the orders placed by dentists' offices, the CUSTOMER database is the main database because each record contains a unique value in the join field, the Customer Number field. In the payroll example, the EMPLOYEE database is the main database, because it contains the unique value (employee number) in the join field of every record.

The database joined to the main database is called the *detail* database. In a detail database, more than one record can have the same value in the join field. For example, more than one record in the ORDERS database will contain the customer number 100, since Dr. Johnson has placed more than one order. Likewise, you will find multiple records in the PAYCHECK database for employee number 1234 if that employee has received more than one paycheck from your company.

Thus, when you use more than one database to solve your business problem, you must keep in mind that you'll need to create a join field in the main database that will contain a unique value.

There's another condition to making the join field the most efficient. While it is not required, it is highly recommended that the join field be defined in both the main and detailed database using the same field type and same field length. For instance, in the CUSTOMER and ORDERS databases, the Customer Number field should be defined as 5 digits, numeric in the CUSTOMER database and as 5 digits, numeric in the ORDERS database. While it is possible to define the customer number in the ORDERS database as a 6-digit numeric value, for example, this makes more work for Approach and could slow down the speed of the program. The name of the field in each database is less important. For instance, the field can be called "Custnum" in the CUSTOMER database and "Customerno" in the ORDERS database without any problem, since you will specifically tell Approach the field names when you join the databases. However, the field *type* must be the same for both fields.

▸▸ Database Relationships

When you join two databases, you create a relationship between the data in the databases. The records in the CUSTOMER database are related to the records in the ORDERS database. The record for Dr. Johnson in the CUSTOMER database is related to the orders in the ORDERS database. By establishing this relationship between two (or more) databases, you create what Approach calls a *relational database application.*

In fact, the term "relational database" is used in many database programs. It simply means that two or more databases are related in some way. In the dentist's office example, the CUSTOMER database is related to the ORDERS database by the Customer Number field. In the payroll example, the EMPLOYEE database is related to the PAYCHECK database by way of the Employee Number field.

The relationships we've discussed to this point are called one-to-many relationships, often abbreviated 1-M or 1-to-M. One record in the CUSTOMER database (for example, the record for Dr. Johnson) can be related to many records in the ORDERS database, since there are many orders in the ORDERS database that were placed by Dr. Johnson's office. If Dr. Johnson places an order once a week for a year, the record in the CUSTOMER database is related to 52 records in the ORDERS database. In this case, one CUSTOMER record is related to many ORDERS records. This relationship is shown in Figure 6.8. Likewise, one EMPLOYEE record is related to many PAYCHECK records.

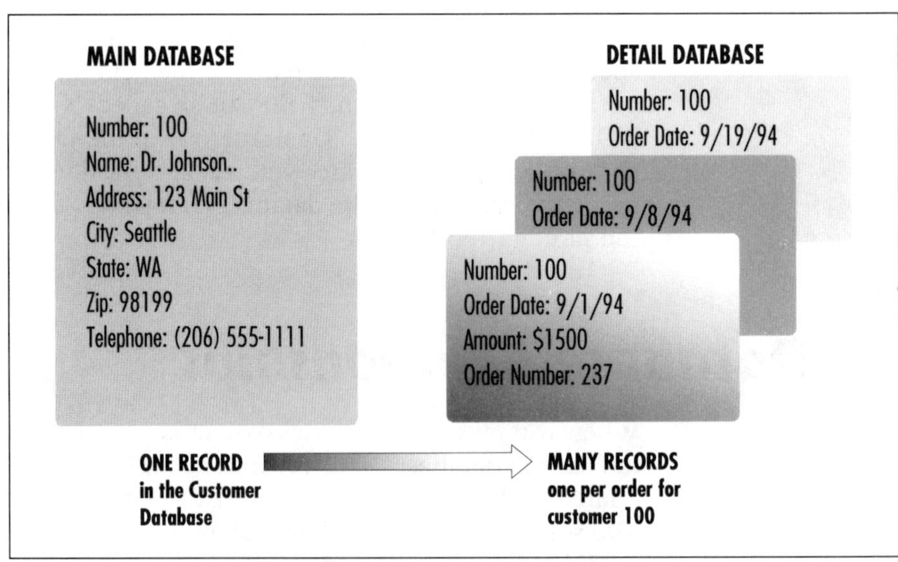

FIGURE 6.8 *The CUSTOMER and ORDERS database form a one-to-many relationship.*

There are hundreds of examples of one-to-many relationships. You can relate (join) a TEACHERS and a CLASSES database: One teacher can teach many classes. Likewise, you can construct a STUDENTS database and a CLASSES database, and join them on the basis of a student identification number. The one-to-many relationship is simple: One student can take many classes. Finally, your bank uses a relational database to maintain its data. There is a record containing your name and address in the CUSTOMER database, and one record for each account you have (a checking account, a savings account, and a car loan, for example). In this case, the one-to-many relationship is between a customer (that's you) and the accounts he/she has.

You can also join databases in a many-to-many relationship. For example, you can have TEACHER, STUDENT, and CLASS databases. A teacher can teach many classes. A student can take many classes. The relationship between teacher and student is many to many—many teachers teach many students. In such a case, Approach uses an intermediate database—the CLASSES database—to create two one-to-many relationships, as shown in Figure 6.9.

FIGURE 6.9

A many-to-many relationship uses an intermediate database and two one-to-many relationships.

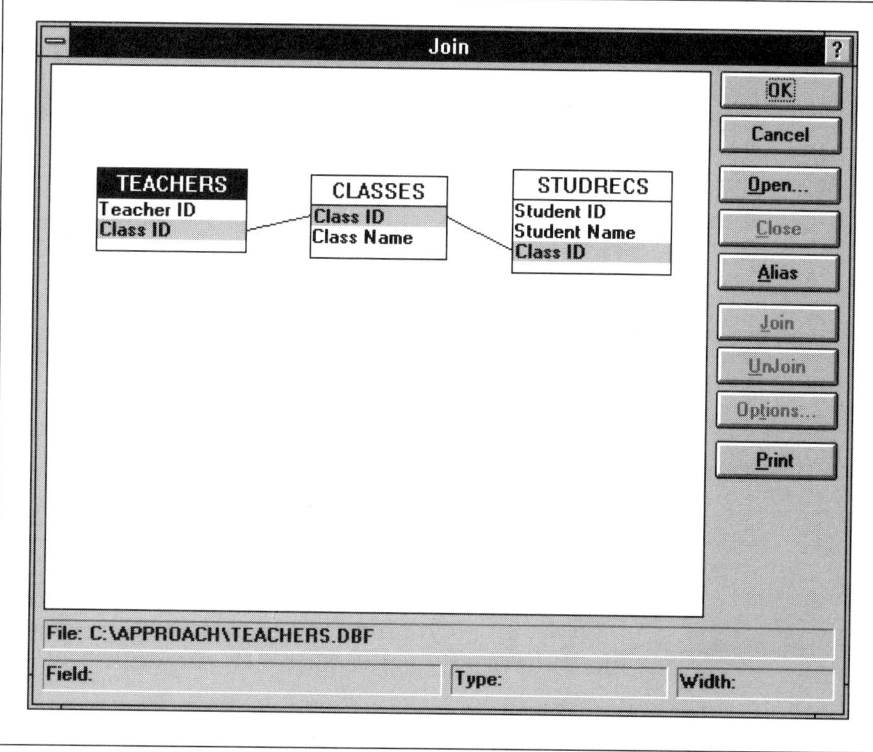

▸ Joining a Database to Itself: Alias Joins

A special relationship can be created from a database to itself. This is called an *alias join* and is rarely used, but it can be just what you need in special circumstances.

In our EMPLOYEE database we've stored the employee number. Suppose we modify the database to add a field to store the supervisor's employee number, and for our example suppose John Mosley has an employee number 1234 and Ruth Scott's record contains the value 2234 in her employee number field. If Ruth is John's supervisor, then the record for John contains the value 2234 in the Supervisor field, as shown in Figure 6.10.

FIGURE 6.10 ▸

The information about John's supervisor can be found in the same database. The supervisor number points to the record containing the data about the supervisor.

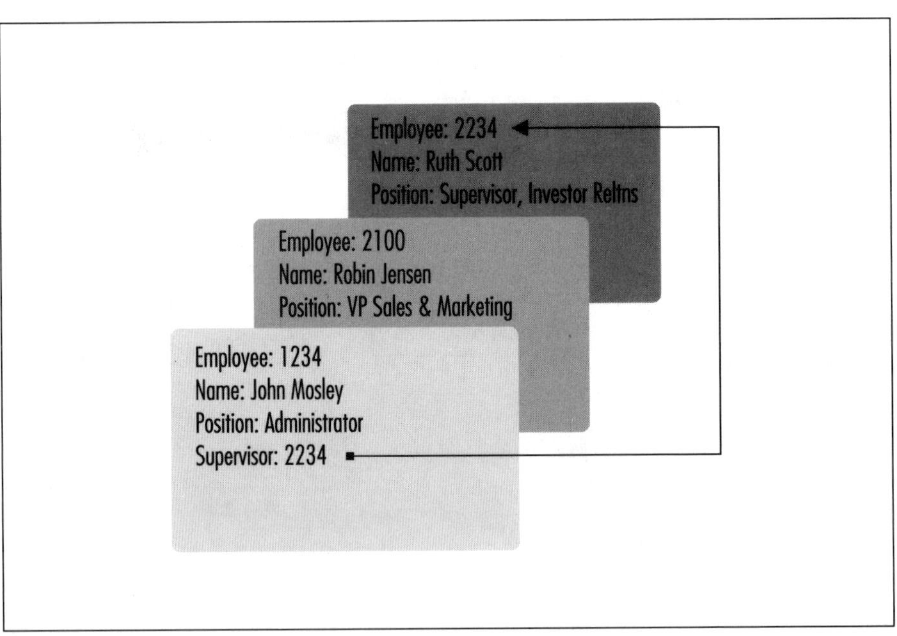

We want to print a report for each employee that lists the name, rather than the employee number, of each employee's supervisor. Thus, we'd like to have a report or form that shows:

```
Name            Title        Supervisor's Name
John Mosley     Inspector    Ruth Scott
```

Obviously the data we need about John's supervisor exists, but in another record in the *same* database rather than in a different database. That's no problem, thanks to alias joins. With an alias join we actually join the database to itself. We'll learn about joins in the next section.

►► How to Join Databases

As you've seen, creating a relationship between two databases is called *joining the databases.* The databases must be separately created, using the techniques described in Chapters 3 and 4. You create or use existing databases independently, keeping in mind that you must define a common (join) field in each database. You then join the databases using the Join command.

A key feature of Approach, and one that is often overlooked, is that Approach can join two or more databases of different file types. In the previous example, the CUSTOMER database (containing information about dentists) can be stored in dBASE format, and the ORDERS database can be stored as a Paradox file. No matter—as long as there is a common field in each database (the Customer Number), Approach can handle the details. Given the complex nature of database file formats, this is a truly remarkable and powerful feature.

Approach can manage up to 255 such relationships, although in practice you'll seldom define a relationship that complex. While Approach can work efficiently with joined databases, each join does require overhead and ultimately slows down the system.

Joins can handle several layers. For example, the main database can be related to a *detail* database, which itself is a main database for another *detail* database. In our dental sales example, a customer (dentist) can place many orders, and the ORDERS database can itself be a "main" database and be related to many Payment records that contain information about the checks received from the dentist fgor that order. Figure 6.11 shows such a relationship.

In order to join two databases, each database must be created individually. Each database to be included in the relationship must include a common field.

FIGURE 6.11

Approach can join up to 255 databases in a relational database application.

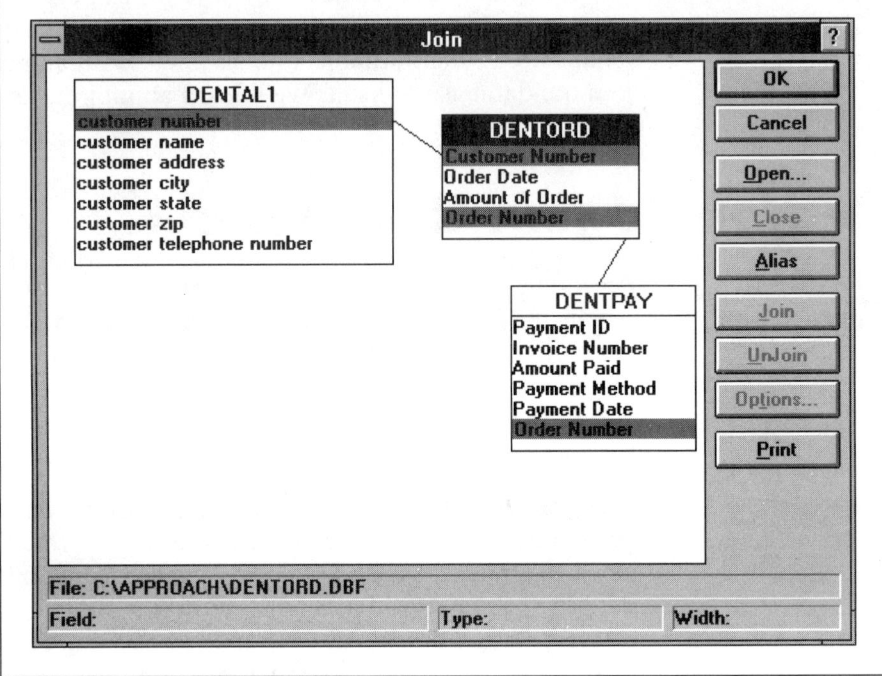

The following considerations are important when creating the main database (the database on the "one" side in a one-to-many relationship):

- The main database must include a field that contains a unique value for each record. This field is called the join field. The value in the join field is "matched" to the same value for records in the join field in the secondary database.
- Once defined, you must not change the value in the join field of the main database or records previously joined (sharing the same value in the join field) will be disconnected (no longer share that value). Although you can add and delete records from the main database, Approach is not able to take the new value in the join field and change all related records in the detail database automatically. Furthermore, changing the value adds to the risk of changing the value to a value that already exists.
- The detail database must contain a field used for the same purpose. If the main database contains a Customer Number field, the detail database must contain a Customer Number field. It is

strongly recommended that the field be defined with the same field type and same field length. Although Approach can make some conversions, this slows down the program and can introduce errors.

- The field names of the join fields in the main and detail databases do not have to be identical, although you may find it easier to use this technique.
- The join field must be a text, numeric, date, or time field. Most typically the field is either a text or numeric field.

The following key considerations should be kept in mind when designing and creating the *detail* database:

- You cannot change the value of the join field in any record in the detail database or the detail records will be disconnected from the record in the main database.
- You can prevent Approach from letting you add records to the detail database that do not have a matching record in the main database. (See the section "Relational Options" later in this chapter.)
- A main database record does not have to have any detail database records. For example, a customer record could contain no detail records in the ORDERS database if the customer has never placed an order. However, a detail database must not contain records that are unmatched in the main database. That is, there can be no records in the ORDERS database with a customer number 1234 if there is no record in the CUSTOMERS database with the same customer number.

▶ Multiple Join Fields

New in Approach version 3.0 is the ability to join two databases by more than one field. For example, suppose you are working with two databases whose structure you cannot change. Both databases contain customer information, including the first name and last name of the customer, but neither includes a field that contains a unique value in each record, such as customer ID. In such a case, you can join the two databases by specifying that the Firstname and Lastname fields in each database are the join fields. Obviously the Firstname fields from each database are related to each other and the Lastname fields are related to each other. Even though the individual fields may not contain unique values—you can have more than one record with the first name John and more than one record with the last name Miller—when you join by these two fields, you will have a unique value, in this case John Miller. (If the combination is not unique, you can not use multiple join fields.) Now you can use Approach to find the data about a customer by combining the data from both databases using the first and last name fields and connecting data based on a match of both fields. You can, for example, tell Approach to combine the data about John Halverson by looking for the value "John" in the first name field of each database and the value "Halverson" in the last name field of each joined database. When you join a database on two fields, both must match.

Thus, you can work with two databases even though there is no *single* field that contains a unique value. This condition is used most often when you are accessing databases that others have created or for which you cannot control the structure (that is, you can't add a Customer ID field, for example).

Follow these steps to set up a one-to-many (1-M) relationship between existing databases in Approach:

▸▸ **WARNING**

Approach does not warn you if the selected fields are of different types or field lengths. It is recommended that you check this information before beginning the join process.

1. Open the Approach file in which you want to join the databases.
2. Switch to a view that uses the database you have selected as your main database.
3. Select Create ➤ Join.
4. Approach displays the Join dialog box, which contains a list of fields from the main database you selected.

5. Select Open and choose your detail database from the Open dialog box, shown in Figure 6.12. Approach displays the field list from the detail database in the Join window. To create an alias join, click on the database displayed in the Join dialog box, and then click on Alias. Approach displays the name of the first database followed by :1, and the name of the second database followed by :2.

FIGURE 6.12

The Join dialog box after selecting the Open button to select the detail database.

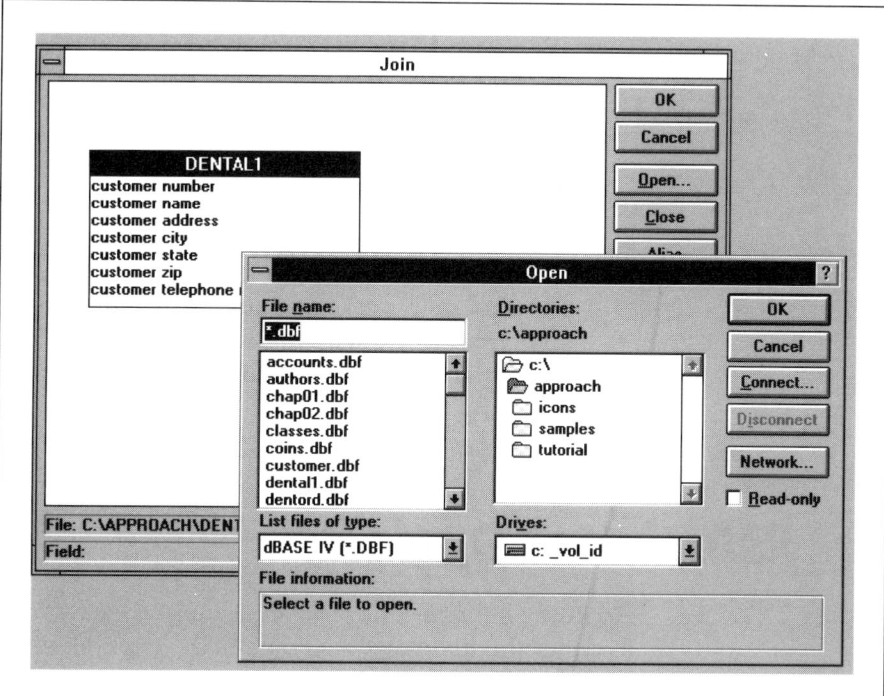

6. Click on the join field in the main database and the corresponding (related) field from the detail database. Select the Join button. Alternatively, click and drag the join field from one database to the other. If you are joining the databases using two fields (such as last name and first name), perform a join on each field.

7. Approach displays a line between the two fields.

8. Select Options to set how Approach handles creation and deletion of records. See the section "Relational Options" later in this chapter.

9. You can join other databases by repeating steps 5 through 8. When all joins have been defined, select OK to update the Approach file.

You can join two databases in only one way. For example, you can join the ORDERS database and the CUSTOMERS database on Order Number or Customer Number, but you can't define two relationships between these databases, one by Order Number and another by Customer Number. It's a one-join-per-two-databases world. If you need to break the relationship, you can delete an existing join. Follow these steps to remove the join:

1. Select Create ➤ Join.
2. Click on the line joining the two fields.
3. Select UnJoin.
4. If there is any database in the Join dialog box that no longer contains a joining line, select the database (click on the list of fields) and choose Close. The database is removed from the dialog box, and Approach warns you it will delete any forms or reports in which that database was the main database.
5. Select OK.

▸▸ Relational Options

Approach lets you control what happens when you create or delete a record in either the main or detail database. Remember that you can create a view that lets you work with only one of the databases, so these options are designed to help you keep the related databases in sync.

Your choices are presented in the Relational Options dialog box. Open this dialog box from the Join dialog box. Click on the line that joins the databases, and then click on Options. Approach then presents the options using the databases you've joined. They are somewhat confusing, so we'll explain these options in some detail.

The first two options shown in Figure 6.13 determine what happens to the main database when you insert or delete a record in the detail database. If you check the first box (Insert), you will be inserting a detail record and here's what happens. First Approach looks to see if there is a matching record in the main database containing the same value in the join field. If there is no record in the main database that matches the value you've entered, Approach will insert a record into the main database with the join value you specified. In our CUSTOMER and ORDER database example, if you add a new order for a Customer Number that Approach cannot find in the main database, say 2443, it will add a new record to the CUSTOMER database with a Customer Number of 2443, leaving all of the other fields blank. Thus, when you open the CUSTOMER database, you will find a record that contains the Customer Number 2443 but no other data. *This option only works on forms in which you have a main database and a detail database in a repeating panel.* Repeating panels display several records from the detail database and are more fully explained in Chapter 8.

FIGURE 6.13

The Relational Options dialog box

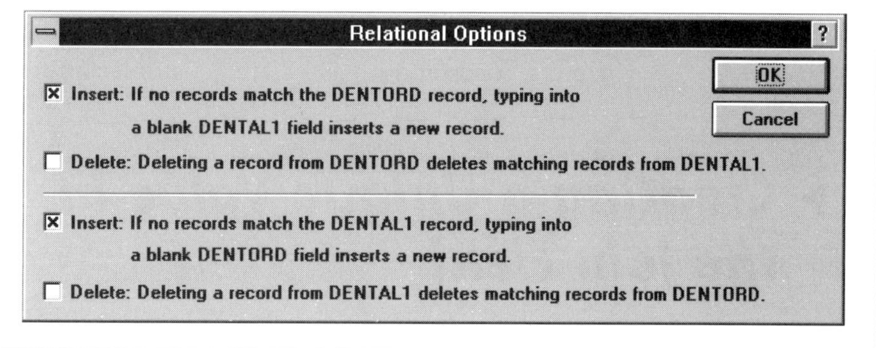

If you check the Delete option, then delete a record from the detail database, the matching record from the main database will be deleted. **This is an extremely dangerous option.** Suppose a customer has placed 10 orders, so there are 10 records in the detail database. There is, of course, one record in the CUSTOMER database, which is the main database. If you select the Delete option, and delete the single order record, Approach will delete the record in the CUSTOMER database also. This leaves you with no customer record to tie to the remaining 9 orders. Approach will display a warning message before proceeding with the deletion.

The remaining two options determine what Approach should do when you insert or delete records into the main database. If you select the Insert option, adding a record to the main database causes Approach to automatically insert a blank record into the detail database. Thus, adding a new Customer Number 3467 will cause Approach to add a record in the ORDERS database for Customer Number 3467. There will be no other information (order date, amount, or order number) for that record, just a single record containing the join value 3467. *This option only works on forms in which you have a main database and a detail database in a repeating panel.* Repeating panels display several records from the detail database, and are more fully explained in Chapter 8.

If you select the last option (Delete), then delete a record in the main database, Approach will delete all related records in the detail database. This option may actually be quite useful. For example, if a customer has not placed an order in some time (say, a year), you may want to delete all records associated with the customer. If you select this option and delete the Customer record, all associated (joined) database records in the ORDERS database will automatically be deleted as well. If you don't check this Delete option, you will have to go through the database and manually delete all the orders for the customer—assuming you remember to do this! If you don't, you'll end up with a database that contains order records and no associated customer information.

▸▸ Creating a Unique Value in the Join Field

In addition to creating the databases, you will have to select a common field in each database. As we've discussed, the common field in the main database must contain a unique value for every record. As you've also seen, you can choose two or more fields, such as the last name and first name, if the combination of values in these fields creates a unique value.

The easiest technique is to create a unique value in the join field of each record, assuming you have control over the design of your databases and are not just using existing databases from another source over which you have no control. Approach has the ability to automatically fill a field with a unique value. This ability, called *serializing* a field, is found in the Design environment using the Field Definition option. To ensure that your join field contains a unique value, let Approach do the hard work. Define a unique join field and tell Approach to use its Serialize function to enter a unique value for each new record in the main database.

Follow these steps to serialize new records in a database:

1. Start Approach and select File ➤ Open. Enter the name of the Approach File that contains the main database. Select OK.
2. Select Create ➤ Field Definition.
3. Select the field you want to serialize. The field should have a field type of numeric. Although it may be defined with decimal places, serial numbers will be whole numbers (integers).
4. Click on Options and select the "Serial number starting at" option on the Default Value tab.
5. If you want to serialize the next new record beginning with 1 and incrementing each new record by 1, proceed to step 8.
6. To begin the next new record with a particular number, enter the number in the "Serial number starting at" text box.
7. To increment this field by a value other than 1, enter the value in the "Incremented by" text box.
8. Select OK to leave the Field Definition dialog box.

►► **TIP**

The increment value must be an integer between -2157583657 and 215783657. In practical terms, the increment value is usually 1.

►► **WARNING**

Serializing only places a unique value in a field for new records. To serialize a field in existing records, see Chapter 16 (Macros) and use the Reserialize Macro.

►► *Using Joined Databases*

You can see several differences when you compare the use of a single database with the use of joined databases in Approach.

When you use a joined database and need to specify a field name, you must also be sure you select the correct database. This is the most significant difference between the use of single and multiple databases. For example, it's no longer enough to select the Customer Number field. You must select the Customer Number field from the CUSTOMER database or from the ORDERS database. Formulas will also include the database name, in the form DATABASE.Fieldname, such as CUSTOMER.Customer Number.

Likewise, when adding fields to a form (or any other view, for that matter), you'll need to be sure the field list presented is shown for the main or detail database. It's an extra step, but not a complicated one.

The overwhelming advantage of joined databases is that Approach allows you to see data from all databases on the same screen. Using a repeating panel, shown in Figure 6.14, you can see the data from the Dental Customers record and all records from the ORDERS database for that customer. (If there are more orders than can be shown on the screen, Approach lets

FIGURE 6.14

Repeating Panels provide views into joined databases.

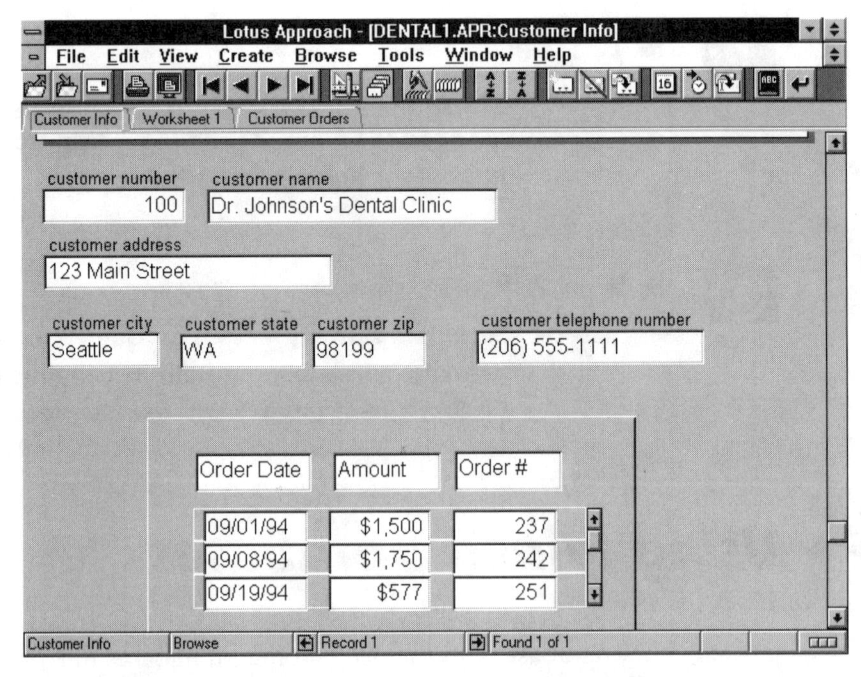

you scroll through the list.) Another advantage of the repeating panel is that you can add records to the detail database (the ORDERS database in this example) by adding another line to the repeating panel. You don't need to create a separate data entry screen to enter new orders. You'll learn more about repeating panels in Chapter 8.

Also keep in mind that just because two databases are joined does not mean you have to use both in a form or report. For example, you can build a worksheet that looks only at the ORDERS database and optionally lists the Customer Number without including the customer name and address on the worksheet. The relational options you set help keep the databases "in sync" by specifying what Approach should do when you insert or delete a record in one of the joined databases.

►► Summary and a Look Ahead

In this chapter you've learned the difference between a flatfile database and relational databases. You've learned when a flatfile database can meet your needs and when it is best to create relational databases. This chapter has also explained the key characteristics of related databases and has shown you how to connect more than one database.

By reading Chapters 3 through 6, you have learned how to create a new database or modify an existing one. Now it's time to learn how to put the database designs to work! In the next chapter you'll learn how to create forms so you can enter your data into your database.

▶ ▶ CHAPTER 7

Creating Forms

▸▸ FAST TRACK

▶ *To begin the five-step process for creating a form* **200**

open the Approach file that will contain the form you want to add. Tell Approach to create a new form. Select the options in the Form Assistant. Modify the resulting form, if desired, then save the form.

▶ *To create a form* ***200***

from the main menu, select Create ➤ Form or click on the Create New Form icon from the SmartIcons toolbar. Approach displays the Form Assistant. Enter the view (form) name, choose the SmartMaster style and layout, then select the Step 2: Fields tab or press the Next key if you are in the Layout tab. Select the database that is to be the source of data for your form if more than one database is defined in the Approach file, then choose each field to be added. If you selected the "Standard with Repeating Panel" option, a third tab will be displayed: Step 3: Panel, from which you must select the database for the panel. Otherwise, select the Done button.

▶ *To add a button to a form* ***220***

select the Macro Button icon on the Drawing toolbar, select the Draw Macro Buttons button on the SmartIcons toolbar, or select Create ➤ Drawing, then choose Macro Button. Use the mouse to draw the button on the form itself. In the InfoBox select the Basics label, and enter a name in the Button Text box. Select the Macros tab and set the macro names and properties for the button's behavior, or click on Define Macro to create a new macro. Use the fonts tab to set the text font for the button's face. Close the InfoBox.

To move an object on a form 225

select the object. Approach changes the pointing mouse cursor into a hand. Drag the object to the new location, then release the mouse.

To align objects to each other or to the grid 229

select the objects. Choose Objects ➤ Align, Ctrl+I, or press and hold the right mouse button on the object and select Align You can also click the Align objects button on the SmartIcons toolbar. From the Align dialog box select the alignment you want in the Align Objects section: To each other or To grid.

Choose the Horizontal and/or Vertical alignment you want. The Distribute horizontally and Distribute vertically options align the objects evenly in the selected direction. Select OK.

To quickly format objects based on the properties of an existing object 239

select the object that has the properties you want to apply to one or more objects. Press Ctrl+M, press and hold the right mouse button as you point at the object and select Fast Format, select Object ➤ Fast Format, or click on the Fast Format icon in the Design default SmartIcons toolbar. The mouse cursor will change to a plus sign and a paintbrush. This indicates that Fast Format has been selected. Click on the object you want to possess the properties of the selected object and repeat until all objects have been selected. Press Ctrl+M, press and hold the right mouse button as you point to the object and select Fast Format, select Object ➤ Fast Format, or click on the Fast Format icon in the Design default SmartIcons toolbar. The icon and mouse cursor will return to their original designs.

▶▶ **Approach's** databases store data—the names, addresses, and telephone numbers of your contacts, for example. Approach takes the data out of the database and displays it in a variety of views, including data entry forms and reports. These views let you actually see and work with the data stored in your database.

In this chapter we'll focus on data entry screens—screen displays that let you add, edit, and delete data, find records, or browse through the database. We'll learn how to create forms for viewing data on your screen. You will learn how to begin the forms design process and use the Form Assistant to help you begin creating a form from scratch. In addition, we will explore how to work with objects—fields, pictures, text, and more—on a form. You will learn about objects and their properties. For example, text fields have a color property for the border, for the font itself, and for shadows around the field. You'll learn more about the properties of fields, and forms in general, in this chapter.

Approach's design is consistent throughout. The techniques described here also resemble those you'll use for building reports, mailing labels, and form letters. In Chapter 8 you'll learn how to set special properties, such as the font and color used in a field, to enhance the visual aspects of your form.

▶▶ Forms

Forms are more than just a way to view data as a simple arrangement of fields on a screen. Forms allow you to add graphical elements to improve or streamline data entry. For example, a Boolean field (one that can contain the value Yes or No) can be displayed on the screen as a text field, a drop-down list, a check box, or a set of radio buttons.

These options are shown in Figure 7.1. When you use a check box, you can simply click on the box to set the value to "Yes." An empty check box corresponds to the "No" value.

FIGURE 7.1 

A Boolean field can be represented on a form in a variety of ways.

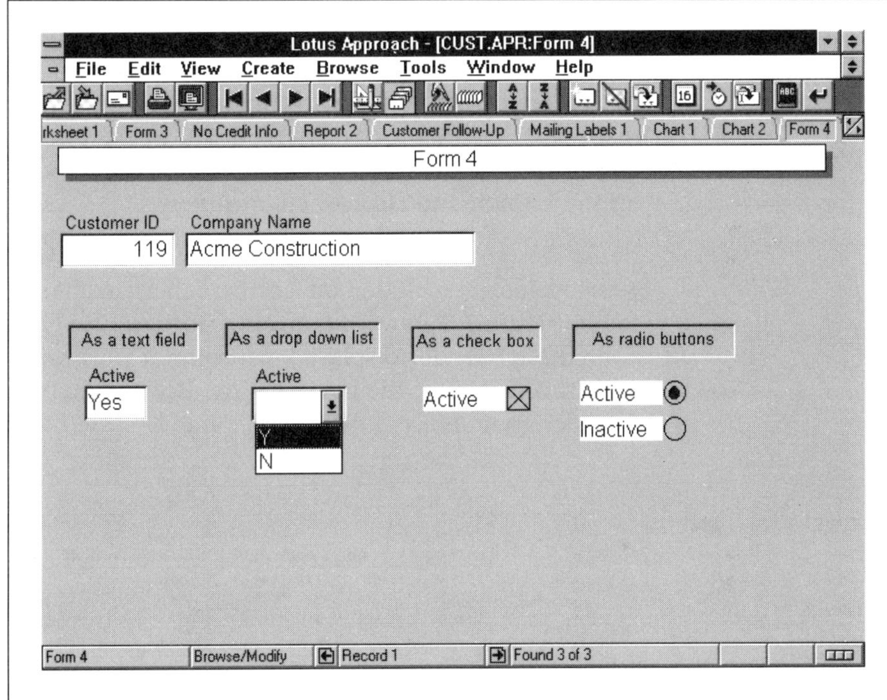

In the same fashion, a field you want to contain one of six values can be displayed on a form using a pull-down list. During data entry, you (or the person using your application) can select from a value in a list you define. Selecting a value from a list is possibly faster (depending on the length of any option text) than typing it each time. However, the principal advantage is that by limiting the options, you ensure field integrity—you ensure that the field contains only the values you expect or permit. Lists also prevent the introduction of errors that can result when a user must type values manually, since typing mistakes can occur.

If you are developing an Approach application, forms provide a method of displaying data (such as an employee identification number) without letting the user modify the data. Thus, while some fields can be modified, others are protected. Furthermore, forms allow you to select which fields from a database are displayed. For example, you can design a form for managers to use that includes an employee's name, title, and salary, then design another form that provides a screen to a different department that shows the employee name, title, and telephone number (since salary is confidential and of no use to someone preparing a company telephone directory—except to satisfy one's curiosity, of course!).

Forms operate in four environments in Approach terminology, which really refer to the modes in which you work. The four environments are Design, Browse, Find, and Preview. In this chapter, we'll concentrate on the Design and Browse environments.

In the Design environment, you work with the layout of a data entry form: which fields are included on a screen, their arrangement, color, size, and so on. Figure 7.2 shows a data entry form in the Design environment. Even though data is displayed, you cannot work with it. It is just displayed to help you arrange the layout. In the Browse environment Approach uses your design and fills in fields with data from the database.

FIGURE 7.2 ▸

A form in the Design environment

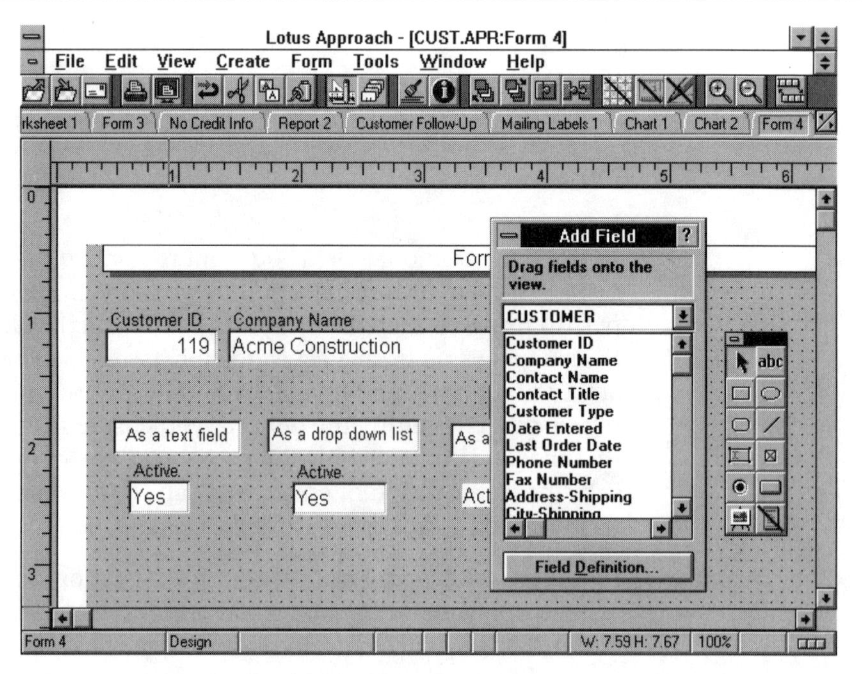

To switch to the Design environment, use any of these methods:

- Select a Design icon from the toolbar.
- Select View ➤ Design.
- Press Ctrl+D.
- Click on the second box from the left in the Status bar and select Design.

There are two Design icons available on the SmartIcons toolbar. The standard icon, which is placed in the standard toolbars when you install Approach, is shown on the left; the optional icon, which you can use instead, is displayed on the right.

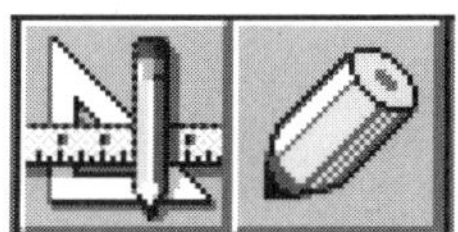

In the Design environment you can view the field names or actual data from the first record(s) in your database, but you cannot modify the data from these records.

To switch to the Browse environment, use any of these methods:

- Select a Browse icon from the toolbar.
- Select View ➤ Browse.
- Press Ctrl+B.
- Click on the second box from the left in the Status bar and select Browse.

There are two Browse icons available on the SmartIcons toolbar. The standard icon, which is used when you install Approach, is shown on the left; the optional icon is displayed on the right.

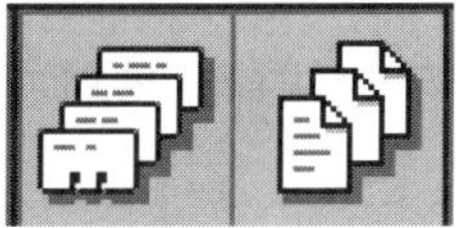

▸▸ Creating a New Form

Approach creates two default views—a Data Entry Form and a Worksheet view—when you open a database for the first time or create a new database. You can create any number of additional forms quickly and simply. Approach adds a tab to its main view for each new form.

Creating a form is a five-step process:

1. Open the Approach file that will contain the form you want to add.
2. Tell Approach to create a new form.
3. Select the options in the Form Assistant.
4. Modify the resulting form, if desired.
5. Save the form.

▸ Step 1: Open the Approach File

From the Main menu, select File ➤ Open and select the Approach file. If you are working with the Welcome dialog box, select Open and then the "an Existing File" option. If the Approach file is currently open, there is no need to close it first and reopen it again. Furthermore, you can create a new form from any environment: Browse, Design, Preview, or Find.

▸ Step 2: Tell Approach You Want to Create a New Form

From the Main menu, select Create ➤ Form or click on the Create New Form icon from the SmartIcons toolbar (shown at left; this icon is not part of the Standard toolbar but may be added to your toolbar). Approach displays the Form Assistant, shown in Figure 7.3. Using this tabbed dialog box you'll make your selections. Form Assistant guides you through the decisions you must make and will generate the form quickly. You can edit any form created by the Form Assistant.

▸ Step 3: Selecting Options in Form Assistant

The first tab of the Form Assistant displays options for the form layout. The layout includes cosmetic elements, such as the background color and 3D look of the form.

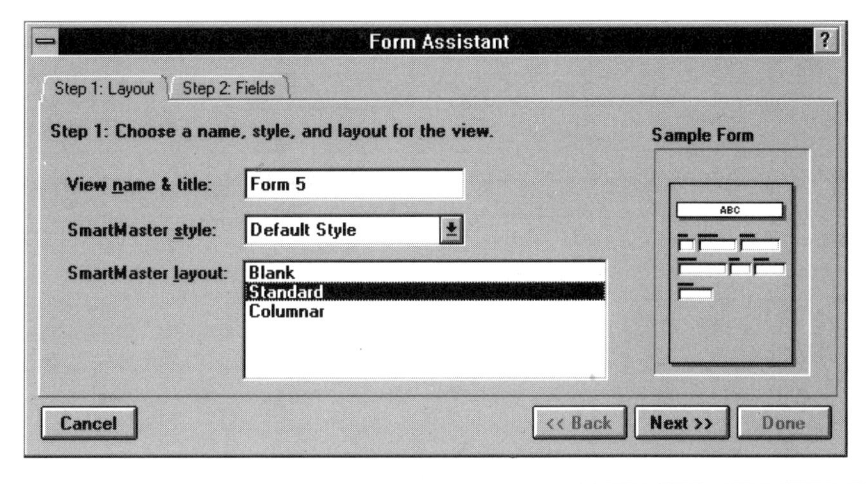

FIGURE 7.3

The Form Assistant

The layout also determines how fields are arranged on a form. Predefined layouts, called *SmartMasters*, make it easy to quickly create standard forms. These SmartMasters are installed when you install Approach. In version 3 of Approach, they cannot be modified, although you can modify the views they help you create.

Approach uses SmartMasters to simplify creating forms. SmartMasters contain details about sample layouts. SmartMaster styles contain 13 different style options, two of which are shown here. A form using the 3D Look1 SmartMaster is shown in Figure 7.4.

A form using the Chisel2 SmartMasters is shown in Figure 7.5.

As you can see, the SmartMasters contain information about the background, and the style used for all fields, including color, borders, font style, and more.

To set the layout, select the "Step 1: Layout" tab in the Form Assistant dialog box if it is not already selected. Then follow these steps:

1. Enter the view (form) name. The name you supply is used in the tab for this view, and can be changed later.
2. Select the SmartMaster style you want. The style includes background and field properties, such as their color and chiseled look. Approach displays a sample layout in the Sample Form box at the right.

FIGURE 7.4

A data entry form using the 3D Look1 SmartMaster

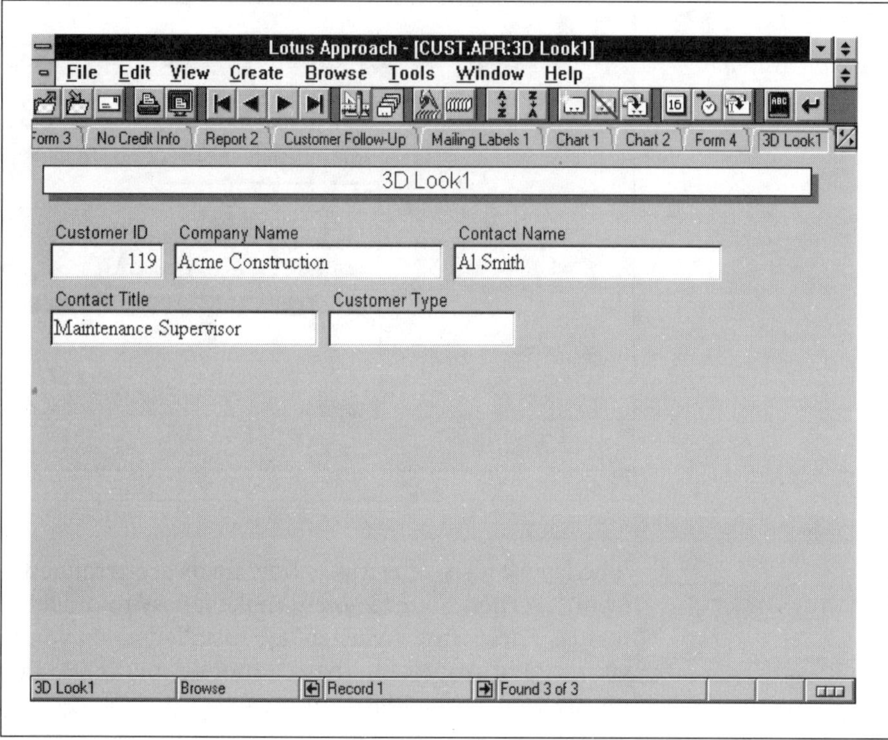

3. Select the SmartMaster layout. This layout determines how the fields will be organized. There are four options, shown here.

SmartMaster Layout Option	How Fields Are Placed on a Form
Blank	Form Assistant will place no fields on the form; you must place all fields on the form manually.
Standard	Fields you select with Form Assistant will be displayed left to right, top to bottom in the order they are selected.

Columnar	Fields you select with Form Assistant will be placed in columns. It creates the first column, then creates column 2 and so on, placing as many fields in rows as will fit on the screen.
Standard with Repeating Panel	Fields from the main (primary) database will be placed in the form. You must select the joined database (called the detail database) and fields from this joined database; these fields will be placed in a columnar layout in a repeating panel and placed at the bottom of the form. See Chapter 6 for more information about joined databases and Chapter 8 for more information about repeating panels on forms.

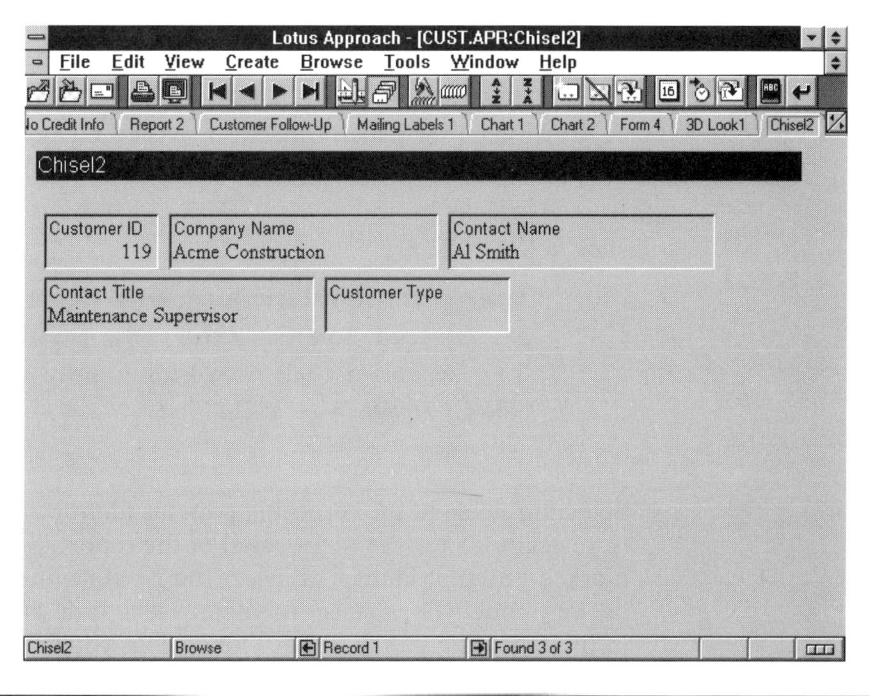

FIGURE 7.5

The same data entry form using the Chisel2 SmartMaster layout

If you selected the Blank layout, you can select the Done button and proceed to the section "Step 5: Saving the Form" later in this chapter. Otherwise, you must select the database and fields for your form.

To select fields to be placed on the new form, select the "Step 2: Fields" tab in the Form Assistant dialog box, or press the Next key if you are in the Layout tab. Then follow these steps:

1. Select the database that is to be the source of data for your form if more than one database is defined in the Approach file.
2. Select the field you want to add to the form. Highlight the field and select the Add button, or double-click on the field. The field is added to the end of the "Fields to place on view" list.
3. Repeat step 1 (if needed) and step 2 until all fields appear in the "Fields to place on view" list. There is no method available for rearranging the fields in this list, so be sure you add the fields in the order in which you want them to appear (left to right, top to bottom for Standard layout [including Standard with Repeating Panel]; or top to bottom, then a second column from top to bottom for Columnar). If you need to rearrange the order of the fields, you must remove them (click on the "Fields to place in panel" option, then click on Remove) and start again, adding the fields in the right order.
4. If you selected the Standard with Repeating Panel option, a third tab will be displayed: "Step 3: Panel," from which you must select the database for the panel. Otherwise, select the Done button and proceed to the section "Step 4: Modifying the New Form" later in this chapter.

▸▸ **WARNING**

Approach will fill the form with fields in the order they are selected. To ensure the order is strictly as you want it to be, select each field individually and add it to the "Fields to place on view" list.

Selecting fields in the repeating panel is identical to the steps you take to select fields for the main panel of the report. Select the third tab, marked "Step 3: Panel," or select the Next key until this panel is the current panel. Then select the database and database fields to include in the repeating panel. Select Done when you are finished. Approach displays your new form in its main window in the Browse environment, filling the fields you specified with data from the current record.

TIP

You can select more than one field in the Database fields list at a time and add them all to the "Fields to place on view" or "Fields to place in panel" list. To select adjacent fields, click on the first field in the list you want to add, then press and hold the Shift key and click on the last field in the list you want to add. Then click the Add button. To select nonadjacent fields, click on the first field, then press and hold the Ctrl key as you click on all other fields you want to include. If you select a field by mistake, click on it again to deselect it. Each selected field is highlighted. When all fields you want are selected, click the Add button.

Step 4: Modifying the New Form

The SmartMaster or Blank form you created using the Form Assistant can be modified. For example, the Columnar layout for a Customer database is shown in Figure 7.6. However, it is customary to see the City, State, and Postal Code fields on the same line. Approach provides all the tools needed to move fields or change their characteristics, including changes to the background and borders of the form itself.

The form editing tools are explained in the section "Work Area Options" later in this chapter.

Step 5: Saving the Form

Although Approach saves all data entered into a database, you must save the Approach file in order to save changes in your form or add new forms to the Approach file.

To save the file, select File ➤ Save Approach File, press Ctrl+S, or click on the Save Approach File icon in the SmartIcons toolbar.

FIGURE 7.6 ▶

When you add fields to a form, they may be displayed on separate lines rather than in the more customary position—all on the same line.

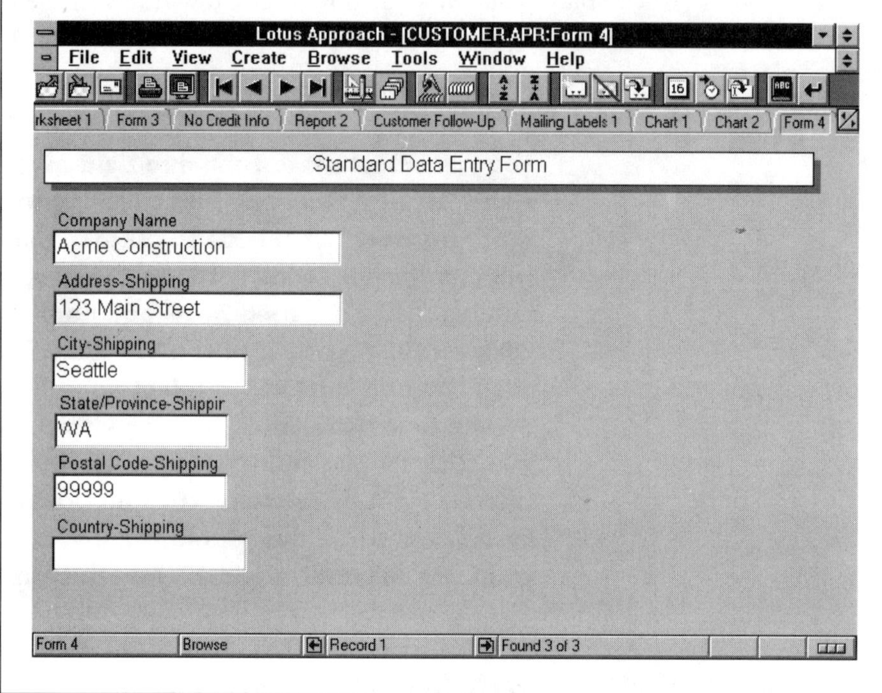

▸▸ Changing the Size of a Form

By default, new forms are the standard size: 8½″ wide and 11″ high, minus space for margins. To change the dimensions of a form, make certain you are in the Design environment and click on the edge of the form. A border will be displayed and the pointer will change to a double arrow. Stretch the form to the new dimension, as you would any other rectangular object in Windows.

The Status bar shows you the new dimensions (W: means width, H: means height).

►► Deleting a Form

If you no longer need a form, switch to the form (click on its tab), and switch to the Design environment. Select Edit ➤ Delete Form; when Approach asks you to confirm your request, select Yes.

If you delete a form by mistake, you may be able to retrieve it. Although there is no Undo feature for deleting forms, you can go back to the last saved version of your Approach file. To do so, close the current Approach file (select File ➤ Close). When Approach asks if you want to save it, select No. Then open the Approach file again. Your form appears as it existed at the last point you saved the Approach file.

►► Copying a Form

If you want to make extensive modifications to a form, you may want to experiment with a new form but leave the existing form unchanged. To do this, copy the form by selecting the original form and switching to the Design environment. Then select Edit ➤ Duplicate Form. Approach creates a new form and names it "Copy of XXX," where "XXX" is the original form name. Now you can make your changes to the copy. When it works the way you wish, delete the original form and rename the copy.

►► Renaming a Form

To change the name of an existing form, double-click on the tab for that form. Approach displays the text in an editable box, as shown in Figure 7.7. Enter the new name and press Enter.

FIGURE 7.7

Editing the Tab Name. Notice the text box in the tab area allows you to type the desired tab name

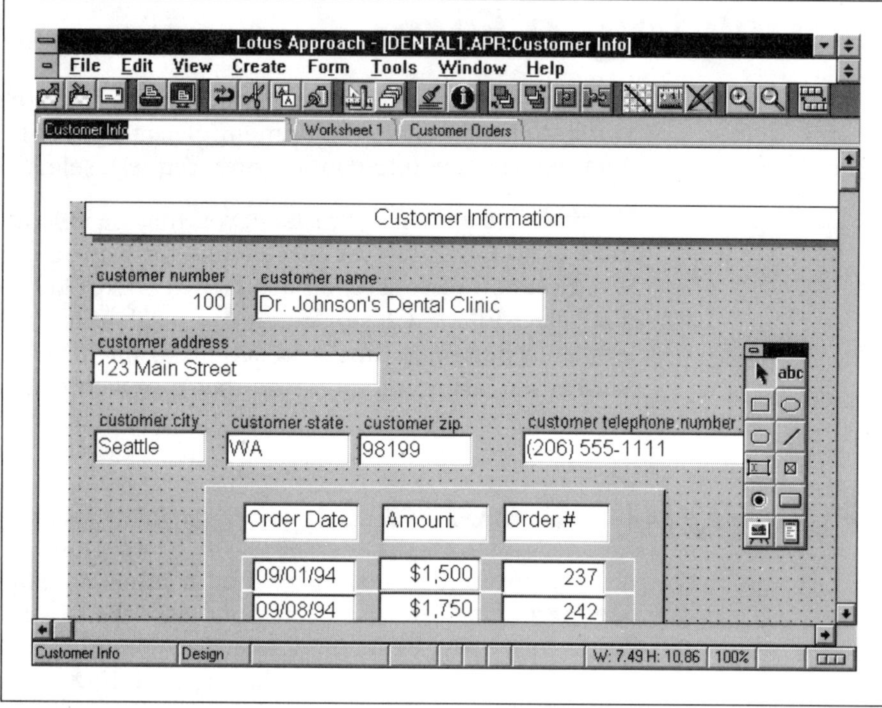

▸▸ The Design Work Area

Before exploring how you modify a form, it's important to understand how the design work area is organized. Approach offers dozens of shortcuts to make modifying a form easy.

To begin editing a form, be sure the form is currently displayed, then switch to the Design environment, as described in the section "Forms" earlier in this chapter. There are two Design icons that may appear on the SmartIcons toolbar. Both icons are shown here.

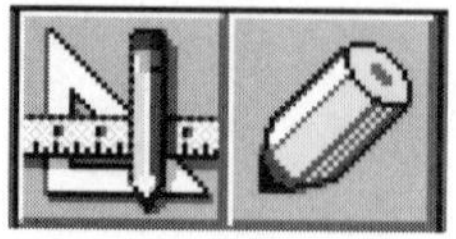

When you switch to the Design environment, Approach changes the SmartIcons toolbar and the menu options, as shown in Figure 7.8. Notice that the important change in the Menu bar is the Form option.

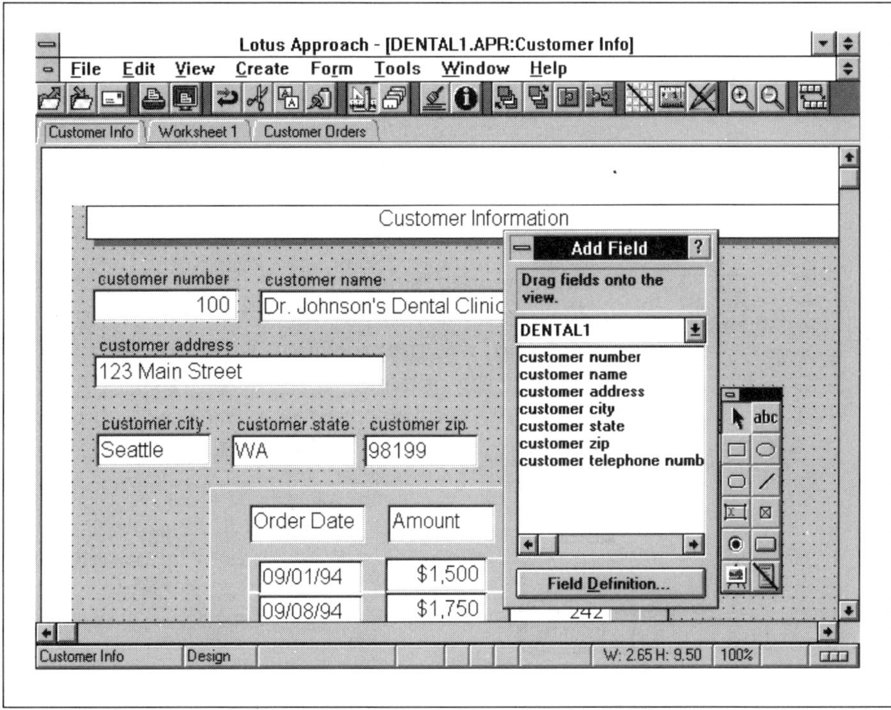

FIGURE 7.8

The Design environment includes a Form option for setting styles, adding fields, inserting special fields (such as the current date), and formatting the form.

The Status bar at the bottom of the screen also changes. It replaces database navigation tools (left and right arrows, for example), with information about the form.

The toolbar and Status bar will change yet again when you select something on the form, which we'll explain in a moment.

The Design environment that appears on your screen may be slightly different from what you see in Figure 7.8. That's because Approach offers several options to customize your work area. Most of these options are set using the View environment menu.

▸▸ Work Area Options

Approach provides several tools to help you align objects on a form. These include grids and rulers.

▸ Grids

Approach can display a grid to help you align elements such as fields and buttons. The grid appears as rows and columns of small dots. If you imagine horizontal and vertical lines connecting these dots, you've just envisioned where the gridlines are.

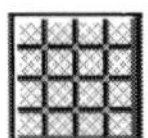

To view the grid, select View ➤ Show Grid or click on the Grid icon in the Design default SmartIcons toolbar. Approach places a check mark to the left of this menu option whenever you select the View menu, indicating that the option is selected (turned on). If the Grid icon is displayed in the toolbar, it appears with a slash through it, signifying that clicking on the button will turn the grids off, the opposite of the current state.

To remove the grids from the screen, select View ➤ Grid again and Approach removes the check mark in the Menu option and removes the grid dots.

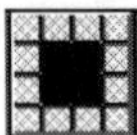

Similarly, you can toggle the Snap to Grid feature by selecting View ➤ Snap to Grid, pressing Ctrl+Y, or pressing the Snap to Grid icon from a SmartIcons toolbar (shown at left). The Snap to Grid option causes fields to be aligned on grid boundaries. If the Snap to Grid option is already selected, a slightly different icon appears, as shown here.

▶ Rulers

Approach can display a horizontal and vertical ruler bar to help align objects. To display the ruler bars, select View ➤ Show Ruler, press Ctrl+J, or click on the Rulers icon in the Design default SmartIcons toolbar. If the Show Ruler option is already selected, the icon appears with a line through it. A check mark to the left of the option shows that Approach is currently displaying the rulers. If there is no check mark, Approach is hiding the rulers. The Show and Hide Rulers are shown in the following graphics.

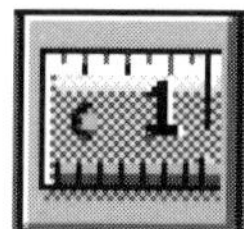

▶ Setting Work Area Defaults

Rather than setting these options for each view, you can tell Approach how you want to view any form in the Design environment by default. Any time Approach opens a form in the Design environment, it will use the options you specify. You can, of course, override them on a temporary basis by using the menu commands previously described.

To set defaults, select Tools ➤ Preferences and Approach displays the Preferences dialog box, shown in Figure 7.9, with the Display tab selected.

To display the grids by default, be sure the Show grid option box contains an X.

To have Approach automatically position an object on a grid boundary when you move it, be sure the Snap to Grid option is selected (the check box contains an X).

To change the units and width of the grid in the Grid section, choose the measurement units (inches or centimeters) and the grid width. To apply these options to the current session, select OK.

FIGURE 7.9

The Preferences dialog box

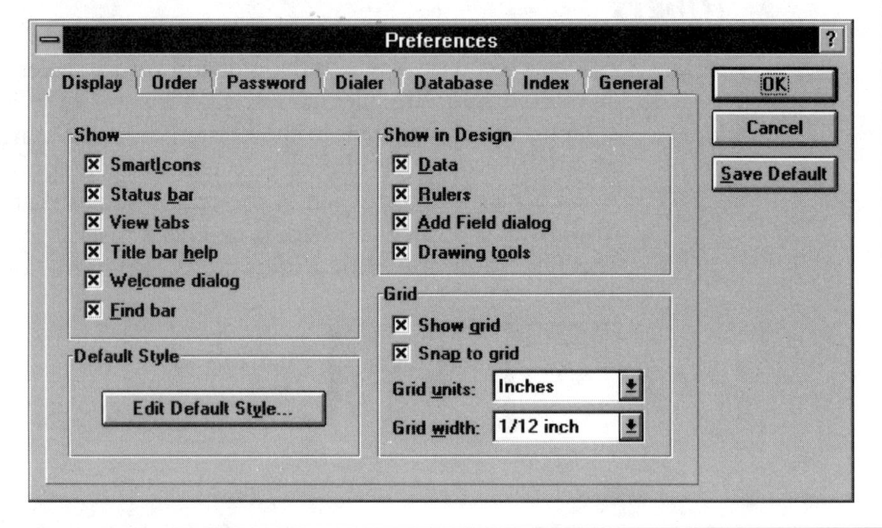

To apply these options to all future sessions (until you change them again), select Save Default, then select OK. This default style will be used whenever you create a new view using the Assistants or can be used to set the style of an individual object on a form.

▸▸ The Design Environment Work Area

Each item you see in the work area is an object. For example, the First Name field is an object. So is the heading, "Customer Information," shown in a box at the top of the form shown in Figure 7.8 earlier in this chapter. In fact, there are many different types of objects. They have one thing in common: You can work with them in the same way. For example, you can click and drag an object to a new location. If you select an object and then press and hold the right mouse button, you'll see a set of options specifically designed to control the object you've selected.

▸ Types of Objects

Everything you see on the screen can be modified by Approach. Each item or element on the screen is called an object. Objects can be classified in these categories:

Objects	Purpose
Buttons	Similar to the buttons you choose in dialog boxes, these buttons are attached to macros that perform repetitive tasks, such as switching to another form or launching a report.
Fields	Fields display data from your database or are used to enter or modify existing data.
Geometric Objects	Lines, circles, rectangles, and other geometric shapes can be used to visually group data of similar characteristics.
Graphics	Images from graphics files can be used to enhance your display.
OLE Objects	Object Linking and Embedding objects are those from other applications that can be linked or embedded in your form. Unlike the other objects on the form, OLE Objects are "connected" to the application that created them. OLE objects can include graphics, word processing documents, sounds, or portions of a spreadsheet. OLE Objects are discussed further in Chapter 20.
Repeating Panels	Repeating panels display data in a table from a detail database that is joined to the main database.
Text	Within this context, text refers to text displayed on the screen but not necessarily connected to a field or other object; text can be used to display instructions (Press Next Key to Select Next Customer, for example) or as a heading on a form.

Even the form itself is an object. In this case, this object can contain other objects (fields, text, OLE objects, and more).

There are several objects in Figure 7.10. For example, the heading "Customer Information" is a text object. The customer number and

FIGURE 7.10

Objects on a form in the Design environment

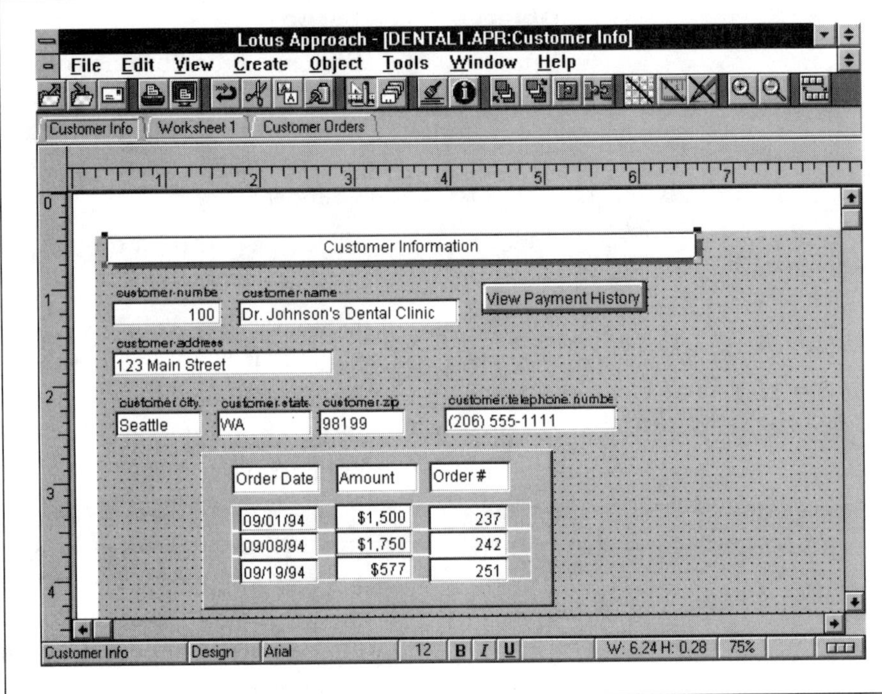

customer city are field objects. The button with the label "View Payment History" runs a macro when you click on it; it is a button object.

Each of these objects can be moved and resized. In many cases you can change the *properties* of each object. Approach calls properties *design settings*, but the more commonly used term (and one also used by Approach) is properties. Properties vary by the type of object, but in general are a property, character, or quality of an object. While most properties are related to visual elements (size, color, and so on), a property may also describe an object's behavior.

For example, you can change the background color of the text and field objects. You set the button object's font properties, changing the font typeface, color, style (bold, italics), and relief (its 3D look), as well as its size and position on the form, and whether the button will print when you print the form.

►► Working with Objects on a Form

Approach lets you add, modify, and remove objects from a form quickly and easily. In this section, we'll describe how to add, move, and remove any of the object types previously described. The process is similar for other views, including reports, mailing labels, and merged form letters.

►► Adding Objects to a Form

To help you quickly add an object, Approach provides the Drawing Tools toolbox, shown in Figure 7.11. Actually this toolbox does more than just add the drawing objects, such as boxes and circles you think of when you hear the word drawing. You can add buttons, fields, and even OLE objects, as well as drawing objects, by dragging items from the toolbox to the work area. If the toolbox, shown in Figure 7.11, is not displayed on your screen, select View ➤ Show Drawing Tools, press Ctrl+L, or click on the Drawing Tools icon in the default Drawing SmartIcons toolbar (the icon contains a picture of a pencil).

To move the toolbox, move the mouse anywhere in the toolbox and press and hold the mouse button and drag the toolbox to the desired location. To remove the toolbox, click on the small button in the upper-left corner (which looks like a minus sign).

FIGURE 7.11 

Drawing Tools Toolbox

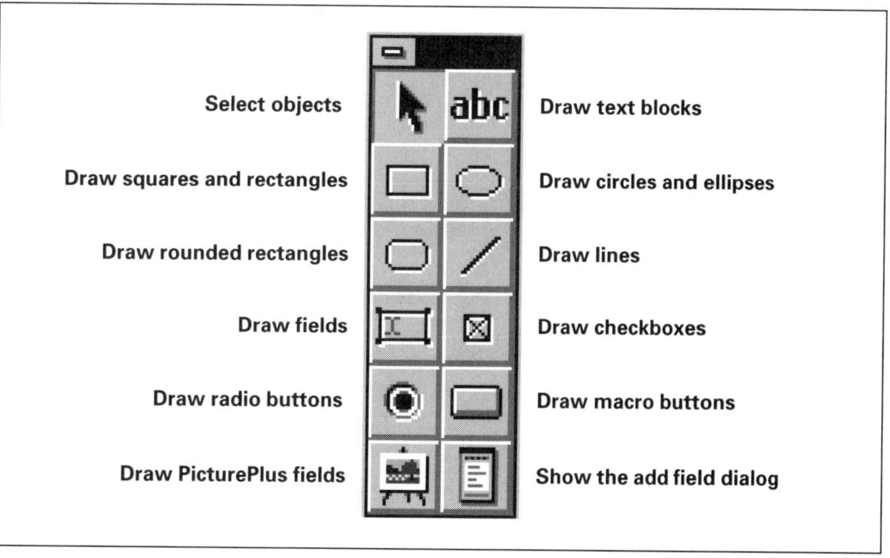

To use the toolbox, move the mouse cursor to the tool you want, then select the tool you want with the mouse. Move the mouse to the work area, and Approach turns the cursor into a crosshair. Move the mouse to the upper-left corner where you want to begin placing the object. Then, with the mouse button still pressed, drag the mouse to the bottom-right corner of the new object. Approach displays a border for this object (a rectangle for fields, for example). Release the mouse button. Approach may display a dialog box asking for information about the object you just created.

►► **TIP**

If you do not remember what each icon on the toolbox represents, press and hold the right mouse button over the icon and Approach will display the name of the object associated with the icon. Moving the pointer over the icon and holding it there for two seconds will also display the descriptive bubble.

You can also add an object using the menu. Select Create ➤ Drawing, then choose the type of drawing you want to add. Figure 7.12 shows the Draw Icons.

FIGURE 7.12 ►

The Draw icons

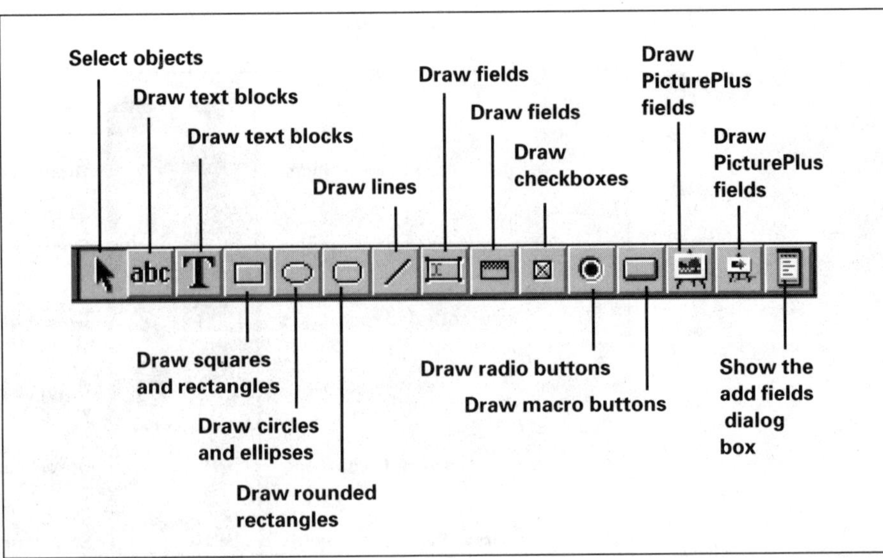

Finally, you can add text, rectangles, ellipses, and lines by adding these icons to the Design SmartIcons toolbar. Modifying the toolbar is explained in Chapter 18. In many cases, there is more than one icon available for a drawing function.

TIP

To draw a square, select the rectangle object and press and hold the Shift key as you drag the mouse over the work area. Likewise, hold the Shift key and select the rounded rectangle to draw a square with rounded corners, or select the ellipse object and press and hold the Shift key to draw a circle. To draw a horizontal, vertical, or diagonal line (at 45°), press and hold the Shift key as you use the line tool.

The icon in the bottom-right corner of the Drawing toolbox shows a small dialog box with a blue title bar and several lines of text. Click this icon, or select Form ➤ Add Field. The Add Field dialog box, shown in Figure 7.13, appears. As with the toolbox, you can drag and position a field from this dialog box onto the form. Fields are described in greater detail in Chapter 8.

FIGURE 7.13 

The Add Field dialog box

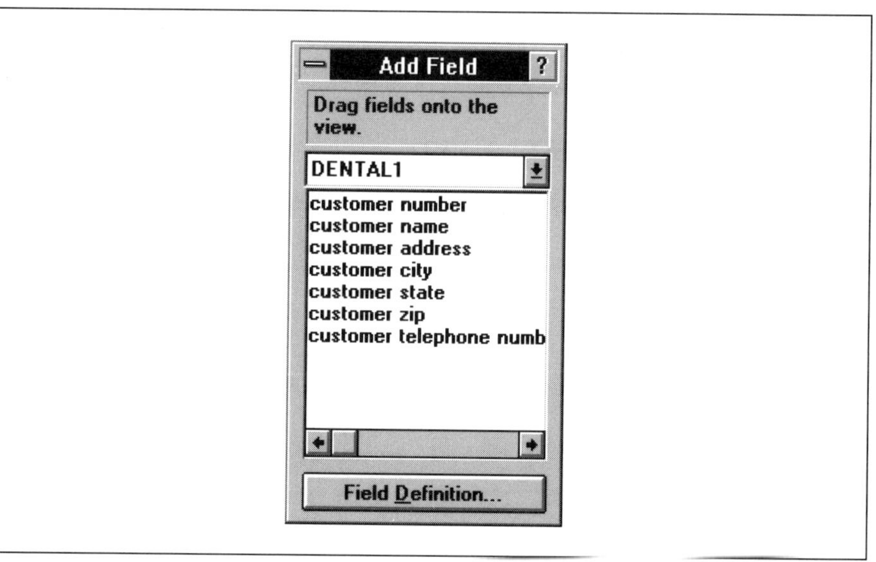

Finally, you can add one of several special objects: the current date, the current time, and the current page number.

To add these special objects, select Form ➤ Insert or press and hold the right mouse button on any object (but not on an empty part of the form itself) and select Insert. Then choose date, time, or page#. Approach adds these fields to the upper-left corner of your form. Drag them to the new location. You can also select from the Insert today's date, Insert current time, and Insert page number icons from a SmartIcons toolbar, as shown in Figure 7.14.

FIGURE 7.14 ▸

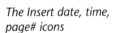

The Insert date, time, page# icons

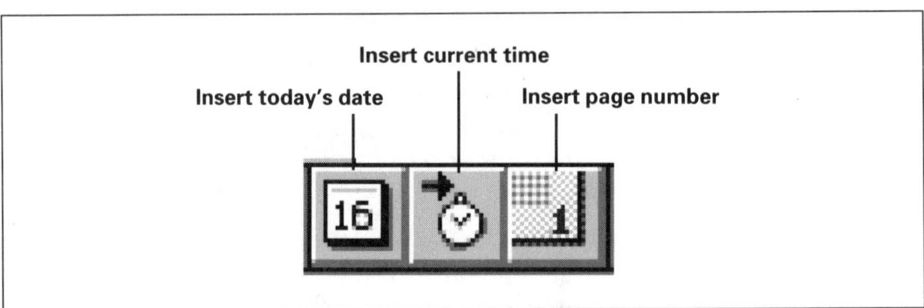

Special fields exhibit special behavior. Take the Date field, for example. When you click on the box (so that the four handles show in the corners), Approach shows the current value of the object (such as 1/5/94). When you click inside the box again, Approach replaces the box with <<DATE>>, the code it uses to remember that the box displays the current date. This field will be displayed on forms, but you cannot edit its value.

▸▸ **TIP**

Should you make a mistake, such as accidentally deleting an object from a form, use Approach's Undo feature. *Immediately* after performing the task you want to undo, press Ctrl+Z, click on the Undo last change button in the SmartIcons toolbar, or select Edit ➤ Undo. The Undo command must be given immediately after the mistaken action is taken. If you perform another task, then realize your mistake, you will not be able to use the Undo command to correct your mistake.

After you have placed objects on a field, you can change most of their properties using the *InfoBox*. The InfoBox, shown in Figure 7.15, is a tabbed dialog box that puts at your fingertips control over what font and color are used, the contents of a field (you relate a text field on your form to the database field that will be displayed in that field), how the field is formatted (does a numeric field contain decimal points and commas, for example), and so on. The InfoBox is the most important dialog box you'll use when building forms.

FIGURE 7.15

The InfoBox

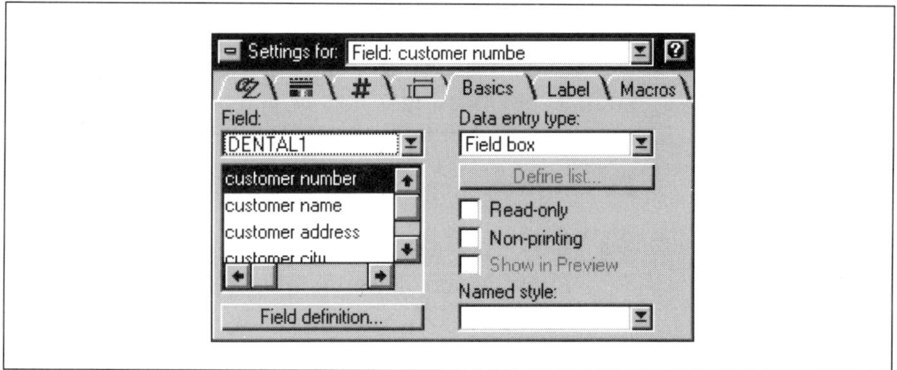

To display the InfoBox, click on the "i" icon in the SmartIcons toolbar. The InfoBox is discussed in greater detail in the section "Viewing and Changing Object Properties Using the InfoBox" later in this chapter. We introduce it here so you can see how it is used with several special field objects we discuss next.

Form Objects

Field objects represent areas of the screen that will display data from your database. For example, in a data entry screen, you'll have a field object to display or enter a customer's first and last name, the company name, credit limit, and other data. Field objects are the most common objects on a form, but they are by no means the only objects.

Although you will probably deal with field objects most frequently, there are three other types of objects that deserve special attention: buttons, graphics, and text objects. These objects provide visual clues about what a form contains or provide your own custom-made shortcuts for performing repetitive tasks. For example, a text object can be added to a form to display the purpose of the form, such as "New Customer Orders" or "Parts On Hand." You can add a graphic object to a form to add color or to position your logo on a data entry screen, which can also be printed when you print the current form. You can add a button to a form so you can quickly switch to a different form by clicking on the button. Let's take a look at these objects, alphabetically, of course.

Button Objects

You can add a button to a form so that when you click it, Approach takes some action. Buttons are connected to macros, so when you select the button, Approach runs the macro to perform a repetitive task, such as performing a sort or generating a report. Macros are discussed in greater detail in Chapter 16.

Follow these steps to add a button to a form:

1. Select the Macro Button icon on the Drawing toolbar, select the Draw Macro Buttons button on the SmartIcons toolbar, or select Create ➤ Drawing, then choose Macro Button. The Draw Macro button is not on the default SmartIcons toolbar, but can be added to the toolbar.
2. Use the mouse to draw the button onto the form itself.
3. In the InfoBox select the Basics label and enter a name in the Button Text box. This is the text that will be displayed on the face of the button. Choose a drop shadow color, printing options, and Named Style properties as appropriate.
4. Select the Macros tab and set the macro names and properties for the button's behavior, or click on Define Macro to create a new macro. Macros are discussed in Chapter 16.
5. The Fonts tab lets you make changes to the text font on the button face. The Dimensions tab lets you adjust the size of the button precisely.
6. Close the InfoBox.

▶▶ NOTE

Named Styles are collections of properties that you can define; using a Named Style lets you apply this collection of properties at once rather than one property at a time. When you change a Named Style, the changes are reflected in all objects with that style—you do not have to change the same property in each object individually.

Graphic Objects

You can add a graphic object, such as a company logo, to the background of a form by pasting the picture onto the form. To paste a graphic object that has been copied to the clipboard from another graphics application (usually using that application's Edit ➤ Copy command), click on the form itself (do not select any other objects already on the form), and select Edit ➤ Paste. The graphic object is added to the form.

You can also add a graphic object that is stored as a file. Select Edit ➤ Paste from File. Approach displays the Paste from File dialog box, shown in Figure 7.16.

FIGURE 7.16 ▶

The Paste from File dialog box lets you select a graphic file for a form.

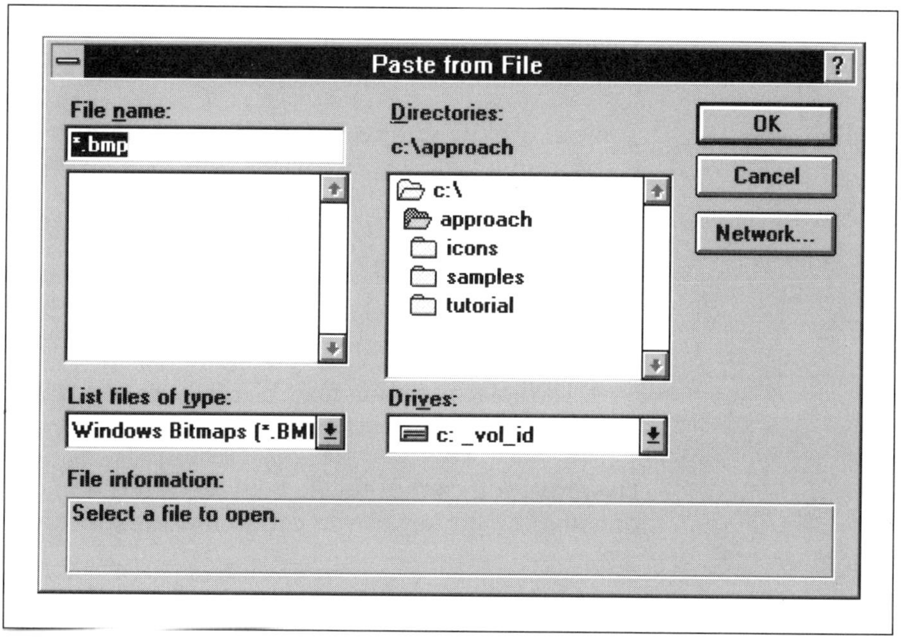

Select the file type, then the file name you want. Approach supports the graphics file formats shown in the following list. Select OK to paste the picture.

File Extension	File Format
BMP	Bitmap
EPS	Encapsulated postscript
GIF	Graphics interchange
PCX	Windows Paintbrush
TGA	Targa
TIF	Tagged Image File Format
WMF	Windows metafile

Text Objects

Text objects—such as form titles or instruction boxes—have special characteristics. When you add a text object to a form, you must also set the size of the object by drawing its boundaries. Then Approach changes to an I-beam cursor, a vertical flashing cursor, inside the box, waiting for you to type the text. When you are done adding the text, click anywhere outside the object.

Select the object, pause, then click on it again. (Double-clicking displays the InfoBox.) Approach places the I-beam inside the text area.

You can use the standard Windows operations to add, delete, or modify text within a text box.

- To add text, position the I-beam where you want to insert text and begin typing.
- To delete text, select the text you want to delete by dragging across it with the mouse, then press Del.
- To replace existing text, highlight the text, then begin typing the new text.

However, you cannot toggle between insert and overwrite mode by pressing the Ins key as you can in most text fields.

Furthermore, you can select the text and use the tools in the Status bar to change the font, font size, and characteristics (bold, italic, and underline). See the section "Viewing and Changing Object Properties with the Status Bar" later in this chapter.

▶ Selecting Objects

To perform an action on an object—such as moving an object or deleting it—you must first select the object. To select a single object, click on it once. Approach places four black squares at the corners of most objects. Line objects are an exception, where squares appear only at the ends. Black squares appear at the outer dimension of round objects, such as circles and ellipses.

Once you have selected an object, the Main menu replaces the Form option with the Object option, shown in Figure 7.17.

FIGURE 7.17 ▶

The Object option

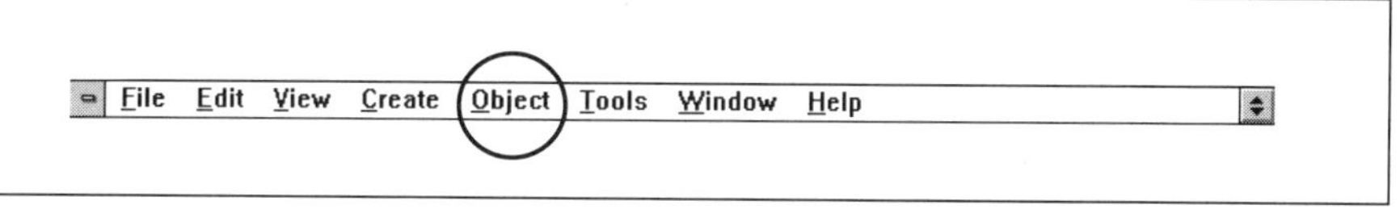

If you selected an object by mistake, click on another object or click anywhere on the form where there are no objects. Approach removes the black squares, indicating that the object is no longer selected.

To select multiple objects, click on the first object, then press and hold the Shift key as you click on the remaining objects. Once multiple objects are selected, they remain selected until you choose another object by clicking on that object without pressing the Shift key or clicking anywhere on the form.

To select all objects on a form, choose Edit ➤ Select All or click on the Select All icon from the SmartIcons toolbar.

TIP

To quickly select multiple objects in an area, click on the arrow tool in the Drawing toolbar or select the Arrow icon from the SmartIcons toolbar (which is not part of the default Design toolbar). Move the mouse pointer to the upper-left corner of the screen region that contains the items you want to select. Drag the mouse to the bottom-right corner of this region and release the mouse. All objects within the region will be selected. To remove an individual object, press and hold the Shift key and click on the unwanted object.

► Grouping Objects

If you need to move two or three objects at once, you can select multiple objects, then define them as a group. When you take any action on an object in a group, such as moving, deleting, or copying an object, the action is applied to all objects in the group.

For example, you can group the customer city, customer state, and customer zip fields on a form. When you select the customer city field and move it, the customer state and customer zip fields are moved as well. Figure 7.18 shows such a group.

To create a group, select the objects, then choose Object ➤ Group, press Ctrl+G, or select the Group Objects button (which looks like two puzzle pieces joined together) from the SmartIcons toolbar. Approach does not indicate the object is part of a group, but when you select an object of a group, Approach places black squares at the corners of the group.

To ungroup the objects, select any object in the group, then choose Object ➤ Ungroup, press Ctrl+U, or select the Ungroup Objects button (which looks like two puzzle pieces that are not joined).

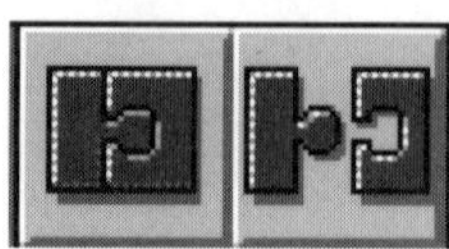

FIGURE 7.18

The customer city, customer state, and customer zip fields are grouped together. When you move one field in the group, all fields are moved at the same time.

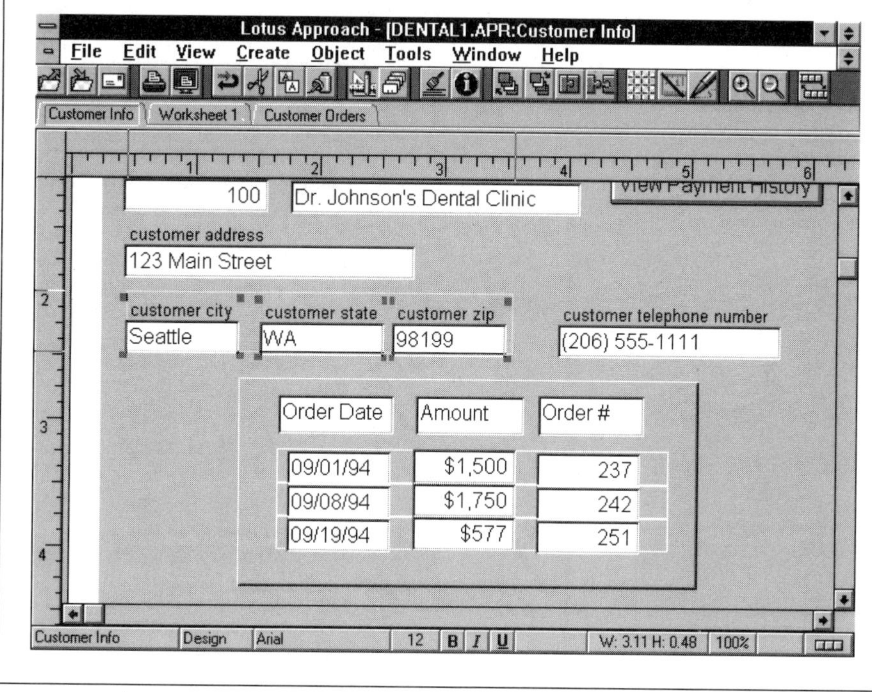

The following procedures apply to working with a single object or multiple objects.

▶ Moving an Object

After placing the object in the work area or working with a form for some time, you may decide you want the object to appear in a different location.

To move an object:

1. Select the object. Figure 7.19 shows the customer address field selected.
2. Approach changes the pointing mouse cursor into a hand.
3. Drag the object to the new location.
4. Release the mouse.

FIGURE 7.19

When a field is selected, Approach places black squares around the boundary of the field and changes the cursor to a hand. Here the customer address field has been selected.

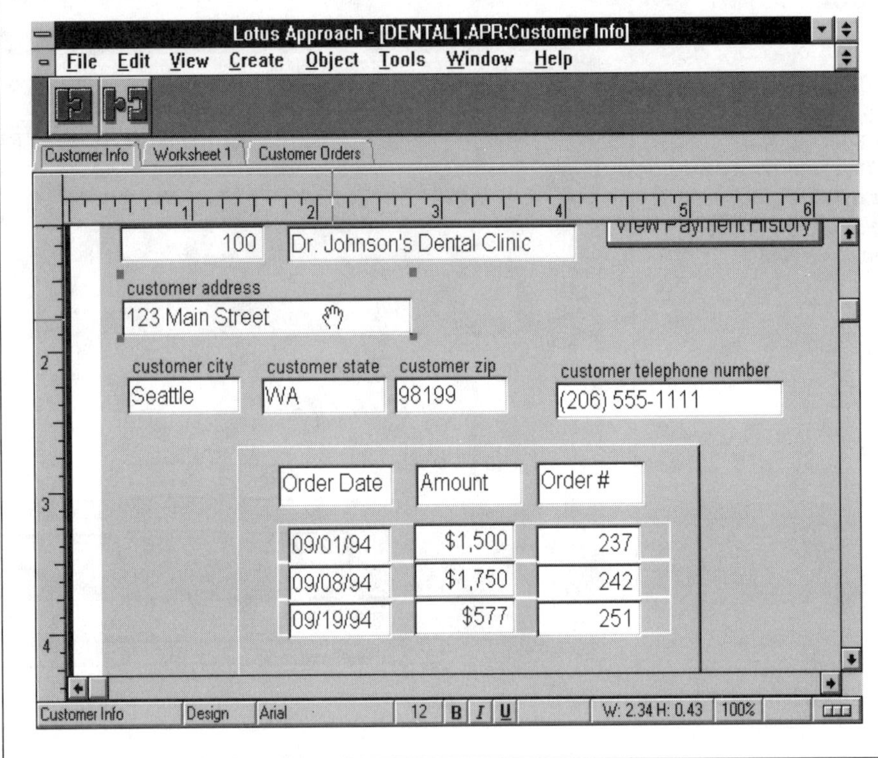

Precise Positioning

If you want to more precisely position one or more objects, you can use one of several options Approach offers to place the object with greater accuracy.

For example, to see the work area in greater detail, you can magnify the area by using the Zoom In and Zoom Out feature. To zoom in on an area, select View ➤ Zoom In, or select the Zoom In icon from the standard Design SmartIcons toolbar. (There is, unfortunately, no keyboard shortcut). Use the scroll bars to move to the desired location. You can now move the object and align it more precisely. When you want to return to the regular view, select View ➤ Zoom Out or select the Zoom Out icon from the toolbar.

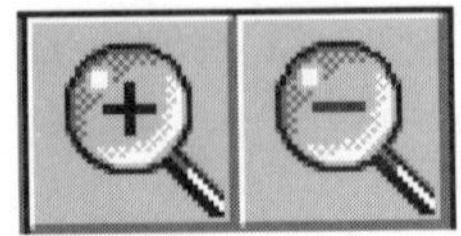

▶▶ TIP

To quickly zoom in and out, select the Zoom box in the Status bar, shown as 100% in the Status bar in Figure 7.19, and select the desired magnification level.

The Snap to Grid option, described in the "Work Area Options" section earlier in this chapter, can be used to position any object along an imaginary grid line so that objects are quickly and easily positioned on the same axis to each other. Note, however, that when you change the grid width, objects already on the form are not moved to align on the new gridlines.

▶ Sizing an Object

An object may be too large, too small, or have the wrong proportion. To change the size of an object, Approach uses the standard Windows techniques that you may have used in other applications to resize an object. First, select it by clicking on the object once. Move the mouse cursor over any of the small black squares Approach displays. The cursor will change into a double-pointing arrow. Press and hold the mouse button as you drag the black square and adjust the dimension of the object.

▶ Deleting an Object

An object may no longer be needed on a form. For example, you may decide that a company logo or a graphic image is no longer needed on a form because it takes too much room. To remove an object from a form, select it by clicking on it once. Approach places black boxes around the object. You can then do any of the following:

- Press the Del key.
- Select Edit ➤ Cut.
- Press Ctrl+X.

- Click on the Cut icon in the SmartIcons toolbar (as shown here).
- Press and hold the right mouse button on the object and select Cut from the Context-Sensitive menu.

▸ Copying an Object

If you need another copy of one or more objects, such as a second text field or a group of text frames, you can quickly copy a current object on the field as the basis for a new object. To copy an object, select it, then choose Edit ➤ Copy, click on the Copy icon in the SmartIcons toolbar, or press and hold the right mouse button and select Copy. Then select Edit ➤ Paste, click on the Paste icon in the SmartIcons toolbar, or press and hold the right mouse button on the form and select Paste. Approach displays the copy immediately on top of the existing object. Click on the object and drag it to a new location to distinguish it from the existing object.

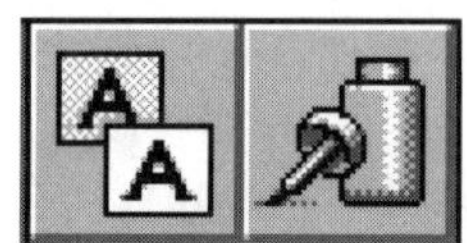

▸▸ TIP

To copy one or more objects quickly, select Ctrl+C instead of using the Edit ➤ Copy command. Then click on the form where the upper-left corner of the objects should appear, and press Ctrl+V. Rather than placing the copies on top of the originals, Approach places them at the location you clicked on the form.

▸▸ TIP

You can copy a field from one form to another. Select the form with the field you want, copy it, then switch to the second form and paste the object in this form. If you select more than one object, you can copy all the objects at once using this method.

▶ Arranging Objects

Objects can be displayed on top of each other. For example, you can create a rectangle with a yellow background, then place a logo on top of it so that the logo appears to be sitting within the rectangle. In fact, these are separate objects (although you can group them, of course). The rectangle is said to "sit in back" while the logo "sits in front." You can change this order by selecting the object, selecting Object ➤ Arrange, and finally choosing one of these options:

- Bring to Front to move the selected object to the top layer
- Send to Back to move the selected object to the bottom layer
- Bring Forward to move the selected object to the next higher layer
- Send Backward to move the selected object to the next lower layer

The default Design SmartIcons toolbar contains buttons that represent Bring Forward and Send Backward, but you can add icons for Bring to Front and Send to Back. See Chapter 18 to learn how to modify toolbars. The Bring Forward button appears with an up-pointing arrow among several layers, and the Send Backward button uses a down-pointing arrow as shown in Figure 7.20.

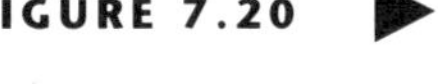

FIGURE 7.20

The Move Layers icons

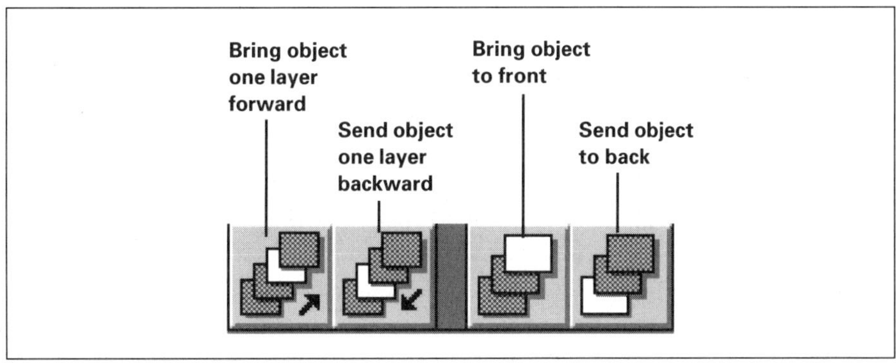

▶ Aligning Objects

After objects are on your work area, you can select two or more and align them with each other along several edges. For example, you can align them vertically along the left or right edge of each object, or horizontally along the top or bottom edge of the selected objects.

Objects may also become unaligned to the grid if you change the grid size.

To align objects to each other or to the grid:

1. Select the objects (see the section "Selecting Objects" earlier in this chapter).

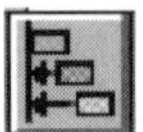

2. Select Objects ➤ Align, Ctrl+I, or press and hold the right mouse button on the object and select Align. You can also click the Align objects button on the SmartIcons toolbar. (This icon is not part of the Standard Design toolbar and must be added.) Approach displays the Align dialog box shown in Figure 7.21.

FIGURE 7.21

The Align dialog box provides all the options needed to place two or more objects in alignment.

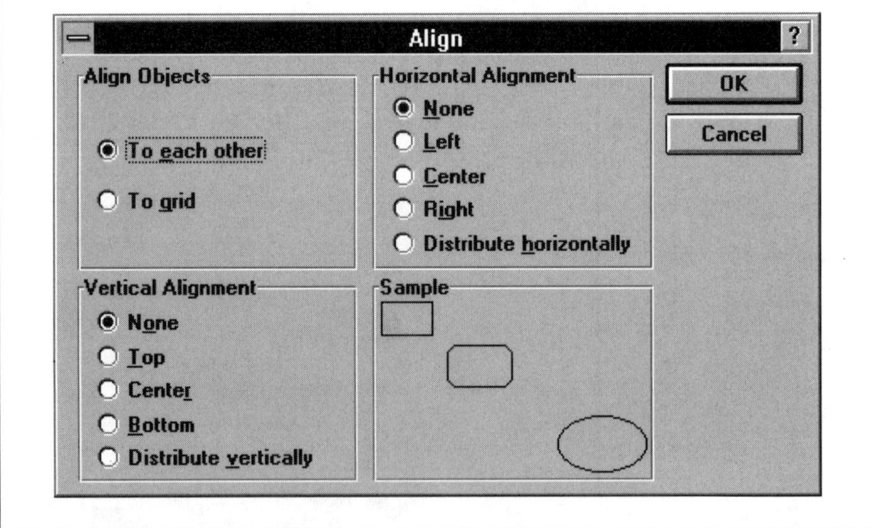

3. Select the alignment you want in the Align Objects section: to each other or to grid.
4. Choose the horizontal and/or vertical alignment you want. As you make your selection(s), Approach displays the result of your

choices in the Sample section of the dialog box. The Distribute horizontally and Distribute vertically options align the objects evenly in the selected direction.

5. Select OK.

►► Viewing and Changing Object Properties Using the InfoBox

In Approach you can view and change an object's properties using the InfoBox. You can select an object, then display the InfoBox and change the properties. However, since the InfoBox can also remain "on top," you can display the InfoBox, then select different objects. As your selection changes, the InfoBox is updated to display the properties of the selected object. Using this feature you can click on several different objects and see the same data (font information or label text, for example) for each object you select.

Follow these steps to view the InfoBox for an object:

1. Click on the InfoBox icon in the Design toolbar.
2. Double-click on the object.
3. Select an object and press Ctrl+E.
4. Select an object, then press and hold the right mouse button and select the Styles and Properties option.
5. Select an object, then select Object ➤ Styles and Properties.

If you don't select an object, Approach displays the InfoBox with information about the form itself.

The contents of the InfoBox change when you select a different object. Using a tabbed format, the InfoBox for a text field offers properties for font, color, format, and size, as well as the name of the database field it relates to (you can even select a field from a different database if you wish), the label font and size, and any associated macros to be run when the field is selected. Settings for the form itself offer options for a color, name, and macros. The InfoBox shown in Figure 7.22 displays the font options for the selected data object, customer city.

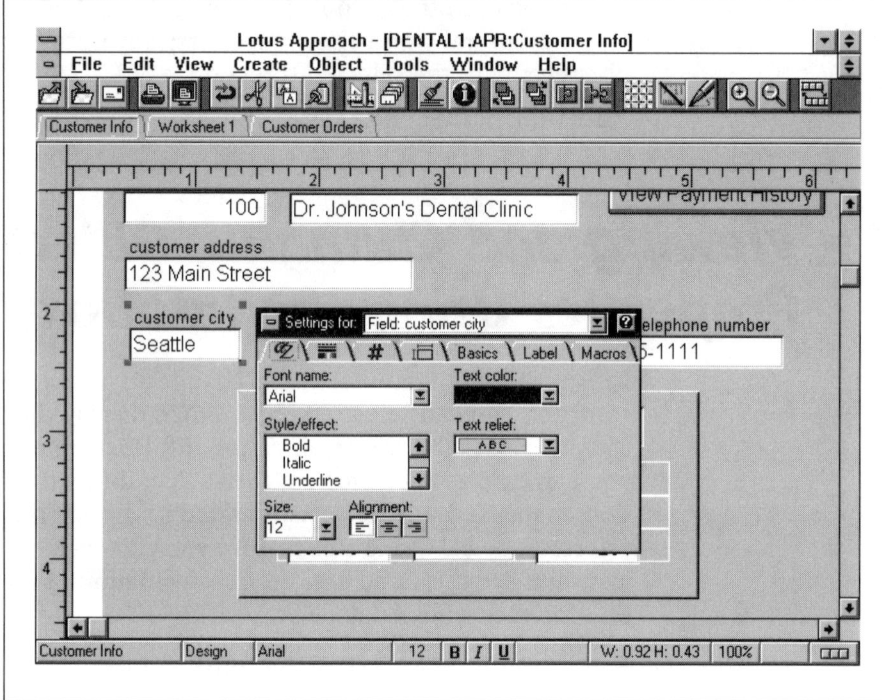

FIGURE 7.22

InfoBox for the Customer City field on a form

To close the InfoBox, double-click on the small icon in the upper-left corner of the InfoBox (the icon looks like a minus sign), or click once on the icon and select Close, or be sure the InfoBox is currently selected (the Title bar displays a color, not white) and press Alt+F4. If you want to move the InfoBox, click on it and drag it to any position on the screen.

To change the property of an object, use the InfoBox as you would any tabbed dialog box. Several options are described in the following sections.

When you select an option, Approach immediately applies the option to the object and displays the result of your choice on the form.

You can select multiple objects and change the same properties on each selected object in one step. Select the objects, then click in the InfoBox. The "Settings for" box displays Multiple Objects. Only those properties that are shared (such as color and font) will be displayed.

TIP

To get more information about any of the options in the InfoBox, click on the Question Mark icon in the upper-right corner.

The Font Tab

The Font tab is labeled with an A and a Z and is shown in Figure 7.22. Options on this tab let you select from the fonts installed on your system. You can also choose the style and effect (bold, italic, underline, and strikethrough) by selecting any or all of these special effects. When a text effect is selected, Approach places a check mark to the left of the effect.

The Font tab also provides options for selecting the font size, its alignment (left, center, right, or full), as well as the text color and relief effect (the three-dimensional look of the object).

Aligning Text

You can align text within a text object by selecting one of the alignment boxes from the InfoBox. In addition, you can choose from the Center, Left, Right, and Justify icons, or the Single, One-and-a-Half, and Double-Space icons from the Design Text SmartIcons toolbar as shown in Figure 7.23. The Justify and One-and-a-Half icons are not on the default toolbar but can be added. See Chapter 18 to learn how to change the toolbars.

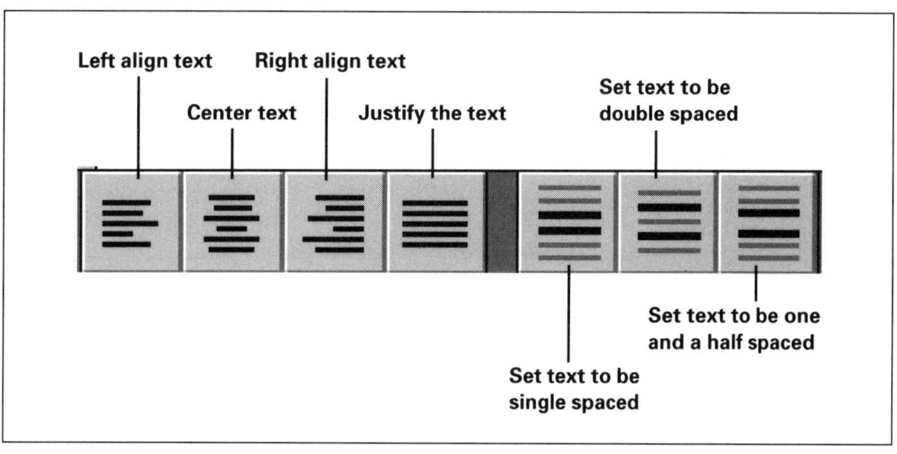

FIGURE 7.23

The Text Alignment and Text Spacing icons

► The Color Tab

The Color tab is labeled with a colored box and is shown in Figure 7.24. Options on this tab are used to select the border size and color, fill color (sometimes called background color), as well as the color of the drop shadow (the color that gives an area a three-dimensional look). In Figure 7.10 earlier in this chapter, the form heading Customer Information has a drop shadow so the text box appears to be rising from the form itself. To eliminate a shadow, select the Shadow color option shown as a white box with a T inside, which stands for Text.

FIGURE 7.24 ►

The Color tab

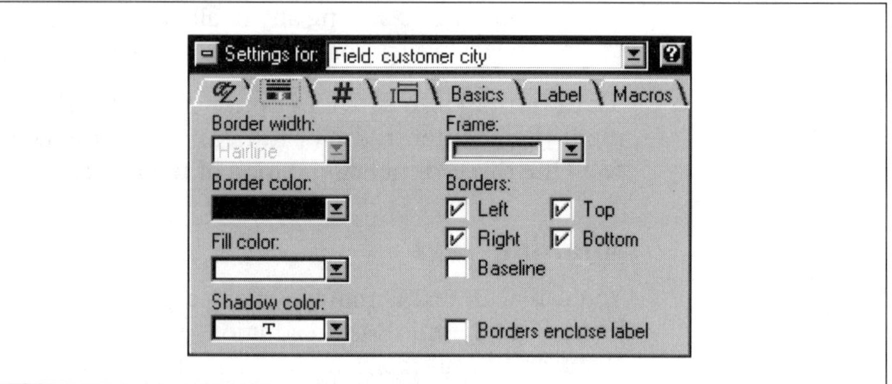

The frame is placed around the outside of the object and is drawn using the line style you select. The frame uses the Border color selected in the first column. If you select "Borders enclose label," the border surrounds both the label and the field. Otherwise, the border is placed around the field only, and the label takes on the background color property of the form itself.

► The Format Tab

The Format tab, labeled with the # sign, provides options that control how the data in a field will be displayed. For example, while a data field may contain a date, you can display the date as Monday, December 5, 1994 or as Mon Dec 5 94. The Format tab is shown in Figure 7.25. Making a selection in the Format type drop-down box determines what other options are displayed on this tab. Formatting is discussed in greater detail in Chapter 8.

FIGURE 7.25

The Format tab

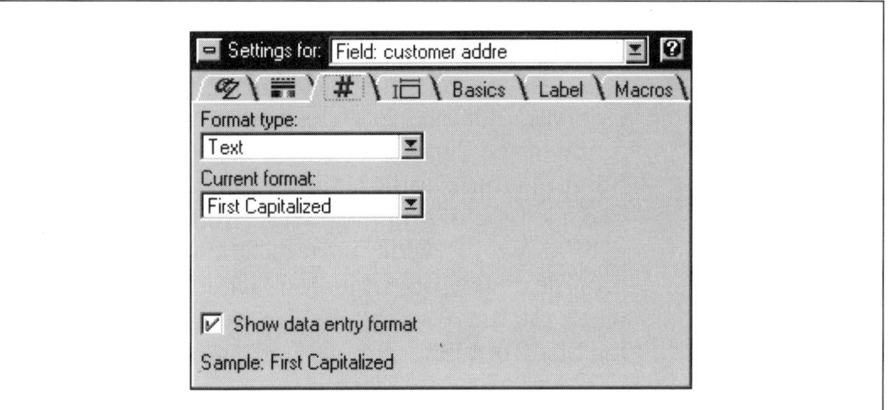

▶ The Dimension Tab

The Dimension tab, labeled with a blue box and red dimension lines, provides options that control the size of the object. You can change an object's size by selecting it and dragging any of the corners, or you can enter precise measurements in this tab.

Field objects have additional options, including how to change the field size during printing. For example, selecting the "When printing, boundaries reduce" option will change the field's boundaries to the size of the data when the form is printed, eliminating white space. Figure 7.26 shows the Dimension tab for a text object.

FIGURE 7.26

The Dimension tab for a Text Field Object

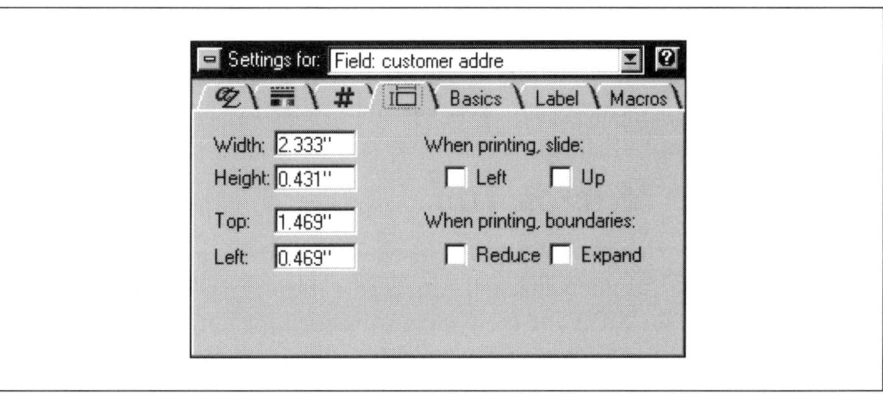

▶ The Basics Tab

This tab controls the "basic properties" of an object, which vary by object type. For example, the basic properties for a data field include the name of the database and the field in that database (you can select another database and/or field here), whether editing should be permitted, and the type of graphical style used to present the data (a text box, a drop-down list, radio buttons, and others). The basic properties of a graphic or text object include whether the object should be shown when the form is printed. You can also access the Field Definition dialog box from here. Figure 7.27 shows the Basics tab for a text object.

FIGURE 7.27 ▶

The Basics tab

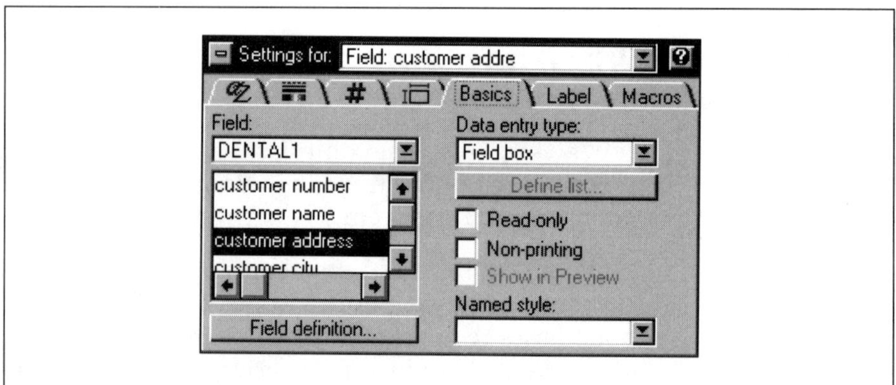

▶ The Label Tab

The Label tab is used for field objects. Options on this tab control the formatting of the label text of a field. For example, in Figure 7.28 the Customer Address field uses the label text "customer address."

▶ The Macros Tab

Approach supports a powerful shortcut for executing instructions called *macros*. A macro can perform a search on a database, switch to a different view, print a record, or sort records on a different form. Macros can be assigned to button, graphic, and text objects so that when you click the object the associated macro begins to run. Macros can also be automatically started when you are working with the form in

FIGURE 7.28

The Label tab

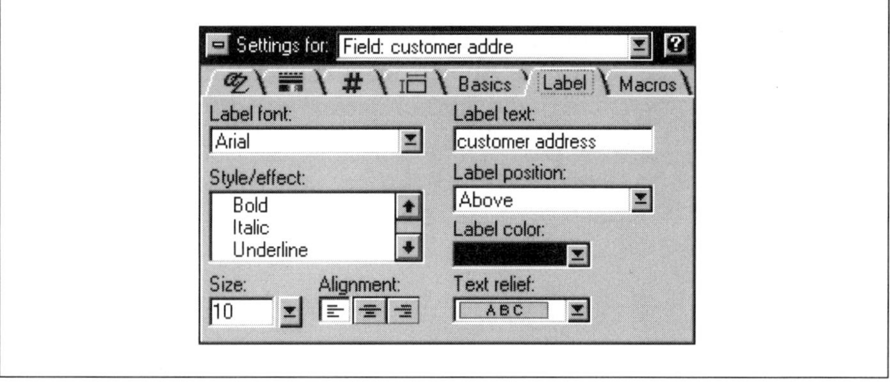

the Browse environment. In the Browse environment, Approach can run a macro when you tab into or out of a field—that is, when you press tab to move into the next field or previous field on a form.

Figure 7.29 displays a Macro tab for a text object, the customer address text field.

FIGURE 7.29

The Macros tab

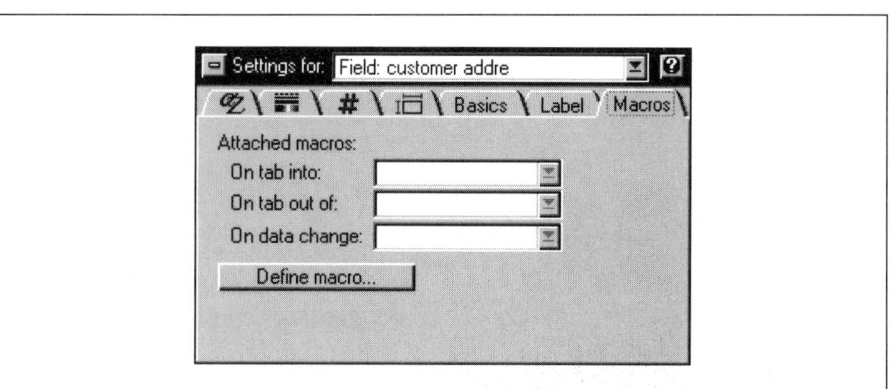

►► Viewing and Changing Object Properties Using the Status Bar

The properties of some objects are displayed in the Status bar. For example, if you add a text object (such as a set of instructions or a title) to a form and select that object, the Status bar changes, as shown in Figure 7.30. In this illustration, we selected the customer city field. The Status bar now displays the font, font size, and font characteristics (bold, italic, and underline), and the Named Style (discussed in the section "Named Styles" later in this chapter). These properties are also shown in the InfoBox.

FIGURE 7.30

The Status bar provides formatting information about the form object you select. Many of the same properties are also displayed in the InfoBox.

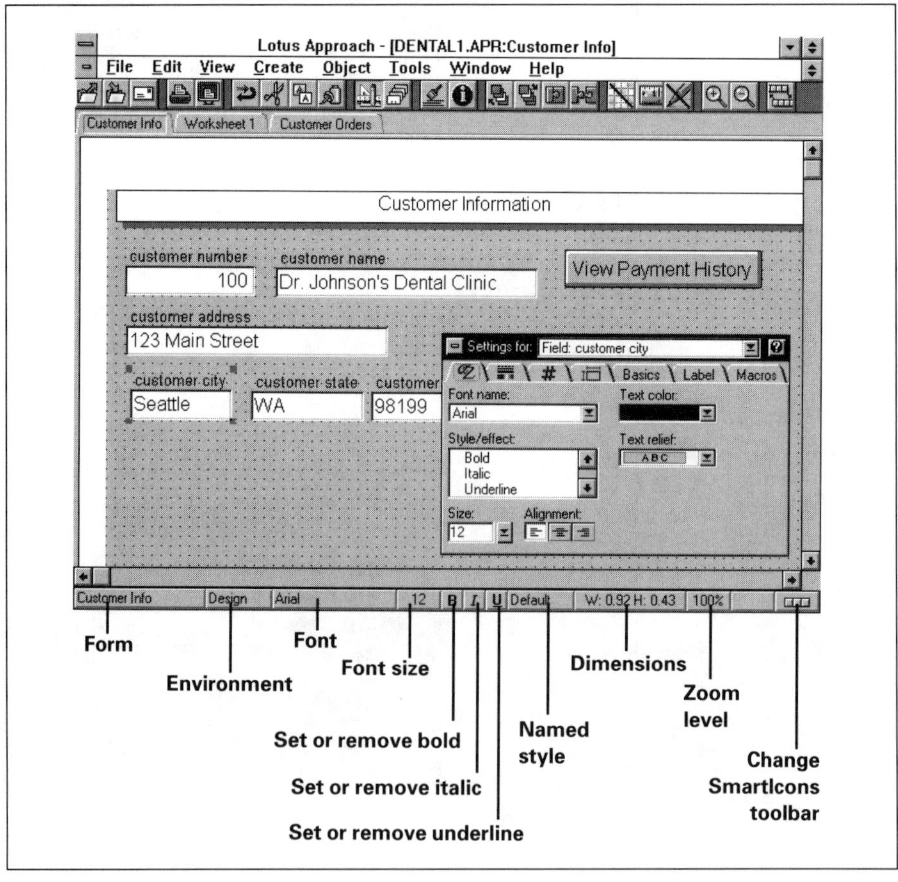

To change any of these properties, click on the box within the Status bar. For example, when you click on the Font property, Approach displays a list of the fonts installed on your system. Select the desired font. To turn the bold, italic, or underline property on, click on the Status bar area corresponding to the property. These areas act as toggles; click them again to turn the property off.

The button to the right of the Named Style shows the dimensions of the selected object. The number to the right of W: indicates the object's width, and to the right of H: is the object's height. Click on this button in the Status bar to see the offset (position) relative to the upper-left corner of the form (L: means left, T: means top).

►► Copying Properties to Other Objects

Approach can quickly copy the characteristics (font, color, size, and so on) from one object to another using its Fast Format feature, a feature shared in other Lotus applications. Using Fast Format, you select the object that has the properties you want to copy, select the Fast Format option, then click on the objects to which you want to apply the properties. Note that all of the properties of the original object are copied—you cannot select which properties are perpetuated using Fast Format.

Follow these steps to use Fast Format:

1. Select the object that has the properties you want to apply to one or more objects.
2. Press Ctrl+M, press and hold the right mouse button as you point at the object and select Fast Format, select Object ➤ Fast Format, or click on the Fast Format icon in the Design default SmartIcons toolbar. If the Fast Format icon is displayed on the toolbar, it is dimmed and a black line appears on the icon. The mouse cursor also changes to a plus sign and a paintbrush. This indicates that Fast Format has been selected.
3. Click on the object you want to possess the properties of the selected object.
4. Repeat Step 3 until all objects are selected.
5. Press Ctrl+M, press and hold the right mouse button as you point to the object and select Fast Format, select Object ➤ Fast Format, or click on the Fast Format icon in the Design default SmartIcons toolbar. The icon and mouse cursor return to their original design.

▶▶ TIP

You can copy properties between forms. In Step 3, switch to the different form before clicking on the objects.

▸▸ Named Styles

Named Styles allow you to save a set of properties, called a *style*, and reuse them throughout a database. You can apply a Named Style to an existing object or use that style automatically when you add new objects.

Named Styles have another advantage—a very strong advantage: objects that use this style are changed automatically. For example, suppose you have ten fields on a form that all use the same Named Style, called Data Field for illustration purposes, which includes the font Arial, 10 point. When you change the Data Field style to use Arial 12 point bold, all fields that use this style are automatically changed to use Arial 12 point bold. Without such a style, you'd have to change one field and use the Fast Format feature to reformat the remaining nine fields on that form. Since styles apply across all fields on all forms in your Approach file, using a Named Style is an excellent way to quickly perpetuate a change everywhere in your application (assuming the objects are all based on this style).

The following are among the properties you can define in a Named Style:

- Field fonts (font name, style, size, color, alignment, and 3D effect)
- Lines and colors, including border, fill, and shadow color, frame style, and border (left, right, top, bottom, and/or baseline)
- Label fonts (font name, style, size, color, alignment, and 3D effect) and label position
- Picture adjustment (crop or shrink image if too big, stretch if too small) and editing (allow drawing inside the PicturePlus object)
- Background properties, including frame, color, and size of border

Not all properties apply to all objects that use this style, for example. You can define a style and apply it to a PicturePlus field and a text field. The picture adjustment settings would be used by the PicturePlus field, while these properties would be ignored by the text field. The properties for field fonts would, however, be used by the text field and ignored by the PicturePlus field. Both text and PicturePlus fields would also use the label properties from the Named Style, since labels are common to both types of fields. In this way, Named Styles are incredibly flexible—they can be assigned to any object type and that object uses only the field properties that make sense.

To add a new style, select Tools ➤ Named Styles and select New, or select the style you want to copy and select Copy. Approach displays the Define Style dialog box shown in Figure 7.31. Enter the style name, which can describe the style using spaces and some punctuation (such as parentheses and dashes).

If you want to copy most of the properties of an existing style, and then change just a few properties, it may be easier to base your style on an existing style. Select the style's name from the "Based on" box. Approach sets that style's properties as the properties of the style you are

FIGURE 7.31 ▶

The Define Style dialog box

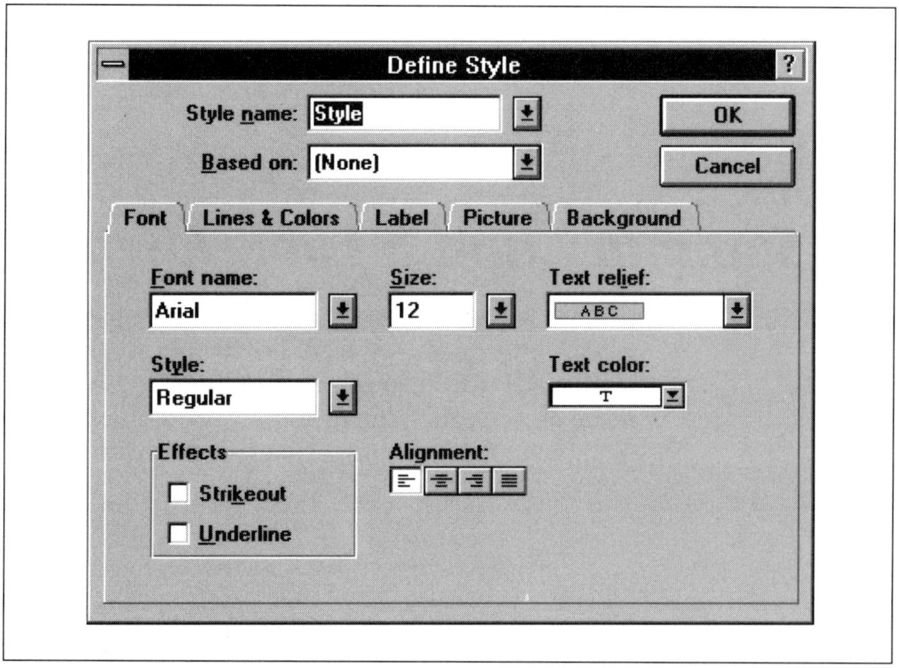

defining. Changes you make are reflected in the new style—the original style is not affected.

Set the font, line, label, picture, and background options, just as you would using the InfoBox. When you are done, select OK. Then select Done from the Named Styles dialog box.

To edit an existing style, choose Tools ➤ Define Style, highlight the style you want to change, and select Edit.

To remove a Named Style, choose Tools ➤ Define Style, highlight the style, and select Delete. Approach asks you to confirm your request. Select OK.

To use an existing style as the basis for a new style, choose Tools ➤ Define Style, highlight the style you want as the model, then choose Copy. Enter the new style name, select the style options, and choose OK.

▸ Using Named Styles

The InfoBox lets you assign a Named Style to an object on a form. For example, select the object(s) on the form to which you want to apply a Named Style, then open the InfoBox to the Basics tab, as shown in Figure 7.32. Select the Named Style from the pull-down list.

Alternatively, select the object(s) on the form to which the style should be applied, then choose Tools ➤ Named Styles, choose the style, and select Apply.

▸▸ Summary and a Look Ahead

In this chapter we've taken an exhaustive look at how to create and modify a form. You've seen the different types of form objects, including fields, buttons, graphics, and drawing objects. You've seen how to move objects, align them, and group and ungroup them. You've also seen how to change properties using the InfoBox.

FIGURE 7.32

The Basics tab of the InfoBox lets you select a Named Style for an object.

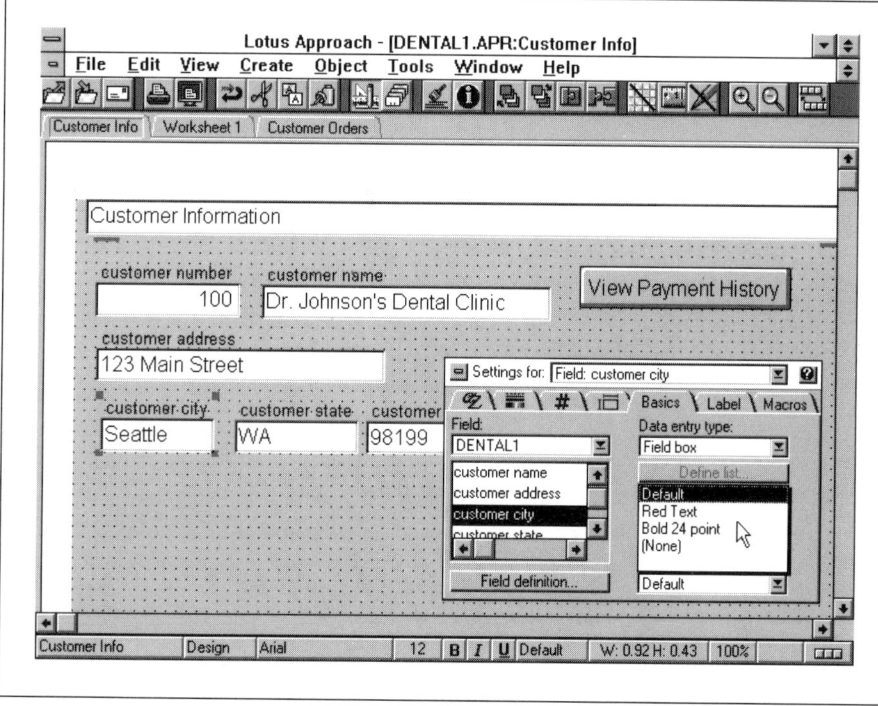

Since the majority of your work with forms will be to display and edit data from your database, we devote the next chapter to looking at how to work with field objects on a form. To learn more about forms, turn to Chapter 8.

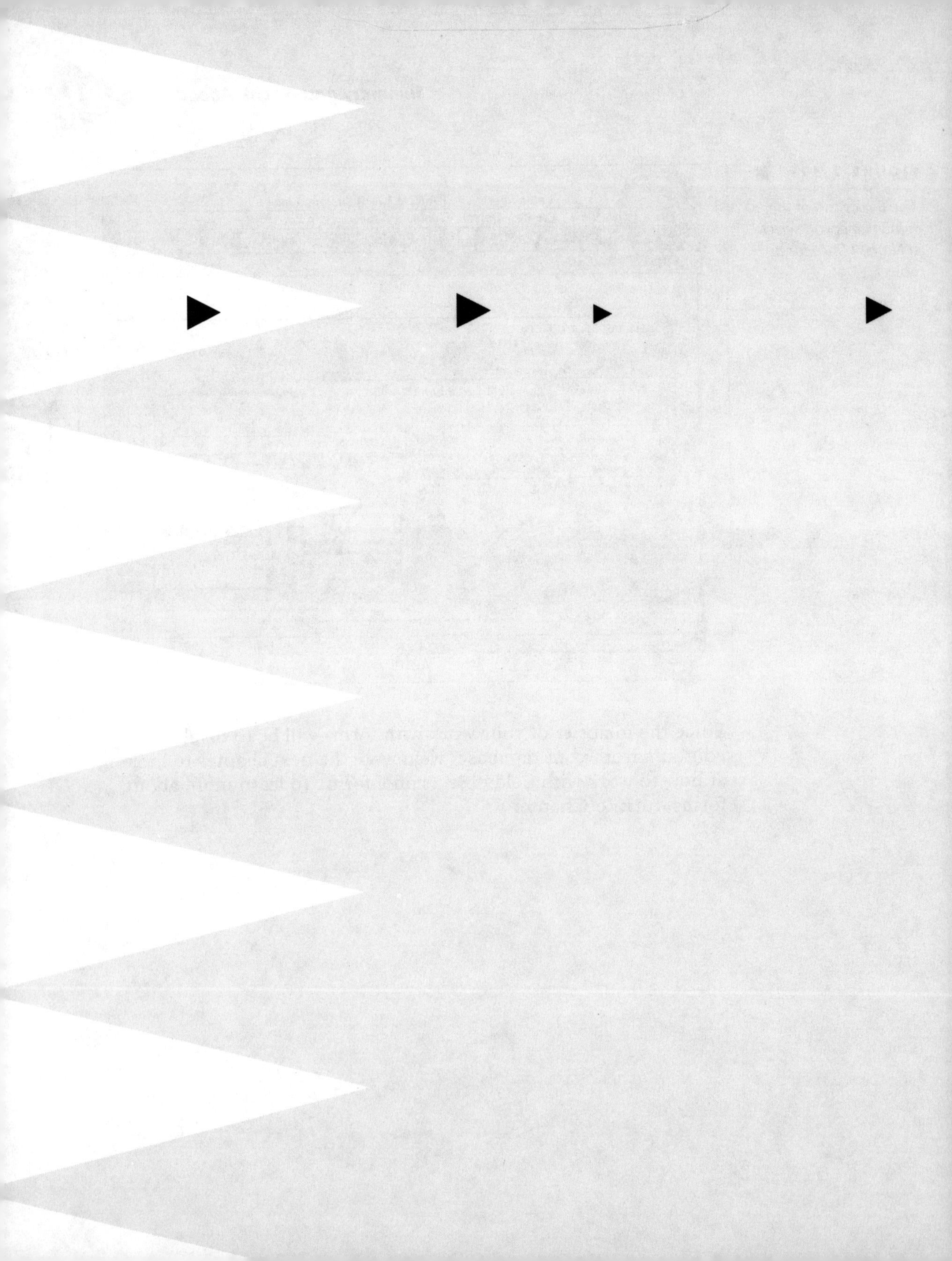

CHAPTER 8

Working with Data and Forms

Fast Track

- ***To display a field as a drop-down list and manually specify the values permitted*** **263**

  select the field and choose the Basics tab from the InfoBox. In the Data entry type drop-down list select Drop-down list. To limit values to those in a list, select Type in list items. Enter the values in List in the order you want the items displayed when the field is selected in the Browse environment. To add an item to the list, click on the item and click Insert. To delete an item, select it and choose the Delete key. Select OK.

- ***To display an existing field on a form using radio buttons*** **276**

  select the field, open the InfoBox, and choose the Basics tab. In the Data entry type drop-down list select Radio buttons. Enter the value to be stored in the database record for the field in the Clicked Value column. Enter the value to be displayed on the form to the right of the button in the Button Label column. To add a button, click on a row, then select the Insert button. To delete a button, select the row and select Delete. To automatically create radio buttons based on existing data in the database, select the Create Buttons from Field Data button. Select OK.

- ***To add a PicturePlus field to a form*** **280**

  select Create ➤ Drawing and choose PicturePlus Field. Drag the mouse cursor across the work area to set the boundaries, then select the PicturePlus field you want to display. Set the Allow Drawing, Non-printing, and Show in preview options if desired. Select the Options tab, then drag the image of the bird to place the image relative to the dimensions of the field. Choose Crop it or Shrink it to adjust an image if the source image is larger than the area defined on the form. Check the Stretch if too small option to enlarge the image and use the Color and Size tabs to set color and dimension options.

➤ *To change the tab order* 281

select View ➤ Show Data Entry Order. To change the tab order, click on the gray square that contains the tab order value, then drag the cursor over the displayed value, which highlights the value, and enter the new tab order value. When you click anywhere else on the form, Approach renumbers all fields with a higher tab order value. To remove the tab order boxes, select View ➤ Show Data Entry Order again.

➤ *To add a summary field* 290

click on the panel and select Panel ➤ Add Field or right-click on the panel and select Add Field. Select the Field Definition button. In the Field definition dialog box, move to the last position (cell) in the Field Name column. Enter a field name and select calculated as data. Select Options to display the bottom portion of the dialog box, then click on Formula and enter a formula that includes a summary function and the field you wish to summarize. When the formula is correct, the formula flag appears without a red X through it. Select OK, then select OK again to add the field to the database. Add this new field to the form.

➤ *To change a repeating panel* 295

click on the top row and drag its borders to the row that has the dimension you want. To increase the row height, click on the bottom border of the top row and drag the mouse pointer downward. To remove a repeating panel, select the top row and press the Delete key.

▶▶ **The** majority of your work in Approach will be performed using fields on a form. Working with fields on a form is similar to working with any other object type discussed in Chapter 7. You can copy, move, group and ungroup fields, align them, change their common properties or use Fast Format to copy the properties of one field to one or more fields of your choice. You can also delete fields and set their properties. There are, however, dozens of properties and characteristics of fields that make them different from the text and graphic objects discussed in Chapter 7.

Fields have several special properties, such as formatting, that control which data is displayed and the format used to display the data. For example, a rectangular drawing object can have a background and border color. So, too, can a date text field. You can also specify how the date in a Hiredate field of a record is displayed (July 25, 25 July, 25 July 1994, or 7/25/94).

These and other special conditions and properties for fields on a form are the subject of this chapter.

▶▶ *Adding a Field to a Form*

You can add any field from a database associated with (defined to) the Approach file, except variable fields.

If you have a single database defined to the Approach file, you can place the fields in any order you wish. However, if you are placing fields from more than one database, you must place the first field from the main or controlling database. This is the database that is on the "one" side of a "one-to-many" relationship (see Chapter 6). When you use the form in the Browse environment and move to another record (next, previous, first, or last), Approach moves to that record in the main database.

▶ Adding a Field Using the Add Field Dialog Box

To add a field to an existing form, use any of these methods:

- Press and hold the right mouse button over any existing object and select Add Field, then drag a field name from the Add Field dialog box to the work area.
- Click on the "Show the add field" button in the Drawing toolbar, then drag a field name from the Add Field dialog box to the work area.
- Click on any object, then select Object ➤ Add Field, then drag a field name from the Add Field dialog box to the work area. Click anywhere on the form's background, then select Form ➤ Add Field. Drag a field name from the Add Field dialog box to the work area.

- Click on the Add Field icon in the SmartIcons toolbar or the Drawing toolbar. Drag the mouse from the upper-left corner of the work area to the bottom-right corner of the new field to define the boundaries of the new field. Select the field name from the InfoBox.
- Select Create ➤ Drawing ➤ Field and drag the mouse from the upper-left corner of the work area to the bottom-right corner of the new field to define the boundaries of the new field. Select the field name from the InfoBox.

When Approach adds a new field, it uses the Default style. You can select the field and display its InfoBox to change the Default style, which is set to Normal when you install Approach. To change the Default style for all future new fields, see the "Named Styles" section of Chapter 6.

Approach tries to approximate the actual size you'll need for the field. However, if you have a very long field, such as a 100-character text field, you may want to make the field smaller so it will fit on the form. As with any other object on a form, clicking a field once places black boxes in the corners of the field. Drag the boxes to resize the field. If the field shown on the form is smaller than the actual length of the field as defined in the database, Approach scrolls the data when you are in the Browse environment. For example, if you have placed a field that can display 20 characters at most on a form, and the field is defined in the database as a 40-character text field, Approach will display only the first 20 characters, although the entire 40 characters will be stored in the database. As you enter characters, the text will scroll to the left and disappear from the screen. However, when you move back to the left, only the first 20 characters will be displayed. You can click on the text and use the left and right arrow keys to move to other locations within the field to view the text.

If, when typing characters in a field, you enter too many, Approach will warn you that your entry is too long. For instance, when you type the 11th character in a field that is only defined as 10 characters long, Approach warns you that you have exceeded the field size.

►► **NOTE**

You cannot place a variable field (explained in Chapter 5) on a form. Since a variable is always the same, and is not directly related to a record, it doesn't really make sense to display it.

You can display the Field Definition dialog box for the selected database by choosing the Field Definition button. You can add a field in the Field Definition dialog box, and when you return to the Add Field dialog box shown in figure 8.1, only the newly added field will be listed. Approach adds a new button—Show All Fields, which changes to Show New Fields when clicked—that toggles the field list between all fields and the one(s) you just added.

►► Switching Between Actual Data and Field Names

If your database contains data, you can show either the field names or the actual data from fields in the first record using the current sort order of the *found set*. The found set is the group of records that meets a condition you specify, such as the records that contain data about customers in California. If you are viewing all data, the found set is the entire database, and Approach displays the first record in your database.

FIGURE 8.1

The Add Field dialog box

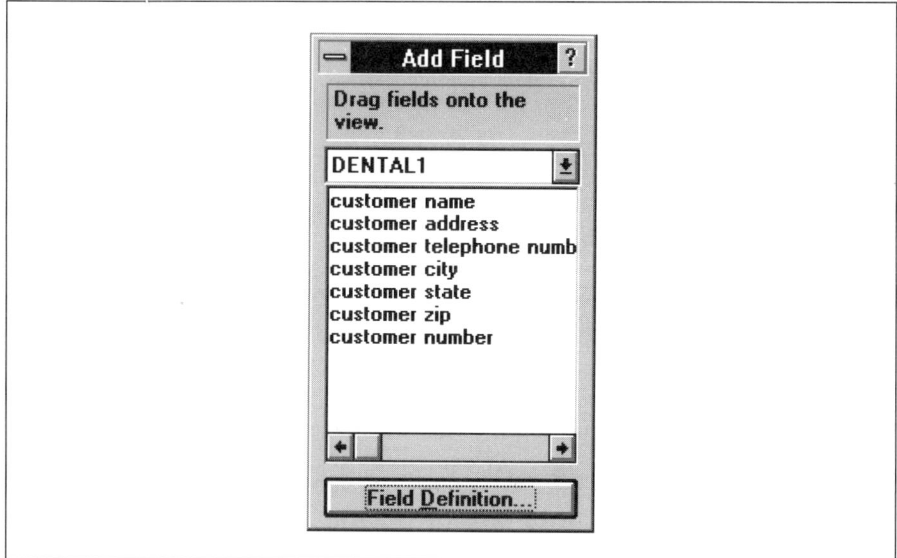

If you have multiple databases defined in your Approach file, the field name is displayed in two parts: the database name, followed by a period, and the field name. For example:

```
CUSTOMER.LASTNAME
```

To show the data, click the Show Data icon from the SmartIcons toolbar, or select View ➤ Show Data. The Show Data icon is not on the default toolbar, but can be added (see Chapter 18). When data is displayed in a field, the Show Data icon contains a black slash through it. To toggle back to showing field names, click the icon or select View ➤ Show Data again.

▶▶ Field Properties

In Chapter 6 we discussed the tabs in the InfoBox that are available for many objects. In this section we'll discuss the tabs that are unique to fields. Exceptions and special conditions are noted for each tab.

▶ The Font Tab

There is no font tab for PicturePlus fields.

▶ The Color Tab

The Borders options (Left, Right, Top, Bottom, and Baseline) and "Borders enclose label" option are available for all fields except PicturePlus.

The Left, Right, Top, and Bottom options arrange the border at the selected positions surrounding a field. Select Baseline to add an underline to the field to show where to type data during data entry. The Baseline option is commonly selected when no other Border option (Left, Right, and so on) is selected.

The "Borders enclose label" option allows you to place the field label inside or outside the frame. In Figure 8.2, the Borders enclose label option was not selected for the customer city field (the label is outside the field area), but was selected for the customer state field (the label and field are contained within the same border).

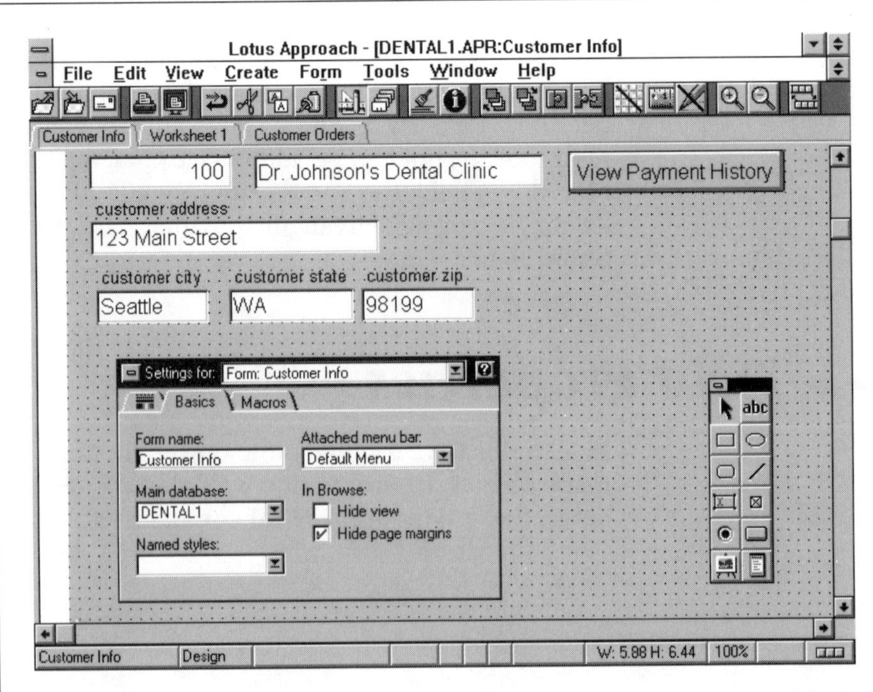

FIGURE 8.2 ▶

The Borders options in the Color tab let you specify where the label appears relative to the field.

▶ The Format Tab

Formatting is unique to fields and is available for date, number, text, time, and calculated fields. When you enter data in a field, you can type data in a blank field or have Approach display part of the formatting for you, such as the slash (/) mark in a date. When you move out of the field (by selecting another field), Approach displays the value of the field according to the format you've specified. For example, you can enter the date 9/3/95 in a blank (empty) field or one that shows you the division between month, day, and year. When you move to another field, Approach displays the field value according to the format string you specified for this date field.

Figure 8.3 shows the same date field displayed using three different format options. The first shows the date when using the default, "Display as entered." The second date is similar, but uses a two-digit month,

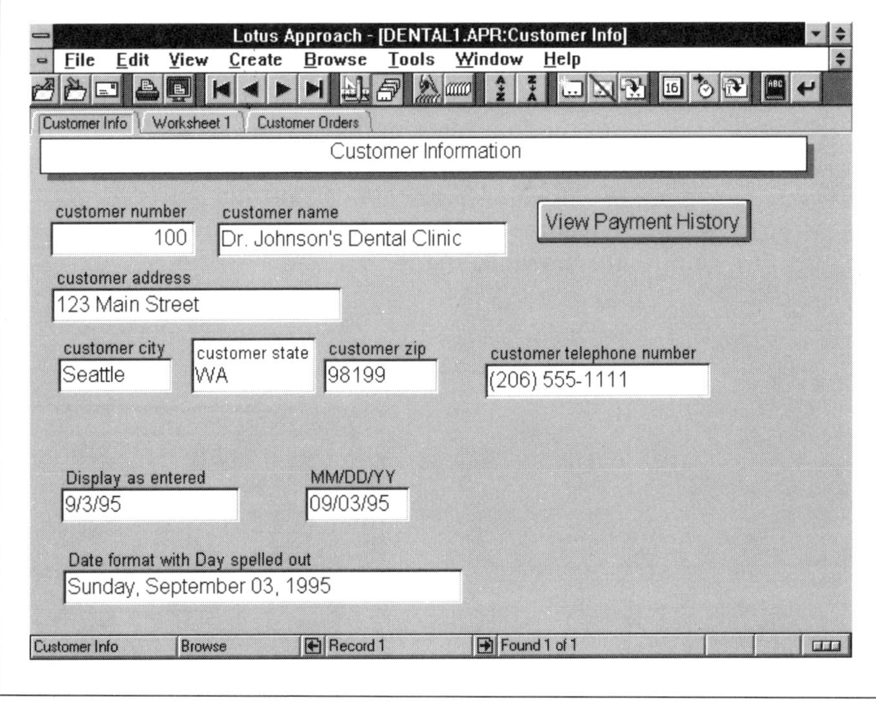

FIGURE 8.3 ▶

The Format options let you specify how a date (or other field type) is displayed. The data in the record is not changed—only the way the data is presented on the screen.

two-digit day, and two-digit year format (MM/DD/YY), displaying leading zeros. The date below uses yet another format and displays the name of the day fully spelled out.

Although Approach stores this data internally in only one format, you can change the way the data is displayed on your form. The default shows the format used to store the data, such as MM/DD/YY for date fields.

To change the format, select a different Format type from the Format tab. The drop-down list displays your options, which vary by field type.

Date Field Formats

Select Date as the Format type and you can select among the following:

- Day-Month-Year
- Month-Day-Year
- Year-Month-Day
- Other

For the first three options, you can then select from the Day of week, Month, Day, and Year display options. For example, when you select Month-Day-Year, you can further select from individual options for the day of the week and the month, day, and year formats. These options are shown in Figure 8.4.

FIGURE 8.4 ►

The Format tab for a date field

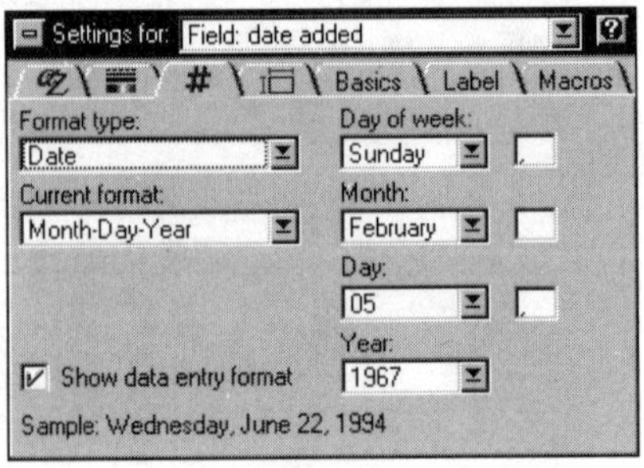

To see the format when you enter data in the Browse environment, check the "Show data entry format" box.

Approach displays a sample of a date at the bottom of the InfoBox.

To select an option, choose from one of the predefined choices in the drop-down list. The first option is always blank, meaning do not include this part of the date in the display. For example, if you select the blank option for Day of week, the date will appear without Monday or Mon for dates that fall on a Monday.

Be sure to select the separator characters that follow the first three options. You can place any character in these boxes. For example, if you place a colon after the Day of week option, the date will display as `Wednesday: June 22, 1994`. By default, Approach uses commas as separator characters.

If these options are not sufficient, you can create a special format by selecting the Other format option from the Current format drop-down list. Approach displays a Format Code box and a list of predefined format codes, as shown in Figure 8.5.

You can select from several predefined format codes (from the right-hand box) or create your own using the Format code test field (the third box in the left column). The following list shows what each component means. To create your own format code, move to the Format code text box and type in a series of format components, as shown in the following list. The format code used in Figure 8.5 includes the components "DDD" so Approach will spell out the day, "YYYY" so it will display the four-digit year, and so on.

FIGURE 8.5 

The predefined Format codes for custom date formats

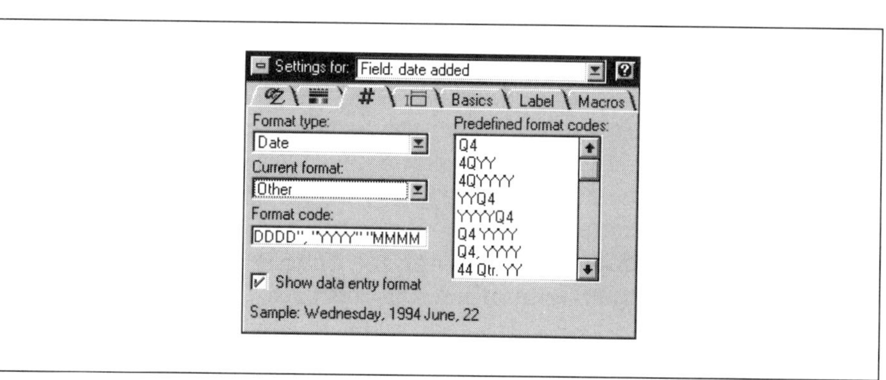

Format Component	Meaning	How July 4, 1994 Appears
4	Quarter in which date occurs	3 (The third quarter of 1994)
44	Quarter expressed as 1st, 2nd, 3rd, or 4th	3rd
444	Quarter spelled out, as First, Second, Third, or Fourth	Third
D	Day Number, no leading zero	4
DD	Day Number, with leading zero	04
DDD	Day of week, abbreviated	Mon
DDDD	Day of week, spelled out	Monday
M	Month number, no leading zero	7
MM	Month number	07
MMM	Month abbreviation	Jul
MMMM	Month spelled out	July
YY	The two-digit year number	94
YYYY	The four-digit year number	1994

Any other text in the format code is displayed as entered. For example, 44 Quarter would be displayed as 4th Quarter. The same July date, when formatted as Q4 would appear as Q3. The "Q" is not a format code, so Approach displays the letter. The "4" however *is* a format code—representing the quarter number—and is replaced by the actual quarter number, 3 in this case.

Numeric Field Formats

Select Numeric in the Format type drop-down box and you can select among the following pre-defined formats:

Integer	No decimal points, separator character (commas) inserted as needed, as in 2,345.
General	Commas inserted as needed, two decimal points (2,345.67).
Currency	Same as Integer, with leading currency symbol ($2,345).
Currency with decimals	Same as General, with leading currency symbol ($2,345.67).
Percent	Whole number with percent sign (15%).
Percent with decimals	Number with two decimals and percent sign (15.46%).
Telephone	If the field contains more than 7 digits (ten is the maximum), the number is displayed in the form (123) 456-7890 (the "extra" digits are assumed to be the area code); otherwise, the number is shown as 456-7890; if less than seven digits, the number is not reformatted.
Social security	In the form of a United States social security number (222-33-4444).
Scientific	In the standard scientific format of a whole number with one digit to the left of the decimal, two to the right, a plus sign, and the two-digit power of "e" (a constant value) following (1.23e+01).
Zip Code	If the field contains more than five digits, the number is formatted as 12345-6789; otherwise the first five digits are formatted as 12345.

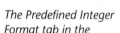

When you select a predefined format, Approach displays the Format code. However, you can create your own custom format by entering the formatting code directly in the Format code box. The Format code consists of two parts: the first code is used to format the number if it is zero or greater; the second code is used to format negative values. The Format code default for an integer is shown in Figure 8.6.

FIGURE 8.6 

The Predefined Integer Format tab in the InfoBox

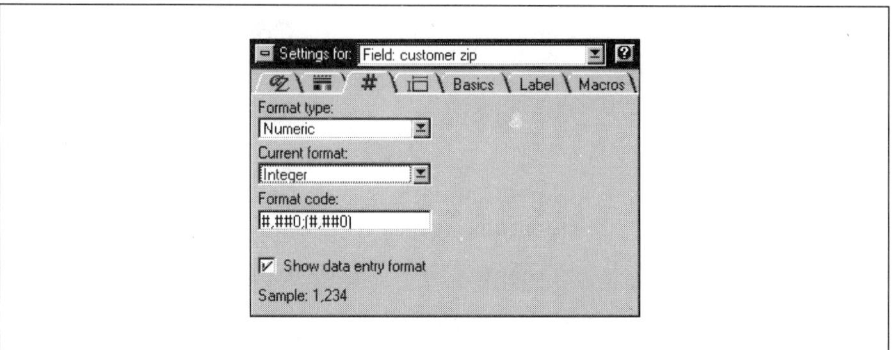

If the second format code is missing, the first format code is used for negative values. The first and second codes are separated by a semi-colon (;).

Use the following characters in your custom format:

This Character	Formats a Digit This Way
#	As the number, or blank if zero
9	An optional digit, it's displayed as itself (zero is formatted as 0)
0	A required digit; the digit is formatted as itself
Any Other Character	The character itself
%	Converts the value to percent

Approach uses the leading characters to format additional characters. For example, you can specify a format of #,### and Approach will format 1234567 as 1,234,567.

Using 0s in the format indicates the digit must be displayed. For example, 0.00 indicates that if the user enters 2.3 the value will be displayed as 2.30; the value 5 will be displayed as 5.00.

Formats can include logic, such as you've seen in the zip code and telephone number predefined formats. The conditions are separated by a vertical line (|, which is the ¦ on your keyboard).

▶▶ TIP

Format strings can also contain only text. For example, if you want to spotlight negative values in a report, assign the format #,##9.99;"OUT OF STOCK" to the QtyOnHand field and positive numbers will appear as digits but negative values will be replaced with the text OUT OF STOCK. (Quotation marks are required in the format code because the text contains spaces.)

▶▶ WARNING

Always be sure your formats agree with the field definition. No matter what your format string, formats cannot override the field definition of a numeric field. For instance, suppose your field is defined as 3.0 (that is, three digits, none to the right of the decimal), and you use the format ##0.00. When in the Browse environment you'll be able to enter 3.45, but Approach will truncate (chop off) the decimal portion of your entry and store the value 3. Approach cannot store the decimal portion (the .45 part of your entry) since the field is defined as a numeric value with no decimal portion allowed.

Text Field Formats

Although most text fields can probably be set to the "Display as entered" format type, you can have Approach change the case of text. For example, you can tell Approach to change the first letter in any word to uppercase, a great time saver that allows you to enter jim powell and have Approach automatically save the value as Jim Powell.

To select one of three text options, select the Text format type, then select Current format. The following table shows what happens to the letters "new York" when entered in a field with a text format option.

Option	Result
ALL CAPITALIZED	NEW YORK
all lowercase	new york
First Capitalized	New York

Time Field Formats

Select Time as the Format type and you can select among four predefined formats. The format tab is shown in Figure 8.7. Unlike the date format, however, you cannot create your own format string. The predefined formats determine how much of the date you'll show (hours, minutes, seconds, and hundredths of seconds). You can also choose between 12- and 24-hour clocks (1PM is the 12-hour representation of 13:00).

If you choose the 12-hour format, you can also choose the time suffix. The default is AM and PM, but you can also enter characters directly, such as am or a.m.

The Display as entered option has a key advantage during data entry: it offers you a great shortcut. With the Display as entered option turned on for a time field, you can type 2 and Approach will interpret this as 2:00 AM.

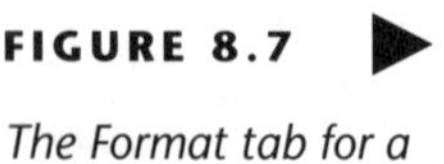

FIGURE 8.7

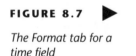

The Format tab for a time field

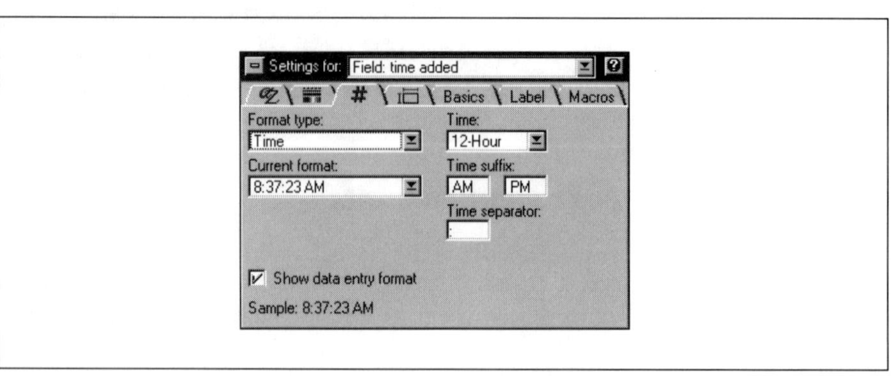

▸▸ Using GUI Elements on a Form

Although text fields may be the standard, you can use several graphical user interface (GUI) elements to help select or quickly enter field values or prevent incorrect values from being entered. GUI elements include:

- Drop-down lists
- Field boxes and lists
- Check boxes
- Radio buttons

The GUI element is chosen using the Data entry type options in the Basics panel of the InfoBox, shown in Figure 8.8.

We'll discuss each GUI element separately below.

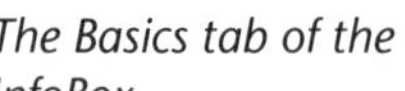

FIGURE 8.8

The Basics tab of the InfoBox

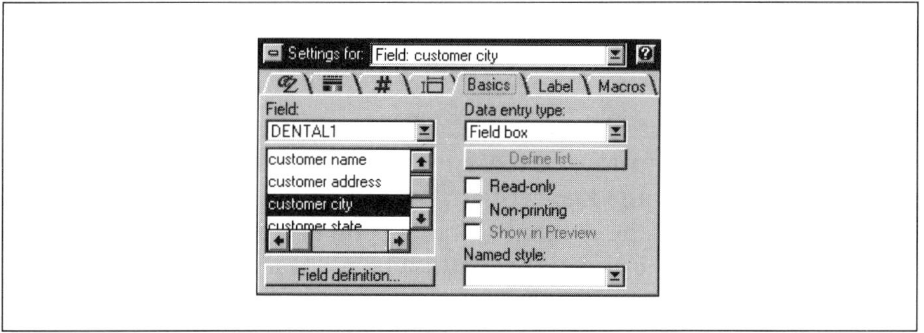

▸ Drop-Down Lists

A drop-down list allows you to select a value for a field from a list displayed as a menu or list box. The list box drops down from the field entry area and displays up to nine options at a time. If more than nine options are defined, Approach adds scroll bars. A drop-down list is shown in Figure 8.9.

Approach offers a variety of options for defining the list box. For example, you can specify the values in the list box manually, or you can create the

FIGURE 8.9

The Region field can be entered by selecting one of four values from a drop-down list.

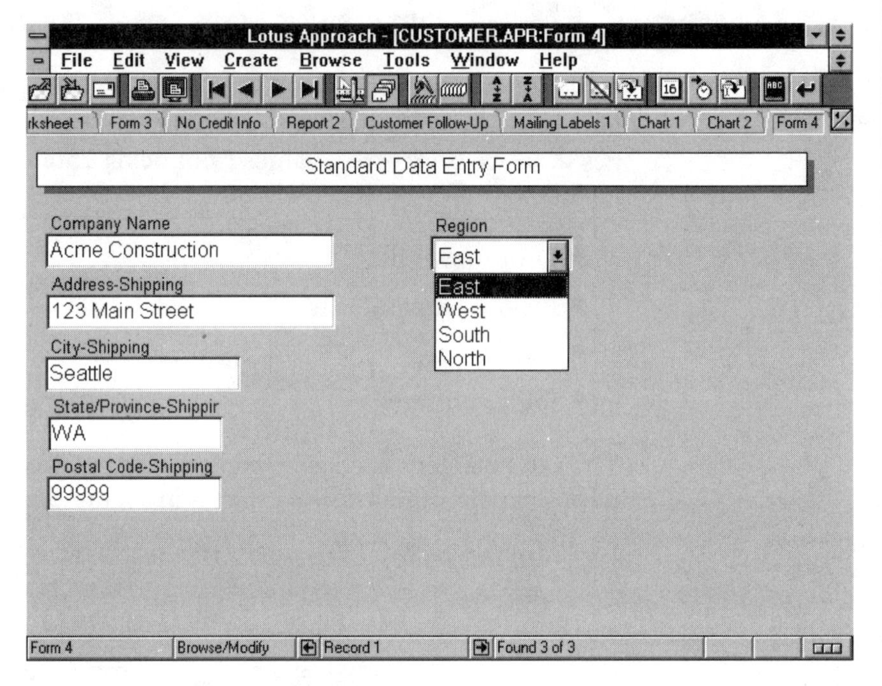

list automatically from values already in a field. For example, if you are using a database created by a coworker and want to limit the entries in the Department field to values that already exist in the Dept field in the database (that is, you can select any Department name that exists but you can't add a new one), Approach offers an option to automatically populate the drop-down list with existing Dept values.

Approach also lets you display values from one field but enter data from another. This somewhat confusing option is best explained by example. Suppose you have a department code and a department description. You can display the DeptCode field as a drop-down list. When you are in the Browse environment and move to the DeptCode field, Approach displays a drop-down list of department *descriptions*. When you select the description, Approach stores the corresponding department *code* value in the DeptCode field. Approach can also let you limit the field values based on the value of another field.

Follow these steps to display a field as a drop-down list, and manually specify the values permitted:

1. Select the field on the form.
2. Open the InfoBox and select the Basics tab.
3. In the Data entry type DROP-DOWN list, select Drop-down list.
4. To limit values to those in a list, select the "Type in list items" box. Enter the values in "List" in the order you want them displayed when the field is selected in the Browse environment. Figure 8.10 shows the Drop-Down List dialog box.

FIGURE 8.10

The Drop-Down List dialog box (without selecting the Options button)

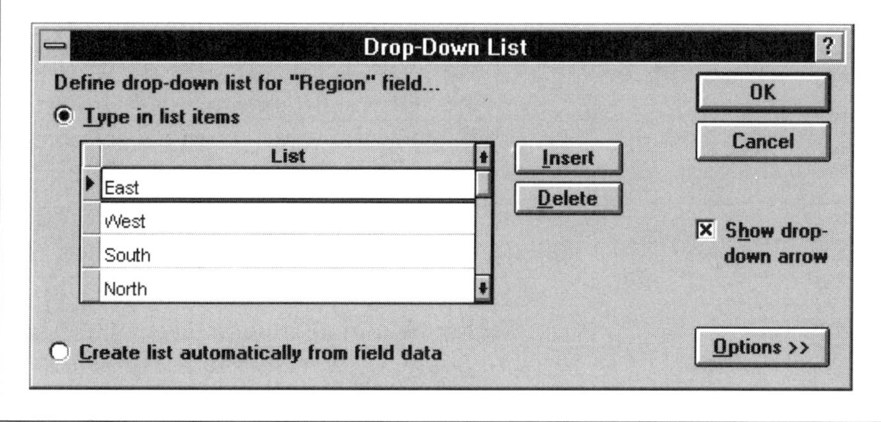

5. To add an item to the list, click on the item and click Insert. (Note that the existing item moves down one row.)
6. To delete an item, select it and choose the Delete key.
7. To move an item within the list, click the mouse button on the gray square to the left of the item and hold the mouse button down. The mouse cursor changes to a hand. Drag the item to the new location and release the mouse button.
8. Select OK.

▶▶ **TIP**

To display a drop-down arrow to the right of the field at all times, check the Show drop-down arrow option. Otherwise, Approach displays the arrow when you select or move to the field during data entry.

Use these steps to display a field as a drop-down list containing values from an existing database field:

1. Select the field, open the InfoBox, and choose the Basics tab.
2. In the Data entry type drop-down list, select drop-down list. If Approach does not display the drop-down List dialog box, shown in Figure 8.10 earlier in this chapter, click the Define list button.
3. Check the "Create list automatically from field data" option. Approach displays the values from the selected field in the List box, as shown in Figure 8.10.
4. To use values from a different field, select the Options button. The full drop-down List dialog box appears as shown in Figure 8.11.
5. Choose the database and field. Figure 8.11 shows that values in the Region field of all records in the Customer database will be used to populate the values in the drop-down list.
6. To show the values from another record in the drop-down list, but use the values from a corresponding field, select the "Show description field" option. An example of this technique is described in Step 7.
7. To display a subset of the list, select the "Filter the list based on another field" option. Approach displays the Define Filter dialog box, shown in Figure 8.12. (If you have joined databases, the Define Filter dialog box displays database and field options.) Select the field that must match. Details of this option are described in the following section. Select OK.
8. Select OK.

FIGURE 8.11

Building a list of values automatically from existing field values

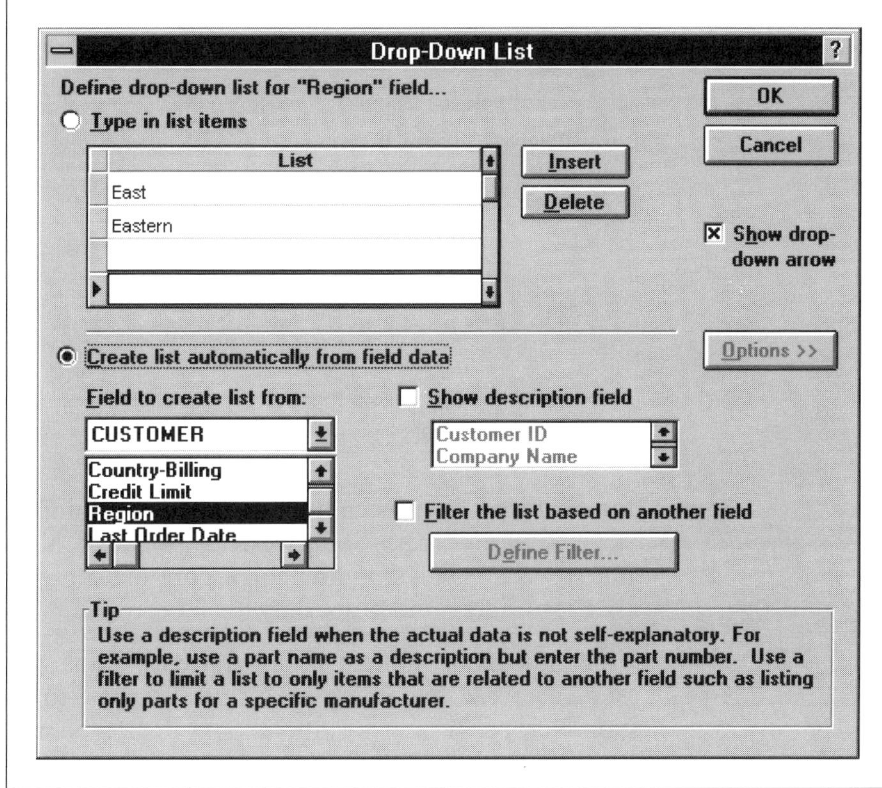

Using Descriptions Previously Step 6 described how to use descriptions in a drop-down list. You might want to use this feature when you store a numeric value in a field but want to let the user select from a list of text options that describe the numeric value. For instance, suppose you have a Region field in your customer database. The Region field is numeric, from 1 to 20. When you add a new customer using the screen shown in Figure 8.13, you want the user to enter a value from 1 to 20, but you know that it is tough for a user to remember if region 2 is the Southwest region or the Northwest region. Therefore, as a substitute

FIGURE 8.12

The Define Filter dialog box

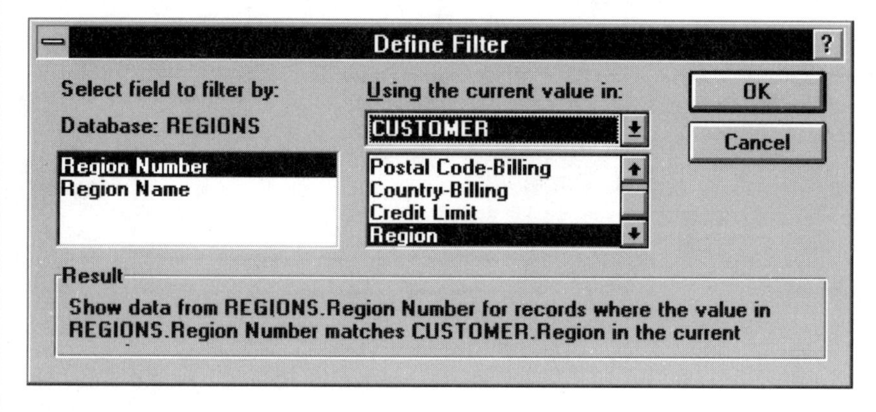

for requiring the user to directly enter the region *number*, the user can select a region name (Southwest, South, West, Northwest, and so on) but Approach will store the corresponding value (1 through 20) for that region in your database field.

To handle this you must set up another database and join it to your existing database. You set up the Region database to contain two fields: Region Number (which is numeric) and Region Name (a text field). There are 20 records in this database, one for each region number/region name combination. For example, the first record contains a Region Number of 1 and the Region Name Southwest. You must also join the region database to your main database (the customer database).

Back on the data entry form for the customer database, select the field containing the descriptions you want to be displayed in the Drop-Down List dialog box. For example, in Figure 8.13, we've set up a drop-down list field to display the region name from the Regions database. When the user picks a region name, the corresponding region number from the Region Number database will be filled into the field. The user will view these descriptive values, then make a selection. For example, the user selects the name Southwest from the drop-down list. Approach stores the value from the Region Number field (1 in our

FIGURE 8.13

Using a field description instead of a field value lets you select from meaningful text (a region name), not numbers or codes (a region number), when you enter a new customer record.

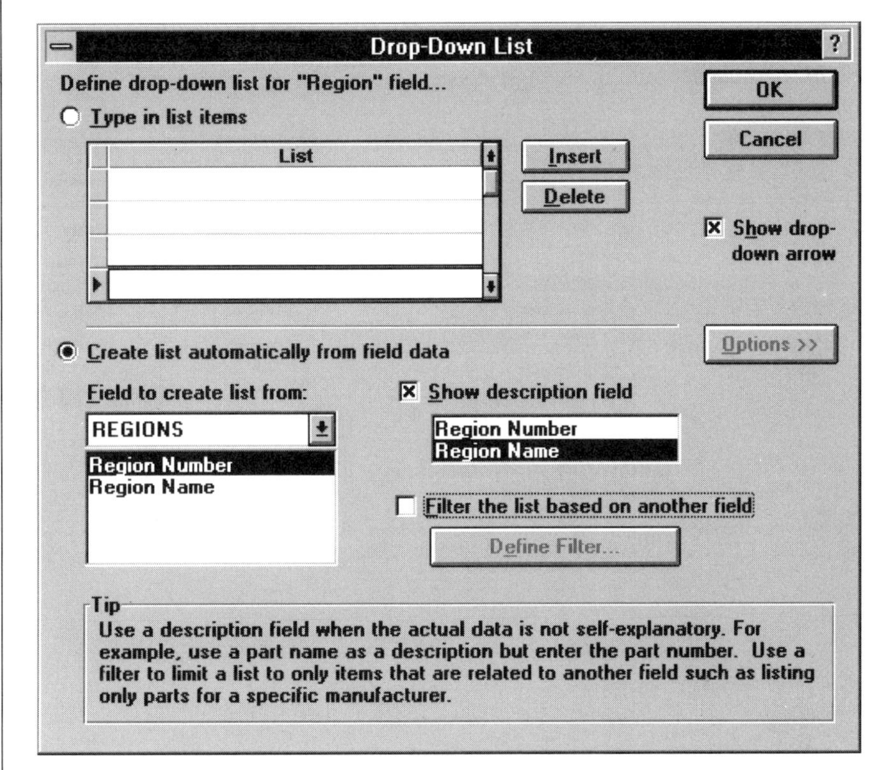

example) in the Regions database. Thus, the net result is that the user selects Southwest but the region field in the new customer record gets the value 1.

In fact, when you move the cursor to the Region field on the form, the drop-down list shows all the descriptions (Southwest, West, and so on), as shown in Figure 8.14.

When you move away from the field, Approach displays the actual value (the region number, or 1, if you select Southwest), as shown in Figure 8.15.

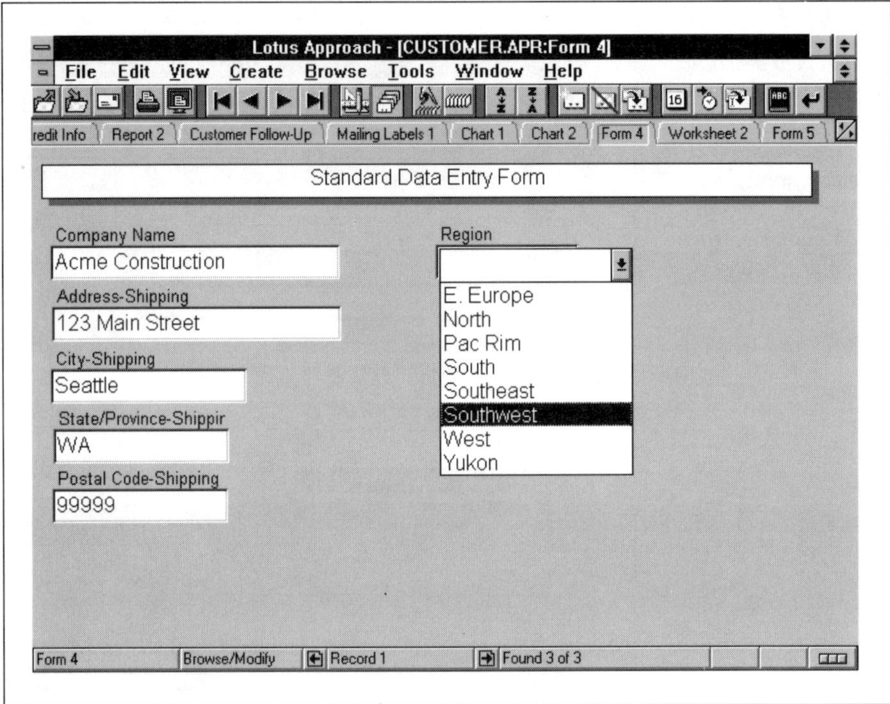

FIGURE 8.14

The drop-down list shows the regional descriptions from the Regions database.

Using Filters

Using the Define Filter dialog box, you can set a filter, which we'll call the Filter field, to display a subset of values shown in a drop-down list box you have specified. By selecting a filter field in the Define Filter dialog box, you are telling Approach that when you edit this field in the Browse environment, you want Approach to display values from a record if the values match the values in your specified list.

For example, suppose we need to enter a division and department number for a new employee into a form. After we enter the division number, we don't want to see a drop-down list of all the department numbers possible. We are only interested in using the department numbers that are associated with the same division. For example, when we add Richard Dalkins and enter division number 100, we know that the only departments we would want to select from are those in division 100—the department numbers used in other records of the same employee database.

FIGURE 8.15

After selecting the region name and moving to another field, Approach substitutes the region number in the field.

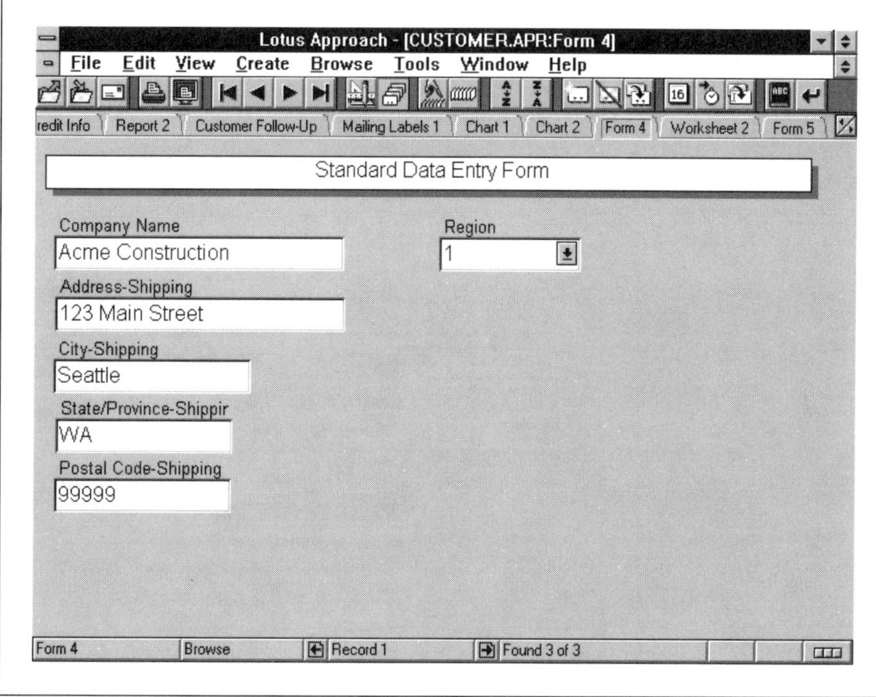

Of course, this technique breaks down if we are adding a new employee to a new department within the division, since it would be the first record to contain this division/department combination. However, when you want to create a drop-down list based on existing values within other records, using filters is a speedy way to go.

Figure 8.16 shows how to define a filter.

Figure 8.17 shows the result of that filter when you perform data entry: The drop-down list shows all of the department numbers where other records in the Employee database also contain a value of 100 in the Division field.

▶ The Field Box and List Option

The Field Box and List option is less restrictive than the drop-down list option. Figure 8.18 shows the Field Box and List option selected for the Department field. It looks identical to the drop-down list option.

FIGURE 8.16

The drop-down List and Define Filter dialog boxes

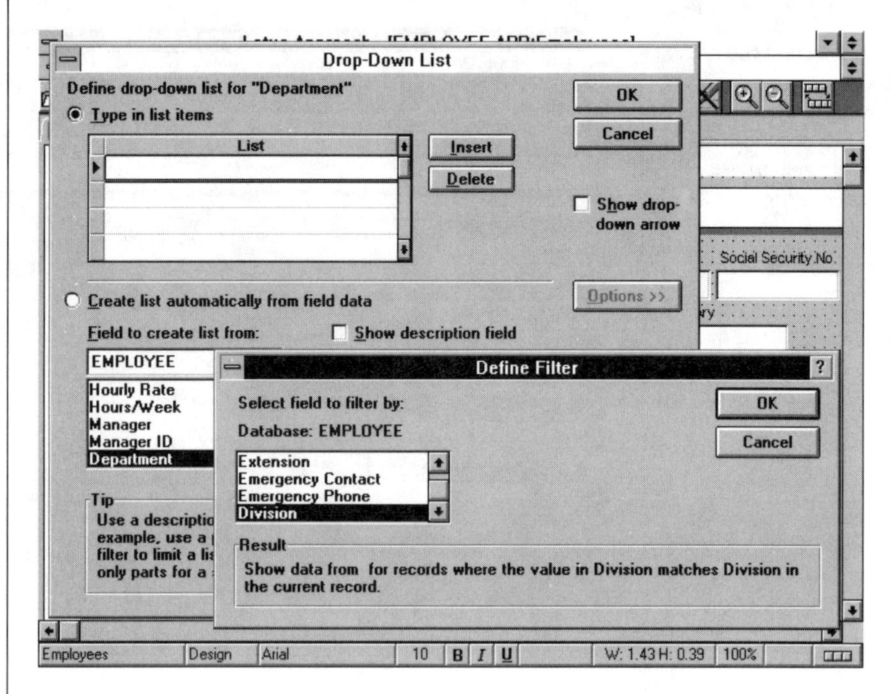

The difference is in its behavior when you are in the Browse environment.

When in Browse, selecting the field will display the existing values from within the database, as shown in Figure 8.19 (just like a drop-down list can) if you select the down-pointing arrow. If you don't select the down-pointing arrow, you can enter any value you like. Thus, the Field Box and List option provides the best of both worlds: You can enter a new value or select from a list of existing values. However, this means that you cannot restrict a user's entry. If you want to confine the user to select from just a list of permissible codes or department numbers, for example, do not use this option. Use the drop-down list option instead. You can apply a filter to a drop-down list box.

FIGURE 8.17

The data entry form shows only values that pass the Filter test.

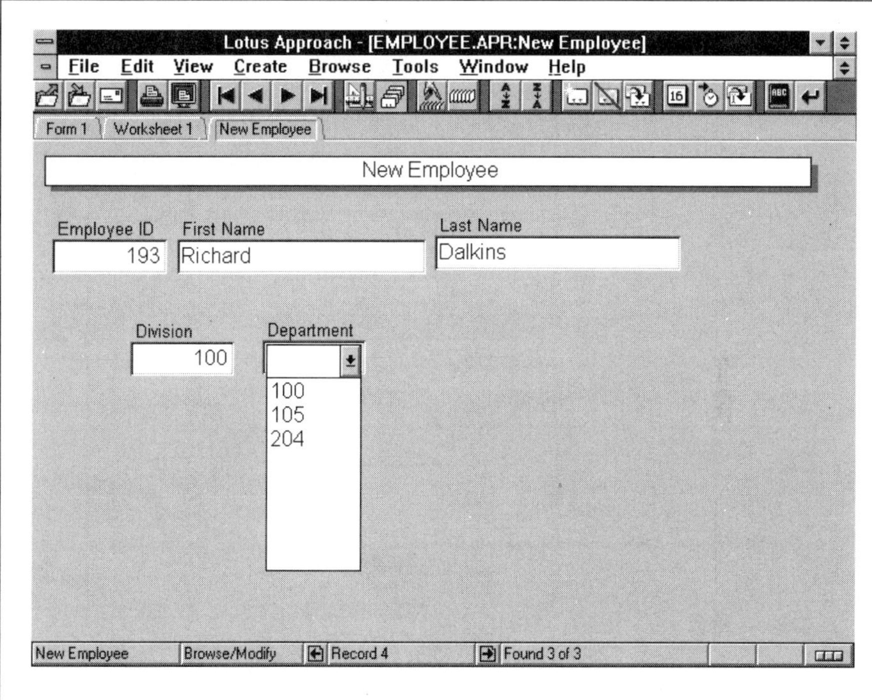

▶ Displaying Field Values with Check Boxes

You can display a field value for a text or Boolean field as a check box. You specify to Approach the value of the field when the box appears with an X inside, and the value when the check box is empty.

For example, suppose your name-and-address database record contains a Type field, defined as a one-character text field with the possible values of B to denote the record as a business contact, and P to mark the record as a personal record. If you display the Type field using a check box, you can tell Approach to display an X in the field if the type is B and leave the check box empty if the value is P.

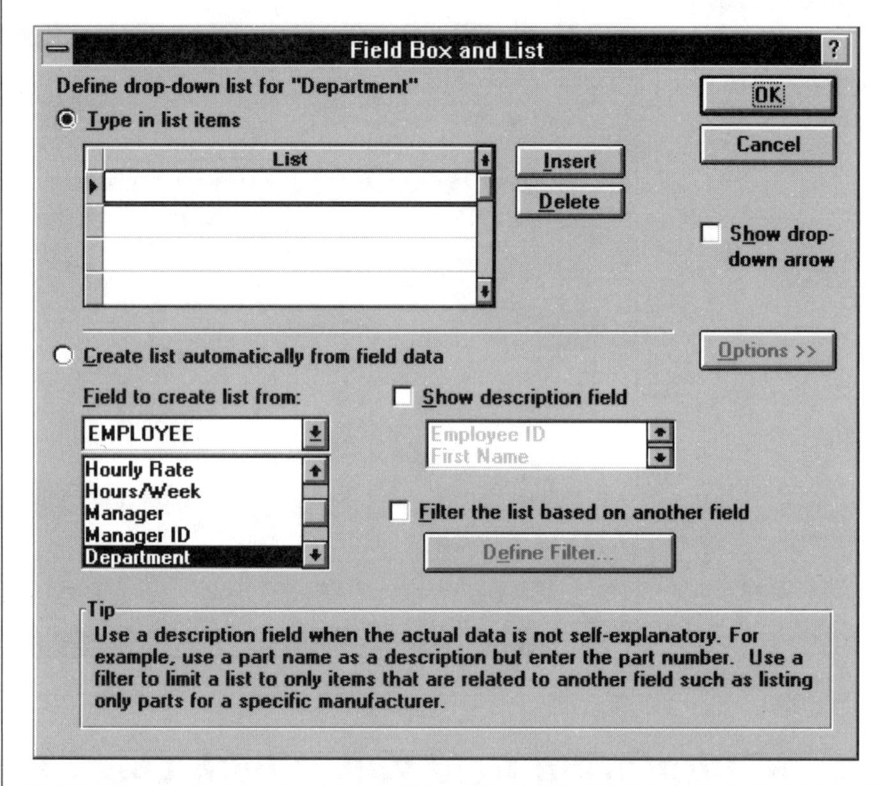

FIGURE 8.18

The Field Box and List Option applied to the department field

You use the Define Checkbox dialog box, shown in Figure 8.20, to set the checked and unchecked values.

The Type field is displayed on the data entry form as a single check box with the label "Business," as shown in Figure 8.21.

Use these steps to display an existing field on a form using a check box:

1. Select the field, open the InfoBox, and choose the Basics tab.
2. In the Data entry type drop-down list select Checkboxes. If Approach does not display the Define Checkbox dialog box, shown in Figure 8.20, click the Define Buttons button.
3. Enter the value to be stored in the field when the check box is checked (contains an X) in the Checked Value cell of the first row.

FIGURE 8.19

When you move to the field, you can enter a new value or select the down-pointing arrow to see a list of values.

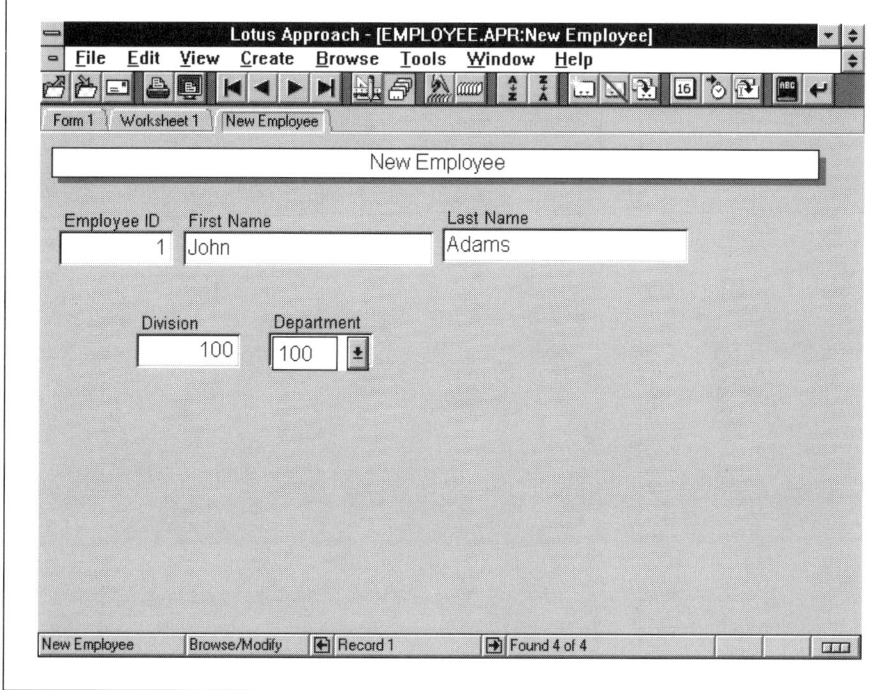

FIGURE 8.20

The Define Checkbox dialog box

Define Checkbox

Edit checkboxes for field "Type" ...

Checked Value	Unchecked Value	Checkbox Label
B	P	Business

OK

Cancel

Insert

Delete

Create Checkboxes from Field Data

Enter the value to be stored in the field when the check box is cleared in the Unchecked Value cell. For Boolean fields, use the values Yes, 1, or True, or No, 0, or False.

FIGURE 8.21

The check box as it appears on the form

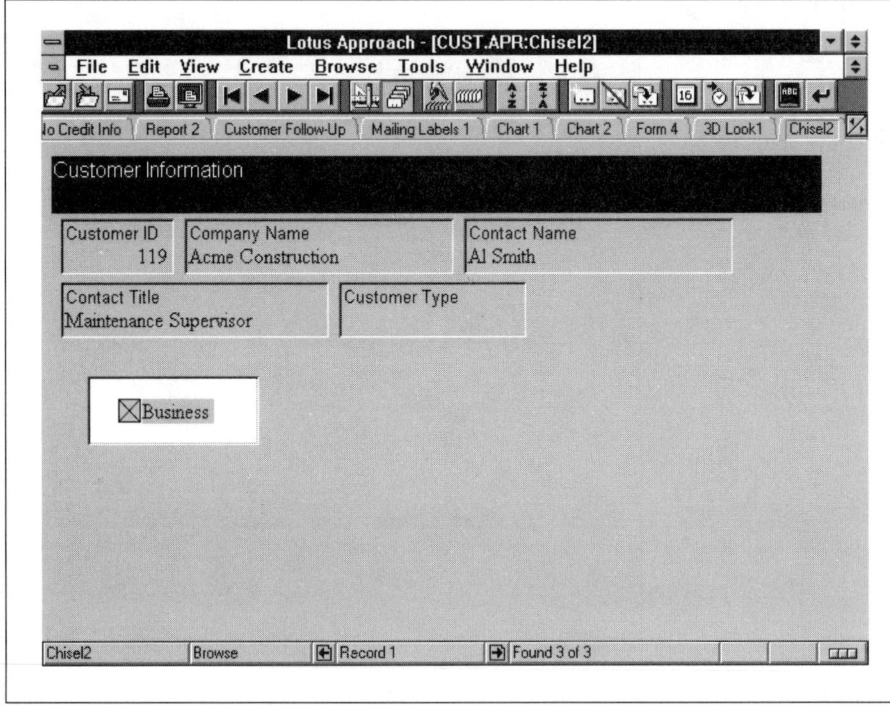

4. Enter the text to appear to the right of the check box in the Checkbox Label cell.
5. To create more than one check box for the field, enter values on succeeding lines or click the Create Checkboxes from Field Data to have Approach examine your database and fill in values from existing records automatically. It is strongly suggested that you do not enter more than one row for a check box (one value for each check box). This is contrary to standard Windows conventions for use of a check box (see the Tip that follows).
5. To insert new values or delete existing ones, select the row and choose the Insert or Delete values. To move a value, select the value. The mouse cursor changes to a hand. Drag the value to the new location.
6. Select OK.

To add a new check box to a form, select Create ➤ Drawing, then select Checkbox, or click on the Checkbox icon in the Drawing toolbox and draw the check box on the form. Approach displays the Define Checkbox dialog box shown in Figure 8.22. Select the field to be displayed by the check box, and follow the directions above for filling in the checked value, unchecked value, and check box label.

WARNING

If the check box is not checked, no value is placed into a field in a new record. Instead, Approach enters a value called the null value, which is not the same as a blank (for a text field) or No for a Boolean field. If you are displaying a value using a check box, it is strongly advised that you use the Default Value settings for the field to fill the field with an initial value, the value of which will be reflected by the check box.

FIGURE 8.22

Use the Define Checkbox dialog box to add fields to a form.

Define Checkbox

Select a field and define the checkbox.

Checked Value	Unchecked Value	Checkbox Label

OK

Cancel

Insert

Delete

Create Checkboxes from Field Data

Select the checkbox field:

CUSTOMER

Customer ID
Company Name
Contact Name

Tip

Use a checkbox with a field that has only 2 possible values, such as "Backordered". In this case, the checked value is Yes and the unchecked value is No.

Approach lets you define more than one check box for a field. Thus, you can define three check boxes for the Status field of an employee database: Active, On-Leave, and Terminated. Whenever one box is checked, that value is stored in the Status field of the database and the other check boxes are cleared (the X is removed). However, this technique is very rare and is contrary to standard Windows behavior, in which check boxes allow you to check one *or more* options simultaneously. Check boxes are usually assigned one per field, so the user has a choice of Business or Personal in one check box (filling the Type field), Active Buyer or Prospect in another (filling the Customer Type field), and so on. When a single choice among several options is needed, use radio buttons, the standard Windows graphical element for choosing between mutually exclusive options.

▸ Displaying Field Values with Radio Buttons

If a field can contain one of several values, you can display the value choices using radio buttons, as shown in Figure 8.23. You specify to Approach the value of each button, and when selected, the field value you specify is stored in the database record. Only one radio button in a group can be selected. When chosen, the currently selected button is unselected (the black dot inside the circle is cleared).

For example, instead of using a check box for a Boolean field, we can define two buttons—one with the value Y (if the Business button is chosen) and the other with the value N (if the Personal button is selected). For a one-character text field as shown in Figure 8.23, we could set a value of B to be stored in the Type field if the user selects the Business button, and store a value of P in the database's field if the user selects the Personal button on the form. (The form that displays the radio buttons is shown in Figure 8.24.)

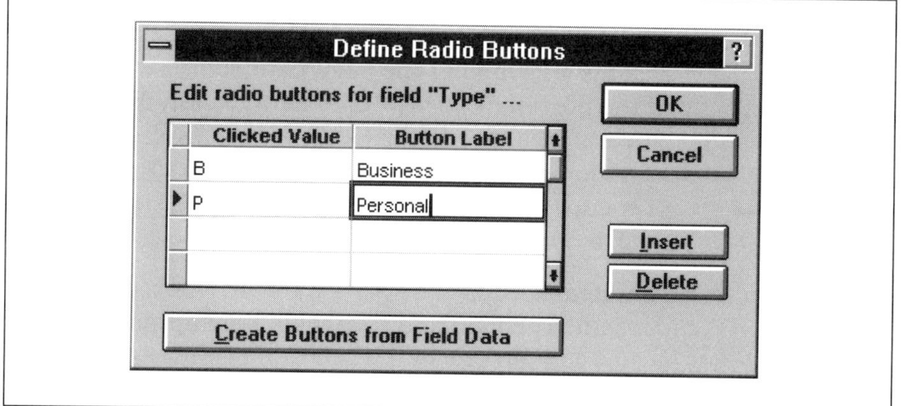

FIGURE 8.23

Radio Buttons for the Customer Type field

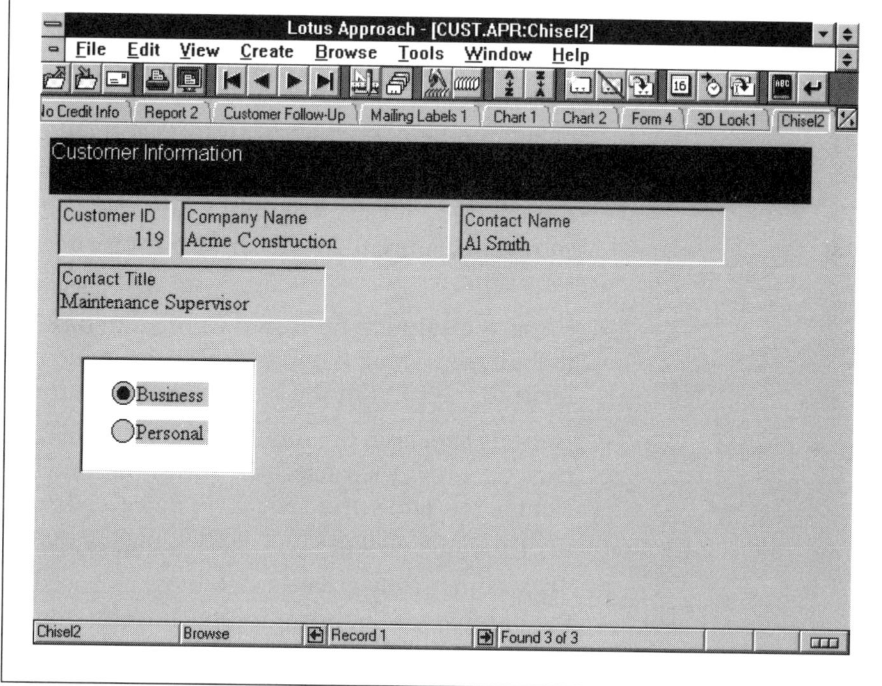

FIGURE 8.24

The form displays radio buttons for the Customer Type field. Here we display the buttons vertically. We added a rectangle in the background to highlight the button group.

Radio buttons are usually placed on a form when a field has three or more values. For instance, suppose your Orders database record contains a PaymentType field, defined as a one-character text field with the possible values of C to denote cash, K for check, M for Mastercard, V for Visa, and D for COD. If you display the PaymentType field using radio buttons, the data entry form lets you select from the options spelled out in words: Cash, Check, Mastercard, Visa, and COD. The selected option is then stored as a single character field in the database.

When Approach displays a record, it examines the value in the PaymentType field and highlights the appropriate button. If the field does not contain one of the valid values (for example, if it contains Y), no button is selected.

Radio buttons are used in place of drop-down lists when there are just a few values (usually no more than six), since choosing a radio button is slightly faster than selecting the same option from a drop-down list.

Use these steps to display an existing field on a form using radio buttons:

1. Select the field, open the InfoBox, and choose the Basics tab.
2. In the Data entry type drop-down list select Radio buttons. If Approach does not display the Define Radio Buttons dialog box, shown in Figure 8.23 earlier in this chapter, click the Define Buttons button.
3. Enter the value to be stored in the database record for the field in the Clicked Value column. Enter the value to be displayed on the form to the right of the button in the Button Label column.
4. Buttons appear in the order displayed in this table. To add a button, click on a row, then select the Insert button. To delete a button, select the row and select Delete. To move a button, select the row. The mouse cursor changes to a hand. Drag the button to the new location.
5. To automatically create radio buttons based on existing data in the database, select the Create Buttons from Field Data button. Approach examines your database and fills in values from existing records automatically.
6. Select OK.

To add a new radio button group to a form, select Create ➤ Drawing, then select Radio Button or click on the Radio Button icon in the Drawing toolbox, and draw the button boundaries on the form. Approach displays the Define Radio Buttons dialog box shown in Figure 8.25. Select the field to be displayed using the radio buttons, and follow the directions previously given to fill the Clicked Value and Button Label columns.

FIGURE 8.25 ▶

Use the Define Radio Buttons dialog box to add fields to a form that you want displayed as radio buttons.

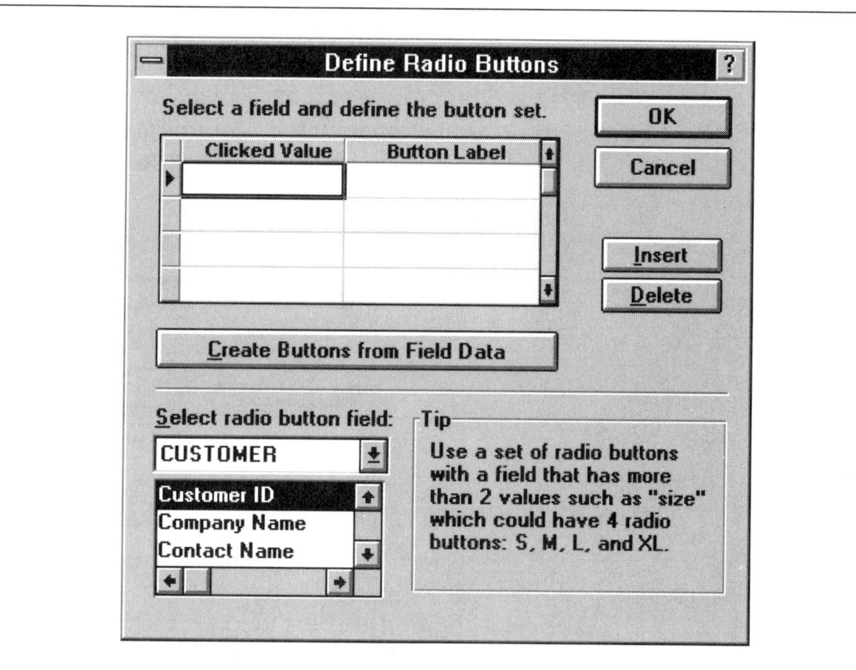

▶▶ PicturePlus Fields

PicturePlus fields can hold graphics, portions of a spreadsheet, documents, sounds—just about anything you can define within Windows. However, because a PicturePlus field can contain graphics, it has some unique features, such as the ability to shrink, stretch, or crop the image within the dimensions you specify on the form.

Because of the unique features of PicturePlus fields, there are special properties and settings for these fields.

As you'd expect, you can change the color, frame, and size of a PicturePlus field. You can move the field, resize it, and delete it, just as with any other object on a form.

▸ Adding a PicturePlus Field

Use these steps to add a PicturePlus field to a form:

1. Select Create ➤ Drawing and choose the PicturePlus Field option, or select the PicturePlus icon from the Drawing toolbar.
2. Drag the mouse cursor (which now displays crosshairs) across the work area to specify the boundaries of the field. Approach displays the InfoBox, shown in Figure 8.26.

FIGURE 8.26 ▸

The InfoBox for a PicturePlus field

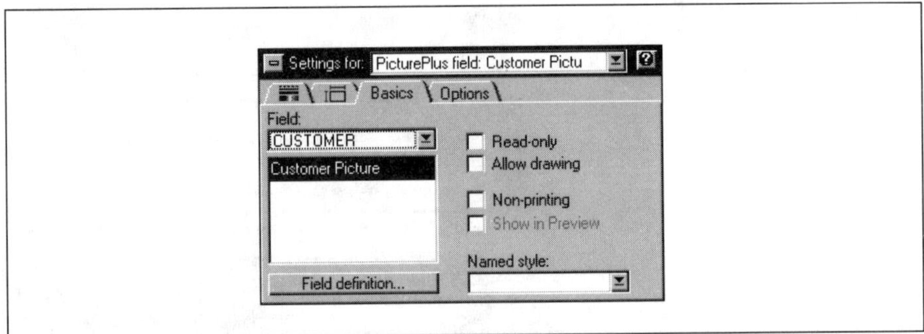

3. Select the PicturePlus field you want to display (select the database if more than one is defined to Approach).
4. Choose Read-only if you want to prevent editing of the field.
5. Choose Allow Drawing if you want to be able to draw over the image with the mouse. (Read-only must not be checked for this option to work.)
6. Set the "Non-printing" and "Show in preview" options as described in the following steps, as you would for any other field on a form.
7. Select the Options tab, shown in Figure 8.27. Drag the image of the bird to any of nine locations within the white box. This places the image relative to the dimensions of the field but has no effect on the picture's size.

FIGURE 8.27

The Options tab lets you specify what Approach should do if the image is too large or small to fit within the field on the form.

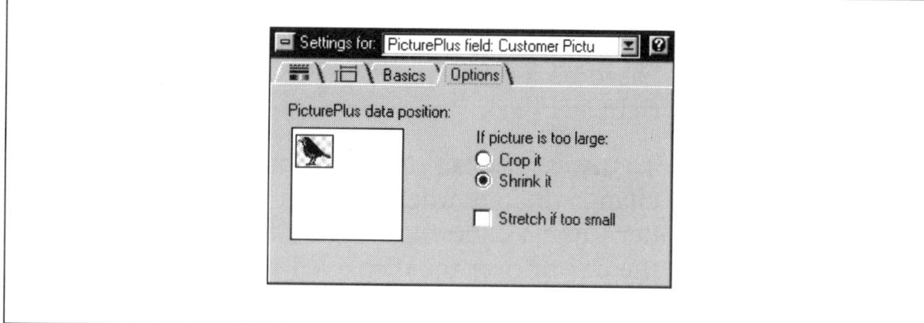

8. Choose “Crop it” or “Shrink it” to adjust an image if the source image is larger than the area defined on the form. Only one of these options can be selected. If you select Crop, Approach will “chop off” any portion of the image that does not fit. If you choose Shrink, Approach will resize the image to fit within the field.
9. If the image is too small and you want Approach to expand (stretch) the image to fill the field on the form, check the “Stretch if too small” option.
10. Use the Color and Size tabs to set color and dimension options.

▸▸ Changing the Tab Order

When you use the form to enter or change data, Approach moves from field to field in what's called the *tab order*. Approach also calls this the *Data Entry Order*. When you press the Tab key to move to the next field, Approach finds the field with the next highest tab order value and moves the cursor to that field. When you move to a form for the first time and press Tab, you'll move to the field with a tab order value of 1. Press Tab again and you'll move to the field labeled 2, and so on. Note that the field with the tab order value of 1 isn't necessarily at the top-left corner of the form.

By default, as you add fields to a form, Approach assigns that field the next highest tab order number. Thus, the first field you add to a form gets a tab order value of 1, the next field gets a value of 2, and so on. If you move a field to a new location, the field retains its tab order value. Therefore, it's possible that if you add fields “out of order” or rearrange them on a form, the fields won't have the tab order you expect. That is, they won't be automatically renumbered from 1 to 10 (for example), based on a field's position on the form from top to bottom or left to right.

To display the tab order, select View ➤ Show Data Entry Order. To change the tab order, click on the gray square that contains the tab order value, as shown in Figure 8.28. Approach displays an I-beam. Drag the cursor over the displayed value, which highlights the value, and enter the new tab order value. When you click in another tab order box, Approach renumbers all fields with a higher tab order value than the number you just entered. Thus, if you select a field and assign it a tab order of 5, fields with the original values of 5, 6, 7, and so on, are assigned the values 6, 7, 8, and so on.

To remove the tab order boxes, select View ➤ Show Data Entry Order again.

FIGURE 8.28 ▶

Tab Order boxes are shown when you select View ➤ Show Data Entry Order. Click inside any of these boxes and change the value to change the order in which Approach moves between fields.

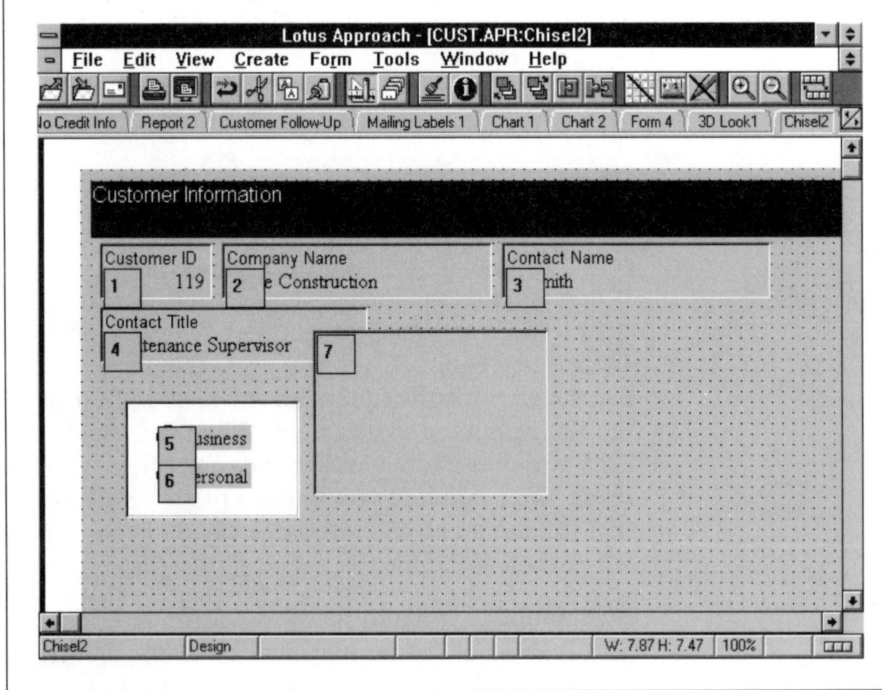

▸▸ Restricting a Field: View Data but Don't Change It

Although you place fields on a form for data entry, you may want to only display the field value. For example, you may want to display an employee's salary field value, but not let a user change it. If you have a serialized field, such as an Order Number or Invoice Number in which the value is automatically entered by Approach using the Default Values of the Field Definition dialog box, you'll want this field to be protected. While you want to see the new Order Number so you can read it back to the customer, you don't want to accidentally change it.

To protect a field from changes, you need to set the Read-only option. Select the field, open the InfoBox, and choose Read-only on the Basics tab. Think of this option as "Display only"—you can view the data of an existing record, or the default value supplied for new records, but you can't change it.

▸▸ Hiding a Field During Preview

In addition to using a form for entering and viewing data, you can also print records using the Print option. However, you may want to suppress printing a field. For example, you might want to use a single form to enter employee name and address information and display the annual salary amount, but when you print the record you do not want to print the salary field.

To suppress printing a field, select the field, open the InfoBox, and select Non-printing on the Basics tab.

If you still want to see the field in Preview mode (the equivalent of Print Preview in many other applications), check the Show in preview option, which is only available if Non-printing is checked.

▸▸ Removing Space Between Fields

When you print a form, each field appears in the same location on your output, just as it appears on the screen. However, during printing you may want to eliminate space between fields. For example, you might want an employee name to read

```
Jim Powell
```

not

```
Jim                    Powell
```

Likewise you may have two address lines in a database record. If the second line is empty, however, you'd prefer to see:

```
Jim Powell
1223 Main Street
Seattle, WA 98199
```

rather than the address with an "empty" line:

```
Jim Powell
1223 Main Street

Seattle, WA 98199
```

In order to eliminate the space between fields of varying width, and to eliminate blank lines, Approach offers the Slide options. Select the field, open the InfoBox, and select the Dimensions tab, which is shown in Figure 8.29. Notice the two options under the "When printing, slide" heading.

FIGURE 8.29 ▸

The Dimensions tab offers options for eliminating excess spaces between fields on the same and different rows when printed.

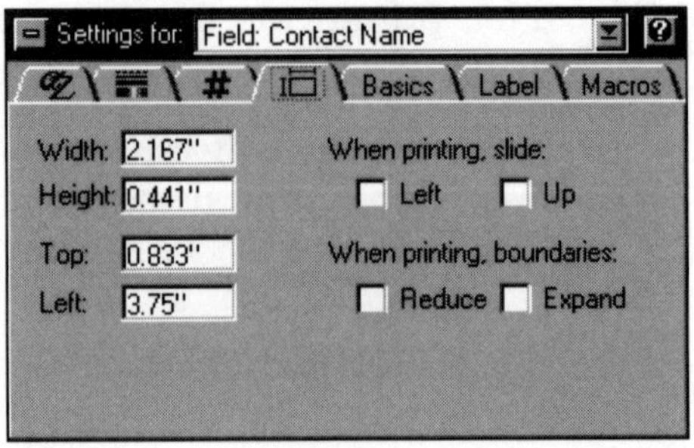

The Left option slides characters together, so the employee name would appear as desired. Both fields (first and last name fields, for example) must be marked "When printing, slide: Left." In addition, both must be aligned on their bottom boundary (border)—use the Object Align command as described in Chapter 6.

The Up option removes a field from printing if it is blank. Note that this assumes that it is the only field in the same horizontal area. Both fields (first and second address lines) must be marked "When printing, slide: Up."

The Slide options are used most when creating forms used as mailing labels. See Chapter 13 for more about mailing labels.

▶▶ **TIP**

Although the slide options are useful, you may not wish to use them if you are printing data on preprinted forms, in which exact field positions are required.

▶▶ Expanding Boundaries

To expand or contract the size of the label boundaries surrounding a field when you print, preview, or view actual data in a form, use the "When printing, boundaries" option.

Select the field, open the InfoBox, and select the Dimensions tab. Check the Reduce or Expand options (or both) as desired.

▶▶ Repeating Panels

If you have joined databases in your Approach file, as explained in Chapter 6, you can add a repeating panel to your form to show records from the "many" side of a one-to-many relationship. For example, if you have a Customers database and an Orders database, you can show several fields from the Customer database (such as name and address) as well as a table that contains data from the Orders database for the selected customer. A repeating panel is shown in Figure 8.30 for order information. The repeating panel will show as many records as possible (or none if there are no records for the main database record), and Approach automatically provides a scroll bar so you can view more records in the panel if necessary.

FIGURE 8.30 ►

A repeating panel shows information about orders on a customer form.

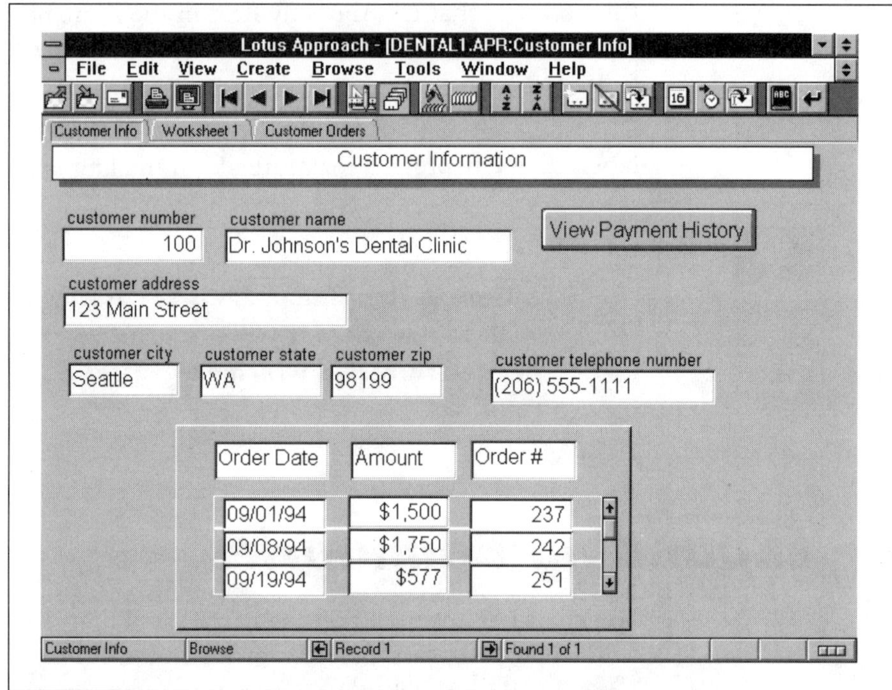

In a form with a repeating panel, the form is driven (controlled) by the main database, and the detail database is displayed in the repeating panel. Each line in the repeating panel displays information from a single record in the detail database and you select which fields are displayed.

►► Creating a Repeating Panel

When you create a new form, the Form Assistant offers a SmartMaster layout style that includes a repeating panel, named Standard with

Repeating Panel. Chapter 5 explained how to create a form. If you select a layout with a repeating panel, the Form Assistant will ask you to select the fields you want to place on the repeating panel, which will be included from left to right on the panel.

Everything we discuss here assumes you are in the Design environment, just as you are when designing and modifying a form. When you want to see the data from a repeating panel, switch to the Browse environment. Data is displayed if Show Data is selected. If data is not displayed, select View ➤ Show Data.

To add a repeating panel to an existing form, display the form in Design and choose Create ➤ Repeating Panel. Approach displays the Add Repeating Panel dialog box, shown in Figure 8.31. Select the fields just as you would from the Form Assistant: Select the database fields to appear in order from left to right in the repeating panel. In addition, you can select the number of lines in the repeating panel (from 1 to 30), choose an alternate color (every other row will use this color as its background), and a sort order for the records within the panel. The Sort Order options are not available from the Form Assistant and will be explained later in this section.

FIGURE 8.31

The Add Repeating Panel dialog box

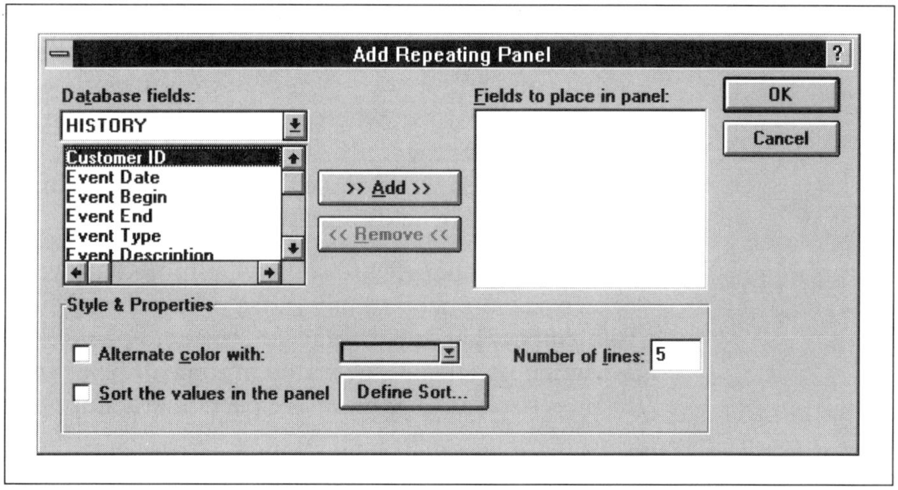

When you select OK, Approach adds a repeating panel to the spot you previously selected on your form. You can then drag the panel to the desired location, change its size, add or remove fields—just like it was a miniature form itself.

You will have to create text fields as column headings for the repeating panel. Add these text fields to the form, not the panel. See "Adding Labels to a Repeating Panel" later in this chapter.

A repeating panel looks and behaves much like any object you add to a form, except that you work with the top row of the panel, not the remaining lines in the panel. When you select the repeating panel itself (by clicking anywhere within the panel that does not contain a field, or on a border), Approach places a dark black border around the panel object. Once selected, you can drag the repeating panel to its new location, or use the InfoBox to set the properties of the panel, such as the number of lines in the panel, the Named Style, and border color and width, and Frame Style. Notice the Menu bar now includes a Panel option.

When you select the top row, the cursor changes to a hand and Approach places a light gray border around the row. You can change the dimension of the row and all rows reflect the new dimension, or change properties using the InfoBox, as we'll describe in a moment. You can also move the entire repeating panel by moving just the top row, although the advantage of selecting and moving the entire panel at once is that you can see the position of the entire repeating panel as it is moved. By contrast, when you move just the top row, you are placing (dragging) that row only—Approach then moves all the other rows accordingly when you release the mouse button, and the entire repeating panel may cover fields already on the form.

Be aware that panels are somewhat more temperamental than regular objects so you need to take extra precautions when working with them. Remember that any change you make to one field in the top row of a repeating panel is perpetuated among all fields in that panel column, so settings such as alignment are particularly important.

▶▶ TIP

Even if your final repeating panel will not use alternate colors, you should turn this feature on to help you build the form. Otherwise you must turn on borders to see the distinct lines in a panel. Also helpful: Turn on the field names so you can see where fields are placed. To do this, select View. If the Show Data option has a check mark to its left, select Show Data to turn this option off and view the field names. Unfortunately, for short fields you may only see the database name for each field, but at least you can see each field's dimension.

▶ *Working with Fields on a Repeating Panel*

You can work with fields just as you do with fields on the main portion of a form. For instance, to add a field, you can drag the field name from the Add Field list just as you do with any field on a form. You can display the Add Field list by right-clicking on the top row and selecting Add Field. Be sure to drag the field name to the top row of the repeating panel. If you drag the field name to any other rows, Approach gets confused and may add it to the form or to the repeating panel. It is always safest to work with the top row only.

To delete a field, click on the field and press the Delete key. To make room for more fields, click on the top row and drag the border to expand the size of the repeating panel. Likewise, you can rearrange fields by dragging them within the top row of the panel: Select one or more fields and align them using the Align Object command (select the fields, then choose Object ➤ Align or press Ctrl+I).

▶ *Summarizing Fields in a Repeating Panel*

Repeating panels give you one more feature not found with fields inan ordinary form: the ability to perform calculations on repeating fields within the panel. For example, in an Orders database, you can summarize the value of the orders by placing a total field in a panel. You can calculate averages, counts (to display the number of records on a repeating panel, for example), or standard deviation, among other functions.

The summary is performed whenever you are in Browse or Preview. In the Design environment you'll see the field but no values.

The Orders repeating panel from Figure 8.30 has been modified to add a summary field to display the total value of all orders. The new repeating panel design is shown in Figure 8.32.

FIGURE 8.32

A repeating panel modified to add the total value of orders for a customer

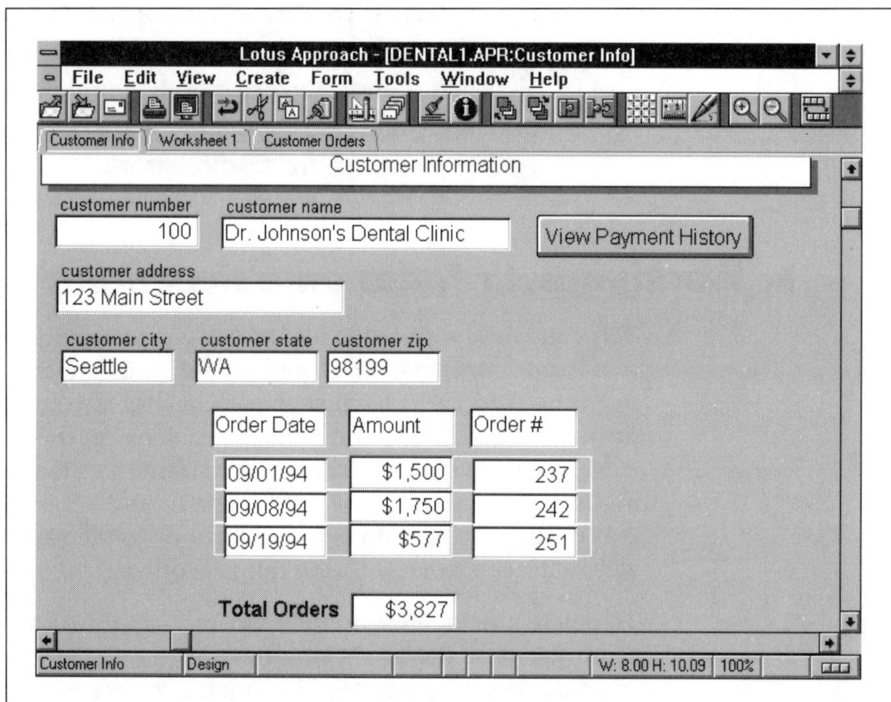

Follow these steps to add a summary field:

1. Display the Add Field dialog box. You can do this by clicking on the panel and selecting Panel ➤ Add Field or right-clicking on the panel and selecting Add Field.
2. Select the Field Definition button. Approach displays the Field definition dialog box for the detail database.
3. Move to the last position (cell) in the Field Name column, since you are going to add a field. Enter a field name and select calculated as the Data Type. The Define Formula tab will be displayed.

4. Enter a formula in the Formula text box that includes a summary function and the field you wish to summarize. Formulas are described in Chapter 19. Some examples include:

SAverage (Orderamt)	Compute the Average of Non-blank Values in a Numeric Field
SCount (ORDERAMT)	Calculate the number of values in the range
SMax (ORDERAMT)	Display the maximum (largest) value in the range
SMin(ORDERAMT)	Display the minimum (smallest) value in the range
SStd(ORDERAMT)	Compute the standard deviation of values in the ORDERAMT field
SSum (ORDERAMT)	Total the values in the ORDERAMT field
SVar(ORDERAMT)	Compute the variance (a statistical measurement) for all values in the ORDERAMT field

5. If the formula is written correctly, the Formula Flag icon will be displayed without a red X through it. Select OK, then select OK again to add the field to the database.
6. Add this new field to the form—not to the repeating panel—as previously described. You may wish to place the field directly underneath the panel column of the field you are summarizing.

▶ Setting Panel Properties

To change the number of lines, fill color, border, or frame properties, select the repeating panel by double-clicking anywhere inside it that does not include a field, or click on the repeating panel and click on the InfoBox icon from the SmartIcons toolbar. Choose the Colors tab or the Basics tab to select the properties, which are similar to those you've seen when working with other fields on a form and won't be described here. (The significant difference is that the Color tab has the option "Alternate fill color.") Remember that the properties you define here apply to the panel itself, not the individual lines within the panel (with the exception of the Alternate color option).

▶ Setting the Sort Order of a Repeating Panel

One special property needs special explanation. In the Basics tab, shown in Figure 8.33, you'll see the "Sort the values in the panel" check box and a Define sort button. (These options also appear in the Add Repeating Panel dialog box shown in Figure 8.31 earlier in this chapter.) When you display records in a repeating panel, Approach can sort the values for you automatically. This sort occurs when, for example, you move to the next or previous record in the main database, but not when you are entering new records within the panel (which uses the detail database, not the main database).

FIGURE 8.33 ▶

The Basics tab for a repeating panel

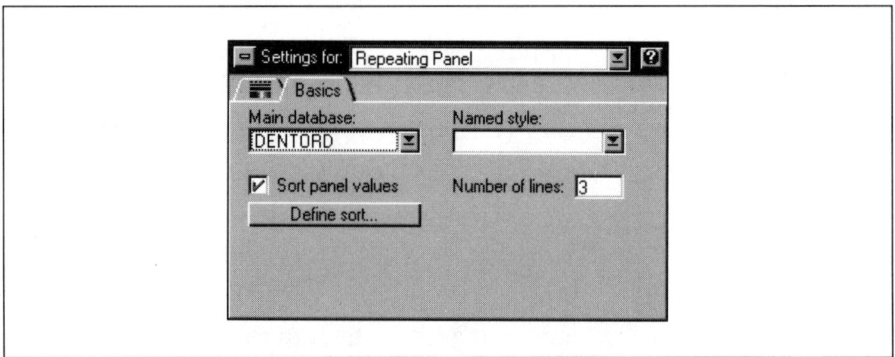

The sort order determines the order in which records are displayed in the repeating panel but does not change the order in which they are physically stored in the database. Sorting is explained more fully in Chapter 12. For purposes of our example, suppose that you enter orders into the Dentord (orders for dental customers) database by date, but you want to display all orders by order amount within the repeating panel so you can see the largest order first. Therefore, you want to create a sort order by order amount in descending order—largest order amount first.

To set the sort order for the first time, check the "Sort the values in the panel" check box or select the Define sort button. Approach displays the Sort dialog box shown in Figure 8.34.

FIGURE 8.34

The Sort dialog box

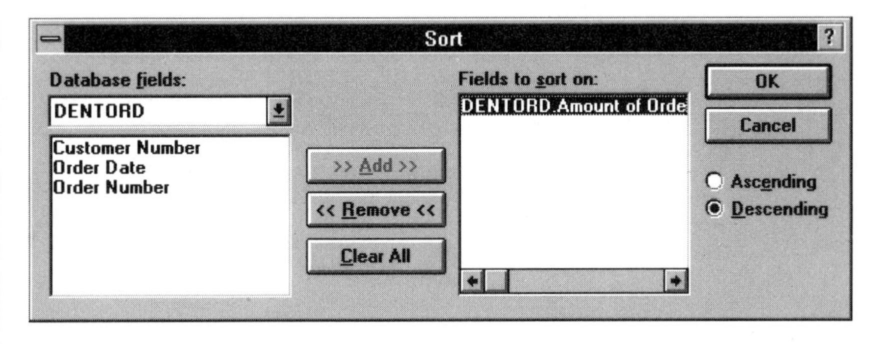

Select the field you want to sort on first by double-clicking its name from the Database fields list. The field will be added to the top of the "Fields to sort on" list. Alternatively, select the field name and select the Add button. Choose Ascending to sort in lowest to highest order, or Descending to sort from highest to lowest. In our example, you will place the Amount of Order from the Dentord database in the "Fields to sort on" list and select Descending, since you want to see the largest value first as shown in Figure 8.35. (One advantage of sorting Ascending is that a blank record will be displayed at the top of the list, handy for data entry.)

If you want to refine the sort more fully, select a second field for the sort. Sorting on primary and secondary fields (and beyond) is explained in Chapter 12. To remove a field from the Fields to sort on list, select that field and click Remove. To remove all fields from this list, click Clear All.

To define the sort, select OK. Since you are in the Design environment, you will not see the actual data re-sorted if you are viewing only field names in your repeating panel. To see the results of your sort (assuming there are records in the detail database), select View ➤ Show Data.

Once the sort is defined, you can check the Sort panel values check box to turn the sort on or off. To view the current sort definition, click the Define sort button.

Sorting values in the repeating panel is now performed automatically when you move to a new record in Browse. However, if you add a record in a repeating panel, the records are not automatically re-sorted. For example, if you add a new order for $1,000 at the end of the

FIGURE 8.35

A repeating panel for Orders has been sorted to show the largest order first.

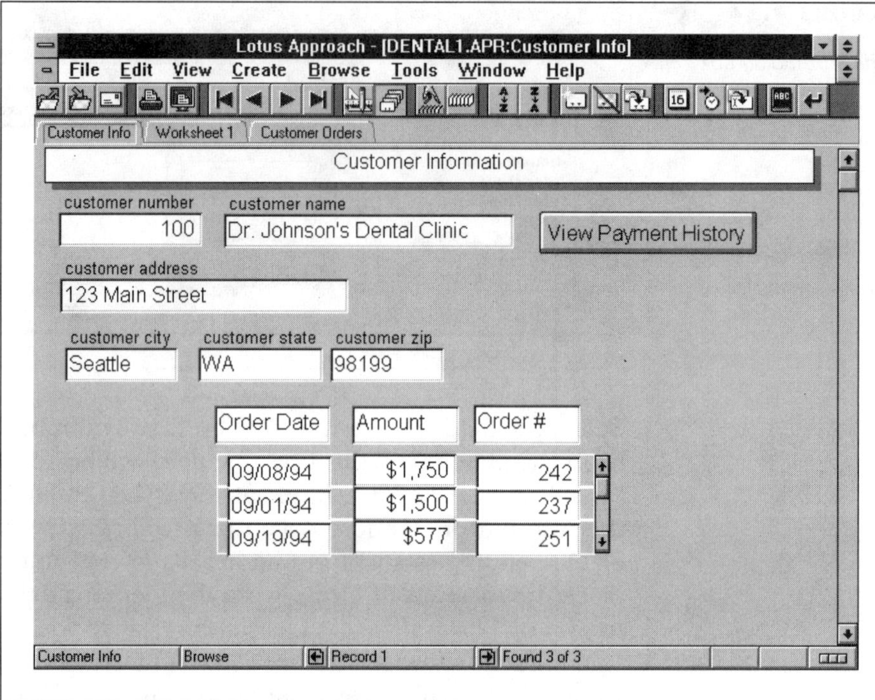

repeating panel for the dental customers, Approach does not place the new order in the appropriate position. Instead you'll have to refresh the display. With the cursor in any field (anywhere on the form, not just within the repeating panel), select Browse ➤ Refresh, or press Ctrl+R. This re-sorts the records displayed in the repeating panel. The data is also re-sorted if you move to another customer record, then return to the customer record you've just changed.

▸ Modifying Fields in a Repeating Panel

Think of a repeating panel as a miniature form—as a form within a form. As such, you can select a field by clicking anywhere on it within the top row of the panel. You can use the InfoBox to change properties of fields, click and drag fields within the top row, and do all the things you can do with a field as though it were placed on the main portion of a form. Remember, however, that what you do on the top row is repeated on each line of the repeating panel.

To change the size of the panel, click on the top row and drag its borders to the row that has the dimension you want. For example, to increase the row height, click on the bottom border of the top row and drag the mouse downward. All rows reflect the new dimension and the grid overall is expanded to accommodate the new heights. Check that the resized repeating panel doesn't cover existing fields on your form.

You can also display more than one field vertically in a row. For example, Figure 8.36 shows a repeating panel in which three fields are displayed. Also note that in this example we don't use column headings but rather field labels. This is accomplished using the InfoBox and selecting the Label tab of the InfoBox for the field, just as with any field on a form.

FIGURE 8.36

A repeating panel can include more than one field.

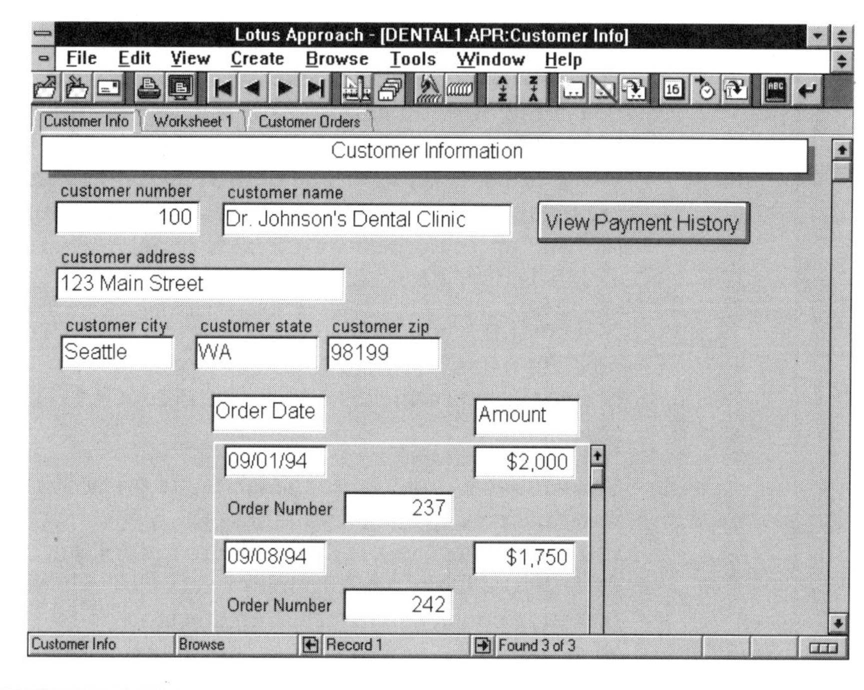

▶ Adding Labels to a Repeating Panel

Note that when you add a repeating panel to a form, Approach does not automatically add column headings. You must do this yourself manually. The more fields you've included in the panel, the more tedious the process. We suggest that you add column titles as the last step of your design—after your form and repeating panel look the way you want them to (without the labels, of course). The following procedure minimizes the hassle of adding labels.

First, be sure you're in the Design environment. Then select the Text tool from the SmartIcons toolbar (the one with the "ABC" on its face) and move the cursor to a position over the column you want to label and click the mouse again. Approach displays a small box with a flashing vertical cursor. Type the label for this text field. Select the properties, such as background color and font from the InfoBox, just as though this were any other text box, since, in fact, it is.

Select the box and choose Edit ➤ Copy or press Ctrl+C, which copies the text box (including all the properties you've set). Select Edit ➤ Paste, or press Ctrl+V. The copy is actually placed on top of the existing text box, so drag the copy over the next column. Click inside the box and enter the text for the new panel. Repeat this procedure until all labels have been created.

Now that the labels exist you'll want to align them. Select the first text box and press and hold the Shift key as you select the remaining text boxes. Choose Object ➤ Align (or press Ctrl+I) and choose the proper alignment.

You're almost done. After the labels are properly placed, you still want to move them as a group if you move the repeating panel itself. To do this, you'll create a group. If the labels are not still selected, select them all, then choose Object ➤ Group or select Ctrl+G. Now when you move the repeating panel, you can click on any label and when you move the labels, all labels will be moved at once, maintaining their relative positions. To individually edit one label, you must choose Object ungroup (or press Ctrl+U), then select the label you want to edit.

Unfortunately, there is no way to group the labels and the repeating panel together.

►► Removing a Repeating Panel

To remove a repeating panel, select the top row and press the Delete key.

►► Summary and a Look Ahead

In this chapter you've learned how to work with form objects that are associated with data fields in your database. You've seen how to add them to, and remove them from, a form. You've seen how field objects are just like other objects: they can be moved, grouped and ungrouped, aligned, and positioned precisely on a form. You've also seen a special case of data fields: repeating panels.

Now that you've learned how to create a form, it's time to learn how to use a form and perform the basic data entry functions: adding records, moving to other records, deleting records, and displaying records. Working with data and moving around through an existing database are the subjects of Chapter 9.

CHAPTER 9

Entering Data in an Approach View

▸▸ FAST TRACK

▶▶ **At** the heart of any database application is the data itself. In this chapter you'll learn how to enter new data records, edit existing data, copy a record (to quickly make a duplicate which you can edit), and delete a record. This chapter also explains how to move between records, such as moving to the first record in the database or to a specific record.

Once you have defined your database records and created a form, you're ready to enter data. You do this in the Browse environment. Browse displays one record per form and performs all the logic you've added using formulas and field properties. In Browse you're working with the data itself, not the background color or dimensions of a field. Unlike working with Design, which requires you to save your Approach file when you make changes, the Browse environment automatically updates the data in your database record when you move to another record.

To switch to the Browse environment, use any of these methods:

- Select the Browse icon from the toolbar.
- Select View ➤ Browse.
- Press Ctrl+B.
- Click on the second box from the left in the Status bar and select Browse.

In the Browse environment, the Approach work area displays a SmartIcons toolbar that enables you to use icons that shorten your tasks. In addition, Approach changes the Status bar and displays the current view name and information about which record you're working on. It also lets you move to the next or previous record.

You can enter data in forms, reports, worksheets, form letters, and mailing labels. The techniques used for entering data are the same. In this chapter we'll specifically focus on entering data in an Approach form.

Chapter 10 discusses worksheets in depth, explaining how to add, change, and delete records in this spreadsheet-like display. Chapter 11 describes how to create a report and explains how to edit records within a report. Chapter 13 explains how to create form letters and mailing labels, which can also display data for editing.

▶▶ Using a Form to Add, Change, or Delete Records

Select the form name from the tabs displayed along the top of your screen, or click on the first box in the Status bar and select the form you want. Also be sure you are in the Browse environment. The Status bar shows the current environment in the second box from the left, and the SmartIcons toolbar will also show the Browse button depressed when you are in Browse.

▶▶ Navigating through the Database

Approach makes it easy to move between records in the database. You can use icons in the SmartIcons toolbar, icons or a pop-up menu in the Status bar, or Menu commands. The Approach work area, with SmartIcons, menus, and the status bar, is shown in figure 9.1.

▶ Moving to the Next Record

Use these steps to move to the next record:

- Select the Next Record icon in the SmartIcons toolbar.
- Select the Next Record icon in the Status bar.
- Press Page Down.

FIGURE 9.1

When you're working in the Browse environment, you can use the SmartIcons toolbar, the Status bar, or Menu commands to move between records.

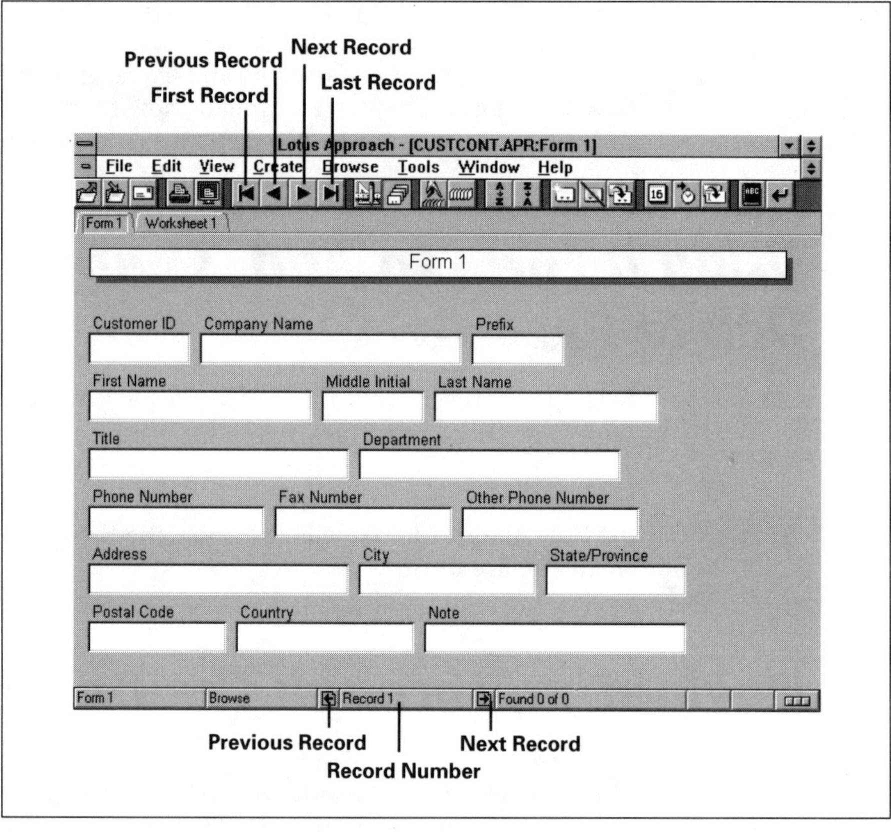

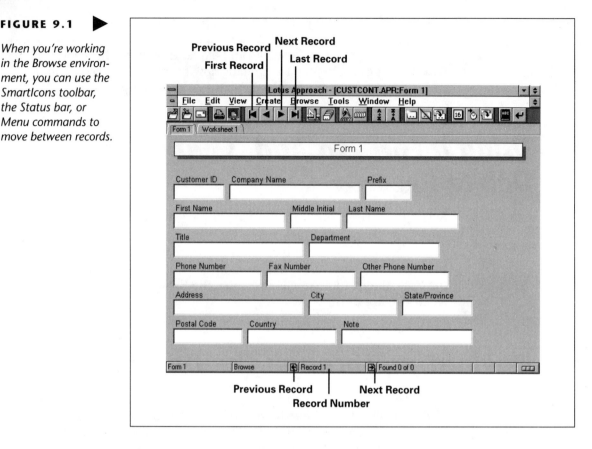

▸ Moving to the Previous Record

To move to the previous record, use any of these methods:

- Select the Previous Record icon in the SmartIcons toolbar.
- Select the Previous Record icon in the Status bar.
- Press Page Up.

▸ Moving to the First Record

Use either of these methods to move to the first record in the database:

- Select the First Record icon in the SmartIcons toolbar.
- Press Ctrl+Home.

▶ Moving to the Last Record

Use either of these methods to move to the last record in the database:

- Select the Last Record icon in the SmartIcons toolbar.
- Press Ctrl+End.

▶ Moving to a Specific Record

To move to a specific record (when you know the record number), click on the Record Number section of the Status bar. Approach displays the Go to Record dialog box, shown in Figure 9.2. Enter the record number and select OK.

FIGURE 9.2 

The Go to Record dialog box

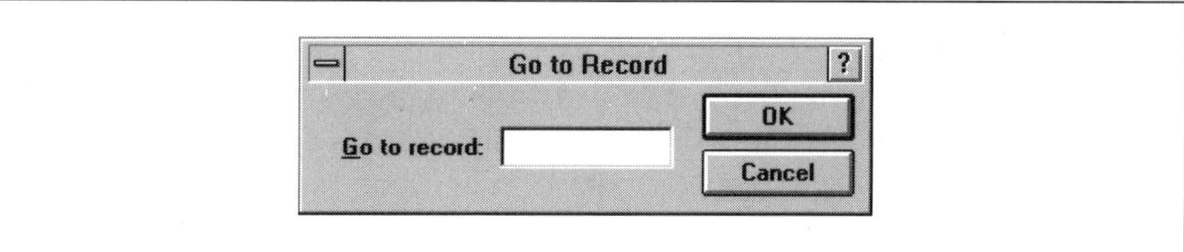

▶▶ Adding a New Record

After you have selected the form and are working in the Browse environment, you can add a record using one of these techniques:

- Select Browse ➤ New Record.
- Press Ctrl+N.
- Select either of the New Record icons from the SmartIcons toolbar. Only the left icon is on the default toolbar, but you can modify the toolbar using the instructions in Chapter 18.

Approach displays an empty form and places the cursor at the first field on the form according to the tab order (see Chapter 8). Remember that you may have fields defined on the form that are display only. Approach will never place the cursor on such a field.

Any field for which you have defined an initial value is filled with that value, although it is possible to override such default values when you edit the field. Editing techniques are described throughout this chapter.

When you are done entering the field values, you can move to another record, or add another record. When you do so, Approach adds the data you've entered as a new record in the database.

The new record is assigned a record number. A new record is automatically given the next available record number. For example, if there are 100 records in your database, Approach will number this record 101 when you add it (by moving to another record or adding another record). This number is used by Approach and is not stored as part of your data. You can use the record number when you move about the database. For example, you can tell Approach that you want to display (move to) a particular record whose record number you provide. This is especially helpful when you have hundreds of records.

▸▸ Adding a New Record in a Repeating Panel

If your form includes a repeating panel, you can quickly and easily add a record to the joined database. Move to a blank line (or use the scroll bars to display additional lines if all rows in the repeating panel contain data) and begin to enter values in the fields. When you move to another row, the non-repeating portion of the form, or another record, Approach adds the record to the joined database.

This technique requires that the join option be set to allow records in a joined database to be added. See Chapter 6 for more information about joining databases.

►► Copying an Existing Record

Many times it is convenient to add a record just like the record currently being displayed, with only a slight modification to a field or two. For example, if you have a name and address database and want to add records for three contacts from the same company, it would be handy to be able to enter the first record, then copy it to another record and change only the first and last name fields (and perhaps the telephone number fields).

To copy an existing record, select the record you want to copy on the screen and be sure the cursor is positioned on a field in this record. Select the Duplicate Record icon from the SmartIcons toolbar, or select Browse ➤ Duplicate Record. Approach displays the duplicate record.

If your form contains a repeating panel, you can duplicate the record in the panel and Approach will add the record to the display. If your form contains a repeating panel and you duplicate the record from the main database (the record shown in the form outside of the repeating panel), Approach creates a duplicate record for that database but does not duplicate the records that are joined to it.

►► Copying a Field Value from the Last New Record

If you are adding a new record, you can copy the value for a field from the last record you added by moving the cursor to the appropriate field, then selecting Browse ➤ Insert ➤ Previous Value, or press Ctrl+Shift+P. Approach fills in the value from the same field of the last record added, not the last record displayed.

►► Deleting a Record

The record displayed on the main portion of the form is filled with data from the main database. Shown in Figure 9.3 is a form that contains data from the Customer database and data from the related (joined) database, called the *detail* database, for Orders.

FIGURE 9.3 ▶

The main database here contains customer data, and the repeating panel shows order data for the customer.

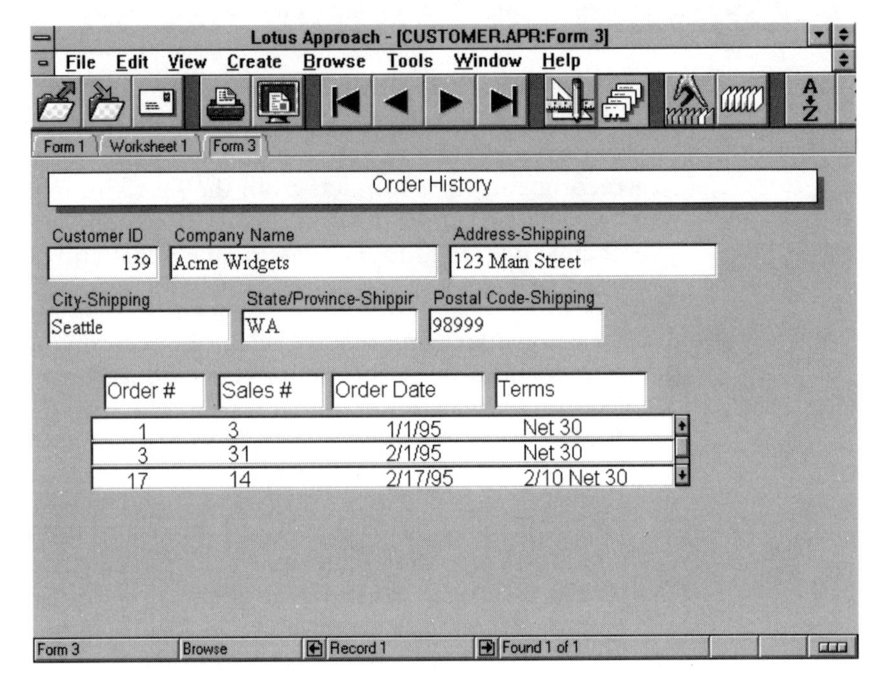

Approach makes it easy to delete a record. First, select a field on the main portion of the form to delete the record from the main database (a record from the Customer database in this example). When you delete the record, all records joined to this record will be deleted if you have this option chosen, as explained in Chapter 6.

To delete a record displayed in the repeating panel, such as a single order from the Orders database, move to any field in the row of the record you want to delete. Next, select Browse ➤ Delete Record, or press Ctrl+Delete, or click on the Delete current record icon on the SmartIcons toolbar. Approach asks if you want to delete the record. Select Yes.

Approach removes the record(s) from the database and displays the previous record in the database (the one you would see if you pressed Page Up).

►► Deleting All Records in the Found Set

If you are displaying a subset of records (called a *found set*) or want to delete all records in your database (if all records are displayed), select Browse ➤ Delete Found Set. Approach will ask you to confirm your request, so select Yes. Found sets are described in detail in Chapter 12.

►► Working with the Data Entry Form

Now that you know how to move among the records in the database, it's important to focus on how you edit data after you've displayed the record you want to change, and how to add data to a blank form.

►► Selecting a Field

You can move to other fields on the form using one of these methods:

- Press Tab to move to the next field.
- Press Shift+Tab to move to the previous field.
- Click on a field to move directly to it without moving through intermediate fields.

You cannot select a field marked as read-only (using the Read-only option in the Basics tab in the InfoBox dialog box from the Design environment), and you cannot select a calculated field.

If you used the Tab or Shift+Tab key method to move to the field, Approach highlights the existing contents. If you begin to type, you'll replace the existing contents. To overcome this problem, either click anywhere in the field (Approach will put your text at the insertion point), or press Home to move to the beginning of the field or press End to move to the end of the field.

If you used the mouse to select the current field, you can move the left or right arrow keys to position the insertion point at the position where you want to enter characters.

If your cursor is at the last field on the form and you press Tab, Approach displays a blank form, ready to create a new record.

TIP

You can move to the next field by pressing Enter, or the previous field by pressing Shift+Enter, by setting the Preferences option to permit this navigation. Select Tools ➤ Preferences. Select the General Tab and check the box marked Use Enter key to move or tab between fields in Browse. When you select this option, the Enter key can be used to move to the next field and Shift+Enter will take you to the previous field, similar to the way Tab and Shift+Tab work.

▸▸ Entering Data in a Field

When you move to a different field, Approach displays the existing data, which may include formatting characters, such as the slashes in a date field (7/25/96). If the field is blank, you may also see these formatting characters to help you enter data properly. When you enter values, Approach does not format your data for you. Instead, it waits until your data entry is complete and you move to another field. It then changes the data to the format you chose when you designed the form and specified the properties for the field using the InfoBox.

Depending on the type of field you have currently selected, Approach uses a different set of rules and offers a variety of special shortcuts.

The key to understanding data entry of different field types is understanding how the Show data entry format option in the Format tab of the InfoBox controls data entry. When this option is checked and you tab into a field, Approach displays formatting characters. For example, for date fields, Approach displays __/__/__ (underscores for values and slashes to separate the month, day, and year). Likewise, for a numeric field defined with a format of Currency with Decimals, tabbing into the field causes Approach to automatically display the dollar sign, underscores for each digit to the left of the decimal point, a decimal point, and underscores for each digit to the right of the decimal point.

If you do not use the Show data entry format option, Approach does not display any formatting characters.

If the Show data entry format option is not selected, or if you select the Display as entered format type option on the Format tab of the InfoBox, you are allowed to enter more numeric characters than are defined for a numeric field. For example, you can enter 1.234 in a numeric field that permits only two digits to the right of the decimal point. However Approach will only save the data according to the field definition. In this case, the "4" will not be saved in the database field .

▶ Entering Data in a Boolean Field

A Boolean field can contain a true or false value. To enter a true value, you can type Yes (and any variation, such as YES or yes), y, or 1. To enter a false value, you can type No, NO, no, n, or 0. Ironically, you cannot enter T or F.

If you display the value as a radio button, the appropriate button is selected. Likewise, if you display the value as a check box, the box is checked if the value is true and unchecked if false. If the Boolean field is displayed as a value in a text field, Approach displays the value as Yes or No. You can shorten the width to show only Y or N, but different monitors and font sizes may not give you the absolute control needed to display just the single character.

▶ Entering Data in a Calculated Field

You cannot change the value of calculated fields. They are for display only.

▶ Entering Data in a Date Field

You can type up to ten characters in a date field (a two-digit month, a two-digit day, and a four-digit year, plus two separator characters), but there are plenty of shortcuts you can use too.

If you selected the Show data entry format option on the Format tab in the InfoBox, Approach displays the separator characters (slashes) between the month, day, and year fields. This format is used no matter what the display format. For instance, even if you want to display the value Tues 1 Dec 94, when you move to the date field, Approach displays __/__/__ and expects you to enter the month, day, and year with numeric characters.

For example, assume that the standard United States date format MM/DD/YY is used—that is, you want to display a two-digit month, day, and year value. Approach also interprets non-numeric characters you type. Thus, when you select the date field, begin by entering the month value for 07/05/94 by typing 7, then pressing the slash key or the spacebar. Approach skips the month field and places you at the beginning of the day field. Enter 5 and press the slash key, then enter the year. Alternately, you can type the digits 070594 (which, in fact, uses the same number of keystrokes). When you fill the month portion of the date, Approach skips over the slash and moves you to the day portion.

To enter the current month, day, or year, press the spacebar when the I-beam is in the appropriate portion of the date field. For example, if today is the 3rd of the month, you can enter a month value, then when Approach moves to the day field, press the spacebar. Approach fills in 03 (the current day) in the day portion of the date. You can continue in this manner: Since the I-beam is now in the year field, press the spacebar again and Approach inserts the current year.

To insert the current system date in a date field, select the Date icon (it appears as a page from a calendar and shows the number 16), or select Browse ➤ Insert, then choose Today's Date.

Approach may require a different order for entering dates, such as DD/MM/YY. This is controlled by the Window Control Panel's International settings. Consult your Windows User's Guide for further details.

►► **TIP**

Approach will substitute the current month and year if you enter only the day value you wish, then move to another field. For example, if the current system date is 10/1/95 and you enter 15 in the date field (you'll actually type this value in the first characters of the date, which are ordinarily used to enter the month) and then press the Tab key, Approach will insert the value 10/15/95 in the date field.

▶ Entering Data in a Memo Field

Memo fields are similar to text fields. When you enter text that cannot be displayed on a single line, however, the text is automatically wrapped to the next line. To insert a new line, press the Enter key. If there are more lines than can be displayed in the field, Approach adds a scroll bar when you move to another field. When you select the field again, you can use the scroll bars to move amid the text.

▶ Entering Data in a Numeric Field

You can type only numbers and two characters in a numeric field. The two characters are a period (to indicate fractional parts) and a minus sign (to indicate negative values). You cannot type commas to separate millions and thousands—Approach will format the field automatically and insert commas as necessary (usually after you have completed your entry and moved to another field).

When you tab into a numeric field, the field is highlighted and you are placed at the rightmost portion of the field (if you have selected Numeric as the Format type and checked Show data entry format on the Format tab in the InfoBox). As you enter the numbers, they are displayed to the left of the decimal point (if you have defined your field using a decimal). After you enter the decimal, the numbers you type are displayed to the right of the decimal point.

As you enter numbers, Approach adds the number you type and moves the rest of the value to the left. Commas and other formatting characters are added as you type.

After you move to another field, the underscores, indicating positions within the field, are removed and the formatting characters are maintained.

The value you enter may be longer than what you have defined for the field length when Display as entered is selected as the format type in the Format tab of the InfoBox or when Show data entry format is not checked in the Format tab of the InfoBox. In this case, Approach will truncate the data. For example, if you have defined the format for a field as ##0.00 (up to three places to the left and up to two decimal places to the right) and enter 23.456 in the field, Approach truncates the final digit (the "6") and displays and stores the value 23.45.

Any digits you do not fill in during data entry are automatically added (with zeros) when you move to another field. For example, you can enter 88 in a field formatted as ##0.00. When you move to another field, Approach displays 88.00. Notice that only significant digits (to the right of existing digits) are displayed; zeros to the left of the leading digit are not displayed. Thus, Approach does not display 088.00, since the first zero in this number is not meaningful.

If you select the Show data entry format in the InfoBox and try to type more digits than you have defined in the field, such as 123456 in a field formatted as ##0, Approach beeps to warn you of the error. This is also true if you try to type too many numbers to the right of the decimal point. For example, if the field is formatted as ##0.00 and you press the decimal point and type two numbers, Approach will accept your entry. When you try to type a third number to the right of the decimal point, Approach will beep and refuse to accept it.

When you place a field on a form, you can select the Show data entry format option. (You can modify existing fields using this option, too.) This displays the fixed characters of a format, such as the decimal point and dollar sign. Approach also provides underlines showing the maximum number of digits you can enter.

To enter a negative value, press the minus sign key (–) at any time. If your format string has been defined to display parentheses when a negative value is entered, the numeric field will be displayed with the left and right parenthesis when you press the minus sign key.

TIP

If the data value is smaller than the format string allows, you can press the period (.) key to move to the fractional part of a number.

▶ *Entering Data in a PicturePlus Field*

To use a graphic in a PicturePlus field, you can draw a picture yourself, paste an existing picture into the field so the database record contains a copy of the graphic, or use OLE to make the graphic appear in the record, even though the image is actually stored on your hard drive as a separate file. Pictures that are too large may be cropped or reduced, depending on the option you set when you added the field to the form.

When you select a PicturePlus field, the Browse menu is replaced by the PicturePlus menu. However, the submenu option, Style & Properties, is only useful if you are drawing inside the field.

To paste the picture, open the application that can edit the picture and select that application's Edit ➤ Copy command. Switch to Approach, select the PicturePlus field, and select Edit ➤ Paste or click on the Paste icon from the SmartIcons toolbar. (Note that the Paste icon is not on the default toolbar but can be added—see Chapter 18.) You can also paste the image using Edit ➤ Paste Special, then select the Paste option. The Paste Special option differs from the Paste option by allowing you to select the object type (if the originating application saves the object to the clipboard in multiple file types) from a list of available options. The Paste Special option also lets you paste a link to the object, so that when the original object changes, the object in your Approach record will be automatically updated when you view the record.

To copy the image from a graphic using the file name, select the PicturePlus field, then select Edit ➤ Paste from File. Approach displays the Paste From File dialog box. Select the graphic type and the file name, then select OK.

To draw an image in the PicturePlus field, hold down the left mouse to draw lines within the border. Make sure Allow drawing is selected on the Basics tab in the InfoBox. To change the pen size and color, select PicturePlus ➤ Style & Properties, or press Ctrl+E. Close the InfoBox before moving to another field. Figure 9.4 shows a freehand drawing in a PicturePlus field.

FIGURE 9.4 

A freehand drawing in a PicturePlus field

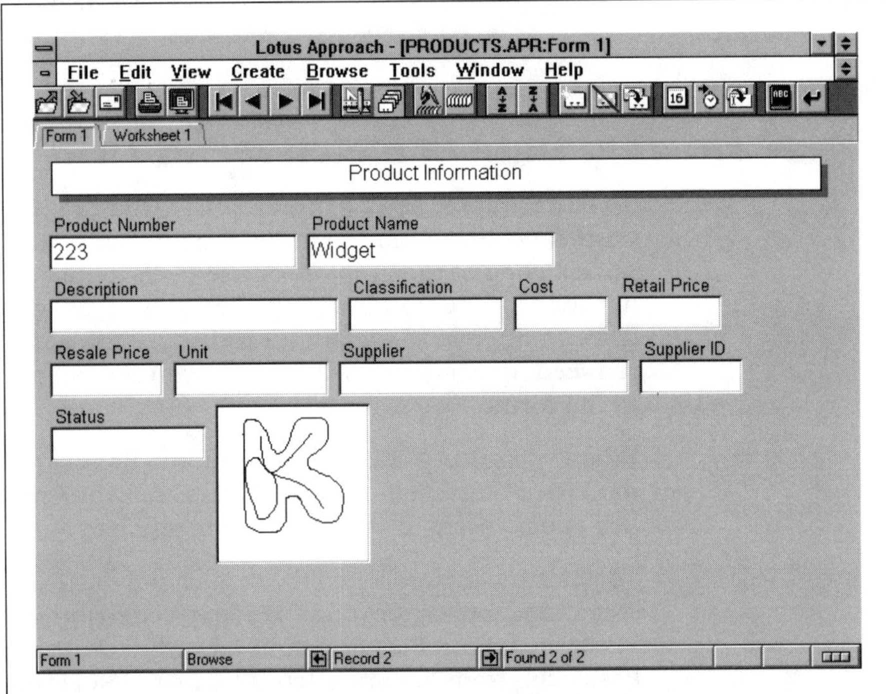

Linking Data to a PicturePlus Field

Windows lets you create a new file or use an existing file in a PicturePlus field. In addition to displaying the image, however, Windows can launch the application that created (or can edit) the image. This ability is dependent on the Registration Database, which is updated and maintained by Windows to keep track of the types of files and which application should be launched for each type. For example, if you store a word processing document in a PicturePlus field, Windows knows if it should launch Word, WordPerfect, Ami Pro, or another word processor you have installed. For more information about the Registration Database, consult your Windows User's Guide.

To insert an object and activate the application that can edit it, select the PicturePlus field, then select Create ➤ Object. Approach displays the Insert Object dialog box, shown in Figure 9.5. In this example we will create a graphic object, but the same instructions can be used to create a spreadsheet object, a sound object, or a word processed object.

FIGURE 9.5 

The Insert Object dialog box appears to help you select the object you want to insert into a PicturePlus field.

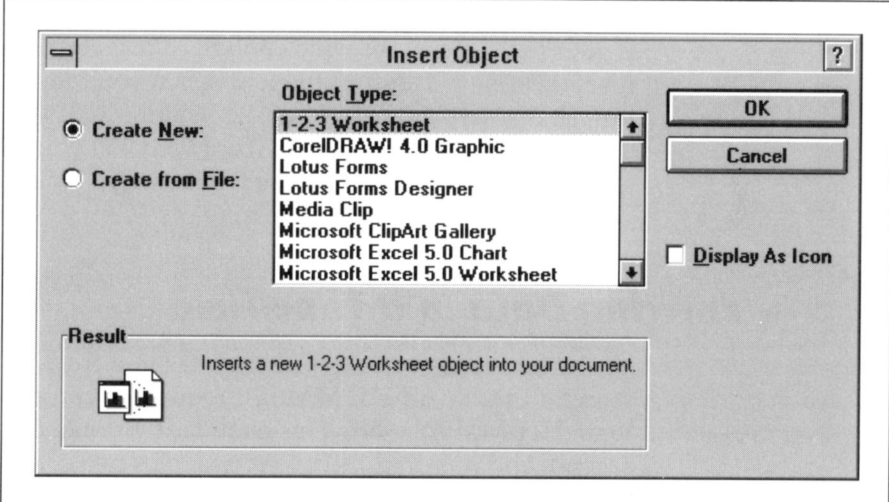

Select Create New to open the application that can create a new document from the list of objects displayed, or select Create from File to open the application and display the file you select. Approach launches the application that can create your graphic or edit the file you've selected.

Create a new image (if you selected Create New) or modify the image you selected (if you selected Create from File), then select Exit and Return from the graphic application's menu. Windows returns you to your Approach form.

When you browse through your database, you can edit the image in the PicturePlus field. To edit the image, double-click on the PicturePlus field and Windows will launch the application, allowing you to edit it. Select Exit and Return from the graphic application's menu to return to Approach.

▸ Entering Data in a Text Field

To enter text in a field, type the character(s) you want. To delete the character to the right of the insertion point, press Del. To delete the character to the left of the insertion point, press Backspace. You can use the left and right arrow keys to move between characters, and the Home and End keys to move to the beginning and end (respectively) of the field.

If your text field is not wide enough to display all the characters you type, the text will shift to the left. When you move to another field, Approach displays the field from the beginning. If the field on the form is drawn to allow multiple lines, Approach will wrap the text to subsequent lines and add scroll bars if necessary. Unlike memo fields, you cannot insert new lines by pressing the Enter key.

▸ Entering Data in a Time Field

You can type up to twelve characters in a time field. Dates are stored in the form HHMMSS00, but you can enter a date in the form HH:MM:SS.00xx. This includes two characters for hour, minute, second, and hundredths of a second, plus two colons and one period as separator characters. The "xx" represents A or P, meaning AM or PM. Many formatting options, including those that do not include the hundredths of a second, allow you to enter AM or PM instead of A or P.

To enter a time value, type the time in any of these ways:

- Hour only
- HH:MM
- HH:MM:SS
- HH:MM:SS.00

Hours can be entered in either 12-hour or 24-hour format. (In addition, you can enter an A or P at the end of the field if you wish.) If you type 8, for example, Approach will store the value 8:00 AM. If you enter an hour smaller than 12, Approach assumes AM. Enter the hour 24 and Approach transforms the value to 12AM. If you enter a value other than AM, PM, A, or P, Approach ignores your entry and examines the value in the hour position to determine AM or PM.

To enter the current time, select the Time icon (the icon has the face of a clock on it) from the SmartIcons toolbar or select Browse ➤ Insert, then select Current Time.

If the Time field uses the Show data entry format option, Approach displays the fields with colons separating hours, minutes, and seconds, and, if appropriate, the period to separate hundredths of a second. To enter the current value from the system time, press the spacebar. For example, if the current time is 8:30AM and the I-beam is positioned at the hour portion of the time field, pressing the spacebar inserts an 8. Pressing the spacebar again will insert 30 in the minute portion of the field.

►► Entering Data in GUI Fields

When you display values using drop-down lists, radio buttons, or check boxes, there are special considerations, since these graphical user interface (GUI) elements have a unique behavior.

► Entering Data Using a Check Box

When you display an existing record, Approach interprets the value in the field and displays the check box with or without a check mark as appropriate. Note that if the field has no value, you cannot assume an unchecked box means the field has the unchecked value.

To select the checked value, click anywhere in the check box or on the check box's label. To remove the X, click on the box or label again.

►► **WARNING**

When you add a new field, an unchecked box does not necessarily mean the field has the "unchecked" value. Instead, it may have what is called the null value—no value at all. To enter the unchecked value, first check the box, then click on it again to remove the X.

▸ Entering Data Using a Drop-Down List

To select a value, click on the down-pointing arrow or press Alt+↓. Use the up or down arrows on your keyboard, or click on the up- and down-pointing arrows in the scroll area to highlight your selection. Press enter or move to another field.

If you are using a field box and list, you can enter the value in the field or select from one of the values in the drop-down list using the techniques just described.

When you leave the field, Approach displays the field value. Approach also removes the down-pointing arrow if the Show drop-down arrow option is not selected in the Drop-Down List dialog box (see the Basics tab of the InfoBox).

▸ Entering Data Using a Radio Button

To select a radio button, click on the button or its label. Only one of the radio buttons in a group can be selected at a time. When you select a different radio button in a group, the original button is unselected.

▸▸ Deleting Data in a Field

As we discussed earlier, if you use the Tab or Shift+Tab key method to move to the field, Approach highlights the existing contents of the field. You can also click the mouse inside a field to move to it. You can double-click the mouse to select (highlight) the word at the cursor, or drag the mouse across the field as you hold down the left mouse button to select the entire field.

When the field's contents are highlighted and you begin to type, you will replace the existing contents. You can also delete highlighted text by pressing the Del key or by selecting Edit ➤ Clear. This is standard Windows behavior.

If you delete a field's contents by mistake, select Edit ➤ Undo or press Ctrl+Z to restore the field value.

▸▸ Copying Data in a Field

You may need to copy the existing contents of a field to another field. For example, you need to change the address of a contact with a new address, but you wish to save the previous address as part of a memo field. You may also need to copy the contents from one field to the same field in another record.

To copy the contents of a field, select the entry either by using the mouse, or by tabbing into the field. Press Ctrl+C select Edit ➤ Copy. You can also select the Copy icon from the SmartIcons toolbar. Move to the destination (another field or the same field in another record) and press Ctrl+V, select Edit ➤ Paste, or choose the Paste icon from the SmartIcons toolbar — the second icon shown in the following graphic. Note that the Copy and Paste icons are not part of the default toolbar but can be added using the directions in Chapter 18.

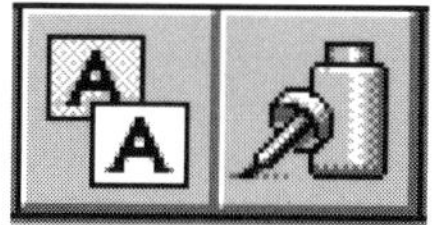

▸▸ Printing

You can print a copy of the current record easily. Select File ➤ Print, or press Ctrl+P. Approach displays the standard Windows Print dialog box, asking you which form you want to print. The default is Current form, which will print the record currently displayed. If you are working with the entire database, you can print a form for each record in the database by selecting All. (If you are working with a subset of records, called the *found set*, selecting All will print only those records in the found set. Found sets are discussed in Chapter 12.) Select OK to begin printing.

Printing is discussed in greater detail in Chapter 15.

▸▸ Summary and a Look Ahead

In this chapter you've learned how to enter new records in your database, and how to navigate between existing records—moving to the next, previous, first, or last record in your database.

In the next chapter you'll learn how to work with data in a worksheet and a crosstab. Forms allow you to view and work with data from a single record at a time. Worksheets let you see a screenful of data at once, and crosstabs help you analyze the data you have. Chapter 10 looks at building and using worksheet and crosstab forms.

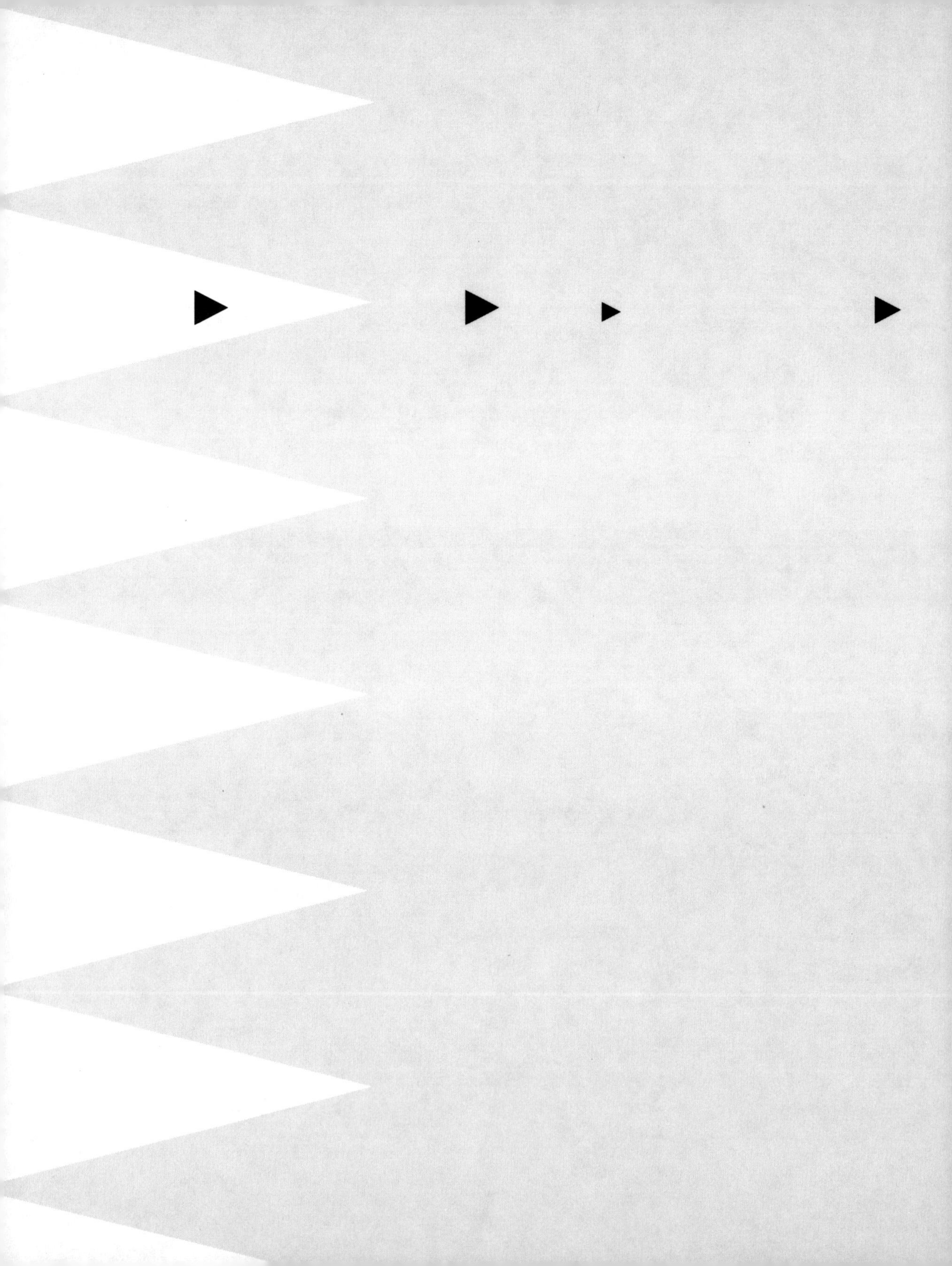

CHAPTER 10

Worksheets and Crosstabs

▸▸ FAST TRACK

▶ ***To create a worksheet*** **331**

select Create ➤ Worksheet or select the Create New Worksheet button from the SmartIcons toolbar. In the Worksheet assistant, select the database and fields you want to be displayed in a worksheet. Select the fields you want in the order you want to see them from left to right in the worksheet, and select Add, or double-click each field to add it to the list. Press the Done button when you have selected the fields. If you are using fields from joined databases, Approach asks you to identify the controlling database—called the main database.

▶ ***To select a cell in a worksheet*** **332**

click on the cell. To select a range of cells, click on the first cell, then drag the mouse to the last cell in the range; all selected cells are highlighted. Click on a column heading or row heading to select all cells in a column or row, respectively.

▶ ***To move around in a worksheet*** **334**

press the Tab key to move to the next field to the right or Shift+Tab to move one cell to the left. During editing, press ↓ to move to the same field in the row immediately underneath, or ↑ to move to the same field in the row above. Press ← or → to move left or right (respectively) in the same row.

▶ ***To create a crosstab*** **350**

select Create ➤ Crosstab. Select the main and/or detail database and the field(s) to include in rows. Click on Next or the Step 2 tab to select fields for the columns. To create a summary report, click on a field in the Database fields list, but do not add it to the Fields to place on view list. Select the database and field you want in the center of your crosstab, and the arithmetic function. Choose Done.

► *To change formatting of cells within a crosstab* **353**

click on the row or column heading containing the cells, then select the InfoBox icon from the SmartIcons toolbar, double-click the mouse, press Ctrl+E, or click on the right mouse button and select Styles & Properties. Be sure the top of the InfoBox reads Settings for Column or Settings for Row.

► *To change a heading in a crosstab* **353**

click twice (don't double-click) on the row or column heading. When you open the InfoBox, be sure the drop-down list at the top reads Settings for Header.

► *To quickly select the cells in the column but not the header* **353**

click on the column heading to select both the column header and the cells underneath. Click on the Cells icon from the SmartIcons toolbar or select Crosstab ➤ Select, then choose Cells Only.

► *To rearrange columns and rows* **354**

drag the column or row to the desired location. For example, you can drag a header to the left side of the crosstab to create a new row. To add a field, drag the field name from the Add Fields dialog box. To remove a field from the crosstab, drag the field to the top of the screen. When the mouse pointer changes to a field name pointing to a wastebasket, release the mouse.

▶▶ **In** Chapters 8 and 9 you learned how to create forms and use them to add, change, and delete data. Forms aren't the only way to work with your data, however. Approach also offers worksheets, which resemble the rows and columns familiar to spreadsheet users. Approach also offers a special analytical tool, called a *crosstab*, that gives you a different perspective on your data.

In this chapter you'll learn how to create a worksheet and how to use it to work with records. If you are familiar with spreadsheets, you'll be creating and working with worksheets almost instantly. You'll see how to create a new worksheet, modify an existing one, and use a worksheet to add, edit, copy, and delete data. You'll also learn how to build and modify crosstabs, which help you organize your data by breaking it down into components that can then be analyzed.

▶▶ Worksheets

Data in a worksheet is arranged in rows—one row per record. If you have a joined database, the worksheet repeats the fields from the main database record as many times as necessary and uses one row for every record in the joined database. A small right-pointing arrow shows which row is selected—that is, the current record in the database.

Worksheets are sometimes the preferred method for entering data in a database because several records are displayed on the same screen, making navigation easier, especially if you are entering data in just a few fields.

To select a row, click anywhere to the left of the first data field, in the gray column to the left of the data.

Figure 10.1 shows a worksheet for a single database. Each column displays a single field. For example, the company field is listed first, then the customer identification number, the contact name, and so on. Approach displays a column heading for each field, which by default is the field name as defined in the Field Definition dialog box.

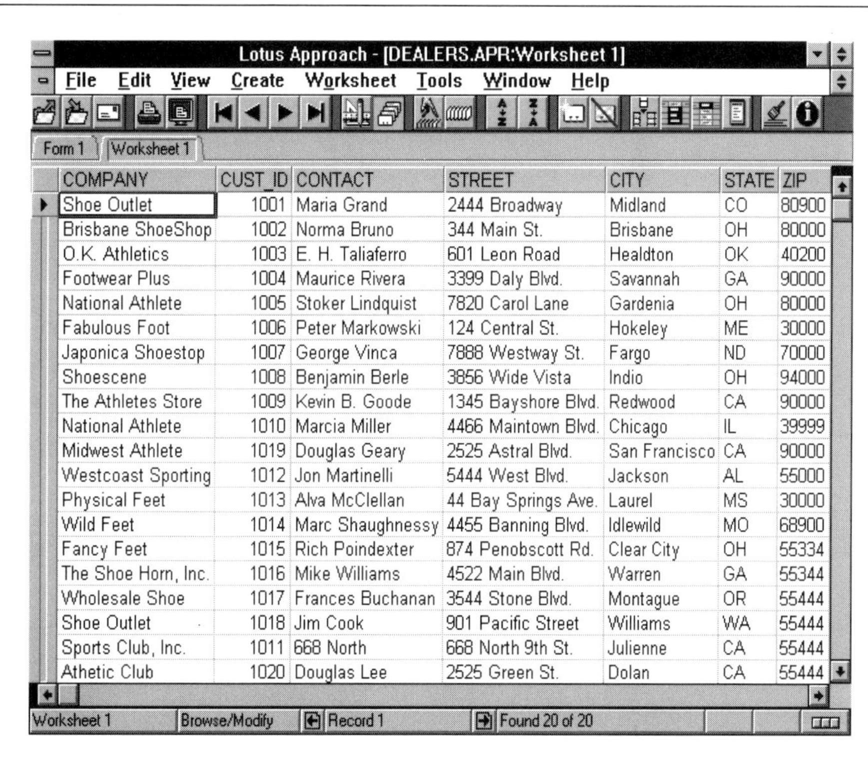

COMPANY	CUST_ID	CONTACT	STREET	CITY	STATE	ZIP
Shoe Outlet	1001	Maria Grand	2444 Broadway	Midland	CO	80900
Brisbane ShoeShop	1002	Norma Bruno	344 Main St.	Brisbane	OH	80000
O.K. Athletics	1003	E. H. Taliaferro	601 Leon Road	Healdton	OK	40200
Footwear Plus	1004	Maurice Rivera	3399 Daly Blvd.	Savannah	GA	90000
National Athlete	1005	Stoker Lindquist	7820 Carol Lane	Gardenia	OH	80000
Fabulous Foot	1006	Peter Markowski	124 Central St.	Hokeley	ME	30000
Japonica Shoestop	1007	George Vinca	7888 Westway St.	Fargo	ND	70000
Shoescene	1008	Benjamin Berle	3856 Wide Vista	Indio	OH	94000
The Athletes Store	1009	Kevin B. Goode	1345 Bayshore Blvd.	Redwood	CA	90000
National Athlete	1010	Marcia Miller	4466 Maintown Blvd.	Chicago	IL	39999
Midwest Athlete	1019	Douglas Geary	2525 Astral Blvd.	San Francisco	CA	90000
Westcoast Sporting	1012	Jon Martinelli	5444 West Blvd.	Jackson	AL	55000
Physical Feet	1013	Alva McClellan	44 Bay Springs Ave.	Laurel	MS	30000
Wild Feet	1014	Marc Shaughnessy	4455 Banning Blvd.	Idlewild	MO	68900
Fancy Feet	1015	Rich Poindexter	874 Penobscott Rd.	Clear City	OH	55334
The Shoe Horn, Inc.	1016	Mike Williams	4522 Main Blvd.	Warren	GA	55344
Wholesale Shoe	1017	Frances Buchanan	3544 Stone Blvd.	Montague	OR	55444
Shoe Outlet	1018	Jim Cook	901 Pacific Street	Williams	WA	55444
Sports Club, Inc.	1011	668 North	668 North 9th St.	Julienne	CA	55444
Athetic Club	1020	Douglas Lee	2525 Green St.	Dolan	CA	55444

FIGURE 10.1

A worksheet for a database of athletic merchandise vendors

When using a worksheet, Approach displays the toolbar shown in Figure 10.2 as the default.

When you create a new database, or open a database file (such as a dBASE file) directly, Approach designs a default worksheet for you. The fields are listed from left to right in the same order as the fields are defined in the database.

FIGURE 10.2

Toolbar for Worksheet in the Browse environment

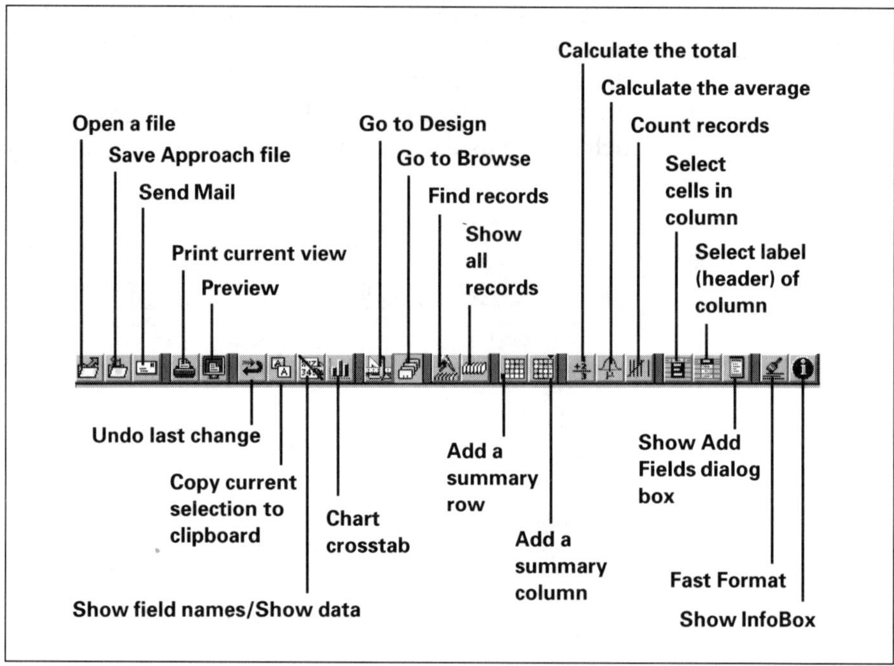

Unlike forms, if your .APR file is not protected with a password, you only work in the Browse environment. In fact, there is no such thing as a separate Design environment for worksheets that have no password. You can make a change directly to the worksheet in either Browse or Design—such as changing the row height or column width—and the format is immediately changed, using the existing records from your database. In fact, when you click on the Design icon in the SmartIcons toolbar, Approach makes minimal changes to the menu options. For databases with passwords, you'll have to switch to the Design environment to make changes to the layout of a worksheet, as described in this chapter. You'll use the Browse environment to edit records and copy data.

Even though worksheets are most useful for quick lists of data, Approach still gives you flexibility for defining how the data is displayed. You can define formatting options, such as color and fonts, just as you can with any form. The techniques described for working with forms (in Chapters 7 and 8)—everything from using the InfoBox to selecting format strings—apply to worksheets as well.

▸▸ Creating a New Worksheet

To create a new worksheet, select Create ➤ Worksheet or select the Create New Worksheet button from the SmartIcons toolbar. Approach displays the Worksheet Assistant, shown in Figure 10.3. The Create New Worksheet button is not part of the default toolbar but can be added to it following the directions in Chapter 18.

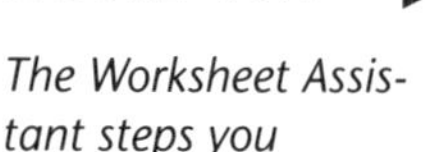

FIGURE 10.3

The Worksheet Assistant steps you through selecting the fields you want displayed in a worksheet.

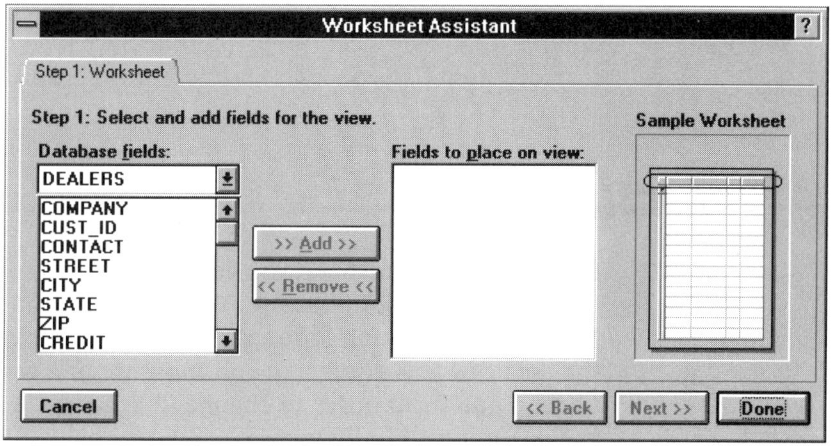

To use the Assistant, select the database and fields you want to be displayed in a worksheet. If you have joined databases in the Approach view and want to display data from a detail database, be sure to select a field from the main database as the first field. You may then select fields from any related database. However, the first (leftmost) field in a worksheet must be from the main database. See Chapter 6 for more about joined databases.

Select the fields you want in the order you want to see them from left to right in the worksheet, and select Add, or double-click each field to add it to the list. You cannot rearrange the fields in the list, so make your selection carefully. Fields are always added to the end of the list. The order of fields *can* be changed once the worksheet is created using the Design environment (for password protected databases) or the Browse environment (if your database does not need a password). You may select a field more than once if you wish.

Press the Done button when you have selected the fields. If you are using fields from joined databases, Approach asks you to identify the controlling database—called the main database. This database controls how you move through records. When you choose the Next or Previous record icon from the SmartIcons toolbar, for example, Approach moves to the next or previous record in the *main* database, not the other (detail) database(s).

After selecting the main database, if necessary, Approach creates the worksheet.

Remember, you must save your Approach file in order to permanently add the new worksheet. Select the File Save icon from the SmartIcons toolbar, press Ctrl+S, or select File ➤ Save Approach File to save the file.

▸▸ Selecting Cells

Similar to a spreadsheet, you can select rows, columns, individual cells, or all cells, then copy them to the clipboard and use the data in another Windows application. You must select a cell or cells in order to change the data the cells contain, a common use of a worksheet. You will also select columns in order to change their layout properties, as explained in the section "Modifying a Worksheet Layout" later in this chapter.

To make a selection in a worksheet, follow these directions:

To Select This	To Perform This Task	Do This
A single cell	Change a cell value	Click in the cell.
A range of cells	Copy the cells to the clipboard	Click on the first cell, then drag the mouse to the last cell in the range; all selected cells are highlighted.

To Select This	To Perform This Task	Do This
All cells in a column (include the heading)	Change the column properties, such as the font or background color	Click on the column heading.
Column heading only	Change the name of the column in the worksheet	Right-click on the column heading, or select the column heading (click on the heading) and click on the label icon from the SmartIcons toolbar.
Cells in a column (exclude the heading)	Change the cell properties such as the display format	Select the column, then click on the Select Cells icon from the SmartIcons toolbar; Approach draws slanted gray lines through the column header.
Multiple columns	Apply changes to more than one column at once	Click on the first column, then drag the mouse to the right or left to select adjacent columns, or click on the first column and press and hold the Shift key and click on the last column in the range; if the cursor turns into a hand when you click the first column, click a single cell, then begin again.
A single row	Copy or delete the record	Click to the left of the row.

To Select This	To Perform This Task	Do This
Multiple rows	Copy or delete multiple records at once	Click in any cell of the first row. Then select the first row and drag the cursor to the last row, or move it to the last row and press and hold the Shift key while you click on the row.
All cells (including the heading)	Apply changes to the entire worksheet, such as the formatting properties, or to copy the data to the clipboard	Click in the upper-left corner of the worksheet (to the left of the first heading) or select Edit ➤ Select All.
All cells (excluding the heading)	Apply formatting changes to the worksheet	Double-click in the upper-left corner of the worksheet or select Edit ➤ Select All, then click on the Select cells of selected column icon from the SmartIcons toolbar (or select Worksheet ➤ Select ➤ Cells Only).

▸▸ Moving Around in a Worksheet

You've seen how to select rows and columns of data. When you select a single cell, you can edit its contents. When you press Tab, the cursor moves to the next field to the right. If you are editing the last column in the row, the cursor moves to the first field in the next row.

When you edit a field and press ↓, the cursor moves to the same field in the row immediately below the current cell. You can press ↑ to move to the same field in the row above, or press ← or → to move left or right (respectively) in the same row.

As with any window, you can use the scroll bars to view other rows or columns. However, you need to click inside a cell to select it; otherwise the current cell remains the last selected cell. Changing your position within the worksheet by scroll bars is not enough—you must select a cell to move the I-beam so you can edit its contents.

Approach lets you view up to four sections of a worksheet. For example, you might want to compare values in the third record in your worksheet with the values in the 100th record. Since a worksheet can't display all the intermediate rows on a single screen, you can use the *splitters* to create independently scrolling panes.

The *splitter bars* are found just above the vertical scroll bar and to the left of the horizontal scroll bar. To split a worksheet, move the mouse pointer to the splitter bar until the mouse changes into a double-pointing arrow. Drag the mouse down or to the right to add a pane. (Likewise, you can drag an existing splitter up or to the left until it disappears to remove a pane.) Figure 10.4 shows a worksheet that has been split horizontally. The currently selected cell, meaning the one you click, is the one just showing a frame, in this case in the upper panel. In this figure the company field for Fancy Feet has been selected in the upper pane.

Each pane works independently—that is, you can move to any record within your database in either pane while the other pane does not change its position within the database. If two panes display the same record, edits you make to a field in one pane are reflected in the other pane when you move to another field.

You can split a screen using both the horizontal and vertical splitter bars at the same time. Doing so splits your screen into four quadrants, which may be useful for larger databases with dozens of fields.

►► Working with Data in a Worksheet

As with forms, you can use a worksheet to change data, add new records, copy existing records, and delete unneeded records.

FIGURE 10.4 ▶

Approach lets you split a worksheet to view two sections of a worksheet. Changes made in one pane are reflected in the other pane immediately if the panes are displaying the same record.

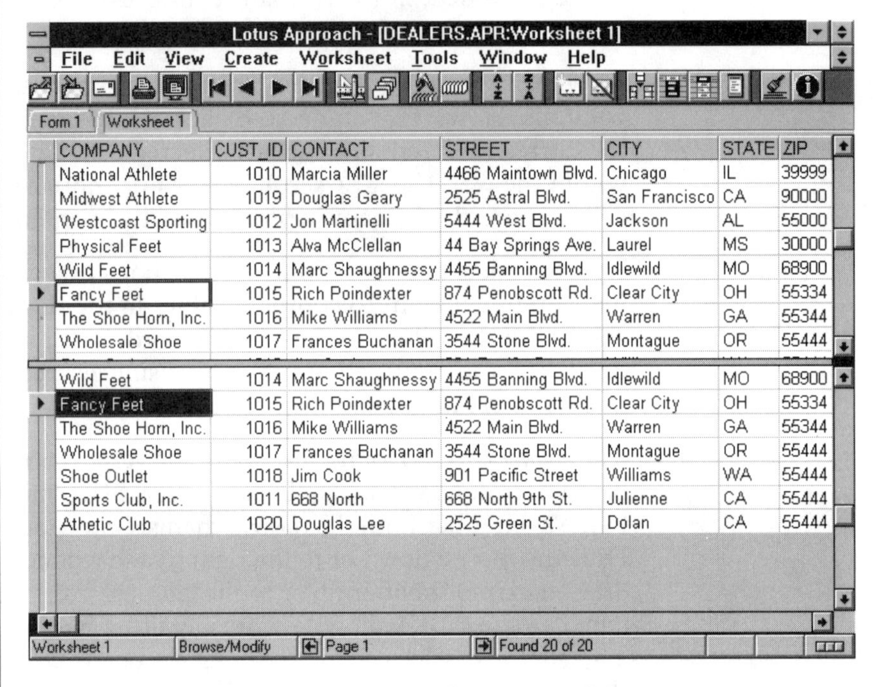

COMPANY	CUST_ID	CONTACT	STREET	CITY	STATE	ZIP
National Athlete	1010	Marcia Miller	4466 Maintown Blvd.	Chicago	IL	39999
Midwest Athlete	1019	Douglas Geary	2525 Astral Blvd.	San Francisco	CA	90000
Westcoast Sporting	1012	Jon Martinelli	5444 West Blvd.	Jackson	AL	55000
Physical Feet	1013	Alva McClellan	44 Bay Springs Ave.	Laurel	MS	30000
Wild Feet	1014	Marc Shaughnessy	4455 Banning Blvd.	Idlewild	MO	68900
Fancy Feet	1015	Rich Poindexter	874 Penobscott Rd.	Clear City	OH	55334
The Shoe Horn, Inc.	1016	Mike Williams	4522 Main Blvd.	Warren	GA	55344
Wholesale Shoe	1017	Frances Buchanan	3544 Stone Blvd.	Montague	OR	55444

Wild Feet	1014	Marc Shaughnessy	4455 Banning Blvd.	Idlewild	MO	68900
Fancy Feet	1015	Rich Poindexter	874 Penobscott Rd.	Clear City	OH	55334
The Shoe Horn, Inc.	1016	Mike Williams	4522 Main Blvd.	Warren	GA	55344
Wholesale Shoe	1017	Frances Buchanan	3544 Stone Blvd.	Montague	OR	55444
Shoe Outlet	1018	Jim Cook	901 Pacific Street	Williams	WA	55444
Sports Club, Inc.	1011	668 North	668 North 9th St.	Julienne	CA	55444
Athetic Club	1020	Douglas Lee	2525 Green St.	Dolan	CA	55444

Unlike forms and reports that you've seen so far, there is little difference between the Design and Browse environments in a worksheet. Almost all of the features described in the following sections can be done in either environment. (The major exception is the ability to delete or duplicate a worksheet.)

▶ Adding Records

To add a new record to a worksheet, select Worksheet ➤ Records, or select either of the Create New Record icons from the SmartIcons toolbar. Only the first icon appears on the default toolbar, but the second can be added using the directions in Chapter 18. Select New. Approach inserts a blank row at the end of the worksheet.

TIP

To enter the value from the last new record you added in the current cell, select Worksheet ➤ Insert, then choose Previous Value. The shortcut for this action is Ctrl+Shift+P.

► Changing Records

Similar to forms, changing and entering data is as simple as selecting the cell and beginning to type. However, there are some important—even critical—differences.

First, any field displayed in a column is editable. Unlike forms, which allow you to display a value but protect it from being modified, worksheets offer no such protection. Thus, if you have a serialized field in a worksheet (one in which a field contains a unique number, in order—such as 1001, 1002, 1003—in a series of records), you may wish to remove it to prevent accidental changes.

If you're working with a PicturePlus field, the field is display only, and if the row size is sufficiently large, Approach displays a thumbnail image of your field. You must use a form to modify the field's contents.

►► WARNING

Calculated fields defined in your database can be displayed in a worksheet. However, when you try to enter a value in a column containing a calculated field, Approach displays the Formula dialog box and asks you to change the formula. If you do, the new formula will replace the field's formula in the worksheet and in the field definition for the calculated field.

▶ Copying Records

To copy a record in a worksheet, select the record (click to the left of the first column in the row) and select Worksheet ➤ Records, then choose Duplicate, or click on the Duplicate current record from the SmartIcons toolbar (which is not on the default toolbar but can be added using the directions in Chapter 18). Approach makes a copy of the record and inserts it at the end of the database, and moves the current row pointer to the new record.

▶ Hiding Records

You can temporarily hide a record from a worksheet by selecting it, then choosing Worksheet ➤ Records ➤ Hide (or press Ctrl+H). To view the record, you must show all records (select Worksheet ➤ Find ➤ Show All, press Ctrl+A, or click on the Show All icon from the SmartIcons toolbar).

▶ Deleting Records

To delete one or more records, select the record or records by choosing the rows containing the records you want to delete (see the section "Selecting Cells" earlier in this chapter). Select Edit ➤ Cut, Edit ➤ Clear, press Ctrl+X, or click on either of the Delete Current Record icons from the SmartIcons toolbar. (Only the left icon is on the default toolbar, but the other can be added following the directions in Chapter 18.) Approach asks if you want to permanently delete the selected records. Choose Yes.

You can also select Worksheet ➤ Delete ➤ Select Records to delete one or more selected rows (records), or press Ctrl+Del (the shortcut key combination). As with the other techniques, Approach asks if you want to permanently delete the selected records. Choose Yes.

To delete all records in the found set (described in Chapter 12), select Worksheet ➤ Delete ➤ Found Set.

▶ Inserting the Current Date or Time

To quickly insert the current system date or time, select the cell and choose Worksheet ➤ Insert. Then choose Today's Date or Current Time. Alternatively, the shortcut for entering the current date is Ctrl+Shift+D. The shortcut for the current time is Ctrl+Shift+T.

▶▶ Modifying a Worksheet Layout

As with forms, you can change how fields (columns) and records (rows) are formatted. In addition, you can make changes to the worksheet itself, changing its background color and name, for example.

To change the properties of a worksheet, select the InfoBox icon from the SmartIcons toolbar, select Worksheet ➤ Style & Properties, press Ctrl+E, or right-click anywhere within the worksheet and select Style & Properties. Approach displays the InfoBox for the worksheet. You will use the InfoBox to make most of your formatting changes. Other changes, such as changing the row height or column width, can be made by directly manipulating cell borders with your mouse.

Remember, you must save your Approach file in order to preserve the changes made to any worksheet. Select the File Save icon from the SmartIcons toolbar, press Ctrl+S, or select File ➤ Save Approach File to save the file.

▶ The Worksheet InfoBox

The InfoBox gives you control over three categories:

- Basics (worksheet name, menu used, and main database name)
- Macros (which macro should be run when moving to or from the worksheet)
- Printing (title, date, and page number options for printing the worksheet)

The Basics Tab

Select the Basics tab, shown in Figure 10.5 from the Browse environment, to enter the worksheet name (to appear in the tab for the view), the Menu bar to use (as a substitute for the main Approach Menu bar, discussed in Chapter 18), and the name of the main database. To hide the worksheet tab, check the Hide view box (but first you must switch to the Design environment for this option to appear). Approach will not display a tab for the worksheet, although you can still switch to it by selecting the worksheet name from the menu in the Status bar (click on the first section of the Status bar to see the menu that pops up from the bottom of your screen).

FIGURE 10.5

The Basics tab lets you specify the name, Menu bar, and main (controlling) database for the worksheet.

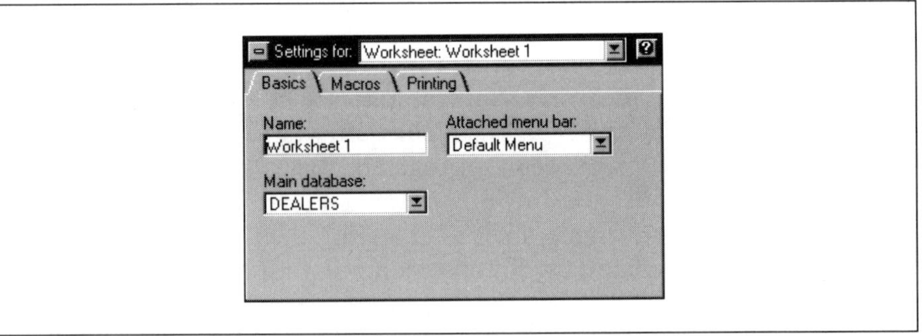

The Macros Tab

Macros let you perform repetitive tasks quickly and are discussed in Chapter 16. The macros tab, shown in Figure 10.6, lets you specify the name of a macro to be executed when you switch to the worksheet, and another macro to be run when you switch to a different view (another form, report, or a different worksheet, for example). You can click on the Define macro button to create the macro without leaving the worksheet.

The Printing Tab

Options on the Printing tab, shown in Figure 10.7, are used when you print the worksheet (using the File ➤ Print command).

Check the Print title box and enter a title. The title will appear in the upper-left corner of the printed output.

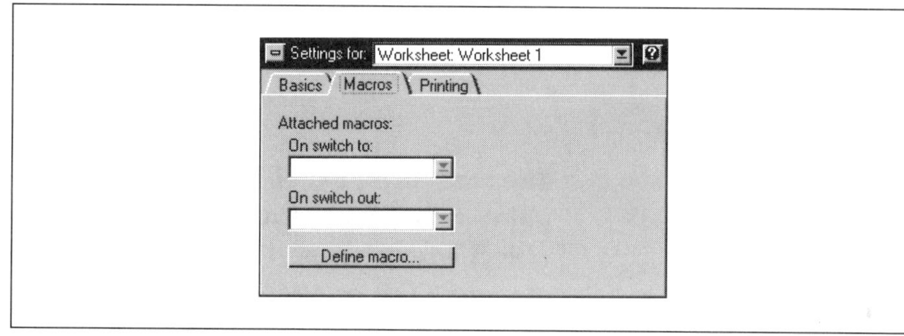

FIGURE 10.6

The Macros tab lets you specify which, if any, macro should be run when you move to the worksheet or away from the worksheet.

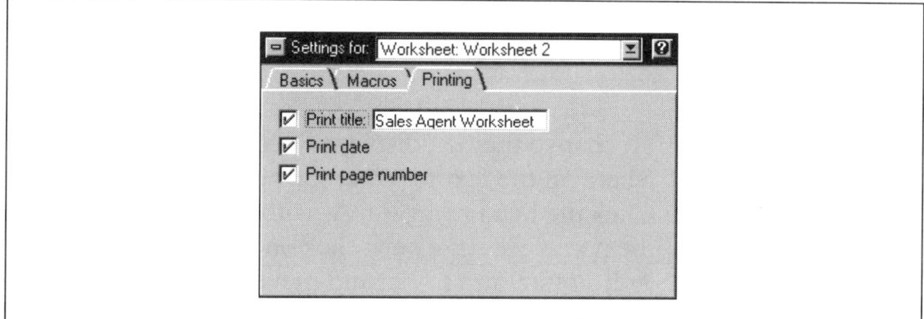

FIGURE 10.7

The Printing tab lets you specify if you want to include a custom title, the page number, and the current (system) date on your printed output.

Select Print date to print a date in the lower-left corner.

Select Print page number to print the page number in the lower-right corner.

▶ Changing Field Properties

To change the properties of the data in a column, click on the column heading, click on the Select Cells icon, then click on the InfoBox icon. Approach displays the InfoBox. Change the properties just as you would for a form. For details, see Chapters 7 and 8.

▶ Changing the Text of a Column Heading

By default, Approach uses the name of the field as the column heading. While this may be sufficient, you may want to change the heading name to something more meaningful. For example, instead of using the field name CUST_ID, you might want to use a more meaningful column heading name such as Customer Number.

▸▸ **TIP**

The Fast Format tool, which works like a "format painter," works just as it does with a form. Select the object whose properties you want to copy, such as a column. Click on the Fast Format icon from the SmartIcons toolbar (or select Worksheet ➤ Fast Format or press Ctrl+M) and select the objects you want to "paint." For more information about the Fast Format tool, see Chapter 7.

To change the text displayed at the top of a column, double-click anywhere on the text to select the heading. The cursor changes to a hand. Click the heading again. As with tab labels, Approach lets you directly edit the name. Alternatively, click on the column heading and select Worksheet ➤ Edit Column Label and make the change in the label area.

▸ *Making Columns Wider or Narrower*

By default, Approach creates column widths that will accommodate the name of the column, which may include the database name if you are using joined databases. This is sometimes far too wide. If the field contains a four-digit customer identification, you probably don't want a heading that reads "CUSTOMER: Customer_ID_Number," which takes considerable space on your screen. Likewise, the contents of an address field may need to be much wider than what Approach displays.

To make a column wider or narrower, move the cursor to the right border of the column you want to adjust. The cursor changes to a two-headed arrow split by a vertical bar, as shown in Figure 10.8 where we are widening the CUST_ID field. A dotted vertical line indicates the column width down the entire screen as you move the mouse to the right or left to widen or shrink the column. Drag the mouse to the right to widen a column or left to make it narrower.

FIGURE 10.8

Change the width of a column by selecting the right border of a column heading. Drag the mouse to the right or left to change the width.

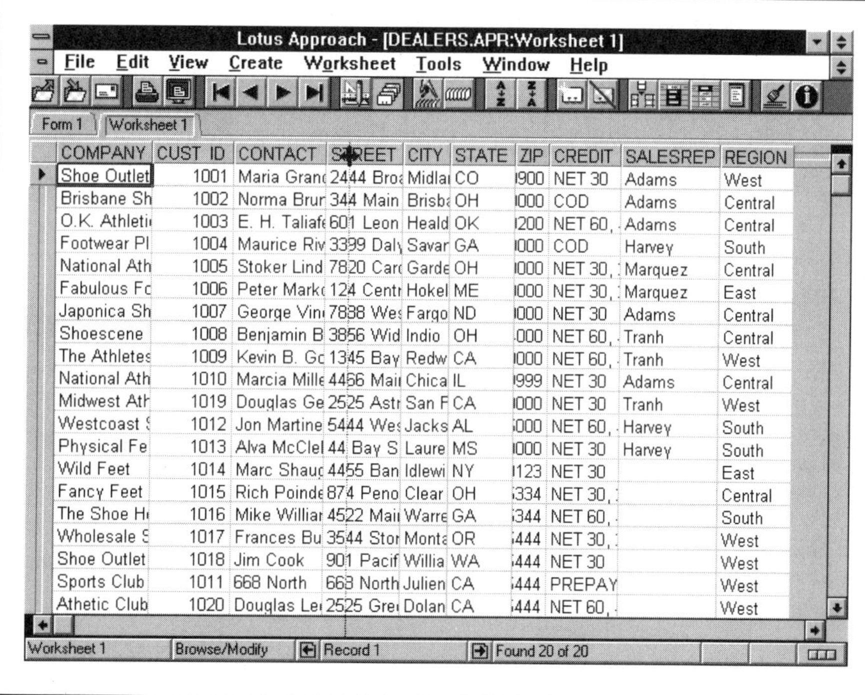

To change the size of several columns at once, select the columns (see the section "Selecting Cells" earlier in this chapter) and resize any column in your selection. All selected columns are resized to the same new width.

WARNING

If you drag the right column border to the left border of the column, Approach will hide the column. To display it again, select the column border and drag it to the right. Often this may not work, since Approach cannot distinguish between your request to un-hide the column and expand an existing column. If this does not work, select a range of columns that includes at least one column to the left of the hidden column and one column to the right, and change the column width of a visible column.

▸ Changing Row Height

To make a row taller or shorter, move the cursor to the bottom border of the row you want to adjust. The cursor changes to a two-headed arrow split by a horizontal bar, as shown in Figure 10.9. Drag the mouse down (to make the row taller) or up (to make it narrower). All rows are changed to the new height.

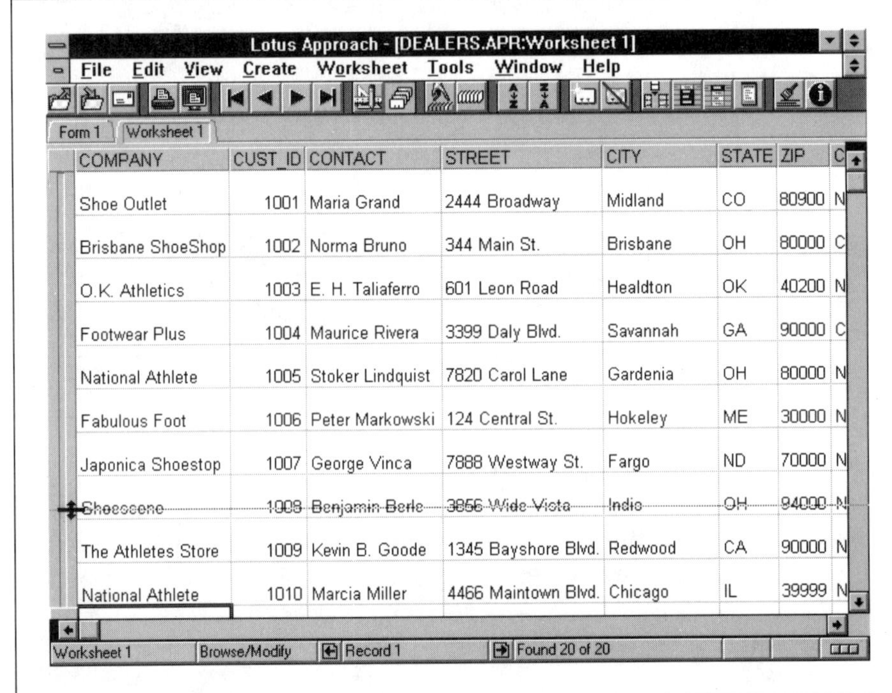

FIGURE 10.9 ▸

Taller rows make it easier to view data. You can use the mouse to adjust the row height—just drag on the lower border of any row. A horizontal dotted line shows you the new height.

▸ Rearranging Fields

As you use a worksheet you may find that the columns aren't in the most convenient order. For example, you may want the customer number to be listed as the first column, followed by the company name, rather than vice versa.

To move a column to a different position in the worksheet, single-click on the column heading. The mouse pointer will change to a hand. Drag the column to the new position. As you do so, Approach displays the name of the column in a box and uses a dark gray vertical bar to show the insertion point (where the field will be added).

▶ Removing a Column

To remove a column, select the column (click on the heading) and drag it up to the tab or menu area. Approach displays the name of the column with an arrow pointing to a trash can, indicating that the column will be deleted. If you change your mind, select Edit ➤ Undo. When you remove a column from a worksheet, you do not remove the data from the database. Instead, you are telling Approach you don't want to *see* the data on your screen. The data is maintained and available for this or any other worksheet (or other view for that matter).

▶ Inserting a Column

Approach offers two ways to insert a column, depending on what you want the new column to contain. You can use drag-and-drop to add a field that contains data from a record, or you can add a blank column to display the results of a calculation rather than the values from an existing field.

Using Drag and Drop

If the Add Field dialog box is not displayed, select Worksheet ➤ Add Field or click on the Add field icon from the SmartIcons toolbar. Select the field and drag it from the Add Field dialog box to the column headings. Approach displays the name of the field in a gray box and displays a vertical gray line indicating where the field will be inserted. Release the mouse when the desired location has been selected.

Adding a Blank Column for Calculations

While most worksheet columns display fields from your database, you can also use a column to perform a calculation, just as you do in a spreadsheet. For example, you can display the employee name and annual salary in columns, then add a third column to compute the effect of giving each employee a 5% salary increase.

To insert a column, move the mouse pointer to any position above the column headings. Notice that the pointer turns into a small pointing block, similar to the base marker for home plate in baseball. Approach calls this the *wedge tool*. Move the wedge tool to the right border of the column where you want to insert the new column and click the mouse. Approach adds a blank column. (Alternatively, move to the right of any cell where you want the new column inserted and select Worksheet ➤ Add Column or click the Insert Column icon on the toolbar. A blank column will be inserted and the Formula dialog box will be displayed. You can then enter a formula, which is described in Chapter 19. You cannot assign a database field to this column.)

Calculations are described in the section "Using Calculations in a Worksheet" later in this chapter.

▸▸ **NOTE**

You can add a blank column as a separator. For instance, insert a column between name and address information, make it narrow, and format it with a distinctive color (such as red). This places a red stripe down a worksheet and helps you better visualize the grouping of name information from address information. Although this is purely cosmetic (no data is displayed or calculations performed), it is a perfectly good use of a column.

▸▸ Using Calculations in a Worksheet

You've seen how to use formulas when defining validation formulas or setting the value of a calculated field. Approach allows you to use formulas in a worksheet column. For example, if you have two dates in a record, you may wish to calculate the number of days between the two dates.

Chapter 19 explains how to create formulas. To enter a formula in a worksheet, add a new, blank column (see the section "Inserting a Column" earlier in this chapter), then enter the formula in the Formula dialog box. For example, you might enter **EndDate-BeginDate** in the cell to calculate the days between the ending date and beginning date fields. Approach inserts the value of the calculation in every record in the worksheet.

Unlike a calculated field, however, the formula is used only in the worksheet and is not available in other views. (A calculated field, on the other hand, which is defined within the database, is computed for every record. This computed value can be used anywhere—on a form, report, form letter, and so on—without having to define the formula. Because the formula is defined in the database itself, Approach lets you place a calculated field in a view.)

▶▶ Printing a Worksheet

To print a worksheet, select File ➤ Print. Remember that the Printing options you selected from the Printing tab in the InfoBox (date, page numbers, and heading) are used on the output.

You can preview your output by selecting File ➤ Preview.

▶▶ Making a Copy of Your Worksheet

To make a copy of your worksheet, switch to the Design environment, then select Edit ➤ Duplicate Worksheet. Approach makes a copy and names it "Copy of XXX," where XXX is the original worksheet name.

▶▶ Deleting Your Worksheet

To remove a worksheet from your Approach file, switch to the Design environment. Select Yes to confirm your request.

▶▶ Crosstabs

A *Cross-Tabulation* view is a powerful analytical tool. A crosstab organizes your data by breaking it down into components that can then be analyzed using various measures. For example, suppose you have the following data, which is also shown in Figure 10.10:

AGENT	PRODUCT	SALES	DATE
Anderson	Widgets	$100	2/1/95
Anderson	Sprockets	$123	2/1/95
Anderson	Widgets	$125	3/1/95
Anderson	Sprockets	$200	3/1/95
Bailey	Widgets	$75	2/1/95
Bailey	Widgets	$100	3/1/95
Bailey	Sprockets	$150	3/1/95
Crockett	Sprockets	$77	2/1/95
Crockett	Sprockets	$99	3/1/95
Crockett	Sprockets	$15	3/1/95
Davis	Widgets	$150	3/1/95
Davis	Doodads	$89	3/1/95

FIGURE 10.10

The sales data entered in a database, shown here in worksheet format. This data will be used to create crosstabs to analyze the performance of the agents. We've used a format of MONTH/YEAR for the SaleDate column.

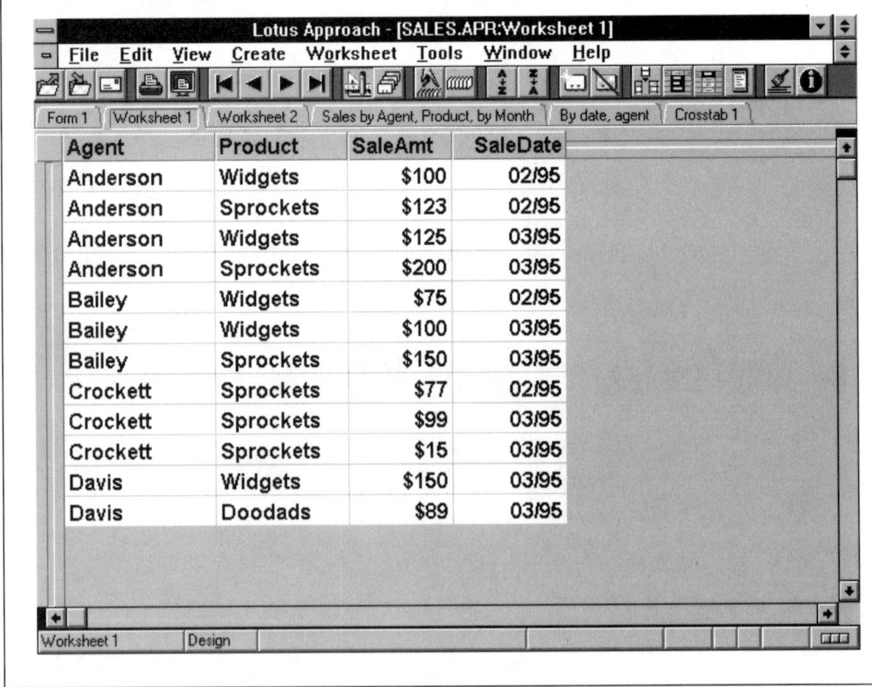

Agent	Product	SaleAmt	SaleDate
Anderson	Widgets	$100	02/95
Anderson	Sprockets	$123	02/95
Anderson	Widgets	$125	03/95
Anderson	Sprockets	$200	03/95
Bailey	Widgets	$75	02/95
Bailey	Widgets	$100	03/95
Bailey	Sprockets	$150	03/95
Crockett	Sprockets	$77	02/95
Crockett	Sprockets	$99	03/95
Crockett	Sprockets	$15	03/95
Davis	Widgets	$150	03/95
Davis	Doodads	$89	03/95

A crosstab can analyze sales by presenting a table showing:

1. Sales by agent for each product, by month
2. Sales by month for each agent, subdivided by product
3. Average sales by product

Figure 10.11 shows the crosstab for the first analysis (we've also added a total column).

FIGURE 10.11

Sales by agent for each product, by month. This crosstab helps you analyze the sales by agent.

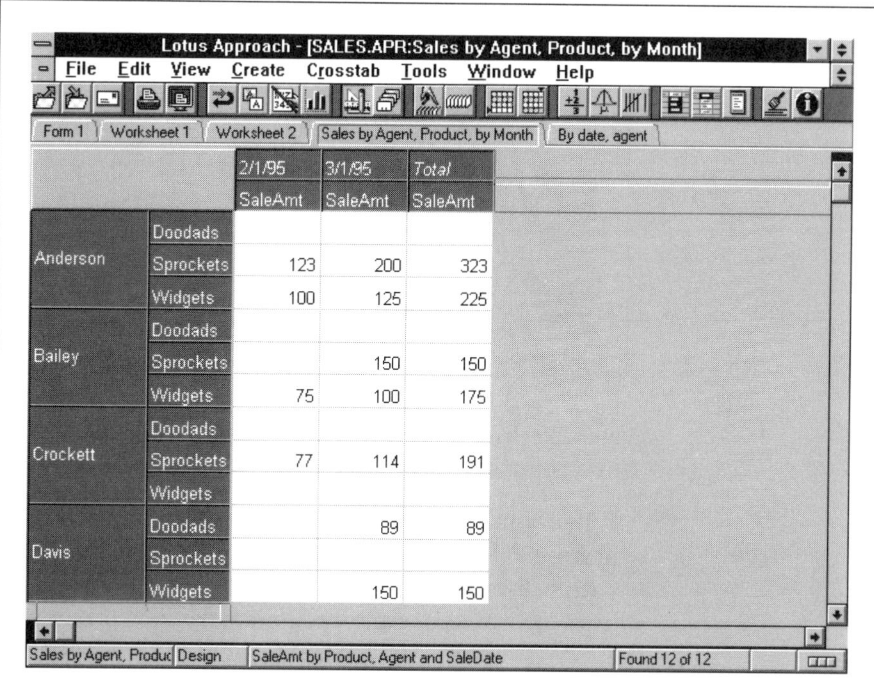

		2/1/95	3/1/95	*Total*
		SaleAmt	SaleAmt	SaleAmt
Anderson	Doodads			
	Sprockets	123	200	323
	Widgets	100	125	225
Bailey	Doodads			
	Sprockets		150	150
	Widgets	75	100	175
Crockett	Doodads			
	Sprockets	77	114	191
	Widgets			
Davis	Doodads		89	89
	Sprockets			
	Widgets		150	150

Figure 10.12 shows a different crosstab for the second analysis (using different formatting options). While the underlying data is the same, each crosstab gives you a slightly different perspective on the data.

Crosstabs are extremely useful when you want to analyze four or more factors. Once you have a crosstab defined, Approach makes it incredibly

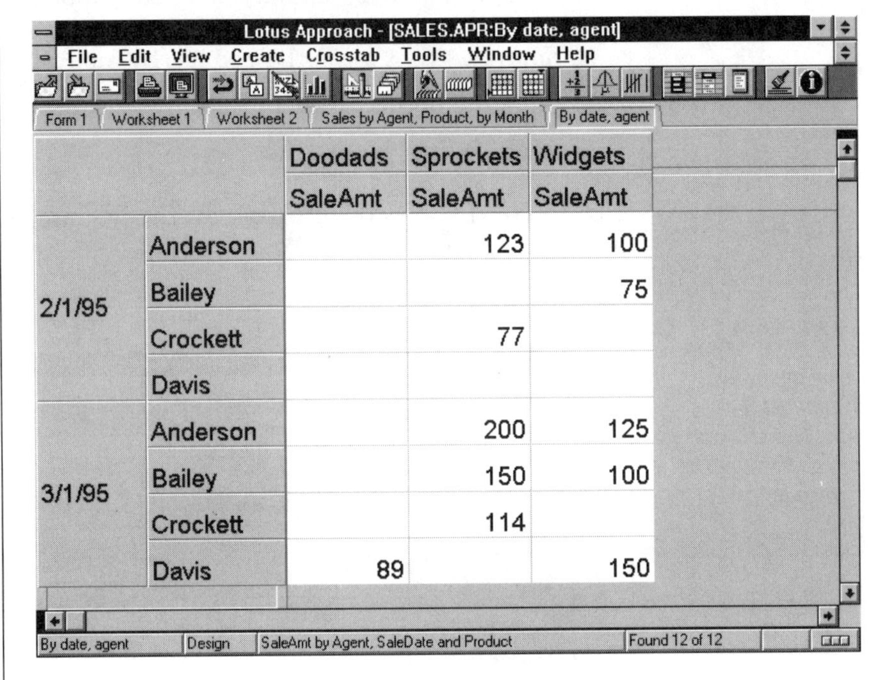

		Doodads	Sprockets	Widgets
		SaleAmt	SaleAmt	SaleAmt
2/1/95	Anderson		123	100
	Bailey			75
	Crockett		77	
	Davis			
3/1/95	Anderson		200	125
	Bailey		150	100
	Crockett		114	
	Davis	89		150

FIGURE 10.12

Sales by month for each agent, subdivided by product; the data is the same as Figure 10.11, but the result helps you view the data organized by date, then within date by agent.

easy to drag and drop field names within the crosstab to view the data in a different way.

When you create a crosstab, Approach searches your database for unique values. Each level in a row or column is automatically filled with values Approach finds. When you rearrange, add, or remove fields in your crosstab, Approach rescans your database and performs a new analysis. Notice that there is one line for Crockett's Sprocket sales for March 1, 1995, even though there were two records for such sales in the original database. The value in the crosstab, $114, is the sum of the two values in the database records: $99 and $15.

▸▸ Creating a Crosstab

Creating a crosstab is an easy, three-step process, thanks to the Crosstab Assistant.

To create a new crosstab:

1. Select Create ➤ Crosstab. The Crosstab Assistant appears, as shown in Figure 10.13.

FIGURE 10.13

The Crosstab Assistant steps you through creating a crosstab from scratch.

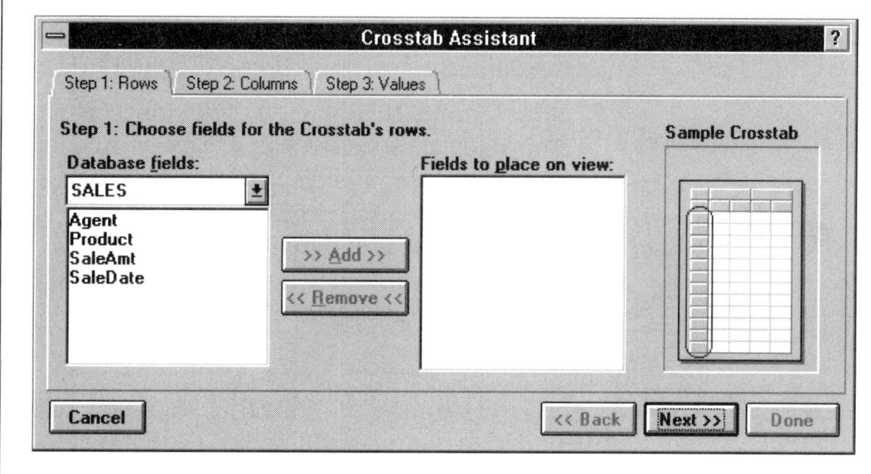

2. Select the main database and the fields to include in rows. (You can also select fields from a detail database.) The first field you select is the outer row. The next field you select subdivides the values from the first field. For example, to build the crosstab shown in Figure 10.11 earlier in this chapter, you would select Agent first, then Product. Each field you add to the list breaks down the data to another level for more detailed analysis. Click on Next or the Step 2 tab to select fields for the columns.
3. If you want to create a summary crosstab, you must click on a field in the Database fields list, but do **not** add it to the "Fields to place on view" list. (This is a minor quirk with the Crosstab Assistant and is necessary to get the Assistant to make the Done button available after you complete Step 4.) Approach will summarize the value for the field you select in the Values tab (in Step 4) if it is numeric, or count the number of values if the field you select is non-numeric (such as a text or date field). Otherwise, to create a regular crosstab, select the fields you want to use as column headers. Select the primary column heading first; the second field you select subdivides the

first field, as with rows. To build the crosstab shown in Figure 10.11, select the SaleDate field. Select Next or the Step 3 tab.

4. Select the database and field you want in the center of your crosstab, and the arithmetic function you want to perform. For example, you can select sum to summarize (total) all values for a field, select the maximum or minimum value, or count the number of values in your database. To build the crosstab shown in Figure 10.11, select the SaleAmt field and choose the Sum function.
5. Select Done. If you are using fields from more than one database, Approach asks you to identify the controlling database—called the main database. This main database controls which database is considered the "main" database and all other databases are considered to be detail databases, containing the "many" records in a one-to-many relationship, such as a Customer database to an Orders database.

After selecting the main database (if necessary), Approach creates the crosstab and displays the InfoBox. Approach will also add total rows and columns (Figure 10.11 shows the total column for SalesAmt; we deleted the row totals created by the Crosstab Assistant).

►► Modifying a Crosstab

Unlike forms and reports that you've seen so far, there is little difference between the Design and Browse environments in a crosstab. Almost all of the features described below can be done in either environment. (The major exception is the ability to delete or duplicate a crosstab.)

Furthermore, there is little difference between a crosstab and a worksheet. In fact, most of the modifications allowed to a crosstab are exactly the same as those allowed for a worksheet. You can select a cell, row, or column and apply changes using the InfoBox, change the column and row heights by dragging the cell borders with the mouse, and click directly on the heading to change the name of the column. Crosstabs, like worksheets, also let you split a window horizontally or vertically using the splitter bars. InfoBox options for Basics, Macros, and Printing are exactly the same for a crosstab as for a worksheet and Approach adds a Formula tab for columns.

You can modify the cells within a crosstab—adding background colors or borders, for example, or setting the display format or font. In addition, you can interactively work with the crosstab, moving column headings to rows, adding new fields, and selecting the calculation performed on any field (such as adding the values or counting the number of values in your database).

▶ Changing Field Formats

When you select a row or column heading, you automatically select similar rows and columns for all other values. For example, when you select and modify the SaleAmt column in Figure 10.11 earlier in this chapter, you change the SaleAmt column for all values in the crosstab, not just the single column you've selected. For example, you would be changing the SaleAmt column for Sales Date 2/1/95 and the SaleAmt column for Sales Date 3/1/95, shown in Figure 10.12 earlier in this chapter.

The higher the level you choose, the more cells you'll select (that is, more cells are selected as you move up the view from the center of the crosstab to the first column headings you encounter, to the column heading above that column heading and so on, or as you move farther left to select a row).

To change the formatting, click on the row or column heading containing the cells you want to format. Then select the InfoBox icon from the SmartIcons toolbar, double-click the mouse, press Ctrl+E, or click on the right mouse button and select Styles & Properties. Be sure the top of the InfoBox reads Settings for *Column* or Settings for *Row*. If the InfoBox reads Settings for Header, you'll change the formatting for the header cell only, not the numeric contents within the crosstab.

To change a heading, click twice (don't double-click) on the row or column heading. When you open the InfoBox, be sure the drop-down list at the top reads Settings for *Header*.

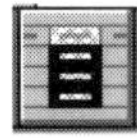

To quickly select the cells in the column but not the header, click on the column heading to select both the column header and the cells underneath. Then click on the Select Cells icon from the SmartIcons toolbar or select Crosstab ➤ Select, then choose Cells Only. Approach places a series of slash marks through the header, but keeps both the header and the cells selected. Changes you make in the InfoBox now apply only to the column cells and not the headers.

To quickly select the header, select the column. Next, choose the Select Label of Column icon from the SmartIcons toolbar or select Crosstab ➤ Select, then choose Header Only.

► Changing Row and Column Fields

Approach lets you move fields from the row headings to columns and vice versa, add new row and column fields, and change the field in the center of the crosstab (the one on which you're performing the calculation).

When you drag a field to the row or column, a new level is added depending on where you drop the field. As you drag a field to a column heading, for example, Approach displays the field name in a box and draws a dark horizontal line around it. If you drag the field so the horizontal line is at the top of the rows, the field is used as the top-level field.

This is best explained using an example. We made changes to the crosstab in Figure 10.12 earlier in this chapter. Suppose instead of the arrangement shown in Figure 10.12 you want to switch the order of the rows. Instead of date subdivided by agent, you want agent further subdivided by date. To switch these rows, click in any of the agent cells (you can click on Anderson, Bailey, Crockett, or Davis). The mouse pointer turns into a hand. Drag the hand to the left, until it is on the left border of the date cells. As you drag the hand, it turns into a clenched fist and Approach attaches the field name (Agent) in a box along with the fist. As you move the fist to the left of the dates, you'll see Approach display a dark vertical line along the date cell's left border. This tells you Approach will use this location when you release the mouse. Be careful that the hand does not change into a picture of the field name pointing to a wastebasket. That icon means the field will be *removed* from the crosstab when you release the mouse. Fortunately, you can use the Undo feature (select Edit ➤ Undo, press Ctrl+Z, or click on the Undo icon in the SmartIcons toolbar) to reverse your last action (removing or repositioning a row or column).

Figure 10.14 shows the screen as you drag the Agent field to the left of the date 2/1/95.

Figure 10.15 shows the resulting crosstab. Notice that now the primary breakdown is by agent. Each agent's data is then broken down by sale date.

FIGURE 10.14

As you drag any agent box to the left of the date cells, Approach displays the cursor as a clenched fist and the name of the field you are moving.

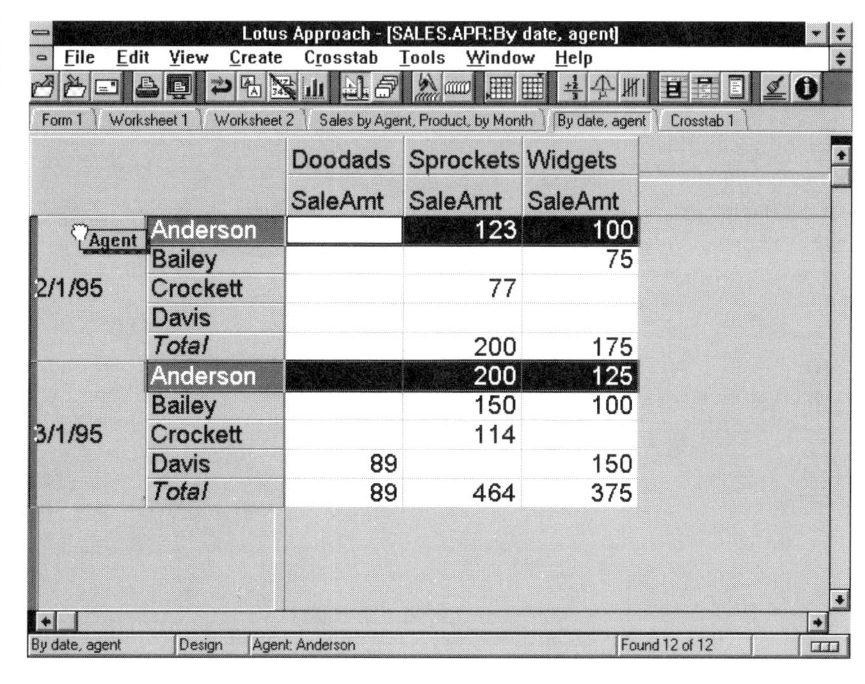

To remove a field from the crosstab, drag the field to the top of the screen. When the mouse pointer changes to a field name pointing to a wastebasket, release the mouse. Approach redraws your crosstab without the field.

You can drag a field from a column to a row and vice versa. For example, we can take the crosstab from Figure 10.15 and drag the date field from its position as a row to a column. To do so, click on any date cell, then drag the cell until Approach displays a horizontal line just under the product columns (the cells marked Doodads, Sprockets, and Widgets). When you release the mouse, the crosstab now appears with a breakdown of products by date, as shown in Figure 10.16. A column will be displayed even if all values in the field have no values. For example, the column for doodad sales for 2/1/95 is empty, but the column is included in the crosstab for consistency.

In addition to moving fields between rows and columns, you can add new fields. Click on the Add Fields icon from the SmartIcons toolbar

FIGURE 10.15

When you release the mouse, the crosstab has been redesigned to show the breakdown by agent first, then a breakdown by sale date.

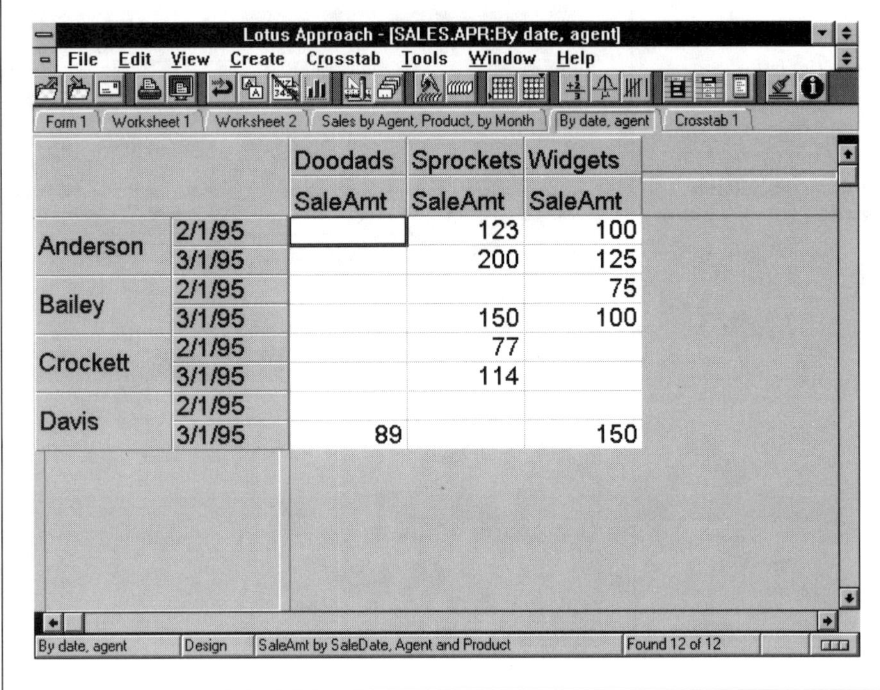

or select Crosstab ➤ Add Fields, then drag a field from the list box to the form. Drag the field to a column or row heading.

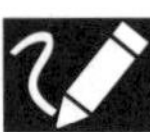

▸▸ **NOTE**

If you drag the field to the center of the crosstab, Approach adds the field to the current fields being calculated. This makes a slightly more complex analysis. If you add a new non-numeric field, such as a text or date field, Approach will automatically count the number of values; new numeric fields are automatically totaled.

As you've seen, Approach uses drag-and-drop to let you rearrange a crosstab. You can also drag on any row or column border to change its width or height.

FIGURE 10.16

Dragging the date from the row breakdown to the column heading further subdivides the figures for products by date.

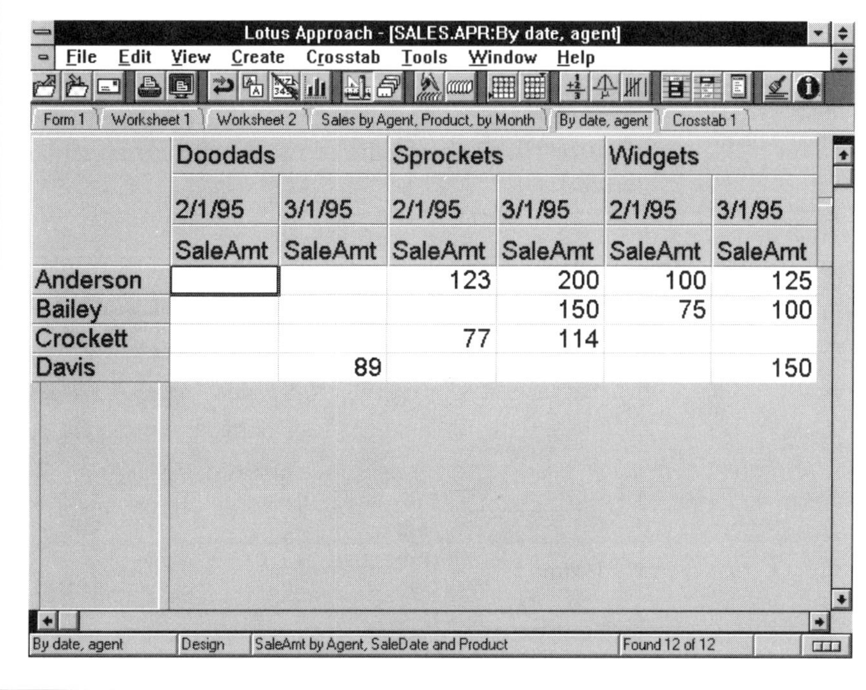

► Adding Summary Columns and Rows

With Approach you can add a new row or column that subtotals or totals values in that dimension. You can use the menu system or the mouse cursor to quickly add summaries.

To add a summary using the mouse cursor, position the cursor in the bottom-left corner of the last field of the level you want to add.

For example, in Figure 10.15 earlier in this chapter, you can add a total line that summarizes sales for all sales agents by moving the cursor along the bottom border of the last agent (Davis) in the crosstab (the mouse pointer changes to a wedge) and clicking the mouse. This technique is often tricky, however, since the mouse can also change to a two-headed arrow for changing the row height. A better technique is to use the menus: Select Crosstab ➤ Summarize Columns or click on the Add a summary row icon from the SmartIcons toolbar. Approach adds a Total row to the bottom of the crosstab and uses the value in the field displayed in the left-most position (Agent Name in this example) to present a sum.

Adding a total column works in the same fashion. Use the Crosstab ➤ Summarize Rows command or click on the Add a summary column icon from the SmartIcons toolbar. Approach adds a total column to your crosstab.

Figure 10.17 shows the crosstab with both row and column totals added.

FIGURE 10.17

A crosstab with both row and column totals.

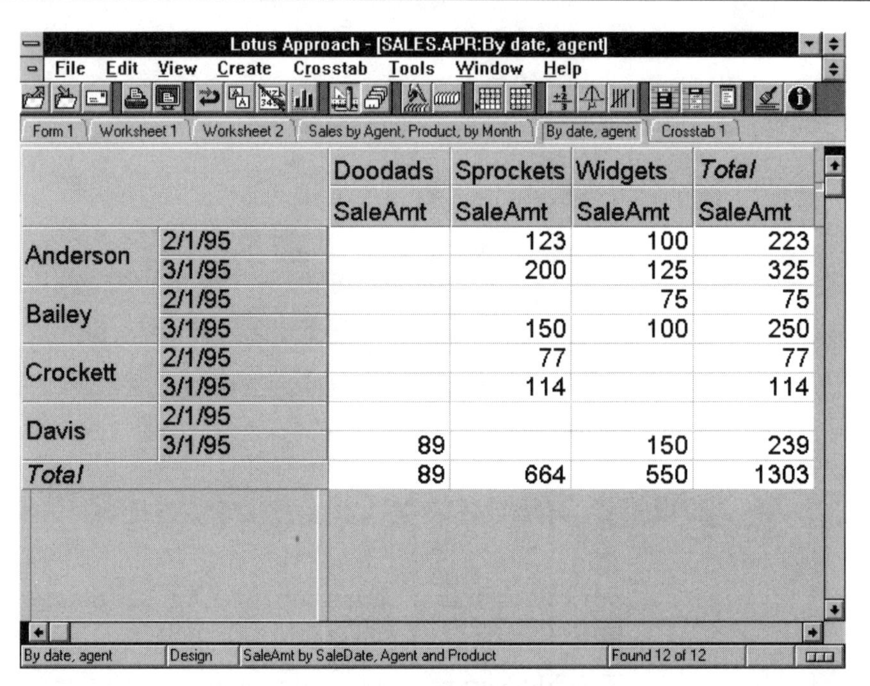

		Doodads	Sprockets	Widgets	*Total*
		SaleAmt	SaleAmt	SaleAmt	SaleAmt
Anderson	2/1/95		123	100	223
	3/1/95		200	125	325
Bailey	2/1/95			75	75
	3/1/95		150	100	250
Crockett	2/1/95		77		77
	3/1/95		114		114
Davis	2/1/95				
	3/1/95	89		150	239
Total		89	664	550	1303

You can add intermediate totals as well as crosstab totals. For example, look at the crosstab in Figure 10.17. To add a total line for each sales agent (to summarize sales for both February and March for each agent), move the cursor until a wedge appears along the bottom border of any date cell (the date field is the level you want to summarize on) and click the mouse button. In this example you could move the mouse cursor until it is positioned along the border between 3/1/95 (for Anderson) and 2/1/94 (for Bailey). When the cursor changes to a wedge shape, click the mouse.

Approach adds a third row to every sales agent, as shown in Figure 10.18.

FIGURE 10.18

Adding a Total Row summarizes sales for each product by agent.

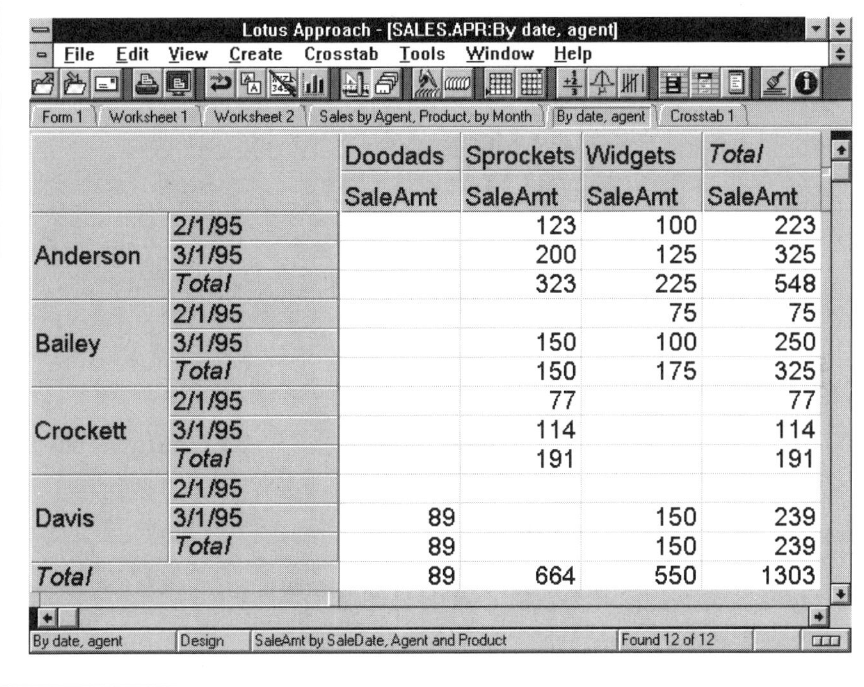

		Doodads	Sprockets	Widgets	*Total*
		SaleAmt	SaleAmt	SaleAmt	SaleAmt
Anderson	2/1/95		123	100	223
	3/1/95		200	125	325
	Total		323	225	548
Bailey	2/1/95			75	75
	3/1/95		150	100	250
	Total		150	175	325
Crockett	2/1/95		77		77
	3/1/95		114		114
	Total		191		191
Davis	2/1/95				
	3/1/95	89		150	239
	Total	89		150	239
Total		89	664	550	1303

To remove the total row, click on the word Total to highlight the row, then press Del.

Adding summary columns works in the same fashion. To add a total for each Doodad, Sprocket, or Widget column shown in Figure 10.16 earlier in this chapter, move the cursor to the intersection of Doodads, Sprockets, 3/1/95 (for Doodads), and 2/1/95 (for Sprockets) until the cursor changes to a wedge, then click the mouse. Approach adds a column summarizing doodads for the two dates. Columns summarizing sprockets and widgets are also shown.

Changing What the Crosstab Calculates

The arithmetic function you selected when in the Crosstab Assistant can be changed using the icons in the SmartIcons toolbar. To change the function, select all cells in the worksheet by clicking on the area of the crosstab above the rows and to the left of the column headings, then select one of these icons:

Icon	**Purpose**
Bell Curve	Average
Tick Marks	Count
1+2=3	Total
Wave with red mark at bottom	Minimum value
Wave with red mark at top	Maximum value
Bell Curve with omega underneath	Standard deviation
Omega squared	Variance

Only the first three icons are on the default Crosstab SmartIcons toolbar, but you can change the toolbar by following the directions in Chapter 18.

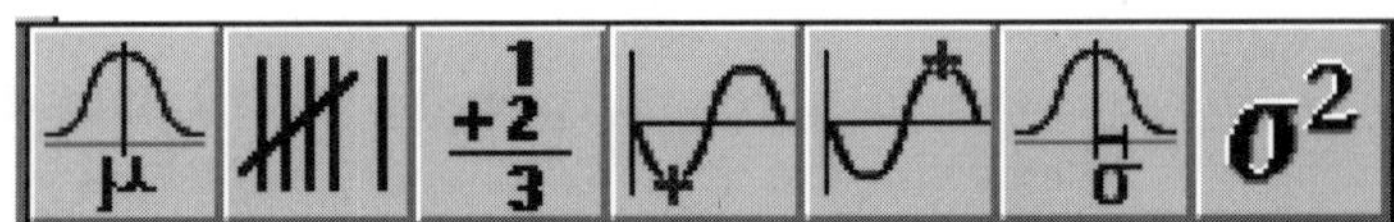

You can also use the InfoBox to change the calculation. For example, to change the calculation for all cells or selected cells, select (click) the bottom-most column label(s) for the cells you want to change. For example, to modify the crosstab shown in Figure 10.18, click on any SaleAmt column heading. This highlights all cells within the crosstab itself. Open the InfoBox (right-click and choose Styles & Properties, press Ctrl+E, or click the InfoBox icon from the SmartIcons toolbar). Be sure the "Settings for" drop-down list is set to Column. Click on the Formula tab, then choose the calculation you want (average, sum, and so on). The Formula tab is shown in Figure 10.19.

FIGURE 10.19

Use the InfoBox to change the calculation the crosstab performs. Select the columns used in the calculation, then open the InfoBox to the Formula tab and choose the calculation you want.

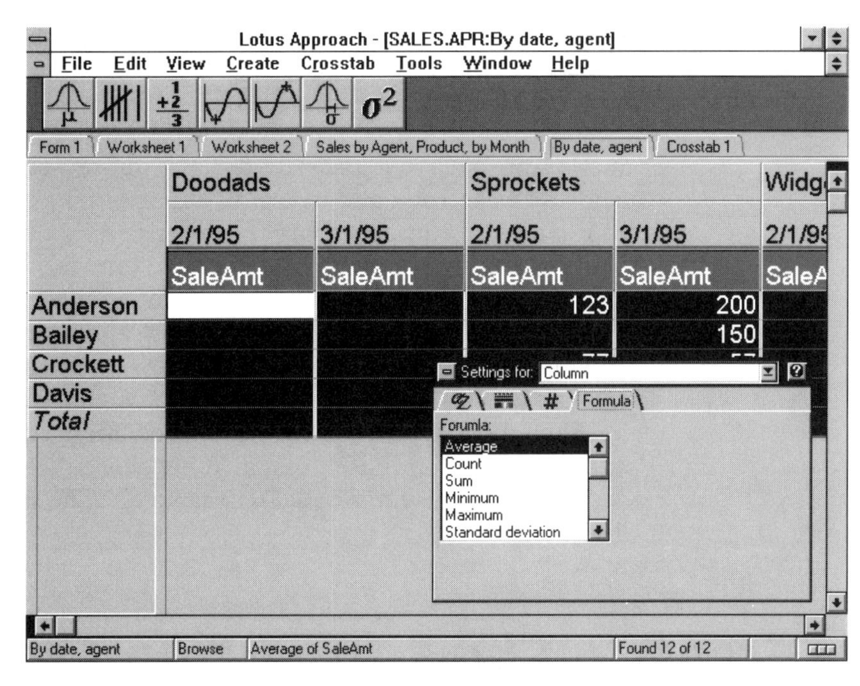

TIP

You can add more than one column to a crosstab to perform multiple calculations. For example, you can add a summary column to calculate the total of the monthly sales by agent, then add another column, change its calculation to Average, and compute the average for the same figures. Another use might be to compare the minimum and maximum values in two adjacent columns, or compare the average with the standard deviation, which gives a measure of the "average" versus how values are actually clustered among the entire set of values.

►► Save Time: View Your Crosstab Design, Not Your Data

While Approach will instantly refresh your crosstab when you move fields between rows and columns, this may take considerable time if your database contains a large number of records. You can look at the field names rather than all the data in a crosstab by deselecting View ➤ Show Data. Toggling this option switches between the full crosstab view (with field values and calculations) and a simple crosstab showing only the fields and where totals will appear. Using this data-less layout, you can quickly switch rows and columns. Since Approach doesn't refresh the display with the data and calculations, designing the crosstab in this fashion is infinitely faster. When you're ready to test your new design, select View ➤ Show Data again and the full crosstab is displayed.

►► Create a Chart from Your Crosstab

Approach has a comprehensive charting tool you'll learn more about in Chapter 14. However, there's a shortcut you can use to turn your Crosstab view into a chart. Click on the Create Chart crosstab icon from the SmartIcons toolbar, select Crosstab ➤ Chart Crosstab, or right-click the mouse and choose Chart Crosstab. Approach creates a default bar chart, similar to the one shown in Figure 10.20. The chart is created as a new view that you can save just like any other view (a form, worksheet, or crosstab, for example).

For more information about how to modify the chart, see Chapter 14.

►► Refreshing Your Crosstab Calculations

When you change, delete, or add new records, Approach automatically recalculates your crosstab. If others are working on the database at the same time you are, and you want the most up-to-date information for

FIGURE 10.20

Approach can create a chart from your cross-tab, as shown here.

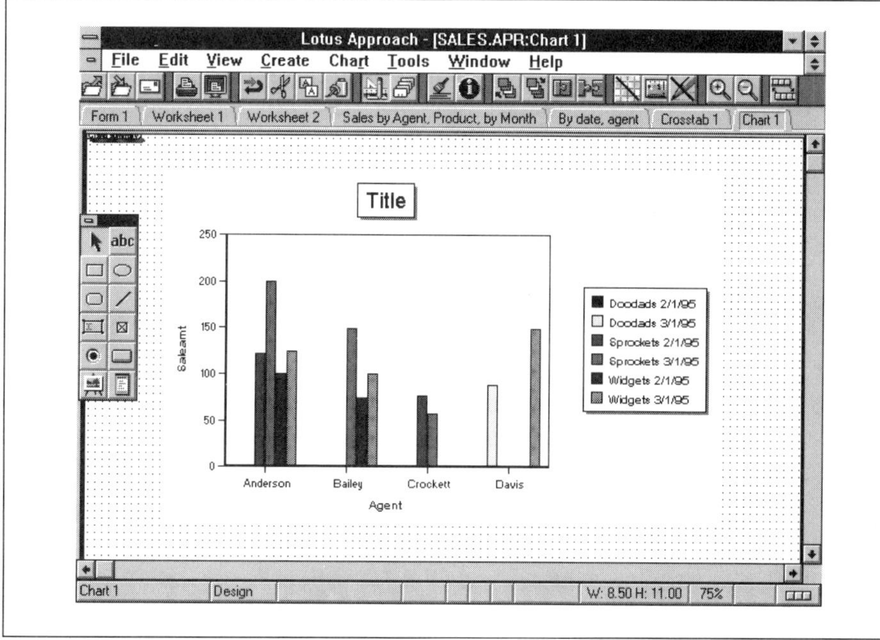

the database, choose Crosstab ➤ Refresh or press Ctrl+R. Approach reads the database and updates your crosstab immediately.

►► Making a Copy of Your Crosstab

Setting up a crosstab can be a simple task if you use the Crosstab Assistant. However, you may wish to modify several characteristics of the default crosstab layout, such as the fonts or field formatting used. If you want to copy this crosstab to a new crosstab view and then make further changes (perhaps rearranging fields in rows and columns), select Edit ➤ Duplicate Crosstab from the Design environment. You cannot copy a crosstab from the Browse environment.

►► Copying Your Data to the Clipboard

You can select any number of cells from the crosstab (or a worksheet), then select Edit ➤ Copy to copy the data to the clipboard. If you select the entire crosstab, you can then select Edit ➤ Copy View (or press Ctrl+C). Approach asks if you want to copy the current view or all views. If you want to include data from a single database, check the Include data box and select the database. You can also select the data you want: the entire database, just the found set, or just the empty databases. Select OK to perform the copy.

▸▸ Deleting Your Crosstab

When the crosstab is no longer of value—or you have made so many changes that it is easier to simply start over—you can delete the current crosstab by selecting Edit ➤ Delete Crosstab from the Design environment. You cannot delete a crosstab from the Browse environment.

▸▸ Turning Your Worksheet into a Crosstab

So far in this chapter you've seen two spreadsheet-like grids that provide access to or analysis of your data. Approach adds one more twist: You can turn your worksheet into a crosstab using the mouse.

▸▸ **WARNING**

Although you can make changes in the crosstab, you *cannot* turn the crosstab back into a worksheet—this is a one-way conversion.

With a worksheet as the current view, click once on the column heading and Approach changes the cursor into a hand. Drag the column heading left—as though you were moving it to an earlier column position in the worksheet—and keep dragging it until Approach displays a vertical dark line in the gutter area (the gray area to the left of the leftmost column). Release the mouse and Approach turns the worksheet into a crosstab. You can then manipulate the rows and columns as you can any other crosstab. However, as we stated above, you *cannot* turn the crosstab back into a worksheet—this is a one-way conversion.

►► Summary and a Look Ahead

In this chapter you've seen how to create a worksheet and a crosstab. Worksheets are spreadsheet-like grids that show one record per row and one field per column. You can hide columns, change their arrangement, and format the fields just like you can in data entry forms. In addition, you can add new records, change the data in existing records, and delete records, including groups of records.

Crosstabs are powerful analytical views that let you organize your data by breaking it down into components that can then be analyzed using average, count, maximum, and standard deviation. You can use the mouse to drag and drop field names between rows and columns, adding finer levels of details. You can also add totals and create charts instantly.

In Chapter 11 we'll take a look at another analytical tool—reports. Reports allow you to print your data in a familiar columnar or structured format. Like crosstabs, reports can summarize and group data for you quickly.

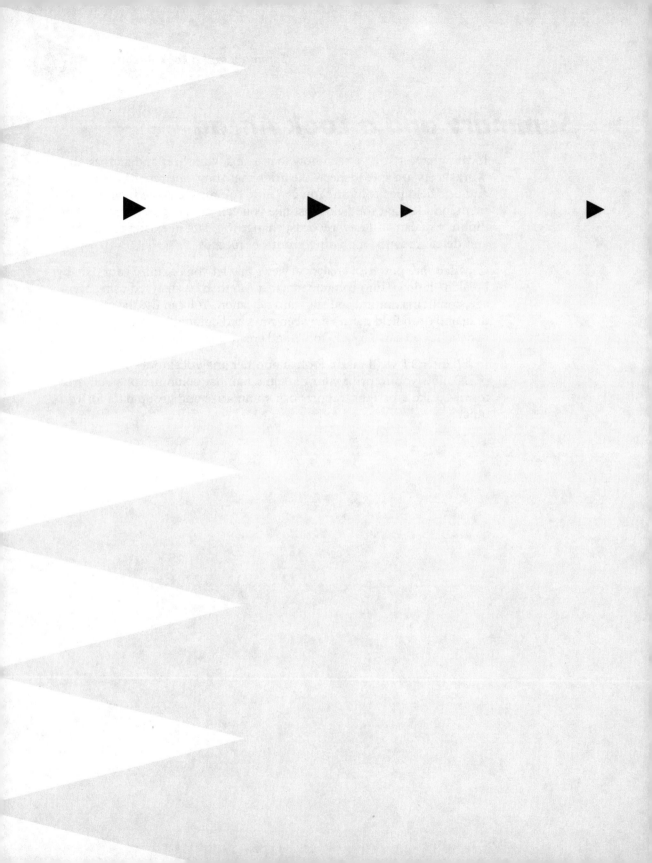

CHAPTER 11

Reports

▸▸ FAST TRACK

▸ *To create a report* **375**

select Create ➤ Report. Enter a title for your report and select the layout, then choose the style and layout. Approach displays a thumbnail of the report layout in the Sample Report shown on the right of the Report Assistant screen. Select Next or the Step 2 tab to select fields for the report. If you selected a SmartMaster layout that includes summaries, select the Step 3 tab, then select the field you want to sort on, calculation (check the "Calculate the" check box and select the type of calculation you want), and choose the field upon which you want to perform this calculation. Select Done.

▸ *To adjust columns quickly in a report* **386**

turn Columns mode on. Select a field in a column and choose Object. If the Turn on Columns option contains a check mark in front of it, Columns mode is on. To toggle the Columns mode, select Turn on Columns.

▸ *To add a summary panel* **388**

select the column within any body section that you want to summarize. Click on the "Group and create trailing summary" button on the SmartIcons toolbar to add a trailing summary section or choose the "Group and create leading summary" button to create a summary section at the beginning of every group when the field value changes. Alternatively, click on the field and right-click the mouse. Select Object ➤ PowerClick, then choose Leading Summary or Trailing Summary. If Approach asks if you want to re-sort the data, select Yes. Approach adds a summary section, but does not add a total field to the section. To create a summary panel using the menus, choose Create ➤ Summary from the main menu and complete the dialog box. To use the PowerClick method, click on the field for which you want to create a summary panel and choose Object ➤ PowerClick, then choose Trailing Summary or Leading Summary.

► *To change the properties of a report* 399

click anywhere on the report, preferably where there is no other object present. If the InfoBox does not display "Settings for: Report" at the top of the dialog box, select this option from the drop-down list. In the InfoBox you can change the report name, change the main database, keep records together on the same screen, or select the number of columns for the report.

► *To sort data on a report on a single field* 403

click anywhere in that field and choose the Sort Ascending icon from the SmartIcons toolbar (to sort from A to Z, 0 to 9) or the Sort Descending icon (to sort in the reverse order). You can also select the field, then choose Object ➤ Sort, then choose Ascending or Descending, or choose Browse ➤ Sort.

► *To print a report* 404

choose the Printer icon from the SmartIcons toolbar. Approach displays the Print dialog box. You can also select File ➤ Print from the Browse or Design environments, or press Ctrl+P.

▶▶ **Approach** provides several views for working with data. Forms let you add, edit, and delete records. Worksheets list data in columns and rows. Crosstabs perform analysis. In this chapter you'll learn about reports, which let you show data from multiple records on one page (or screen). Reports can quickly sort and subtotal information, such as sales by region.

Reports are most often associated with printed output. Reports are designed to create a piece of paper on which information from your database is displayed and/or summarized. Reports offer a permanent record of the state of your database at a particular time. For example, the report you run today of average salary per employee may be different from next month's report because in the interim you may add or terminate employees, other employees may quit, and you may give raises to one or more employees. Printed reports provide a good historical record of the data in your database at a particular point in time.

Reports are a bit like combining the features of worksheets and crosstabs. Reports allow you to display multiple records on a page or screen, just as you can with worksheets. However, reports go far beyond worksheets because they can create subtotals and totals, sort records, and perform calculations on intermediate results. Similar to a crosstab, you can ask for summaries (counts, averages, smallest and largest value). As with other forms, reports let you select the fields and the presentation of the data.

In this chapter you'll learn how to create new reports and modify existing ones. You'll learn how Approach's Report Assistant makes it easy to get the basics into a Report view, and how the program's Design environment for reports is similar in principal to the Design environment for forms.

Approach is unique among database programs, however. In addition to displaying data on your screen in a report, Approach actually lets you edit the data on a report. This provides a tremendous increase in your productivity. For example, suppose you create a list of employees that includes their employment status and annual salary. When you review a report, you may see an error in the data—an employee's annual salary may be $3,000 when you know it should be $30,000. Rather than having to switch to another view, find the record, and make the correction, you can actually click on the field in the report and make the change *immediately*, with an absolute minimum of fuss. (There is one obvious and natural exception to editing report data: You cannot edit summary fields, such as subtotals and totals.)

You may wish to mark corrections on the physical, printed output when you're away from your computer, then transcribe your changes from the printed report to the actual data, perhaps using a data entry form.

►► Report Styles

There are several report styles that you can create in Approach. We'll review several of them here.

To begin, suppose you have a database that contains information about the dealers who sell your product. We'll use the sample database supplied with Approach for the reports in this chapter, and add a credit limit field that uses a numeric field type. The tutorial file we used was stored in the C:\APPROACH\TUTORIAL\FILES\DEALERS.APR directory. The fields include the following. Next to the fields appear the field names as listed in the Dealers database. These field names appear in the figures in this chapter:

- Company Name (COMPANY)
- Customer ID (CUST-ID)
- Contact Name (CONTACT)
- Street Address (STREET)
- City (CITY)
- State (STATE)
- Zip Code (ZIP)
- Credit Terms (CREDIT)

- Sales Representative Name (SALESREP)
- Sales Region (REGION)
- Credit Limit (This is our new field.)

The version of this database came from a beta version of Approach and may not resemble the final data in the shipping product. We also modified some of the data within this database to produce more interesting reports.

The report shown in Figure 11.1 was created to list several fields from every record. It is similar in style to a worksheet, and is called a columnar report, since the data is arranged in columns. The report is displayed in the Preview environment, which is similar to Print Preview modes of most Windows applications. Notice that the mouse cursor changes to a mouse and magnifying glass, telling us that when we click the left mouse button we'll zoom in on the report, and when we click the right mouse button we'll zoom out.

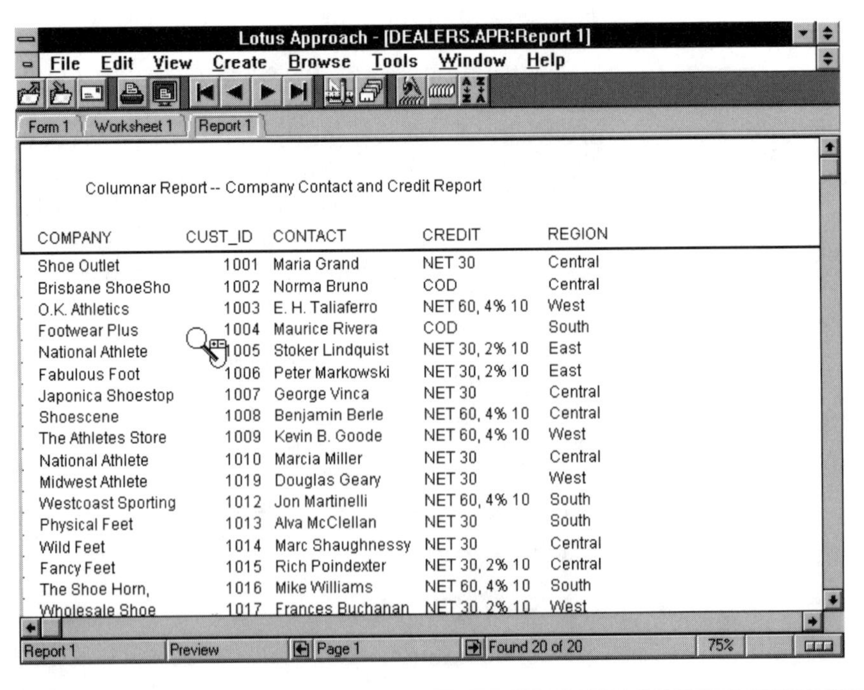

Columnar Report -- Company Contact and Credit Report

COMPANY	CUST_ID	CONTACT	CREDIT	REGION
Shoe Outlet	1001	Maria Grand	NET 30	Central
Brisbane ShoeSho	1002	Norma Bruno	COD	Central
O.K. Athletics	1003	E. H. Taliaferro	NET 60, 4% 10	West
Footwear Plus	1004	Maurice Rivera	COD	South
National Athlete	1005	Stoker Lindquist	NET 30, 2% 10	East
Fabulous Foot	1006	Peter Markowski	NET 30, 2% 10	East
Japonica Shoestop	1007	George Vinca	NET 30	Central
Shoescene	1008	Benjamin Berle	NET 60, 4% 10	Central
The Athletes Store	1009	Kevin B. Goode	NET 60, 4% 10	West
National Athlete	1010	Marcia Miller	NET 30	Central
Midwest Athlete	1019	Douglas Geary	NET 30	West
Westcoast Sporting	1012	Jon Martinelli	NET 60, 4% 10	South
Physical Feet	1013	Alva McClellan	NET 30	South
Wild Feet	1014	Marc Shaughnessy	NET 30	Central
Fancy Feet	1015	Rich Poindexter	NET 30, 2% 10	Central
The Shoe Horn,	1016	Mike Williams	NET 60, 4% 10	South
Wholesale Shoe	1017	Frances Buchanan	NET 30, 2% 10	West

FIGURE 11.1 ▸

A standard columnar report lists selected fields for every record. There are no calculations in this report, which is shown in the Preview environment.

Figure 11.2 is a variation of this report. We want to have a listing of customers by Sales Representative, so we'll sort the database data first by sales representative, and then by company name. This report places the agent's name in what Approach calls a *leading summary panel*, which we'll discuss in a moment, so that an agent's name is listed only once for a group of records. Then, the companies assigned to this agent are listed under the agent's name, in another panel called the *body panel*.

FIGURE 11.2

Leading grouped summary shows all customers by sales representative. We've added totals by agent for the credit limit field, which tells us the total credit available to customers assigned to each representative. You may wish to change the heading to Credit Limit to distinguish this column from the Credit Terms field.

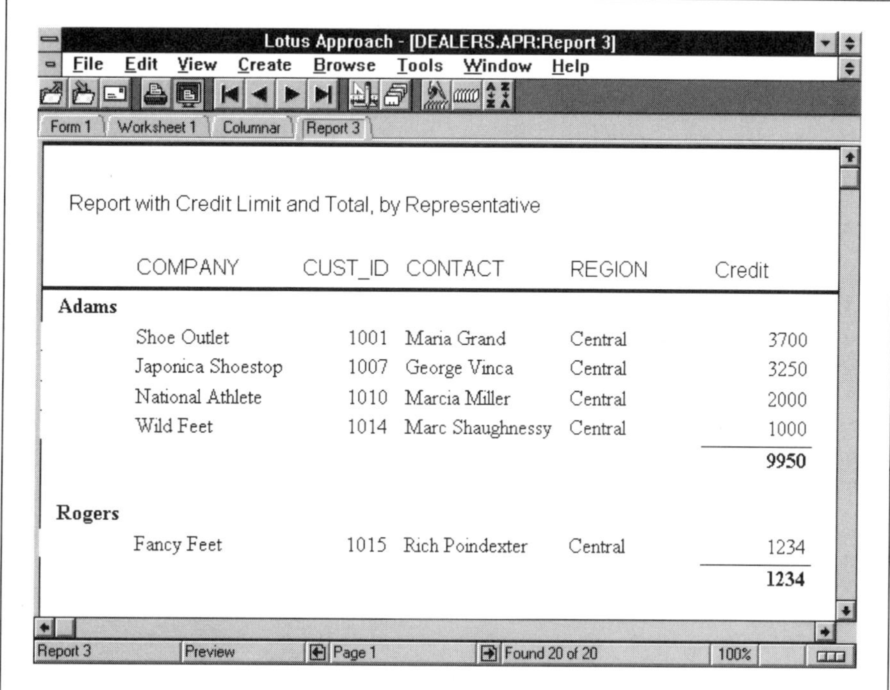

Figure 11.2 also adds calculations. This report will not print the credit terms but will include the credit limit assigned to the company. Every time the name changes in the leading summary panel, the report calculates the total of the available credit for all customers that are assigned to a given representative.

Finally, in Approach we have the option to perform one more calculation. We can add a grand total that totals the sales for all agents.

In addition to columnar reports, Approach can create reports that more closely resemble forms. These reports use the Standard Smart-Master layout, positioning data fields anywhere on a report. Thus, they are sometimes called free-form reports. You can use more than one row to display data in a free-form report. Typically, you'll put the data from one record on a single printed page, to resemble paper forms that are familiar to you. In fact, such forms are most often compared to data entry forms, since a single page on a report is similar to a single screen of a data entry form.

For example, your free-form report can display the agent's name on the first line, contact name and address information on subsequent lines, and the credit terms and credit limit on yet another line. A free-form report is shown in Figure 11.3.

FIGURE 11.3 ▶

A report created using the Standard Smart-Master layout and Chisel2 SmartMaster style to add interest. One database record is printed on each report page.

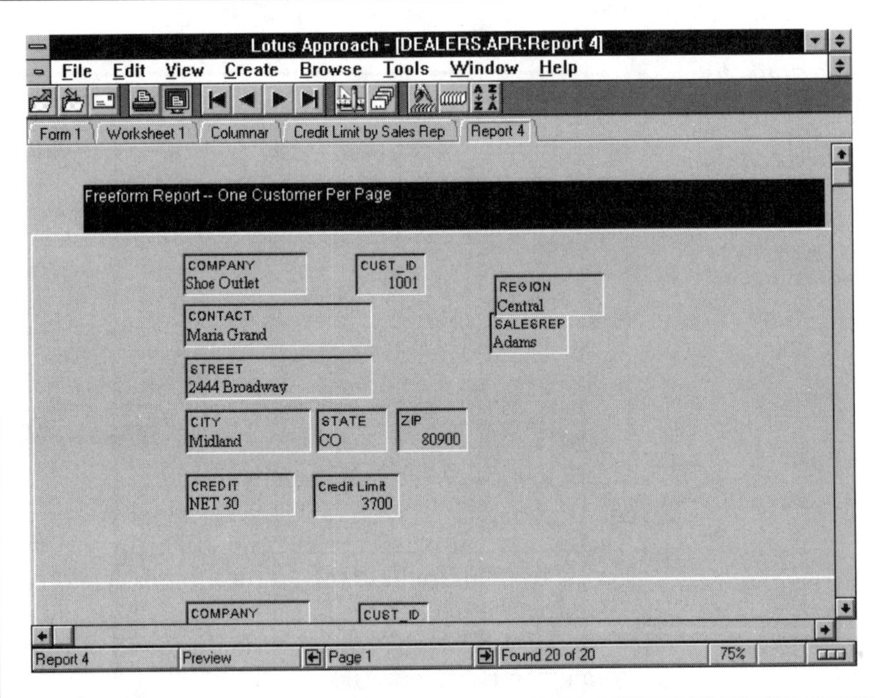

In this chapter you'll learn how to use the Report Assistant to create these reports, and you'll learn about the sections of a report, including the title, body, and summary panels.

▸▸ Creating a New Report

The Report Assistant helps you create a new report by asking you to select the style and layout of a report, then select the fields you'll need to place on the report. The Report Assistant is similar to the Form Assistant, described in Chapter 7. Terms such as *SmartMaster style* and *SmartMaster layout* are described in that chapter. Because the Report Assistant and Form Assistant are so similar, we'll only highlight the differences here.

To create a new report, select Create ➤ Report. Approach presents the Report Assistant, shown in Figure 11.4. Enter a title for your report and select the layout, then choose the style. (By default the SmartMaster layout is set to *Blank*, and the SmartMaster style has nothing to show, so select a layout other than blank to see the result of your SmartMaster style selection.) Approach displays a thumbnail sketch of the report layout in the Sample Report shown on the right of the Report Assistant screen.

FIGURE 11.4 ▶

The Report Assistant helps you through the various steps necessary to create a variety of report styles.

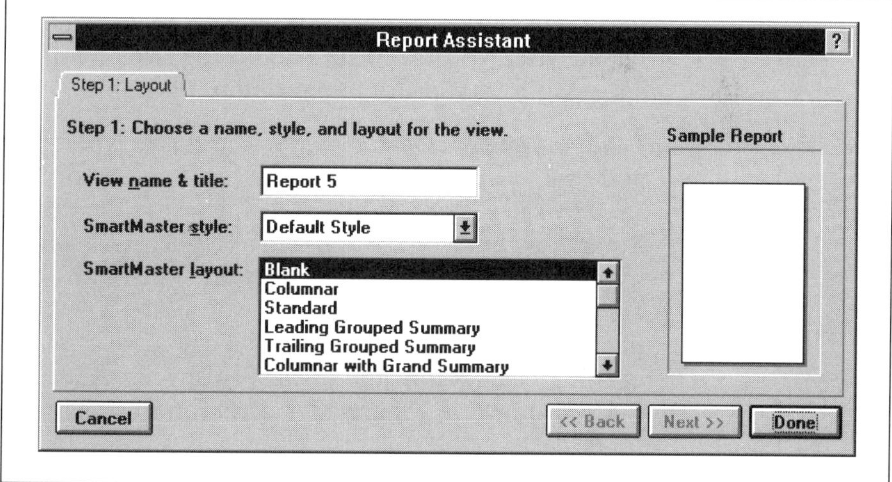

SmartMaster Layout Options

Approach offers several predefined SmartMaster layouts. These layouts provide the easiest way to include subtotals and sorting on a report. Trust me—if ever there was a reason to use a template, these SmartMaster report layouts are it.

Columnar reports show one field per column, one record per row. They look very similar to a worksheet. Columnar reports are good for quick listings where no summarization is needed. However, be aware that if you select more columns than will fit on a single page, Approach creates a second page and includes the "overflow" fields on the second page. Therefore, when selecting columnar reports be sure to include just a few columns or use small font sizes. (You may also wish to print your report in landscape mode [sideways] to make it wider—select File ➤ Print Setup, then choose the Landscape orientation.) To see if your report has spanned multiple pages, choose a small zoom ratio (such as 25%) and click on any section of a report (called a *panel*), such as a *body line* (an individual line on a report) or the *header* (such as the report name and current date shown at the top of each page) of your report. If the boundary spans pages, your report data does too.

Standard reports are a variation of data entry forms. Fields are displayed across the first row. If more fields are selected than fit in one row, Approach uses another line and begins to fill that line with the remaining fields you selected. Approach will add as many lines as needed to display all selected fields from each record. This option is usually preferred when you are unsure about the size of a line and do not want to span pages, as the Columnar option permits.

Leading grouped summary reports are used when you want to sort data and display subtotals. For example, suppose you want to summarize all sales by sales agent. When you choose the Leading Grouped Summary SmartMaster layout, Approach's Report Assistant will ask you to specify the field that you want to sort on. The report displays the field value once for every group of records containing a matching value. When the field value changes, Approach will calculate a summary (sum, average, or other calculation) for a field you specify. A leading grouped summary is shown in Figure 11.2 earlier in this chapter.

Trailing grouped summary reports are also used when you want to sort data and display subtotals. They are similar to leading grouped summary reports, with one important difference. The *key value* (the field you're sorting on) is displayed on the same line as the total (or other calculation) rather than at the beginning of the data group. When you choose the Trailing Grouped Summary SmartMaster layout, the Report Assistant will ask you to specify the field you want to sort on.

When the field value changes, Approach will calculate a summary (sum, average, or other calculation) for a field you specify. A trailing grouped summary is shown in Figure 11.5.

FIGURE 11.5

A trailing grouped summary puts the changed value on the same line as the calculation. Here the sales representative's name is on the same line as the total credit limit for the companies assigned to the representative.

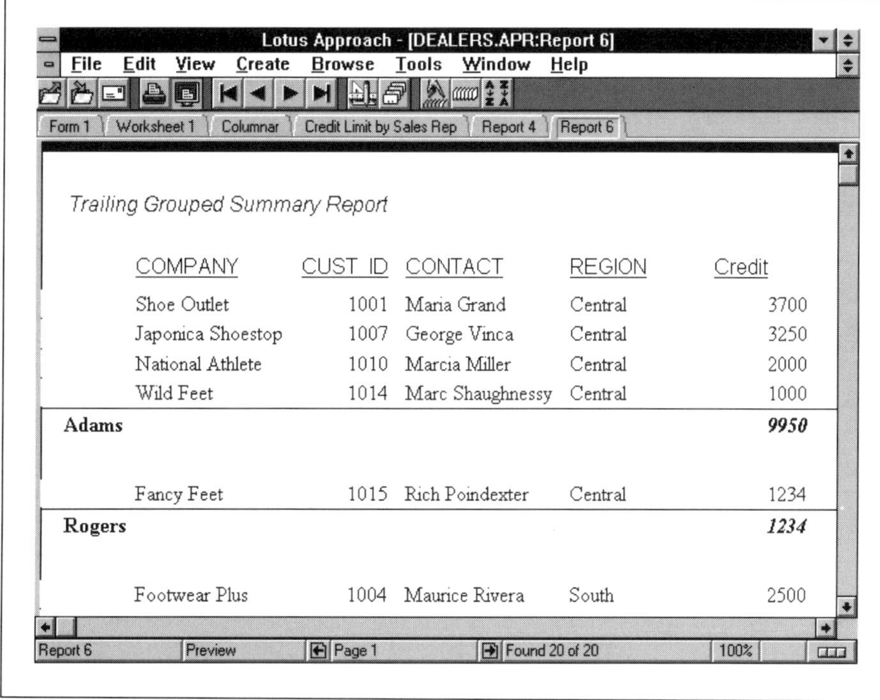

You can create multiple trailing grouped summaries (as well as multiple leading grouped summaries) on a report. For example, you can summarize a report by credit limit within region for each salesperson. This creates subtotals every time the salesperson name values change in the data display and again every time the region value changes. A sample of a trailing grouped summary report that breaks and summaries on two fields is shown in Figure 11.6.

Columnar with grand summary reports are best suited to long lists of data in which you need to perform a calculation, such as a grand total, average, or standard deviation. There is a single grand summary at the end of the report. There are no intermediate subtotals in a grand summary report.

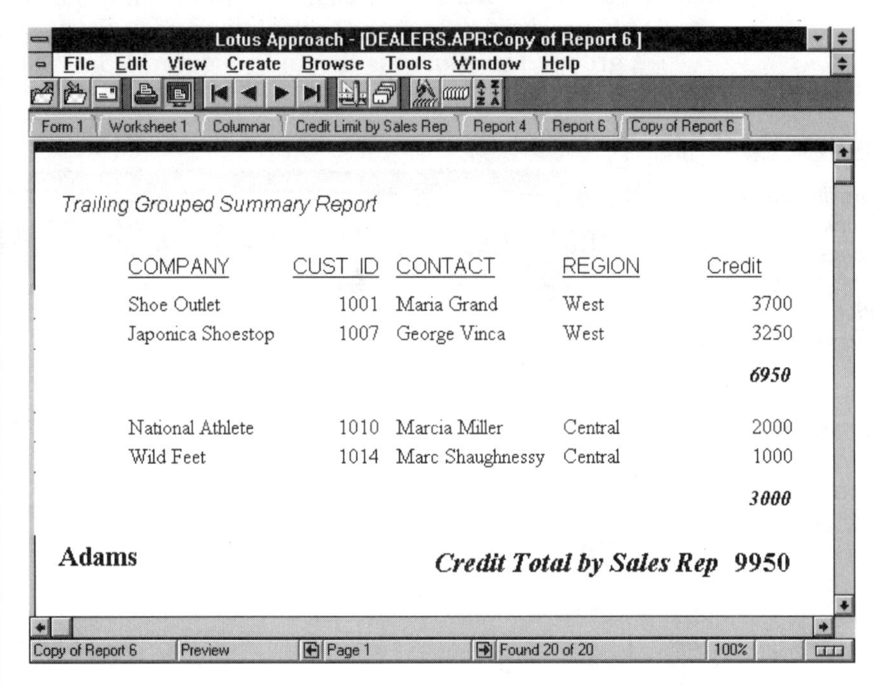

FIGURE 11.6

A trailing grouped summary using two field values for subtotals and sorting. Here the report will summarize the credit limit for companies in the western region, then the credit limit for the central region, then the report totals the credit limit for all companies for the sales representative (in this case, for Adams).

Summary only reports show a single calculation (count, average, sum, largest value, and so on) of your database. There are no individual records shown. The purpose of this report is to compute the desired number (count, average, and so on) quickly. If you need to know the total amount of sales or the average sales by all sales agents, a Summary only report will provide the answer quickly.

Repeating Panel reports are similar to forms with repeating panels and are available if you have joined databases in your Approach file. You identify a main database and a detail database, then include as many records from the "many" side of the one-to-many relationship as are connected to the main database record.

▶ Selecting Fields for a Report

After you have selected the layout, the Report Assistant adds tabs to the dialog box, depending on the style selected. Select Next or the Step 2 tab to select fields for the report, as shown in Figure 11.7. If you've

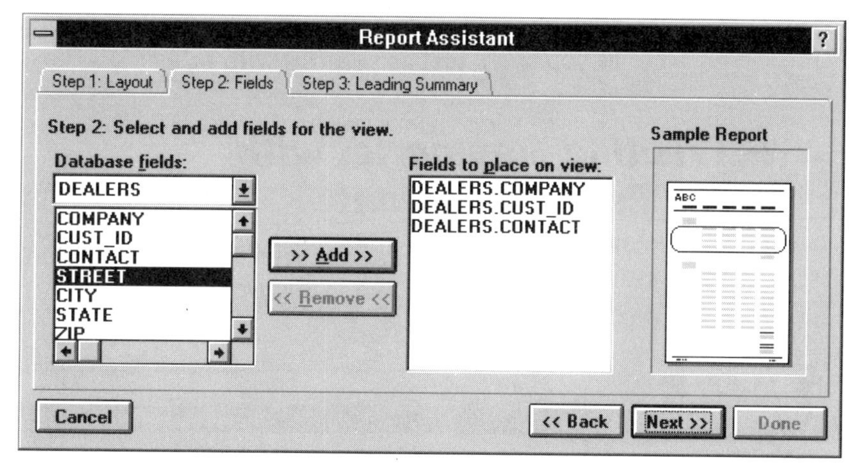

FIGURE 11.7

The Report Assistant's Step 2 tab is used for selecting fields for the report. Each field selected is added to the end of the "Fields to place on view" list at the right of the dialog box. The Sample Report thumbnail shows you the area you're defining.

selected a report layout with a summary (for counts, subtotals, averages, or totals), you must also select the summary characteristics by selecting Next (again) or the Step 3 tab.

Using the Step 2 tab, select the database and fields you want to include on the view. Note that the Sample Report thumbnail shows you how the fields will be placed.

The order in which you select fields is important. Select the fields in the exact order you want them to appear, left to right, on the report. If an additional line is needed to display the fields, remaining fields will appear on the next line, once again left to right, until sufficient rows have been added. Since selecting additional fields adds them to the *bottom* of the list only, you must select the fields in order carefully. Referring to Figure 11.7, the report will include the company, customer identification number, and contact name (in that order). If you select another field, it will be displayed on the report to the right of the contact name (for columnar reports) or on the next line (for the standard report layout).

If you add a field by mistake, you can select it from the "Fields to place on view" list, then select the Remove button, or double-click on the field name in the "Fields to place on view" list.

Once your report has been created, you can switch to the Design environment and make corrections, inserting, moving, or removing fields as you wish, just as you can with other views.

▸ Creating Summaries with the Report Assistant

If you selected a SmartMaster layout that includes summaries, select the Step 3 tab, shown in Figure 11.8.

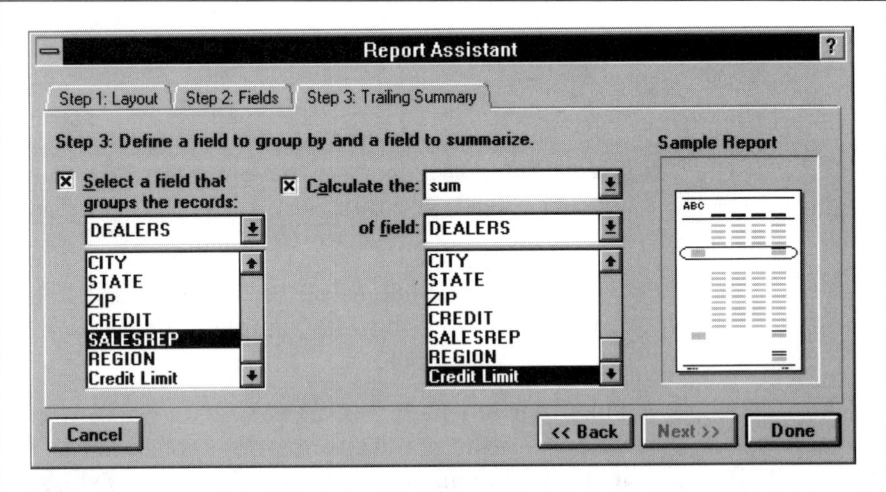

FIGURE 11.8 ▸

The Report Assistant's Step 3 tab, which varies by the type of summary you select in Step 1. The Step 3 tab for a trailing grouped summary report is shown.

First, select the field you want to sort on. This field will be placed at the beginning (leading summary) or end (trailing summary) of each block of values that contains the same value. For example, if you select the Leading Summary layout and choose the SALESREP field, the Report Assistant will display a unique agent name, then all the columns you selected, and finally a total when all records for this agent have been printed. If you select the Trailing Summary layout and choose the SALESREP field, your report will show all columnar data for an agent, followed by a line containing the agent's name and the total (or other calculation) you requested.

The calculation is specified on the Step 3 tab, too. To create a calculation, check the "Calculate the" check box and select the type of calculation you want. Your choices include average, number of items (which is the same as counting the number of items in the group), sum, smallest item, largest item, standard deviation, and variance. The last two calculations are statistical measurements that are explained in the Approach User's Guide.

Finally, if you want to perform a calculation, you must select the field upon which you want to perform this calculation. If you also want to see the value of this field for each record (as in Figure 11.5 earlier in this chapter), you must also select this field in the Step 2 tab.

Select Done. Approach may ask for permission to sort by the grouped field. Click Yes. If your Approach file contains joined databases, and if you selected fields from more than one database, you will be asked to select the main database, which controls the order of the report. For example, if you have a one-to-many relationship and are reporting on the "one" side, be sure to select the database corresponding to the "one" side as your main database. Joined databases are discussed in Chapter 6.

Report Assistant will create a new report using the options you have selected. The program creates the report layout and displays the report in the Design environment.

►► Working with Existing Reports in the Design Environment

Although the easiest way to create reports is to use the Report Assistant, you can also modify existing reports or build your own using the Design environment. Reports are just like any other form in Approach: You can select fields, move them, add graphics, and use the InfoBox to set properties. However, there are some special characteristics about reports that we'll discuss here.

▶ Panels

The first special characteristic that separates reports from other views is that reports include several panels. There are a variety of panels on any report. For example, you can have a panel that contains headings (a report title), a panel for each line in the body of a report, another panel for group breaks (to show changes in the sales representative or state values), and a panel to display footer information, such as the current date or page number. We'll look at several of these panels, some of which are shown in Figure 11.9.

FIGURE 11.9 ▶

A trailing grouped summary report with panel labels showing. Panel labels help you understand which section of a report you are working with: the header, body (individual records), or summary panels (which contain calculations). The report is shown in the Design environment. The Footer panel, although part of the report, is not shown.

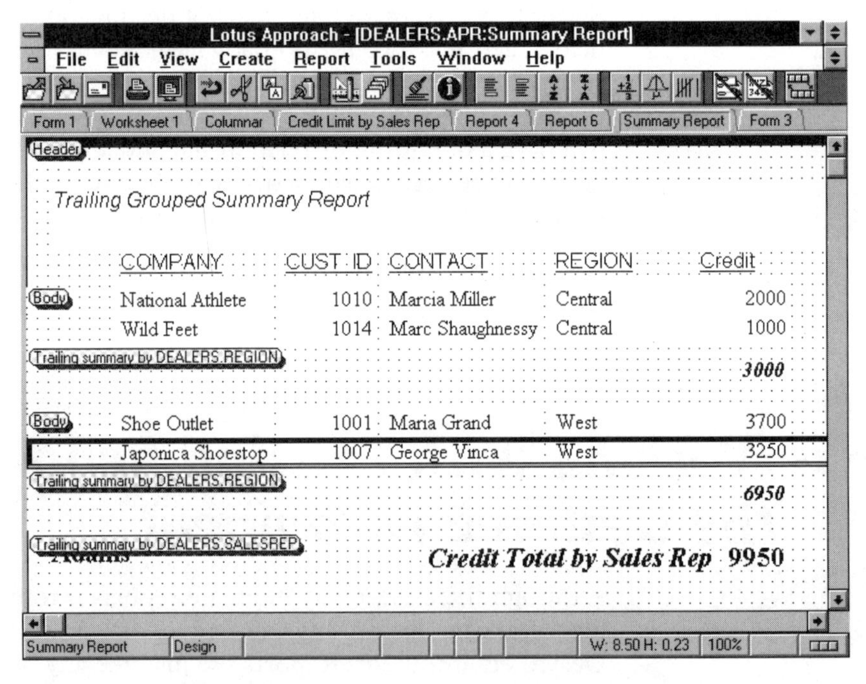

In Figure 11.9 we have a header panel that contains the report title, Trailing Grouped Summary Report. It also contains the columnar headings for company, customer identification number, and so on. Although you cannot see the dimensions of the header panel, when you click anywhere within the panel, Approach surrounds the panel with a thick black line, indicating the size of the panel. You can drag the borders of the panel to change its size.

Figure 11.9 also includes panels for the body, one per line. For example, there is a body panel for National Athlete, and another for Wild Feet, and still another for Shoe Outlet, and a fourth for Japonica Shoestop (which has been selected; its panel is surrounded by the black border just described). There is another panel that appears whenever the Region value changes. For example, there is a trailing summary panel when the records for the Central region are all printed, and another trailing summary panel when the records for the West region are printed. Yet another summary panel appears on the report when the value in the SALESREP field changes. That panel contains the text "Credit Total by Sales Rep" and the total field (which contains the value 9950—the total credit limit for this sales representative).

Not all report panels will be in every report. For example, for simple columnar reports there may be no grand summary, or you may omit the header if you only need a quick list of a few records.

When you work with a report, it's important to know which section you're working on, since the actions you take apply only to the section you're in. To show the section names, as shown in Figure 11.9, click on the Show report panel labels button in the SmartIcons toolbar or select View ➤ Show Panel Labels. When selected, small yellow boxes appear that indicate the beginning of the panel. To turn the boxes off, click on the same button.

Let's look at each of the panels in further detail. We'll examine the panels (sections) used to create the report shown in Figure 11.9.

The Header Panel

The *header panel* is used for the report header, which usually consists of a title for the report that will print at the top of each page. You can place the page number, current (system) date, and current time in this area as well. The header is printed at the top of each new page in the report and at the top of each screen.

The header is also used to contain column headers for fields that use a columnar layout.

Approach's Report Assistant automatically creates headers for you (unless you select the *Blank* SmartMaster layout). To add your own header panel, select Report ➤ Add Header. To remove the header from the report, select Report ➤ Add Header a second time.

To place the current date, time, or page number in the header, click anywhere within the header or if you have the panel labels displayed, click on the panel label. Approach places a dark border around the header, indicating its size and position. Choose Panel ➤ Insert. Choose Date, Time, or Page#, and Approach places the object in the header. As with any object on a form, drag the object to the desired location within the header panel. You can expand its size if the default size is not large enough. To change the properties of an object in the header, select the object and open the InfoBox.

If you've created a report using the Report Assistant, Approach has already placed individual text fields, one per column, in the header as column headings. You can manipulate these labels any way you like, just as you can with any object on a form: You can move, resize, and delete the labels, use the InfoBox to change the color(s) and fonts, and align the labels. Note one important difference between these labels and the columnar data underneath: When you move a label, you do not move the associated data in the columns. However, when you move the data columns, the headings are automatically repositioned.

Note, too, that you should only move the object within the boundaries of the header panel. If you move the field to another location, such as a body panel, the object will appear as part of that panel. In a body panel the object would appear on a line for every data record, as you will see in the next section.

The Body Panel

The *body panel* is the main section where individual records are displayed. The best way to see your report as you modify its design is to select View and choose Show Data if it does not have a check mark in front of the option. This lets you view the actual data in your database rather than guess if the field widths and positions are correct.

The body panel appears once for each data record. Thus, if you use the Show Data option, you'll see one line for each record in your database. If you don't use this option, you'll see how each panel is composed by viewing the field names, not the actual data. This view may be more useful in the Design environment if you are working with large databases, as it compresses the report display to a very small space—usually fewer than two screens.

There is one important difference between fields in the body of a report and the fields you place as objects on a form. When you select a column or individual field, you are selecting all occurrences of that field. Thus, in a columnar report, clicking on any column highlights the entire column. If you move the position of any field in a body panel, you are changing the position of all such fields in the report. (To change the position of an object, work with the object just as you would any object on a form: Drag the object to the new location.)

Notice that if you drag a column to the right, all columns to its right are moved as well. Approach does not allow you to cover over a field. Likewise, you cannot drag a field (column) to the left so that it overlaps with a field that is currently displayed on the report.

When you move the field, the heading moves with it if you've used one of the columnar SmartMaster layouts.

Columns Mode Controls How Fields on a Body Panel Are Manipulated
It's worth taking a short side trip here to discuss the two special modes of Approach reports: *Columns On* and *Columns Off*. The *Columns mode* controls what you can change about a field as well as how other columns behave when you make changes. When the Columns mode is *on* and you click on a field in a columnar report, Approach highlights the selected column in reverse video. You can drag the entire column to the right, and columns to the right of the selected field (column) are pushed to the right. In other words, dragging a column with the Columns mode on bumps all fields to the right of the selected field farther to the right. With the Columns mode on you can also change the size of the field by moving the mouse to the right border and dragging the border to the left or right. All fields (columns) to the right of the selected field (column) are moved as well. Thus, if you make a field smaller (drag the mouse to the left), all fields to the right of the selected field are moved over to the left to eliminate the extra inter-column space that would otherwise result.

When the Columns mode is off, you are working with fields just as you would on a form. When you change the dimension of a field, it's possible that your new dimension and position will overlap an existing field. When you widen a field, fields to the left or right remain in their original position—they are *not* moved a corresponding distance to the right.

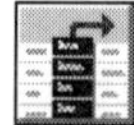

To turn Columns mode on or off, select a field in a column and choose Object. If the Turn on Columns option contains a check mark in front of it, Columns mode is on. To toggle the Columns mode, select Turn on Columns. (When you choose Object again, you'll see that the check mark has been removed.) Alternatively, select the Manipulate Objects as Columns icon from the SmartIcons toolbar to toggle between Columns mode. You can tell when Columns mode is on: When you select a field in a column, Approach uses reverse video to show the field (column) has been selected.

Summary Panels

Each summary that you create will use its own summary panel. For example, in the report shown in Figure 11.6 earlier in this chapter, there is a trailing summary panel for the change in region and another summary panel when the sales representatives' names change. The summary panel for the region field automatically calculates the credit limit total for the records immediately above it—that is, it totals the credit values for the companies assigned to the SALESREP for the region. In the report shown in Figure 11.6, there is a summary panel created after the first two records, since these two records have the same value for sales representative and region. Likewise there's another summary panel created when data for the West region for the sales representative named Adams is listed. While there are two summary panels shown, you actually only create one summary panel, specifying that the panel appear when the region changes.

The summary panel for the SALESREP field summarizes all the records in the group—that is, it computes the total of all credit limits for companies assigned to the sales representative.

A leading summary group and a trailing summary group will each have its own summary panel.

The summary panel usually contains a calculated field that is used to display the result of a calculation, such as a total, average, or standard deviation. You've seen functions in earlier chapters and you can learn more about formulas in Chapter 19. Just keep in mind for now that these fields use what are called the "S" (for summary) functions to make their calculations. A summary does not necessarily mean a total or subtotal, however. A "summary" function in Approach terminology means a calculated result that summarizes the data records immediately above it in the same group. The average, sum, count, minimum value, maximum value, or standard deviation are all considered "S" or summary functions. You'll learn more about summary functions and fields in the next few pages.

You will usually add text to summary panels, such as the word "Subtotal" or "Total." In Figure 11.6 earlier in this chapter, text is not included in the summary panel displayed when the region value changes. However, the text "Credit Total by Sales Rep" is used in the summary panel generated when the SALESREP field changes to help explain what the figure to its right represents. The text is just an ordinary text object.

The Footer Panel

Approach's Report Assistant automatically creates footers for you (unless you select the *Blank* SmartMaster layout) that usually contain the page number and often the report name. To add your own footer panel, select Report ➤ Add Footer. To remove the footer from the report, select Report ➤ Add Footer again. The Footer is not shown in Figure 11.9.

►► Choosing Panels

As we've said, when you want to make a change to a panel in the Design environment, you need only click on it, and Approach will surround the panel with a black border. What is confusing to some Approach users is that there is really only one panel defined for each item. For example, there is only one actual body panel defined for the report. The panel is repeated for each data record in your database. Likewise, there is only one "Trailing Summary by DEALERS.REGION" panel defined, but every time the region field changes value Approach adds a panel and fills it with the necessary data. Thus, you define a single panel and Approach inserts the panel in the report as often as necessary.

►► Changing or Removing a Panel

You can remove a header or footer panel by selecting the Report option from the Main menu. If the Add Header option is checked, the header will be displayed in the report. Select Add Header to remove the header. Likewise, if the Add Footer option is checked, the report will print the footer. To turn the footer off, select the Add Footer option (which removes the check mark when you view the option again).

You can select the panel by clicking anywhere within the panel where no field exists. For example, you can click in the blank space between fields in a panel, or click in the left margin (to the left of the leftmost object in the desired panel). When selected, Approach places a black border around the panel to indicate it has been chosen.

To remove a summary panel, click on the summary panel. Then press the Delete key.

To change the dimension of a panel, use the mouse to drag the border in any direction. If, for example, you drag the lower border downwards, you will increase the size of the panel. The dimension will change for each panel on the form. If you change the dimension of the body panel, the data for each record will appear in a larger area since each record appears in a separate body panel. When you are using the Show Data feature, changing any body panel changes them all. This features gives you immediate feedback so you'll know the dimension of each line of data.

▸▸ Adding a Summary Panel

You can add additional summary levels. However, unlike the ease with which you can add a summary level using the Report Assistant for a brand new report, adding a summary level to an existing report is much trickier. Hold on to your hat and we'll explain how to add a panel in the most efficient way.

You can add a new summary panel by clicking directly on a field in the report, in which case Approach makes some assumptions about what you need based on the field you selected. Another method lets you use the main menu to create a summary panel. A third option is a combination of the two and is called the *PowerClick feature*. This feature provides a powerful shortcut for creating summary panels and adding the appropriate value to the panel. Because it is so radically different from the first two procedures, although much simpler, it will be discussed last. In fact, if you want to do things the easy way, skip the next two options and proceed directly to PowerClick!

When you add a panel, Approach assumes that you are adding a new summary that is secondary to the existing summary or summaries. For example, if your report already summarizes by division and you add a new summary for the department field, the report will be modified to summarize by department *within* division. If you want to summarize by department, then division, you will have to remove the division summary panel and begin the report by defining the department summary, then adding another summary panel for the division field.

▶ Adding a Summary Panel by Clicking on the Report

To add a summary panel, select the column within any body section that you want to summarize. Click on the "Group and create trailing summary" button on the SmartIcons toolbar to add a trailing summary section for this field (one that appears at the end of all records for the group), or choose the "Group and create leading summary" button to create a summary section at the beginning of every group when the field value changes. Alternatively, click on the field and right-click the mouse. Select Object ➤ PowerClick, then choose Leading Summary or Trailing Summary.

If the fields have not been sorted in the proper order, Approach will ask if you want to re-sort the data. Select Yes. Approach adds a summary section, but does not add a total field to the section. To add a field, click on the summary section so that Approach surrounds the area with a gray border. You may wish to enlarge the area temporarily so your placement of the field can be positioned with greater accuracy. Choose a field from the Add Field list and drag it to the panel. (To display the Add Field list, select Panel ➤ Add Field, or click on the Add Fields icon from the SmartIcons toolbar, which is not part of the default toolbar but can be added following the instructions in Chapter 18.)

Which field should you add? We'll discuss that question in a moment. First, we need to take a detour and explain how to add a summary panel using the Main menu.

▸ Adding a Summary Panel Using the Menus

To take more control over how the summary panel is added, choose Create ➤ Summary from the Main menu. Approach displays the Summary dialog box shown in Figure 11.10.

FIGURE 11.10

The Summary dialog box can be used to create new summary panels. You can specify the interval for the summary, such as every 10 records, for all records (a grand total, for example), or when a field value for a group changes.

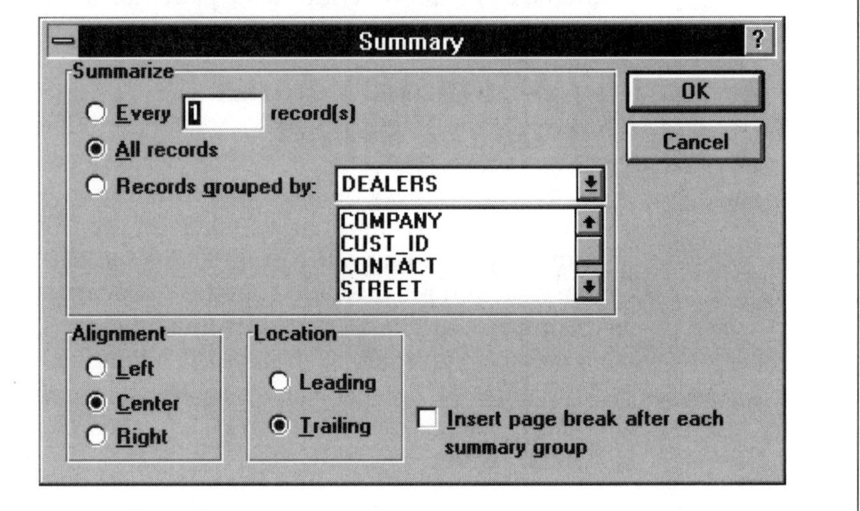

Select how often the summary is to be created. You can select:

- Every x record(s)—a new summary will be calculated after the number of records you select. This option is useful if you want to subtotal a field value after every 10 records (or some other multiple that is meaningful).
- All records—Approach will add a grand summary at the end of the report.
- Records grouped by—this is the usual choice if you want to add a new group. Select the database and field name you want to summarize the data on which. Choose the desired alignment (Should the value be printed at the left, center, or right portion of the panel?) and the location (Will the summary panel be displayed at the beginning of each new group or at the end?).

NOTE

If you are counting records, do not select the "every x record(s)" option unless you carefully define the summary field, since all summary panels except the last panel will, by default, contain the same value—the number of records you've selected! For example, if you select "every 5 records," an SCount field (which counts the number of records for this summary panel) will always be 5, except for the last group, which may contain the value 1 to 5. To avoid this problem, use the Field Definition dialog box, choose the calculated field, choose Options, and click on the Define Summary tab. Select "Summary of all records in all databases." Check the "Make calculation a running summary" option and the summary field will continue to be incremented at each group interval. Thus, the first summary field will show 5, the next 10, the third will show 15, and so on.

To add a page break after each new group, check the Insert page break after each summary group check box.

Choosing Calculation Fields for the New Summary Panel

Whether you've added the summary panel by clicking on the form or by using the menus, your next task is to add fields to the panel. Summary panels must be calculated fields. Select one of the fields displayed in italics in the Add Field dialog box. These fields begin with Auto (such as Auto_Count_of_Description, Auto_Sum_of_Costs, Auto_Average_of_ProductPrice) if Approach automatically created them, which it does when you define summary fields on other reports. The calculated fields you've already defined are also shown in italics in the Add Field dialog box.

If the calculated field you want to position on the report is not in the list, it is easy to create one. Select the Field Definition button from the Add Field list, then add a new field name (with the data type "Calculated") to the end of the list. Define a formula using one of the "S" functions. For example, in Figure 11.11 you'll see a new definition of a field named Count_customers. The formula uses one of the "S" functions, which stands for summary. We've selected SCount("Credit Limit") to summarize (in this case, count) the number of the entries in the Credit Limit field. We could also have created SAverage("Credit Limit") to calculate the average of the field, or use any of the other S functions: SMax (largest value), SMin (smallest value), SSum (total), SStd (standard deviation), or SVar (variance). Notice that the formula flag is black, meaning that the formula syntax is correct.

FIGURE 11.11

An S function is used to count the number of records containing a credit limit.

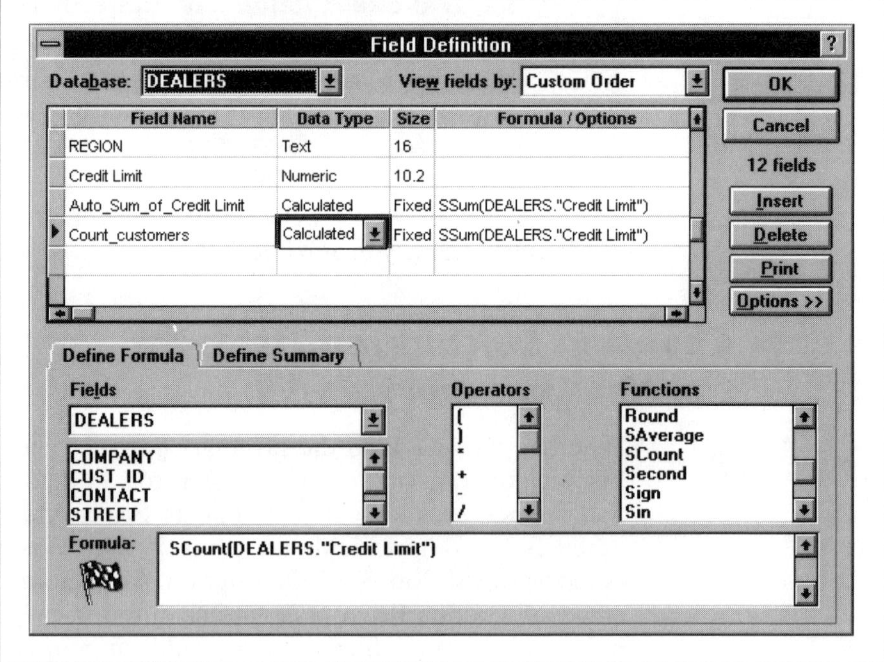

Approach automatically knows which fields to include in the summary because you have created a summary panel at the appropriate level. That is, because you are going to place this Count_customers field in the panel that appears when the region value changes, Approach knows you want to include in the count only those customers in the group. In the report shown in Figure 11.6 earlier in this chapter, if we place the Count_customers field in the panel that changes when the region value changes, the count value would be 2 for the West region and 2 for the Central region.

To ensure this, click on the Define Summary tab in the Field Definition dialog box. The "Summarize on" list provides several options. Choose the "Summary panels where this field is placed" option and Approach will automatically base the summary (count, average, total, and so on) on the records within the section. Other options let you compute the value for all records in all databases or for all values in any of the joined databases. Use the former for grand totals on reports. The remaining options limit or control which database records are included in calculations and are self-explanatory. Still more options are created depending on summary panels defined in reports. You can, for example, specify that a field be calculated only in trailing summaries of records based on a particular grouping. This ensures absolutely, positively that the computation is what you expect.

However, it is usually safest—and the most efficient—to select the Summary panels where this field is placed. Why? It's because this allows you to place the same field in two different panels, such as the "break on region" and the "break on sales" representative. By its position within each panel, Approach knows what you want to summarize, so you can use one field in two places rather than having two fields. It is also easy to move fields between panels and know that the calculation you intend—what's natural to assume—will be the calculation Approach makes, all automatically without any further definition by you.

You can include several calculated fields at the same level. For example, you could include a subtotal for a cost and a retail price field, assuming both summary fields were defined in the database definition.

To add text or other field types to a summary panel, select the panel, then choose the text tool from the Drawing tools toolbar and add the field to the panel. However, sometimes the panel dimensions are small. You can add the field to the main form and format it as desired, then move the field to a summary panel. When placed, the field will be added to each summary panel (you'll see multiple occurrences of the field if two or more summary panels are visible in the Design environment).

For example, to add the text field shown in the trailing summary group panel for the sales representative (Adams in our example) in Figure 11.6 earlier in this chapter, we first added the label to the form itself, then moved the label to the first summary panel. In fact, we could move it to any of the panels shown on the screen and it would be added to all occurrences of the summary panel. Similar to creating a summary panel, it is often most helpful to enlarge the section before you begin to add or position fields in the section. After the fields are placed as you wish, you can then change the dimension of the panel.

As with any other object, you can select a summary panel and use the InfoBox to change its properties, such as the background color.

▸ *Adding a Summary Panel Using PowerClick*

You can use the PowerClick feature of Approach to create a summary panel and add a new calculated field in just a few clicks of the mouse.

To begin, be sure the panel labels are displayed. This will help you follow these instructions and provide a clear indication of what Approach is doing. We'll also use a new example to show how easy it is to create a summary with the PowerClick method. We've created a columnar report, as shown in Figure 11.12 in the Design environment, using the Report Assistant.

To begin, click on the field for which you want to create a summary panel. In this case we'll select the Region field. Approach highlights the entire column—all fields in the column are selected (as shown in Figure 11.12)—if you selected Objects ➤ Turn on Columns, or Approach places black boxes around each Region field if the Columns option is turned off. Choose Object ➤ PowerClick, then choose Trailing Summary or Leading Summary, depending on which summary you want to create. To create the summary panels shown in Figure 11.13, we selected leading summary so that the Region summary panel will appear at the beginning of each group.

FIGURE 11.12

A new report sorted by region. We'll use the PowerClick feature to create a trailing summary whenever the region value changes.

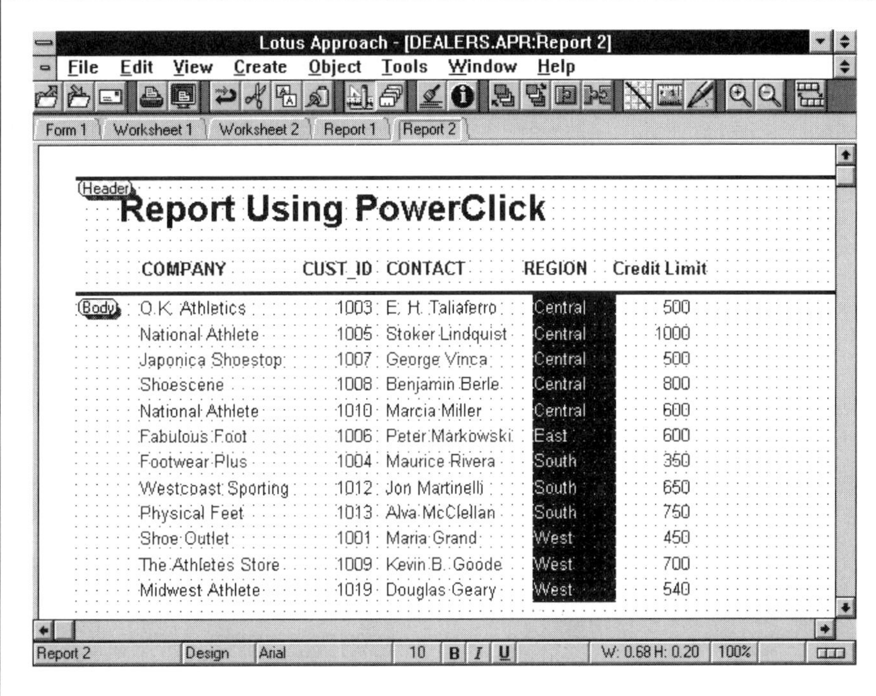

Approach automatically creates a new summary panel, although, ironically, the summary panel is empty. This is one of the confusing actions of Approach—you've created a summary panel, but there is nothing in the panel, although you might expect there to be.

Be sure the Columns option is turned off. (To check the status of the Columns option, select the field on the report, then select Object from the Main menu. The Turn on Columns option should not be checked. If it is, select it.) Click on the field you selected to group data by (the Region field in our example) and Approach surrounds each field with black boxes. Now click on one occurrence of the field—any Region field in a body panel is fine—and drag the field to the summary panel. The field is removed from the columnar report, as shown in Figure 11.14, and is now part of the Leading Summary by DEALERS.SALESREP summary panel at the beginning of each group. You may wish to remove the label REGION and move the next field (credit limit) to the left and remove the blank spaces. Also you'll probably want to move the actual

FIGURE 11.13

The leading summary panel has been created, but it is empty.

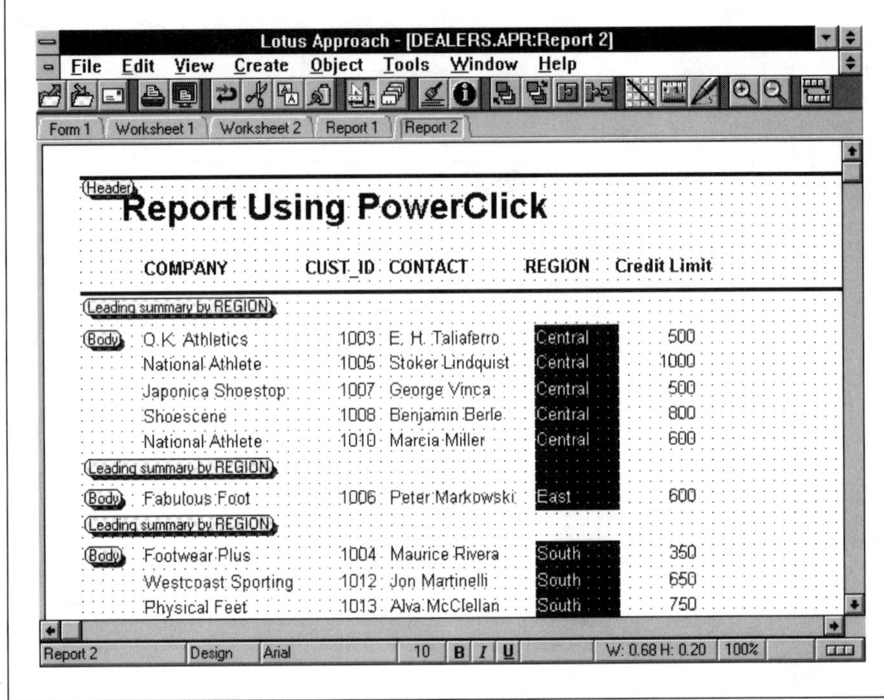

region field in the summary panel to the left. We've placed it so you can see both the panel label and the field value in Figure 11.14.

Sum
Average
Count
Minimum
Maximum
Standard Deviation
Variance
Leading Summary
Trailing Summary

Note that you can do more than just move a field from a column to a summary panel. You can add a calculation to your new summary panel when you select Object ➤ PowerClick. Click on the Credit Limit column, then choose Object ➤ PowerClick. Notice that calculation options sum, average, count, minimum, maximum, standard deviation, and variance are available. Select the calculation you want to perform, such as count or sum. Alternatively, select the field and click on the sum, average, or count icons from the default SmartIcons toolbar. Other buttons can be added to this toolbar, including icons for calculating the minimum, maximum, standard deviation, or variance. These icons are the same as those used for creating calculations in a crosstab.

Approach creates a new field definition (if necessary) and places the field on the summary panel. Thus, if we chose the Credit Limit field in the report shown in Figure 11.14, then the Sum option, Approach would add a new field at the bottom of the Credit Limit field that

FIGURE 11.14

The leading summary panel now contains the field value, which is the value for the group.

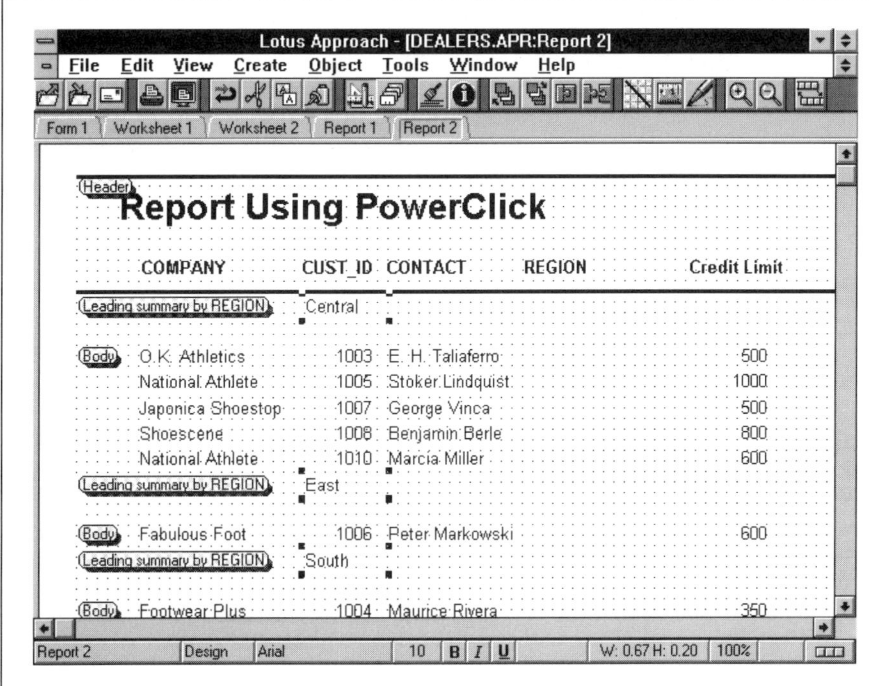

would total the credit limit every time the region value changed. You can repeat this process for another field: Click on any other field upon which you want to perform a calculation, then choose Object ➤ PowerClick. Continue in this manner until all desired fields have been added to your summary panel.

▶ Removing Repeating Values

You can quickly turn a columnar report into one that includes a leading summary panel. The easiest technique combines using the mouse and setting up a leading summary panel.

If you create a leading summary, you can move the field you've selected for grouping and move it to the leading summary panel. Select the field, then choose Object from the main menu. If the Turn Columns On option is checked, select the option to turn the feature *off*. Now drag the field from the body panel to the summary panel.

▸ Changing a Summary Panel Field Using the InfoBox

The Summary dialog box provides options for creating summaries, and once a summary is created, changing its options is easy. First, select the panel you want to change. Open the InfoBox and you'll see the tabbed dialog box shown in Figure 11.15. Compare this Summary dialog box with the one shown in Figure 11.10 earlier in this chapter and you'll see many of the same summary options. If you choose the Display tab in the InfoBox, you can set the alignment (left, center, right) and the location (leading or trailing).

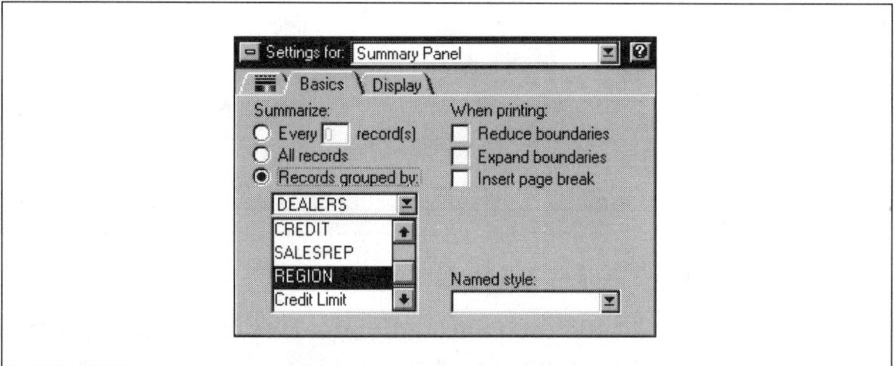

FIGURE 11.15 ▸

The tabbed dialog box for summary panels lets you change options for panels already on your form.

▸▸ Modifying and Enhancing Reports

As with any other form, the key to changing objects on a report is the InfoBox. To open the InfoBox, click on the InfoBox icon in the SmartIcons toolbar, press Ctrl+E, double-click on the panel, or right-click on any object and select Style & Properties.

The objects on a report are similar to those on any other form: You can select fields, graphics, text, or drawing objects (lines, circles, and rectangles). In addition, there are several new panels, each of which is an object. To change the properties of a field or graphic object, click on the object and use the tabbed dialog boxes as appropriate.

In this section we'll look at some of the tabbed dialog boxes from the InfoBox for objects that are unique to reports. All panels share one feature: You can change the dimension of any panel by dragging on the border of the selected panel. For example, to display records as though they were double-spaced on the report, click on the body panel until the black border surrounds the panel, then drag the bottom border down to stretch the height of the panel. The data in this panel remains centered at the top of the panel, so the extra space appears as blank space between records.

► Properties for the Report

To select the form, click anywhere on the report, preferably where there is no other object present. If the InfoBox does not display "Settings for: Report" at the top of the dialog box, select this option from the drop-down list.

In this InfoBox tabbed dialog box you can:

- Change the report name, which will appear on the tab for this report.
- Change the main database, which is the controlling database for joined databases; records are sorted according to the main database fields.
- Keep records together; this option is used for reports that include multiple lines for the same record. Checking this box keeps all fields from the same record together on the same page or screen. It also ensures that records are not split between columns if you use multiple columns.
- Select the number of columns for the report. By default, the value is 1. However, if you have selected only two or three columns, Approach can create a report showing more than one column per page. Figure 11.16 shows a report with two columns. Approach fills out the first column with the report, then adds a second column on the same page and includes the next set of records in this column.

FIGURE 11.16 ►

You can automatically create columnar reports by choosing the Number of columns option in the InfoBox for the report. In this two-column example, the data (which is sorted by company name) is printed down the first column, then remaining records are printed in the next column.

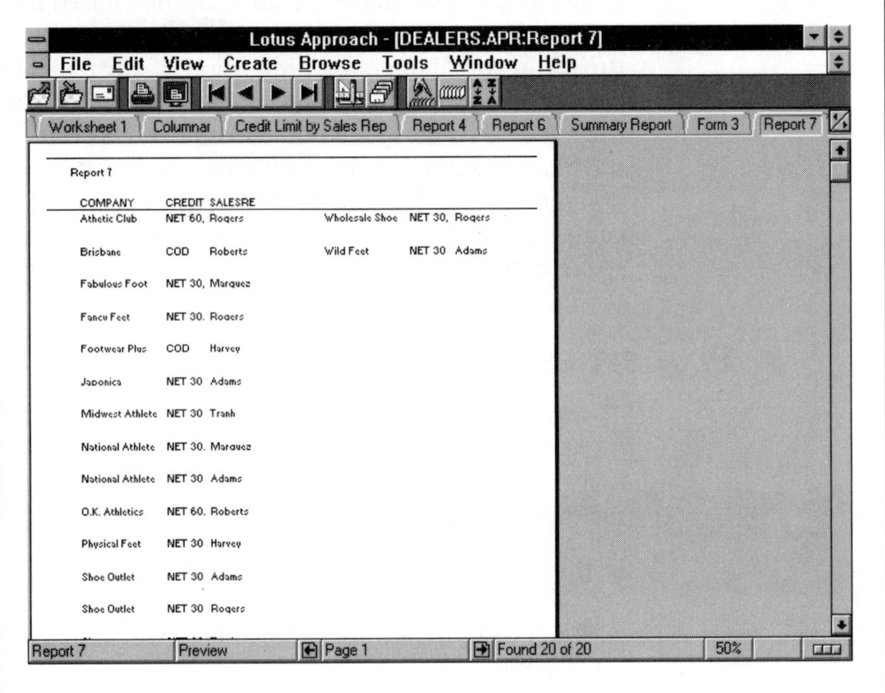

- Select the menu options available from this report; see Chapter 18 for creating and using custom menus.
- Remove the tab for this report from the set of tabs for this Approach file (the set of tabs at the top of the Approach work area that lets you jump between forms, worksheets, reports, and so on). You can select this option if you want to keep the report "hidden" from your end users. However, you (or your end users) can still move to this report by selecting the report from the list of views from the menu that appears when you click on the first box on the Status bar.

Click on the Macros tab in the InfoBox and you'll see the dialog box for macros. You can change the macro executed when you switch to this report or switch to another form. You might want to set the "On switch to macro" option to run a filter so that the report only prints data for selected records.

▶ Properties for the Header and Footer Panels

To select the header or footer panel, click anywhere within the panel until a dark border surrounds the object. The InfoBox options change to those shown in Figure 11.17. The options are self-explanatory and are similar to those used for any text field.

FIGURE 11.17

The InfoBox options for the header panel. The InfoBox for footers is identical.

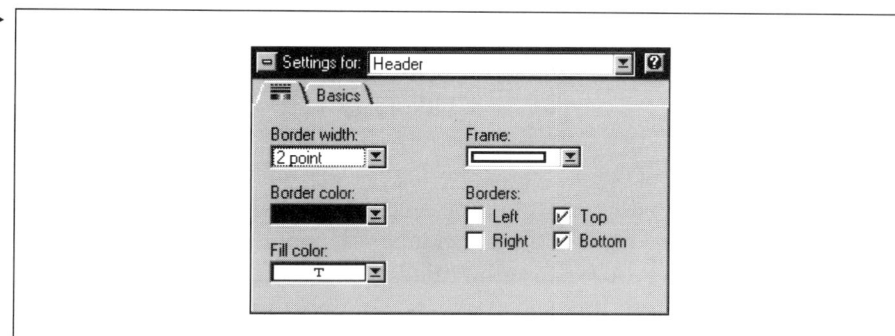

▶ Properties for the Body Panel

To select the body panel, click anywhere within the panel until a dark border surrounds it. Be careful to click on an area not occupied by a field, since clicking on the field will select the field or column, not the body panel. The InfoBox options change to those shown in Figure 11.18. The options are self-explanatory and are identical to those for header/footer.

FIGURE 11.18

The InfoBox options for the body panel let you specify the properties for borders and frames and select a named style.

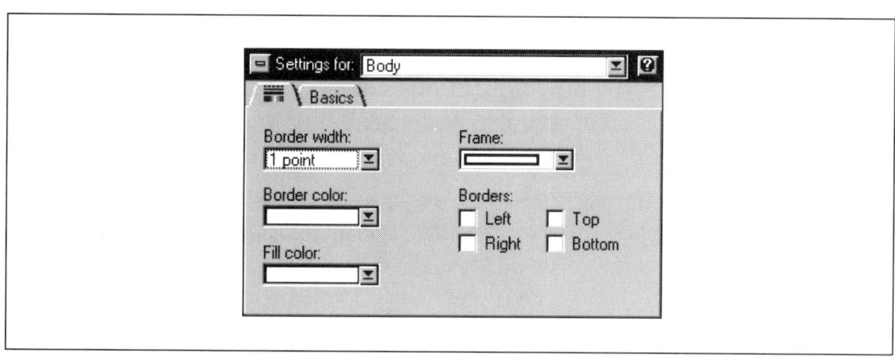

▸▸ Adding a Title Page

In some cases you'll want to display a title page to your report. A title page prints once, at the beginning of a report, to separate your report from others that may be printed on the same output device.

A title page includes all the form data just as any other page, but it adds a blank header and footer panel. A title page can be edited only in the Design environment, not in the Preview environment.

To add a title page be sure you are in the Design environment and select Report ➤ Add Title Page. Now the very first header panel on the report becomes the title page header. The header on the second page of the report is the header that will begin on page 2 and continue until the end of the report. These headers are independent panels, even though Approach displays the panel label "Header" for both. You can make any changes you wish to the title page header, such as making the panel a full page or adding text (such as the report title and current date).

To switch between displaying title page header and report page header, select/deselect Report ➤ Add Title Page.

▸▸ How to Avoid Breaking Data between Two Pages

Sometimes your report layout may cause a data record to print at the end of one page and continue on the beginning of the next page.

To prevent "widows" and "orphans," as such splits are called in word processing applications, open the InfoBox and in the "Settings for" pull-down list choose Report. Click on the Basics tab and check the "Keep records together" box.

▶▶ Sorting Data in a Report

Reports are easier to use if the data they contain are arranged in order. It's easier to locate a name in a customer report if that is how the report lists the data—alphabetically by customer name. Reports using leading and trailing summaries are already sorted by the field used to group the data.

You can sort data from the Preview, Design, or Browse environments. To sort a report on a single field, click anywhere in that field and choose the Sort Ascending icon from the SmartIcons toolbar (to sort from A to Z, 0 to 9) or the Sort Descending icon (to sort in the reverse order). You can also select the field, then choose Object ➤ Sort, then choose Ascending or Descending, or choose Browse ➤ Sort.

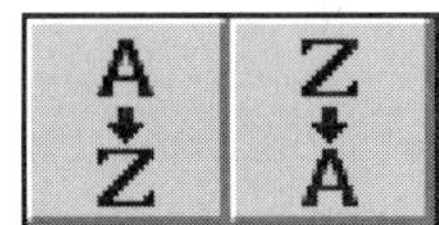

To sort on multiple columns, you'll need to use the Object ➤ Sort ➤ Define option, which is more fully explained in Chapter 12. Click the Open Sort Dialog Box icon from the SmartIcons toolbar (if available), press Ctrl+T, or select a field and choose Object ➤ Sort ➤ Define Sort (in Design) or Browse ➤ Sort ➤ Define (in Browse). Choose the fields you want to sort on and select OK.

▶▶ Editing Data in a Report

You can edit data in the Browse environment by clicking on any field and entering the new value. The Browse environment is slightly different from the Preview and Design environments, since it does not include summary breaks or panels. In the Browse environment you see your data, but not the other calculated fields, such as subtotals and totals. This minimizes the distractions on your screen. Remember that you can switch between the Preview environment (which shows all calculations and groupings) and the Browse environment.

▸▸ Deleting a Report

To remove a report you no longer need, switch to the Design environment and choose Edit ➤ Delete Report, then select Yes to confirm your request.

▸▸ Copying a Report

To use a report as the basis of another report, switch to the Design environment and choose Edit ➤ Duplicate Report. Approach makes a copy and names it Copy of XXX, where XXX is the original report name.

▸▸ Printing a Report

To print a report, choose the Printer icon from the SmartIcons toolbar. Approach displays the Print dialog box. You can also select File ➤ Print from the Browse or Design environments, or press Ctrl+P.

Printing is discussed in greater detail in Chapter 15.

▸▸ Summary and a Look Ahead

In this chapter you've learned how to create reports. You've seen how the Report Assistant can help you build the basic report structure, and how you can modify the report further to meet your individual needs. You've also seen how reports are divided into panels, and how you can create additional leading and trailing summary panels to print subtotals when a value in a field changes.

In the previous chapters you learned how to create forms and other views to list and display information. In Chapter 12 you'll learn how to maximize the usefulness of your data by limiting the records displayed. You will learn how to search for individual records or groups of records (all customers in Michigan, for example), and then learn how to work with this subset of data. For example, you may want to print a list of only customers with credit limits above $10,000 and send them a form letter (which you'll learn about in Chapter 13) about special purchase opportunities.

▶ ▶ CHAPTER 12

Finding and Sorting Data

▸▸ FAST TRACK

▶ *To find a value for a field on a view* **412**

from the Browse environment you can select Browse ➤ Find, press Ctrl+F, or select the Find icon from the SmartIcons toolbar, or click on the second box from the left in the Status bar and select Find from the pop-up menu. (If you are working in a Worksheet view rather than a form, select Worksheet ➤ Find ➤ Find.) In the view, move to the field for which you want to select values, then enter the value you want to find. Select OK.

▶ *To view all records in a database* **414**

click on the Show All icon from the SmartIcons toolbar, select Browse ➤ Show All, or press Ctrl+A. (If you are working in a Worksheet view, select Worksheet ➤ Find ➤ Show All.)

▶ *To find a precise value* **416**

precede your search string with the equal (=) sign. Otherwise, Approach will find all values that begin with the specified value (for example, it will find "Mary" if your search criteria is "Mar").

▶ *To find more than one value in a field* **417**

separate individual search criteria values with a comma. To search for records that contain a value within a range of values, use the … (ellipsis) operator (such as 1…150).

▶ *To find records that are missing a value in a field* **421**

use an equal sign in the field. To find records that do contain values, use the less-than and greater-than symbols: <>.

▶▶ **T** *o* this point you've been learning about how to work with all the records in a database. Although you can go directly to a record if you know its record number, it's increasingly unlikely you'll know that number as the number of records in your database grows.

To help you locate one or more records, Approach offers the Find environment. In this environment, Approach will quickly search the entire database looking for one or more records that meet the criteria you specify. For example, you may wish to display only those records for customers living in California. You may wish to find a specific customer (locate the data for John Anderson, for example). Find can also locate fields using a combination of conditions. For example, if there is more than one John Anderson in your database, you can ask for just the records for customers named John Anderson who live in Stockton, California.

Find is one of the most powerful features in Approach. The Find environment lets you concentrate on a group of records—a meaningful subset of data so you can focus on specific data. You can also use Find to look for data that is out of bounds or out of the ordinary, such as annual salaries larger than $1,000,000 or less than $10,000.

According to Approach's Technical Support department, using the Find environment is the second most frequently misunderstood topic, right behind joining databases (which was described in Chapter 6). Therefore, this chapter takes the subject slowly and provides plenty of examples of the various ways you can use the Find environment to locate specific data.

In addition to finding records, you can also sort them. This allows you to quickly locate records yourself. For instance, you can create a worksheet and list the next payment due date for your customers. If the worksheet is listed by customer name, it's easy to find a customer by scrolling through the list alphabetically. However, you can also sort the records by date. This way the first records you see are those with the earliest Next Payment Date. If the date in this field is earlier than today, the payment is late and you may wish to call the customer and ask when you may expect payment.

Sorting can also be a benefit for mailing lists. The United States Postal Service offers discounts on postage if you have sufficient numbers of letters going to the same zip code. Of course, you'll have to sort labels by zip code—which is something that Approach can do for you quickly and easily!

In this chapter you'll learn how to find records, work with the records you find, and sort records in a view.

►► Finding Records

Approach is very flexible when it comes to finding records. It can find a single record or groups of records. You can search for records from any view—from a worksheet, form, or mailing label, for example. While Approach works in a slightly different fashion depending on which type of view you are working with, the principle is the same: You specify what you want Approach to find, and Approach returns with the record(s) that match(es), displaying only that record(s).

To give you a flavor for a simple Find, suppose you know that your customers in California are buying larger quantities of widgets than you expected. To analyze this further, you'll want to view information about only the customers in California to see if you recognize a pattern. For example, you may discover that your customers in California have a larger credit limit (and thus can buy more at one time).

► Example

There are four steps to finding a set of records. In this example, we're storing records of dealers who sell our products. Data about these dealers has been stored in an Approach file named DEALERS. We want to find the dealers located in California while working in the Browse environment, using the form shown in Figure 12.1.

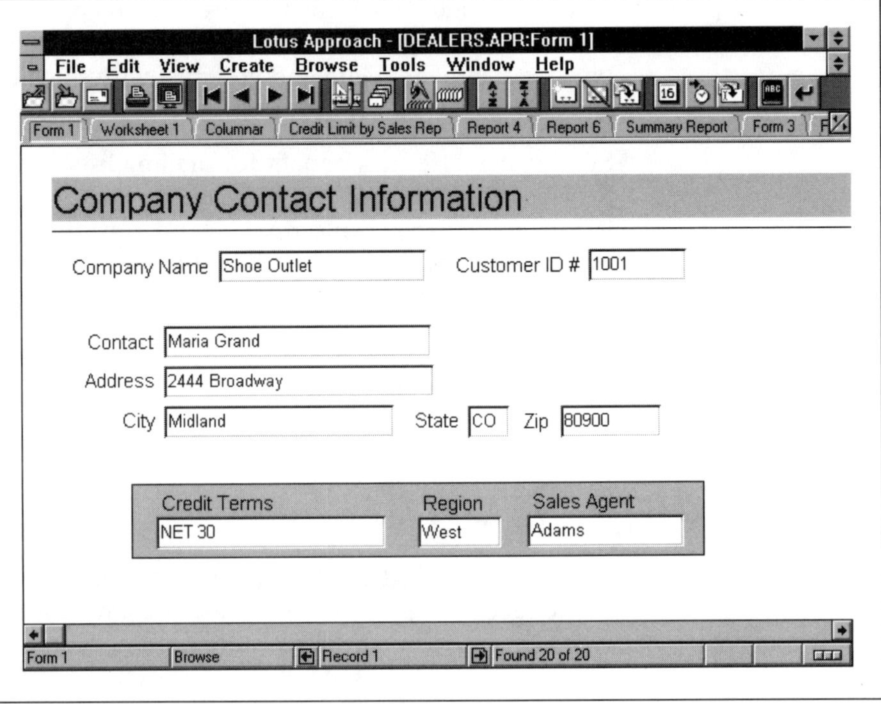

FIGURE 12.1

The Browse environment for a name and address database of dealers that sell our products

In the DEALER database, the State field is defined as a two-character text field. Notice that as we begin there are 20 records in the database: the Status Bar displays Found 20 of 20 (that is, it is displaying all records).

Use these steps to find dealers with offices in the state of California:

1. Issue the Find command. From the Browse environment you can select Browse ➤ Find, press Ctrl+F, or select the Find icon from the SmartIcons toolbar. (There are two possible Find icon buttons—each has fingers walking across a set of records.) You can also click on the second box from the left in the Status bar and select Find from the pop-up menu. (If you are working in a Worksheet view rather than a form, select Worksheet ➤ Find ➤ Find.)

2. Approach displays a blank Form view as shown in Figure 12.2—all of the fields are empty. Approach adds four buttons to the top of the form and changes the SmartIcons toolbar. We'll ignore the buttons in the toolbar for this example. Move to the field for which you want to select values. For example, to select all customers in the state of California, move to the State field.

FIGURE 12.2

The same form in the Find environment. Notice the four new buttons at the top of the form. The default SmartIcons toolbar has also changed.

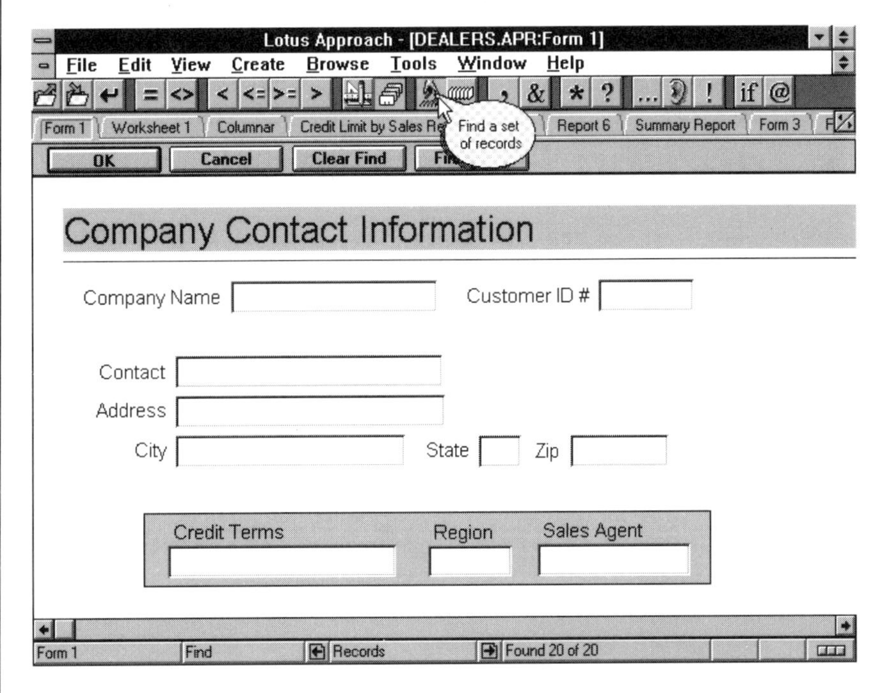

3. Enter the value you want to find, which is called the *Find criteria*. Setting Find criteria is described in greater detail in the following section, since there are many options. In this example, we want to find records that contain the value CA in the State field. Therefore, type CA in the State field.

4. Select OK.

Approach displays a form with the first record from the *found set*. Now when you move between records, you are only working with the record(s) in the found set. Although Approach keeps track of the other records—nothing is lost—you can only view the records you've selected.

To view all the records, click on the Show All icon from the SmartIcons toolbar (there are two icons possible), select Browse ➤ Show All, or press Ctrl+A. (If you are working in a Worksheet view, select Worksheet ➤ Find ➤ Show All.)

▸▸ Entering Find Criteria

To help you understand the seemingly limitless ways to specify the records you want, we'll use a set of sample data to see the results of several Find criteria. We'll use the databases containing commissioned sales information for the sales agents that service the dealers in our DEALERS database.

Suppose we have the following records for sales agents in a database called SALESCOM (for Sales Commission). The commission amount is a numeric field. The date field stores the date the sale was made (the commission is due at the same time). An agent may work full or part time, indicated by Yes (full time) and No (part time) in a Boolean field.

FirstName	LastName	Commission Amount	Sale Date	Full-Time
Harry	Andersen	$145	10/1/94	Y
Richard	Anderson	$200	11/2/94	Y
Mary	Andrews	$229	10/5/94	N
Vicki	Appex	$320	11/6/94	Y
MaryAnn	Basehart	$100	12/7/94	N
Rocky	Burns	$211	12/9/94	Y
Cynthia	Capehart	$95		N

Note in our sample that Cynthia Capehart does not have a value in the Sale Date field.

The form in Figure 12.3 shows the first record. Note that the Status bar shows "Found 7 of 7," since there are seven records. We'll use this form to find several conditions, exercising most of the Find criteria Approach supports. In each case we'll assume you're viewing the entire database, then issue the Find command (see Step 1 in the previous section).

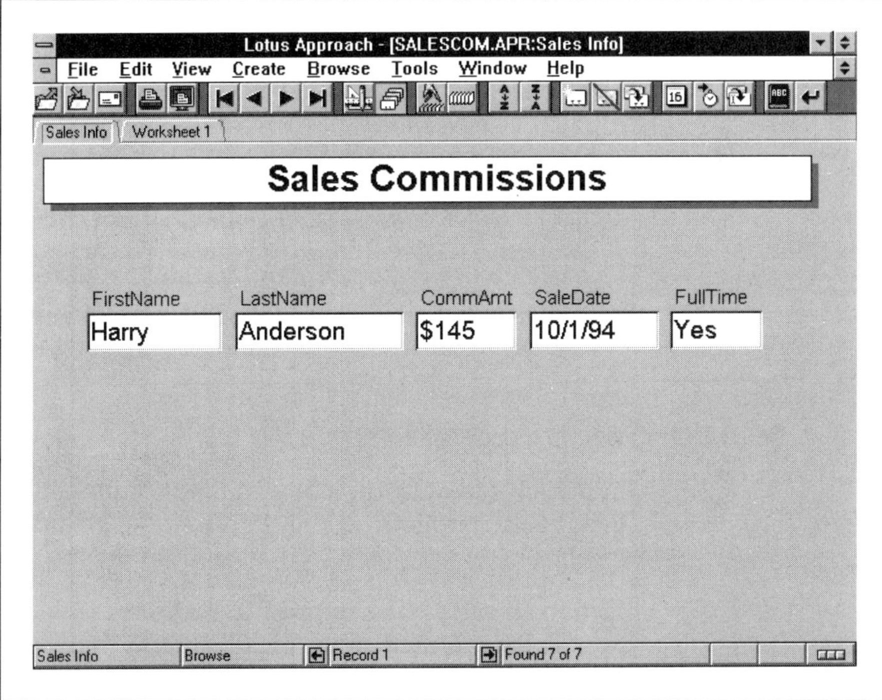

FIGURE 12.3

A simple form for recording sale and commission information.

Search #1: Find Richard Anderson

Issue the Find command. To find a particular record using a value in a text field, enter as many characters as needed to make the search unique. For our example, you can enter **Anderson** in the LastName field, since there is only one person with that last name.

If you were unsure of the spelling, you could enter **Ander** in the LastName field and the first few characters, such as **Rich** or **Ric,** in the FirstName field. Because there is only one employee whose last name begins with Ander and whose first name begins with Rich or Ric, Approach displays the desired record. The Status bar shows "Found 1 of 7."

To view all records again, press Ctrl+A or click on the Show All button in the SmartIcons toolbar.

▶ *Search #2: Find All Agents Whose Last Name Begins with "And"*

In the first search you were looking for a specific record. In this scenario you need to find an agent whose last name is "Anderson." Since you don't know the employee's first name, you could enter the characters A,n,d,e,r,s,o,n in the LastName field. However, if you do this, you'll miss seeing the record for Andersen (notice the slight variation in spelling), which may be the person you want to find.

The safe choice is to enter **And** in the LastName field, then select OK to begin the search. The Status bar shows "Found 3 of 7," since three last names in the database begin with the letters And.

▶ *Search#3: Search for "Vicky"*

Approach can perform a *Sounds Like* search. Since you aren't sure how Vicki spells her name (it may be Vicky, Vicki, or Vickie), you can use a special character, the tilde, ~, in front of the characters you want to find.

To find all values that sound like Vicky, press the tilde character on your keyboard, then enter **Vicky**. Alternatively, click on the ear button from the SmartIcons toolbar, then type the name **Vicky**. Your search will look like Figure 12.4. Select OK to begin the search.

▶ *Search #4: Search for Exact Text: Find Mary but Not MaryAnn*

If you want to perform an exact search, you can precede your search string with the equal (=) sign. For example, if you enter **Mary** in the FirstName field, Approach will match all names that begin with the characters M, a, r, and y. Both Mary Andrews and MaryAnn Basehart

FIGURE 12.4

A Sounds Like search uses the tilde character to indicate the value entered "sounds like" what you want to find. You can enter the tilde character yourself or click on the Sounds Like SmartIcon, which displays a picture of an ear.

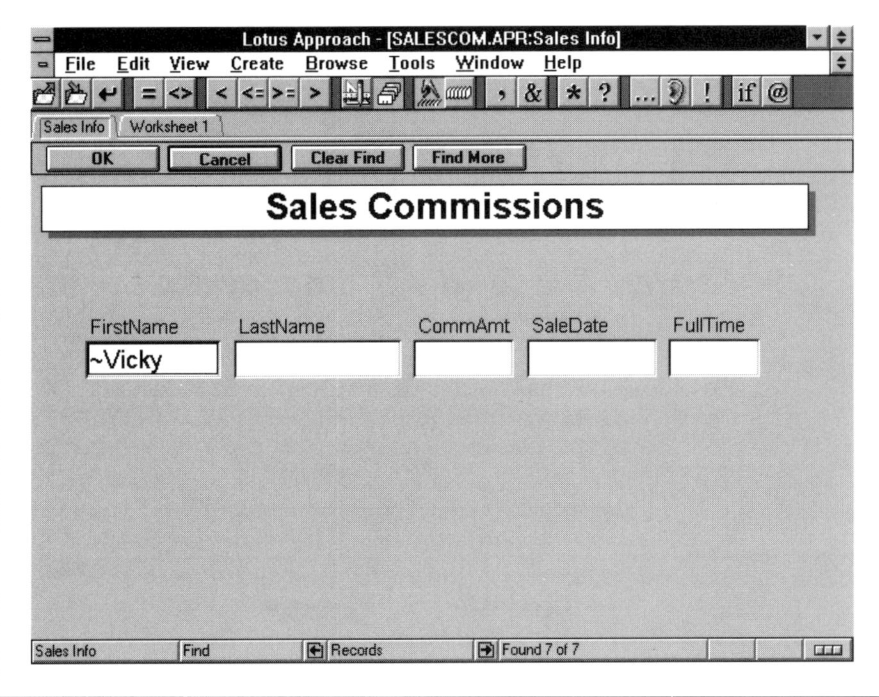

meet those criteria. Therefore, to find only the records with exactly the characters Mary (and no more) in the FirstName field, enter the criteria as **=Mary**. You can enter the equal sign yourself, or click on the Equal Sign icon from the SmartIcons toolbar. Select OK to begin the search.

▶ *Search #5: Find Appex and Burns*

You want to compare the commission information of Vicki Appex and Rocky Burns. You can individually select each record, write down the information, and then make changes to the data if necessary, or ask Approach to retrieve both records at once.

To search for two values at once, separate the values with a comma. For example, to find Appex and Burns, enter

```
Appex, Burns
```

in the LastName field. You could also enter

```
Vicki, Rocky
```

in the FirstName field, since these values are also unique in the database.

You can enter the comma yourself, or click on the Comma icon from the SmartIcons toolbar. Select OK to begin the search.

▶ *Search #6: Find All Employees Earning Over $200*

Now that you've worked with text fields, it's time to work with the numeric fields. In this search, we'll examine the Commission amount field.

Approach uses several operators to limit your searches. These operators work on text, numeric, date, and time fields.

Operator	**Purpose**
<	Less than
≤	Less than or equal to
>	Greater than
≥	Greater than or equal to
=	Equal to
<>	Not equal to
&	And (two conditions in the same field)

Two special conditions apply to the equal and not-equal-to operators. If entered alone in a field in a view, the equal sign causes Approach to look for blank fields. If the not-equal-to operator is used alone in a field, Approach finds non-blank fields.

To return to the search at hand, enter **>200** in the CommAmt field to find records for commissions over $200 (that is, $200.01 and above). The Status bar shows that 3 records meet this condition. Richard Anderson earned exactly $200, so his record does not match the Find criteria.

▶▶ NOTE

When entering search criteria in numeric fields, enter the value without special characters, such as the currency symbol or commas. A decimal point is acceptable if you want to find a value that includes a decimal portion, but is not needed if you assume a decimal portion of zero. That is, you can enter 1 and Approach understands you are looking for the value 1.00. However, do *not* enter 1,000. Approach does not know how to handle the comma separating the one from the zeroes that follow.

▶ Search #7: Find All Employees Earning between $1 and $150

To find records that contain a value within a specified range, use the ... (ellipsis) operator. To find amounts between $1 and $150 (including the end points of the range, $1 and $150), enter the value $1...$150 in the Amount field.

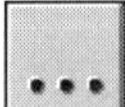

You can enter the ellipsis yourself or click on the Range icon in the SmartIcons toolbar.

As an alternative, you could use the "&" symbol to search based on two criteria. In the CommAmt field you can enter

```
>=1&<=150
```

This finds all records in which the amount field is greater than or equal to 1 and less than or equal to 150. The results are exactly the same, although using the ellipsis is faster to enter and easier (and more natural) to read because it is consistent with range selections from other Windows applications and is similar to the range specifications used in spreadsheets.

When you use the ellipsis, you cannot use *wildcards* (which let you substitute a character in place of one or more characters, and are explained in the next section) or Find operators (equal, not-equal-to, less than, and so forth) in the same Find criteria.

Harry Andersen, MaryAnn Basehart, and Cynthia Capehart are the found set of Search #7.

▸ Search #8: Find All Employees Earning Commissions in October

To search for all October 1994 dates, enter 10/*/94 in the date field. The * is a wildcard, as is ?—wildcards let you substitute a character in place of one or more characters. The * wildcard matches any number of characters (including no characters). The ? wildcard matches one and only one character.

All dates in October are in the form 10/xx/94, where "xx" represents a one or two digit value. (You can also use a dash instead of a slash mark: 10/1/94 can be entered as 10-1-94.) If we use the search criteria 10/??/94, we would miss the dates in our data (10/1/94 and 10/5/94) because the day portion of the date field is a single digit. So, when you don't know how many characters are contained in your field's value, use the * wildcard.

Note that you must enter all characters in a month and day field (or use the wildcard *). For example, if you enter 10/94, Approach will not return October dates. However, if you omit the year field, Approach will assume the current (system) year.

You can enter the * or ? wildcards manually using the keyboard or insert them by clicking on the appropriate icon from the SmartIcons toolbar.

▶▶ **TIP**

Wildcard searches work much like DOS file name searches. Use the question mark to match one and only one character (which must be present). Use the asterisk to search for zero to many characters. The asterisk is a useful place holder when you don't know how many characters may precede the text you're trying to find. For example, you can enter *ann to find MaryAnn. The Approach User's Guide includes several additional examples of wildcard searches.

▶ *Search #9: Find Missing Values in Text Fields*

Enter = in a blank field to find all records that contain no value in the field. This search is most useful when you are trying to find records that are missing key values. For example, in our data, each record should have a sale date entered. Entering a single equal sign (=) in the Sale Date field will locate Cynthia Capehart's record because this record contains no value in the sale date field.

Enter <> alone in the blank field to find all records that *do* contain a value (the search excludes records containing a blank value in the field). You can enter the <> by typing the < key followed immediately by the > key, or by selecting the Not Equal icon from the SmartIcons toolbar.

▶▶ *Finding Values in Other Field Types*

There are some special rules for finding values in other field types, such as Boolean and time fields.

▶ *Boolean Fields*

Enter any of these values for no:

```
0, N, n, no
```

Enter any of these values for yes:

```
1, Y, y, yes
```

Note that you can use any combination of uppercase and lowercase letters

▸ Date Fields

To use the current date in a Find criteria for a date or calculated field, enter a comparison operator (greater than, less than, equal to, and so on) and the special value **@Today()**. *@Today()* stands for the current system date.

Date fields are strictly limited to entering dates in the format MM/DD/YY (or YY/MM/DD depending on your International setting in the Control Panel—Control Panel settings are usually available from an icon in your Main program group in Program Manager). You cannot, for example, enter Thursday to find all dates that fall on a Thursday. However, you can use an *If statement* to find such dates, as explained later in this chapter.

▸ Time Fields

To find a value in a time field, enter the value in 12-hour or 24-hour format, and separate hour, minute, and second portions with colons. You can also take some shortcuts. For example, you can enter 2PM for 02:00PM.

▸▸ Finding Values in Fields Using Check Boxes

Recall that when you add a new record that contains a field displayed using a check box (see Chapter 8 for adding records in which fields are displayed using check boxes), Approach does not save a value in the field by default. To store the "checked value" you defined, you must check the box. To store the "unchecked value" you defined, you must check, then uncheck the box. If you do not check the box, Approach stores a value called the null value, which is neither Yes (True) nor No (False) for a Boolean field for example.

To find records that contain the checked value, select the check box, which places an X in the box. To find records that contain the unchecked value, select the check box twice—once to enter an X and again to remove it.

There is no way to check for null values in fields displayed using a check box. Instead, use a worksheet and enter the equal sign (=) in the field, or create another form that does not use a check box to display the field's value and use the equal sign (=) operator.

►► Finding Values in Fields Using Radio Buttons

To find records containing a set of radio buttons in the field display, you can select a single radio button to find all records with the value in the selected field. If you need to check for more than one condition, perform an *Or search*. (See the sections "Complex Searches" and "Widening a Search: Entering Or Criteria" later in this chapter.) For each "or" condition you can select one radio button value. You cannot, however, select more than one radio button on a single Find screen.

When Approach reads through your database, it selects a record if the value for that field matches the value indicated by the radio button(s) selected. In Figure 12.5, Approach will select any record in which the Payment Method field contains the value associated with Check. Remember that the radio button displays a label you define, not the value stored within the field. The database record might contain "1" in the Payment Method field, which you've associated with the meaning "Check" for the radio button.

To find all records where the payment method is cash or check, select the Cash button, then choose the Find More button and select the Check button. Select OK to perform the Find.

►► Case-Sensitive Searches

Ms. MaryAnn Basehart's first name has an uppercase A in the middle. If we search for this name by entering the Find criteria Maryann,

FIGURE 12.5

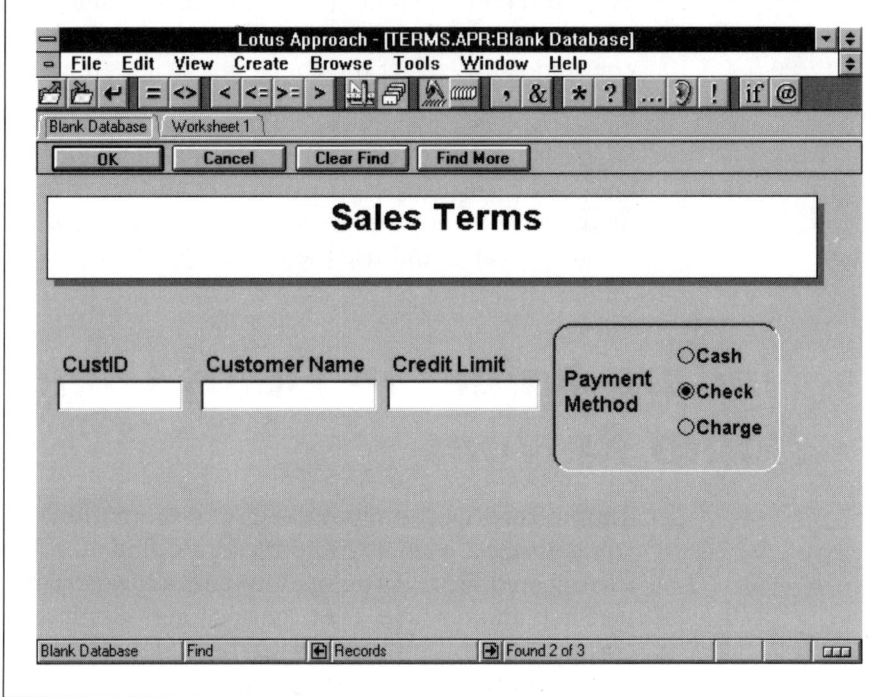

You can select records that match a value in a field using radio buttons. To find records meeting two or more radio button values, use an "or" search, described in the sections "Complex Searches" and "Widening a Search: Entering Or Criteria" later in this chapter.

Approach will still find the name if our database is dBASE, FoxPro, or Paradox 4.0. However, if the file type is Paradox 3.5, an SQL database, or one opened using Open Database Connectivity (ODBC), the search is case sensitive, meaning that to find MaryAnn you have to enter the "A" in Ann in uppercase.

In a dBASE, FoxPro, or Paradox 4.0 file you can limit your search to be case sensitive. For example, suppose you know your database contains MaryAnn Basehart and Maryanne Peters. To find Ms. Peters, enter **!Marya** in the first name field. Note that you need enter only as many characters as needed to make the search unique. You could also enter **!Maryann** to find the same record.

To find Ms. Basehart's record, enter **!MaryA** (or **!MaryAn** or **!MaryAnn**). You can enter the exclamation mark from the keyboard or click on the Case Sensitive button from the SmartIcons toolbar. Approach conducts a search and matches each letter to the appropriate letter in your field and gets a match only if the case of each letter also matches.

▸▸ Complex Searches

Now that you know how to search for records using simple search criteria, it's time to plunge into more complex searches. In this section, you'll learn how to narrow or widen your search by entering multiple search criteria.

▸ Finding Records That Meet More Than One Condition

As you've seen, you can enter a value in a field and Approach returns all records that match the criteria you specified. However, you can enter Find criteria in more than one field at a time to limit your search.

For example, to find agents who were paid no more than $200 in October 1994, you would enter the Find criteria shown in Figure 12.6. Here we've entered **<=200** in the amount field, and **10/*/94** in the date

FIGURE 12.6 ▸

Finding records with values less than or equal to $200 in the CommAmt field and a SaleDate in October 1994

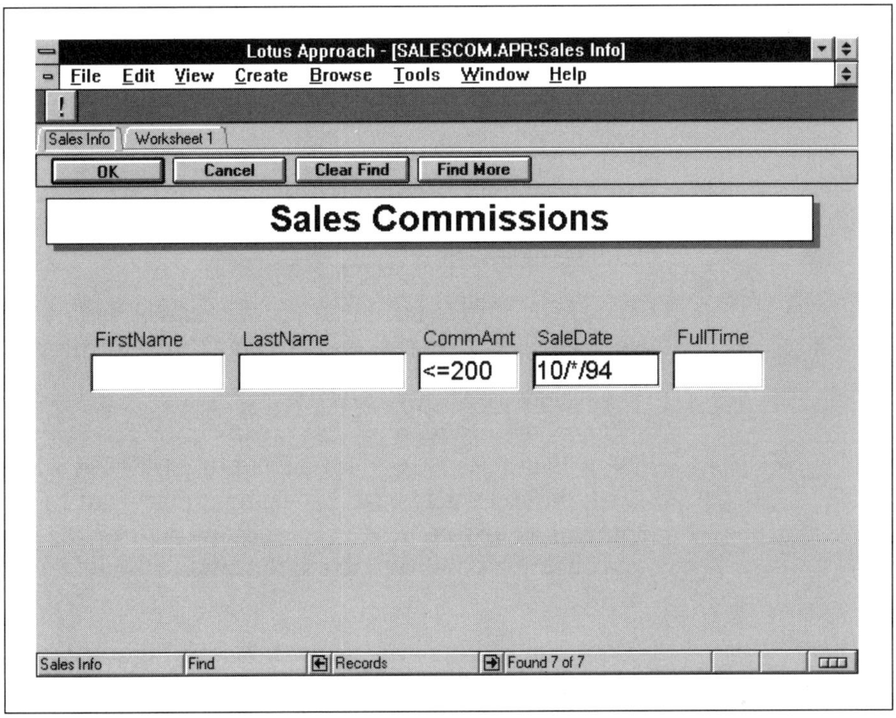

field. When Approach searches through the database, it checks both conditions before it considers the record a match. In our sample data, Harry Andersen's record matches both conditions. However, while Mary Andrews earned a commission in October, her commission amount exceeds the $200 limit, so Approach will not return her record. The found set includes only one record: Harry Andersen.

Note that when you enter values in two different fields on the same view (form, worksheet, and so forth), all conditions must be met for a match to occur. In the next section we'll see what happens when you enter multiple conditions but use more than one view.

▸ Widening a Search: Entering "Or" Criteria

You've already seen that you can use the comma within a single field to find two values. You were able to find Vicki and Rocky by entering two values in the FirstName field (or the LastName field, depending on your preference). By separating the values with a comma, Approach understood you wanted both Vicki and Rocky.

Ironically, you've just used an "or search" to return two records: Vicki and Rocky. In English we use the word *or* to mean one thing or another, but not both. When you conduct searches, however, "or" takes on a completely different meaning. When you use "or" in a search, it means you want both conditions.

In Approach the comma is used to indicate an "or condition." We want Approach to match the FirstName field on the values Vicki or Rocky, and return both records.

Once you understand that an *or condition* means you'll see more, not fewer, records, you're on your way to using Approach's powerful search feature.

You've already seen how to create an or condition using the comma. Now you'll see how to specify an or condition when you want to work with different fields. In this example, we want to look for part-time employees or anyone who earned more than $300. This means we'll be specifying a condition using the FullTime field and the CommAmt field.

If we entered the criteria as shown in Figure 12.7, Approach would return no records at all. Why? If you specify two conditions on the same

FIGURE 12.7

Approach finds no records in our Sales Commissions database because no records meet all criteria entered on the screen. Here we ask for part-time employees who earn more than $300.

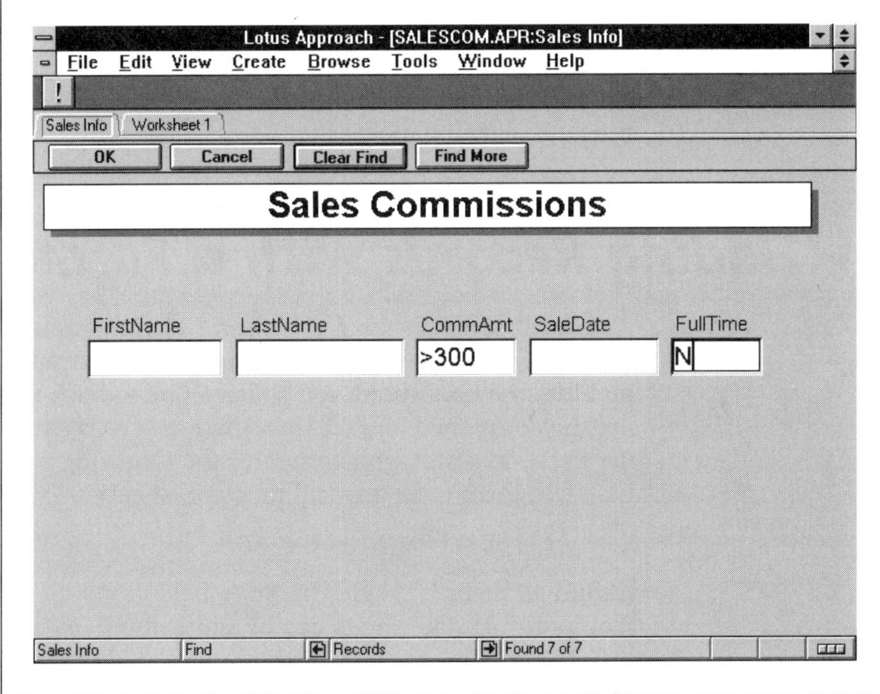

form, Approach won't match a record until all conditions are met. By placing both conditions on the same form, we've asked Approach to show us part-time employees *and* those who earned more than $300.

Instead, we'll use the Find More command in Approach to widen the search. To search for multiple conditions, use the or condition—records must meet one criteria or another (or a third and so on). Use these steps to set the or condition to find employees who earned more than $300, or who are part time, or both:

1. Issue the Find command (press Ctrl+F or click on the Find button from the SmartIcons toolbar).
2. Enter the first criteria. For instance, enter N in the FullTime field.
3. Select the Find More button, select Browse ➤ Find More, or press Ctrl+F. Approach appears to erase your first Find criteria and presents you with another blank view.
4. Enter the next criteria: type > (or click the > button on the SmartIcons toolbar) and type **300**.

5. You can repeat Steps 3 and 4 until your criteria are all entered. At this point our criteria have been entered, so select OK.

None of the records in our data meets the specified criteria of part time and earning more than $300.

▸▸ Finding Records with a Formula

Approach provides the *If statement* to help you find data using a formula. Approach will display the record(s) you select if each record matches the conditions you specify. Going back to our example involving the company Contact Information screen shown in Figure 12.2 earlier in this chapter, you can enter the following search criteria in any field in a form or in any cell in a worksheet:

```
If (DEALERS.State='CO')
```

to find all records where the State field contains the value CO (for Colorado). If statements can be quite complex, as you'll soon see.

The If statement is unique in that you can enter the search criteria in any unused field on the form. You can also combine the If statement in a field (such as the City field) with criteria in another field. For example, you can enter the **If (DEALER.City='Denver')** statement in the City field and enter **Adams** in the SalesAgent field to find all customers in Denver whose sales representative is Adams.

The format of the If statement is more fully explained in Chapter 19. The format is similar to other formulas you write when creating validation rules (see Chapter 5 for validation rules). For example, the If statement can include multiple conditions. Each condition must be surrounded by parentheses, and the entire If statement must itself be surrounded by another set of parentheses. For example, you can enter the following statement in any field on a form or cell in a worksheet:

```
If( (DEALERS.State='CO') And (DEALERS.Salesrep =
'Adams'))
```

This example is shown in Figure 12.8, with a slight modification. We have not capitalized the Colorado abbreviation, since our database is in dBASE format and thus searches are case insensitive.

FIGURE 12.8

You can find a record using a formula. The formula can be entered in any field on the form.

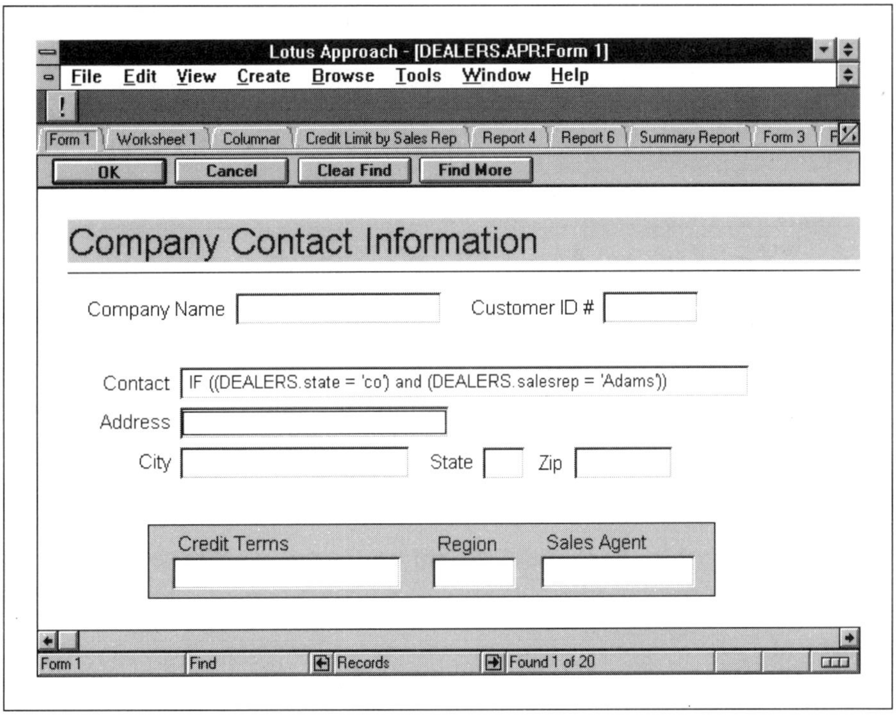

Notice that if your Approach file contains more than one database, you must include the database name in every field reference, but the database name need not be written using all UPPERCASE letters, as is the default format when writing formulas. Approach expects to find the database name, a period, then the field name when more than one database is defined within the Approach file. You must place a field name in double quotation marks (") if the field contains a space or any of these characters:

. , / # + - < > ( )

Also notice that constant values, such as text, date, and time values (the value CO, for example), are placed within single quotes. Numeric values, such as the value 300, do not need to be placed in quotes.

►► Shortcuts for Finding Records

When you work with a found set, you can change values in fields, add records, and do all the tasks you would normally do if you were working with all records. However, when you add records, you may be adding records that don't match the Find criteria. You may also want a quick way to modify the current search. In either case, select Browse ➤ Find Again and Approach will display the original criteria from your last Find request. To clear the Find criteria, select the Clear Find button.

▸▸ Finding Unique Records

Approach lets you display one record for each value in the field or fields you select. For example, suppose in our database Harry Andersen earned another commission on November 1. You want to create mailing labels for each agent so you can send a notice about the new commission schedule. If you select all records, Andersen will get two copies of the notice—a waste of paper.

Approach lets you find one record for each employee. Use these steps to select unique records:

1. Select Browse ➤ Find Special. Approach displays the Find Special dialog box shown in Figure 12.9. (If you are working in a Worksheet view, select Worksheet ➤ Find ➤ Find Special.)
2. Check "Find unique or distinct records in the current found set."
3. Select the field(s) that must be unique. If you select more than one field, Approach looks at the combined values to create a unique key. This combined value is then checked against all other records in the database.
4. Select OK.

▸▸ **NOTE**

Approach displays the first record ever entered (chronologically) for the duplicate value. (Remember that each record added is assigned a record number in the order entered. Thus, if record numbers 10 and 20 contain the same value, Approach returns record 10 as the unique record.)

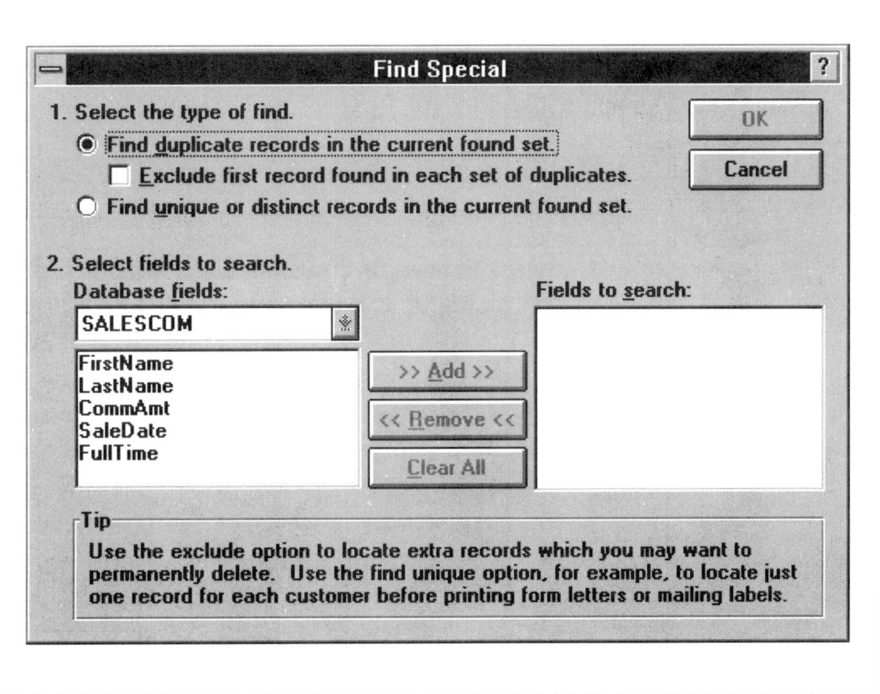

FIGURE 12.9

The Find Special dialog box lets you find duplicate or unique records.

►► Finding Duplicate Records

Approach can also use the Find Special dialog box to find duplicate records. Suppose, for example, that we only want one record for each agent. The Find Duplicate option lets you locate records that do not belong in your database. Approach gives you the option of viewing all occurrences of the repeated value or just records that contain the repeated value (and hiding the first record that contains the repeated value).

For example, suppose record number 10 in your database is

LastName	FirstName	Amount	Date	FullTime
Andersen	Harry	$145	10/1/94	Y

and that record number 25 is

LastName	FirstName	Amount	Date	FullTime
Andersen	Harry	$155	11/1/94	Y

You want to save only one record per agent. Use these steps to find the duplicate record:

1. Select Browse ➤ Find Special. Approach displays the Find Special dialog box shown in Figure 12.9 earlier in this chapter. (If you are working in a Worksheet view, select Worksheet ➤ Find ➤ Find Special.)
2. Select the "Find duplicate records in the current found set" option. This will show both records for Harry Andersen.
3. To limit the Find to the second (and succeeding) occurrences of duplicate values, check the "Exclude first record found in each set of duplicates" option. In this case, only record 25 will be displayed.
4. Select the field(s) that must be unique. If you select more than one field, Approach looks at the combined values to create a unique key. This combined value is then checked against all other records in the database.
5. Select OK.

▸▸ Deleting Found Records

After you display selected records using the Find or Find Special commands, you can delete the records in the found set. For example, you can select all employees whose status is "I" (for inactive), then remove them from the database. You can also select the duplicate records and exclude the first record for each duplicate value, then delete the found set—only unique values from the original found set remain.

To delete the found set, select Worksheet ➤ Delete ➤ Found Set if you are working in a worksheet, or Browse ➤ Delete Found Set from any other view. Approach will display a message asking for confirmation. Select Yes.

►► Sorting Records

By default, Approach lists records in the order in which they were added to the database. While this may be fine when records are added sequentially, such as data in an Orders database, it is often more useful to see records in a different order, called the *Sorted Order*. For example, it is easy to find a customer name when the list is arranged alphabetically by last name. Approach lets you sort data by one or more fields in your database, either ascending (A to Z) or descending (Z to A). Approach can sort on any field except PicturePlus, memo, and variable fields. For example, you can sort on a date field and display your records chronologically.

You can also define the Sort Order on more than one field. For instance, you can sort your list of records by last name, then by first name. In this way, if you have two records with the name Smith, Approach will sort Bob Smith before James Smith. In this example, LastName is the primary sort key, because all records are sorted on LastName first. The FirstName is the secondary sort field, because after all records are sorted by LastName they are then sorted within LastName by FirstName. Approach lets you have several levels of sorts, so you can sort by LastName, then FirstName, then AmountDue, for example. Remember, however, that the greater the number of levels of sort, the more time it takes Approach to display your data.

Sorting only changes the way you view the data. It does not change the way the data is stored in the database.

You can also perform several sorts on the same database without fear. For instance, you can sort your customer list by LastName in order to find Bob Smith, then sort the data by AmountDue so you can call customers who owe the largest amount. You can later sort the same database by zip code to create mailing labels in sorted zip code order, and thus possibly qualify for postage discounts.

When you are working with the found set, the sort you specify applies to the records in the found set, not the entire database. However, it is just as easy to specify a Sort Order for a found set as it is for the entire database.

► Sorting Data on a Single Field

To tell Approach how to sort your data, display the form or worksheet containing the data you want to view.

To sort on a single field on a form, move to that field and select the Ascending Sort icon (it contains an A at the top and a Z underneath) or the Descending Sort icon (it contains a Z at the top and an A underneath) from the SmartIcons toolbar. Approach automatically sorts data based on the selected field.

To sort one or more columns that appear together (called *contiguous* columns) in a worksheet, click on a single column heading (or drag the mouse across contiguous column headings), then select the Ascending Sort icon or the Descending Sort icon from the SmartIcons toolbar. Alternatively you can select Worksheet ➤ Sort, then choose Ascending or Descending. Approach automatically sorts data based on the selected column(s). Approach sorts the left-most column first, then the second, and so on.

► Sorting Data on More Than One Field

Simple single-field sorts (for forms) or single or contiguous column sorts (for worksheets) may provide everything you need. However, when your needs are greater, you can sort on many fields at once.

Use these steps to sort by more than one field:

1. If you are using a form, select Browse ➤ Sort, then choose Define. If you are using a worksheet, select Worksheet ➤ Sort, then choose Define. For both forms and worksheets the shortcut key is Ctrl+T. You can also select the Open the sort dialog box icon from the SmartIcons toolbar, although it is not on the default toolbar (but it can be added using the directions in Chapter 18). Approach displays the Sort dialog box shown in Figure 12.10.

FIGURE 12.10

The Sort dialog box lets you sort on multiple fields, defining whether each field should be sorted in ascending or descending order.

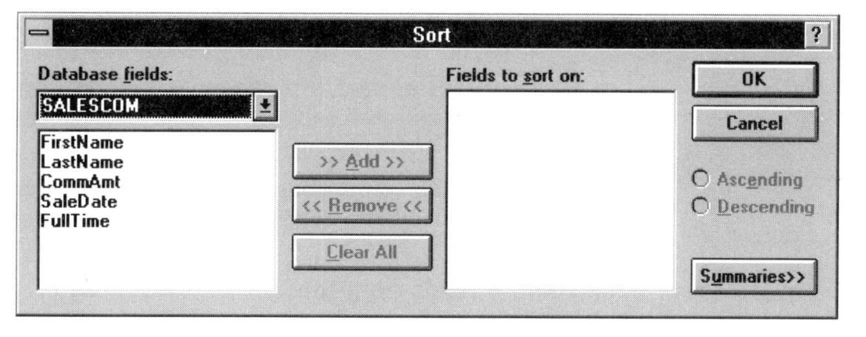

2. Select the primary sort key (the one you'll sort on first) by selecting the database and field, then clicking on the Add button. Approach moves the field name to the top of the "Fields to sort on" list. Choose Ascending or Descending to sort from A to Z or Z to A. (If the text field has letters and numbers, the sort order is 0 to 9, then A to Z.) Non-text fields are sorted as you expect. For example, numeric fields are sorted as 0, 1, 2, and so on for ascending sorts and 2, 1, 0 for descending sorts.
3. To further refine the sort (to sort all records further after they have been sorted by the field selected in Step 2), repeat the process. You can select as many fields as you wish, but the more you select, the slower Approach will be. You can sort the fields in different order. For example, you can sort primary field in ascending order and the secondary field in descending order and so on.
4. To remove a field from the sort specification, select it from the "Fields to sort on" list and choose the Remove button. To start over, select Clear All.
5. If you want to sort on a Summary field (explained in Chapter 5), select the Summaries button, then select the summary field you want included in the "Fields to sort on" list. If the Summary field is used on more than one Summary Panel, select the desired "Summarized On" option.
6. Select OK to perform the sort.

▸▸ **NOTE**

If you have previously sorted the database by a field, that field is already displayed in the "Fields to sort on" list.

Since Approach remembers the last sort you performed, it's easy to change the sort order. Simply select Browse ➤ Sort, then choose Define or press Ctrl+T. The Sort dialog box is restored. You can now add or remove fields from the list. To change the order, select the field from the "Fields to sort on" list and choose Ascending or Descending. Select OK to re-sort the data.

▸ Showing All Records in Their Original Order

To remove the effect of your sort, click on the Show All icon from the SmartIcons toolbar. (There are two icons for Show All. One contains the picture of cards arranged in order, the other icon contains a picture of a sunrise breaking over your database.)

You can also:

- Select Worksheet ➤ Find ➤ Show All or press Ctrl+A if you are working in a worksheet.
- Select Crosstab ➤ Find ➤ Show All or press Ctrl+A if you are working in a crosstab.
- Select Browse ➤ Show All or press Ctrl+A if you are working in a form.

Note that if you have sorted records in a found set, this removes the Find criteria and shows all records, not just those in the found set.

►► Summary and a Look Ahead

In this chapter you've learned how to find an individual record or multiple records, called a found set. You've also seen that once you display a found set, you can navigate through the found set just as you do through the entire database. You've also seen how to turn off a filter and display all records.

In addition, you've seen how to sort records and display them alphabetically or in descending order (from Z to A). You've seen how to quickly sort records in a worksheet (by clicking on the header and choosing the Sort icon from the SmartIcons toolbar), as well as how to define more complex sorts that sort records on multiple fields.

In previous chapters we've focused on forms, worksheets, and reports, since these views are the most frequently used and allow you to display and edit data. Approach can create two other types of forms: form letters (for creating personalized letters) and mailing labels (for attaching to the envelopes of those letters). You'll learn more about those views in Chapter 13.

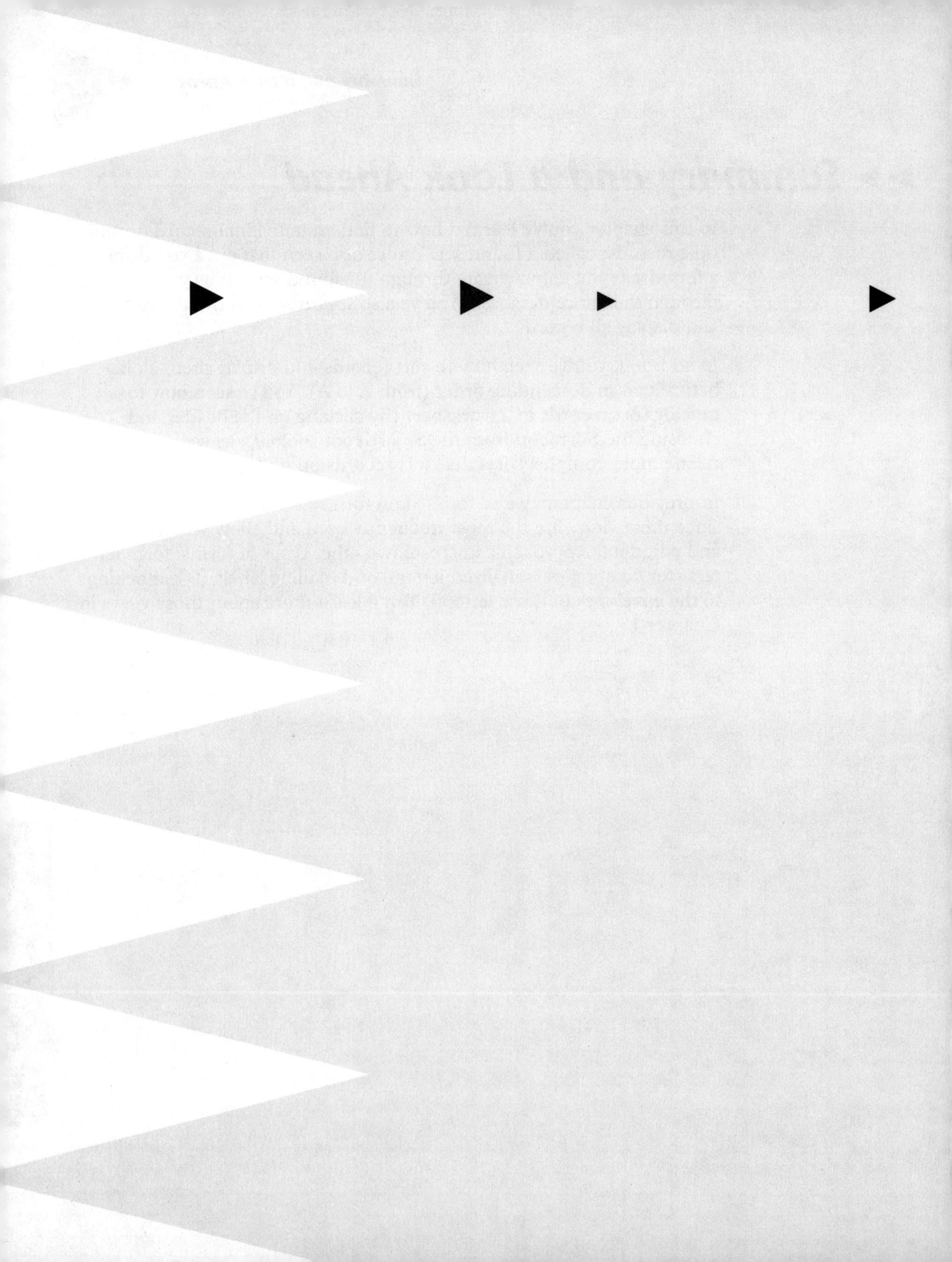

▶ ▶ CHAPTER 13

Form Letters and Mailing Labels

▸▸ FAST TRACK

▸ *To create a form letter* **444**

select Create ➤ Form Letter or select the Create Form Letter icon. Using the Form Letter Assistant, enter the name of the form letter in the View name & title box of the Step 1 tab. Select the SmartMaster Style and layout. Select the Return Address tab or press Next and enter the return address, then click on Next. In the Step 3 tab, select the fields that match the positions in your layout, then choose Next and select the fields for the salutation if desired. Using the Step 5 tab, enter the closing text. Click on Done.

▸ *To add text to your form letter* **448**

click twice anywhere within the text object (that is, anywhere in the form letter). Approach changes the mouse into a vertical blinking bar. Enter or edit the body of the letter. To add a field, move the insertion point to the location where you want to insert the field. Select Text ➤ Insert, then chose Field, or click on the Insert field icon from the SmartIcons toolbar. Approach displays the Add Field list. Double-click on the field you want to add.

▸ *To change the text properties of the form letter* **450**

select the text and click on the left-, center-, right-align, or full justification icons in the SmartIcons toolbar. To change the spacing, click on the Single Space, Double Space, or One-and-a-Half icons. Text options on the Main menu and the Font tab in the InfoBox also let you select font properties.

▶▶ A form letter combines fields from a database record with predefined text. For example, a letter informing a customer of the contents of an accompanying package (brochure, price list, order form) can be merged with the customer's name and address to create a letter that appears to be written individually to that customer. A form letter is a special type of form, with many of the same characteristics of a data entry form you saw in Chapter 7. A sample form letter is shown in the Design environment in Figure 13.1.

A mailing label is another type of form provided by Approach to create labels you can paste on the outside of an envelope.

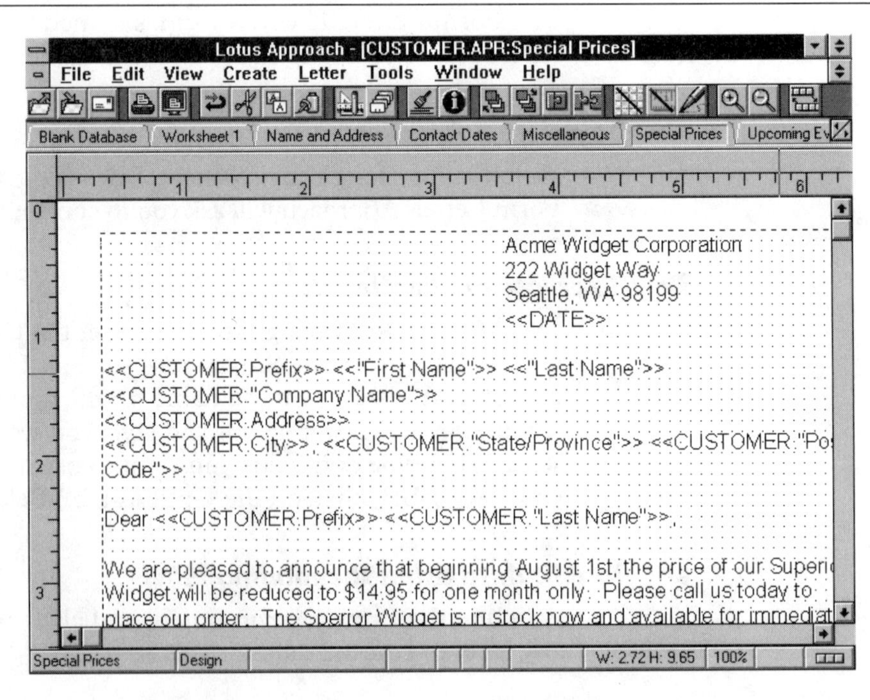

FIGURE 13.1 ▶

The Design environment for a form letter lets you create or modify a form letter, merging fields from your database with fixed text.

Both form letters and mailing labels use Assistants to get you started quickly. You can then edit the design created by the Assistants to suit your special needs.

▸▸ Form Letters

Form letters can combine the current date, a customer's name and address, an opening or salutation, such as Dear Mr. Smith, the body of the letter (including any database fields you select to merge with the text), and a closing (such as: Sincerely yours). If your database includes a product the customer has called your company about, such as the Super Widget 3000, you might store the product name in a field called "Product." You can then generate a form letter at the end of the day (or immediately, if you wish). Your form letter design includes the following:

```
Thank you for your interest in our <<PRODUCT>>.
```

When you print the form, Approach creates one form letter for every database record in your found set, replacing the field name Product with the value from that field in each database record. In our example, your form letter will read:

```
Thank you for your interest in our Super Widget 3000.
```

By default, all text in a form letter is automatically shifted to the left or up one line to eliminate gaps in the finished product. Unnecessary spaces are a tip-off that your letter has been generated by computer.

For example, if you include two fields on your form letter form, <<CUSTOMER.First>> and <<CUSTOMER.Last>>, Approach will "trim" the first name field to the necessary number of characters and remove unwanted spaces, then print the customer name as

```
James Powell
```

not

```
James      Powell
```

Remember that this affects how the data is printed on the form letter, *not* how the data is stored within the database record itself.

►► Creating a Form Letter

To create a form letter, select Create ➤ Form Letter or select the Create Form Letter icon from the SmartIcons toolbar. Approach displays the Form Letter Assistant shown in Figure 13.2. As with other Assistants, you can complete the information on each tabbed screen and select Next or Back to move to the next tab, or directly click on the tab to fill in the parameters. You can select Done to create the form only when all tabbed screens have been filled in.

Enter the name of the form letter in the View name & title box. This name will appear on a tabbed index when the letter is complete.

Select the SmartMaster style from the pull-down list. The style defines the look and feel of the letter. When you select a style other than the Default Style, the Sample Letter will be displayed with a magnifying glass, letting you see the type of font used. You can then choose from the layout, which determines the positioning of key elements, such as the salutation and closing.

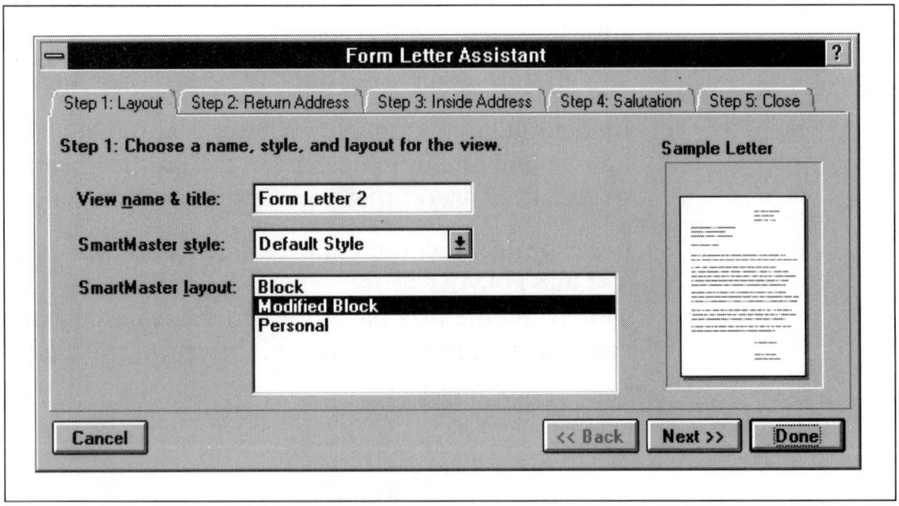

FIGURE 13.2 ►

The Form Letter Assistant presents a tabbed dialog box in which you can specify the parts of your form letter quickly and easily.

Select the Return Address tab or press Next to define the text of the return address, as shown in Figure 13.3. Many SmartMaster styles include a place for the return address, but you can skip it by selecting None. To enter a multi-line return address, click anywhere in the text area and type the first line, then press Enter to move to the next line. When you have completed the return address information, click on Next.

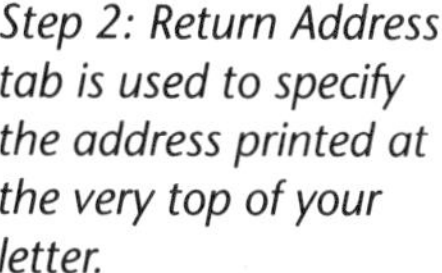

FIGURE 13.3

Step 2: Return Address tab is used to specify the address printed at the very top of your letter.

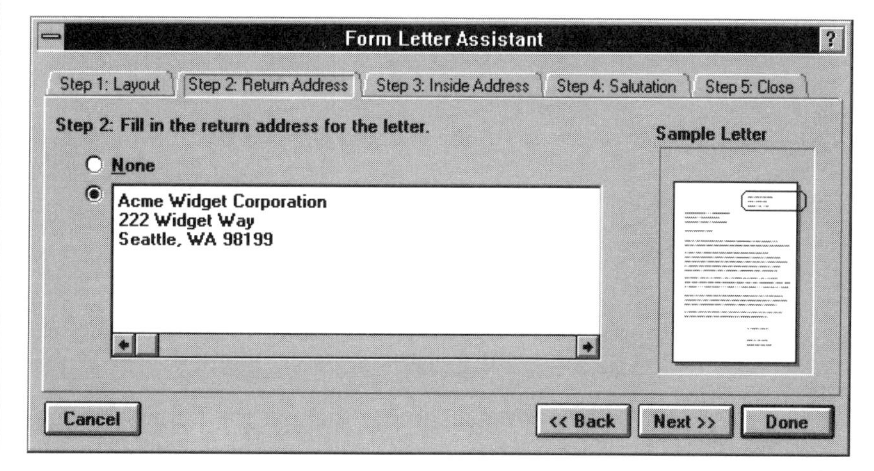

Step 3 of the Assistant, shown in Figure 13.4, asks for information about the Inside Address—that is, the address of the person to whom you are addressing the letter. Select the "Address layout" at the top of the screen. In the middle of the screen, Approach displays the locations within the address where you can assign fields in the "Fields for the address" sample. The layouts vary by the number of lines as well as the position of fields, such as zip code, the inclusion of a field for title (Mr., Ms., Mrs.), and so on. Select the address layout that is best suited to the fields you have in your database.

Your job in Step 3 is to match a field in the layout with a field from your database. Approach highlights the field in the upper-left corner of the address block. Select the database field that you want to fill this spot by double-clicking on the field or by highlighting the field and pressing the Add button. As you select the fields, Approach includes

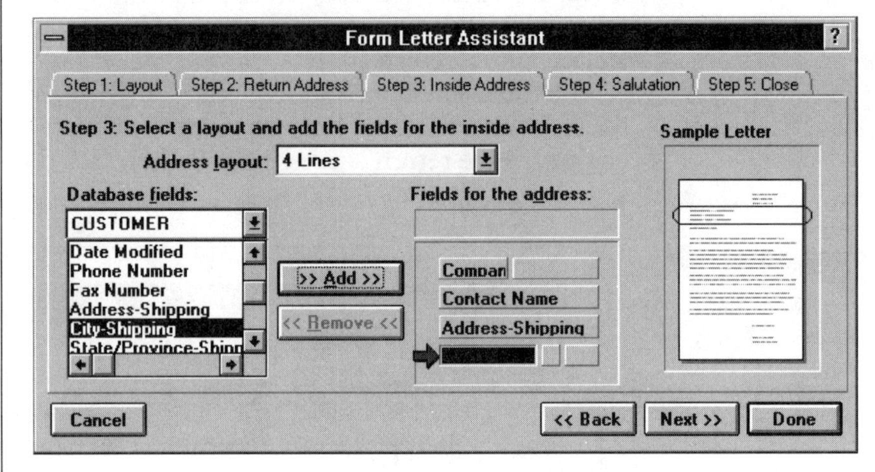

FIGURE 13.4

Step 3: Inside Address tab allows you to enter the address of the person you are writing to. You can select from a variety of label styles and layouts, then choose which field goes in each predefined field position. Approach offers layouts for a variety of address formats, including international addresses.

the field name in the box, or as much of the name as will fit. You can skip a field you don't need by clicking on the next field. To remove the field from the inside address, highlight the block and select Remove.

When you are done matching the fields with the inside address layout, select Next.

The Salutation tab lets you select how you want to open the letter. It is shown in Figure 13.5.

You can select two fields in addition to fixed text, such as Dear or To. For example, you can define a salutation to read:

```
Dear Mr. Smith:
Dear John,
To Betty Smith:
Attention Ms. Smith:
```

assuming you have stored your data in individual fields for the title (Mr., Mrs., and so forth), the first name, and the last name.

Select the form of salutation you wish to use, including the punctuation at the end of the salutation (commas and colons are the common

FIGURE 13.5

Step 4: Salutation tab is used to include an opening, customizable greeting to begin your letter.

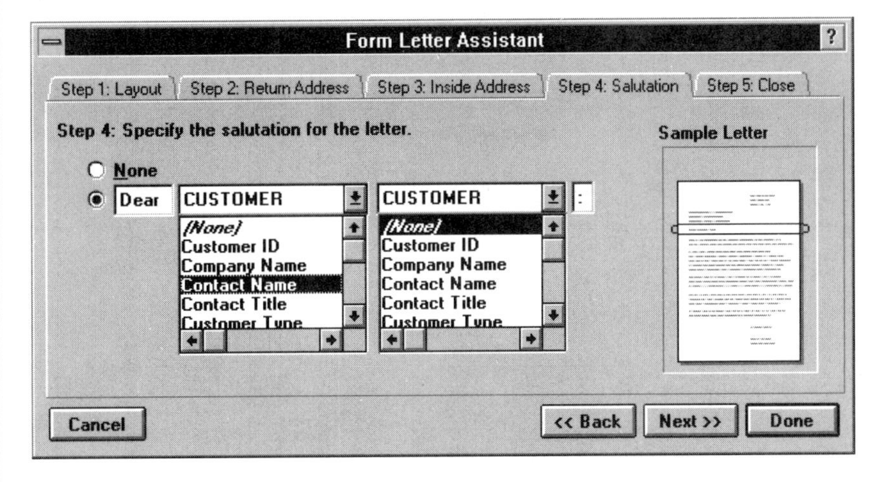

marks used to end a salutation). You can customize your salutation by typing the salutation you want and/or changing the punctuation. If you do not want a salutation, click on the None button. Click Next when you have selected the form of the salutation, or click on the Step 5 tab to enter the closing text.

The closing text appears at the bottom of the letter, and is usually of the form:

```
Very truly yours,
Sincerely yours,
Best regards,
```

followed by three or four lines (to give you room to sign your name) and then your printed name. Type any closing text you wish in the text box. The dialog box for entering closing text is shown in Figure 13.6.

Click on Done and Approach creates the form letter for you. A sample is shown in Figure 13.1 earlier in this chapter. Notice that we have also added some content to the letter, something the Form Letter Assistant does not provide. Instead the Assistant creates a skeleton view, which closely resembles a form.

FIGURE 13.6

Step 5: Close tab includes a closing for a signature block. The closing can include text but not a graphic image of your actual signature.

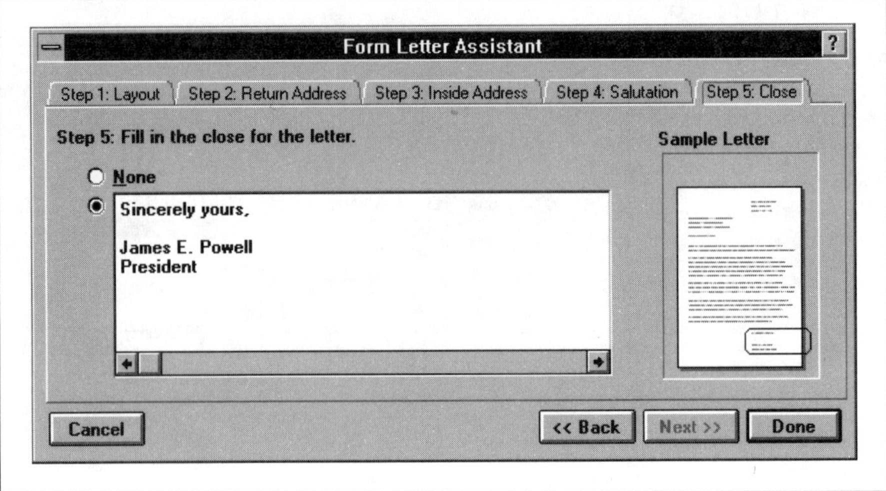

►► Adding Text to Your Form Letter

Now that you have the basics of the form letter in Approach, it's time to add the text and any special objects, such as a company graphic of your logo, as well as merging information from the database record. Using our previous example, at this point we add the text thanking the customer for requesting information about a particular part our company sells.

The text in your letter is actually one large text object—or you can create several text objects and place them on the same form. As with any text object, you can cut, copy, and move text. Also note in Figure 13.1 earlier in this chapter that the Ruler bar shows the left and right margins and tab settings, much as a word processor does. These were also available from smaller text fields when placed on a data entry form, but the area within such text areas was usually so small that the Ruler bar and Tab settings were not needed.

To begin editing, click twice anywhere within the text object, meaning anywhere in the form letter. Approach changes the mouse into a vertical blinking bar, indicating that you are in edit mode within the text object.

▶ Adding a Field to a Form Letter

Adding a field is very similar to the technique you use to add a field object to a form. Move the insertion point (the vertical flashing cursor) to the location where you want to insert the field. Select Text ➤ Insert, then choose Field, or click on the Insert field icon from the SmartIcons toolbar. Approach displays the Add Field list. Double-click on the field you want to add, and Approach inserts the field at the insertion point.

You can format a field just as you can any field on a data entry form. Select the field, including the opening and closing marks (<< and >>), then open the InfoBox or right-click on the field and select Styles & Properties. Proceed to set the options you wish as though it were any field on a form. (For more details on setting field properties, see Chapters 7 and 8.)

▶▶ **NOTE**

If you know the name of the field, you can type it directly by including opening angle brackets (<<), the database name (in ALL UPPERCASE CHARACTERS), a period, and the field name, followed by closing angle brackets (>>).

▶ Using the Ruler Bar to Adjust Text

You use the Ruler bar to set tabs and margins. The Ruler bar in Figure 13.1 earlier in this chapter shows that the return address begins at about 3.5 inches from the left margin of the letter, which has a quarter-inch margin from the left side of the physical page. To move these settings, highlight the text (the entire return address, in this example), and drag the top triangle to the left margin (or any other location along the line). When you release the mouse button, the text is repositioned.

▶ Editing Text

To enter text, click the mouse in the area in which you want the text to appear, and begin to type. You can highlight text and then begin typing to replace existing text.

Unfortunately, text is not like other objects on a form—you cannot drag it from one position to another to move it. Therefore, to move a section of text, select it, choose Edit ➤ Cut, move the cursor to the new location, and select Edit ➤ Paste. In order to move a field in the form letter, select the entire field name, including the double open (<<) and closing (>>) angle brackets.

You can set text properties using the SmartIcons toolbar, the Text menu, or the icons on the toolbar. For example, you can select text and click on the left-, center-, right-align, or full justification icons in the SmartIcons toolbar to adjust the text's position. (The justification icon is not on the default toolbar but it can be added using the directions in Chapter 18.)

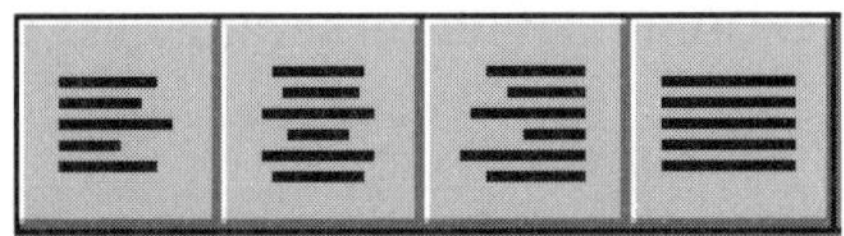

You can also change the spacing between single and double lines by selecting the text and clicking on the Single Space, Double Space, or One-and-a-Half icons from the SmartIcons toolbar. (The One-and-a-Half icon is not on the default toolbar but it can be added using the directions in Chapter 18.)

The text options on the Main menu and the Font tab in the InfoBox let you select font properties. For example, select the text you want to change and choose Text from the Main menu. The list of options that change the font style and effect includes Normal, Bold, Italic, Underline, and Strikethrough.

Likewise, you can highlight the text and select these same font settings, plus choose the font name, color, size, alignment, and spacing by displaying the InfoBox. The InfoBox appears in Figure 13.7 and is similar to that used for any text field, except that in this case you are applying the properties to a section of text, not the entire text within the text object. You can also select the font name and size and the bold, italic, and underline options from the boxes on the Status bar.

FIGURE 13.7

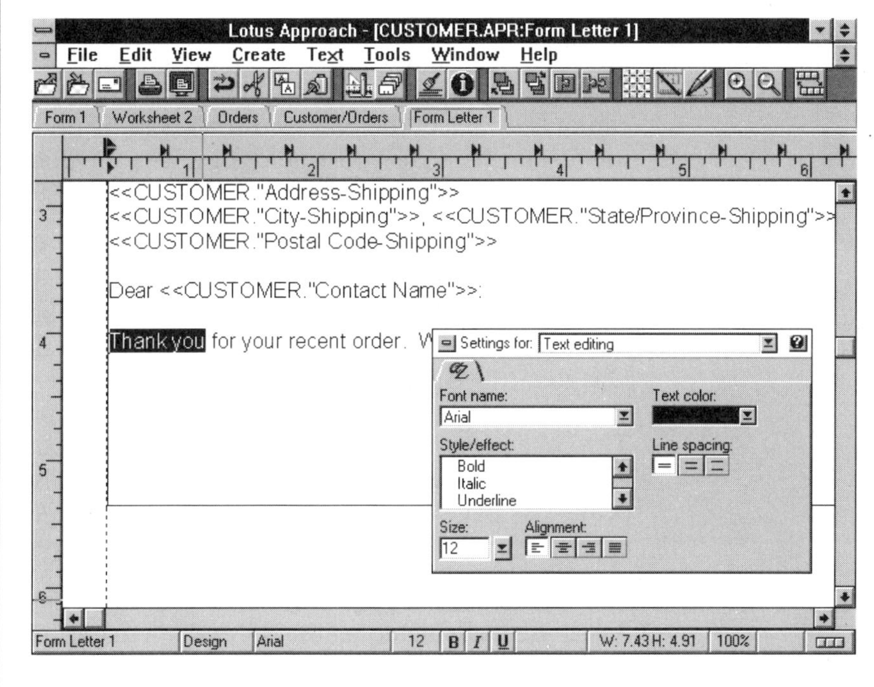

The Font tab of the InfoBox for editing text within your form letter.

▶ *Adding Special Fields: Date, Time, and Page Numbers*

To insert the current system date or time, or the page number in your letter, move the cursor to the desired location and select Text ➤ Insert, then choose Date or Time to insert a special field marker in your text. For date you'll see

```
<<DATE>>
```

which is replaced by the current date when you print the form letter. Likewise, time is represented by

```
<<TIME>>
```

and is replaced with the system time at the time you print or preview the form letter. You can also insert the date and time place holders by selecting the Date and Time icons from the SmartIcons toolbar.

You can change the format of the date and time just as if each field were placed on a data entry form: Select the field (including the opening << and closing >> markers), then open the InfoBox, or select the field and right-click on the field and choose Style & Properties. (You can quickly select the date and time field by double-clicking on it.) Set the format string as you would for a date or time field on a form. (See Chapter 8 for more details.)

To insert the page number, move the cursor to the desired location and select Text ➤ Insert and choose Page #. Alternatively, click on the Page Number icon from the SmartIcons toolbar. (The Page Number icon is not on the default toolbar but can be added to it using the directions in Chapter 18.) Approach inserts the place holder <<#>> and will substitute the page number value when you print or preview the form letter. The page number is always relative to 1 for each record. For example, if you have three customers in your found set, the page number will be printed as page 1 for each customer's form letter, not 1 for the first customer, 2 for the second customer, and 3 for the third customer.

You can format the page number as you would any other numeric field. Select the field, including the << and >> marks, then open the InfoBox, or right-click on the field and select Style & Properties. Set the format you wish. For more details about formatting numeric fields on a form, see Chapter 8.

▸▸ **TIP**

You can enter <<DATE>>, <<TIME>>, or <<#>> directly rather than using the menus or SmartIcons from the toolbar if you wish.

▸ *Adding Graphics to Your Form Letter*

You can add a graphic image to your form, thus eliminating the need to print your letter on letterhead. Instead, simply include the graphic from your letterhead on your form.

Adding a graphic to a form letter is accomplished in exactly the same way as adding a graphic image to any other form. See Chapter 8 for further details.

▶▶ Viewing Your Form Letter

To see what your form letters will look like before you print them, select File ➤ Preview, press Ctrl+Shift+B, or click on the second box in the Status bar at the bottom of the page and select Preview.

In the Preview environment you can move to any record in your found set, zoom in or out of the image, and even re-sort your data.

When you switch to Preview, Approach changes the SmartIcons toolbar, as shown in Figure 13.8. Notice the familiar VCR-like controls for moving to the next, previous, first, and last records. In addition, you can select a subset of records (the found set, discussed in Chapter 12) by clicking on the Find icon or selecting Find from the Browse menu, quickly print the form letter, or send it as electronic mail.

The Preview environment is discussed in Chapter 15.

FIGURE 13.8 ▶

The SmartIcons toolbar changes when you preview your form letter.

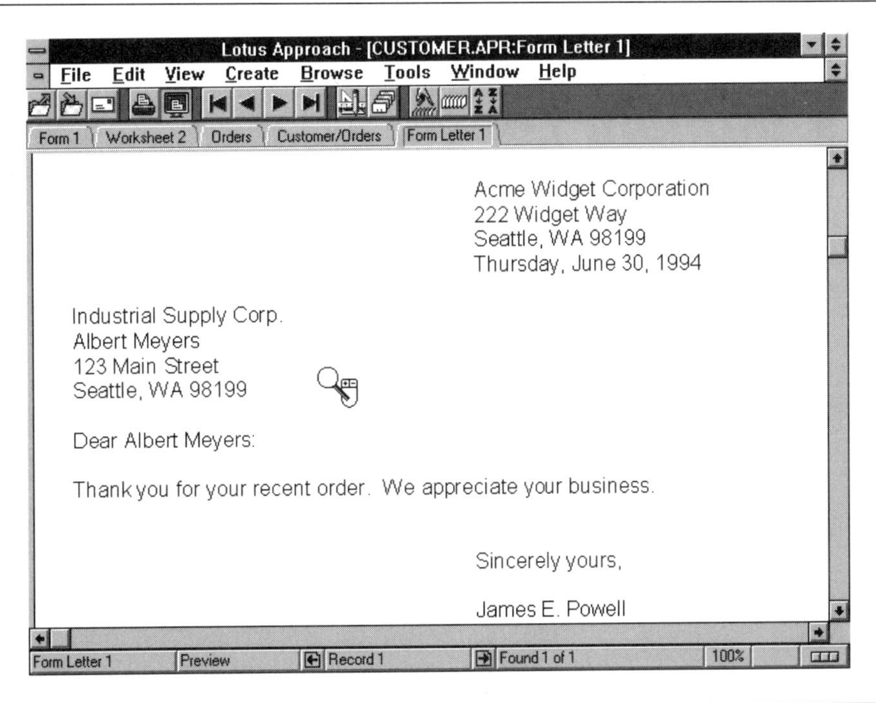

Form letters can't be edited in the Browse environment as you can with reports, but you can perform most other functions (sort, find, delete records) in the Browse environment.

▸▸ Copying a Form Letter

To create a duplicate copy of a form letter, switch to the Design environment and select Edit ➤ Duplicate Form Letter. Approach then copies the form to a new form, named Copy of XX, where XX is your original form letter name.

▸▸ Deleting a Form Letter

If you have a form letter in your Approach file that you no longer use, move to the form and switch to the Design environment. Select Edit ➤ Delete Form Letter. Approach will ask you to confirm your request.

▸▸ Mailing Labels

If you've created a form letter, you've already seen how easy it is to pick the fields from your database and create an inside address. With the Mailing Label Assistant you'll also choose which fields are to be included on an address label. Like the Form Letter Assistant, Approach offers a variety of addressing styles.

Mailing labels are also special in that you want to print several labels to a page. Approach has predefined several dozen Avery label formats for your use, or you can create your own layout. You can view the results of your design by using the Preview environment.

To create mailing labels:

1. Select Create ➤ Mailing Label or select the Create a new mailing label icon from the SmartIcons toolbar. Approach displays the Mailing Label Assistant, shown in Figure 13.9.

FIGURE 13.9

In the Mailing Label Assistant you select the label format, then fill in the predefined fields in the label layout.

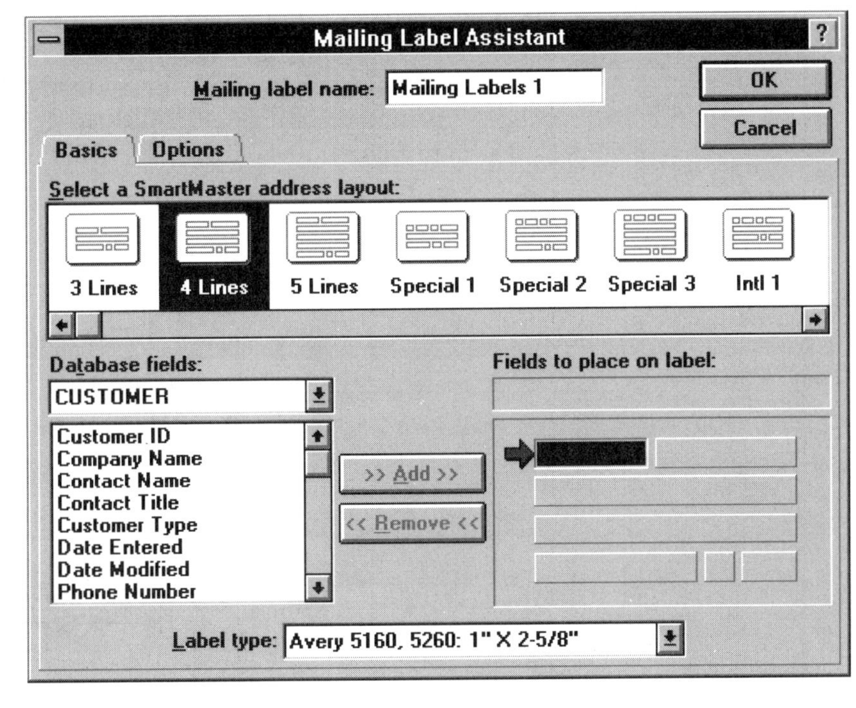

2. Enter a name for the mailing label. This description will appear in the tabs for the Approach file.
3. Select the SmartMaster layout you want. Approach displays a thumbnail sketch of each layout. When you make your selection, the "Fields to place on label" layout changes to reflect the number of lines and open positions for each field.
4. Select the database field for the first position on the label—a red arrow is pointing to this position. Double-click the field name in the "Database fields" list or highlight it and select Add. The red - arrow moves to the next field. To skip a field or move about the label, click on the space you want to fill.
5. Repeat Step 4 until all fields have been defined.
6. Select the label type you want to use. This type has the physical dimensions built in, including the size of the label, the number of labels per row, the space between labels, and so on. If you want to

define your own label, click on the Options tab, enter a name for the label, specify all dimensions and options, then select Add. The name of the custom label you create will appear in the Label type box on the Basics tab the next time you use the Mailing Label Assistant. The options are clearly reflected in the Sample label box, as shown in Figure 13.10.

7. Select OK to create the mailing label form.

FIGURE 13.10

To create custom label layouts in the Mailing Label Assistant, select the Options box and provide the dimensions and details shown here.

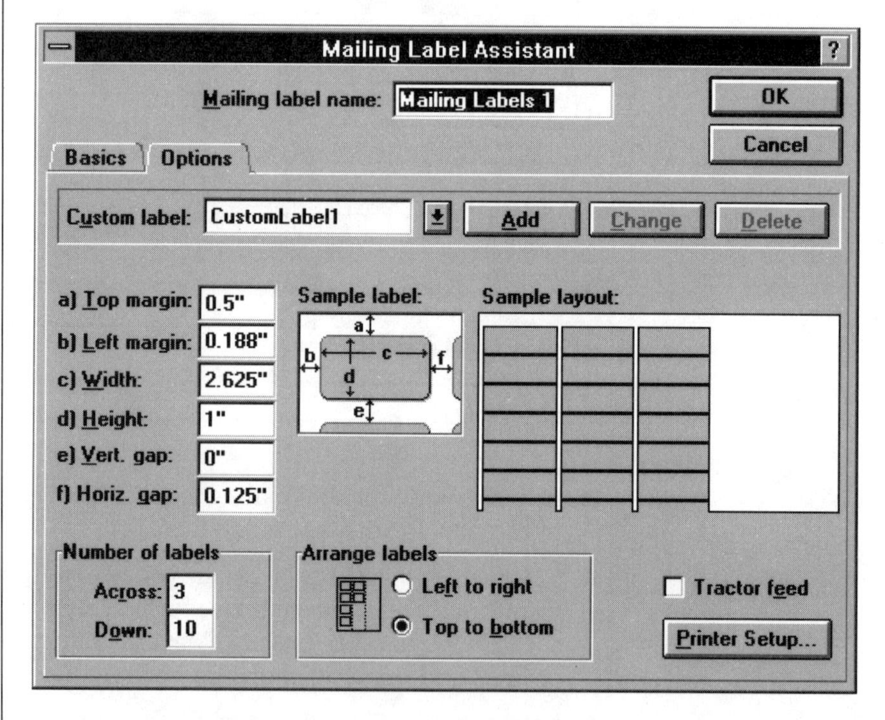

Once you've created the mailing labels, you can work with the definition just as you can with any other form. A mailing label form in the design environment is shown in Figure 13.11. For instance, you can switch to the Design environment and use the InfoBox to set the properties of fields, add fields, move and align fields—all the tasks you can perform with any other form.

Figure 13.12 shows the label in the Browse environment.

FIGURE 13.11

Labels in the Design environment look much like any other form. You can choose View ➤ Show Data to see live data instead of field names, as shown here. The Show Data mode also displays one label for each record in the found set.

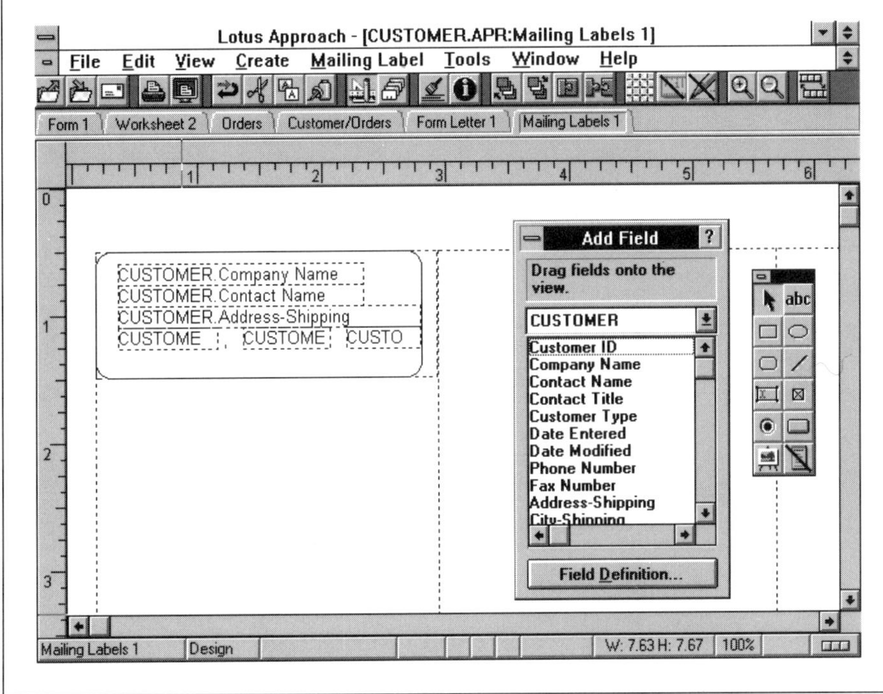

There is a special property that Approach uses in all mailing labels to slide the fields together in order to eliminate extra blank spaces. Your labels will print

```
Seattle, WA 99999
```

rather than

```
Seattle,      WA      99999
```

To see how this is done, or change the property to eliminate sliding, switch to the Design environment. Select the field and choose the Dimensions tab (the one with the blue box and two red dimension markers). Notice the options marked "When printing, slide." When the Left box is checked, text slides to the left to eliminate spaces, as in the Seattle, WA 99999 example. When the Up box is checked, text slides up if the line above contains no text. If, for example, your label contains two fields named Address1 and Address2, and there is no data in Address2, then the City, State, and Zip Code will be moved up one line, essentially taking the place of the otherwise empty Address2 line. Your label

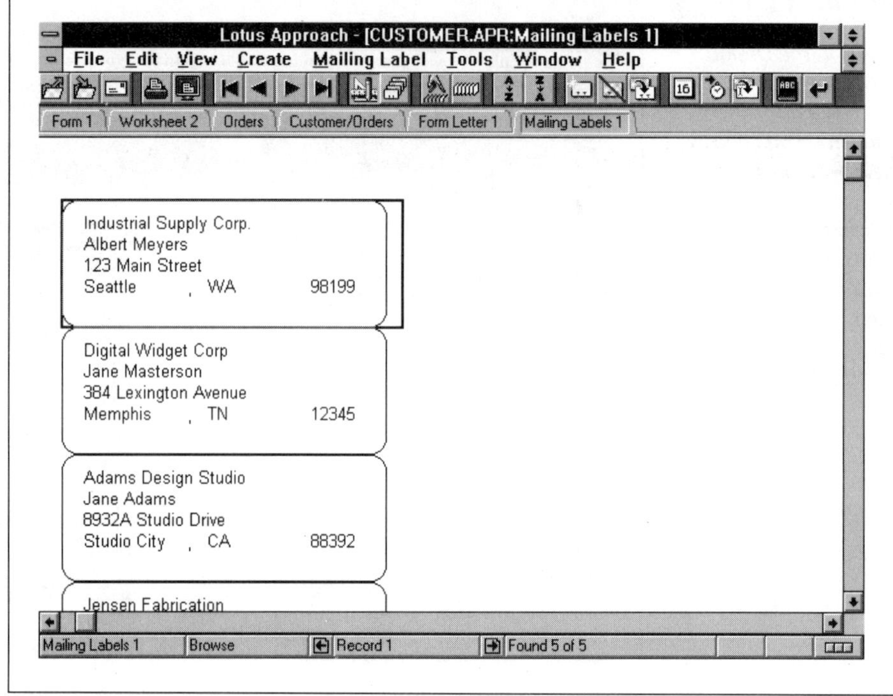

FIGURE 13.12

Labels in the Browse environment show one label for each record in your found set. You can edit data directly by clicking on any field, just as you can in a form or report.

will look like:

```
Jim Powell
234 Main Street
Seattle, WA 99999
```

not this:

```
Jim Powell
234 Main Street

Seattle, WA 99999
```

You may want to see these properties when you add fields to the mailing label, since the options are not set by default.

Notice that when you view the labels in the Browse environment, shown in Figure 13.12 earlier in this chapter, the fields don't seem to slide. That's because the sliding takes place only when you print the labels, not when you view them. To see how the mailing labels will look when printed, select File ➤ Preview. Printing and Preview are described in Chapter 15.

►► Changing Special Label Layouts

If you want to change the special label format you've created, select the mailing label form and switch to the Design environment. Open the InfoBox and from the pull-down menu for "Settings for" choose "Mailing Labels" followed by the name of your labels. Choose the Basics tab and click on the "Edit label options" button. The mailing label options are presented in a dialog box that looks much like the screen used by the Mailing Label Assistant. The dialog box is shown in Figure 13.13. Select the Custom Label name, make your changes, click on Add to add a new label definition, or click Change to save your changes under the current label name, then select OK.

FIGURE 13.13 ►

The Mailing Label Options dialog box lets you set the special dimensions and properties of your label.

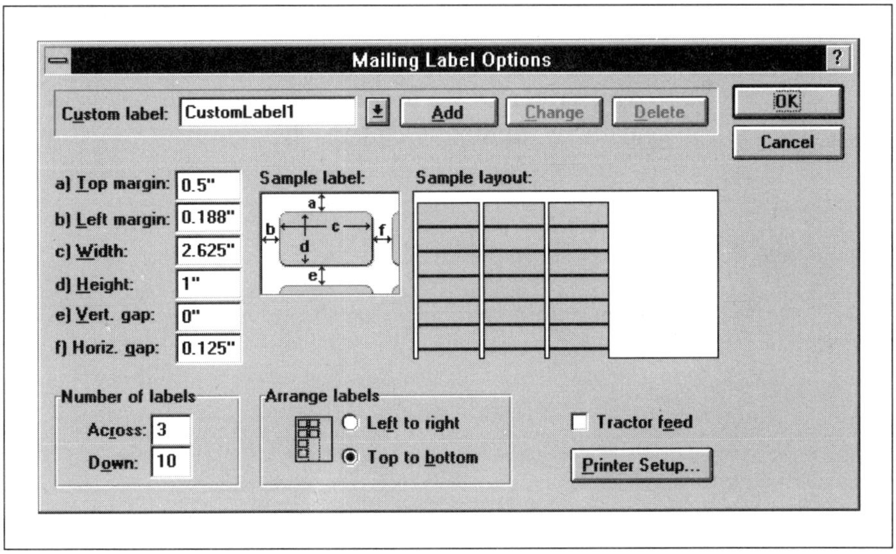

▸▸ Editing Data in Mailing Labels

As with any other form or worksheet, mailing labels let you edit the data within your database. For example, when you switch to the Browse environment, you'll see the labels filled in with data from your database. You can click on any field in any label and edit the data if it is incorrect. For example, when you are looking at labels in the Browse environment, you may notice that a zip code is missing or a city name is misspelled. Simply click on the field and edit the data directly. There is no need to switch to a form, find the appropriate record, and make the change.

▸▸ Summary and a Look Ahead

In this chapter you've learned how to create customized form letters, including how to merge data from any field from your database into a letter. You've also learned how to create mailing labels using an Assistant that is very similar to the opening address of your form letter.

In chapter 14 we'll examine how to display your information graphically by looking at Approach's powerful charting capabilities.

▶ ▶ CHAPTER 14

Creating Charts and Graphs

▸▸ FAST TRACK

▸ ***To create an area, bar, or line chart*** **473**

switch to the Design environment and select Create ➤ Chart or click on the Create Chart icons from the Smart-Icons toolbar. Use the "Step 1: Layout" tab in the Chart Assistant to enter the name and title of your chart. Select a SmartMaster style and layout. Select the "Step 2: X Axis" tab or select the Next button. Select the field to be displayed along the x-axis. Select the "Step 3: Y Axis" tab or select the Next button and select the field for the y-axis. To plot multiple values along the x-axis, select the "Step 4: Series" tab or select the Next Button and select the field to be plotted. Select Done.

▸ ***To create a new pie chart*** **475**

switch to the Design environment, then select Create ➤ Chart or click on the Create Chart icons from the Smart-Icons toolbar. Using the "Step 1: Layout" tab in the Chart Assistant, select a SmartMaster style and choose Pie chart from the SmartMaster layout list. Select the "Step 2: Pie fields" tab and choose the field to be graphed in each pie wedge. Select the field to be represented by each slice from the "Show a new wedge for each value of" list. Choose the value you want to plot for each wedge in the "Of field" list box. In the "Each wedge shows the" option, select the calculation you want for each field. Select Done.

▸ ***To change the fields or calculation used in a chart*** **476**

select Chart ➤ Chart Data Source or right-click anywhere in the chart area and select Chart Data Source. Approach displays the Chart Data Source Assistant, which includes three of the four tabs found in the Chart Assistant for area, bar, and line charts or one of the two tabs found for pie charts. Choose the x- and y-axis fields or the series field for area, bar, or line charts or pie fields for pie charts. Make your changes, then choose the Done button.

➤ *To change chart properties* 477

double-click on any chart element, such as the title, legend, or plot area (the area in the center of the chart), click on the InfoBox icon from the SmartIcons toolbar, or right-click the mouse anywhere inside the chart area and select Style & Properties, select Chart ➤ Style & Properties, or press Ctrl+E.

➤ *To change the title of a chart* 485

double-click on the title area and enter the new text. You can move the title (and subtitle) by dragging the text to the desired position. You can also open the InfoBox for the chart, then click directly on the title. When you choose the layout option in the InfoBox, however, the title is repositioned to one of the five standard positions.

➤ *To change labels on your chart* 490

such as adding the value to each plot point or adding the percentage value for each point, choose the Series Layout option of the InfoBox. Properties can be set for each series. For pie charts, the Slice Labels option acts much like the Series Labels for area, bar, and line charts. You can show the value each slice represents and its percentage, and use the legend to further clarify the source of the data. To explode pie slices by a uniform percentage, select the Options tab of the Chart InfoBox and select a percentage. To explode one or more slices manually, click on the slice and drag it away from the center of the chart.

***Y*ou've** seen how to use forms to view individual records, and how to use worksheets and reports to work with multiple records at a time. Approach offers yet another way of looking at your data. Charts (sometimes called graphs) live up to the expression "A picture is worth a thousand words." When you examine your data with a chart you can:

- Spot trends (e.g. sales are increasing over time).
- Compare values (sales agent A is selling more than sales agent B).
- See abnormal values (unusually high or low sales).
- Examine which records in your database account for the greatest percentage of the whole (which region is selling the most widgets).

Charts are often preferred over reports as an analysis tool because you can quickly see trends and values rather than looking through pages and pages of numbers in a report. Charts can help you pinpoint your business progress—or problems—as demonstrated by your data.

Similar to charts generated in spreadsheet applications, Approach charts are recalculated and redrawn when the data they display changes. For example, if you create a bar chart such as the one shown in Figure 14.1, then add a new sales agent, the new agent will appear in the chart when you switch to the Chart tab.

In this chapter you will learn how to create charts and graphs from scratch, such as the bar chart shown in Figure 14.1. You'll also learn how to modify existing charts using the Lotus Chart module included in Approach.

FIGURE 14.1

This bar chart is typical of the type of chart you can easily create from data in your Approach database.

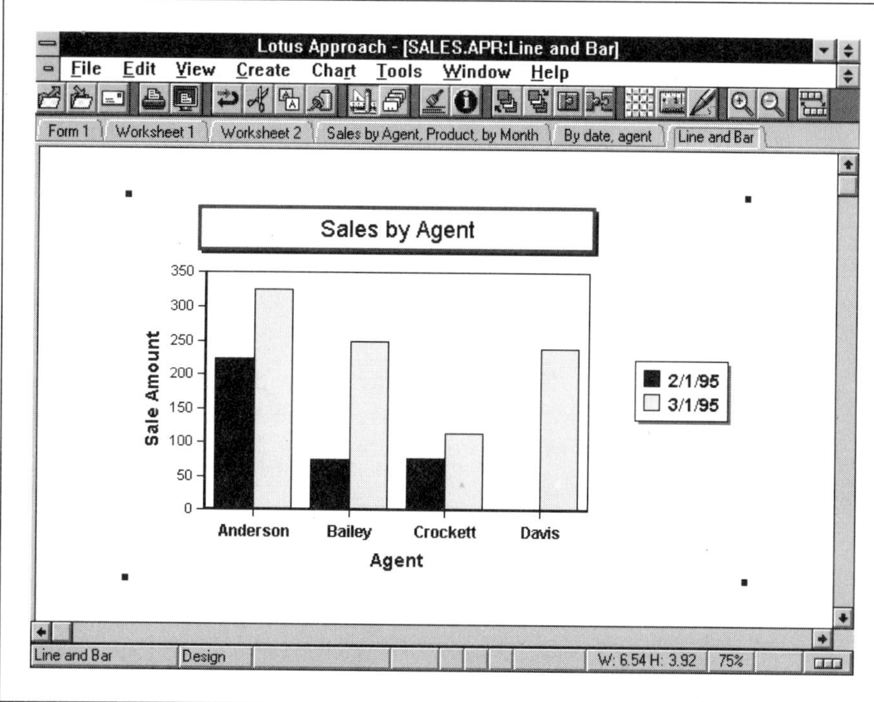

▶▶ Chart Fundamentals

Approach can create four types of charts:

- Area
- Bar
- Line
- Pie

The first three are remarkably similar, while pie charts are distinctive. We'll cover area, bar, and line charts first.

▶ Area, Bar, and Line Charts

These charts display, or plot, data using a horizontal axis called the *x-axis* and a vertical axis called the *y-axis*. For example, in Figure 14.1, we plotted sales data for each sales agent, using the agents' names as the x-axis and the amount of the agent's sales as the y-axis, noted by tick marks for every $50. We've told Approach to plot the sales amount for 2/1/95 in one set of bars, and the sales amount for each agent for 3/1/95 in a second set of bars. We can, and should, have a title for each axis. The x-axis title is Agent, while the y-axis title is Sale Amount.

As you'll see in this chapter, you have complete control over all aspects of a chart. You can change the colors and fonts used in each bar, specify the height and markings for the y-axis, and specify the text of the x- and y-axis labels.

The data for this chart came directly from our Approach database. The following records display the same values we used in our crosstab examples in Chapter 10.

Agent	Product	SaleAmt	SaleDate
Anderson	Widgets	$100	2/95
Anderson	Sprockets	$123	2/95
Anderson	Widgets	$125	3/95
Anderson	Sprockets	$200	3/95
Bailey	Widgets	$75	2/95
Bailey	Widgets	$100	3/95
Bailey	Sprockets	$150	3/95
Crockett	Sprockets	$77	2/95
Crockett	Sprockets	$99	3/95
Crockett	Sprockets	$15	3/95
Davis	Widgets	$150	3/95
Davis	Doodads	$89	3/95

As you can see, the chart has summed the sales for each agent by date. For example, Anderson's total sales in February 1995 are $223, and her sales for March 1995 are $325. Rather than add up the values from our database and view them on a report, we can see from the chart in Figure 14.1 earlier in this chapter that sales for Anderson are rising. In fact, this trend (rising sales) may be more important than the value of the sales. There are also no sales for Davis in February, which is why there is only one bar for Davis in the chart.

The legend at the right of the chart displays two lines. Each box is filled with a color or pattern, and the text to its right indicates what is represented by the bar of the same color and pattern. For example, the dark bar for each agent represents the sales for February, and the lighter bar is used to plot the March sales data.

The title at the top of the chart is also customizable. There is an optional second line you can add to the title. For example, to this chart title we might add the subtitle "By Date" to emphasize that the two bars for each agent represent different time periods.

▶ Pie Charts

In contrast, pie charts don't have x- and y-axis. Instead, a pie chart is used to highlight the percentage of the whole each value represents. Unlike the bar chart shown in Figure 14.1 earlier in this chapter, which showed sales for two time periods, a pie chart can display information from one field only, but not subdivide it. For example, you can plot the total sales for each agent, but we would have to filter the database for February sales in order to limit our pie chart to show the percentages for just February. The pie chart in Figure 14.2 shows the total sales by agent.

The labels for each pie slice show the total sales dollars and the percentage that amount represents of the total sales by all agents. Like the bar chart, we can create a title. This chart also includes the subtitle "Shown as a Pie Chart." Pie charts can also include legends.

▶▶ Choosing the Right Chart Type

The bar chart shown in Figure 14.1 earlier in this chapter is a traditional chart style. There are several variations to this style, including a three-dimensional look. Each bar represents a value in a series. In Figure 14.1 we have a series based on date. The first series of bars (the dark-colored bars) represents sales for February, and the second series (the light-colored ones) shows values for March.

Bar charts are the easiest chart types to read, in part because the bars are large and bold, and because they are the most common type of

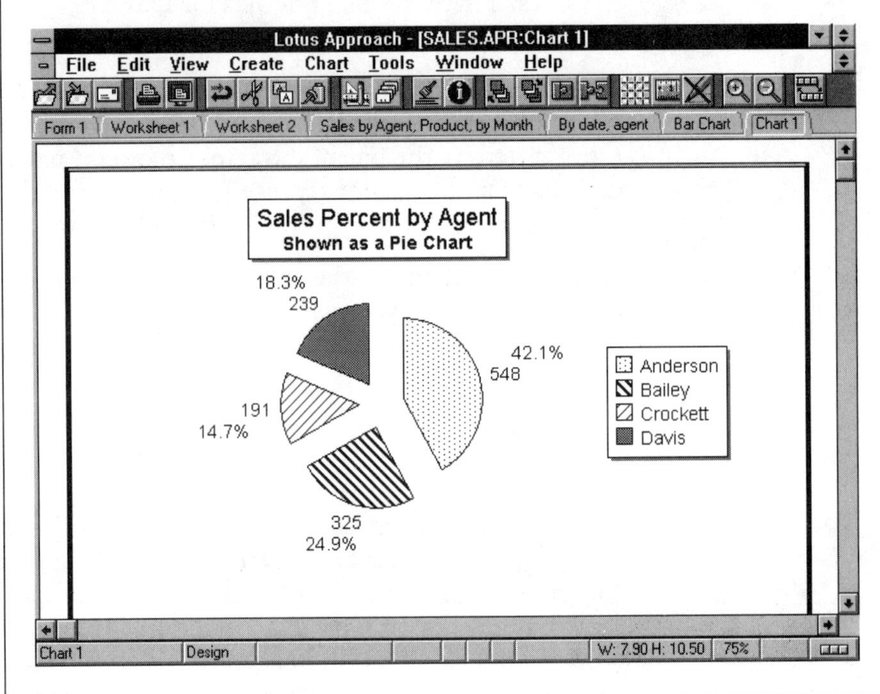

FIGURE 14.2

Pie charts can show each agent's sales as a percentage of total sales. However, pie charts cannot break sales down by month, as is possible with the bar chart style.

business graphic. Bars are a good choice when you want to compare values, but your choice of the x-axis and y-axis is important. The chart in Figure 14.1 is designed to compare sales for each agent. With a few changes, as shown in Figure 14.3, the same data can be displayed to make it easy to compare agent sales by looking at the sales date. (We also added the 3-dimensional look to this chart.) The data is the same—only the chart properties have been changed.

Line charts, such as the chart shown in Figure 14.4, are traditionally used to show changes over time. The line chart would be more meaningful if we had more dates—such as sales for a six-month period. In fact, line charts should be used instead of bar charts when the number of values along the x-axis is large. The more points you have, the skinnier the bars on a bar chart must be in order to show all data. However, you don't have to worry about the thickness of points in a line chart, so if you have several values along the x-axis, a line chart is the more suitable chart type.

Each point in a line chart is plotted to show the value for that date, just as the height of a bar indicates the value of sales for that period.

FIGURE 14.3

By changing the x-axis field, you can examine sales by date and compare how each agent is doing for the same period.

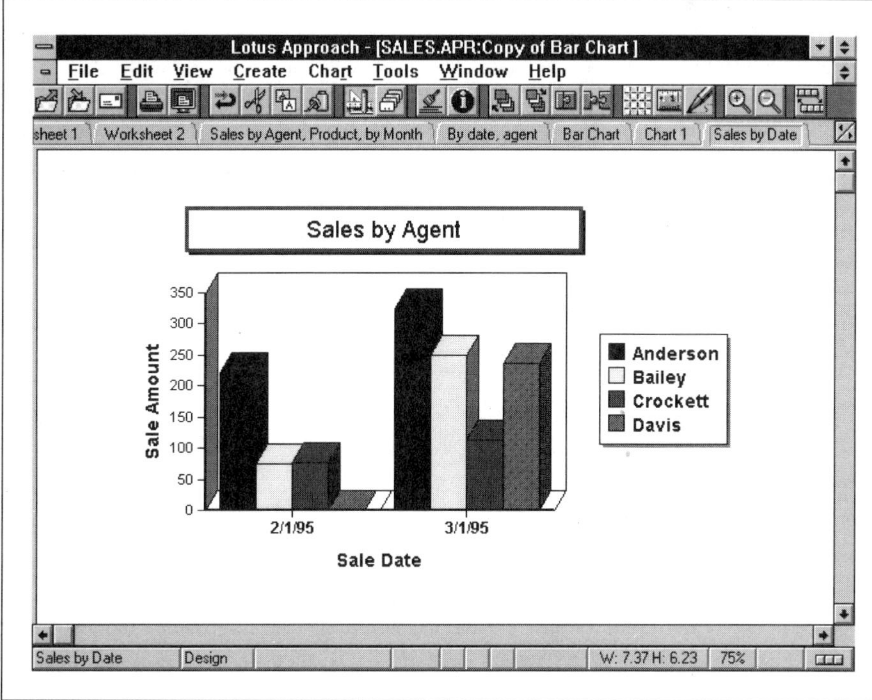

To help distinguish lines, you can use a variety of colors. As you can see here, however, printing a chart in black and white erases any benefit of color. Therefore, Approach lets you choose not only the line style (solid or broken) but use markers—small graphics at each plot point. For instance, values for Anderson are indicated by a small solid dot and are connected by a broken line. Even markers have their limits, however, since it is difficult to distinguish markers when the values they indicate are the same (Bailey and Crockett's February values are the same).

Area charts, like the one shown in Figure 14.5, are also used to show trends over time. However, unlike line charts, which show distinct points connected by lines, area charts emphasize the *area* under a point. These charts are best used when you want to illustrate trends and show the difference between sets of values. Points are plotted differently from line charts, however. Instead of plotting each value beginning from 0 along the y-axis, each series is plotted beginning at the ending value of the previous series.

For example, Anderson's 2/1/95 sales were $223, so the portion of total sales is illustrated by the area of the chart under the value $223.

FIGURE 14.4

A line chart showing the same data as the bar chart in Figure 14.1. Line charts are more beneficial as the number of values plotted along the x-axis grows.

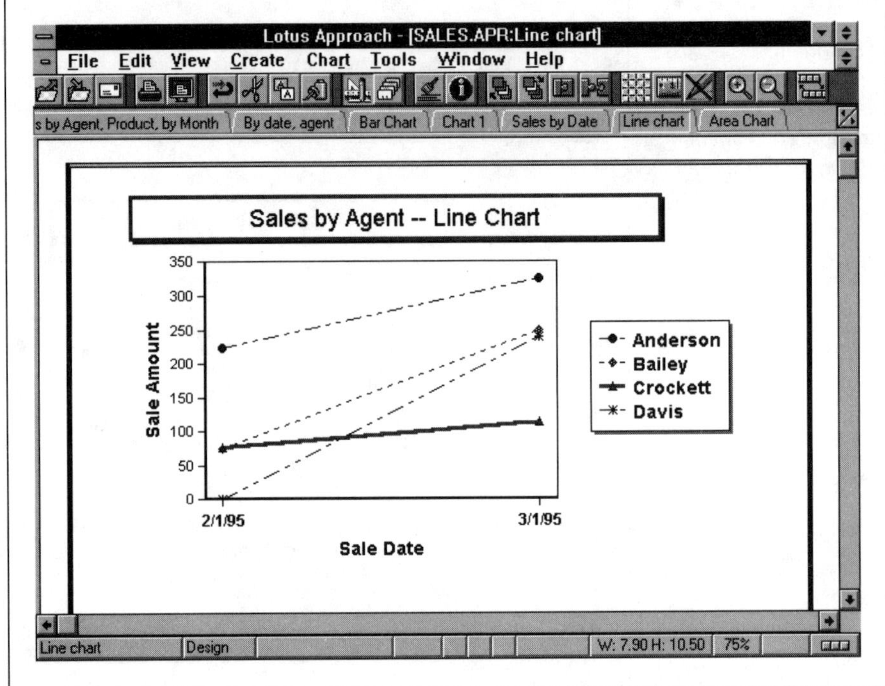

Bailey's sales were $75. Bailey's sales are plotted beginning at $223 and extending to $298. Crockett's sales are plotted beginning at $298 and extending to $375 (298+77=375). Since Davis had no sales in February, there is no plotted area for this agent. So in Figure 14.5 we see the total sales (375) and each agent's contribution to this amount. In this regard, area charts combine pie charts (showing relative percentages of a whole), bar charts (areas are distinctive), and line charts (they show a trend).

Pie charts, as shown in Figure 14.2 earlier in this chapter, are best used to show relationships of individual values to a whole. Each value (agent sales, in this example) is represented by a "slice" of the pie. In Figure 14.2 the slices are "exploded"—that is, the pie slices have been cut and partially removed from the pie in order to emphasize the borders. You can also create pie charts where the slices all touch, and you can add a three-dimensional effect to pie charts for interest.

FIGURE 14.5

Area charts combine the properties of bar charts, line charts, and even pie charts. The sales agent values appear here as an area chart. The data is identical to that of Figure 14.4.

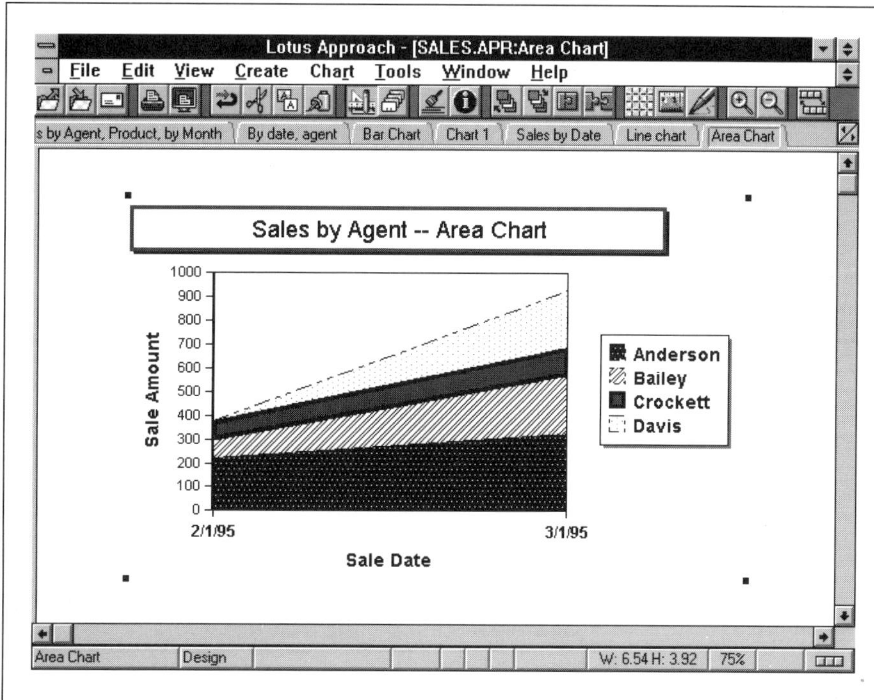

▶▶ Creating Charts

You already saw in Chapter 10 that you can create a chart directly from a crosstab. In this chapter we'll look at how to create a chart using the Chart Assistant. After a basic chart has been created, either from a crosstab or using the Chart Assistant, you can modify most of the properties of the chart. We'll explain how to modify charts later in this section.

The Chart Assistant is similar for area, bar, and line charts. Pie charts are unique and the Chart Assistant uses a separate set of tabbed dialog boxes to create them. Therefore, we'll divide our directions into two groups. First, we'll explain how to create area, bar, and line charts. We'll follow those instructions with an explanation of how to create a pie chart.

▶ Creating Area, Bar, and Line Charts

To create a new area, bar, or line chart, switch to the Design environment and follow these steps:

1. Select Create ➤ Chart or click on the Create Chart icons from the SmartIcons toolbar (although not part of the default toolbar, it can be added using the directions in Chapter 18). Approach displays the Chart Assistant shown in Figure 14.6.

FIGURE 14.6

The Chart Assistant steps you through the option selections for creating charts from your database records.

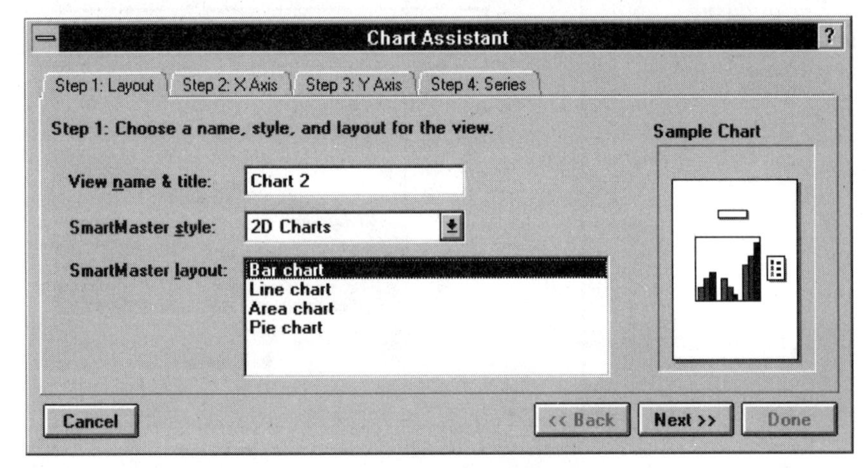

2. The Chart Assistant is similar to the other Assistants within Approach. You can select a tab at any time, but information on all tabbed dialogs must be completed before the Assistant will create your chart. The Step 1: Layout tab asks you to select the name and title of your chart. This name will be used in the tabbed dialog box for the Approach file.
3. Select a SmartMaster style. As you make your selection, Approach displays a thumbnail layout in the Sample Chart box.
4. Select the SmartMaster layout: Bar chart, Line chart, or Area chart.
5. Select the Step 2: X Axis tab or select the Next button. Here the Assistant needs to know which field you want to select for the x-axis. For the line chart in Figure 14.4, we selected the SaleDate field. Each of these field values was plotted along the x-axis. In our database there were two distinct values through all the records in the database: 2/1/95 and 3/1/95. For the bar chart in Figure 14.1 earlier in this chapter, we chose the Agent field. There were four distinct values in our database for agent, so there will be four sets of bars for this chart.
6. Select the Step 3: Y Axis tab or select the Next button. Here you'll tell the Assistant the value you want to plot along the y-axis. In

the line chart in Figure 14.4 and the bar chart from Figure 14.1 earlier in this chapter, we selected the SaleAmt field. Any value plotted in the chart represents the value of this field from the database. Remember that values from multiple records for the same field (such as Anderson's two records for sales in February 1995) were added together before they were plotted in the line chart. Likewise, Crockett's two records for sprocket sales in March were added together before being plotted in the bar chart. Select the type of calculation from the "Chart the" drop-down list.

7. If you want to plot multiple values along the x-axis, select the Step 4: Series tab or select the Next Button and proceed to step 8. Otherwise choose the Done button and Approach will build the chart.
8. The Series tab lets you plot more than one value for each x-axis value. For example, in the bar chart in Figure 14.1 earlier in this chapter, we selected the Agent field as the x-axis and a series based on the SaleDate field. Each date is represented by a separate bar. In the bar chart shown in Figure 14.3 earlier in this chapter, we selected the Sale Date as the x-axis field and chose the series based on the Agent field.
9. Select Done and the Chart Assistant will build your chart.

The chart created by the Assistant is now displayed in the Design environment. From here you can select any element on the chart and change its properties, as we'll discuss shortly.

▶ Creating Pie Charts

To create a new pie chart, switch to the Design environment. Then:

1. Select Create ➤ Chart or click on the Create Chart icon from the SmartIcons toolbar. Approach displays the Chart Assistant shown in Figure 14.6 earlier in this chapter.
2. The Chart Assistant is similar to the other Assistants within Approach. You can select a tab at any time, but information on all tabbed dialogs must be completed before the Assistant will create your chart. The Step 1: Layout tab asks you to select the name and title of your chart. This name will be used in the tab dialog box along the top of the Approach work area.
3. Select a SmartMaster style. As you make your selection, Approach displays a thumbnail layout in the Sample Chart box.

4. Select the Pie chart in the SmartMaster layout list.
5. Select the Step 2: Pie fields tab. Here the Assistant needs to know which field you want to select for each wedge. Each value in this field will be represented by a separate pie slice. Select the field to be represented by each slice from the "Show a new wedge for each value of" list. In the pie chart shown in Figure 14.2 earlier in this chapter, we selected the Agent field. There is a pie slice for each agent in the database.
6. Select the value you want to plot for each wedge in the "Of field" list box. For example, in the pie chart in Figure 14.2 we selected the SaleAmt field, since we want Approach to calculate and plot the values found in the SaleAmt field of all records. In the "Each wedge shows the" option, select the calculation you want for each field. We selected sum, because we want to add the total value of all SaleAmt fields for each agent slice. You can also tell Approach to calculate the average, compute the number of items, plot the smallest or largest value, or compute the standard deviation or variance for the field (SaleAmt in our example).
7. Select Done and the Chart Assistant will build your pie chart.

▸▸ Changing What You've Charted

If the chart created by the Assistant or from a crosstab doesn't show the data you want, you can change the options for the x-axis, the y-axis, and the field used to plot series values.

▸▸ NOTE

Unlike other views, charts offer only the Design and Preview environments. There is no such thing as a Browse environment when working with charts.

To change the fields used in the chart, or the calculation used (for pie charts):

1. Select Chart ➤ Chart Data Source or right-click anywhere in the chart area and select Chart Data Source. Approach displays the Chart Data Source Assistant, shown in Figure 14.7, which includes

3 of the 4 tabs found in the original Chart Assistant (for area, bar, and line charts) or 1 of the 2 tabs found for pie charts.

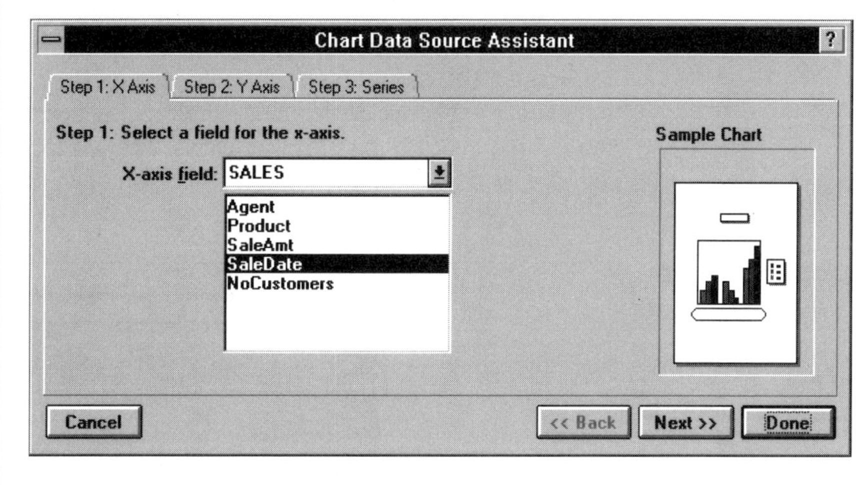

FIGURE 14.7 *The Chart Data Source Assistant includes 3 of the 4 tabs found in the original Chart Assistant (for area, bar, and line charts) or 1 of the 2 tabs found for pie charts.*

2. Choose the x- and y-axis fields or the series field (area, bar, or line charts) or pie fields (pie charts).
3. Choose the Done button.

►► Changing Chart Properties

Approach's Chart module lets you modify the characteristics of many parts of a chart. What you can modify depends, of course, on the type of chart, but the technique for modifying the chart is the same. We won't cover every modification possible within Chart—the possibilities are almost endless—but we will cover the main features. We'll also discuss some of the less obvious possibilities, especially such items as a second y-axis.

To change an item, display the InfoBox for the chart. You can do this in several ways:

- Double-click on any chart element, such as the title, legend, or plot area (the area in the center of the chart).
- Click on the InfoBox icon from the SmartIcons toolbar.

- Right-click the mouse anywhere inside the chart area and select Style & Properties, select Chart ➤ Style & Properties, or press Ctrl+E.

If you click *outside* the chart area (the area surrounded by a border or four black squares at the corner of the chart), you'll open the InfoBox for the chart, not the InfoBox for the chart properties. The Chart InfoBox, which appears in Figure 14.8, should be familiar. It controls the name of the chart, the main database, the Named Style, the Default menu, and whether you want to see a tab for this view among the other views. The Macro tab of the Chart InfoBox lets you specify a macro to be run when you open or close the view.

FIGURE 14.8

You can open two types of InfoBoxes. Here is the InfoBox for the chart as a whole. It resembles the InfoBoxes used in other views.

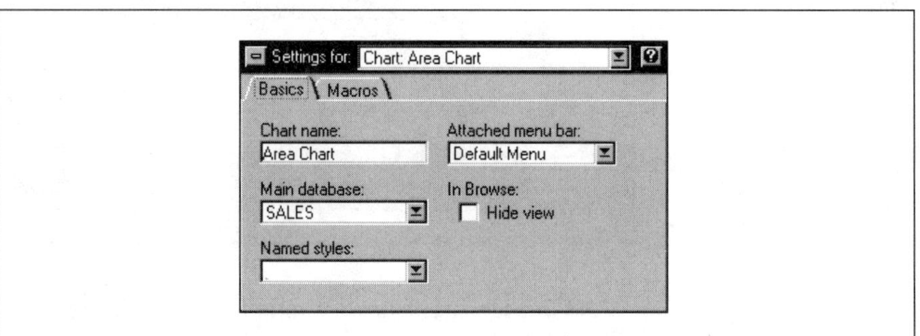

The InfoBox for chart properties is shown in Figure 14.9. This looks and behaves differently from the InfoBox for the chart. At the top is a drop-down list of the elements you can change. Figure 14.9 currently shows Chart as the element selected. Within the Chart InfoBox, Approach shows that we have selected an area chart and the layout includes a chart with a legend to the right.

Along the bottom are the familiar tabs for the Basics (chart type and layout), Options (unique by chart type: for bar charts we can select the gap between adjacent bars, the overlap for multiple bars, and the color used for negative values), and Data (which, for series, switches the series and x-axis fields).

We can change the chart type from area to, say, pie chart, by clicking on the Area button in the Basics tab. Likewise, we can change the type of area chart by clicking on the Layout tab and choosing where we want the legend and if we want horizontal grid lines.

Other options from the drop-down list vary by chart type. In general, however, you can select the title, legend, x- and y-axis, series and series labels,

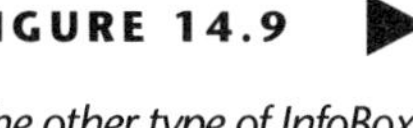

FIGURE 14.9

The other type of InfoBox applies to the chart elements themselves. Here we show the InfoBox for the area chart. You click on the Area button or the Layout button to choose different chart styles.

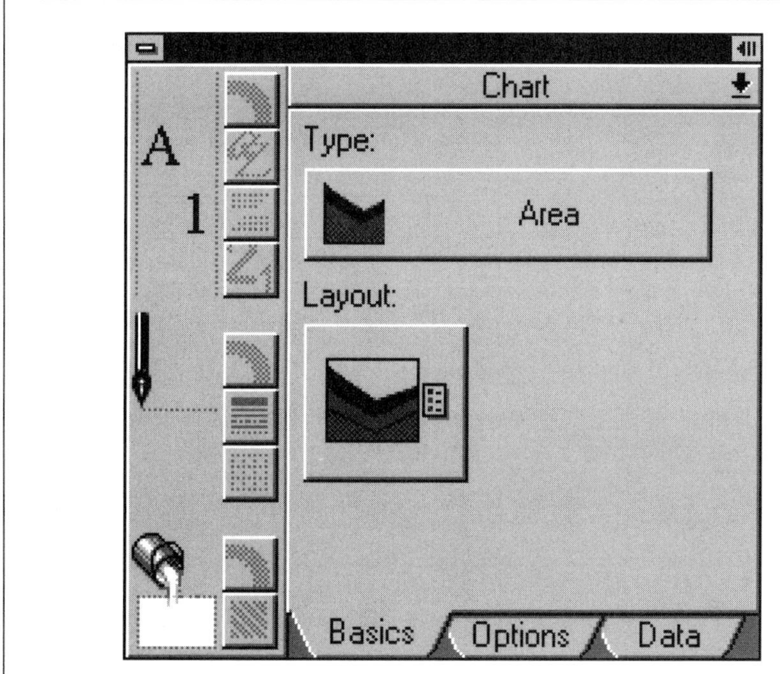

plot (which when selected, returns the chart to a default size and proportion), and Note (for adding a floating note, which is much like having an additional title box that you can place anywhere on the chart).

To change an element on a chart, you must select it. You can select any element by choosing it using the InfoBox drop-down list (chart, title, and so on, as just explained), or by double-clicking on the element (such as the title or a bar in the chart itself), which automatically opens the InfoBox to the appropriate tab and option.

Each dialog box within the InfoBox is different. However, the common style elements are shown along the left side of the Chart InfoBox. The first set of four icons controls the text color, font, alignment, and numeric format, respectively. The next group of three icons controls the color, line size, and shadow for lines. The last group of two buttons controls the fill color and pattern, which is generally used for the plotted areas (bars and area sections). The dialog box and style properties work as a team. For example, when you select the Title option from the drop-down list in the InfoBox, shown in Figure 14.10, you can then select

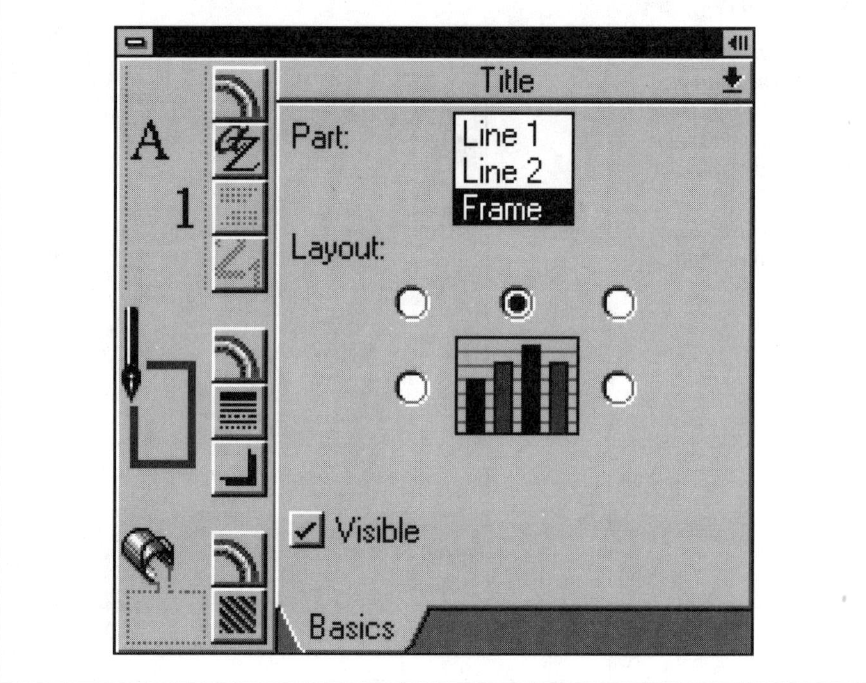

FIGURE 14.10

The Title option in the Chart InfoBox

what part of the title you're going to change (the first line, second line, or frame), then choose the text, line, or fill style for that part.

Let's take a closer look at some of the options within the Chart InfoBox.

▸▸ **TIP**

You can shrink the InfoBox by clicking on the left-pointing arrow in the small box in the upper-right corner of the InfoBox. This leaves the options at the far left visible (for text, line, and fill color) but hides the options. You can then move the InfoBox to any location on the screen. To expand the InfoBox, click in the upper-right corner again.

▸ The InfoBox Chart Properties

The Chart section of the InfoBox lets you select different chart styles, as shown in Figure 14.11.

FIGURE 14.11

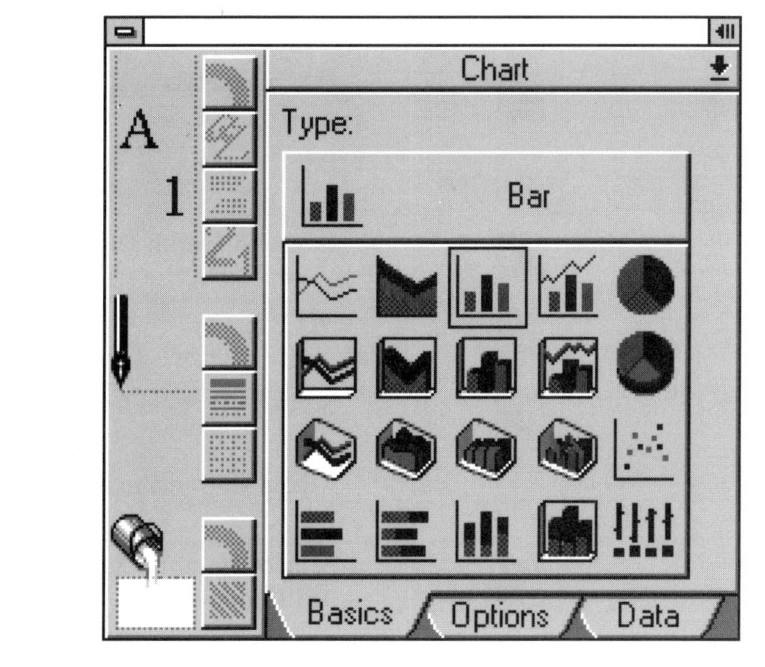

The Chart section of the Chart InfoBox provides 20 chart types.

You've already seen area, bar, line, and pie chart options. The icons represent the following chart types:

Line

 Line with Depth (3D Chart but Short 3rd Dimension)

 3D Line

 Stacked Horizontal Bar

 Area

 Area with Depth (Short 3rd Dimension)

3D Area

Horizontal Bar

Bar

Bar with Depth (Short 3rd Dimension)

3D Bar

Stacked Vertical Bar with Depth

Mixed Bar and Line

Mixed Bar and Line with Depth (Short 3rd Dimension)

3D Mixed Bar and Line

Stacked Vertical Bar with Depth

Pie

Pie with Depth (Short 3rd Dimension)

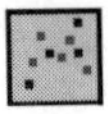

Scatter

High/Low/Close/Open

Beware the High-Low-Close-Open Chart

While the "High-Low-Close-Open" (HLCO) chart is used in other Lotus products, it's a misnomer in Approach. This chart type is used to plot four points for every value, such as the opening and closing price of a stock and its price at the beginning (open) and end (close) of a trading session. Unfortunately, there is no way in Approach to designate these values.

Instead, use an HLCO chart to plot the minimum and maximum values for a plot point.

Figure 14.12 shows an HLCO chart for the sales data we have used in previous examples. Approach plots both the high value and the low value for each sales agent. For example, Anderson's sales (the first vertical line) range from a low of $223 (for February) to a high of $325 (for March). Likewise, Davis' sales went from zero in February to $239 in March. The "open" and "close" values are not defined in Approach charts.

FIGURE 14.12

High-Low-Close-Open charts are misnamed in Approach. These charts show only the minimum (low) and maximum (high) values using vertical lines.

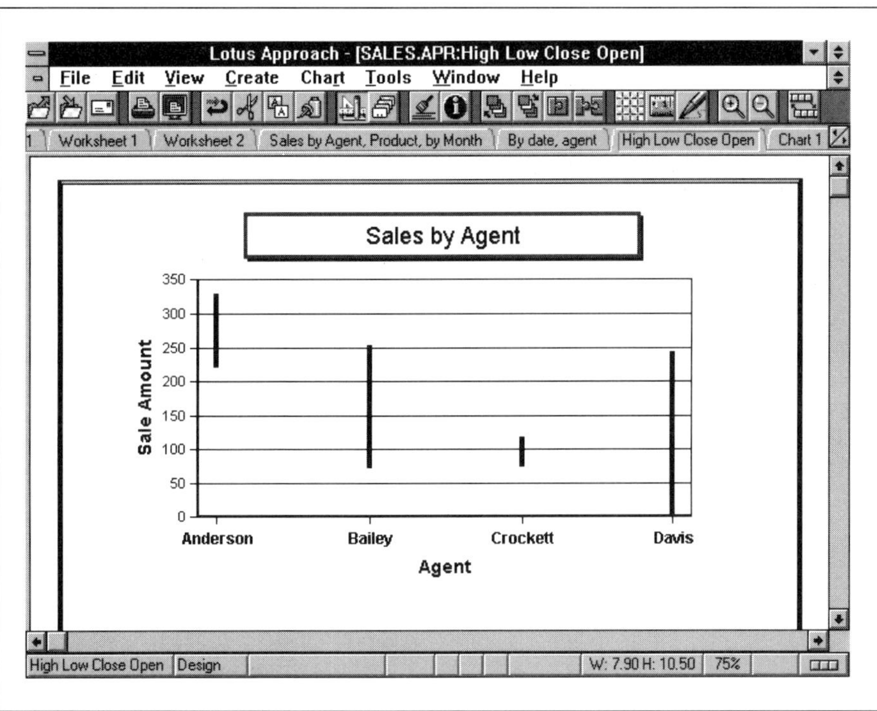

Since you can't create an HLCO chart directly using the Chart Assistant, create a bar chart, then use the Chart InfoBox to change its type to HLCO.

A Word about Scatter Charts: Don't Use Them

Scatter charts look at plotting points along two distinct axes. Do not select this type of chart in Approach because Approach offers no way to define two different fields for use by such charts.

Mixed Chart Types

Approach lets you chart two fields using different styles (one bar, one line, for example) in what is called a *mixed chart*. It's easy to turn any bar, line, or area chart into a mixed chart. Select the Series option from the Chart InfoBox drop-down list. Choose the series value you want to change, and choose the type of chart element you want from the "Mixed type" option.

For example, Figure 14.13 takes the chart shown originally in Figure 14.1 earlier in this chapter and displays the 2/95 sales amount as a line and the 3/95 sales figures as a bar.

FIGURE 14.13 ►

A mixed chart type lets you select the type of chart for each series. Here we have combined a line and bar chart for sales figures. The 2/95 figures are shown as points on a line chart superimposed on a bar chart depicting the 3/95 figures.

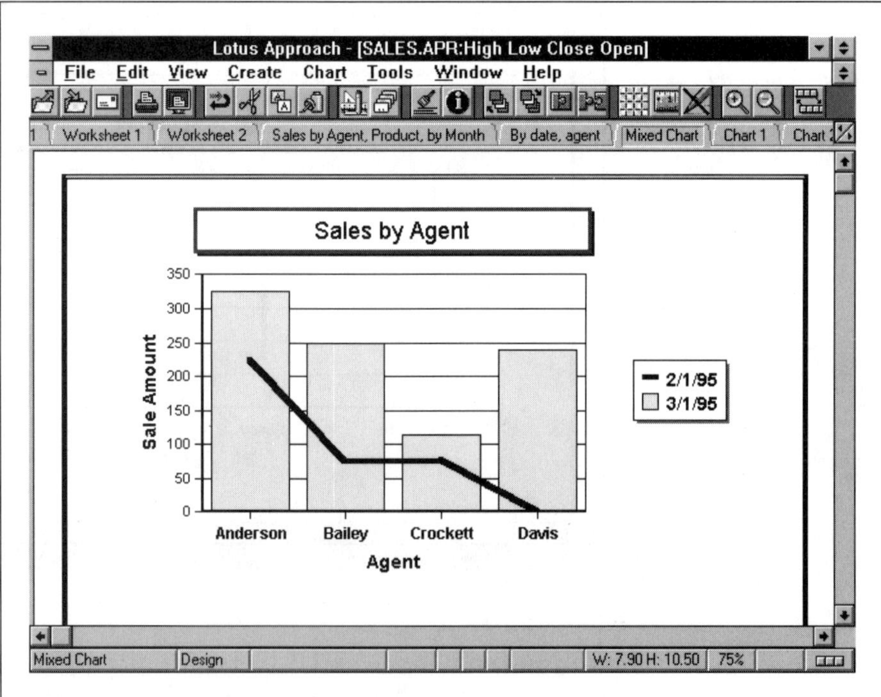

►► Using the InfoBox Properties

As you select a property from the Chart InfoBox, Approach highlights the corresponding element in the chart. For example, if you select the

Title section of the Chart InfoBox and then choose the Line 1 option, Approach places black selection boxes around the first line of the chart's title. Likewise, you can click anywhere within the chart and Approach changes the Chart InfoBox to the appropriate section.

When you change the property, the chart is immediately redrawn to reflect your selection.

▶ The InfoBox Title Properties

In this dialog box you can change the characteristics of the two-line title (title and subtitle) or frame, choose the position of the title relative to the chart, and select whether you want the title and subtitle visible.

You can also click and drag the title area itself and move it to any position on the chart. When you choose the layout option in the InfoBox, however, the title is repositioned to one of the five standard positions.

To change the title or subtitle, double-click on the text itself. Approach displays the text in a separate text editing box, with the entire text highlighted. To replace the text, begin typing. Otherwise press the End or Home key, then use the Backspace, Delete, Insert, or Arrow keys to move about the text, just as you would when editing a value on a form.

▶ The InfoBox Legend Properties

In this dialog box you can change the characteristics of the text (the words to the right of each legend symbol) or the frame containing the legend blocks and text. The legend in Figure 14.13 has two legend symbols: one for the line (2/1/95 data) and the other a block (for the bar showing 3/1/95 data).

You can change the text of any legend text by double-clicking on it. Approach displays the text in an edit box.

Choose the "Place inside plot area" option to move the legend inside the chart, rather than place it on the outside of the plot area. When you select the inside option, the layout buttons determine where within the plot area the legend appears. You can click and drag the legend to any area manually.

The last option on the dialog box lets you show or hide the legend.

▶ The InfoBox X Axis Properties

The X axis InfoBox, shown in Figure 14.14, contains a multitude of options. As you select a part (title, subtitle, line and so on), Approach changes the x-axis options. We'll explore only a few of the options here, since most are self-explanatory.

The part option "Tick mark labels" refers to the labels for each x-axis value. In Figure 14.13, the tick marks are the agent names (Anderson, Bailey, Crockett, and Davis). When we add more agents, as shown in the chart in Figure 14.15, not all the agent names can fit on the same line.

Approach uses the "Overlapping labels" feature to address this problem. This feature offers three options:

- Auto lets Approach automatically decide when to display labels on the same line and when to stagger them.
- Stagger forces Approach to stagger the labels.
- Vertical displays the labels vertically (at a 90 degree angle) rather than horizontally.

If you want labels to show at specific intervals, which is useful when the x-axis displays dates or numeric values, enter a value in the "Place labels every x ticks" box, shown in Figure 14.14, where x is the value you enter.

If the x-axis labels are too long, shorten them by checking the "Shorten to x characters" box, and enter a value in the box. By default, labels are 14 characters long.

You can change the text of any label along the x-axis by double-clicking on it. Approach displays the text in an edit box.

The Major grid lines option of the Part scrolling list lets you show (when the Visible box shown in Figure 14.14 is checked) or hide vertical grid lines. For most bar charts, grid lines are usually hidden. They may, however, be useful for line and area charts.

When you select the Scale tab in the X axis InfoBox, you can change the scale type, selecting minimum and maximum values, and intervals for the tick marks. Such intervals are usually adjusted only on the y-axis, or when you use horizontal (rather than the standard vertical) bar chart style. (We discuss scales and adjustments in the y-axis section which follows.) Of special interest on the Scale tab is the "Scale type"

FIGURE 14.14

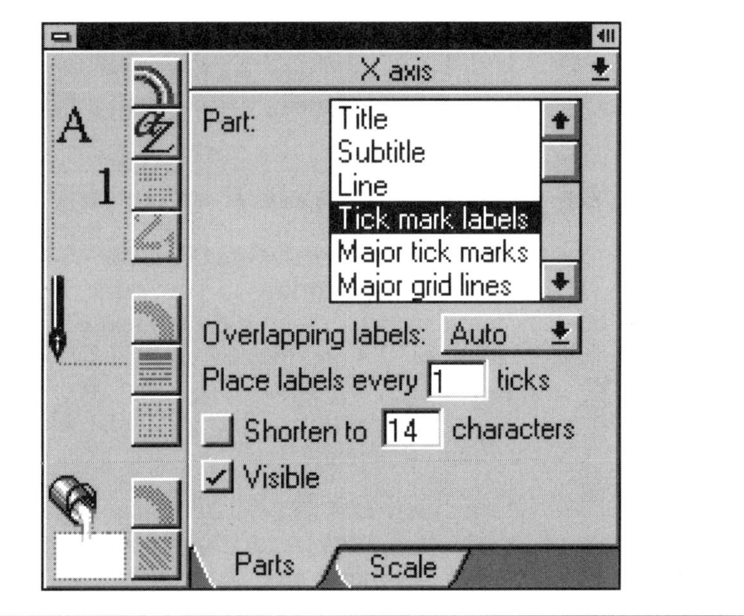

The X axis section of the Chart InfoBox offers a variety of settings that control the way labels are displayed along the horizontal axis.

FIGURE 14.15

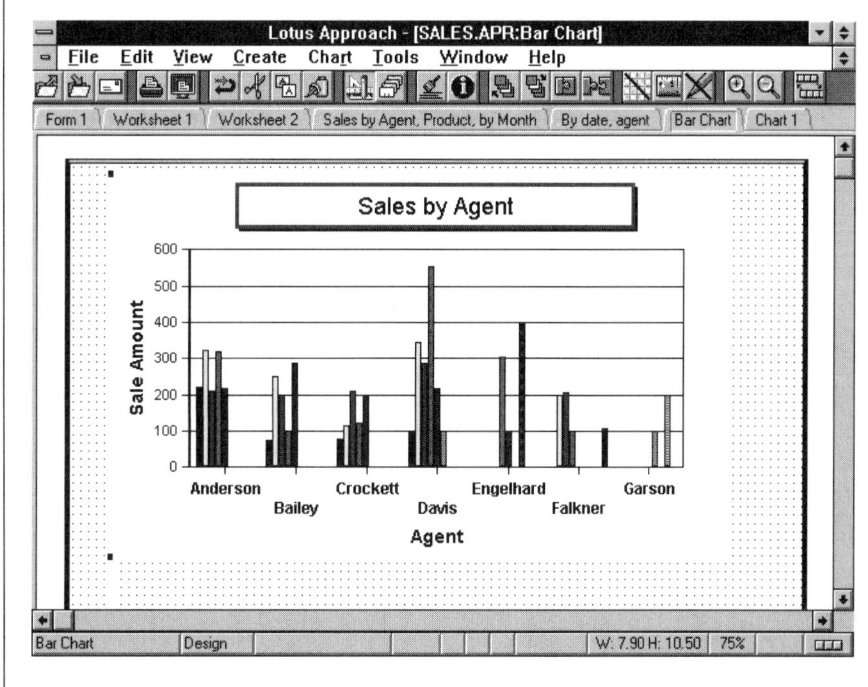

When you have a large number of values along the x-axis, Approach can stagger them on two lines, as shown in this chart.

option. Select Ascending and the x-axis values are displayed in ascending order. For instance, Figure 14.15 earlier in this chapter lists the agent names alphabetically. If you select Descending, the order is reversed (Garson would come first, followed by Falkner, and so on).

▸ The InfoBox Y Axis Properties

The y-axis properties are similar to those for the x-axis. The Title, Subtitle, and Line options are the same. Note that if you want to change the y-axis title, clicking on the text displays the text in a box for editing. However, the box may be very narrow, because Approach will use the horizontal dimension of the vertical text as the width of the text box. When you are done editing the text, click anywhere else and Approach redraws the vertical text.

Along the y-axis you can have major and minor tick marks. Major tick marks might be placed at significant intervals, such as every 1,000 units. Minor tick marks are used to subdivide the major ticks; you might place minor tick marks at every 500 units. You can have grid lines for either major or minor tick marks, or both, although you may wish to change the line settings (particularly the width or pattern) for minor grid lines. Often minor tick marks are used without displaying the grid lines for each tick mark. You set which marks and grid lines you want from the Parts tab, and set the intervals for these marks using the Scale tab. You can also select a layout for tick marks from the Parts tab.

When you select the Scale tab, you'll see two buttons at the top. The first lets you choose the scale for the y-axis. The scale can be linear (even increments for each tick mark), Log (a logarithmic scale is used), or 100%. The 100% option changes the values along the y-axis from their numeric values to a percentage. Thus, the highest value on the y-axis that reads 500 with the Linear option will read 100% using the "100%" option. This option combines the visual appeal of bar charts with the analytic power of a pie chart, which is used to show relationships to a whole.

The Ascending/Descending button lets bar, area, and line charts show values rising from the horizontal axis (Ascending) or dropping from the top of the chart (Descending).

The Scale manually options provide complete control over all scaling. You can change the Intercept (the value on the y-axis through which the x-axis will appear), for example.

To change the y-axis labels by hundreds, thousands, or other units, choose the appropriate Units measure. If the highest value is 1,000 and you select Thousands for the "Units" value, the y-axis label will read 1, not 1,000, since it has been adjusted to reflect the number of thousands. You can also select the format of the y-axis values by clicking on the Format button in the Style Panel. You can add a percent sign, commas, dollar signs, and surround negative values with parentheses using this option. You can also select how many decimal points you want to display, up to a maximum of 15.

▶ *The InfoBox 2nd Y Axis Property*

This property is available if you select the Series option, then choose a series and check the "Plot against 2nd Y axis" option. Approach displays a y-axis to the right of the charting area. In charting applications such as spreadsheets, you can use a different y-axis grid. For example, you can plot sales amount as a bar chart using the x-axis values and plot the number of customers using the y-axis scale. However, in Approach, the scale of both y-axes must be the same. Thus, the value of the 2nd Y axis property is used to specify a different set of tick markings. For example, the primary (first) y-axis (on the left of the chart) could use tick marks for every $50 increment, while the 2nd Y axis could use tick marks positioned at every $100 increment.

Typically, however, you will not use the 2nd Y axis grid, since its scale must be identical to the primary y-axis grid.

▶ *The InfoBox Series Properties*

These options let you select the series you want plotted against the 2nd Y axis, which appears at the right of the chart.

The marker option is available for line charts only and lets you select a symbol at each plot point, such as a square or circle. This helps your reader find the plotted value, rather than interpret the value along the lines connecting the plot points.

To show only the plot points and not the connecting lines in a series on a line chart, do not use the "Connect points" option.

▸ The InfoBox Series Labels Properties

Use these properties to add the value to each plot point or add the percentage value for each point. The "Layout" option lets you choose the position of the value display (above the top of the plotted point or below it). The properties can be set for each series. Since such values often clutter the chart, you should use these properties only when the number of plot points is small.

▸ The InfoBox Slice Labels Properties—Pie Charts

For pie charts, the Slice Labels option acts much like the Series Labels for area, bar, and line charts. You can show the value each slice represents and its percentage, and use the legend to further clarify the source of the data. The legend text for the pie chart in Figure 14.2 shown earlier in this chapter is the agent's name (Anderson, Bailey, and so on). If you use the legend text in the chart, you can eliminate the legend box, which repeats the same information.

Incidentally, to explode pie slices by a uniform percentage, select the Options tab of the Chart InfoBox and select a percentage. To explode one or more slices manually, click on the slice and drag it away from the center of the chart.

▸ The InfoBox Plot Properties

You can adjust the plot area by clicking on it and dragging the border. If you wish to default to the standard view size, check the "Default plot position and size" box.

▸ The InfoBox Note Properties

To add a free-form note in a box, similar to the text found in the title, select the Note section of the Chart InfoBox. Select the Visible box and choose the options for the two lines of text and the position relative to the chart. Double-click on the note box and type the text you want to display.

►► Summary and a Look Ahead

In this chapter you've seen how to create a chart from scratch using the Chart Assistant. You've also seen the variety of styles available to you, and have learned how to change the properties of your chart. Charts, whether created using the Chart Assistant or from a crosstab, offer an excellent way to summarize data, indicate trends or unusual conditions, and compare values to each other or as part of a whole.

In Chapter 15 we'll look at how to print charts and all other views. While charts and other views are valuable tools for viewing on screen, you may find it helpful to keep a printed record for your files, or share a view with a coworker who does not have a copy of Approach.

CHAPTER 15

Printing

▸▸ FAST TRACK

▶ ***To print any view*** **496**

switch to the view. Select File ➤ Print, press Ctrl+P, or click on the Print icon from the SmartIcons toolbar. From the Print dialog box, select the Setup button if the printer you want to use is not displayed in the Printer section. Select the range of the view you want to print, which varies by view. (The All option prints all the records for the database. If you are displaying a found set—a subset of the entire database — the All option prints only the records in the found set.) Use the pages option to print a continuous set of pages, such as 4–7 to print pages 4 through 7. If you are printing a form, choose the Current Form option to print the data from the form currently displayed on your screen.

▶ ***To keep information from a record on the same page of a report*** **499**

use the InfoBox's Basics tab and choose the "Keep records together" option.

To select a printer **499**

select File ➤ Print, then choose the Setup button in the Print dialog box or choose File ➤ Print Setup from the main menu. You can also select the Configure Printer icon from the SmartIcons toolbar. (Although this icon is not on the default toolbar, it can be added using the directions in Chapter 18.)

To view your form at different zoom levels in the Preview environment **500**

select File ➤ Preview, press Ctrl+Shift+B, or click on the second box in the Status bar and select Preview. You can also click on the Preview button from the SmartIcons toolbar. After entering the Preview environment, the mouse cursor changes from a pointer to a magnifying glass with the image of a mouse. To zoom in, click the left mouse button. To zoom out, click the right mouse button. You can also change the zoom level, one level at a time, by selecting View ➤ Zoom In or View ➤ Zoom Out. To see the view at the 100% zoom level, select View ➤ Actual Size, or press Ctrl+1.

►► ***You've*** seen how to use forms to view individual records and how to create worksheets, crosstabs, and reports to work with multiple records. You've also seen how to create, manipulate, and view charts. Up to this point, however, you've only been working with these views on your screen. Sometimes you need to print a copy of what you see. A coworker may need to include your chart in a report for top executives, for example. You may need to print a form and include it in a file folder as part of an employee's permanent record. For these and other reasons, Approach's printing feature lets you create output from what you see on your screen.

You can print any view in almost the same manner.

1. Select what you want to print (which page or range of pages).
2. Select where it should be printed (which printer) or send the output to a file.
3. Start the printing process.

►► Getting Your Data from Screen to Printer

To print any view, you must first select the view. You can't print a view other than the one currently displayed.

To begin the print process, select File ➤ Print, press Ctrl+P, or click on the Print icon from the SmartIcons toolbar. (Note that there are two possible icons in the toolbar for printing.)

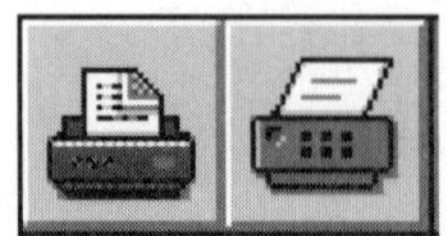

Approach displays the Print dialog box, shown in Figure 15.1. This dialog box is similar to the dialog box found in many Windows applications.

FIGURE 15.1 

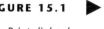

The Print dialog box lets you specify the destination and pages of the view you want to print.

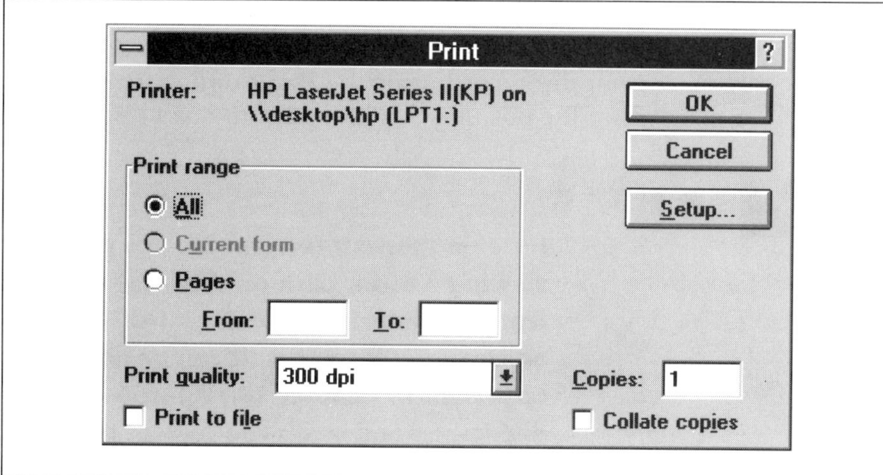

If the printer you want to use is not displayed in the Printer section at the top of the dialog box, select the Setup button. See the section "Setting Up Your Printer" later in this chapter for details.

Select the range of the view you want to print. This varies by the type of view. For example, you can select All (to print all pages of the view) or select the Pages button and enter the starting and ending page number. The All option prints all the records for the database. If you are displaying a *found set* (a subset of the entire database), the All option prints only the records in the found set.

The Pages option lets you print one range of contiguous pages at a time. If you want to print pages 4–7 and 9–11, you will have to create two print jobs—that is, you will have to print pages 4 through 7, then repeat the procedure and select pages 9 through 11. You can print all records beginning from a selected page by entering a large number (such as 999999) in the "To" range. If you enter a value in the From box and no value in the To box, Approach prints a single page (the page number specified in the From box).

If you are printing a form, the Print dialog box offers you an additional option: Current Form. This allows you to print the data from the form currently displayed on your screen. The All option will print all records in the database, or in the found set if you are using one. The Pages option associates one form with a page. For example, the first record displayed on a form is considered to be page 1, the next form is page 2, and so on. Examine the third box from the left in the Status bar (Record x). The "x" value shows you the record number you are viewing, relative to the first record in the database or found set. If you wanted to print this record using the Pages option, you would enter the "x" value from the position box in the From box of the Print dialog box.

▸▸ TIP

Here's a shortcut for printing the current record when viewing a form. Click on the Print Current Form icon from the SmartIcons toolbar. (Although the icon is not on the default toolbar, it can be added using the directions in Chapter 18.) Approach bypasses the Print dialog box and sends the current page to the printer directly.

If your printer offers several print quality settings, you can select the desired quality from the Print dialog box.

The Copies option lets you create multiple copies using one Print command. If you select more than one copy, Approach will print each page of the report multiple times. For example, Approach will print three copies of page 1, then three copies of page 2, and so on. To print collated copies, check the "Collate copies" option. When you check this box and request 3 copies, Approach will print page 1, then page 2 of a 2-page report, then print page 1 and page 2 (for the second copy), and finally page 1 and page 2 (for the third and final copy). When you remove the pages from the printer, all you need to do is staple the pages in groups. You do not need to collate them.

If you want to print to a text file, check the "Print to file" box. When you select OK, Approach asks you to provide the output file name. Your view will be directed to the file and will not be printed. To both create printed output *and* send the view to a file, you must issue two separate print commands: one for the printed output and the other to direct the printing to a file.

▸▸ What You See May Not Be What You Print

When you print a view Approach will automatically calculate any formulas, such as subtotals and totals on a report or in a crosstab. It displays summary totals for repeating panels, and shows the proper page number, date, and time (if these fields are used in headers or footers) as you move through pages in the Preview environment. Therefore, any calculated fields you've included in a view, and which are displayed on a view in the Browse or Design environments will be printed on the report.

There is an exception to the What-You-See-Is-What-You'll-Print rule. Remember that on a form you can include a button. However, while that button may activate a macro, you don't necessarily want that button to be included with your printed output. In the InfoBox for macro buttons you can select the Non-printing option from the Basics tab. When this option is chosen (which is the default for all new buttons), the button will appear on your form in the Browse and Design environments, but not in the Preview environment, so it won't appear on your printout. There is also a Show in Preview option that will show in Preview but will not be printed.

If there is a macro button on your view, you can click on it in Preview to run the macro.

Printing respects the "Keep records together" option set in the report view using the InfoBox's Basics tab. It also slides fields to the left if you've selected that option for fields on mailing labels.

▸▸ Setting Up Your Printer

By default, Approach displays the default printer in the Print dialog box. This printer is set using the Printer feature of the Control Panel within Windows. However, you can define several printers to Windows, then choose between them without having to jump to the Control Panel and select or configure the printer.

If the printer shown in the Print dialog box is not the one you want to use, you can select the Setup button in the Print dialog box or choose File ➤ Print Setup from the main menu. You can also select the Configure Printer icon from the SmartIcons toolbar. (This icon is not on the default toolbar but can be added using the directions in Chapter 18.) Approach displays the Print Setup dialog box shown in Figure 15.2.

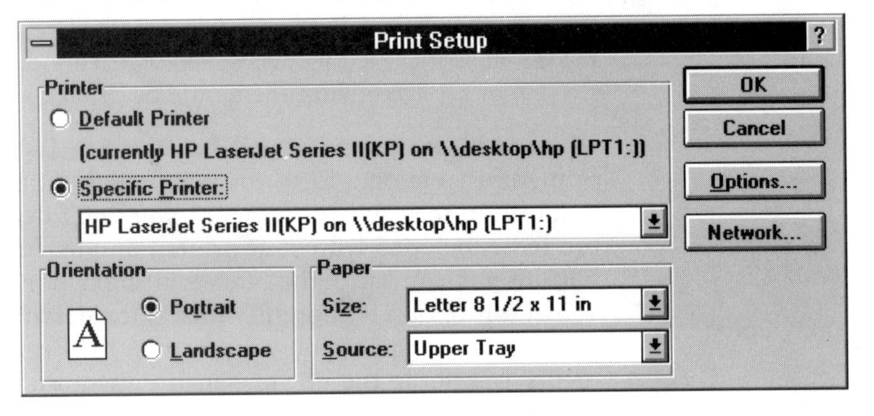

FIGURE 15.2 ▶

The Print Setup dialog box lets you specify the printer you want to use. It is similar to the Printer Setup dialog box used by the Printer feature of the Windows Control Panel, and looks like many of the Printer Setup dialog boxes in other Windows applications.

In this dialog box you can select the default printer (set by the Printers feature of the Windows Control Panel) or another printer defined to your system, including network printers. You can also select the orientation (portrait is the traditional direction; landscape prints "sideways"), paper size, and paper source. If there are other options you can set (which is determined by your printer driver), select the Options button.

When you have selected the printer options, choose OK.

▸▸ Look Before You Leap—Previewing Your Output

It's easy to print your output using Approach, but you may be wasting paper if the printout does not appear as you expect. You can use the Print Preview feature of Approach to make sure that what you print is what you want to see.

To view your form in the Preview environment, select File ➤ Preview, press Ctrl+Shift+B, or click on the second box in the Status bar and select Preview. You can also click on the Preview button from the SmartIcons toolbar. (Note that there are two possible icons for Preview in the toolbar.)

A report for the Sales database is shown in Figure 15.3 in the Preview environment.

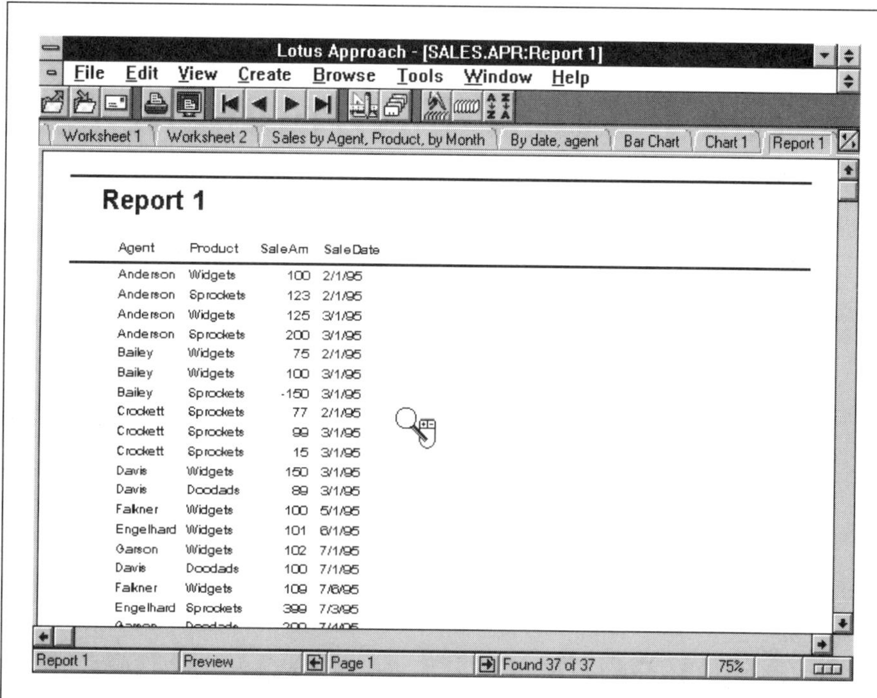

FIGURE 15.3

This report is shown in the Preview environment. Notice that the mouse pointer has changed to a magnifying glass. Now you can click on the left or right mouse button to zoom in or out of the report.

When you enter the Preview environment, notice that the mouse cursor changes from a pointer to a magnifying glass with the image of a mouse. To zoom in and see greater detail, click the left mouse button. To zoom out and see a larger perspective, click the right mouse button. As you do so, the

Status bar displays the new zoom level. The available zoom levels are 200%, 100%, 75%, 50%, and 25%. You can also change the zoom level, one level at a time, by selecting View ➤ Zoom In or View ➤ Zoom Out. To see the view at the 100% zoom level, select View ➤ Actual Size, or press Ctrl+1.

The zoom setting affects only how you view your printout on the screen. Approach will print the view at 100%.

Notice, too, that the toolbar has changed. The VCR-like buttons in the Browse environment work by navigating among records. In the Preview environment, these buttons move you to the first, previous, next, or last page in your form. Likewise, the Status bar left and right arrows move to the previous and next page. When you click on the Page section of the Status bar, Approach displays the Go to Page dialog box, in which you can enter the page number you want to jump to.

▸▸ The Preview Environment Let's You Do Even More

Although you can't use the Preview environment to change data as you can in the Browse environment, you can do more than just see what your printed output will look like.

You can use the toolbar and menu option to perform many of the same actions you would perform in the Browse environment. For example, you can click on the Define Sort button and resort the data. You can perform a Find and limit the preview to a subset of records meeting a condition. (Sorting records and finding records are described in greater detail in Chapter 12.)

▸▸ Summary and a Look Ahead

In this chapter we looked at how to print views, whether you need one page, a range of pages, or all pages in your view. You've seen how to print a form or report, how to set the printer options, and how to use the Status bar tools and toolbar for moving between pages. You've also learned how to zoom in and out of the preview window so you can see various levels of detail.

Chapter 15 ends Part I of *Mastering Approach*, which looked at the basic operating principles of Approach. Part II looks at advanced topics—features you may rarely use but that provide exceptional power and flexibility. You'll learn how to automate your work with macros, build sophisticated queries, modify your environment (including toolbars and menus), write formulas, and work with data in other formats and with other applications.

More Advanced Techniques

PART TWO

▶ ▶ CHAPTER 16

Streamlining Your Work with Macros

▸▸ FAST TRACK

▶ *To build a new macro* 513

choose Tools ➤ Macros or click on the Define macro button in an InfoBox. Select New from the Macros dialog box. Enter the name of the macro in the Define Macros dialog box; use the name *Open* to automatically execute the macro when you open the Approach file. Choose a shortcut function key if desired. As you choose commands, the bottom portion of the Define Macro dialog box displays the options for the command. Choose the option(s) you want. Enter each command on a separate line, in order, and select OK when your macro is complete. Click the Done button.

▶ *To change a macro's set of commands from the Define Macro dialog box* 514

insert a line in your macro by selecting the line (click in the small gray box to the left of the command), then select Insert. To remove a line, select it and select Delete. To start over (delete all lines), select Clear All. To move a command line within a macro, click to the left of the command, then move the mouse pointer over this small gray box. The mouse pointer turns into a picture of a hand. Drag the command to the desired position (indicated by a dark horizontal line) and release the mouse.

▶ *To assign a macro to a macro button on a form* 528

switch to the Design environment, then select the macro button (or add one by dragging the button icon from the Drawing Tools toolbar onto the form) and open the InfoBox. Click on the Macros tab, decide where you want to attach the macro, and choose the macro from the drop-down list.

If you need to define a new macro, you can click on the Define Macro button; Approach displays the Macros dialog box and you can proceed to build your macro as described previously.

▶ To run a macro 529

choose one of these methods. If you assigned the macro to a button on a view, click the button. If you assigned a function key to the macro, press the function key. If you checked the "Show in menu" option from the Macros dialog box, select Tools ➤ Run Macro and select the macro from the cascading macro list. You can select Tools ➤ Macros, highlight the macro, and select Run. If the macro is assigned to a view or an object on a view (such as a field or graphic), the macro will be run automatically based on the condition for which the macro is assigned, such as "On tab into."

▶ To stop a running macro 529

press the Esc key.

▶ To create a looping macro 529

choose Tools ➤ Macros or click on the Define Macro button in an InfoBox. Select New. Enter the macro name and select a keyboard function key (a shortcut key that, when pressed, will execute the macro) if desired. In the first and subsequent command lines, enter the commands you want the macro to execute for each record. In the next command line, select the Records command and choose the Next Record option from the choices at the bottom of the dialog box. In the last command line, choose the Run command. Choose the Run macro option and enter the macro name of the current macro.

▶▶ **Macros** are a familiar feature in word processing and spreadsheet applications. Macros allow you to repeat steps or tasks quickly. For example, if you regularly select records for all customers from California and run a report for this found set, you can create a macro to perform these steps and assign the macro to a button. Then all you need to do is click on the button and Approach will run the query, create the found set, and print the report. You can modify the macro to create a found set for a different group of customers (such as those with a credit limit over $1,000) and create a different macro to run mailing labels.

Macros can also be used to control behavior when you switch to or from a view. For example, you can assign a macro to a form that will perform a query before displaying the form.

Likewise, you can assign a macro to a field so that the macro executes when you move into or out of a field. You can even have one macro call another macro to string together a series of commands.

In this chapter you'll learn how to create new macros, modify existing ones, and assign macros to buttons and menu options. In addition, you'll see how macros can turn ordinary Approach databases into powerful applications.

▶▶ *Anatomy of a Macro*

As you'll recall from previous chapters (especially Chapters 7 and 8), you can assign a macro to a view or a field by selecting the Macros tab of the InfoBox. For example, in Figure 16.1 you can specify the macro to run when you tab into a field, when you tab out of a field (when you press the tab key to move to another field), and another macro to run if the data changes.

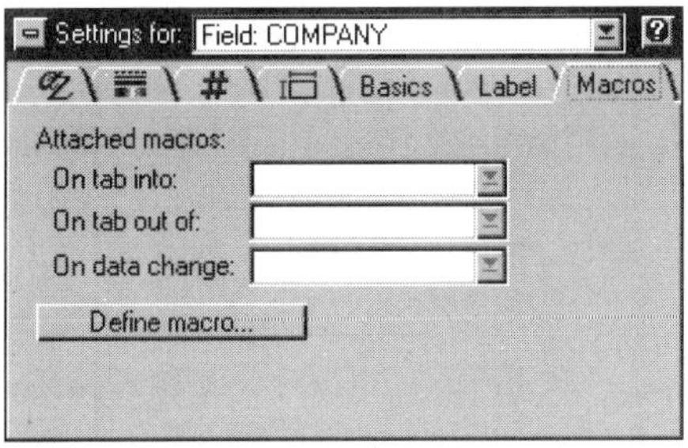

FIGURE 16.1

The Macros tab in the InfoBox is available for many objects in a view. Here the Macros tab lets you specify three conditions that will execute a macro (the same or different macros in each case).

Settings for: Field: COMPANY
Basics | Label | Macros
Attached macros:
On tab into:
On tab out of:
On data change:
Define macro...

Notice the Define macro button. This button provides a quick and easy way to move to the Macros dialog box, shown in Figure 16.2. You can also display the Macros dialog box by selecting Tools ➤ Macros.

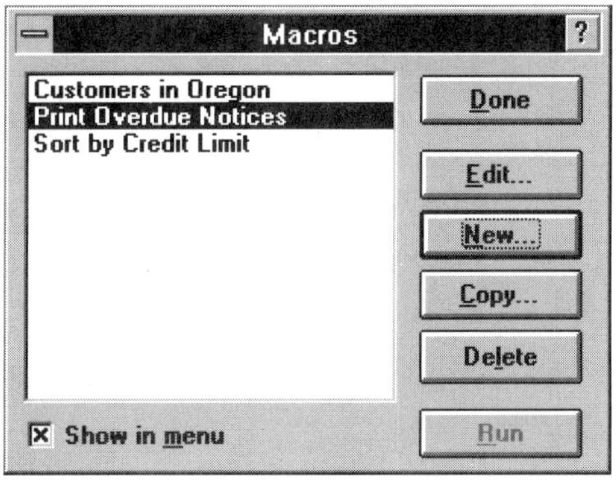

FIGURE 16.2

The Macros dialog box lets you select from existing macros (for editing) or build new macros.

Macros
Customers in Oregon
Print Overdue Notices
Sort by Credit Limit
Done
Edit...
New...
Copy...
Delete
Run
Show in menu

To build a new macro, click on the New button. Approach displays the Define Macro dialog box, shown in Figure 16.3. Approach fills in the first line automatically, depending on your current action in the form. For example, if you are working with a form in the Design environment and begin to define a macro, Approach will display the View command. The Options will specify "Switch To" and the macro will substitute the current form name. If, for example, you just performed a sort, the first line of the macro will use the View command to switch you to the currently displayed form, and the second line will supply the macro command to perform the sort you just performed. Thus, you can execute a command, then build a new macro to see the equivalent macro commands. However, such steps may be unnecessary, as macros are incredibly easy to build.

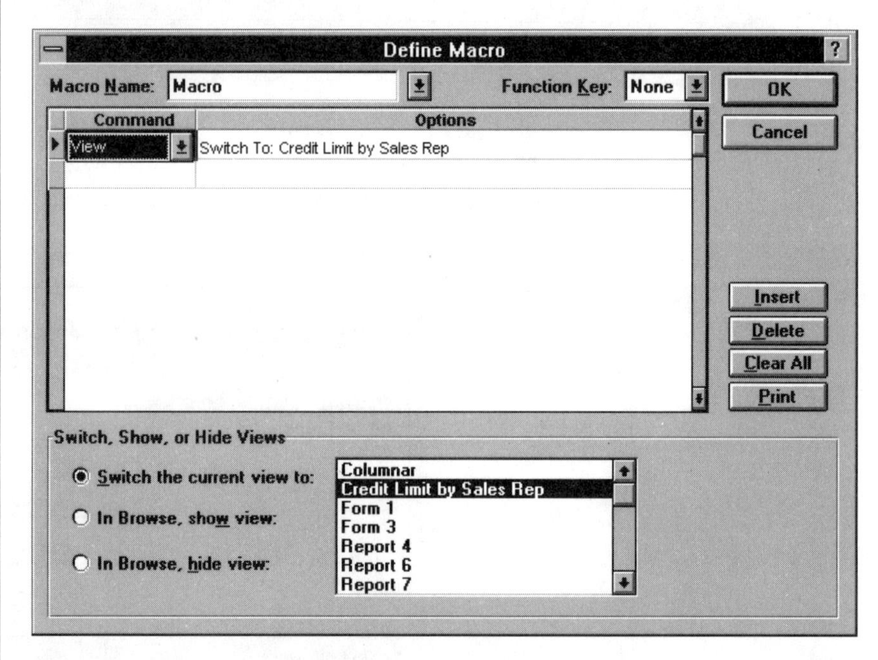

FIGURE 16.3 *The Define Macro dialog box displays the list of commands the macro will execute. You can also assign the macro name and function key shortcut.*

You can name a macro and assign it to one of the 12 function keys, so that pressing the function key executes the macro. The lines in the macro are executed in order, beginning with the top line. Like programming languages, a line in a macro can also execute another macro or perform special processing. You'll learn about these conditions in a moment.

Each line consists of two parts: a command and the command parameters. For example, in Figure 16.3 the first (and only) line to be executed will switch the user to the Credit Limit by Sales Rep form. After displaying this form, the macro finishes and returns control to the user.

The commands in the first column are selected from the drop-down list. Click on the down-pointing arrow to the right of the command to see the list, as shown in Figure 16.4. The macro names closely correspond to the commands you can issue from the menu or by clicking an icon from the SmartIcons toolbar. A few, such as Enter and Run, serve a special purpose, which we'll describe shortly. As with other dialog boxes in Approach, such as the Field Definition dialog box, you can insert and delete lines at any point in the two-column grid.

FIGURE 16.4

Approach displays the list of available commands using the drop-down list shown here. Each command has a separate set of options that is shown in the bottom portion of the Define Macros dialog box.

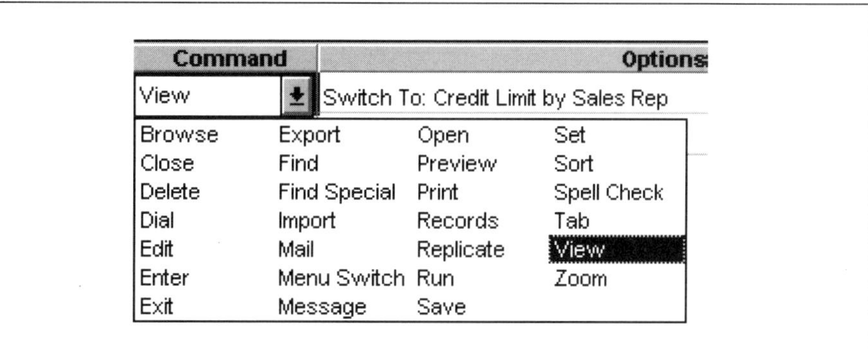

After you select a command, the bottom portion of the Define Macro dialog box changes to reflect the options available for the command. Each command is described in greater detail in the section "A Macro Command Encyclopedia" later in this chapter.

▶ A Step-by-Step Guide to Building a New Macro

Now that you've seen what a macro looks like, we'll provide the step-by-step instructions you need to build a new macro:

1. Choose Tools ➤ Macros or click on the Define macro button in an InfoBox. Approach displays the Macros dialog box, shown in Figure 16.2 earlier in this chapter.
2. Select New. Approach displays the Define Macro dialog box, shown in Figure 16.3 earlier in this chapter.

3. Enter the name of the macro. You can use a meaningful name of up to 21 characters and can include spaces in the name. If you want the macro to automatically execute when you open the Approach file, enter the name Open. If you want the macro to automatically execute when you close the Approach file, use the name Close.
4. If you want to execute the macro by pressing a function key, choose the function key from the drop-down list provided following the label Function Key at the top of the Define Macro dialog box.
5. Select the first command. You can enter the first letter of the command (or enter it again if two or more commands begin with the same letter), or display the drop-down list of commands and select the command you want to execute.
6. The bottom portion of the Define Macro dialog box displays the options for the command you selected in Step 5. Choose the option(s) you want.
7. Move to the next line and repeat Steps 5 and 6. Repeat this until all commands have been entered.
8. When your macro is complete, select OK. Approach displays the Macro dialog box again. If you want the macro to appear in the drop-down Tools ➤ Run Macro menu, check the "Show in menu" box.
9. When you are done defining macros, click the Done button.

You can insert a line in your macro by selecting the line (click in the small gray box to the left of the command), then select Insert. The selected line is moved down one line and a blank line appears. To remove a line, select it and select Delete. To start over (delete all lines), select Clear All.

To move a command line within a macro, click to the left of the command, then move the mouse pointer over this small gray box. The pointer turns into a picture of a hand. Drag the command to the desired position (indicated by a dark horizontal line) and release the mouse.

▶▶ TIP

If you are having problems with your macro, or want a printed copy for documentation purposes, you can select the Print button to print the list of commands in your macro. The Print dialog box will be displayed. The only option available in the Print range is All.

▶▶ A Macro Command Encyclopedia

Each macro command closely mimics what you can do using the menus or the toolbar. However, there are some special conditions that exist that must be taken into account. Here we'll look briefly at each of the commands, noting any special conditions you may need to know in order to use the command effectively.

▶ Browse

The Browse command has no options. When you issue this command, Approach switches to the Browse environment.

▶ Close

When you select the Close command, Approach closes the current file. You may choose the "Automatically disconnect from server" option if your database is accessed via a network server.

▶ Delete

The Delete command can delete the current record or all records in the found set. In addition, you can delete a file (click on the Files button if you do not know the complete file name, including drive and directory). If you check the "Don't show warning dialog before deleting" option, Approach will delete the record without prompting you with a message to confirm the delete.

▸ Dial

The Dial command will dial the telephone number stored in the field you specify. The Dial command is explained in Chapter 20.

▸ Edit

Editing commands include the ability to cut, copy, paste, or select all items on a form. In addition, you can specify that Approach open the Paste Special dialog box, which will wait for a user selection and paste the selection to the current view. The Edit commands are shown in Figure 16.5.

FIGURE 16.5 ▸

The Edit commands include the standard Windows commands for cutting, copying, and pasting to and from the Clipboard.

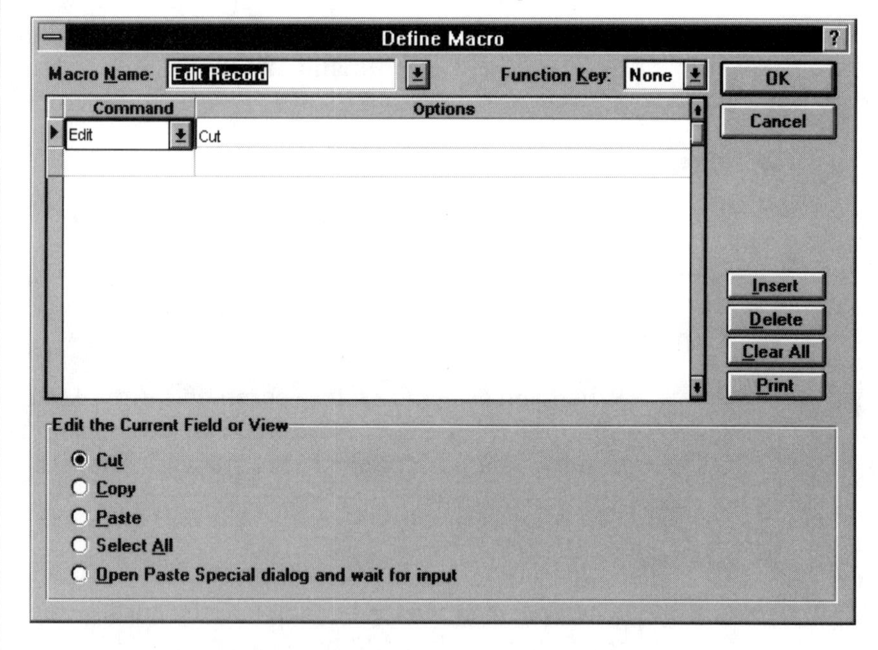

Enter

Choosing the Enter command is the same as if you pressed the Enter key from your keyboard. The command has no options.

Exit

The Exit command has no options. When you issue this command, Windows exits the Approach application. If you have made changes to your Approach file, you'll be asked if you want to save them.

Export

The Export command lets you send data from your databases to an external file for use by another application. There are two options. The first, "When macro is run, open Export Data dialog and wait for input," specifies that the export setup will be performed at run time (when the macro is executed). If you want to use a constant (predefined) export layout, you can specify it using the "Set Export Data options now and automatically export when macro is run" option. Click on the Edit Export button and specify the criteria in the Export Data dialog box. Exporting is described in further detail in Chapter 20.

Find

The Find command offers several custom options, as shown in Figure 16.6.

Perform Stored Find When Macro Is Run

The "Perform stored find when macro is run" command lets you predefine the search criteria. If you have just performed a Find, Approach highlights the Edit Find button and allows you to refine the search. Otherwise the New Find button is enabled. Click the button and you'll be placed in the Find environment for the current view. Enter the find criteria, as described in Chapter 12, and click on OK when your criteria are complete. Your criteria are saved with the macro.

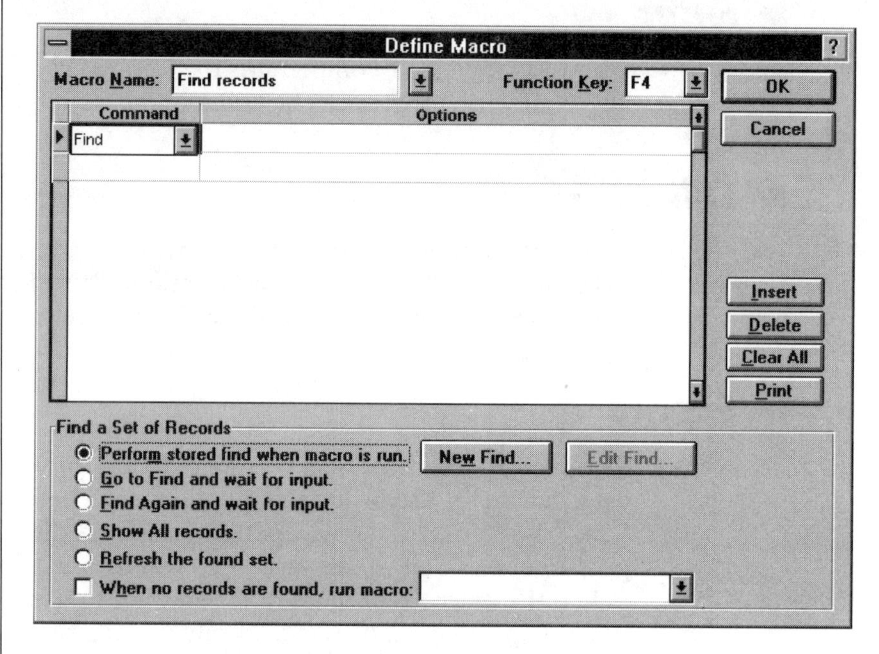

FIGURE 16.6 ►

The Find command options let you predefine the Find criteria, or prompt the user for them when the macro is run.

Go to Find and Wait for Input

The "Go to Find and wait for input" command is the macro equivalent to selecting Find from the Main menu. For example, it is the same as selecting Worksheet ➤ Find if the current form is a worksheet. You are placed in the Find environment when the macro executes, and you must then fill in the find criteria.

Find Again and Wait for Input

The "Find Again and wait for input" command is the macro equivalent to selecting Find Again from the Main menu. Using this command is the same as issuing the command Browse ➤ Find Again for a form. You are placed in the Find environment (with the last Find criteria shown) when the macro executes, and you must then fill in the new or revised find criteria.

Show All Records

The "Show All records" command is the macro equivalent of selecting the Show All command, such as Browse ➤ Show All when a form is displayed.

Refresh the Found Set

The "Refresh the found set" command is the macro equivalent of choosing the Refresh command, such as Browse ➤ Refresh when a form is displayed.

When No Records Are Found, Run Macro

The "When no records are found, run macro" command is a special option that lets you specify another macro to execute if the Find defined previously returns no records. For example, you might want to display a special screen that indicates that no customers with overdue balances were found, and thus no reports will be generated.

► Find Special

The "Find Special" option is the macro equivalent of selecting the Find Special command from the Main menu, such as Browse ➤ Find Special when viewing a report. You can specify the special criteria by choosing the Edit Find Special button. Your criteria are saved with the macro.

You can specify a macro to run if no records are found. For example, you can run a macro that uses the Message command to display an error message indicating that your search was unsuccessful.

► Import

The Import command lets you use data from another source in Approach. There are two options. The first, "When macro is run, open Import Data dialog and wait for input," specifies that the import setup will be performed at run time (when the macro is executed). If you want to use a constant (predefined) import layout, you can specify it using the "Set Import Data options now and automatically import records when macro is run" option. Click on the Define Import File button and specify the criteria in the Import Data dialog box (which asks for the data file name) and then displays the Import Setup dialog box where you match the files between your input dataset and fields in an existing Approach database. If you've just imported a file, the import setup can be edited by selecting the "Edit Import Setup" option.

Importing is described in further detail in Chapter 20.

▸ Mail

The Mail command lets you prompt the user at run time for the mail parameters, or predefine these parameters by clicking the Edit Send Mail button. Procedures for sending mail are described in Chapter 20.

▸ Menu Switch

The Menu Switch command lets you change the menu displayed by Approach. You can also select a custom menu you've already defined and use the Customize Menus command to edit a menu. Custom menus are described in Chapter 18.

▸ Message

The Message command allows you to create a quick pop-up dialog box, including a title and message text. For example, if a Find does not return any values, you can branch to another macro in which you define a Message command explaining that no records were found, then return to the original macro.

The Message command is an excellent way of notifying users of what has just been performed. The Message command, shown in Figure 16.7, will display the dialog box shown in Figure 16.8.

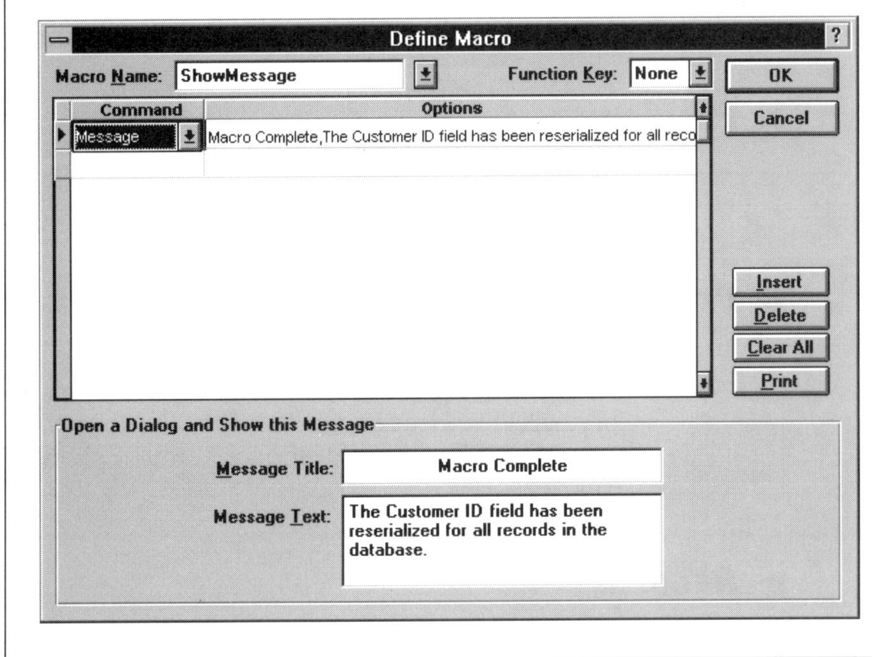

FIGURE 16.7 *The Message command is a simple way to display a dialog box showing your user what has occurred.*

FIGURE 16.8 *The dialog box that is displayed when the macro in Figure 16.7 is run*

▶ Open

The Open command is equivalent to the File ➤ Open command. You can request the file name at run time or specify the file name in the command so the File Open dialog box is not shown. To use the second option you must enter the complete path and file name; if you don't know it, select the Files button (to the right of the File Name text box at the bottom of the Define Macro dialog box) to choose the file.

▶ Preview

The Preview command has no options. When you issue this command, Approach switches to the Preview environment.

▶ Print

The Print macro command is equivalent to the File ➤ Print command. You can request the print options at run time or specify them in the command by selecting the "Set Print options now and automatically print when macro is run" option. To make changes later on, click Edit Print.

▶ Records

The Records command is used to navigate the database. It offers options to move to the current record, first, previous, next, or last record, or to a specific record number. It can also create (insert) a new record, hide the current record, or duplicate the current record.

▶ Replicate

The Replicate command is used to replicate (copy) a Notes database on your local hard drive. You can prompt for the parameters at run time or specify them within the macro by selecting the "Set Replication options now and automatically Replicate when macro is run" option, then set the specific options by clicking on the Edit Replicate button. You can change the options in the future by selecting the Edit Replicate button. Working with Lotus Notes is described in Chapter 20.

▶ Run

The Run command controls how a macro's steps are executed. Because of its complexity, it is described in greater detail in the section "Controlling How Your Macro Executes" later in this chapter.

▶ Save

The Save command lets you specify whether the Save As dialog box is used (prompting the user at run time to specify the file name) or whether the current Approach file is saved without additional prompting.

▶ Set

The Set command lets you place a value in a field. You must select the database and field name, then enter a value, as shown in Figure 16.9. The value can be the result of a calculation—just click on the Formula button to open the Formula dialog box and enter the calculation you wish to make. All records in the database can have the field replaced if you use a looping macro. See the section "Controlling How Your Macro Executes" later in this chapter for more information about looping macros.

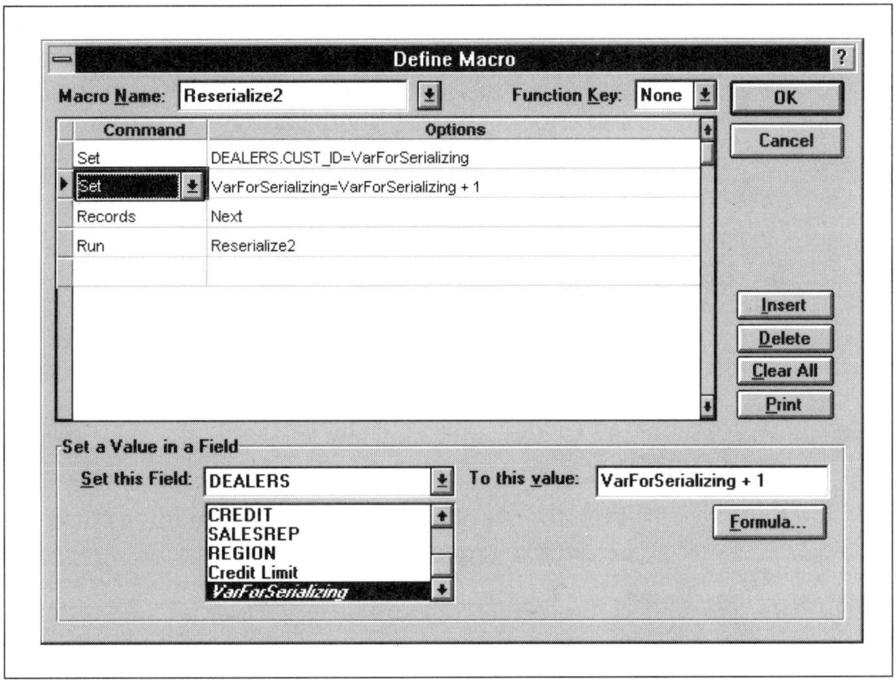

FIGURE 16.9 ▶

The Set command lets you assign a value to a field or increase a variable field using a formula, as shown here.

▶ Sort

The Sort macro command lets you display the Sort dialog box at runtime and ask the user for the parameters, or you can specify them within the Define Macro dialog box. To set the sort, click on the second option and add one or more fields to the right-hand box. To specify summary fields, click on the Summaries button in the bottom-right corner of the Define Macro dialog box and enter the summary fields and the summary technique (choose it from the "Summarized on" drop-down list).

▶ Spell Check

The Spell Check command opens the Spell Check dialog box and has no options. Spell checking is discussed in Chapter 17.

▶ Tab

Using the Tab macro command is the same as clicking on a specific field in a view. You must supply the tab position (data entry order number). To find this number, open the view in the Design environment and choose View ➤ Show Data Entry Order. Approach displays the number of each field. Use this number in the Tab command of your macro.

▶ View

The View command lets you switch to a different view, or show or hide a view. You must specify the view you want the View command to work on.

▶ Zoom

The Zoom command lets you zoom in or out one step, or move to the actual size (zoom ratio is 100%).

▸▸ Modifying or Deleting an Existing Macro

To modify an existing macro, open the Macros dialog box by selecting Tools ➤ Macros. Select the macro you want to edit, then select Edit. You can change any line by choosing a command, insert or delete a single line, or delete all lines (using the Clear All button).

To copy an existing macro as the basis of a new macro, choose the existing macro and select Copy. Approach fills in the command lines. Enter a new macro name, make the changes to the macro, and select OK.

To delete a macro, select it from the Macro dialog box and choose Delete. Approach prompts you to confirm your request. Select Yes.

▸▸ Controlling How Your Macro Executes

As you've seen, the macro commands are usually executed in order, from the first line to the last. However, there are times when you want to execute another macro in the middle of your current macro, then return to your macro.

For example, suppose you want to create a macro and print all records in a database. You can create a found set, then run a *looping macro* (one that continues to execute once for each record in the database or found set). However, you may also want to add a condition, such as checking to see if the customer's account is overdue, before you run another macro to print an overdue notice.

The Run command is used to interrupt the line-by-line execution order of a macro. It allows you to check for a condition before executing the next line in the current macro. The options are described below.

▶ Run Macro

The Run Macro option lets you run another macro defined within the current Approach file. If you check "Return to the next line" in this macro, the current macro will execute another macro and then execute the next line in the current macro. This is called a *branch and return*, since Approach branches off to another macro, executes it, and returns to the next line in the current macro.

▶ If

The "If Run" option checks the value of a formula you specify, then takes action based on the result. For example, suppose you want to send a special notice of a sale to customers whose credit limits are $500 or above. These are your special customers and you want to invite them to spend even more money at your store. The Define Macro dialog box shown in Figure 16.10 shows how you would set up such a macro.

FIGURE 16.10

The Run macro command lets you specify what macro you want to run if a condition is met. You can also specify the macro to run if the condition fails.

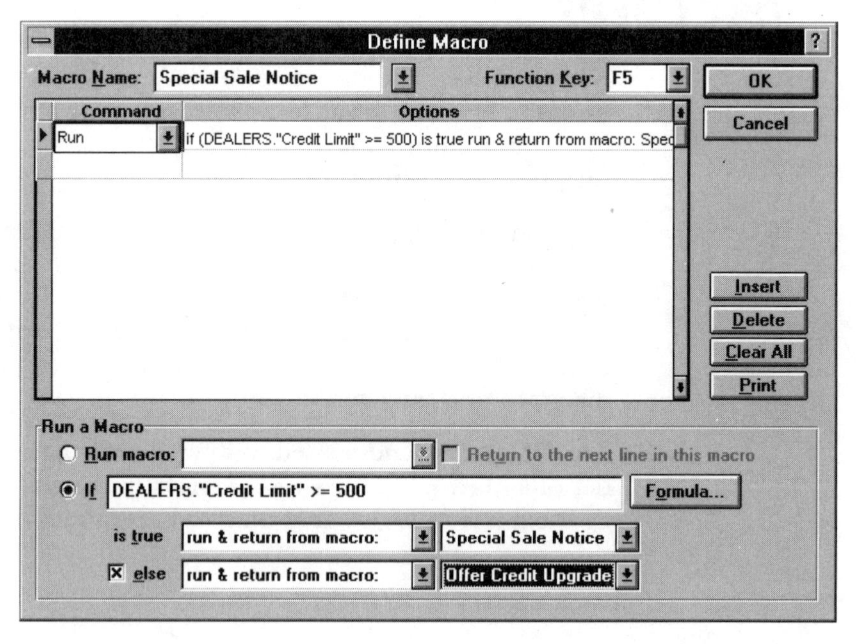

Check the If option. Enter the formula in the text box to the right, or click on the formula to open the Formula dialog box. (Formulas have been discussed in earlier chapters and are more fully described in Chapter 19.) We've entered the formula DEALERS."Credit Limit">= 500. Here the database name is in ALL CAPITAL LETTERS. The dot separates the database name from the field name, which is placed in quotation marks because the field name contains a blank. The comparison operator, greater than or equal to, compares the value in the Credit Limit field with the constant value 500. The formula we enter here will be evaluated as True or False. The formula is not used to calculate a value and substitute the calculated result in a field.

The next line in the Define Macro dialog box tells Approach what to do if the record being examined meets this criterion. The macro can:

- Run another macro but not return to the next line of the current macro
- Run another macro, then return to the current macro and execute the next line
- Continue to the next line within the current macro
- End the current macro immediately and return control to the user

We've selected the second option. You make this selection by clicking on the "is true" drop-down list. We want to run the Special Sale Notice macro, which we've created to switch to the form letter view, print the letter, and then stop. When the letter has been printed, the Special Sale Notice macro ends and control is passed back to our macro, which proceeds to run the next command within the macro.

You can also specify what happens when the formula evaluates to false. For example, if the user's credit limit is less than 500, we want to run the "Offer Credit Upgrade" macro, which we've separately defined as opening a different view (a different form letter view), printing the letter (offering to upgrade a customer's credit limit if they supply additional information), then stopping. The "else" condition also lets us specify the four run options noted above. So if the current record being examined by the macro has a credit limit of $400, the macro will open the Offer Credit Upgrade macro, run the commands it contains, then return to the next line of our current macro.

▸▸ Adding a Macro to a View

The most common way of executing a macro is to assign it to a macro button on a form. To do this, switch to the Design environment, then select the macro button (or add one by dragging the button icon from the Drawing Tools toolbar onto the form) and open the InfoBox. Click on the Macros tab, decide where you want to attach the macro and choose the macro from the drop-down list. If you need to define a new macro, you can click on the Define Macro button; Approach displays the Macros dialog box and you can proceed to build your macro as described previously.

You can attach a macro to any object, including a field, on a form in much the same way. Select the object in the Design environment, open the InfoBox, and choose the Macros tab. Decide where you want to attach the macro and choose from the list of existing macros by using the drop-down menus, or click on the Define Macro button to build a new macro.

Macros can also be assigned to a view. Click on the background of the view (any place where there is no object). Open the InfoBox and choose the Macros tab, as shown in Figure 16.11. Select a macro to be executed when you switch to the view and/or a macro to be executed when you switch to another view.

FIGURE 16.11 ▸

The InfoBox for a worksheet lets you tell Approach what macro you want to run when the view is opened and what to run when you switch to a different view.

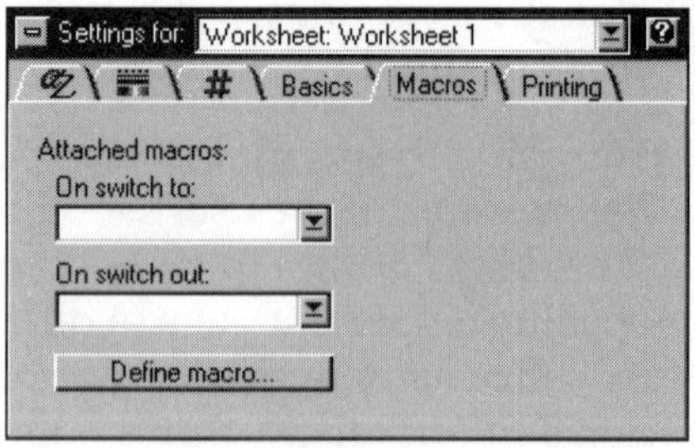

►► Running a Macro

You must be in the Browse or Preview environment to run a macro.

There are several ways to run a macro:

- If you assigned the macro to a button on a view, click the button.
- If you assigned a function key to the macro, press the function key.
- If you checked the "Show in menu" option from the Macros dialog box, select Tools ➤ Run Macro and select the macro from the cascading macro list.
- Select Tools ➤ Macros. Highlight the macro and select Run.
- If the macro is assigned to a view or an object on a view (such as a field or graphic), the macro will be run automatically based on the condition for which the macro is assigned. For example, if you assigned the macro to the "On tab into" condition, Approach will execute the specified macro when you move to the field.

►► Stop That Macro!

To stop a macro from running, press the Esc key.

To display a reminder of this fact while the macro is running, select Tools ➤ Preferences. Choose the General tab and check the box marked "Show the Cancel Macro dialog when running macros." Now when you run a macro Approach displays a message box saying it is running the macro, and you can press Esc to cancel the macro.

►► Looping Macros

The Run command is also used when we want to perform a macro on every record in our database or in the found set (if we've executed a Find command). The trick to a looping macro, as this special kind of macro is called, is to combine the Run command with the Records command in just the right order.

Here's an example: Suppose that we want to write a macro to increase every customer's credit limit by 10%. We could go through this process by hand, but it's far too tedious to do this for every customer. Using the Set command by itself to change the value of the Credit Limit field won't work, because that command works only for the current record, and we want to update every customer's record. Therefore, we have to find a technique for looping through the database—starting from the first record and working our way to the end—changing the Credit Limit field for each record.

Here's how we create a looping macro to do just that. Figure 16.12 shows the macro that will do the trick.

Use these steps to create the macro:

1. Choose Tools ➤ Macros or click on the Define Macro button in an InfoBox. Select New.
2. Enter the macro name and select a keyboard function key (a shortcut key that, when pressed, will execute the macro), if desired.

FIGURE 16.12

A looping macro lets you perform the same action on multiple records in the database. However, a word of warning: the macro begins at the current record, so when you run the macro you must be sure you are positioned at the first record in the database if you want to update all records.

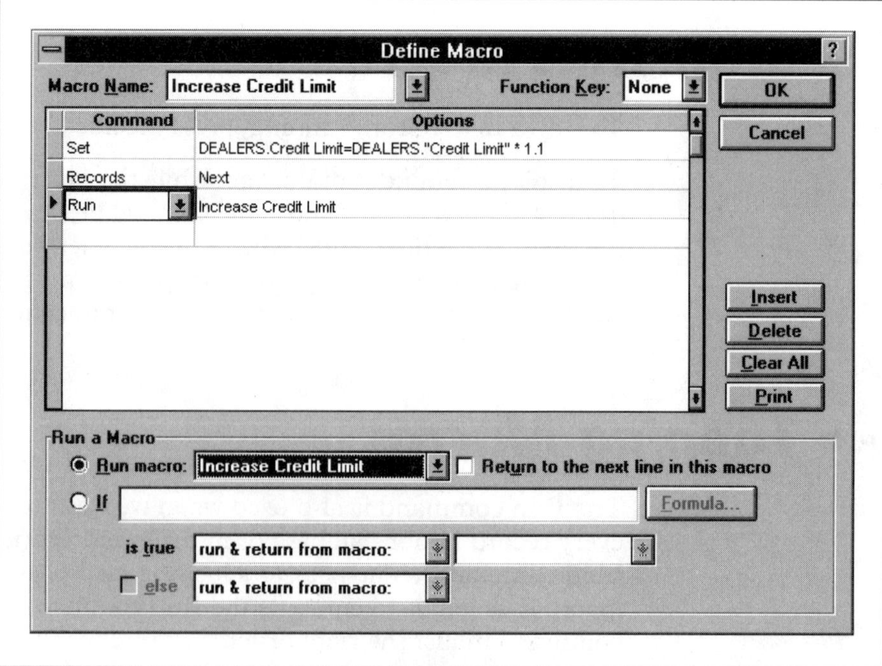

3. In the first and subsequent command lines, enter the commands you want the macro to execute for each record.
4. In the next command line, select the Records command and choose the Next Record option from the choices at the bottom of the dialog box.
5. In the last command line, choose the Run command. Choose the Run macro option and enter the macro name of the current macro (the name you entered in Step 2).

WARNING

To run the macro, be sure you are positioned at the beginning of the database, since the macro begins at the current record and runs until it reaches the end of the database. There is nothing in the macro to tell Approach to begin at the first record.

Reserializing a Field

When you create a serialized field, Approach automatically looks for the largest value in the field and increments it by one when you add a new record. Over time, however, you may delete records from the database and wish to reserialize all the records so there are no gaps in the numbering scheme.

The reserializing process shown here uses two macros and a variable field. You must add a variable field to the database, as explained in Chapter 5.

The first macro, called Reserialize1, is shown in Figure 16.13. It:

1. Moves to the first record in the database.
2. Sets the variable field to 1 (or the number you want for the first serial number).
3. Runs the second macro.

FIGURE 16.13

Reserialize1 is the first of two macros used to update a serialized field for all records in a database. This macro moves to the first record, sets the first value for the serialized field, and then calls Reserialize2.

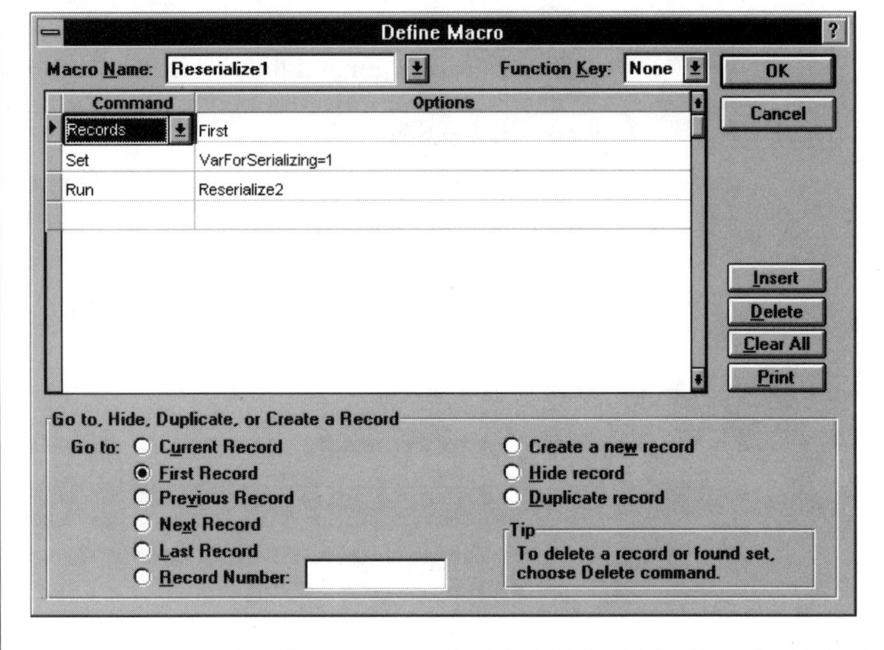

The second macro, called Reserialize2, is shown in Figure 16.14.

Reserialize2:

1. Sets the field you want serialized to the variable value.
2. Increases the variable value by 1. You can change this to another value, such as 10, if you want the serial numbers to be incremented by a different amount.
3. Moves to the next record.
4. Runs the second macro again.

The second macro is a looping macro that eventually stops when it runs out of database records. Since the first macro's Run command did not instruct Approach to return to the first macro when the second macro was finished, the process is complete and the database field is reserialized.

FIGURE 16.14

Reserialize2 is called by Reserialize1 and performs the database update.

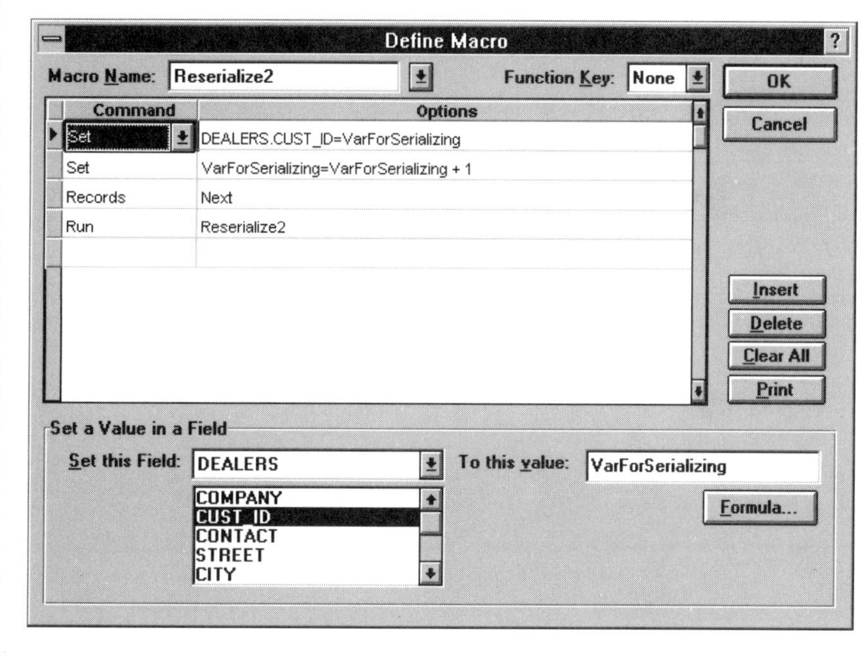

▶▶ Summary and a Look Ahead

In this chapter we looked at how to create macros, including macros that loop through your entire database and macros to reserialize a field. You've seen how to create a new macro or edit an existing one, and how to assign a macro to a button, to an object on a view, or to the view itself.

In Chapter 17 we'll tackle the subject of queries. You learned in Chapter 12 how to find a single record or sets of records. In Chapter 17 you'll learn about Approach's powerful searching features that let you perform mass updates to a database, and you'll learn more about using formulas to find values.

CHAPTER 17

More Data Searches and Updates

▸▸ FAST TRACK

▶ ***To change the value in a field for multiple records*** **539**

issue a Find to create a found set (or use the Show All option to change the value for all records). Move to the field containing the value you want to replace, and select Browse ➤ Fill Field. Approach displays the Fill Field dialog box. Enter the value you want Approach to place in the field. Select OK. To access the Fill Field dialog box from a worksheet, click on the column heading so the entire column is selected, then choose Worksheet ➤ Fill Field. In a report or mailing label, select Browse ➤ Fill Field. The Fill Field command is not available from crosstabs.

▶ ***To change the value in a field in multiple records using a macro*** **540**

create a looping macro. Display the found set (finding all records that contain the value you want to replace), then execute the looping macro that includes the Set command.

▶ ***To change a value for records that contain no value in a field*** **541**

create a looping macro using the IsBlank command.

▶ ***To hide a record*** **543**

you must be in the Browse environment. To hide a record, select it (if you are working with a worksheet or report) or make it the current record (when working with a form). You can use Shift+Click to select multiple contiguous records. If you are using a Worksheet, select Worksheet ➤ Records ➤ Hide. If you've selected a PicturePlus field, select PicturePlus ➤ Hide Record. From any other view select Browse ➤ Hide Record. The shortcut key is Ctrl+H.

➤ *To view all records* 543

select a Show All Records icon from the SmartIcons toolbar. Alternatively, press Ctrl+A, choose Browse ➤ Show All, PicturePlus ➤ Show All, Worksheet ➤ Find ➤ Show All, or Crosstab ➤ Find ➤ Show All.

➤ *To spell check text in a database record* 544

switch to the Browse environment. To spell check a portion of a record, select the text you want to check. Select Tools ➤ Spell Check, press Ctrl+K, or click on the Check Spelling icon. The options in the Check section vary depending on your current work. To set the speller options, select the Options button. To choose the language you want to spell check (American English or British English, for example), select the Language Options button, enter the path of the dictionary and the language you want to use, and select OK. If you want to check the text in a memo field, which usually contains free form text, and skip all other fields, check the "Memo fields only" box. Select OK to begin.

➤ *To edit your spell checker's dictionary* 546

switch to the Browse environment. Select Tools ➤ Spell Check, press Ctrl+K, or click on the Check Spelling icon. Select the Edit Dictionary option. Choose the word from the Edit Dictionary dialog box. Enter a new word and select Add to add the word to the dictionary. Select a word from the Current words list and select Delete to remove it. When done, choose OK, then choose OK from the Spell Check dialog box to begin a spell check, or Cancel to return to your view.

▶▶ **In** previous chapters you have seen how to find individual records and groups of records called *found sets*. Now suppose you want to update your database with new credit terms. For example, while you used to extend Net 30 terms, where the payment is due 30 days from the receipt of the invoice, your competition is offering Net 45 terms. You want to update the Credit Terms field in all customer records where the current value is Net 30. If most of your customers are on Net 15-day terms, and only a handful are granted Net 30, it is probably easy to change the data in this small found set. Problems arise, however, when you need to change data from dozens, hundreds, or even thousands of customer records. If Net 30 is your most common credit term, changing to Net 45 by manually accessing the individual records for 10,000 customers could be a daunting task.

Fortunately, Approach makes it easy. In fact, Approach offers you several ways to update your database. In this chapter we'll explore some of those ways, and in so doing provide a deeper insight into some of the searching capabilities and functions available in Approach.

▶▶ A Quick Review

In order to find a single record or set of records you'll issue the Find command, which was discussed in detail in Chapter 12. The Menu command varies based on what view you are using, but you can always click on the Find icon from the SmartIcons toolbar or press Ctrl+F. (Note that Approach provides two icons for finding records.)

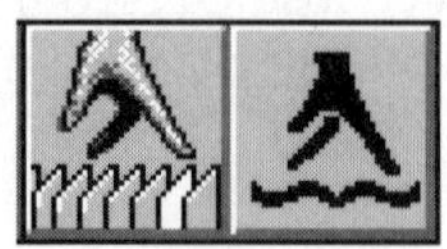

Approach then displays your current view with a new 4-button strip across the top and a different toolbar. The OK and Cancel buttons are self-explanatory. The Clear Find erases any previously entered conditions and criteria, while the Find More displays an additional screen for entering more conditions.

►► Changing Values with the Fill Field

To change the credit limit field in all records offering Net 30 credit terms, you can issue a Find and enter **Net 30** in the credit limit field. Approach will display only those records matching the condition you specified. If there are only a few records matching this condition, you can choose to edit each record individually. However, there is a shortcut you can use. Instead of entering the data for each record, move to the field containing the value you want to replace, and select Browse ➤ Fill Field. Approach displays the Fill Field dialog box shown in Figure 17.1.

FIGURE 17.1 ►

The Fill Field dialog box asks you to enter the field value you want to place in every record.

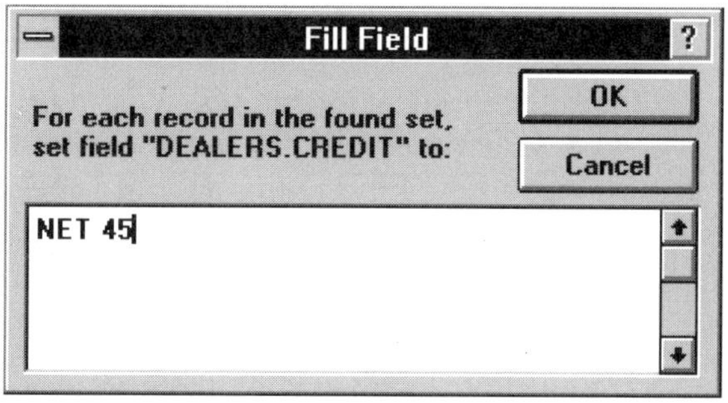

Enter the value you want Approach to place in the field. Notice that the dialog box indicates the field name, including the database name if your Approach file contains joined databases (joins are described in Chapter 6). Select OK.

You can also access the Fill Field dialog box from a worksheet. Click on the column heading so the entire column is selected, then choose Worksheet ➤ Fill Field. In a report or mailing label, select Browse ➤ Fill Field. Fill Field is not available from crosstabs.

The Fill Field function has dozens of uses. For example, suppose you have a name and address database. Within the record of each client is the company name and address. Suppose you have 20 clients within the Acme Widget Company, and Acme moves to a new location. You can use a Find command to create a found set of all Acme employees, then choose each field that has changed (Street, City, State, and Zip) and update the client records in one fell swoop. This is much faster than updating the data individually, and eliminates not only time but potential typing errors.

Likewise, if there is an error, such as a misspelling in the address field, you can select a found set containing this value and replace it for all incorrect records. If you notice that some records contain the address 123 Maine Street, but the address should read 123 Main Street, you can select the found set based on the value 123 Maine Street, then use the Fill Field to make the correction to all incorrect records at once.

►► Filling Fields with a Looping Macro

In Chapter 16 you learned how to create a looping macro. Once you have a found set (for all records containing the credit term Net 30), you can use a looping macro to refine your replacement.

For example, suppose you want to extend the credit terms only to your best customers—those with credit limits over $1,000. While you could issue a new Find command and specify two conditions (one for the credit term and the other for the credit limit field), you could use your current found set and a looping macro that uses criteria to accomplish the same things.

Figure 17.2 shows the macro as well as the formula used in the Set command. Just behind the Formula dialog box we've told the macro line to set (fill) the field DEALERS.CREDIT. You can see this in the Options section of the first line of the macro. We use the If command to determine the value we'll use in the Set command. The function asks if the Credit Limit Field of the Dealers database contains a value that is greater than or equal to 1000. If the answer is true, then the first value (Net 45) is used. Otherwise, Approach will use the Net 30 value.

There's an important consideration when creating looping macros. You'll want to move to the first record in the database before running the macro, since the macro ordinarily begins at the current record and

FIGURE 17.2

This macro will fill the field using the Set command. The macro uses the If command to make a decision and give the longer credit terms to customers with the higher credit limits.

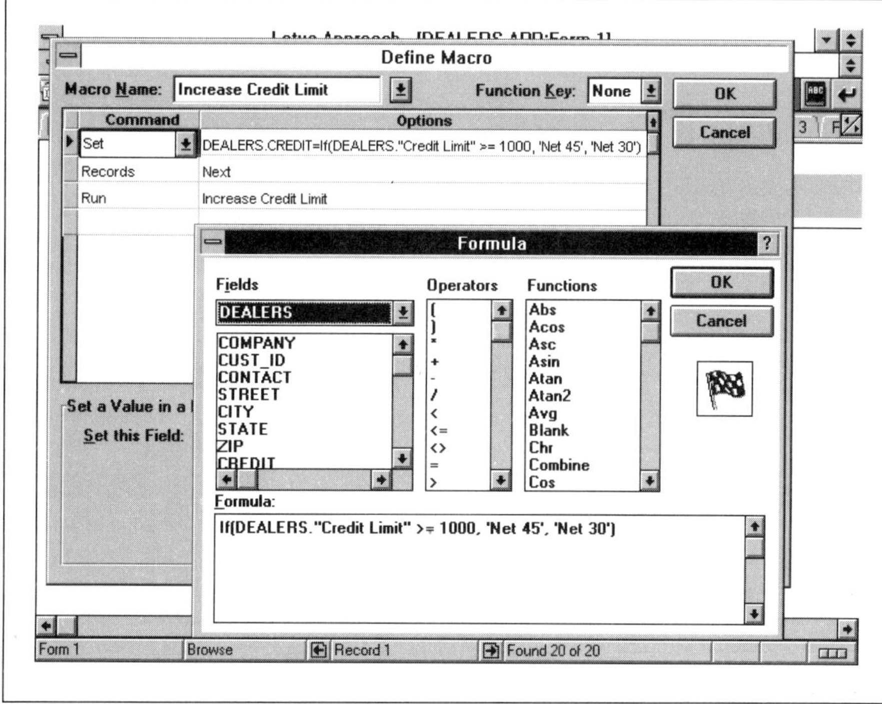

moves to the end of the database. The Reserialize1 and Researialize2 macros in Chapter 16 showed you how to overcome this limitation and ensure that all database records are changed by using two macros (one calling another).

▸▸ Filling Fields with Default Values

Another important function that you can use in a looping macro bears mentioning: IsBlank. IsBlank checks to see if the field contains a value. You might use this function to ensure that all customers have a credit limit established, for example. If there is no limit (value) in a record, the looping macro shown in Figure 17.3 can set a default limit of $500. Notice that the macro uses the If command, which requires two values: one to use in the Set command if the condition is met (the field is blank), and another value if the condition is not met (that is, the field contains a value already). If the limit exists, we don't want to replace it, so we must include a replacement value in the formula: We tell Approach to replace the value with the value already in the field.

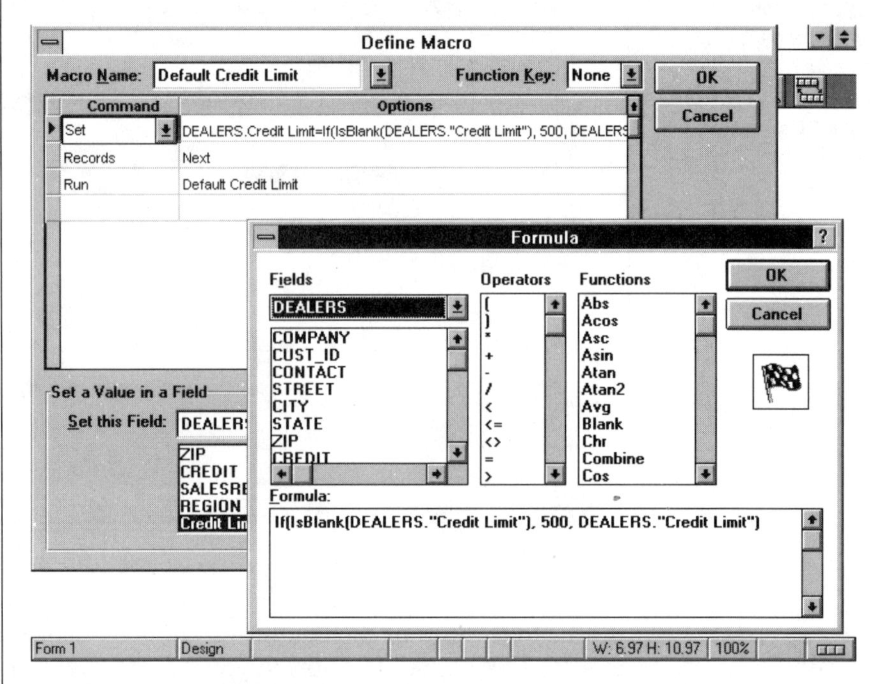

FIGURE 17.3

This macro uses the IsBlank command to fill fields with a default value if they contain no value. If there is already a value in the field, that field value is not changed.

While you could have entered this as a validation criteria or default value in the Field Definition dialog box, it's often the case that such conditions are recognized or needed only after some records have already been added to the database.

Note that the IsBlank function looks for records in which the field does not contain a value—a field that was skipped during data entry, for example, or one in which you highlighted and pressed the Backspace key in order to remove any value already present. Thus, if a customer has a credit limit of 0, this looping macro will not change its value. Zero is a legitimate value and is not the same as a field that contains no value (called *null*).

▶▶ Hiding and Showing Records

When you issue a Find command, Approach returns the individual record or group of records that meets your criteria. Sometimes, however, you want to exclude an individual record from the found set without issuing another Find command. For example, you might issue a Find command to display all records of customers in Wisconsin so you can change their tax rates. However, as you browse through the found set you notice that there are two non-profit corporations within Wisconsin that pay no tax whatsoever. Therefore, what you really want your found set to list are all the Wisconsin companies with a tax rate greater than zero.

Rather than issue a new Find command, you can hide the records from view. This does not delete the records—it simply makes them temporarily disappear from the found set. When you perform an update or search, Approach does not include the hidden records when looking through your database.

To hide a record, you must be in the Browse environment. Select the record (if you are working with a worksheet or report) or make it the current record (when working with a form). You can also use Shift+Click to select multiple contiguous records. If you are using a Worksheet, select Worksheet ➤ Records ➤ Hide. If you've selected a PicturePlus field, select PicturePlus ➤ Hide Record. From any other view select Browse ➤ Hide Record. The shortcut key is Ctrl+H.

To view all records, click on the Show All Records icon from the SmartIcons toolbar. Alternatively, press Ctrl+A, choose Browse ➤ Show All, PicturePlus ➤ Show All, Worksheet ➤ Find ➤ Show All, or Crosstab ➤ Find ➤ Show All.

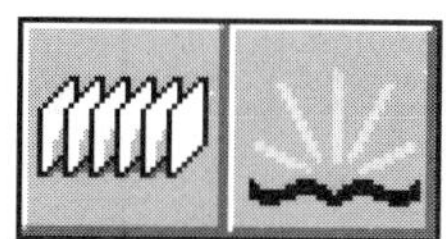

If you are working with a found set, you can quickly jump to the Find criteria by selecting Browse ➤ Find Again, PicturePlus ➤ Find Again, Worksheet ➤ Find ➤ Find Again, or Crosstab ➤ Find ➤ Find Again.

▸▸ Correcting Records Using the Spelling Checker

The built-in spell checker can be used to check the spelling of data within your database as well as the spelling of text in field labels and text objects, such as text within the body of a form letter.

As with most spell checkers, Approach supplies a default dictionary that contains the most common words. The spell checker will also look for words in a user dictionary, which you specify and which contains words not found in the default dictionary. Your user dictionary may contain technical terms or proper names important to your business, for example.

To spell-check the text within a record:

1. Switch to the Browse environment.
2. Select the text you want to check, or skip this step to check the text in the entire record.
3. Select Tools ➤ Spell Check, press Ctrl+K, or click on the Check Spelling icon from the SmartIcons toolbar. Approach displays the Spell Check dialog box shown in Figure 17.4 (in this example the spell checker was requested for a form). This dialog box is shown when you request a spell check for a

FIGURE 17.4 ▸

When you begin the spell checker, Approach asks you to specify what you want to check.

form, a report, or mailing labels. The options in the Check section vary depending on your current work. For example, if you are working with a worksheet, your options are limited to Selection and Entire Worksheet.

4. To set the speller options, select the Options button. Here you can:
   - Check for or skip repeated words.
   - Check for or skip words that contain numbers (such as 3rd).
   - Check for or skip words with Initial Caps (which usually indicate proper names, such as company names or the first or last names of clients, customers, employees, and so on—names that are unlikely to be in your dictionary).
   - Include alternatives from your user dictionary.
5. To choose the language you want to spell check (American English or British English, for example), select the Language Options button. Enter the path of the dictionary and the language you want to use, and select OK.
6. If you want to check the text in a memo field—which usually contains free form text—and skip all other fields, check the "Memo fields only" box.
7. Select OK to begin.

When Approach encounters a word that it cannot find in its dictionary or your user dictionary, it displays the dialog box shown in Figure 17.5, which includes the misspelled or questionable word.

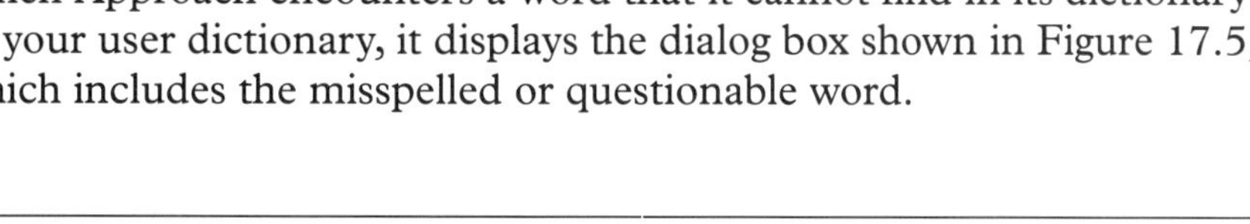

FIGURE 17.5

When Approach finds a word that is not in its dictionary or your user dictionary, it asks you what you want to do.

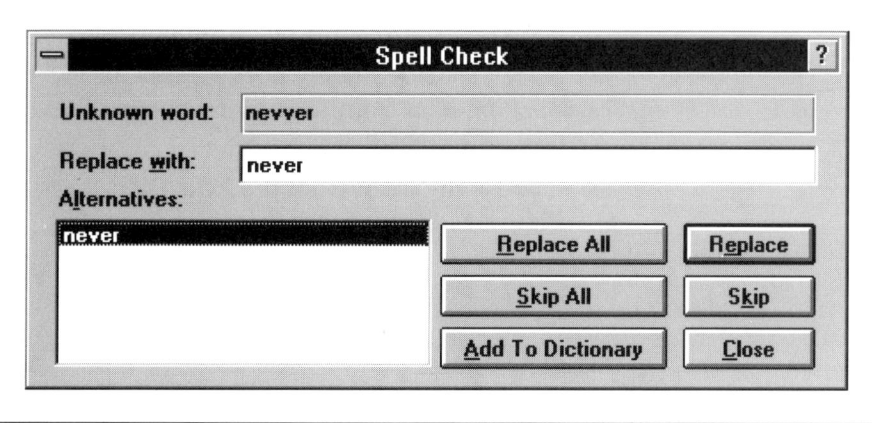

In the Spell Check dialog box you can:

- Select an alternative spelling, then select Replace to replace the single occurrence or select Replace All to change all occurrences of the misspelled word.
- Type a replacement in the "Replace with" box and select Replace or Replace All.
- Skip the word during the remainder of the spell check (the Skip All option).
- Skip the word this time only, but flag the word if it is found again later in the database (the Skip option).
- Add the word to your user dictionary (the Add to Dictionary option).
- Stop the spell checker (the Close option).

▸ *Editing Your User Dictionary*

Over time you may wish to remove a word from your user dictionary. This usually happens when you've added a word to the dictionary in error. For example, if we add the word "nevver" to the user dictionary, we need a way to remove the word so that future spell checks don't accept this misspelling.

You may also want to add a series of technical terms to your user dictionary rather than adding them as each is discovered by the spell checker.

To add or remove a word from the user dictionary:

1. Switch to the Browse environment.
2. Select Tools ➤ Spell Check, press Ctrl+K, or click on the Check Spelling icon from the SmartIcons toolbar. Select the Edit Dictionary option.
3. Choose the word from the Edit Dictionary dialog box, shown in Figure 17.6.

FIGURE 17.6 ▶

You can use the Edit Dictionary dialog box to change the spelling of existing words, or add new words to any dictionary.

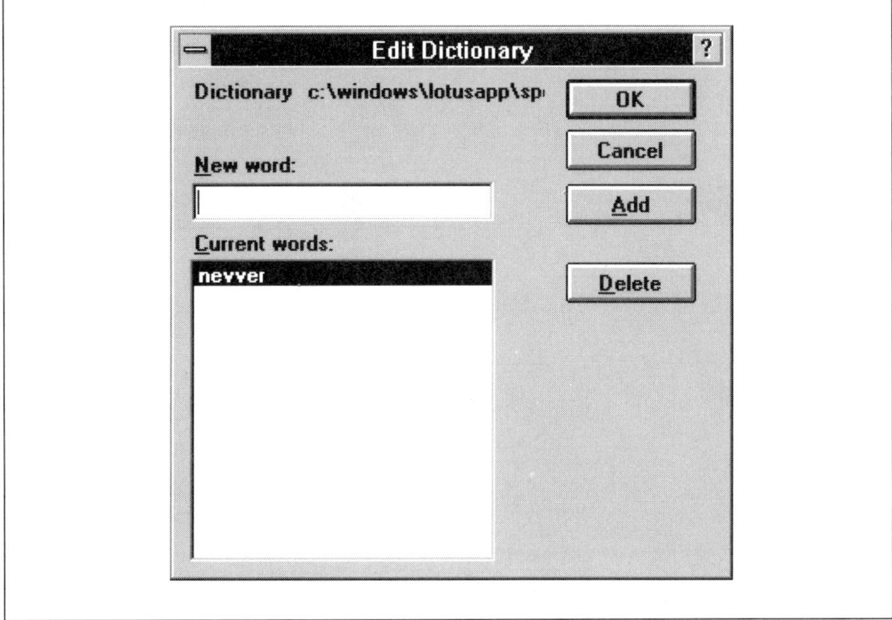

4. Enter a new word and select Add to add the word to the dictionary. Select a word from the "Current words" list and select Delete to remove it.
5. Select OK when you are done. Select OK from the Spell Check dialog box to begin a spell check, or Cancel to return to your view.

▶▶ Summary and a Look Ahead

In this chapter we looked at some techniques for replacing values in multiple records using the Fill Field command and using formulas and macros. We also looked at how to hide and view records, and how to use the spell checker to correct data.

In Chapter 18 we'll look at how to customize Approach. With all its flexibility, there are many ways to have Approach work the way you want it to, including displaying a custom set of toolbars and menus.

CHAPTER 18

Customizing Approach

▸▸ FAST TRACK

▶ *To set display options* **553**

select Tools ➤ Preferences. The Display tab is selected by default. Select the desired options, then select OK to use these settings during the current session only, or select Save Default and then OK to use them in this and future sessions. The Display tab controls what appears on your screen, the default styles, design options, and grid properties.

▶ *To work more efficiently with Approach* **557**

select Tools ➤ Preferences, then select the General tab.

▶ *To change the default display order for records in your database* **559**

select Tools ➤ Preferences and select the Order tab. Select the database from the "Maintain default sort for" drop-down list. Select the field from the Database fields list to sort on, then select the Add button. Select the sort order for the field, either ascending or descending. Repeat this process until all fields have been selected for the selected database. Select OK.

▶ *To set a database password* **561**

select Tools ➤ Preferences, then select the Password tab. Select the database you want to protect. Check the read/write password box and enter a password. Approach replaces your keystrokes with asterisks. When you move out of the field, Approach asks you to confirm your password. Enter the password again, then select OK.

To set an Approach file password 563

select Tools ➤ Preferences, then select the Password tab. Check the "Password for the Approach file" checkbox and enter the password in the text field to the right. When you move out of this field you must re-enter the password, then press OK. Select OK to close the Preferences dialog box.

To change an existing SmartIcons toolbar 572

switch to the environment (Design, Browse, or Preview) or task (Find, Preview) that uses the toolbar you wish to change. Select Tools ➤ SmartIcons. Select the SmartIcons toolbar you want to change by clicking on the down-pointing arrow in the text box at the top of the right column. To add an icon, drag it from the Available Icons column to the second column. To remove an icon, select the icon and drag it off the toolbar. To rearrange icons in the second column, drag the icon to the desired position in the list. Select the location for the toolbar using the options in the Position drop-down list. Top, Bottom, Left, and Right options anchor the toolbar to that position of the screen. To display bubble help when you move the mouse pointer over an icon, check the "Show Icon Descriptions" box. Choose the Icon Size button to switch between medium- and large-sized icons. Select OK.

To assign a menu to a view 581

select the view, click anywhere on the view (but not on an object on the view) and open the InfoBox. Select the Basics tab and select the Menu bar name from the "Attached menu bar" drop-down list. Save the Approach file to make your menu-view assignment permanent.

While Approach is easy to use, you may find that you want to "tweak" the program to work a little bit differently. You can tailor how to work with Approach in a variety of ways. For example, you can determine if the Add Fields dialog box appears in the Design environment. You can specify how the SmartIcons toolbar looks and its position. You can even change the menus so that you can control the access your end user has when working with an application you build in Approach.

In previous chapters we've mentioned how some default settings can be changed. In this chapter, we've collected all the customizable features.

The default settings you select and save are stored in a file called APPROACH.INI, which is located in the Windows subdirectory on your hard disk. Typically this directory is C:\WINDOWS. You can directly edit this file if you wish, but we strongly recommend that you use the techniques described in this chapter to set your defaults. Using Approach to set defaults ensures that Approach will always start properly, and that no unexpected conditions will be encountered when it reads (and tries to use the settings in) APPROACH.INI.

It is interesting, of course, to explore APPROACH.INI. You can open the file using Notepad or another text editor, but be sure you do not save the file when you are done looking at it. The purpose or use of many options listed in APPROACH.INI is obvious. For example, sRecentFile1=C:\ APPROACH\DEALERS.APR provides the name of the file that will appear in the pull-down list from the Welcome screen. Others, such as icon_desc=4 are less clear—all the more reason to use Approach to modify your default values.

►► Setting Preferences

Many of the preferences are set using the Tools ➤ Preferences menu option. SmartIcons and Menu settings will be described later in this chapter (see the sections "Changing the SmartIcons Toolbars" and "Creating Your Own Menus"). In most cases, the options are set using a check box. When the check box contains an X, the option is set. When the check box is empty, the option is not set. Other options, such as the Default style, require you to select a button and make additional choices. In any event, the preferences last from session to session if you choose the Save Default button from the options panels. Conversely, if you use the settings for the current session only, when you launch Approach again, Approach will read the original APPROACH.INI file settings and restore the original values.

►► Setting Display Preferences

The first category of preferences control what you view on the screen. The more options you choose, the less screen space you may actually have to work with. However, many of these options, such as the Smart Icons toolbar, significantly reduce the time it takes to perform a task, or at least make it easier than selecting the equivalent commands from the cascading menus.

To set display options, select Tools ➤ Preferences. The Display tab, shown in Figure 18.1, is selected by default. You can set the options you want for any tab, as described below, then select OK to use these settings during the current session only, or select Save Default and then OK to use them in this and future sessions (until they are changed again, of course).

► Changing What's On Your Screen

The following options control what Approach features are displayed on your screen and are set using the Display tab in the Preferences dialog box.

This Option	Controls This Feature
SmartIcons	Displays the SmartIcons toolbar.
Status Bar	Displays the Status bar at the bottom of the screen.

FIGURE 18.1

The Display tab lets you set what Approach displays on your screen, from displaying the SmartIcons toolbar and rulers to the spacing between grid points.

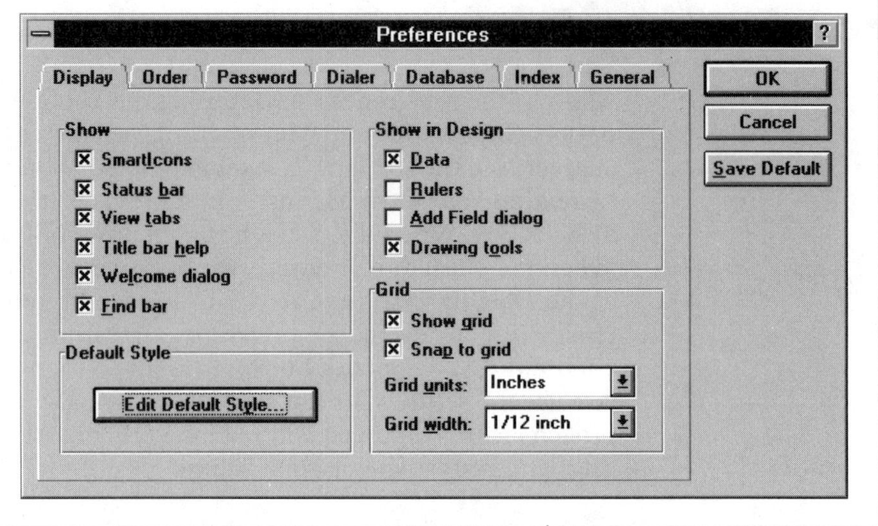

View Tabs	Displays each view using a separate tab; you can also navigate to other views if you display the Status bar and click on the first box (which displays a list of all available views).
Title Bar Help	Displays a command description when you select a menu using the mouse or keyboard. The Title bar temporarily replaces the application name (Lotus Approach) and the current Approach file name and view name with a description of what the menu command does.
Welcome Dialog	Displays the Welcome dialog box after launching Approach; if you select Cancel from the Welcome dialog box, it will not appear again during the session unless you open, then close an Approach file.
Find Bar	Displays the OK, Cancel, Clear Find, and Find More buttons during a Find. I highly recommend you set this option.

▶ Changing the Default Style

When you use an Assistant to create a new view, the Assistant uses the Default style, which contains properties about the background, foreground, and objects, such as colors and fonts.

To change the Default style, select the Edit Default Style button. Approach displays the Define Style dialog box, shown in Figure 18.2. Choose the default style from the "Based on" pull-down list, and select OK.

FIGURE 18.2 ▶

The Define Style dialog box lets you define the properties that will be used for new objects on a view.

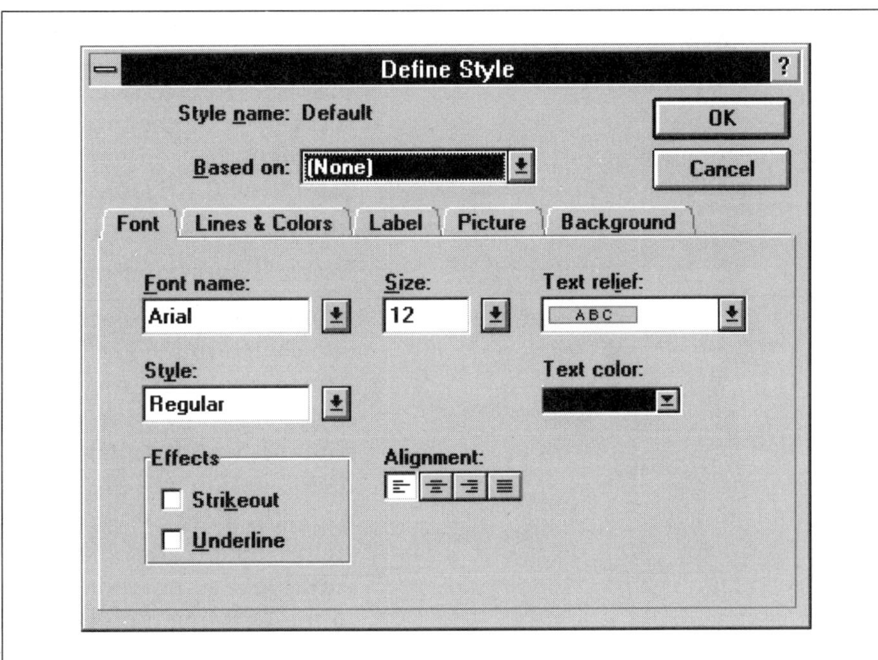

▶ Changing Design Options

The following set of options, found in the Show in Design section of the Display tab, controls what you see when you are working in the Design environment.

This Option	Does This
Data	Displays the actual data value from the first record in the found set (or the first set of records for worksheets and reports). If checked, you can see if the field dimensions are appropriate—a last name won't be fully readable if your field is too short. If unchecked, you'll see the field name (and database name for joined databases), which is sometimes too cryptic. At other times, fields are too narrow to display the field name, such as a Boolean field named Overdue. You may be able to see Y or N on the form (if the Data option is checked), but you probably can't view CUSTOMERS.Overdue in the same space.
Rulers	Displays horizontal and vertical ruler bars.
Add Field dialog	Displays the Add Field dialog box when you switch to the Design environment. Alternatively, you may wish to use this dialog box only occasionally, in which case it is wise to uncheck the Add Field dialog option and display the dialog box using the Form ➤ Add Field command, right-click on any object and select the Add Field command, or click on the icon in the Drawing tools palette.
Drawing Tools	Displays the Drawing Tools palette.

► Changing Grid Options

Grids are the evenly spaced dots you see in the Design environment. They help you align objects, calculate the dimensions, and set the automatic spacing between objects (when used with the "Snap to grid" option).

This Option	Does this
Show Grid	Displays the grid points.
Snap To Grid	Makes selected objects align their borders with a grid. Snaps occur when you create new fields or move or resize existing objects.
Grid Units	Sets the unit of measure (either inches or centimeters).
Grid Width	Sets the distance between points.

►► Making Your Work with Approach More Efficient

Approach hides some of the most productivity-enhancing options under the General tab of the Preferences dialog box. These options can save time and keystrokes by performing some tasks automatically. To set them, select Tools ➤ Preferences, then choose the General tab. The options are shown in Figure 18.3.

FIGURE 18.3 ►

The General tab is a dumping ground for those "miscellaneous" settings that control everything from record sharing to how the Enter key behaves in the Browse environment.

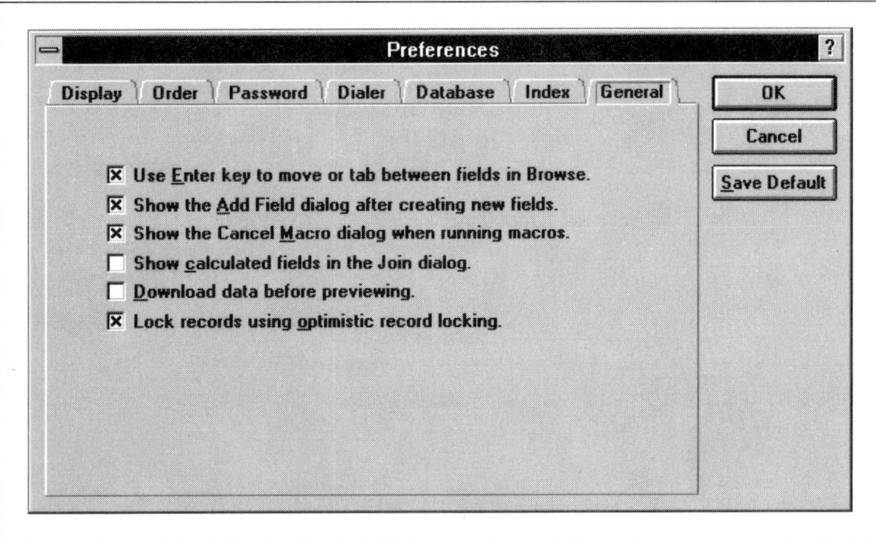

These options can be used as follows:

Check This Box	To Do This
Use Enter key to move or tab between fields in Browse	This makes the Enter key work just like the Tab key in the Browse environment: Press Enter and you'll move to the next field. If this option is not checked, Enter accepts the characters you type in a field but keeps the cursor in the field.
Show the Add Field dialog box after creating new fields	Like it sounds, but better; Approach will automatically display the Add Field dialog box that lists only your new or modified field, so it's easy to find the field in the dialog box (it's the only one listed!) and drag it onto a form. The Add Field dialog box includes a new button (Show All Fields) that lets you list all field definitions, too. This option is highly recommended.
Show the Cancel Macro dialog box when running macros	If a macro takes a while to run, you'll want to let your user (or you) cancel the macro in progress. Check this box and Approach will display a small dialog box that tells you the macro is running and lets you press a Cancel key to stop it.
Show calculated fields in the Join dialog	Does what it says it does; calculated fields appear in italics in the field list of the Join dialog box.
Download data before previewing	For files on a network, you may wish to download a copy of the data set when you preview your work so you'll have the most up-to-date data available. This ensures that what you preview is what you print.

Lock records using optimistic record locking	If you're on a network and want to let two users edit the same record at the same time, check this box. If someone else is changing the record, Approach will ask if you want to overwrite their changes with your own. This may be dangerous. However, the option makes Approach run faster because there is less overhead than the alternative: If this option is not checked, Approach uses full record locking. With full record locking, Approach will let two users view the record but only one can edit it at a time. If you try to edit the record being edited by another, Approach will tell you that you have to wait. With full record locking, the other user's changes are written to the database; then you can make your changes and both sets of changes are incorporated into the database record.

►► Setting the Record Display Order

By default, a form view lists records in the order in which they were created. This is sometimes called the creation order, or more frequently referred to as record number order, since Approach assigns each new record a unique, ascending number, as each record is added. Thus, showing records in the order in which they are added is the same as listing them by their record number. You can change this order by sorting the records, but the underlying order (by record number) is not changed.

You can change the default display (sort) order for any database in your Approach file, but this does not change the physical order of the records in your database. You can continue to sort records in different ways, but when you select the Show All command, the order returns to the order set by the Order option we're about to describe. Think of the Order option as a default sort order. The records are always displayed in this order, although the underlying database doesn't actually change.

Use these steps to change the default order:

1. Select Tools ➤ Preferences and select the Order tab. The Order tab is shown in Figure 18.4.

FIGURE 18.4

The Order tab lets you override the display of records by specifying a default sort order. The records in the database are not rearranged.

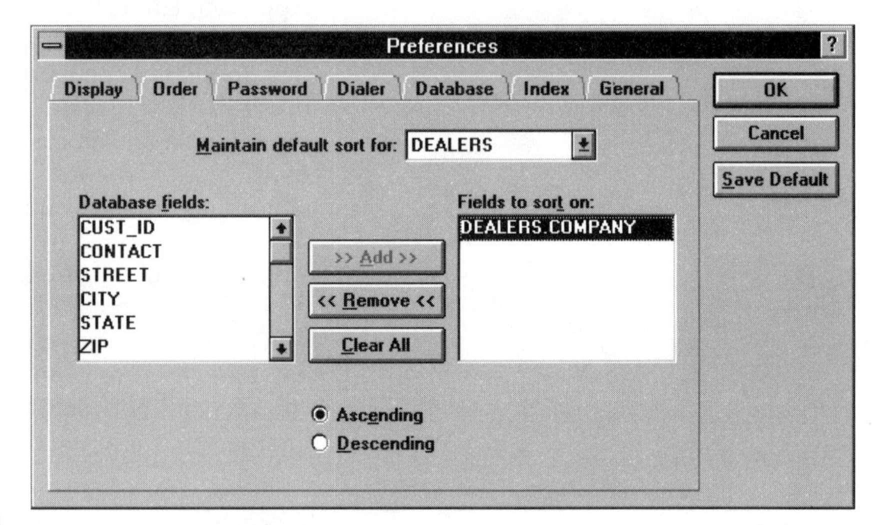

2. Select the database from the "Maintain default sort for" pull-down list.
3. As with any sort, select the field from the Database fields list. When the field is highlighted, select the Add button. Alternatively, double-click on the field name to add it to the "Fields to sort on" list. If you make a mistake, click on the field in the "Fields to sort on" list and select Remove, or double-click on the field you want to remove. To remove all fields, select Clear All.
4. Select the sort order for the field, either ascending or descending.
5. Repeat Steps 3 and 4 until all fields have been selected for the selected database.
6. Repeat Steps 2 through 5 for any other database whose sort order you wish to change.
7. Select OK.

►► Setting Passwords

Passwords provide you a level of security—you can restrict who has access to your database, who can modify data, and who can create or modify additional views.

There are two types of passwords: database file passwords and Approach file passwords. A word of warning about both types of passwords is in order first, however.

►► WARNING

You must save the Approach or database file for the password to take effect. If you close the file but do not save it, the previous password (if any) is still in effect.

► Database File Passwords

With a database file password you can restrict who has access to your file. A read/write password lets a user have complete access to the file—anything is possible if the user has the read/write password. He or she can add, change, or delete records, create new views and change reports, and join databases to the Approach file. A read-only password lets a user view the data (as in a report or form) but that user can't modify the data. A read-only password is a valuable tool for providing access to information with the safety of knowing the person cannot add additional records, change values, or delete records.

It's easy to set a database file with a read/write password. If you want to set a read-only password, however, you'll also have to set a read/write password, since someone (presumably you) must have full access to the database.

Another word of warning: if you assign a database file password (either a read/write or both a read/write and a read-only password), Approach will encrypt the file. This means that other users in your organization will not be able to use your database files in their native format. For example, if you assign a password to the DEALERS.DBF database file, another user in your company cannot use another database tool or application that can read dBASE files and open the DEALERS.DBF file. Thus, your database file is no longer sharable. You can, of course, make an unprotected copy of your file (using the File ➤ Save As command). Don't assign a password to this new file.

Use these steps to set a database password:

1. Select Tools ➤ Preferences, then select the Password tab shown in Figure 18.5.

FIGURE 18.5

The Password tab is the place for setting database and Approach file security.

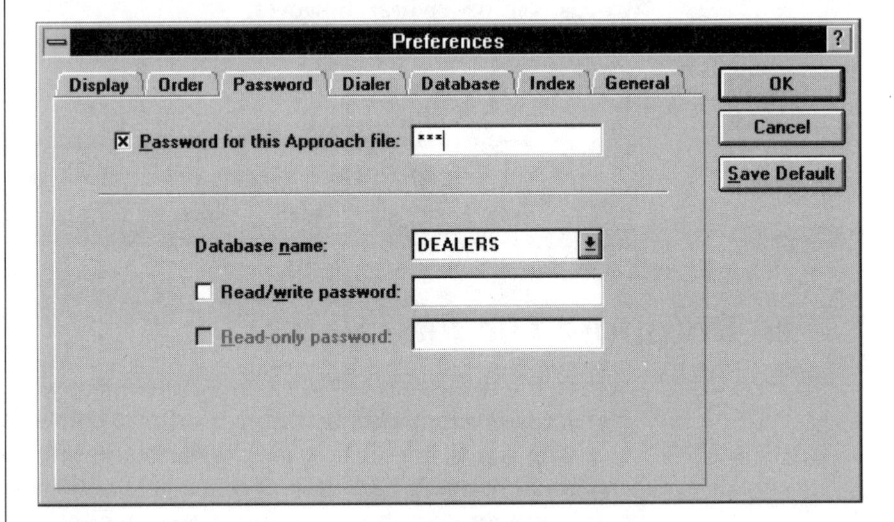

2. Select the database you want to protect.
3. Check the read/write password box and enter a password. Approach replaces your keystrokes with asterisks. When you move to another field (by pressing the tab key or selecting another tab, for example), Approach asks you to confirm your password, as shown in Figure 18.6. The password can be up to 16 characters long and is not case sensitive (the password KeepOut is the same as KEEPout).
4. Approach enables the Read-only Password option. Check it and enter a password if desired. Approach replaces your keystrokes with asterisks. This password is also case insensitive and can be up to 16 characters long. You will be asked to re-enter the password.
5. Select OK.

FIGURE 18.6

The Confirm Password dialog box is used to make sure you don't enter a password incorrectly. The password you enter here must match the password you originally typed.

Setting an Approach File Password

You can protect the design of your views. By assigning a password to the Approach file, you ensure that a user cannot add, change, or delete views, join databases, or use an Assistant to create a new view. In fact, the user cannot even switch to the Design environment unless he or she enters the correct password.

Use these steps to set an Approach file password:

1. Select Tools ➤ Preferences, then select the Password tab. The tab is shown in Figure 18.5 earlier in this chapter.
2. Check the "Password for the Approach file" check box and enter the password in the text field to the right. The password can be up to 16 characters long, and the password is not case sensitive. Approach replaces your keystrokes with asterisks.
3. When you move out of this field (by pressing the tab key or clicking on another field or a different tab), Approach asks you to reenter the password, as shown in Figure 18.6 earlier in this chapter. Do so and select OK.
4. Select OK to close the Preferences dialog box.

To remove a password, uncheck the "Password for the Approach file" check box. Approach does not ask you to confirm this change.

▸▸ **WARNING**

Don't lose or forget your password! If you do, you will not be able to open the files, and there is no recovery of this data if the password is lost or forgotten.

▸▸ *Setting Dialing and Modem Preferences*

Approach can use a telephone number in a field and dial the number for you automatically. To use this feature, however, you must specify the parameters for your modem and communications. You'll find these preferences in the Dialer tab of the Preferences dialog box. Standard modem settings for Hayes-compatible modems are provided. However, if your modem does not conform to the Hayes standard, you can enter special command strings manually using the Dialer options.

Use these steps to set the Dialer options:

1. Select Tools ➤ Preferences, then select the Dialer tab. The Dialer tab is shown in Figure 18.7.

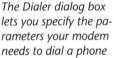

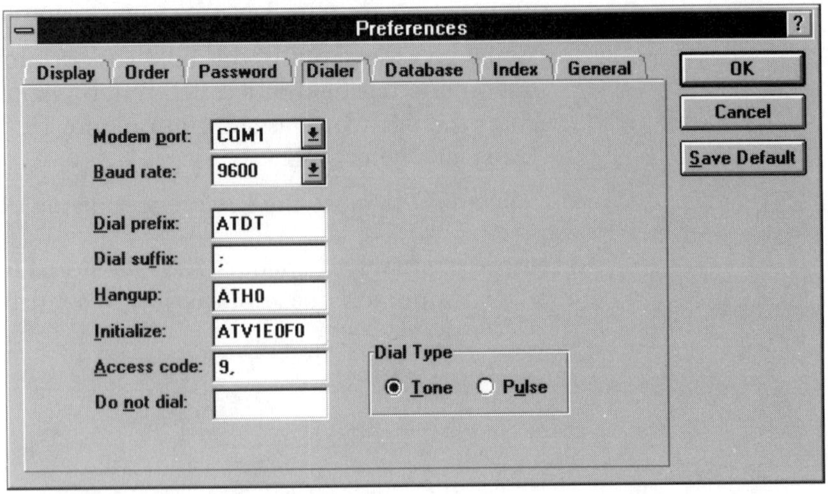

FIGURE 18.7 ▸

The Dialer dialog box lets you specify the parameters your modem needs to dial a phone number from within Approach.

2. Enter the options that suit your needs.
3. Select OK to accept your settings and close the Preferences dialog box.

The options work as follows:

This Option	Controls This
Modem Port	Sets which serial port is used with your modem; COM1 and COM2 are the most common settings.
Baud Rate	Sets the speed at which your modem can communicate; this is the maximum speed your modem can support, but your actual communications speed is set by the highest speed shared by both modems; if your modem supports 9600 baud but you dial a modem that has a maximum speed of 2400 baud, your communications will occur at the 2400 baud rate.
Dial Prefix	Sets the character string to use with your modem before dialing the number; ATDT (attention, dial tone) is the most common setting.
Dial Suffix	Sets the character string to use with your modem after you dial the telephone number; this is usually a semicolon (;).
Hangup	Sets the character string Approach should send to your modem to cause it to break the connection (hang up).
Initialize	Sets the character string command for initializing your modem; this is usually blank or ATV1E0F0.

Access Code	Sets any numbers you must dial to access your telephone system; in businesses this may mean dialing 9, then pausing for a dial tone. The character string for this is 9, (9 and a comma, which pauses briefly in order to wait for the dial tone).
Do Not Dial	Sets any numbers that should not be dialed, such as an area code for local calls.
Dial Type	Selects Tone (the most common setting used for touch-tone telephones) or Pulse (for rotary dial telephones).

►► Changing Database Options

In the section "Setting Passwords" earlier in this chapter, we discussed how to protect access to a database. You can also make a database file read-only. In addition, you can specify settings that control the character set options, case sensitivity, and cache options, depending on the file format used for the databases in your application.

► Changing Options for dBASE and FoxPro Database Files

For dBASE and FoxPro database files, you can:

- Make the file read-only so others can view the database records but not add, change, or delete them.
- Use either the DOS character set or the Windows character set, which controls special characters (those not on your keyboard).
- Compress the database. In FoxPro and dBASE, records you delete are marked as deleted but are not physically removed from the database until you "pack" or compress the database. Although Approach does not allow you access to a deleted record, other applications that use the dBASE file format may. Therefore, if you have deleted a large number of records, you may want to compress the database to save hard disk space and prevent access to the deleted records by other database applications.

Use these steps to set options for dBASE or FoxPro files:

1. Select Tools ➤ Preferences, then choose the Database tab (shown in Figure 18.8).

FIGURE 18.8 ▶

The Database tab, shown here for dBASE and FoxPro files, varies by the database file format of the database you select.

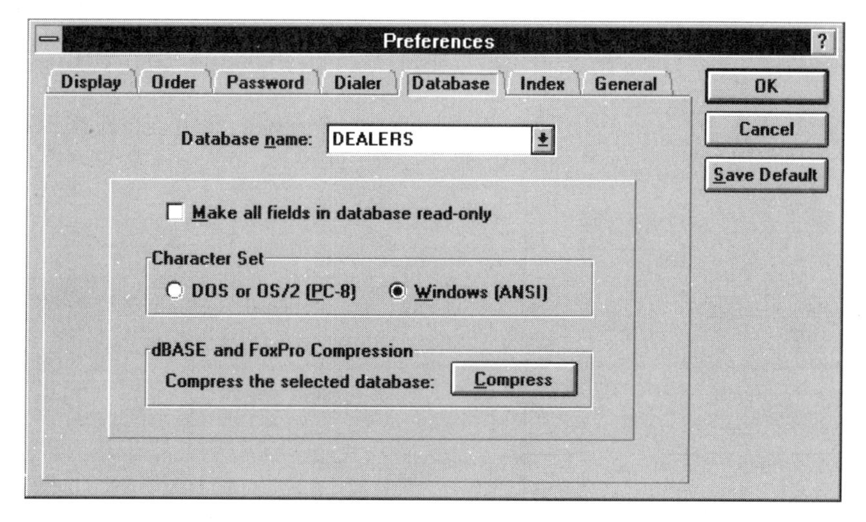

2. Choose the database from the Database name pull-down list at the top of the screen.
3. Check the "Make all fields in database read-only" box to prevent changes to the database.
4. Select the character set you want to use.
5. To compress the database, select the Compress button.
6. Select OK to return to the Approach work area. Approach will compress the database but does not provide a progress indicator. When the hard disk light on your computer stops flashing, it's a good bet the compression is complete.

▶ Maintaining dBASE and FoxPro Indexes

Approach creates its own index for dBASE and FoxPro tables. However, if you are using a dBASE or FoxPro file that uses its own index files, you may want Approach to maintain those indexes, so that when another user opens the file in a different application, he or she will not have to re-index the file. Maintaining external indexes is more than just a courtesy: If you are sharing a dBASE or FoxPro file that uses an external index with another user, and that user is working with the database using another application, that user's application may not perform properly if the index does not match the data.

To maintain an existing external index for a dBASE or FoxPro database file:

1. Select Tools ➤ Preferences and select the Index tab, which is shown in Figure 18.9.

FIGURE 18.9 ►

The Index tab is used to maintain external indexes as you update your database. These indexes are used by other applications but not by Approach.

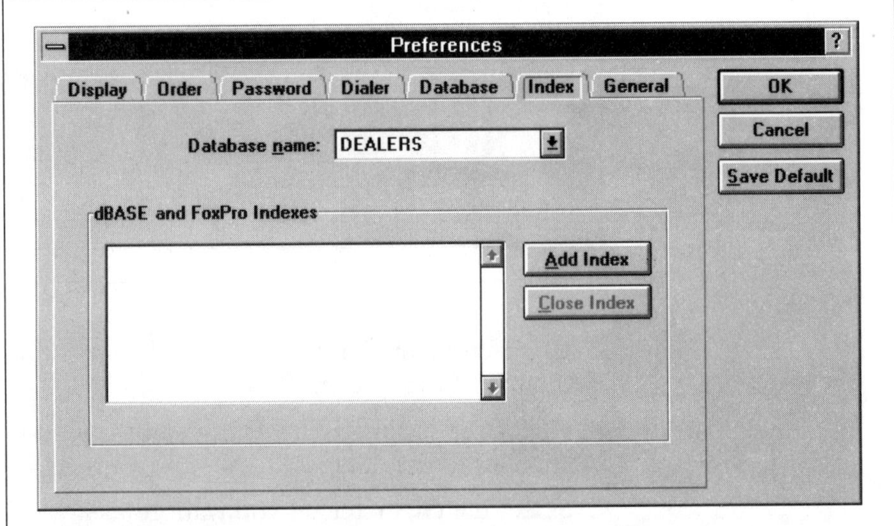

2. Choose the database from the Database name pull-down list.
3. Select the Add Index button, then choose the index file from the Add Index dialog box. Select OK to add the index. Approach returns to the Index tab.
4. Repeat Step 3 until all indexes have been added.
5. To remove an index from the list, select it and choose the Close Index button.
6. Select OK to return to the Approach work area.

▶ Changing Options for Paradox Database Files

For Paradox database files, you can:

- Make the file read-only so others can view the database records but not add, change, or delete them.
- Use either the DOS character set or the Windows character set, which controls special characters (those not on your keyboard).
- Make searches case sensitive or not (for Paradox 4.0 and greater files).

Use these steps to set options for Paradox files:

1. Select Tools ➤ Preferences, then choose the Database tab, as shown in Figure 18.10.

FIGURE 18.10 ▶

The Database tab for Paradox files lets you specify case sensitivity, among other options.

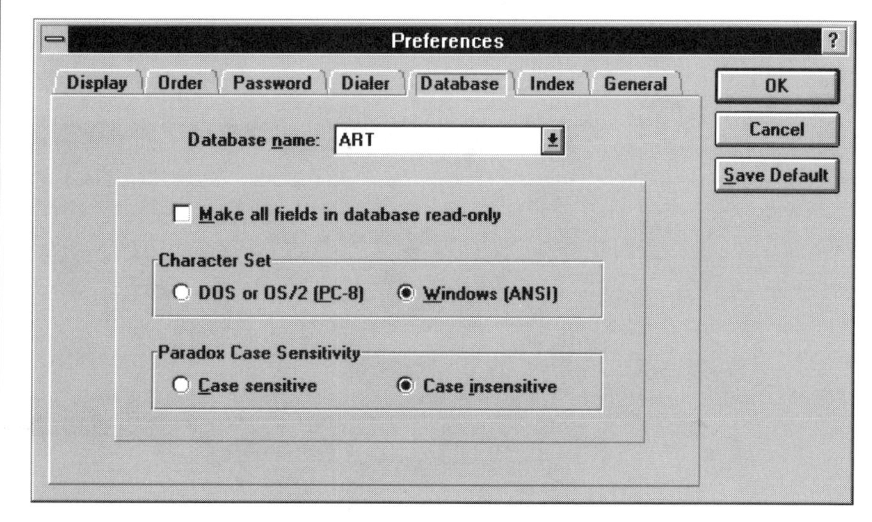

2. Choose the database from the pull-down list at the top of the screen.
3. Check the "Make all fields in database read-only" box to prevent changes to the database.

4. Select the character set you want to use.
5. If you are using a Paradox file using the Paradox 4 format, you can select the desired search option: Case sensitive or Case insensitive.
6. Select OK to return to the Approach work area.

▸ Creating a Secondary Index for a Paradox Database

When you create a database using the Paradox file format, Approach asks you to define the key field. (See Chapter 3 for details.) Paradox creates an index based on this key field, but you can create additional indexes, called secondary indexes, for the same Paradox file. All indexes are then updated when you make changes to the database.

Use these steps to create a secondary index for a Paradox file:

1. Select Tools ➤ Preferences, then choose the Index tab, as shown in Figure 18.11.

FIGURE 18.11 ▸

The Index tab for Paradox files lets you create secondary indexes.

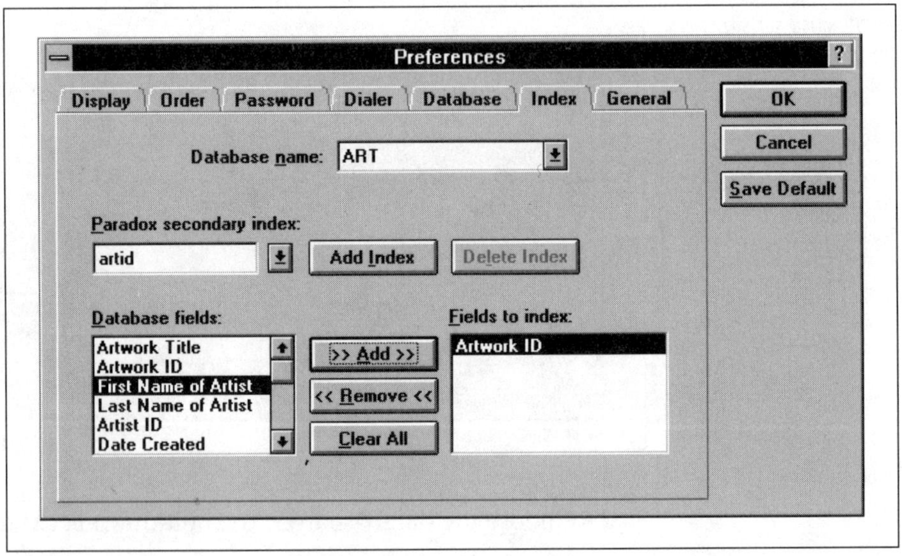

2. Choose the database from the Database name pull-down list at the top of the screen.
3. Enter the index name in the Paradox secondary index text box. Select the field(s) from the list displayed under Database fields on which to index (select the field and choose Add, or double-click the field name). To remove a field from the index, select it and choose Remove, or double-click on it in the "Fields to index" list. Click on Add Index.
4. Select OK to return to the Approach work area.

To remove an index, select its name from the Paradox secondary index list and choose the Delete Index button.

▶ Changing Options for Access, Lotus Notes, ODBC, and SQL Database Files

For Access, Lotus Notes, ODBC, and SQL database files, you can make the file read-only so others can view the database records but not add, change, or delete them.

For Access, ODBC, and SQL database files (but not Lotus Notes), you can:

- Display SQL system tables in any dialog box that displays file names.
- Cache the names of these tables so that display of the tables is quick.

The settings for Access, Notes, ODBC, and SQL files apply to all files in your Approach file, not just a single database.

Use these steps to set options for Access, Lotus Notes, ODBC, and SQL files:

1. Select Tools ➤ Preferences, then choose the Database tab.
2. Choose the database from the Database name pull-down list at the top of the screen.
3. Check the "Open all SQL tables as read-only" box (the last check box on the screen) to prevent changes to the database.

4. Check the "Show system tables in open dialog" box to include system tables in dialog boxes that show file names.
5. Check the "Cache table names for use in open dialog" box to implement name caching for speedier access on subsequent uses.
6. Select OK to return to the Approach work area.

Note that no indexes can be created or modified for these types of databases.

►► Changing the SmartIcons Toolbars

The SmartIcons toolbar provides a quick and easy way of performing tasks or navigating through your database. By clicking on a single icon, you can switch between the Design, Browse, and Preview environments, print a form, move to the last record, perform a sort, or open a new file.

When you install Approach, there are several SmartIcons toolbars installed by default. A different toolbar is displayed when you are in the Browse, Design, Preview, or Find environment or when working with Crosstab or Worksheet views.

In this section you'll learn how to customize the SmartIcons toolbar to suit your needs.

► Customizing the SmartIcons Toolbar

Use these steps to change an existing SmartIcons toolbar icon set:

1. Switch to the environment (Design, Browse, or Preview) or task (Find, Preview) that uses the toolbar you wish to change.
2. Select Tools ➤ SmartIcons. The SmartIcons dialog box appears, as shown in Figure 18.12.
3. Select the SmartIcons toolbar you want to change by clicking on the down-pointing arrow in the text box at the top of the right column. Approach displays the icons and descriptions in the second column. The first icon listed in this column is the first icon displayed in the toolbar (from left to right).

FIGURE 18.12

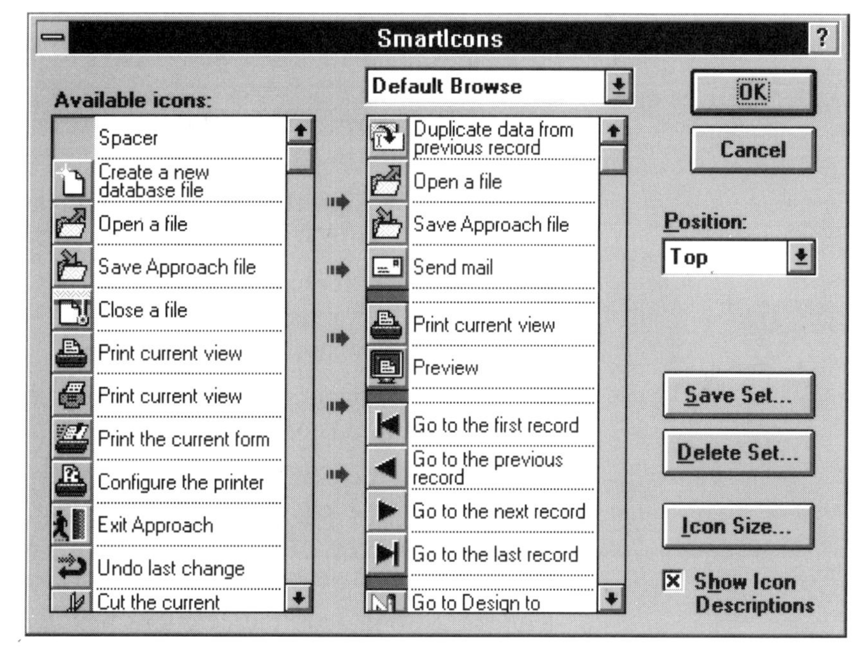

The SmartIcons dialog box is at the heart of customizing your SmartIcons toolbars.

4. To add an icon, drag it from the Available Icons column to the second column. The icon will be inserted at the new location. To remove an icon, select the icon and drag it off the toolbar. You do not have to drag the icon to the Available icons column. To rearrange icons in the second column, drag the icon to the desired position in the list.
5. Select the location for the toolbar using the options in the Position pull-down list. Top, Bottom, Left, and Right options anchor the toolbar to that position of the screen. Floating creates a window that floats on top—it can be moved (dragged) anywhere within the Approach window, resized (dragging the borders of the toolbar to the new dimension), and is always visible until you close it (by clicking on the small horizontal bar in the upper-left corner of the toolbar).
6. If you want to display bubble help (yellow balloons containing a description of what each icon does) when you move the mouse pointer over an icon, check the "Show Icon Descriptions" box.
7. Choose the Icon Size button to switch between medium- and large-sized icons.

8. Select OK.

Use these steps to create a new SmartIcons toolbar icon set:

1. Switch to the environment (Design, Browse, Find, or Preview) where you want to add the toolbar.
2. Select Tools ➤ SmartIcons. The SmartIcons dialog box appears, as shown in Figure 18.12 earlier in this chapter.
3. Select the SmartIcons toolbar that will serve as the model for your new toolbar. You must perform this step even if you wish to create a completely new toolbar from scratch.
4. Make the modifications as necessary, adding icons from the Available Icons columns or removing them from the second column.
5. Select the position (where the SmartIcons toolbar will be positioned). Floating lets you place the toolbar anywhere on your screen and move it wherever you like. Choose the Icon Size button to switch between medium- and large-sized icons.
6. Check the Show Icon Descriptions box to display bubble help.
7. Select Save Set. Approach displays the Save Set of SmartIcons dialog box shown in Figure 18.13.

FIGURE 18.13 ▸

The Save Set of SmartIcons dialog box lets you give a name to your toolbar.

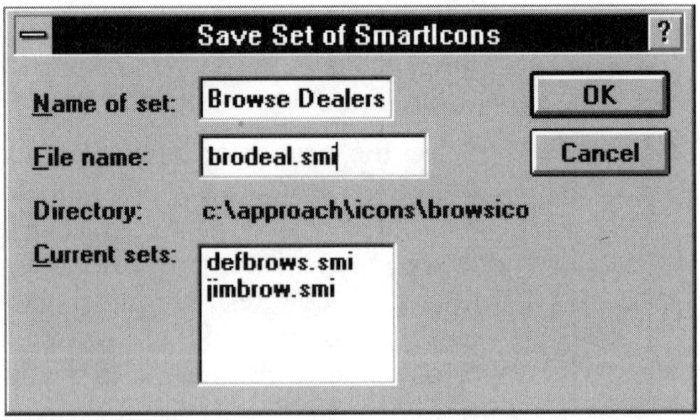

8. Enter the description for this set in the Name of set text box. Enter a file name in the File name text box (Approach will add the .SMI file extension for you). Select OK.
9. Select OK again to return to your current view.

To delete an icon set, switch to the environment (Design, Browse, Find, or Preview) where you created the custom toolbar and select Tools ➤ SmartIcons. Select Delete Set, highlight the set(s) you wish to delete, and select OK.

WARNING

Be careful when you select a toolbar to be deleted. You can accidentally delete the default toolbars.

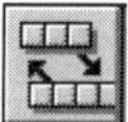

Add the Show the Next SmartIcon™ bar icon to your SmartIcons toolbar. This icon allows you to switch between the defined toolbars for the environment (or task) you're working in with just one click of the mouse. This is much faster than selecting the desired toolbar from the menus.

Displaying the SmartIcons Set

When you are working in Approach, the program will display one of the icon sets you have defined, depending on the environment in which you are working or the task you are performing. To change which icon set is displayed in the SmartIcons toolbar, use any of these methods:

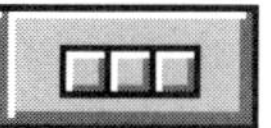

- Click on the SmartIcons button in the Status bar (the right-most box in the Status bar) and select the SmartIcons set you want.
- Select Tools ➤ SmartIcons and choose the toolbar (icon set) from the pull-down list. You can select the position (where the SmartIcons toolbar will be placed) and choose the Icon Size button to switch between medium- and large-sized icons if desired. Select OK.

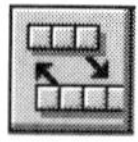

- If your SmartIcons toolbar itself contains a Show the Next SmartIcon™ bar button, click on it to move to the next SmartIcons set defined for the current environment.

▸▸ Creating Your Own Menus

When you use Approach to build an application, you'll often want to customize the toolbars to remove features such as the Design environment you don't want users to venture into. Likewise, you'll want to customize menus to prevent access to features like Hide Record, which could get a novice user into trouble, or Delete Record, which could compromise your data. Custom menus also let you place macros on a pull-down menu. Approach lets you create menus and assign them to views so that when your users open the forms, the menu they see is the menu you designed especially for the Browse environment current application. You can only create menus for the Browse environment.

You can base your custom menu on an existing menu, or build a menu from scratch. Since Approach has two sets of menus (the default menu includes all options, while the short menu includes the most commonly used tasks and is designed for data entry tasks rather than design tasks), you may wish to base your application menu on the short menu, then add or remove the commands necessary to suit your needs. Building a menu from scratch may be tedious, but once complete, you can create other menus based on your custom menu—you might want to have a custom menu that looks just like the menu you designed but does not include the Find command, for example.

The Define Custom Menu bar dialog box, shown in Figure 18.14, is at the heart of the menu definition process. The list at the left, called the top-level menu list, includes a grid that contains one line for every option that will be displayed across the top of the user's screen. The Menu Type controls what information is displayed for the pull-down list of options for each top-level menu option, while the Menu Name is the actual text that will appear on the menu. The possible Menu Types will be listed in just a moment.

Figure 18.15 shows a simple menu structure we've built as shown from the Browse environment for a data entry form, and Figure 18.14 is the corresponding Define Custom Menu Bar dialog box for that menu. The first line of the top-level menus in Figure 18.14 has a menu type of Menu + Files, which means you'll be able to include all the standard Approach commands in the pull-down options for this top-level menu option. In addition, Approach adds the last files accessed to this menu

FIGURE 18.14

The Define Custom Menu Bar dialog box is used to set up the top-level menu options (the options that are displayed horizontally at the top of the screen) and the list of options for each top-level menu item.

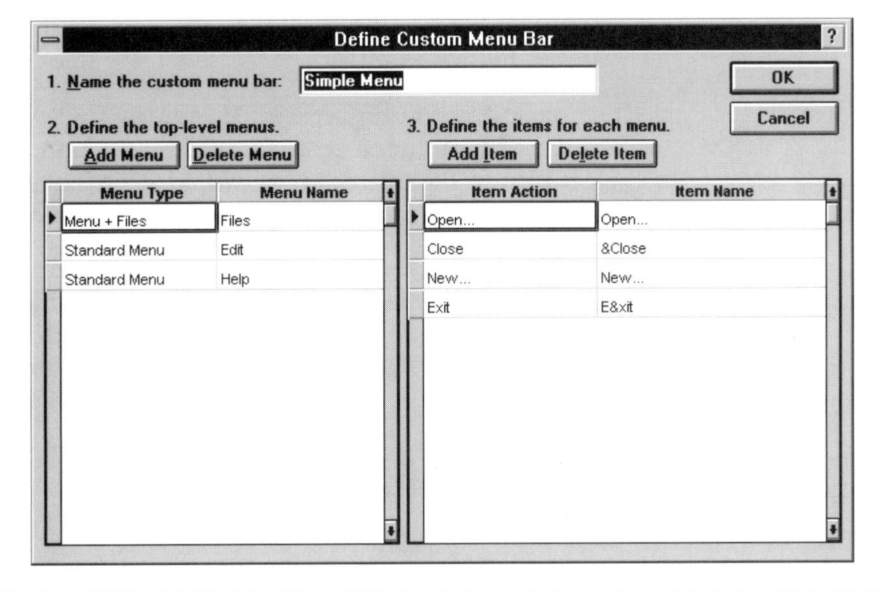

FIGURE 18.15

This is the simple menu structure that results from the definition shown in Figure 18.14. Since we specified Menu + Files, Approach adds a list of the last Approach files opened at the end of the drop-down menu.

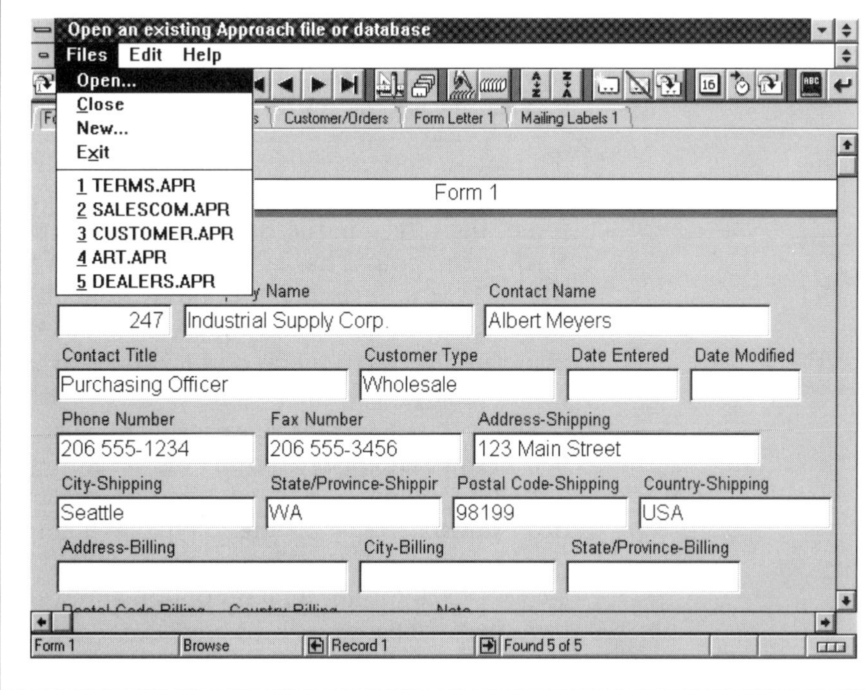

option, as you can see in Figure 18.15. The Menu Name of this option is Files in Figure 8.14, and that's the first menu option in the top-level menu in Figure 18.15.

The second line in Figure 18.14 is for the Edit option. It uses the Standard Menu menu type, and the Menu Name, Edit. If we were to select Edit in Figure 18.15, we would see a list of menu options, including New Record, Edit Record, and Delete Record.

The third line in Figure 18.14 is for the Help option. It, too, uses the Standard Menu menu type, and the Menu Name, Help. Although you can't see it in the figure, we've told Approach that the Help pull-down menu will have three options: Function Help, How Do I?, and Search.

Use these steps to create a custom menu:

1. Switch to the Design environment.
2. Choose Tools ➤ Customize Menus. Approach displays the Customize Menus dialog box.
3. Select New to build a menu from scratch, or highlight a menu on which you want to base your new menu and choose Copy. Approach displays the Define Custom Menu Bar dialog box, shown in Figure 18.14 earlier in this chapter.
4. Enter the name of the menu in the text box at the top of the screen.
5. The menu options shown in the list at the left, called the top-level list, correspond to the Main menu options displayed across the top of the screen in the Browse environment of your application. Each menu option has a Menu Type and a Menu Name. The Menu Type is described more fully in the following text and specifies the type of commands that can be listed in the pull-down list associated with the menu option, and may include automatically generated options, such as the last files accessed, the windows open, or the macros or views available. The Menu Name is the text string that appears on the top-level menu. Select the Menu Type by clicking in the field. Click on the arrow to display the drop-down list, select a menu type, and enter a Menu Name you want to appear across the top of the screen in Browse. Repeat this step for each top-level menu option you want to have on your custom menu bar.

6. Select a top-level menu option and add the corresponding pull-down menu options (called Item Actions) by building a list of options in the grid at the right of the screen. (Skip this step if the Menu Type is Macro List or View List, which Approach automatically controls.) Each item in the grid at the right will appear as a separate line in the pull-down list for the menu option in the top-level list. Click on the Item Action to choose from the list of predefined actions. Enter an Item Name in the second column. Use the ampersand (&) before a letter and Approach will underline that letter when displaying the option. For example, &Help appears as Help. Enter the keystroke shortcut in this area, too, such as Ctrl+H, following at least one space after the Item Name text. Select the '----' option (the second option in the Item Action pull-down list) to add a separator bar to the menu. Select Add Item to insert a new item.
7. Repeat Step 6 until all action items are included. Select another top-level menu option and repeat step 6 for that menu option, and so on until your menu is built.
8. Select OK to save your work and return to the Approach work area.

► Menu Types for Top-Level Menus

The top-level menu grid asks you to select a menu type. The menu type not only defines what options are available in the Item Action for each pull-down menu option, but the option may also add several options by default. Choose from the following:

Menu Type	Includes the Following Options
Standard Menu	Any Approach commands you can select.
Menu and Files	Any Approach commands you can select; in addition, Approach lists the last files used at the bottom of the pull-down list (Figure 18.15 earlier in this chapter shows this option in action).

Window Menu	Any Approach commands you can select; when displayed, Approach also automatically adds a list of open Windows so you can switch between Approach files.
Context Menu	Approach adds this menu depending on the view you're working with. For example, Approach will add a worksheet menu to Worksheet views automatically, allowing the user to add fields or columns, find or sort, or change the style and properties of the worksheet. When you select ContextMenu, Approach displays ReadOnly in the Menu Name, meaning that you cannot change the text for this menu option.
Macro List	A list of available macros; the list is built automatically by Approach. Approach fills in the pull-down list and displays the macro names in the same order as the Macros dialog box (use Tools ➤ Macros to see this list). This option is limited to macros; you cannot add any other commands.
View List	A list of the currently available views; the list is automatically built by Approach. This option is limited to views; you cannot add any other commands.

► Item Actions for Pull-Down Menus

Approach handles all the details for you. For example, if you select Open, the menu option will automatically display the File Open dialog box and then open the file selected. All you need to do is select the action (Open) you want to take.

The actions are listed alphabetically. Click on the down-pointing arrow to open the list, and press the first letter of the option to jump to the actions that begin with that letter. Press the letter again to see the next option beginning with that letter.

There are no actions available for the Context Menu, Macro List, and View List Menu Types. That's because Approach automatically fills in the pull-down options for you.

►► Making Changes to a Menu

You can also modify an existing menu by selecting the menu name in the Customize Menus dialog box and choosing the Edit button. The Define Custom Menu bar dialog box appears, and the directions for modifying an existing menu are identical to those for building a new menu bar, as described earlier in this chapter. You can insert an item in either the top-level or pull-down menu list by selecting the line in which you want the new item to appear and selecting the Add Menu or Add Item button. Likewise, you can remove an item by selecting it and choosing the Delete Menu or Delete Item button.

►► NOTE

You cannot edit the Default Menu or Short Menu, which are predefined by Approach. You can use these menus as the basis for your own custom menus.

To delete a menu, select it from the Customize Menus dialog box and choose the Delete key.

►► Attaching Your Menu to Views

Once you've created your custom menu, you can easily attach it to a view. When you switch to that view in the Browse environment, Approach will use your custom menu instead of the Default Menu, which (as you can tell by its name) is the default menu Approach uses for all new views.

To assign the menu, select the view, click anywhere on the view (but not on an object on the view) and open the InfoBox. Select the Basics tab and select the menu bar name from the "Attached menu bar" pull-down list, as shown in Figure 18.16. Be sure to save the Approach file to make your menu-view assignment permanent.

FIGURE 18.16

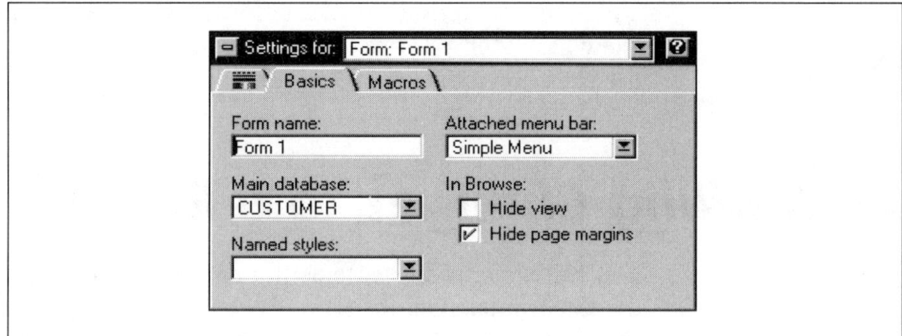

The InfoBox is the place where you assign a custom menu to a view. Here we're assigning the Simple Menu to a form named Form 1.

▸▸ Summary and a Look Ahead

In this chapter you've seen how to customize Approach. You've seen how easy it is to change the working environment—everything from controlling how the Enter key works to setting database properties. You've also seen how to edit SmartIcons so you have your own custom toolbar, and how to create menus so you or your application user can be limited to the commands you specify.

In Chapter 19 we'll look at another way you can control what Approach does—this time, at the field level. Formulas and functions let you specify sophisticated validation criteria, control the operation of a macro, and compute the value of calculated fields.

▶ ▶ CHAPTER 19

Formulas and Functions

▸▸ FAST TRACK

combine one or more operands and operators. The operands are the elements in a formula that contain values you will use to calculate a value and can be constants, variables, or functions. Operators can perform actions using arithmetic, logical operations, or comparisons.

use the function Today(). Functions are predefined routines that return a value. The parentheses are part of the function, and indicate that you don't need to specify additional parameters—data the function needs to perform its task.

▶ *To properly use parameters for functions* **595**

use constants or field names. Constants must be enclosed in single quotes for date, time, and text values. Field names must include the database name if the Approach file uses joined databases, and the field name must be enclosed in double-quotation marks if it includes special characters, such as a space, comma, period, or any of these characters: +–/*()<>.

▶ *To use multiple parameters for functions* **595**

enter the parameters in the proper order and separate parameters by commas. You can include spaces between parameters to make your function more readable.

A formula is a set of operators, operands, and functions that, when combined, return a result. The result can be a numeric value, a text string, a date, or a Boolean value (Yes or No).

In previous chapters you've seen how to use formulas in validation criteria, macros, and calculated fields. You can enter a formula from the Field Definition dialog box or a macro line, but you'll always use the Formula dialog box shown in Figure 19.1. When your formula is free of errors, the checkered flag is shown. If anything is wrong, the flag is grayed out and has a red X through it.

FIGURE 19.1

The Formula dialog box is where you'll combine fields, operators, and predefined functions into formulas that compute a single value.

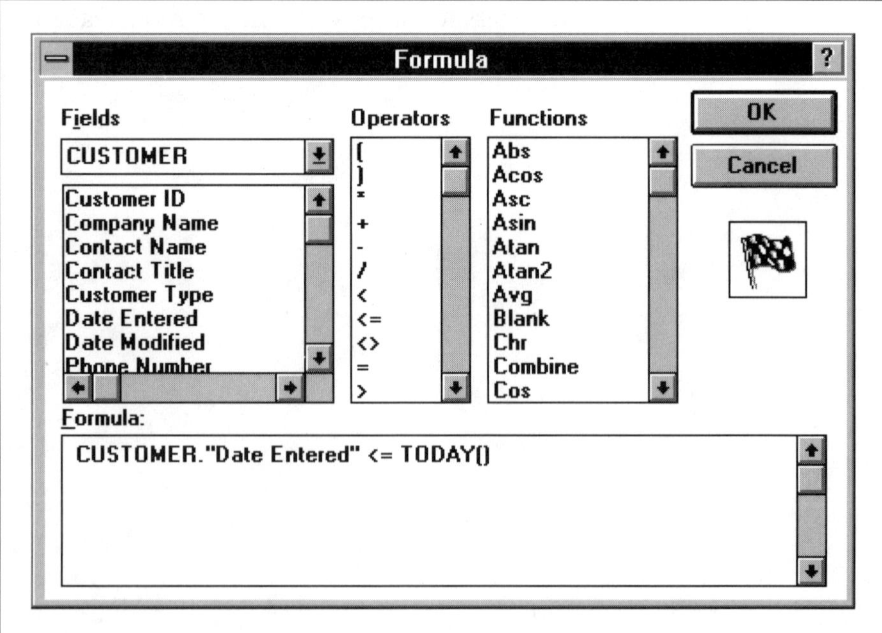

Of course, just because you write a formula doesn't mean the formula does what you expect. The purpose of this chapter is to take a closer look at the parts of a function, describe the functions available in Approach that you can use in formulas, and provide examples of how to build some sophisticated formulas.

►► Parts of a Formula

At its most fundamental level, a formula combines operands and operators. For example, the formula

```
Price * Quantity
```

has two operands (Price and Quantity) and a single operator, the multiplication symbol. Assuming both price and quantity are numeric fields, the result is a numeric field containing the value of the multiplication (called the product). Likewise,

```
OrderDate + 30
```

is a formula with a date field operand (OrderDate) and a numeric constant (30). The result is a date field containing a date that is 30 days past the order date. If Order Date contains 1/1/95, the result of this formula is 1/31/95.

► Operands

The operands are the elements in a formula that contain values you will use to calculate a value. Operands can be constants, variables, or functions. However, because Approach uses the the special Field type called *variable* (described in Chapter 5), we call variable operands *field operands*, since the operand represents a value from a field in a database.

Constants

Constants are fixed values that do not change. For example, you can use a formula to compute the tax on a purchase. If the tax rate is 8.2%, the formula

```
Price * 0.082
```

computes the tax on an amount stored in the Price field. The 0.082 in the formula is a constant, since it doesn't change.

You can have constants for text, time, and date values, too, by enclosing them in single quotation marks. The formula

```
'1/1/95' + 30
```

uses a date constant and adds 30 to it (the result is 1/31/95).

When entering a numeric constant, enter only digits and the separator (. for the U.S.; , in many other countries). Do not include formatting. For example,

```
Quantity * 1234
```

is acceptable, but

```
Quantity * $1,234
```

is not, because neither the dollar sign nor the comma (the thousands separator) can be used.

Fields

Price, on the other hand, varies from one record to the next. In Approach, a field is a variable in a formula, since its value for record number 1 is probably not the same as the value in record number 2.

A field name must be surrounded by double-quotation marks if the name includes a space, comma, period or special character:

```
+-/*()<>
```

Furthermore, if your Approach file includes joined databases (described in Chapter 6), you must include the database name in the formula, unless the field is a calculated field or a variable field. For example, to multiply the Price field in the Dealers database by the tax rate of 8.2%, use the formula:

```
DEALERS.Price * 0.082
```

You must write the database in uppercase letters and separate the database name and field name with a period. If the field contains special characters and is part of an Approach file with joined databases, you must use the database name and double-quotation marks:

```
DEALERS."Unit Price" * 0.082
```

Functions

An operand may also be the result of a function. A function is a predefined routine that returns a value. For example, the function Today() returns the current (system) date. The open and close parenthesis are part of the function, and indicate that you don't need to specify additional parameters (data the function needs to perform its task). Sometimes the number of parameters is fixed. For example, the absolute value function, ABS, needs only one parameter. To compute the absolute value of a number, you just place the number between the parentheses. ABS(5) returns the result 5, while ABS(–100) returns the value 100, since the absolute value of a negative number is its positive "equivalent."

Still other functions take as many parameters as you provide. The Avg function computes an average of the parameters you pass it. For example, Avg(2,6,16) returns 8 since the average of 2 and 6 and 16 is 8. Avg(1, 3, 5, 7) is 4. Notice that the Avg function is the same—only the number of parameters (3 in the first example, 4 in the second) has changed. We'll discuss functions in greater detail throughout this chapter.

▶ Operators

There are three types of operators: *arithmetic* operators, *logical* operators, and *comparison* operators.

Arithmetic Operators

Arithmetic operators are probably the most familiar: They perform a calculation on two operands. Price * Quantity uses the multiplication operator to compute the product of two field values: price and quantity.

Arithmetic operands include:

+	Addition
–	Subtraction
*	Multiplication
/	Division

Arithmetic operators aren't limited to use with numeric fields, however. You can perform arithmetic on date fields, for example. The expression Today() + 30 returns a date value 30 days from today's date.

Logical Operators

Logical operators are used to combine two or more expressions and are used with the *If* function or in an evaluation expression (for validation expressions, for example; validation rules are explained in Chapter 5). Suppose that two conditions must be met in order to set the Overdue field to true. You could write the following formula—an evaluation expression—using the logical operator *And*:

```
AmtDue > 0 And DueDate < Today()
```

The logical operator And is used to specify that both conditions must be true to return a value of Yes.

Logical operators include:

And	Returns Yes if both conditions are true
Or	Returns Yes if either condition is true
Not	Returns Yes if the condition is false

The Not operator is often confusing. Examples will help to illustrate its purpose. Suppose you want to create a SendLetter field, which can contain Yes or No based on the value in the AmountDue field. If the value in the PastDue field is greater than $1,000, you want to set the SendLetter field to Yes. (You'll use the SendLetter field in a Find command to create a found set, then send reminder letters to those customers who have an outstanding balance.)

There are two ways to write the expression. PastDue > 1000 is the most obvious and straightforward. The other way is to write the expression using the Not operator:

```
Not PastDue ≤ 1000.
```

You can also use the Not operator on a Boolean field. For example, suppose you have a field named Business. If Yes, the customer record is a business contact. If No, the customer record is a personal contact.

You can use the Not operator to select the personal contacts by using the formula:

```
Not Business
```

However, mixing Ands, Ors, and Nots can be confusing. It is usually a good idea to rewrite your formula to avoid the Not operator if at all possible.

Comparison Operators

Comparison operators are used to evaluate the relationship between two operands. The result of a comparison operator is a Yes or No value. For example,

```
DueDate < Today()
```

compares the date in the DueDate field with the current (system) date, and returns Yes or No depending on the value in the DueDate field and the current date. If the DueDate contains 1/1/95 and today's date is 1/2/95, then the formula returns Yes.

Comparison operators include:

=	Equal to
<>	Not equal to
<	Less than
<=	Less than or equal to
>	Greater than
>=	Greater than or equal to

►► Using Parentheses

So far you've seen a variety of formulas that are simple: they involve two operands. However, your formulas can be quite complex. Approach uses some built-in rules for determining the order in which it evaluates a formula. For example, the formula

```
10 + 6 / 3
```

evaluates to 12. That's because Approach performs multiplication and division before it performs addition and subtraction. Looking from left to right, Approach first sees the division symbol, so it computes the value using the two adjacent operands, which in this case are 6 and 3. Having divided 6 by 3, the formula now looks to Approach like:

```
10 + 2
```

Looking left to right, it finds the first operand (a plus sign) and computes the value using the two adjacent operands. The result is 12.

You can use parentheses to control the order in which a formula calculates a result. Approach looks for these symbols and computes the value inside the parentheses before performing any other calculation. Thus,

```
(10 + 6) / 3
```

returns 5.333. That's because Approach looks left to right and sees the parentheses. It evaluates the expression contained between the "(" and the ")" first (which is 10 + 6 or 16). Then, internally at least, the formula looks like this:

```
16 / 3
```

which is a simple division, the result of which is 5.333.

Our original expression can be rewritten as

```
10 + (6 / 3)
```

which still yields 12. This points out an important property of parentheses: You can always add them even if they aren't strictly needed. They won't hurt and may increase readability.

▸▸ Functions

A function returns a single value—a number, text string, Yes/No value, date, or time. For example:

Function Example	Returns
ABS(–10)	The absolute value of –10, which is 10 (a number)
Today()	1/1/95, a date, if the current system date is January 1, 1995

Function Example	Returns
CurrTime()	13:02:03.0 if the current time is 1:02:03 PM
Combine('abc , 'def')	abcdef, a text string
If (DueDate < '6/30/95')	Yes, if the value in the DueDate field is less than (earlier than) June 30, 1995, and No otherwise
Proper(FullName)	If the FullName field contains the value 'jim powell', the Proper function returns 'Jim Powell'

As you've seen, some functions require a parameter (the value placed between the pair of parentheses). Other functions, such as Combine, require two or more parameters, while others, such as Today() don't require any parameter at all (although you *must* include the parentheses).

The following rule applies for all parameters: Parameters can be constants or field names. Constants must be enclosed in single quotes for date, time, and text values. Field names must include the database name if the Approach file uses joined databases, and the field name must be enclosed in double-quotation marks if it includes special characters, such as a space, comma, period, or any of these characters: +–/*()<>.

For functions that require two or more parameters, the following rules apply:

- The parameters must be entered in the proper order. The Date function requires three parameters: month number, day number, and year number. The parameters must be entered in that order. Date(10,5,1995) is different from Date(5,10,1995). Furthermore, Date (1995, 1, 1) makes no sense since the month "number" must be between 1 and 12.
- Parameters must be separated by commas. Date(10,5,1995) is acceptable. Date (10 5 1995) and Date (10/5/95) are not.
- You can include spaces between parameters to make your function more readable. Date (10,5,1995) is the same as Date(10, 5, 1995). This property is especially useful when you combine functions to make complex formulas.

▸▸ Complex Formulas

Operands, operators, and functions can be combined to produce some complex and powerful formulas. When you use parentheses, you'll also enhance readability, making it easier for another user to quickly grasp what your function does and make modifications as necessary.

Functions afford the greatest opportunity for building complex formulas. For example, consider the following. Your database contains a Full-Name field in which the customer's name is listed as

```
Lastname, Firstname
```

There is a single space after the comma.

You want to reverse the order of the first and last names. Remember, however, that your customer's name is in a single field, not two fields. Fortunately, your field has a comma indicating where the last name ends and the first name begins. This helps you know that

```
Powell Jr., Jim
```

contains a first name of Jim and a last name of Powell Jr., and that

```
Van Dyke, Homer
```

has a last name that contains two "names." Without the comma you would have to conclude that

```
Van Dyke Homer
```

referred to Mr. Van, whose first name was Dyke and middle name was Homer.

You can use a combination of the Position, Combine, Right, Length, and Left functions to reverse the order of data in a field. Full descriptions of each function are provided in the section "Function Reference," later in this chapter. You may wish to refer to each function in this reference as we use it.

Although it is not necessary, your function will be much more readable if you add a calculated field type to your database and use the Define Formula to specify the formula, such as Position(FullName, ',' 1). We'll call this field PosComma (for position of the comma).

We'll build the formula one step at a time. For the purpose of this example, we'll assume that the FullName field contains the value *Smith, Trevor*. PosComma contains 6 (the comma is the sixth character in the name).

1. We need to extract all the characters from the comma to the end of the field. We'll use the Right function. Right requires two parameters: the name of the field and the number of right-most characters we want to extract. That's the correct function, but we know only the position of the comma at this point.
2. To calculate the number of right-most characters we need, we'll use the Length function. This function returns the number of characters in a field. Length(FullName) returns the number of characters in the name. In our example, it is 13: 6 for Smith and the comma, 1 for the space, and 6 for Trevor.
3. Now we can use the Length and the Right functions to extract Trevor:

   ```
   Right(FullName, Length(FullName)-PosComma-1)
   ```

   Approach evaluates this as:

   ```
   Right(FullName, 13-6-1)
   ```

   Since 13 – 6 = 7, and 7 – 1 = 6, the Right function asks Approach to get the right-most six characters from the FullName field. The result: Trevor. So now we have the first name.
4. To get the last name, we'll use the Left function. Similar to the Right function, Left needs two parameters: the text string or field we want to extract characters from, and the number of characters we need. We know that the comma is at the position just to the right of the last character we need, so we need PosComma – 1 characters. Thus, we'll write the Left function as:

   ```
   Left(FullName, PosComma - 1)
   ```

   Notice that we've included an arithmetic expression as one of the parameters—just one more way you can combine functions, operators, and operands.

5. Now we need a way of putting the first name and last name together. We'll use the Combine function, which lets you include as many parameters as needed. Combine takes each text string (or field) and concatenates it—that is, it strings together the parameters into one long text string. Our final formula is:

```
Combine (Right(FullName, Length(Fullname)-PosComma-1),
  ' ', Left(FullName, PosComma - 1))
```

6. Whew!

Here's another example of what we can do, this time focusing on the *If* function. The If function returns a Yes or No value, and is frequently used in macros and validation formulas.

Let's assume we want to set the payment terms for our customers. We have a PaymentTerms field, a CreditLimit field, and a LastOrderDate field.

The PaymentTerms are Net15, Net30, and Net60. That is, the customer must pay within 15, 30, or 60 days, depending on how we rate the customer. We perform this rating by looking at whether they are a frequent customer and how much credit we have extended to them (another indication of their credit worthiness).

The LastOrderDate field contains just what you think it does—the date the customer placed the last order. A customer who has not ordered within the last 90 days will get credit terms of Net15—we want our money as soon as possible.

The CreditLimit field contains the amount of credit we can extend to a customer. If the credit limit is less than $1,000, we'll extend 30 days of credit. If the credit limit is $1,000 or above, we'll extend credit for 60 days.

Here's the formula for the PaymentTerms field written in words:

- Condition 1: If the LastOrderDate < 90 days ago, set the field to Net15; that is, if the LastOrderDate is earlier than (less than) 90 days ago, the field is set to Net15.
- Condition 2: Otherwise, if the CreditLimit < 1,000, set the field to Net30.
- Condition 3: Otherwise, set the field to Net60.

Let's create the formula one piece at a time:

1. If the LastOrderDate is more than 90 days in the past, we'll assign the term Net15. The current date can be accessed using the Today() function. Ninety days ago is Today() – 90.
2. We'll use the If statement, whose structure is:

   ```
   If (Condition, true value, false value)
   ```

   We'll fill in the first part of the formula:

   ```
   If(LastOrderDate < Today()-90, 'Net15', false value)
   ```

   This satisfies condition 1.
3. Now what if the LastOrderDate is within the last 90 days? A single false value isn't enough. We need yet another If statement to look at the CreditLimit amount. We need an If statement such as the following:

   ```
   If(CreditLimit < 1000, 'Net30', 'Net60')
   ```

   In fact, that's exactly the expression we'll use for the false value.
4. Here's the complete formula:

   ```
   If(LastOrderDate < Today()-90, 'Net15',
           If(CreditLimit < 1,000, 'Net30', 'Net60'))
   ```

Here's how Approach evaluates this formula:

```
If the LastOrderDate is older than 90 days, then re-
turn the value Net15. Otherwise, evaluate the false
value. The false value says check the CreditLimit,
and if it's less than 1,000, use Net30 terms, and if
the CreditLimit is not less than 1,000 (that is, if
it is 1,000 or above), use the term Net60.
```

The possibilities for combining functions, operands, and operators is almost limitless. Best of all, Approach provides the checkered flag in most formula windows to show you when the syntax of your function is correct. If you leave out a matching parenthesis, Approach won't let you save the formula. It's one more way Approach ensures everything is correct.

▸▸ Function Reference

In this section the functions available in Approach are listed in alphabetical order. Each function description includes an English-language name, what it returns plus any special notes or hints about using the function, the format of the function, and some examples of its use.

ABS The Absolute value function returns the absolute value (positive) of a number.

Syntax: `ABS(number)`

Examples:

This	Returns This
`ABS(-5)`	`5`
`ABC(0)`	`0`
`ABS(10.2)`	`10.2`
`ABS(CreditLim)`	`100 if the CreditLim field contains the value -100 or 100`

Acos The Arc cosine function returns the trigonometric arc cosine of a number between −1 and 1 in radians, from 0 to Pi.

Syntax: `Acos(number)`

Examples:

This	Returns This
`Acos(1)`	`0`
`Acos(0.5)`	`1.0471975`
`Acos(-1)`	`3.1415926`

ASC The ASCII function returns the ASCII numeric value of a character, from 1 to 255. If a string, rather than a character, is provided, ASC returns the ASCII value of the first character in the string.

Syntax: `ASC(character)`

Examples:

This	Returns This
ASC('d')	100
ASC('DOG')	68
ASC('#')	35

Asin The Arc sine function returns the trigonometric arc sine of a number between –1 and 1 in radians, from –Pi/2 to Pi/2.

Syntax: `Asin(number)`

Examples:

This	Returns This
Asin(0.5)	0.5235987
Asin(-0.5)	-0.5235987

Atan The Arc tangent function returns the arc tangent of a number, from –Pi/2 to Pi/2.

Syntax: `Atan(number)`

Examples:

This	Returns This
Atan(0.5)	0.4636476
Atan(-2.0)	-1.1071487

Atan2 The Arc tangent 2 returns the arc tangent of number1 divided by number2, as radians (between –Pi and Pi).

Syntax: `Atan2(number1, number2)`

Examples:

This	Returns This
Atan2(1,2)	0.4636476
Atan2(-2,3)	-0.5880026

Avg The Average function returns the average of values in a list. Blank values are not included in the calculation.

Syntax: `Avg(number1, number2, number3...);Avg(number list)`

Examples:

This	Returns This
`Avg(1, 2, 3.5)`	`2.16666`
`Avg(number1, number2, number3)`	`0.8333 if number1 equals 1, number2 equals -2, and number3 equals 3.5`
`Avg(number1, number2, number3, number4)`	`returns 0.8333 if number1 equals 1, number2 equals -2, number3 equals 3.5, and number4 is blank`

Blank The Blank function returns the value you specify if the field is blank, or it returns the value in the record if the field is not blank.

Syntax: `Blank(field, value)`

Examples:

This	Returns This
`Blank(Credit-Limit, 1000)`	`1000 if the CreditLimit field is blank`
`Blank(Credit-Limit, 1000)`	`2,000 if the CreditLimit field contains 2000`

CHR The Character function returns the ASCII character corresponding to the number you specify.

Syntax: `CHR(number)`

Examples:

This	Returns This
CHR(100)	d
CHR(68)	D

Combine The Combine function returns a text string consisting of all strings concatenated in the order in the list.

Syntax: `Combine(string1, string2, string3...)`

Examples:

This	Returns This
Combine('Acme', 'Widgets')	AcmeWidgets
Combine('Acme ', 'Widgets')	Acme Widgets
Combine('Acme', ' ', 'Widgets')	Acme Widgets
Combine(FirstName, ' ', LastName)	John Jones, where the FirstName field contains John and the LastName field contains Jones

Cos The Cosine function returns the trigonometric cosine of an angle (in radians). The result will always be between –1 and 1.

Syntax: `Cos(angle)`

Examples:

This	Returns This
Cos(PI())	-1
Cos(1)	0.5403023

CurrTime The Current time function returns the current (system) time.

Syntax: `CurrTime()`

Example: `CurrTime()` returns 13:14:15 when the system time is 1:14:15PM.

Date The Date function returns a date value consisting of the month, day, and year. Also see the "Today()" function.

Syntax: `Date(month, day, year)`

Examples: `Date(1,2,1996)` returns January 2, 1996.

DateToText The Date To Text function converts a date to a text string. This function is used when you need to output a date in a format other than the field's predefined format.

Syntax: `DateToText(date, formatstring)`

Example: `DateToText(Today(),'MMM DD, YYYY')` returns Feb 3, 1996 if the current (system) date contains 2/3/1996.

Day The Day function returns the day portion of the date, from 1 to 31. Also see the Month and Year functions

Syntax: `Day(date)`

Examples:

This	Returns This
`Day('12/30/96')`	`30`
`Day(BirthDate)`	`25, where the BirthDate field contains 7/25/96`

DayName The Day Name function returns, in text form, the name of the day. The day of week used must be between 1 (Sunday) and 7 (Saturday).

Syntax: `DayName(dayofweek) or DayName(date)`

Examples:

This	Returns This
`DayName(2)`	`Monday`
`DayName('7/24/94')`	`Sunday`
`DayName(BirthDate)`	`Sunday, where BirthDate contains 7/24/94`

DayOfWeek The Day of Week function returns the number of the day of the week, from 1 (Sunday) to 7 (Saturday).

Syntax: `DayOfWeek(date)`

Examples:

This	Returns This
`DayOfWeek('7/25/94')`	`2`
`DayOfWeek(Today())`	`7, where the current date is 1/1/94`

DayOfYear The Day of the Year function returns the number of days since January 1st of the year of the date.

Syntax: `DayOfYear (date)`

Examples:

This	Returns This
`DayOfYear(HireDate)`	`15 if the HireDate contains 1/15/96`
`DayOfYear('2/1/95')`	`32`

Degree The Degree function converts a number from radians to-degrees.

Syntax: `Degree(radians)`

Examples:

This	Returns This
`Degree(PI())`	`180`
`Degree(10)`	`572.95779`

Exact The Exact function returns Yes if the two strings match, character for character; No if they don't. The string comparison is case sensitive ("A" does not match "a"). Also see the Like function, which performs a case-insensitive search.

Syntax: `Exact(text1, text2)`

Examples:

This	Returns This
`Exact(Type, 'Business')`	`Yes if the Type field contains Business`
`Exact('ABC','Abc')`	`No`

Exp The Exponentiation function returns the constant 'e' (2.718281828545904) to the power of a number.

Syntax: `Exp(number)`

Example: `Exp(2)` returns e to the second power (e squared), or 7.389056099.

Factorial The Factorial function returns the factorial of a number.

Syntax: `Factorial(number)`

Example: `Factorial(5)` returns 120 ($5 \times 4 \times 3 \times 2 \times 1$).

Fill The Fill function returns a text string that repeats text the number of times in *number*

Syntax: `Fill(text, number)`

Example: `Fill('XX',2)` returns XXXX.

FV The Future Value returns the future value of an investment.

Syntax: `FV(payment, rate, number of periods)`

Example: `FV(100, 0.01, 18)` returns 1961.47, which is the value of a $100 investment, invested at the rate of 1% per month (12% per year) for 18 months.

Hour The Hour function returns the hour portion of a time field.

Syntax: `Hour(time)`

Examples:

This	Returns This
`Hour('10:11:12')`	`10`
`Hour(CurrTime())`	`1 where the current (system) time is 1:02:03.`

Hundredth The Hundredth function returns hundredths of a second of the time field.

Syntax: `Hundredth(time)`

Examples:

This	Returns This
`Hundredth('12:13:14.15')`	`15`
`Hundredth(LoginTime)`	`30 if the LoginTime field contains 12:13:14.30`

If The If function returns True value or False value, depending on the evaluation of the condition. You can nest If statements and add conjunctions in the If formula, including And and Or.

Syntax: `If(condition, true value, false value)`

Examples:

`If(State='WA',8.5, 0)` returns 8.5 if the State field contains WA, or 0 if it does not.

`If(HireDate≤Today()-30,100, 200)` returns 100 if the HireDate field contains a value that is less than or equal to 30 days prior to the current (system) date, and 200 if it is not.

`If(CreditLimit<5000,'Net 30',If(CreditLimit<10000,'Net 60', 'Net 90'))` returns the credit term "Net 30" if the credit limit is less than 5,000, "Net 60" if the credit limit is 5,000 to 9,999.99, and "Net 90" if the credit limit is 10,000 or more.

`If(CreditLimit≤5000 And Type='Business',100, 200)` returns 100 if *both* conditions are true, and 200 if they are not.

`If(CreditLimit≤5000 Or Type='Business', 100, 200)` returns 100 if *either* condition is true, and 200 if both conditions are false.

IsBlank The Is Blank function return Yes or No. Use IsBlank for looping macros, this function is used to find missing values.

Syntax: `IsBlank(field)`

Example: `IsBlank(Type)` returns No if the Type field contains a value, Yes if there is no value in the Type field.

IsLastRecord The Is Last Record function returns Yes if the current record is the last record in the database or found set (according to the current sort order), and No if it is not. IsLastRecord can be used in looping macros to terminate processing or branch to another macro when the last record is encountered.

Syntax: `IsLastRecord()`

Example: `IsLastRecord()` returns Yes if you are positioned at the last record in the found set.

Left The Left function returns a text string containing the specified number of characters, beginning at the left of the text string. Also see the Right function.

Syntax: `Left(text, number)`

Examples:

This	Returns This
`Left('Business', 1)`	`B`
`Left('11/1/94',2)`	`11`
`Left(DateToText(Today(), 'MMM DD, YYYY'),3)`	`Jan if the current date is in January`

Length The Length function returns the number of the characters (including spaces and special characters) in the text string.

Syntax: `Length(text)`

Examples:

This	Returns This
`Length('Widget')`	`6`
`Length('Acme Widget')`	`11 (4 for Acme, 6 for Widget, and 1 for the space between the two characters)`

Like The Like function returns Yes if text1 matches text2 (character for character), and No if it does not. The string comparison is case insensitive ("A" matches "a"). Also see Exact, which performs a case-sensitive search. You can use wildcards in text2, such as * to match any number of characters or ? to match a single character.

Syntax: `Like(text1, text2)`

Examples:

This	Returns This
`Like('Acme','acme')`	`Yes`
`Like('Acme','Ac*')`	`Yes`
`Like('Acme', 'Ac?e')`	`Yes`
`Like('Acme', 'acmm')`	`No`

LN The Natural Logarithm function returns the natural logarithm (base e) of a number.

Syntax: `LN(number)`

Example: `LN(100)` returns 4.605170186.

Log The Logarithm function returns the logarithm (base 10) of a number.

Syntax: `Log(number)`

Examples:

This	Returns This
`Log(100)`	`2 (because 10 to the second power equals 100)`
`Log(1000)`	3 (because 10^3 equals 1000)

Lower The Lowercase function converts all characters in text to lowercase. Also see Proper, Upper.

Syntax: `Lower(text)`

Examples:

This	Returns This
`Lower('Acme Corp')`	`acme corp`
`Lower(terms)`	`net30 if Terms field contains NET30`

Middle The Middle function returns characters from *text* string, beginning at *start*, for *length* number of characters.

Syntax: `Middle(text, start, length)`

Example: `Middle('widgets', 3,2)` returns `dg`.

Minute The Minute function returns the minute portion of a time field.

Syntax: `Minute(time)`

Examples:

This	Returns This
Minute('10:11:12')	11
Minute(CurrTime())	2 when the current (system) time is 1:02:03

Mod The Modulus function returns the remainder of division of number1 by number2. The second of the following examples can be used to determine if the quantity ordered is in dozens. If the Mod function returns 0, the customer has ordered a multiple of a dozen. Mod can also be used to determine odd and even.

Syntax: `Mod(number1, number2)`

Examples:

This	Returns This
Mod(4,2)	0
Mod(quantity, 12)	5 if quantity contains 17
Mod(number, 2)	0 if number is even, 1 if it is odd

Month The Month function returns the month portion of the date, from 1 to 12. Also see Day and Year.

Syntax: `Month(date)`

Examples:

This	Returns This
Month('12/30/96')	12
Month(BirthDate)	7, where the BirthDate field contains 7/25/96

MonthName The Month Name function returns text containing the name of the month. Note that the monthnumber must be between 1 and 12.

Syntax: `MonthName(monthnumber)` or `MonthName(date)`

Examples:

This	Returns This
`MonthName(2)`	`February`
`MonthName('7/24/94')`	`July`
`MonthName(BirthDate)`	`June, when BirthDate contains 6/24/57`

NPeriods The Number of Periods function returns the number of periods necessary to eliminate principal at a given rate and payment amount.

Syntax: `NPeriods(rate, principal, paymentamt)`

Example: `NPeriods(0.01, 500, 25)` returns `23`. It will take 23 periods (nearly 2 years) to return the $500 principal, with interest accumulating at 1% per month, paying $25 per month.

NumToText The Number to Text function converts a numeric field to a text string. NumToText is useful in converting a number to a text string that is part of a larger text string. See the following Combine example.

Syntax: `NumToText(number, formatstring)`

Examples:

This	Returns This
`NumToText(100,'##0.00')`	`the text string 100.00`
`Combine('Quarterly Sales of ', NumToText(sales, '$#,###'))`	`Quarterly Sales of $4,000 if the sales field contains 4000`

Pi The Pi function returns 3.14159.

Syntax: `Pi()`

Example: `Cos(PI())` returns –1.

Pmt The Payment function returns the payment required to pay a loan principal, given the interest rate (per period) and number of periods.

Syntax: `Pmt(principal, interestrate, numberofperiods)`

Example: `Pmt(1000,.01, 18)` returns $60.982047895. It will take 18 payments of approximately $60.98 to pay a $1,000 loan over 18 months, where the loan interest rate is 1% per month (12% per year). Rounding up is sometimes used (payments would be $60.99) with a final payment slightly less than the monthly payments.

Position The Position function returns the position of a string within text, beginning at the start position within text. If the string is not found, the function returns 0.

Syntax: `Position(text, string, start)`

Examples:

`Position('San Diego, CA', ' ', 1)` returns 4, because beginning at the first character of the city, the first space is found in the 4th position.

`Position('San Diego, CA', ' ', 5)` returns 11, because, beginning with the "D" in Diego and looking to the right, the first space is in the 11th position of the text.

Pow The Power function returns a number1 raised to the power of number2 (e.g., $\text{number1}^{\text{number2}}$).

Syntax: `Pow(number1, number2)`

Examples:

This	Returns This
`Pow(3,2)`	`9, since 32 = 3 × 3 = 9`
`Pow(4,3)`	`64, since 43 = 4 × 4 × 4 = 64`

Prefix The Prefix function returns yes if the characters in text1 match the beginning characters in text2, or No if they do not.

Syntax: `Prefix(text1, text2)`

Examples:

This	Returns This
`Prefix('Net', 'Net 30')`	`Yes`
`Prefix(Status, 'Action')`	`No when the Status field contains 'Activ'`

Proper The Proper function changes the first letter of each word in the text to uppercase, and all other letters to lowercase. Also see Lower and Upper.

Syntax: `Proper(text)`

Examples:

This	Returns This
`Proper('angela smith')`	`Angela Smith`
`Proper(City)`	`San Diego if the City field contains san diego`

PV The Present Value function returns the present value of an annuity in which payments are made at equal intervals. The rate is often referred to as the discount rate.

Syntax: `PV(paymentamt, rate, numberofperiods)`

Example: `PV(100, 0.12, 5)` returns 360.477620235. The present value of an annuity that pays $100 per year for 5 years, discounted at 12% (the "inflation rate" of 12% will decrease the value of future payments in terms of today's value) is $360.48. Thus, if you were to choose $400 today or an annuity (assuming the 12% rate), you'd have more money (in today's terms) taking the $400 than the $500 ($100/year for five years) over a period of five years.

Radian The Radian function converts a number from degrees to radians.

Syntax: `Radian(degrees)`

Example: `Radian(90)` returns 1.5708.

Random The Random function returns a random number between 0 and 1. The Trunc function is used to remove the fractional portion of the random number.

Syntax: `Random()`

Example: `Trunc(Random()*100)+1` returns a random number between 1 and 100.

Replace The Replace function returns a text string that replaces the characters in *text* beginning at the start position (relative to the first character) replacing the number of characters (specified in *length*) in *text*, with the *replacement* text. The replacement text does not have to be the same length as *length*. Unlike other functions that *return* a value, Replace actually *replaces* the field value in the current record.

Syntax: `Replace(text, start, length, replacement)`

Examples:

This	Returns This
`Replace('Back Order', 1, 4, 'Out of')`	`Out of Order`
`Replace(PartNum, 4, 7, 'xx')`	`the PartNum value with 890xx, assuming PartNum originally contained 8901234568`

Right The Right function returns a text string containing the specified number of characters, beginning from the *right* of the original string. Also see Left.

Syntax: `Right(text, number)`

Examples:

`Right('Approach',5)` returns roach.

`Right(City, Length(City) - Position(City,' ',1))` returns Francisco, when the City field contains San Francisco. In the second example, the function finds the first space within the city name (in this case, the space occurs at the 4th position). Assuming the length of the

City field is 20, the Right function then looks at the City field and extracts the rightmost 16 (20 minus 4) characters.

Round The Round function rounds the number to the decimal precision specified. If *decimals* is 0 or omitted, Round assumes no decimals and rounds to nearest integer.

Syntax: `Round(number, decimals)`

Examples:

This	Returns This
`Round(12.3456,2)`	`12.35`
`Round(12.3456)`	`12`

SAverage The Summary Average function returns the average for values in a summary range, excluding fields with no value. SAverage is used to compute the average in a summary range of records.

Syntax: `SAverage(field)`

Example: Suppose the Sales database contains four records in a summary range of records, such as a report subtotal or a repeating panel. Assume the SaleAmt field in a database contains the values 100, 300, 400, and 700. `SAverage(SaleAmt)` returns 375, the average of the four values.

SCount The Summary Count function returns the number of nonblank values in the summary range. SCount is used to compute the number of records in a summary range.

Syntax: `SCount(field)`

Example: Suppose the Sales database contains four records in a summary range of records, such as a report subtotal or a repeating panel. Assume the SaleAmt field in a database contains the values 100, 300, 400, and 700. `SCount(SaleAmt)` returns 4, since there are 4 nonblank values in the range.

Second The Second function returns the second portion of a time field.

Syntax: `Second(time)`

Examples:

This	Returns This
`Second('10:11:12')`	`12`
`Second(CurrTime())`	`3 when the current (system) time is 1:02:03`

Sign The Sign function returns –1 if the number is negative (<0), 0 if the number is 0, and 1 if the number is positive (>0).

Syntax: `Sign(number)`

Examples:

This	Returns This
`Sign(-123)`	`-1`
`Sign(123)`	`1`

Sin The Sine function returns the sine of an angle in radians.

Syntax: `Sin(angle)`

Examples:

This	Returns This
`Sin(1)`	`0.841470985`
`Sin(Pi())`	`0`

SLN The Straight-Line Depreciation function returns the amount of depreciation per period, given the cost, salvage value, and expected life.

Syntax: `SLN(cost, salvage, life)`

Example: `SLN(1000, 100, 15)` returns 60. The depreciation amount for an asset purchased for $1,000, with a salvage value of $100, is $60 per year for each of 15 years.

SMax The Summary Maximum function returns the maximum value for values in a summary range. SMax is used to compute the largest value in a summary range of records. The field can be a number, date or time field.

Syntax: `SMax(field)`

Example: Suppose the Sales database contains four records in this summary range, such as a report subtotal or a repeating panel. Assume the SaleAmt field in a database contains the values 100, 300, 400, and 700. `SMax(SaleAmt)` returns 700, the largest of the four values.

SMin The Summary Minimum function returns the minimum value for values in a summary range. SMin is used to compute the smallest value in a summary range of records. The field can be a number, date or time field.

Syntax: `SMin(field)`

Example: Suppose the Sales database contains four records in this summary range, such as a report subtotal or a repeating panel. Assume the SaleAmt field in a database contains the values 100, 300, 400, and 700. `SMin(SaleAmt)` returns 100, the smallest of the four values.

SNPV The Summary Net Present Value function returns the net present value of an investment. The cash flows are contained in the value field on the database. A negative value in the value field indicates an investment (payment or deposit), while a positive value indicates a withdrawal (a dividend).

Syntax: `SNPV(value field, discountrate)`

Example: `SNPV(Flows, 0.12)` returns –480.1263, assuming the following values in the Flows field of adjacent records:

- The initial investment, made one year from today, is 1,000.
- The investment earns a dividend of $100 one year after that.
- The investment earns a dividend of $200 in the next year.
- The investment earns another dividend, this time of $300, in the following year.

- The net present value of an investment one year hence, followed by three dividends in succeeding years, is 480.13, using the annual discount rate of 12%.

Note that the initial deposit (investment) is entered as a negative number in the Flows field of the database record. All dividends are stored as positive numbers. The database records must be sorted in the order in which the investments and withdrawals (dividends) are made.

SoundsLike The Sounds Like function returns Yes if text1 "sounds like" text2.

Syntax: `SoundsLike(text1, text2)`

Examples:

This	Returns This
`SoundsLike('read', 'red')`	Yes
`SoundsLike('snow', 'goose')`	No

Span The Span function returns the number of characters in text1 that are also in text2, looking from left to right. Span counts the characters until a character is found in text1 that is not in text2. Also see SpanUntil.

Syntax: `Span(text1, text2)`

Examples:

This	Returns This
`Span('abc', 'abcde')`	3 (all characters in text1 are in text2)
`Span('abcabd', 'abc')`	5 (the first 5 characters in text1 are found in text2, the 6th character in text1 is not in text2)
`Span('abc', 'def')`	0 (first character in text1 is not found in text2)

SpanUntil The Span Until function returns the number of characters in text1 that are *not* in text2, scanning left to right until a character in text1 matches a characters in text2. Also see Span.

Syntax: `SpanUntil(text1, text2)`

Examples:

This	Returns This
`SpanUntil('abc', 'defg')`	3 (all characters in text1 are not in text2)
`SpanUntil('abcd', 'defg')`	3 (the first 3 characters in text1 are *not* found in text2, but the fourth character [the letter d] *is* in text2)
`SpanUntil('abc', 'abcde')`	0 (first character in text1 is also found in text2)

SQRT The Square Root function returns the square root of a number.

Syntax: `SQRT(number)`

Examples:

This	Returns This
`SQRT(4)`	2
`SQRT(100)`	10

SStd The Summary Standard Deviation function returns the standard deviation for values in a summary range. Sstd is used to determine the standard deviation—a statistical measure—of a summary range of records.

Syntax: `SStd(field)`

Example: Suppose the Sales database contains four records in this summary range, such as a report subtotal or a repeating panel. Assume the SaleAmt field in a database contains the values 100, 300, 400, and 700.

`SStd(SaleAmt)` returns 216.5064, the standard deviation of the four values.

SSum The Summary Sum (Total) function returns the total for values in a summary range. SSum is used to compute the total (sum) in a summary range of records.

Syntax: `SSum(field)`

Example: Suppose the Sales database contains four records in this summary range, such as a report subtotal or a repeating panel. Assume the SaleAmt field in a database contains the values 100, 300, 400, and 700. `SSum(SaleAmt)` returns 1,500, the total of the four values.

Std The Standard Deviation returns the standard deviation of the values in the list.

Syntax: `Std(numberlist)`

Example: `Std(100, 300, 400, 700)` returns 216.5064.

SVar The Summary Variance function returns the variance for values in a summary range. SVar is used to compute the variance—a statistical measure—in a summary range of records.

Syntax: `SVar(field)`

Example: Suppose the Sales database contains four records in a summary range, such as a report subtotal or a repeating panel. Assume the SaleAmt field in a database contains the values 100, 300, 400, and 700. `SVar(SaleAmt)` returns 46875, the variance for the four values.

Tan The Tangent function returns the trigonometric tangent of an angle in radians.

Syntax: `Tan(angle)`

Example: `Tan(1)` returns 1.557407725.

TextToBool The Text to Boolean function returns No if the first character in the text field is F, f, n, N, or 0, or it returns Yes otherwise. Note that the TextToBool function returns Y even if the value in the text field is not "true" (T, t, y, Y, or 1).

Syntax: `TextToBool(text)`

Examples:

This	Returns This
`TextToBool('no')`	No
`TextToBool('apple')`	Yes

TextToDate The Text to Date function converts text to a date value for use with date functions and arithmetic. The text string must contain a date in the format MM/DD/YY (or the format specified in the Windows Control Panel's International settings).

Syntax: `TextToDate(text)`

Example: `TextToDate('1/1/95') + 10` returns 1/11/95 (a date value).

TextToTime The Text to Time function converts text to a time value for use with time functions and arithmetic. The text string must contain a time value in the format HH:MM, HH:MM:SS or HH:MM:SS.00, and may optionally have AM or PM at the end of the text string. The time separator, usually a colon (:), is determined by the International settings in the Windows Control Panel.

Syntax: `TextToTime(text)`

Example: `TextToTime('1:15PM')` returns 13:15:0.0

Time The Time function returns a time value using the hours, minutes, seconds, and hundredths parameters.

Syntax: `Time(hours, minutes, seconds, hundredths)`

Example: `Time(1,2,3,0)` returns 1:02:03.0.

Today The Today function returns the current (system) date. Also see Date.

Syntax: `Today()`

Example: `Today()` returns 7/25/95 if the system date is July 25, 1995.

Translate The Translate function replaces all occurrences of character1 in text with character2. Note: If the first parameter is a field name, Approach *replaces* the field value with the translated value in the current record.

Syntax: `Translate(text, character1, character2)`

Example:

This	Returns This
`Translate('Part 123-456', '-','/')`	`Part 123/456`
`Translate(PartNum, '-', '/')`	`replaces the field PartNum with 123/456, assuming it originally contained 123-456`

Trim The Trim function returns a text string with all leading and trailing spaces removed. Note: Many programming languages have an RTRIM and LTRIM (to trim the right-most and left-most spaces) from a text string. Approach has only the Trim function, which is the same as RTRIM(LTRIM(text)) in other languages.

Syntax: `Trim(text)`

Example: `Trim(' New York ')` returns `New York` (8 characters).

Trunc The Truncate function truncates a number to the precision specified. If the decimal position is 0 or omitted, Trunc returns an integer. Note: The Trunc function does not perform any rounding. It simply "cuts off" the decimal digits.

Syntax: `Trunc(number, decimals)`

Examples:

This	Returns This
`Trunc(123.456,2)`	`123.45`
`Trunc(1.234)`	`1`

Upper The Uppercase function converts text to a string of all uppercase characters. Also see Lower and Proper.

Syntax: `Upper(text)`

Example: `Upper('Wa')` returns WA.

Var The Variance function returns the variable for values in the list. Also see SVar.

Syntax: `Var(number list)`

Example: `Var(100, 300, 400, 700)` returns 46875.

WeekOfYear The Week Of Year function returns the number of weeks since January 1 of the given year.

Syntax: `WeekOfYear(date)`

Examples:

This	Returns This
`WeekOfYear('1/1/1995')`	1
`WeekOfYear('1/10/1995')`	2

Year The Year function returns the year portion of the date. Also see Month and Day.

Syntax: `Year(date)`

Examples:

This	Returns This
`Year('12/30/96')`	1996
`Year(BirthDate)`	1947, when the BirthDate field contains 7/25/47

▸▸ Summary and a Look Ahead

In this chapter you've learned more about functions and formulas, including looking at the parts of a formula and the ways in which parentheses can control how calculations and evaluations take place.

In the next chapter you'll learn more about how to share your data with other programs, including how to import, export, and merge data, create mail messages, and work with Lotus Notes.

▶ ▶ CHAPTER 20

Working with Other Data and Applications

▸▸ FAST TRACK

▸ ***To add imported data as new records*** **631**

select File ➤ Import, then choose the "Add imported data as new records" option, Approach will add all records from the imported database to your existing database. The records will be added to the end of the database, unless you have specified a custom sort order using the Tools ➤ Preferences ➤ Order command.

▸ ***To import a database into an existing database*** **632**

open the existing database. Switch to the Browse environment and select File ➤ Import Data. Select the file type, choose the drive and directory where the file is located, enter the file name, and select OK. If you selected file type Text - Delimited, specify the separator character, whether the first row (record) contains field names, and the character set, then select OK. If you selected file type Text - Fixed Length, specify the field name, field type, starting position, and length for each field. For each field that you want to import or update, click in the middle column under the blue arrow. A blue arrow appears when the fields are matched. Select the type of import you want(see above), then choose OK.

▸ ***To export a database*** **635**

open the database you want to export and switch to the Browse environment. Select File ➤ Export Data. From the Export Data dialog box select the drive, directory, and file type; then enter a file name and in the bottom of the dialog box, select the database fields in the order you want them in the exported file. Select which records you want exported with the "Records to Export" box and select OK. If you selected the Text file type, you will have to specify the field separator character, the character set, and whether you want to include each field name in the first exported record. If you select the Text - Fixed Length file type, specify the field name, type, beginning position, and length, plus the character set. Select OK.

▶ *To create an Approach OLE object* 641

switch to the Browse or Preview environments and select the view that you'll use in the OLE object. Select Edit ➤ Copy View. Choose "Copy current view only" to copy the view you just selected or select "Copy all views" to use all views in the Approach file. If you want to include data, check the Include data box and choose the amount of data you want from the drop-down list. Select OK. Switch to the application that will use this object and select that application's Edit ➤ Paste command, Edit ➤ Paste Special ➤ Paste, or Edit ➤ Paste Special ➤ Paste Link.

▶ *To create an Approach view within a Lotus 1-2-3 spreadsheet* 643

from within 1-2-3, define a 1-2-3 database table. Select the database table by highlighting the entire range, including column headings. Select Tools ➤ Database, then choose Form, Report, Dynamic Crosstab, or Mailing Label. Select OK and the Lotus Assistant for the view type is displayed. Windows then launches Approach and displays the appropriate Assistant. Create the view, then choose File ➤ Exit and Return to return to 1-2-3 and close Approach. If you want to leave Approach running in the background, select File ➤ Close and Return.

►► **In** Chapter 4 you learned how to open an existing database in a different format. For example, you learned how to open a dBASE file or an ASCII text file when there was no corresponding Approach file.

In this chapter you will learn how to *import* data from these and other file formats. When you open a file, you work with only the records in that database. When you import a file, you add the records from the imported file into your existing database. Approach also provides an option that lets you update records in your existing database with values from an imported database if the records in the existing and imported database have the same values in fields you specify. For example, you can replace an address in your database with an address in an imported database if the records in both databases match on first name, last name, and zip code.

You'll also learn how to copy the views from one Approach file to another, create an Approach OLE object for use in other applications, and use an Approach view in your Lotus 1-2-3 spreadsheet.

►► Importing Data from Other Files: The Options

You can import data from the database file formats introduced in Chapter 4. If your data resides on a server, you will be asked for the appropriate connection information (the server name, your name and password, and so on).

To begin the process, you must decide the type of import you want to perform.

▶ Add Imported Data as New Records

If you select the "Add imported data as new records" option, Approach will add all records from the imported database to your existing database. The records will be added to the end of the database unless you have specified a custom sort order using the Tools ➤ Preferences ➤ Order command.

▶ Use Imported Data to Update Existing Records

The "Use imported data to update existing records" import option lets you specify which field(s) in the imported record should be matched with the field(s) in the existing record. If there is a match, Approach will then update the existing database with the value in a field you specify in the imported database.

For example, suppose you are importing records from a Customer database called CustCredit that contains the most up-to-date credit limits. This database contains several fields, but of particular interest is the Customer ID field and the Credit Limit field. (The imported database may also contain fields for the customer name and customer address, but we'll ignore those fields during this importing process.) The existing Approach file contains a database called CUST.DBF, which contains several dozen fields, too, but of interest to us are the CustID field and the CreditLim field.

During the import process you want Approach to match records based on the value in the Customer ID field in the imported database (CUSTCREDIT) with the CustID field in the existing database (CUST). If the values are equal (that is, when Approach finds a match), Approach should replace the value in the CreditLim field in the CUST database with the newer value found in the CreditLimit field in the CUSTCREDIT database. At the end of the import process, your original CUST database has been updated with values from the CUSTCREDIT database. All other data remains untouched.

Keep in mind that if the CUSTCREDIT database contains a customer not found in the existing database CUST, the customer is **not** added. Furthermore, only the records in CUST that have a match in the CUSTCREDIT database are updated with the fields you specify (the credit limit field, CreditLim, is replaced in the record in the CUST database, for example). If there is no matching record in CUSTCREDIT, the original value is not changed (to zero, for example).

▶ Use Imported Data to Update and Add to Existing Records

The "Use imported data to update and add to existing records" import option combines the previous two options. If a match between the existing and imported database is found, the specified field(s) is updated. If a record exists in the imported database that does not have a matching record in the existing database, the record is added. Records in the existing database that have no matching records in the imported database are not affected—they remain in the database.

▶▶ **WARNING**

You cannot update existing records from an import file if the import file is a text or spreadsheet file—that is, if it has the file extension .TXT, .WK*, or .XL*. You must use Approach to import these file types, create a dBASE file, and use the dBASE file as the import file.

▶▶ Importing the Data

Use these steps to import a database into an existing database:

1. Open the existing database. Use the File ➤ Open command. (See Chapter 4 for more details.)
2. Switch to the Browse environment and select File ➤ Import Data. Approach displays the Import Data dialog box.
3. Select the file type, then choose the drive and directory where the file is located. Enter the file name or select it from the list. Select OK. If your file resides on a network, you will need to click on the Network button, then you will be asked for the appropriate server name, user name, and password in order to access the file. If you

want to share the database, select the Connect button and choose the desired sharing options.

4. If you selected a file type of Text - Delimited in Step 3, you must specify what character separates records. You can also specify whether the first row (record) contains field names, and you can specify the character set used when creating the imported file. Select OK. Text Delimited files are discussed in Chapter 4.
5. If you selected a file type of Text - Fixed Length, you must specify the field name, field type, starting position, and length for each field. See the section "Creating a Database from a Fixed-Length Text File" in Chapter 4 for more information about working with fixed-length text files.
6. Approach displays the Import Setup dialog box shown in Figure 20.1. The field names from the imported database are shown in the column on the left, while the field names from your existing database are shown in the column on the right. If your Approach file uses joined databases, you may need to select the proper database from the pull-down list following "Fields in." (If you are importing a spreadsheet, the left column contains the values from the first row. If you are importing a delimited text file, the word "Field" appears repeatedly in the left column if you did not specify that the first row contains field names.) To see the actual data records, click on the left or right arrows at the bottom-left corner of the dialog box.
7. For each field that you want to import or update (for updating selected fields in the existing database), click in the middle column under the blue arrow. A blue arrow appears when the fields are matched. If the fields are not properly aligned, click and drag the field from the right column to match up with the field name or data in the left column. Press Clear to erase all blue arrows. Click the blue arrow to remove a single arrow and "un-match" the two fields.
8. Select the type of import you want (see the section "Importing Data from Other Files: The Options" earlier in this chapter). If you select the second or third option (which includes updating existing records), a fourth column appears with a check mark in the heading. Click in this column for each field you want to use to match values between the imported and existing database. The fields marked with a blue arrow will be updated in the existing database.

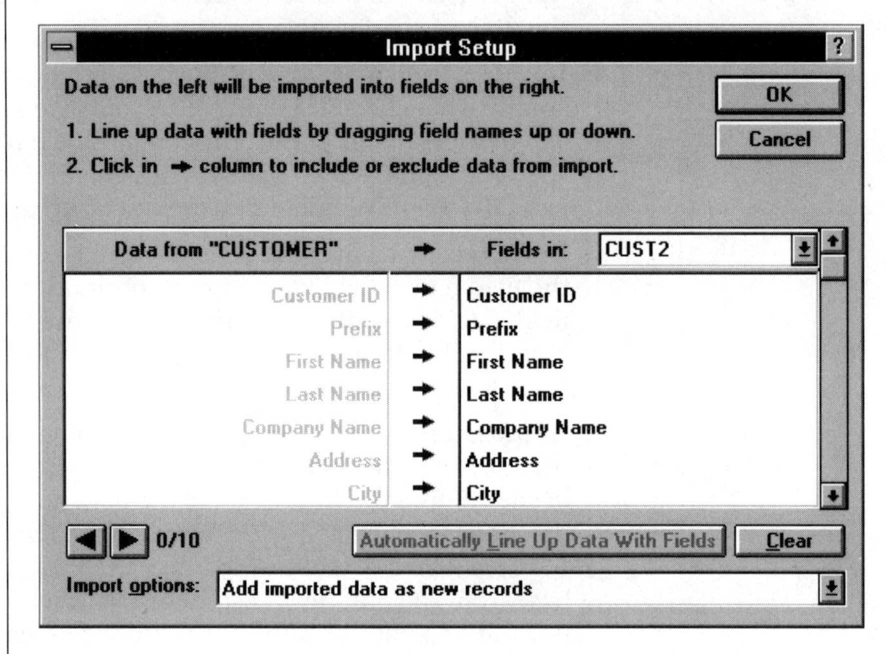

FIGURE 20.1 ►

The Import Setup dialog box displays field names from the imported database file in the left column and from the existing database in the right column. The blue arrows show which fields are "mapped" to each other. Like-named fields are automatically mapped by Approach.

9. Select OK. Approach performs the import or update and the Found box in the Status bar will display the new number of records.

►► Copying Approach Views between Approach Files

To copy views from one Approach file to another, use a variation of the Import command. After you *map* (match) the fields from an existing Approach file (the file to be "imported") to the current Approach file, Approach will make the translation and create copies of the views that refer to the corresponding fields in the current Approach file.

For example, suppose you have an Approach file named OLD-CUST.APR that contains a view called WORKSHEET1 that references to a field named CustomerID. You want to import

WORKSHEET1 into your current Approach file, named NEWCUST, but in this file the customer identification number field is called CustID. During the import process you'll tell Approach that the CustomerID field in WORKSHEET1 matches the CustID field in the current file, NEWCUST. Approach will make a copy of the WORKSHEET1 view, changing the reference to CustomerID to CustID in the NEWCUST file.

Use these steps to import Approach file views:

1. Open the current Approach file and switch to Design.
2. Select File ➤ Import Approach File.
3. Select the Approach file you want to import, then select OK.
4. Approach displays the Import Approach File Setup dialog box. Fields from the imported Approach file are displayed in the left column, and fields from the existing Approach file are shown in the rightmost column. Fields that are identically named have blue arrows in the middle box, indicating a match. If the corresponding fields are not aligned in the same row, drag the field name in the right column up or down until it is properly aligned with its corresponding field, then click the middle column to display a blue arrow. (Click the blue arrow to remove the arrow if you want to "un-match" the two fields.)
5. Select OK. Approach will import all views from the imported Approach file.

►► Exporting Data

Approach uses industry-standard file formats, such as dBASE. There will be times, however, when you will want to share data with someone who cannot use the format you are using. For example, if you are storing data in a dBASE format, you may need to share data with a coworker whose application can only use ASCII text in comma-delimited format. In such a case, all you need to do is export the data.

There are some limitations with exports:

- You can export calculated fields, but their values are converted to text, numeric, date, or time fields and will contain the calculated value at the time of the export; they will not be updated in the application that imports this file, even if that application is Approach.

- You can export a variable field, but its value will be the same in every record you export.
- You cannot export a calculated field that performs a summary function.
- You can export PicturePlus fields, but they can only be read by Approach. (To save the contents of a PicturePlus field to a file, see the section "Saving a PicturePlus Field to a File," later in this chapter.)
- You cannot export macros, custom menus, or other data, such as preferences.

Use these steps to export a database:

1. Open the database you want to export and switch to the Browse environment.
2. Select File ➤ Export Data. Approach will display the Export Data dialog box shown in Figure 20.2.
3. Select the drive, directory, and file type, then enter a file name or select an existing file name. In the bottom of the dialog box, select the database (if your Approach file uses more than one database) and select the database fields in the order you want them in the exported file. Select whether you want to export just the current found set or all records by choosing this option in the "Records to Export" box.
4. Select OK.
5. If you selected the Text file type, you will have to specify the field separator character, the character set, and whether you want to include each field name in the first exported record.
6. If you select the Text - Fixed Length file type, you'll have to specify the field name, type, beginning position, and length, plus the character set. (See the section "Creating a Database from a Fixed-Length Text File" the in Chapter 4 for more information about working with fixed-length text files.)

FIGURE 20.2

The Export Data dialog box lets you specify the name and location of the exported file. You can choose a different file type if you wish. You must select the database fields you want included in the output file at the bottom of the dialog box.

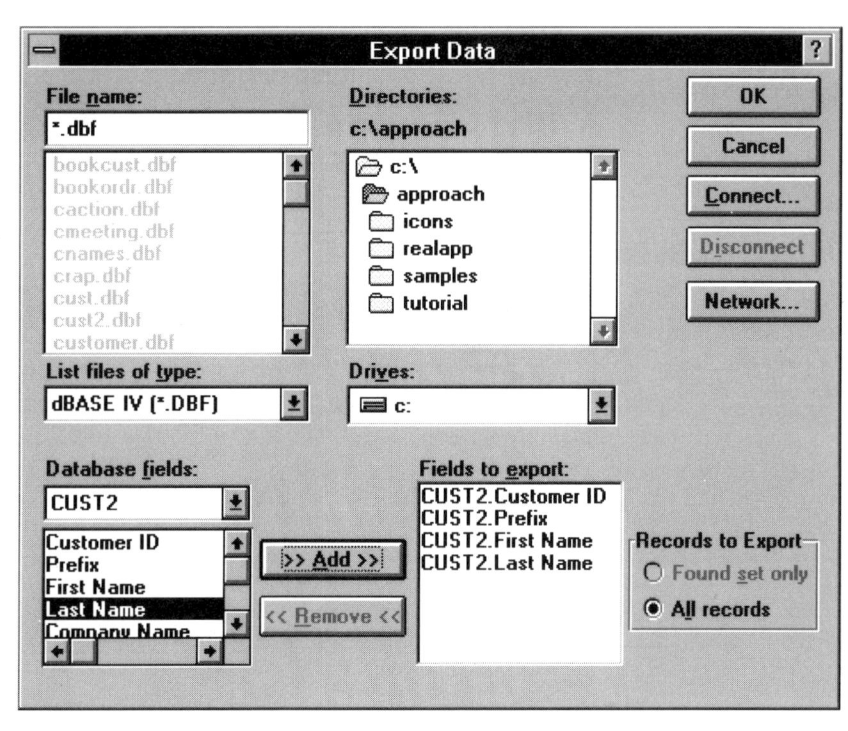

▶▶ Saving a PicturePlus Field to a File

Although you can include a PicturePlus field in a database export, its contents can't be read by any application except Approach. However, you can copy the contents of a PicturePlus field to a new file (or replace an existing file).

Use these steps to copy the contents of a PicturePlus field to a file. Note that you can only copy the contents if the PicturePlus contents were pasted from an existing file or drawn using the mouse. If the contents are linked to another file, you cannot copy the contents.

1. Switch to the Browse environment. Move to the record whose PicturePlus field you want to copy, then click on the PicturePlus field to select it.

2. Select Edit ➤ Copy to File. Approach displays the Copy to File dialog box, shown in Figure 20.3.
3. Select the drive, directory, and file name, then choose a file type.
4. Select OK. Approach performs the copy and returns you to the Browse environment.

FIGURE 20.3

The Copy to File dialog box is used to copy the contents of a PicturePlus field to a separate file.

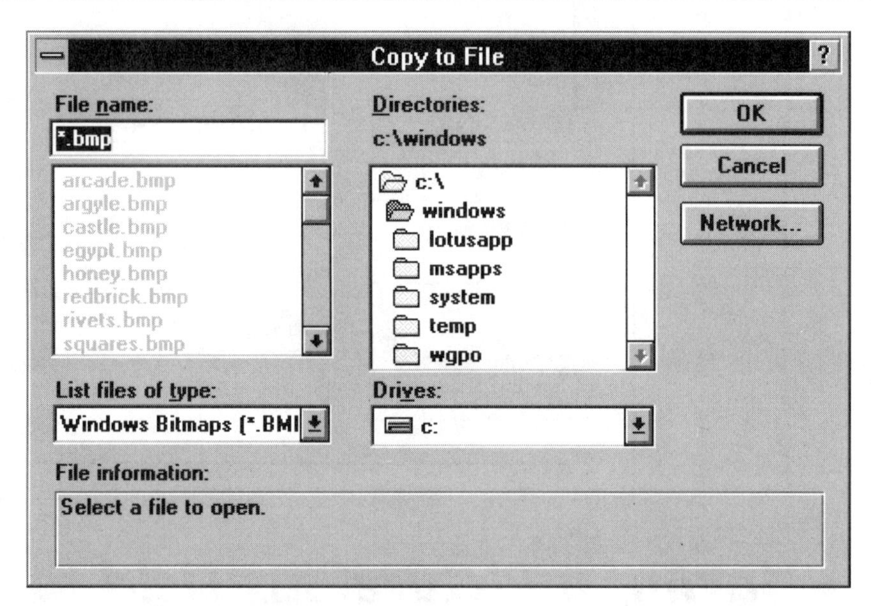

▸▸ Sending Electronic Mail in Approach

If you are using a VIM-compliant mail system (cc:Mail or Notes), you can send a picture (a Windows MetaFile image) of the current view. If you are using a VIM-compliant mail system or a MAPI-compliant mail system, such as Microsoft Mail, you can include all or part of the current Approach file in an electronic mail message.

Use these steps to send an e-mail message:

1. In the Browse environment, move to the record you want to send, or use the Find command to create the found set if you want to send selected records. If you want to send all records, use the

Show All Records command (for example, click on the Show All Records icon from the SmartIcons toolbar).

2. Select File ➤ Send Mail. The Send Mail dialog box, shown in Figure 20.4, appears.

FIGURE 20.4

The Send Mail dialog box lets you specify what you want to send via electronic mail.

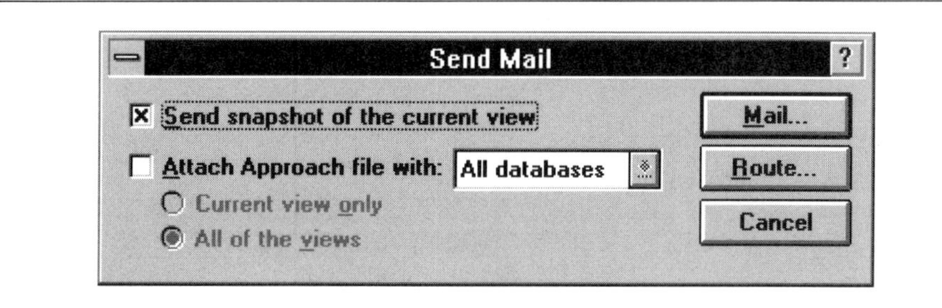

3. To send a Windows MetaFile snapshot of the current view using a VIM-compliant mail system, check the "Send snapshot of the current view" box.
4. To send the current Approach file with the views and the selected data, check the "Attach Approach file with" box, then choose which databases you want to include (you can choose All Databases to copy all databases in the Approach file, for example). Next, select Current view only or All of the views, depending on which views you wish to include in your message.
5. If you have a VIM-compliant mail system, you can select Route to choose the recipients who will receive your message, one after the other. Click OK to return to the Send Mail dialog box, then choose Mail. Approach launches your mail system. You may be asked to enter your user identification and password. The Send dialog box appears, depending on which mail system you have. The Send dialog box for Lotus Notes is shown in Figure 20.5. The Send Note dialog box for Microsoft Mail is shown in Figure 20.6.

FIGURE 20.5

The Lotus Notes Send dialog box.

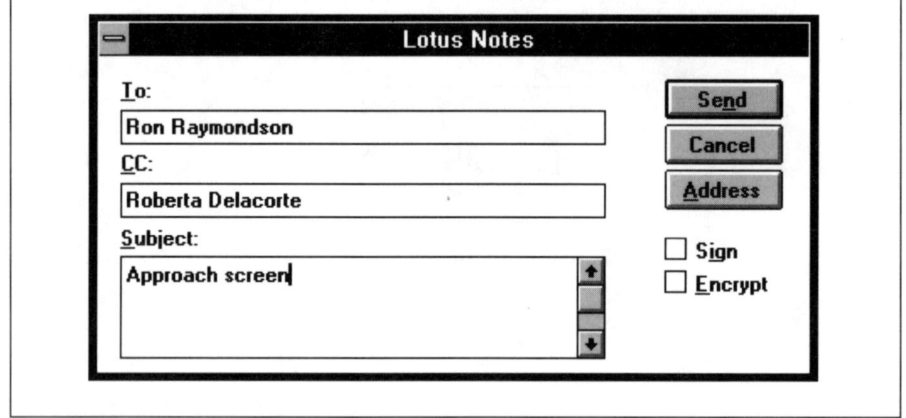

FIGURE 20.6

The Microsoft Mail Send Note dialog box. We've chosen to attach all databases to this note, hence the icon in the message area.

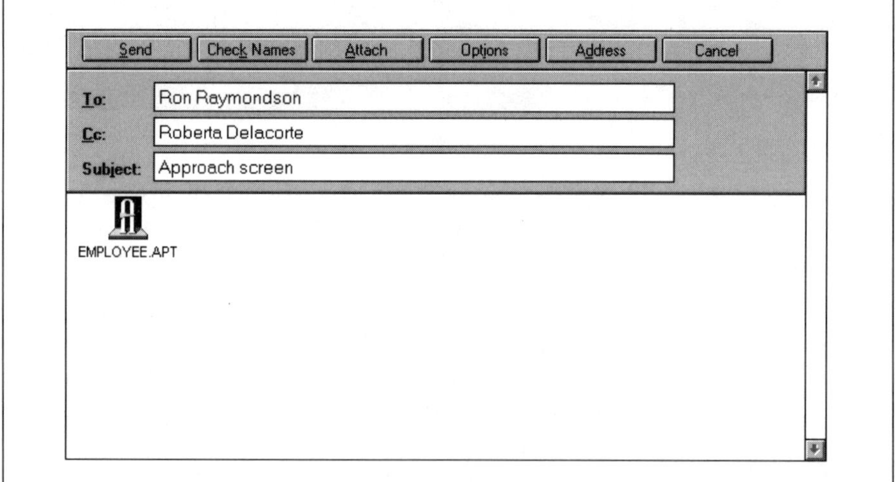

6. Follow the instructions from your mail system, or see your mail administrator, for directions on how to address and send mail from this point.

▸▸ Working with OLE

In Chapter 9 you learned how to link data from another application into a PicturePlus field. (See the "Linking Data to a PicturePlus Field" topic in the section "Entering Data in a PicturePlus Field" in Chapter 9.)

In this section you'll learn how to do the opposite: how to create an Approach OLE object for use by another application.

There are two types of OLE objects you can create: a Data object and a View object. As their names imply, a Data object is a worksheet or crosstab that can be dragged into an OLE 2 target application. For example, by pressing Ctrl and using the left-mouse button, you can drag a section of a crosstab into a spreadsheet. A View object can be either a single view within an Approach file or all views within the file, with or without the data.

Use these steps to create an Approach OLE object:

1. Switch to the Browse or Preview environment and select the view that you'll use in the OLE object. Be sure that you have selected no field in the view.
2. Select Edit ➤ Copy View. Choose "Copy current view only" to copy the view you just selected or select "Copy all views" to use all views in the Approach file. If you want to include data, check the Include data box and choose the amount of data you want from the pull-down list. If you include data, Approach embeds the actual records in your object. If you do not include data, Approach includes pointers to the data, which will remain valid as long as the databases remain in their current location and you do not change the Approach file name(s).
3. Select OK.
4. Switch to the application that will use this object and select that application's Edit ➤ Paste command (to view the data as a picture), Edit ➤ Paste Special ➤ Paste (to paste the data in the application and permit editing by clicking on the object), or Edit ➤ Paste Special ➤ Paste Link (to insert the contents of the Clipboard).

▸▸ Creating an Approach OLE Object from within Another Application

You can create an Approach OLE object while you are working in another OLE-compliant application by following these steps:

1. Use the application's Insert ➤ Object (or a similar command to insert an OLE object), then choose the desired object from the list.
2. The Object dialog box from Microsoft Word 6.0 is shown in Figure 20.7. Choose the database you want to use from the Open dialog box.

FIGURE 20.7 ▸

The Object dialog box in Microsoft Word lets you select the type of object you want in your document.

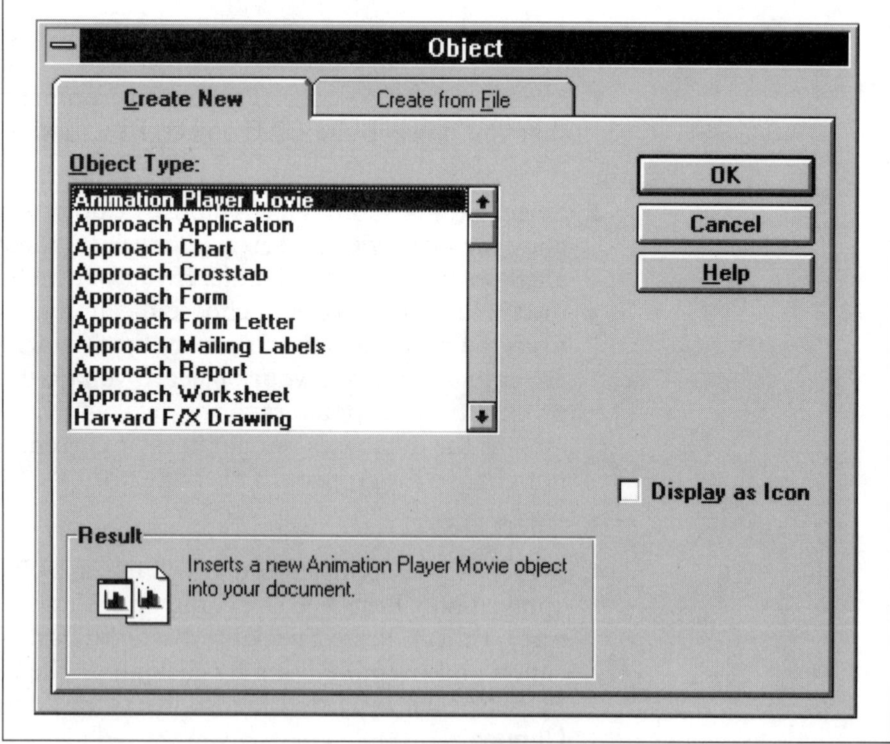

3. Use the appropriate Assistant (depending on which object you selected in Step 1) to create the desired object.

4. Select File ➤ Close to exit Approach and create the object, which will appear as an icon in your application.

▶▶ Using Approach Forms in Lotus 1-2-3

In Chapter 4 you saw how to open a Lotus 1-2-3 spreadsheet and use the data it contains in Approach. In this section we'll look at the reverse: using Report, Form, Crosstab, or Mailing Label views within 1-2-3. For example, you'll see how to use an Approach form to view and modify data in your 1-2-3 spreadsheet, all without leaving 1-2-3.

Use these steps to create an Approach view within a 1-2-3 spreadsheet:

1. If necessary, define a 1-2-3 database table. See your 1-2-3 User's Guide for details.
2. Select the database table by highlighting the entire range, including column headings.
3. Select Tools ➤ Database, then choose Form, Report, Dynamic Crosstab, or Mailing Label.
4. Select OK and the Lotus Assistant for the view type selected in Step 3 is displayed, as shown in Figure 20.8. Windows then launches Approach and displays the appropriate Assistant. In the example shown in Figure 20.8, when you select OK, Approach displays the Form Assistant.

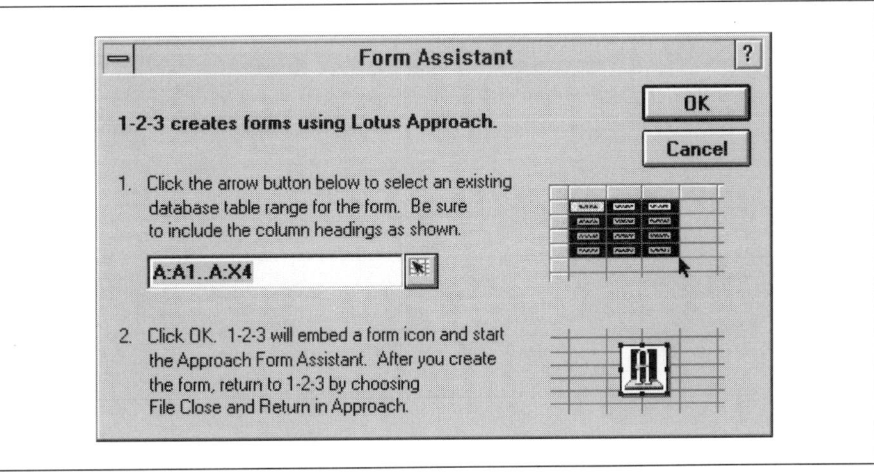

FIGURE 20.8 ▶

The Form Assistant in Lotus 1-2-3 helps you create a form for the correct range of cells.

5. Create the view, then choose File ➤ Exit and press Return to return to 1-2-3 and close Approach. If you want to leave Approach running in the background, select File ➤ Close and Return.

Lotus 1-2-3 displays an Approach icon in the worksheet, as shown in Figure 20.9. Click on the icon to open the form and work with your spreadsheet data. From the Approach view select File ➤ Exit and press Return to return to 1-2-3 and close Approach, or File ➤ Close and press Return to leave Approach running in the background.

FIGURE 20.9 ▶

1-2-3 creates an Approach icon in the worksheet. Click on the icon to launch Approach and use the form.

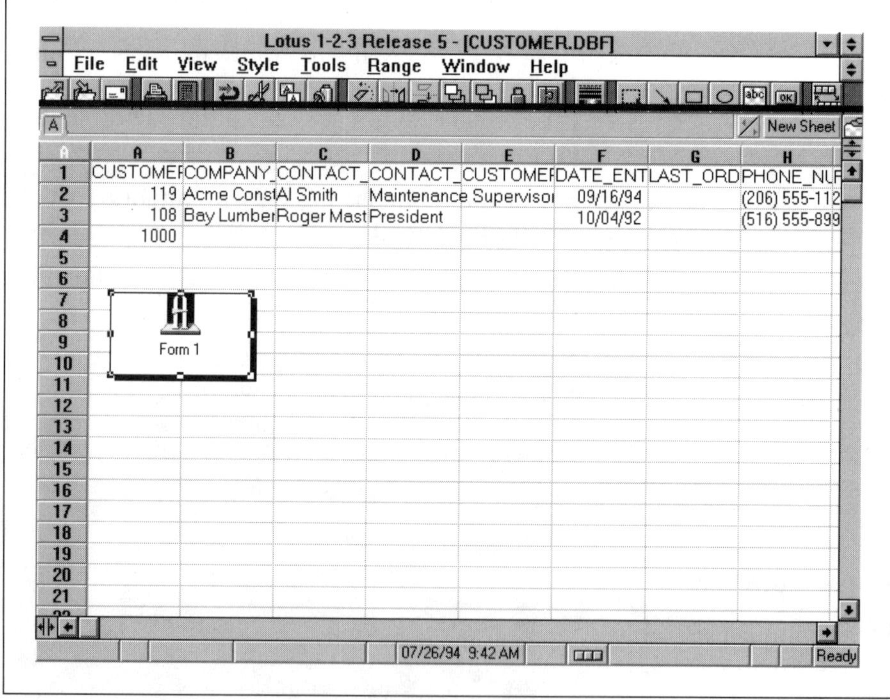

▸▸ Summary and a Look Ahead

In this chapter you've learned how to import and export data with Approach, save a PicturePlus field to a separate file, and create and use Approach OLE objects. You've learned how to copy views between Approach files. You've seen how to work with Approach forms in Lotus 1-2-3 and how to send Approach data in an electronic mail message.

In Part III, you'll learn how to build an application from start to finish. You'll learn not only the principles behind effective and efficient application design, but you'll actually build an application using a variety of Approach features, such as forms and macros.

Building an Application

PART THREE

CHAPTER 21

Creating Applications in Approach

▸▸ FAST TRACK

▶▶ In Part III we focus on putting all the "pieces" together from earlier chapters. Step by step we'll build an application that helps us keep up to date with customers and keeps us on track with the things we have to do. The application we'll build will manage names and addresses of customers, as well as a contact log that will keep track of when we met or spoke with each customer. In addition, we'll keep a "to-do list" to make sure that tasks not directly connected to a customer, such as picking up our laundry, don't "fall through the cracks."

The primary purpose of this chapter is to help you understand how to analyze a problem and "build" a solution. We will assume that you've read the earlier chapters, or that you will refer to them when an unfamiliar technique or subject is discussed. However, we'll also go behind the scenes to explain some of the tradeoffs you have to make when using Approach. This discussion is borne of practical experience with Approach, as well as good application design principles we've gathered from actual application development.

It's tempting to skip this chapter, which contains more theory than instructions. However, this chapter is vital because we will show you how and why we made some of our design decisions. It's easy to say, "Sure, that looks good," when you see the finished design, but it's tougher to understand why a developer did what he or she did. Chapter 21 explains how to plan your project so you'll have an application that meets your needs, not one you must constantly change. We'll go through each phase of an application development cycle, explaining the theory and giving you practical examples. We'll show you the questions we asked and the decisions we made when designing our application.

▶▶ Designing Applications

Before you work with Approach to solve a business problem, it's important to understand the steps you should go through to be sure your solution works. While drawing the layout of your final report on a cocktail napkin is a great way to start your design juices flowing, it is not the way to create an application. Too frequently drawing the "final product" puts the cart before the horse. Doing so may blind you to understanding the data your database must contain, and lead to short-circuiting proper application development rules.

The steps provided in this chapter will guide you through developing an application in Approach that is efficient and accomplishes what you set out to do. The steps take a top-down approach. That is, we'll start by detailing an overview of the project and stating its purpose; then we'll provide the specifics in levels of increasing detail.

▶ Step 1: Develop a Statement of Purpose

Before you begin working with Approach, it's important to understand and properly state your business problem. What are you trying to accomplish? It may be that Approach is not the right tool for the job. For example, if your goal is to keep better track of your appointments, using a calendar or appointment book rather than a series of yellow sticky notes may accomplish the task without using a database.

It's also important to state the business problem and goal clearly, not state the solution. Writing down the solution makes everything seem like a foregone conclusion. You also need to be explicit about the problem. "Use a database to track customers" doesn't say why you want to do this, or what you hope to accomplish by doing this. What data about a customer do you want to track? Just their name and address? A better statement of the business problem might be: "Customer follow-ups are not performed within two days of an initial order. The solution derived from the data must notify salesman of which customers are to be contacted."

You may also want to provide some high-level specifications in your statement that are not only vital to your business but keep the focus on key elements you'll need. For example, a customer contact system may need to "provide a method of notifying salesmen of which customers must be contacted and provide historical data about previous contacts." Notice that this statement doesn't say how the solution is to be implemented, and it sets only a few requirements on the design. Instead, the business statement is created to make sure all involved understand the goal of the project. A simply stated goal helps all team members know the direction in which they are headed.

In our application, we looked at how we were working with names and addresses. We found that we weren't always recording data promptly, that mailing lists were difficult to prepare, and sometimes we were missing upcoming appointments. Therefore, our statement of purpose could be something like this:

```
Our current methods of entering customer data and
tracking appointments is inefficient. Customer data
may not be current and appointments may be missed.
The new application must allow easy update of cus-
tomer data, notify the user of upcoming
appointments, and store the history of all previous
contacts (dates and subjects). In addition, it will
maintain a salesperson's personal "to-do" list.
```

Notice that we haven't said how we'll implement this requirement. Although we're headed down the road toward building an Approach application, we may find that after further analysis the best solution would be a better set of index cards. Our statement is generic in the sense that we aren't phrasing it so that an Approach application is a foregone conclusion.

▸ Step 2: Organize and Analyze Your Data and Work Flow

Many organizations find it important to detail the work flow of the current situation and the desired solution. For example, you can diagram how a sales representative follows up with a customer now. Where does the sales data come from? Does the customer phone in the order to the Sales Department, or does the sales representative write up an order from an in-person visit? After the order is written up, how is communication handled? How does the representative know to follow-up with the customer and when?

You may also want to analyze what data you currently have about a customer. For example, what data do you need to make a follow-up call? Is that data currently available to the sales representative?

In our example, we were using sticky notes to update customer data. Of course, this wasn't efficient because those notes frequently got lost or buried under other papers on someone's desk. However, sticky notes were close at hand throughout the day.

Thus, we also studied how we performed our work. We discovered that most of our changes to existing data were made throughout the day, rather than bunched up at one time. This told us that access to different parts of the application (maintaining customer data, previous appointments, and our to-do list) must be flexible. We must be able to jump around to all sections of the program since we don't enter customer data for one hour, then work with appointments for the next 10 minutes.

▶ Step 3: Create Functional Specifications

Similar to stating the purpose of the project and the nature of the business problem to be solved, functional specifications are kept at a high level (we don't consider the nitty gritty details at this point). A functional specification defines what you want to happen. For example, in the sales follow-up system, you probably want:

1. Shared databases accessible by all sales representatives for tracking customer name and address data.
2. Complete customer meeting (contact) data, including a record of all contacts (date, time, subject) and who met with the customer.

Notice that there is still plenty of flexibility for designing an Approach database. A functional specification notes that customer data is to be maintained, but the specification does not detail the exact fields to be created. How many lines of a company address do you need? How many telephone numbers, and should each contain an extension number? These questions are answered in Step 4, when you create detailed specifications.

Your functional specifications are not limited to the database design alone. You must think of all aspects of your work. How and when does data comes into the system? Who (the name of the position, not the individual) is authorized to access it? What does the person do with the data? Where does the data go after that person has worked with it? Will the new system change the manual procedures? If so, you'll need to write down what the new procedures will be, and how the transition from the old system to the new system will be handled.

Functional specifications are also used at the end of the project to evaluate the final solution. Functional specifications serve as a list of the features your Approach solution must embrace.

In our customer name and address/to-do list, we asked literally dozens of questions. Notice the familiar who, what, when, where, why, and how questions. Most of the questions you'll ask in this step naturally fall into these categories. For instance, in our example we have defined the following:

Who will use the system?	The designer (you) will also be the end-user. Only one user will be working with the application.
What data will you store?	You want to store customer names, addresses, telephone numbers, notes, and appointments, and a list of things we need to do.
What do you want to do with the data?	You'll add, change, and update customer data and appointments; dial any telephone number; add, change, update previous contact data, and set the next meeting date.
When do you want to work with the application?	You'll work with the data throughout the day; there will be random access to any part of the application.
Where will the data be saved?	You'll use your our own hard disk, rather than a network drive, since you are not going to share this database with other users.

Why do you keep this data?	The data will be used to help you maintain regular contact with your customers, thus improving customer service. This data will replace all data currently stored on sticky notes. (You don't have to worry about importing data from an existing system, but you will have to be sure that manual conversion—by typing all the data into the system—can be accomplished in a short period of time. Otherwise, you'll be working with an Approach database for part of your customers and the sticky notes not yet converted for the others.)
How will the data be used?	You want to view the data and change it online, produce hard copy reports with name and address data (to create a printed address book), and produce a chart showing how many appointments are upcoming. The data will be for the user exclusively—it does not have to be designed to mimic a current company-standard report.

We need to look at the environment and ask questions about the user(s). To simplify our application development, we're going to assume that you are the end-user, and we'll assume for simplicity that you work in a one-person office. These answers make our design much easier. For example, because you know how to use Approach, you don't need custom menus. We don't need to enforce strict security, since you are the only one using the system. We don't need to forbid changes to designs, for example, and we can create, modify, or delete forms if we need to. Since you are the only user on the system, we don't have to worry about tracking which salesperson made a call on a customer—you did. In Chapter 26, however, you'll get some ideas on how to modify the application to take multiple users into account.

Now we'll admit that many of our questions and answers reflect a limited view—we're building a simple application from scratch and are not working with some of Approach's more complex features, such as designing a form to match a company's existing layout, or importing existing data from another file. To build an application from start to finish, we had to limit our scope—or we could write another book on the subject! Where appropriate in the next few chapters, we'll explain some of the design decisions you can make to take into consideration needs such as sharing a database with multiple users.

► Step 4: Create Detailed Specifications

When you build detailed specifications, you convert the functional specifications into a design that you can implement in Approach. Answers to questions such as those raised in preceding chapters (How many lines for a company address?) are specified in this step of the application development process. You'll also specify the length of a field: Should the name field be 20 or 30 characters long? Do you want to keep the first name separate from the last name? If so, you'll need to create two fields instead of one.

Describing where the data will come from is another key task in writing detailed specifications. If you are converting data from an existing database, or plan to use Approach to access a database, this is the time and place to say it in writing.

In this step you specify every field, record, and database you need to create and maintain. If you are *joining* (relating) databases, you need to specify which field the databases share. In fact, your specifications must be so specific as to make it possible for a different person on the team—perhaps an Approach expert—to develop your application solely on the basis of reading the specifications.

In many application development efforts, the team takes each functional specification and *maps* it to a detailed specification. That is, you'll examine each functional specification and make sure that somewhere in your detailed specification you've met the requirement. For example, our functional specification noted that we want to store names, addresses, and telephone numbers. In the detailed specification we'll expand upon the requirements for those fields:

Field Needed	Purpose/Notes
Prefix	Mr., Mrs., Ms., Dr., and so on
First Name	Customer's first name
Last Name	Customer's last name
Company	Company name where customer works
Address	Single line address for now; may consider 2-line address later
City	Company's location
State	Company's location
Zip	Company's location
Country	Optional, Company's location
Telephone Numbers	Three fields: office, home, and fax, including area code. (The office phone number should have a four-digit extension.)
E-mail Address	Customer's name on an electronic mail service, such as MCI, CompuServe, Prodigy, or the Internet
Next Contact Date	Date of next appointment
Next Contact Time (Beginning)	Time of next appointment
Next Contact Time (Ending)	Time of next appointment
Next Contact Type	Meeting or telephone call (use a single code: M or T)
Next Contact Description	Explain why next contact has been arranged.

Those are the essential fields. We can also add fields unique to our business. For example, if referrals are an important way for us to get new business, we'll want to keep track of who referred this customer. Therefore, we'll also need a referral field. You may wish to add additional fields, such as the name of the product the customer buys from you, the customer's birthdate or anniversary date, a credit limit, shipping address, alternate address (perhaps a home address), and so on.

We also want to keep track of the date the customer was added to our system, and the date the record was last modified. Approach can keep this data updated automatically, but we must define the fields to store the data.

Finally, we'll add a Notes field to store text of any type. It may be free-form notes, or special data that doesn't fit into a neat and tidy category.

Using this data, we'll add these fields to our list:

Referred By	Name of customer referring this customer
Date Entered	Date customer was added to our database
Date Modified	Date record was updated
Notes	Free-form text

Remember that one of our functional specifications was to keep track of the last contacts we had with our customer. Therefore, we'll need to keep track of:

Last Meetings	Include the date, time (beginning and ending), type, description, and notes (for free-form text that recaps the events at the meeting)

For our to-do list, we'll need:

Priority	From 1 (high) to 10 (low)
Description	What is the task
Due date	When task must be completed
Complete Date	Date task was completed

When we listed functional specifications for the data, we asked: What do we want to do with this data? The answers are reflected in the following specifications for views within our application:

Need	Use
Customer Contact Screen	Add, change, delete customer information; with button (?) to dial a telephone number
Customer History Screen	Show next and all previous appointments
Upcoming Appointments Report	Show all future appointments

Our to-do list must include:

To Do Entry Screen	For adding, changing, and deleting tasks
To Do List	List all items in the database
Overdue List	List all items that are past due
Tasks by Date and Priority	A crosstab showing the number of tasks due by date and by priority
Task Chart	A chart of the data in the crosstab to graphically illustrate how many tasks are due

You'll want to sketch out each view formally. Then for each field on a view, list the field within the database that will contain the data you want displayed. If you plan to use joined databases, you'll want to specify the database name as well as the field.

In the next chapters we'll show illustrations of our final design, then explain how to create each view. Rather than use paper and pencil, we created a sample database, then used the database to create mockups of each screen. This prototyping is a key feature of Approach, making it easy to develop and test your ideas before you develop a full-scale application.

▶ Step 5: Build the Database Application

In this step the rubber meets the road. Defining the database, the data entry forms, reports, and macros are all accomplished in this step, using the detailed specifications as the road map. The remaining chapters of this book explain how to build the application.

▶ Step 6: Test Your Application

After you build the application, it's time to test it. This usually involves a set of test data that has been created while the database application was being built. The test data can be written down (writing out each customer's name and address to be input, for instance), or records can be used from an existing database or extracted from another source.

Testing and building are a cycle. When you find a "bug" in the application, you may revise the application yourself, or give the application back to the developer(s) as you test other areas. For example, you may uncover a problem during data entry because a field validation rule is improperly set up. After notifying the developer (assuming you didn't develop the application yourself), you can continue testing—perhaps testing a report (to approve the layout, calculations, or summaries) or a macro, keeping in mind that the data field may contain incorrect data.

You may find it helpful to have another person test your application—even if he or she doesn't know anything about your application. Another set of eyes can help you improve your user interface as well as catch bugs. Remember that another person (or your eventual end-user if you are developing this application for someone else) will work with the application in ways that are different from how you work. Another computer user may try to add incomplete records—something you didn't test because, after all, you'd never do that! However, if you want to make your application truly bullet proof, don't rely on yourself to do everything. Get a second opinion!

▶ Step 7: Implement Your Solution

Start using your application for your daily work. You may wish to phase in use of your application—adding in only a portion of each day's work, for example, to make sure that all the bugs have been worked out. Another advantage of a cautious approach is that you can become more comfortable using smaller amounts of data than using large amounts of data right from the start. The disadvantage is that you have to keep track of which data is in the database and which is still being processed "the old way."

In either case, it's important to switch to your solution as soon as possible. You may find that your database solves most, but still not all, of your business problems. After you have worked with the database for some time (and the amount of time varies by the complexity of the application you develop), it's time to start with a new project and a new statement of purpose. That's right—you're back to Step 1 of a whole new development cycle.

►► Using the Seven Steps

Note that these seven steps are useful even if you work alone. If you are the only team member—if you are the designer, developer, tester, and implementation specialist all in one—it's still important to follow all the steps. It's tempting to skip the analysis steps and get right into Approach to design the databases "on the fly." *Don't do it.* Be sure you fully understand what you're trying to do before you begin. While Approach makes it easy to change a database design, there are limits to its flexibility. You'll find that macros, for example, can become extremely complex if they are not planned out carefully in advance.

It's tempting to skip the analysis phases. Once again, we must emphasize—don't succumb to the temptation!

►► Some Rules of the Road

While the steps described above are the standard steps you'll see in any textbook on application design and development, there are some things that you won't find in a list of project phases. Here are four guidelines to developing an application that come from my experience in developing applications for over 17 years. They apply to just about any project you can imagine, and particularly to database applications. They can help you prepare for the development process, or make the most of your time as you build an application.

► Allow Extra Time for Revisions

Development is a cyclical process. One method of cutting down development time is to use a prototype—a "mockup" that doesn't contain all the details but gives you a general idea of how the database will work. For example, when you create a database, Approach creates a standard form for data entry. It's a simplistic form—one field per line—and you'll probably want to create your own form. However, you can use the default form to enter some test data, then create sample reports and test them. You may find that you cannot create the reports you need because your database does not contain all the necessary fields. You can change the database definition, use the new default form for data entry, and revise your reports. Since during this mockup process you don't invest a lot of time in developing data entry forms, such revisions to the database cause less overall disruption to the entire application. If radical changes to a database design are needed, such as splitting a database into two databases that must be joined, the savings are greater still.

If you are building an application for another person or group of users, be sure to have some process in place for managing changes, or you'll be revising your application up to the last minute. One advantage of going through the functional and detail specification phases is to get everything in writing. Users who see in detail what they are asking for and how it will be used are more likely to approve the end product than if you merely try to explain what they are getting and how it will work. Paper records (with the signatures of users) are much more reliable than any developer's memory. Furthermore, the end-users often think they have told you, the developer, about a requirement, when, in fact, they only thought about telling you. Putting everything in writing can resolve disagreements about who said what.

► Work on Small Sections at a Time

As in the previous rule, working on small sections—such as a data entry form with small amounts of data—gives you a sense of what you need to change in your design. Small amounts of data also help you compare the expected results (such as a calculation in a report) with the actual output of a report.

When building this application, we worked first on the section for customer name and address, then on the to-do list manager. We worked on building small sections at a time (we chose the simplest screens first), and built the macros bit by bit, testing just one or two lines at first to make sure we had the right idea. The smaller the pieces of work, the faster you'll see results, which can be a great boost to your ego (and your productivity)!

▶ Have Patience

If you are the developer, expect users to change their minds repeatedly during a project. If you're the user, you can shorten the development process by creating your own mockups for the developer(s). The biggest problem in developing specifications is from users who have little experience with such projects, but who "will know the end result when they see it." Again, the benefit of prototypes becomes obvious here.

Remember that building an application as you learn Approach can be doubly frustrating, since you're trying to work with a new application (Approach) that you don't fully understand while you develop an application that has changing requirements. Take frequent breaks, and, if possible, put your work aside when you run into stumbling blocks. Returning to your work after a break gives you a fresh perspective.

▶ Your First Efforts May End Up Unused

The benefit of using Approach is its ability to let you create applications quickly. However, building applications is still a learning process, and although databases can be changed and forms can be revised, there may come a point when starting over makes the most sense. Don't be dismayed—this happens to everyone. There's a saying in project management classes: Your first project is built to be thrown away. A learning curve takes some sacrifice. Don't be so attached to your first application that you fear throwing it away and starting over. If it makes sense, do it, and profit from what you have learned.

In fact, as we developed the name and address application, we tried to solve a problem by being clever. We tested our theory on a small set of data, then realized that our clever design wasn't going to work. That's just as well, since clever applications are also the most difficult to update later. (Things may seem clear now, but when you look at what you did six months from now, it's doubtful you'll remember how the trick works or why you even used it in the first place.)

There is a lot to be gained by trying your ideas out on a small database—perhaps one with only two or three fields so you can see if your idea about a report or crosstab is practical. Then you can incorporate your idea into the real application. It's also appropriate to completely throw out your first effort when you realize you've developed yourself into a corner.

▸▸ Summary and a Look Ahead

In this chapter you've seen the steps necessary to design and develop an application in Approach. You've also seen an example of this theory as we've explained some of the functional and detailed specifications for the name-and-address application. In Chapter 22 we'll begin the actual development of this application.

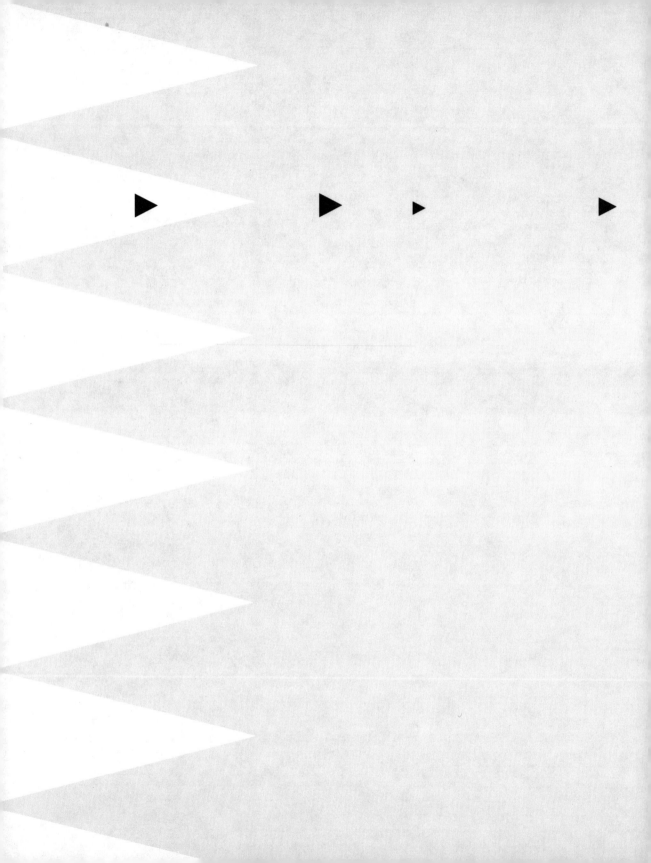

▶ ▶ CHAPTER 22

Building the Customer Application

▸▸ FAST TRACK

Join the customer and history databases 686

so that the Customer ID in a Customer record will point to the history for that customer by looking for the same Customer ID value in the Customer ID field in the History database. We've named the joined fields the same in both databases. Although this is not strictly necessary, it tends to reduce confusion if you refer to the same field name in both records. Select Create ➤ Join. Approach opens the Join dialog box showing the Customer database. Select Open and choose the History database. Click on the Customer ID field in the History database, then click on the Customer ID field in the Customer database. Select Join and Approach draws a line between the two fields. Select OK.

Create the To Do database 687

which keeps track of the things that we need to do that are not directly related to a customer. To-do items include reviewing a budget proposal or picking up library books. Use the field definitions detailed in this chapter.

▸▸ **I***n* this chapter we'll take a closer look at the functional and detailed specifications of our application. Assume at this point that we have sketched out a sample of the reports and screens we want and have created a list of the fields we want to maintain to get our work done. Of course, as we put these ideas and requirements into practice, we have to refine them. Therefore, consider this chapter an overview: It's what we start out with, but not what we'll end up with by the end of Chapter 25.

Why the disparity between what we want and what we get? In part, there are some limitations of Approach. For example, we really would like to incorporate several database files into a single Approach file, but in reality Approach can't handle multiple databases unless they are joined, and the databases we wanted to include had no logical relationship.

Another limitation is physical: We may want our screen to include 30 fields of data so that we use only one screen; however, putting 30 fields on a screen creates a data entry form that is hard to read (we must use small fonts, making the screen difficult to use).

Finally, we may discover that while our design looks good on paper, it either doesn't do the job or we could do the job better by revising the design. As you'll see, we will add a calculated field (combining first and last names) because we want to provide more feedback on a form. While everything looked good when we sketched out our screen layout on a piece of paper, when we looked at the computer screen we realized we had missed this helpful piece of data.

▸▸ *Defining the Data Fields*

In Chapter 21, we decided on the types of data we wanted to store. Now it's time to define specific properties for each field. However, as may be apparent, our application will use joined databases. Recall from Chapter 6 that when you have repeating data, such as past appointment data, it's important that you don't repeat the static (or unchanging) data for each contact. For example, if we have met with a customer 20 times, we don't want to keep 20 copies of the customer's name and address. Instead, we want to keep the customer contact data separate, and use a joined field to connect the name and address data with the historical contact data.

Therefore, we'll need two databases: a name-and-address database and a meetings database. Each database will include the join field (joins are described in Chapter 6). Typically this is a unique number or code. We'll use Approach's serialization feature (described in Chapter 5) to ensure a unique value and define this join field as a numeric value of five digits.

We'll discuss each field in each database individually. In each case we'll discuss some design decisions and special considerations for the field within the application.

▸▸ Data Fields for the Name and Address Database

For simplicity, we'll name the name-and-address database the Customer database. We'll also name the application the Customer application. The Customer database contains—what else—all the data about customers. We will use this database as the main database for most forms within the application.

Let's take a look at some of the fields within the Customer database.

▸ Customer ID

We must have a unique identifier for each customer. Since we don't expect to have more than 99,999, a five-digit numeric field is sufficient. Because the value must be unique, and to eliminate the necessity of entering a unique value, we'll use the Default Value tab within the Creating New Database dialog box to specify the beginning serial number (1) and the incremental value (also 1).

▶ Prefix

This field stores the courtesy title, known as a *prefix* in Approach, to a person's name, such as Mr., Mrs., Ms., Dr., and so on. We can use a pull-down list on a form so we can select the value. However, since we never know what new prefix might be added, such as "Dr." and "Mr.", we'll allow new entries in this field. Therefore, we'll want to keep in mind that when we display this field on a form, we'll use a display type of "Field box and list."

▶ First Name

We'll keep the first name and last name separate. Because of the "When printing, slide left" feature that permits Approach to move fields together to eliminate spaces on mailing labels and in form letters, we don't need to be concerned that we'll end up with

```
Jim  Powell
```

instead of

```
Jim Powell
```

We also need to keep the last name in a separate field in case we want to alphabetize the list on last name. See the following "Last Name" section for a detailed discussion of this situation.

▶ Last Name

Nothing complicated here. However, if the name includes a designation or *suffix,* such as Jr., Sr., or III, include it in the Last Name field. For example, for John Anderson III, enter Anderson III in the Last Name field.

Separating First and Last Names

The most important piece of data is the customer name, of course. If you're new to databases, you may be tempted to create a single text field for a customer name. This field could contain the last name, a comma, and the first name, and even a middle initial. When you sorted the records, they would appear in alphabetical order by last name, which is the usual way you'd expect to see such a list. Since it's unlikely you'd ever have to sort by the customer's first name, there seems to be no problem.

Unfortunately, you'll run into problems when you try to use the field for other reports. For example, if you want to create mailing labels, you'd probably prefer the address to read Marsha Cunningham, not Cunningham, Marsha (which is an obvious clue that the contents of the envelope were probably computer generated, and impersonal). Although Approach provides functions that let you split apart the first name from the last name, this takes considerable work and is fraught with problems, especially when you add a suffix like Jr. or spaces in a name, such as Van Dyke.

There's yet another reason to split the name apart. Suppose you want to find a customer's record and you only know his first name is Alonzo. Approach can search for this text much faster if it looks for it in a short First Name field, rather than looking for the same text in a longer Full Name field.

It's always best to split apart a field when you know you'll need to display a field's contents differently from the way you enter the data. Another example of a field you might want to split is a telephone number, separating the area code from the rest of the number. Working with the area code separately may be important if you need to determine if a telephone number is long distance (the area code field does not match your own area code) or if you want to select customers in a particular area code to receive a special mailing.

Not all fields need to be split, however. An address field can contain 123 Main Street without splitting this into a numeric portion and a text portion if it is unlikely you'll sort records based on the street name or perform math on the numeric portion.

▶ Company Name, Address, City, State/Province, Postal Code, Country

Enter the name of the company the contact works for, as well as the address data. We'll define the State field as a 15-character text field, since we want to be able to handle international addresses, such as Canadian Provinces. Likewise, the zip code will really be called Postal Code in our database and will be 10 characters long to handle international addresses. Note, however, that since 99.9% of our customers are in the U.S., the form we design in subsequent chapters can use the label Zip Code. We will enter the Postal Code for international customers in the field labeled Zip Code, even though the data we type will be stored in the Postal Code field.

Why not just use the Zip Code designation in our database to start with? Our business may expand, and it's better to plan for expansion than to have to make modifications throughout a system when we change our minds.

▶ Office, Home, Fax Telephone Numbers

We'll have three telephone numbers in this database. We could define each as a 20-character text field, which is the default definition in many of the Approach sample database templates. A 20-character field allows you to have the format

```
(206) 555-1111 x1234
```

However, we chose a numeric definition with the telephone number fields defined as 10-digit fields and the extension as a 4-digit field for several reasons:

- Numeric definitions allow for automatic formatting using the Telephone format.
- The definitions are shorter, thus taking up less hard disk space for each record.
- There are no extensions for home and fax telephone numbers, so using 20 characters when 10 numeric digits will suffice is a waste of space.

▶ E-mail Address

We chose an arbitrary length of 30 characters for this field to store E-mail addresses. If we encounter a longer name, we can put it in the Notes field or simply expand the field size using the Field Definitions dialog box.

▶ Next Contact Data

The data we want to collect includes the date of the next contact (meeting or telephone call), the beginning time (if known), the ending time (if known), the type of contact (Is it a meeting or a telephone call?), and a text description of the contact. We chose the arbitrary field length of 30 for the text description.

▶ Referred By

Since referral data is important to us, we'll keep track of who is referring whom. As you'll see when we modify this field of the form (refer to Chapter 26), we can list the values of the customers' names in this field and choose from existing customers, reducing data entry.

▶ Notes

We'll use a memo field to allow virtually unlimited text entry for a customer. We can use the field to track important data that varies from customer to customer, as well as random thoughts about the customer that don't fit neatly into any other field. Since we may want to keep significant amounts of text, we will use a memo field. Text fields are limited (to about 250 characters), which may not be enough space to keep everything we want to record about this customer.

▶ Date Entered, Date Modified

Keeping track of the date data is entered or modified creates an audit trail, which can be helpful in monitoring database maintenance needs. Fortunately, Approach can automatically fill in these fields for us.

▶▶ Fields We Didn't Include

There are other fields we could have added, but to keep the application simple we have omitted them. If you are working with a database that keeps name-and-address data, consider including the following fields:

- Salutation (what follows "Dear" in a letter)—this is useful if you want some form letters to be addressed formally and others more personally.
- Middle Initial—this often helps you clearly distinguish a customer's first name.

- Cellular telephone field—cellular phones are becoming more widely used.
- Multiple E-mail address fields—separate fields for each online service.
- Spouse data.
- Additional address data, such as a home address.

▸▸ Creating the Customer Database

To begin the database application development, start Approach. If you see the Welcome screen, select the Blank Database option from the Create a new file section, then select OK. If the Welcome Screen does not appear, select File ➤ New.

We chose not to use the Customer template from Approach for several reasons. First, it includes a number of fields we don't need, and omits several that we will need. Second, it creates a form and worksheet that we'll have to modify extensively, and it's simply easier to create our own database and have Approach create the default form from our database definition. In the case of this application, it probably is six-of-one, half-a-dozen-of-the-other. We could make extensive modifications or build an application from scratch. Keeping these directions to a minimum is one of our goals, so building from scratch is a better choice.

Approach displays the New dialog box. Be sure the directory is pointing to the proper location. We'll create everything in the C:\APPROACH directory, but you may wish to use a different location. We've selected the dBASE IV format because of its universal support in other applications which we—or coworkers—may wish to use with our data.

The "List files of type" box should show dBASE IV (*.DBF). We'll use the industry-standard dBASE file format for this database. dBASE has a number of benefits. Chief among them is that the format is readable by hundreds of other applications, so if we decide that we need to share our data with other users who are working with different applications, we can do so easily.

In the File name box enter the name of the database. We'll use Customer, so enter **CUSTOMER** (or **customer**—upper and lowercase text are identical to Approach). You don't need to enter the period and DBF; Approach will add them for you. Select OK. If Approach warns you that you already have a Customer database file, select No and change the directory location. You may need to switch to the Windows File Manager to create a new directory for this application, such as C:\APPROACH\CUST.

Approach next presents the Creating New Database dialog box, shown in Figure 22.1, and the Title bar includes the new database name, CUSTOMER. Select the Options button to open the dialog box to its full size.

FIGURE 22.1

The Creating New Database dialog box is used to specify each database field. Be sure to click the Options button to expand the dialog box to its full size.

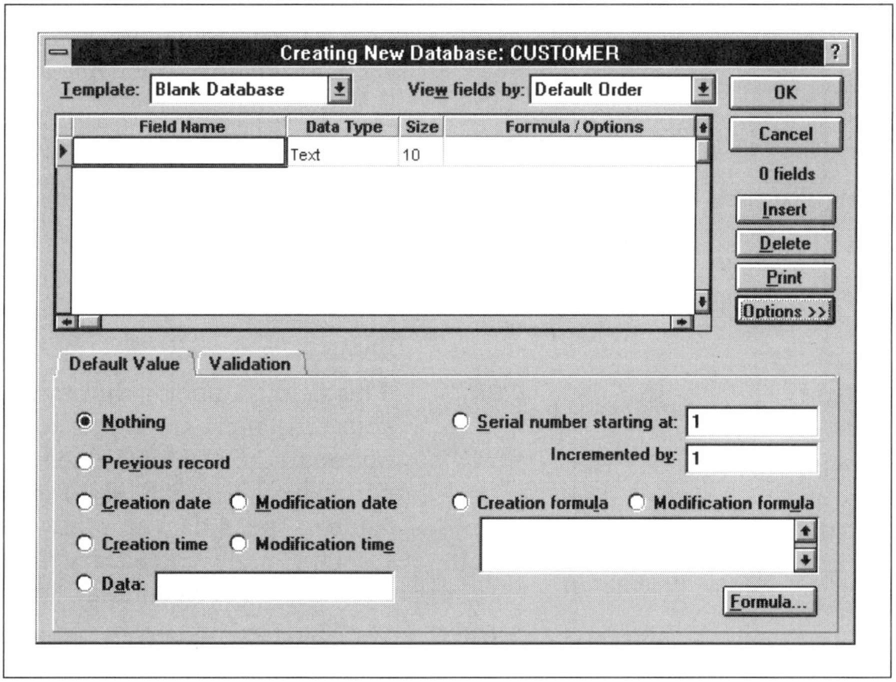

If you are unsure about how to enter data in the Creating New Database dialog box, see Chapter 3. Create the fields as defined in the following list. Note: When the size is displayed as Fixed, it cannot be changed.

Field Name	Data Type	Size	Notes
Customer ID	Numeric	5	Check the "Serial number starting at" option in the Default Value tab. Use 1 for the beginning and incremental values. When you move to another field, Approach displays "Auto-enter Serial" in the Formula/Options column.
Prefix	Text	10	---
First Name	Text	15	---
Last Name	Text	25	---
Company Name	Text	30	---
Address	Text	40	If you need two lines for address, you can change your definition to include Address1 and Address2, then add the Address2 line in the view designs as described in Chapter 23.
City	Text	20	---
State/Province	Text	15	---
Postal Code	Text	10	For U.S. addresses this will contain the zip code. It can accommodate Zip+4 codes (e.g., 98199-0123), but you'll need to add the dash during data entry.
Country	Text	20	This field is optional during data entry. If most of your customers are in one country, use the Data option in the Default Value tab and enter the country, such as U.S.A. We entered this default value to speed data entry. By doing so, Approach displays "Auto-enter Data" in the Formula/Options column.
Office Phone	Numeric	10	You can also enter 10.0 for the size. The .0 refers to the number of digits to the right of the decimal. In a telephone number, there are no fractional parts. The telephone number (123) 456-7890 will be stored internally as 1234567890, but you can use the formatting strings to display the field on a form using the parentheses and dash.

Field Name	Data Type	Size	Notes
Office Ext	Numeric	4	---
Home Phone	Numeric	10	---
Fax Number	Numeric	10	---
E-mail Address	Text	30	If your customers have complex electronic mail addresses (especially on the Internet), you may wish to expand the length of this field; if only a few customers have addresses, you may wish to store this in the Notes field, since the field takes 30 bytes of storage for every customer in your database, a waste of space if only a few customers have such addresses.
Next Contact Date	Date	Fixed	---
Next Contact Begin	Time	Fixed	Beginning time of the appointment.
Next Contact End	Time	Fixed	Ending time of the appointment.
Next Contact Type	Text	1	We must restrict the values to M (for meeting) and T (for telephone call). Choose the Validation tab, check "One of," and enter the value M (in the text area to the right of "One of") and select Add. Enter T in the text area and select Add. Be sure to use an *uppercase* M and T. Approach displays "Value List" in the Formula/Options column.
Next Contact Description	Text	30	Use for a short description of the purpose of the meeting or telephone call.
Referred By	Text	30	---
Notes	Memo	Fixed	---

Field Name	Data Type	Size	Notes
Date Entered	Date	Fixed	Select the Default Value tab and choose Creation Date. Approach displays "Creation Date" in the Formula/Options column.
Date Modified	Date	Fixed	Select the Default Value tab and choose Modification Date. Approach displays "Modification Date" in the Formula/Options column.

The first six fields are shown in Figure 22.2. Notice that Approach shows the number of fields in the database under the Cancel button. If you have created a database exactly as we described, you should have 24 fields.

Select OK to create the database. Approach creates a default data entry form and a worksheet. We'll work with forms and views in the next chapter.

Approach displays the default form on your screen, shown in Figure 22.3. At this point you don't actually have an Approach file until you save your work. Therefore, it's important to use the File ➤ Save Approach File command (or press Ctrl+S). Approach displays the Save Approach File dialog box, suggesting the name CUSTOMER.APR for your file in the same directory as the CUSTOMER.DBF file. Select OK.

Our Customer database contains the customer data related to future contact with our clients (meetings or telephone calls) in the Next Contact Begin, End, and Type fields. We also want to keep track of when we last spoke to or met with a customer. To store this historical data about previous contacts, we need to create a History database. Let's do that now.

▸▸ Creating the History Database

Next we'll create the History database, which stores data about past meetings and telephone calls.

FIGURE 22.2

The Creating New Database dialog box is shown here with the first six fields detailed. The Customer ID field will be filled automatically when a new record is added. The first new record will contain an ID of 1, the second will contain 2, and so on.

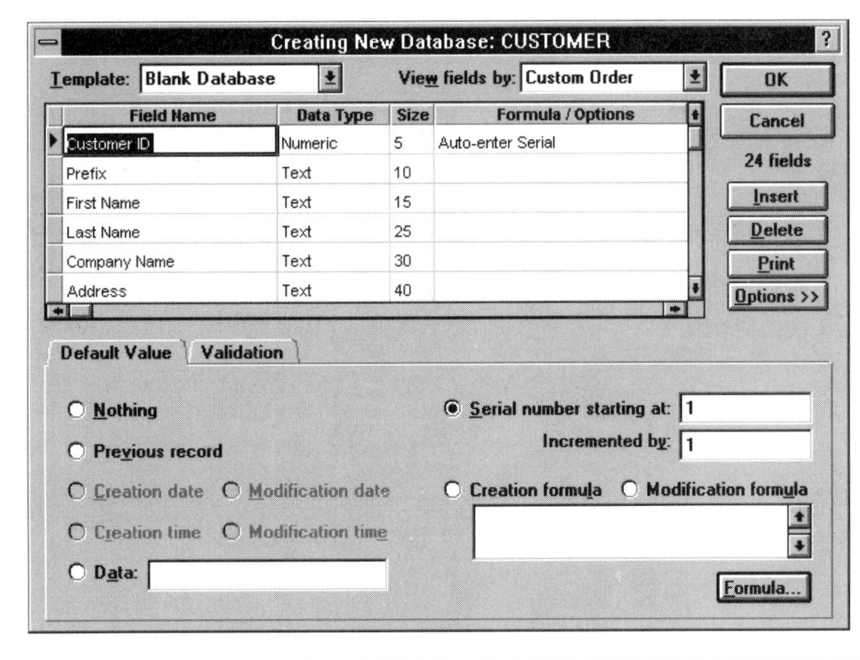

We need the following fields:

Customer ID	This is the join field and its value must be identical to the value in the customer's record in the Customer database to which the events refer.
Event Date	The date the event took place.
Event Begin	The time the event started.
Event End	The time the event ended.
Event Type	The type of event (M for meeting, T for telephone call).
Event Description	A short description of the event.
Event Notes	Free-form text describing the event, what was discussed, what remains to be done and so on.

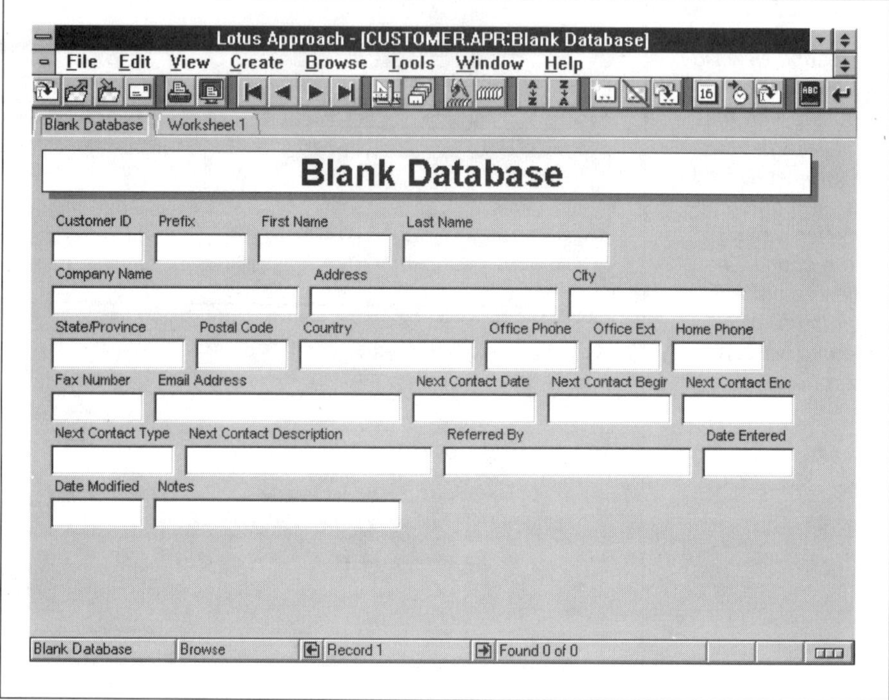

FIGURE 22.3

Approach creates a view with all fields included. We'll work with views in Chapter 23.

The Customer ID is an important field, and should have the same definition as the corresponding Customer ID field in the Customer database.

When you created the Customer database, Approach created two default views and put you in the Browse environment. You saved the Approach file as CUSTOMER.APR. We'll do something slightly different with the History database. We need to create the History database, but we do **not** want to create an Approach file (by default, named HISTORY.APR). The HISTORY.DBF (database file) will be joined to the CUSTOMER.DBF file and used within the CUSTOMER.APR Approach file, which stores all the details of our application: the forms, reports, mailing label layouts, the databases joined together (CUSTOMER.DBF and HISTORY.DBF), and how those databases are joined (using a field called Customer ID in the CUSTOMER.DBF file and a like-named field in the HISTORY.DBF file). Therefore, in creating the History database, we'll skip the step when Approach asks if we want to create a History Approach file.

Select File ➤ New. Approach displays the New dialog box. Enter the name **HISTORY** (in uppercase or lowercase letters or a combination of the two—it doesn't matter) in the File name text box, and select the dBASE IV file type. You will probably want to use the same drive and directory as you did for the CUSTOMER.DBF file. Select OK.

Once again you'll see a Creating New Database dialog box, this time with the name HISTORY in the Title bar. Add the following fields:

Field Name	Data Type	Size	Notes
Customer ID	Numeric	5	There is no need to check the "Serial number starting at" option. We'll use the History database records in a repeating panel. In doing so, Approach will automatically enter the correct value in the Customer ID field.
Event Date	Date	Fixed	---
Event Begin	Time	Fixed	Beginning time of the event (meeting or telephone call).
Event End	Time	Fixed	Ending time of the appointment.
Event Type	Text	1	We must restrict the values to M (for meeting) and T (for telephone call). Choose the Validation tab, check "One of," and enter the value M (in the text area to the right of "One of") and select Add. Enter T in the text area and select Add. Be sure to use an *uppercase* M and T. Approach displays "Value List" in the Formula/Options column.
Event Description	Text	30	Use for a short description of the purpose of the meeting or telephone call.
Event Notes	Memo	Fixed	---

The first six fields in the History database are shown in Figure 22.4. There are seven fields in the database.

Select OK to create the database. Once again Approach will create a default form and a default worksheet.

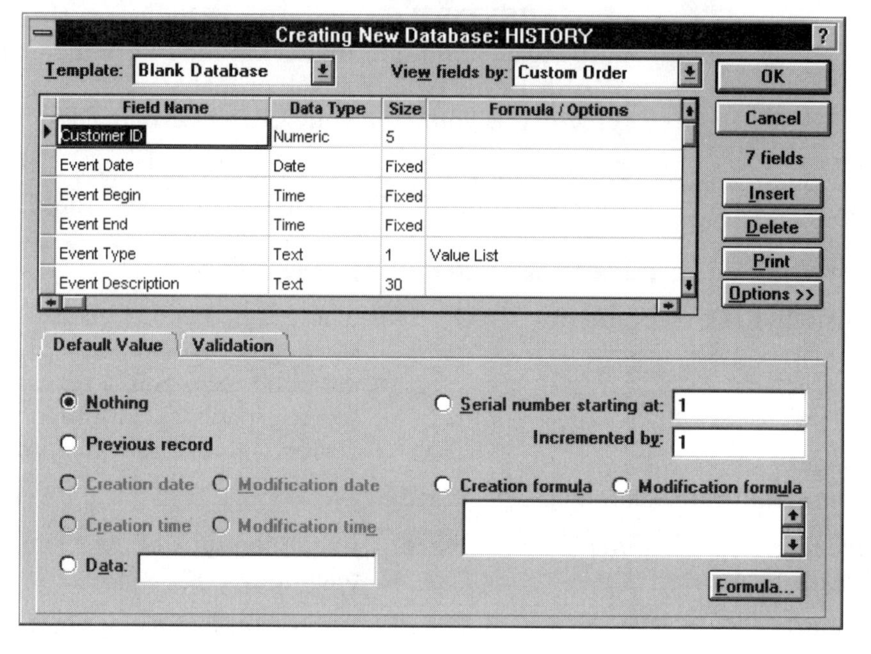

FIGURE 22.4 ▶

The Creating New Database dialog box is shown here with the first six fields detailed for the History database. The Event Type field must be selected from a list of acceptable values, as indicated by the entry in the Formula/Options column.

Select File ➤ Close. Approach will ask you if you want to save the Approach file. Select No. By using the Creating New Database dialog box, you have created the HISTORY.DBF (database file). You don't need the associated Approach file, because you are going to use the History database as part of the Customer Approach file.

Approach returns you to the Customer Approach file and displays the default data entry form.

▸▸ Joining the Databases

Next you'll want to join the Customer and History database. When you do, the Customer ID in the Customer database record will "point to" the history for that customer in the History database by looking for the same Customer ID value in the Customer ID field of the History database. Remember that there may be more than one record in the History database that contains the same Customer ID.

For example, suppose you have a customer from Acme Cement Corporation. You assign the customer a Customer ID number of 8762. There is one record for this customer in the Customer database. Over the course of the next few months you meet with the customer four times. When you look at the History database, you'll find four records for this customer. Each of these four records will contain the value 8762 in the Customer ID field of the History record.

We've named the joined fields the same in both databases, although this is not strictly necessary. However, it tends to reduce confusion if you refer to the same field name in both databases.

To join the databases, select Create ➤ Join. Approach opens the Join dialog box showing the Customer database, the only database it knows about at this point. Select Open and choose the History database. Approach now displays a list of fields from the History database. Click on the Customer ID field in the History database, then click on the Customer ID field in the Customer database. Select Join and Approach draws a line between the two fields, as shown in Figure 22.5. Select OK to close the dialog box and return to the Browse environment.

►► Creating the To-Do List Database

Our work is almost done. Our last job is to create the to-do list database—the database that will keep track of the things that we need to do. These items are not connected to a customer. For example, we may have to review a budget proposal with a colleague, pick up library books, or renew our driver's license. These are all tasks that we want to keep track of, but they are not associated with a particular customer in the Customer database.

The fields we include in the to-do list database are very similar to those we used for customer contact:

Priority	From 1 (high) to 10 (low)
Description	What is the task?
Due date	When is it needed?
Complete Date	When was the task completed?

FIGURE 22.5

The Customer database is known to the Customer Approach file. When you add the History database, you can then join the two databases on the common, or join field. Although the fields are named the same in both databases, this is not necessary in order to create a join.

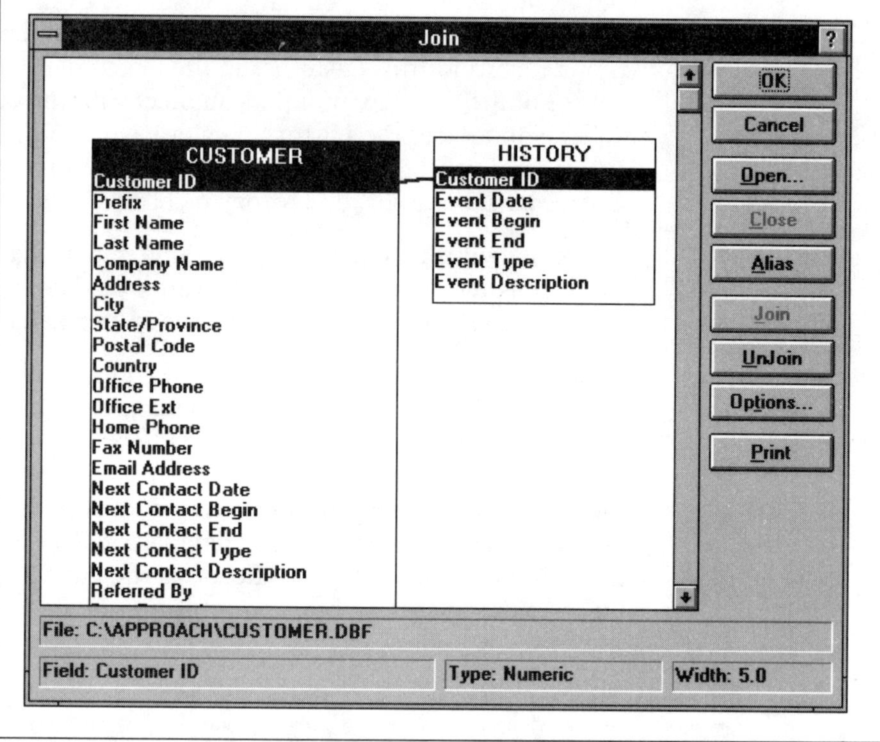

Since to-do items are short, we won't include a memo field for free-form notes.

To create the to-do list database and a to-do list Approach file, which we'll call TODO, we'll first exit the Customer file. Select File ➤ Close. Since we've made changes since the last save, Approach will ask if you want to save them. Select Yes or No as appropriate.

If the Welcome screen is displayed, select Create a new file, chose Blank Database, and select OK. If the Welcome Screen is not shown, select File ➤ New instead.

Approach displays the New dialog box. Enter the name TODO in the File name, and select the dBASE IV file type. You will probably want to use the same drive and directory as you did for the CUSTOMER.DBF file. Select OK.

Once again you'll see a Creating New Database dialog box, this time with the name TODO in the Title bar. Select the Options button, then add the following fields:

Field Name	Data Type	Size	Notes
Priority	Numeric	2	To restrict values from 1 (high) to 10 (low), choose the Validation tab and select the From box. Enter **1** in the first text box to the right and **10** in the second text box. This limits the values from 1 to 10.
Description	Text	30	---
Due date	Date	Fixed	---
Complete date	Date	Fixed	---

Select OK to create the file. Approach creates a default form and worksheet. We'll accept them for now. Select File ➤ Save Approach File, and accept the default name TODO.APR to create an Approach file that includes the form and worksheet definition.

►► Summary and a Look Ahead

In this chapter you've created the databases necessary to track customer names and addresses, a historical record of all previous contacts, and a to-do list database for tracking tasks that must be accomplished that are not directly related to a customer.

In Chapter 23 we'll look at creating forms for these databases.

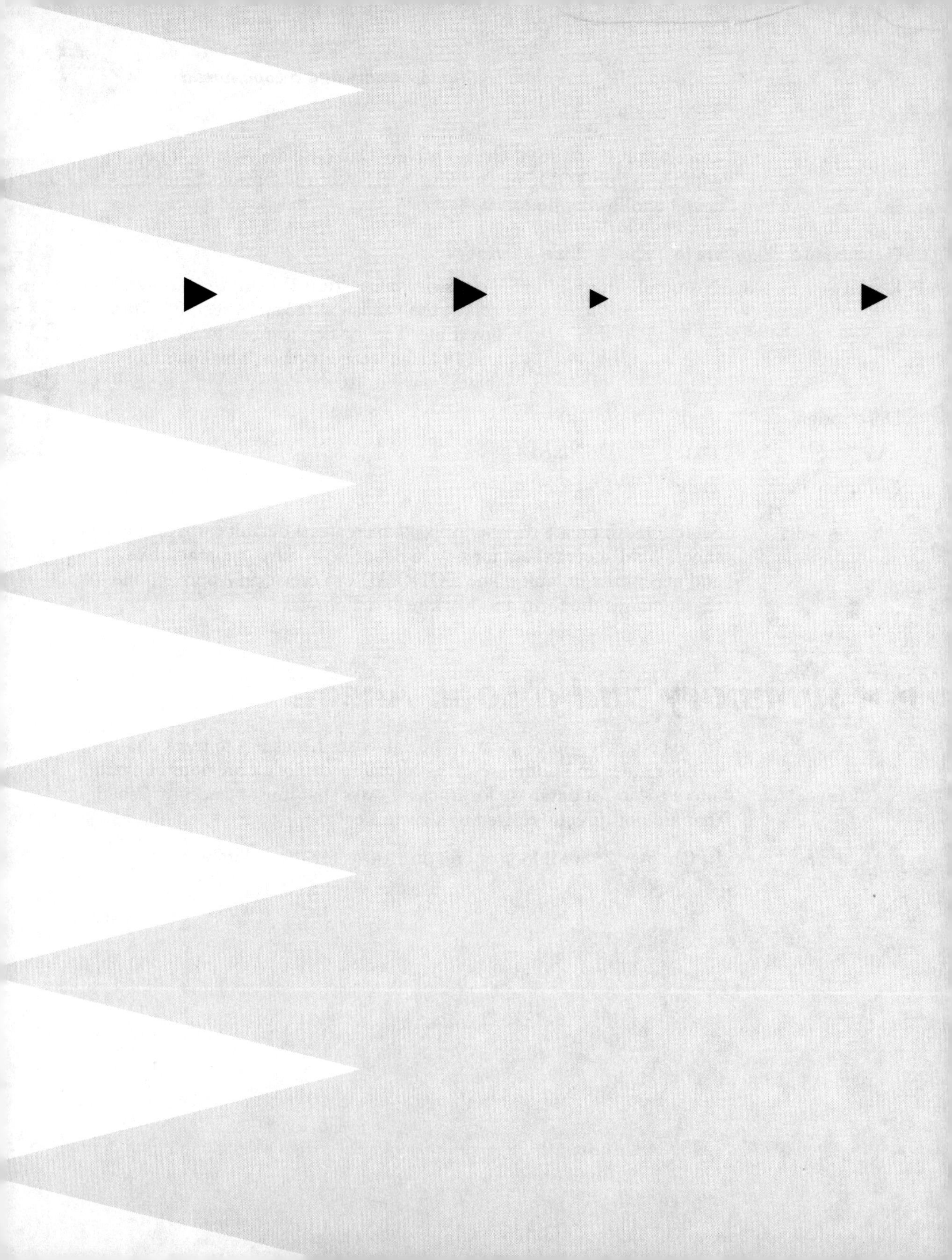

▶ ▶ CHAPTER 23

Building Forms

▸▸ FAST TRACK

▶ *To create the main database form for the customer database* ***698***

switch to the Design environment and select Create ➤ Form. (Switch to the Design environment by selecting the Design icon from the SmartIcons toolbar, select View ➤ Design, or press Ctrl+D). Using the Form Assistant, enter Name and Address in the "View name & title" text box. Select the Default style for the SmartMaster style, and choose the Standard tab to move to the next step. Select the Customer database, then select the Customer ID field and choose Add (or double-click on Customer ID). Make changes to the form's basic properties, then add the rest of the fields.

▶ *To add fields to the form* ***700***

use the Add Field window. If the window is not already displayed, click on the Add Fields icon in the Drawing Tools palette (display the palette by selecting View ➤ Show Drawing Tools or press Ctrl+L), or select Object ➤ Add Field.

▶ *To change label properties* ***701***

double-click on the Prefix field and choose the Label tab. Select the desired position. Change the height by dragging either of the lower square boxes up (or either of the upper square boxes down) to resize the field. To perpetuate your changes to other fields, select the fast format icon from the SmartIcons toolbar (the one that looks like a paintbrush), then click on all fields on the form.

▶▶ **Approach's** default forms offer a great advantage: They're automatically set up and ready to use. Default forms are usually acceptable in a pinch, or for databases with just a few fields. For example, the default forms need only a small modification or two for the to-do list database. However, for our Customer database, we want to create new forms that are easier to use.

In this chapter we'll build several new forms for the Customer application. The forms will include graphical user interface (GUI) elements, graphics, and a repeating panel. We'll show you some tricks for creating attractive forms and provide some hints along the way for creating visually appealing forms.

This chapter looks only at data entry forms. We'll work with the other view types—reports, mailing labels, form letters, worksheets, charts, and crosstabs—in Chapter 24.

Let's start by taking a look at the default form Approach created for us. Open the CUSTOMER.APR file: From the Welcome screen select CUSTOMER.APR from the Open pull-down list, then choose OK. Alternatively, select "an Existing File" from the Open pull-down list and select OK, then choose the CUSTOMER.APR file.

The default form is shown in Figure 23.1. The form was created using the default style when you defined the database in Chapter 22. The default style is a good choice. However, there are many problems with the way the form looks.

For example, there is no balance to the form. The fields simply appear in a seemingly random order. There is some logic (thanks to the order in which we defined the fields): The Prefix, First Name, and Last Name fields appear together. However, the city, state, postal code, and country

FIGURE 23.1

After creating the fields for the Customer database, Approach creates a default data entry form that includes each field, in the order it was defined, top to bottom, left to right.

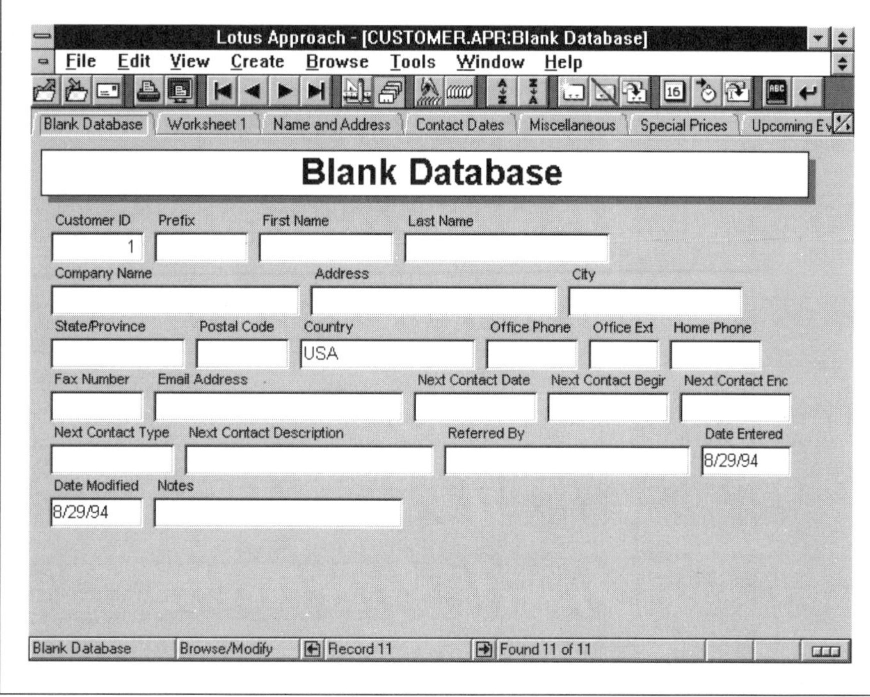

are on different lines. The telephone numbers are split between two lines, as is the next contact data. The Notes field appears small (remember we can use it to store significant amounts of text). Fortunately, the default values we assigned (USA to the Country field, as well as the date entered and modified values) are reflected in this new record.

A better design—and the form we're going to create in this chapter—is shown in Figure 23.2.

It's simpler, in part, because it contains fewer fields. Where are the other fields? They have been placed on two other forms. These other forms are shown in Figures 23.3 and 23.4.

By separating the fields into smaller groups, we keep the user's focus on the important details of the set of fields on the current form. For example, in Figure 23.2 the user need only concentrate on entering name, address, and telephone number data.

FIGURE 23.2

The main screen for entering customer name and address data is uncluttered.

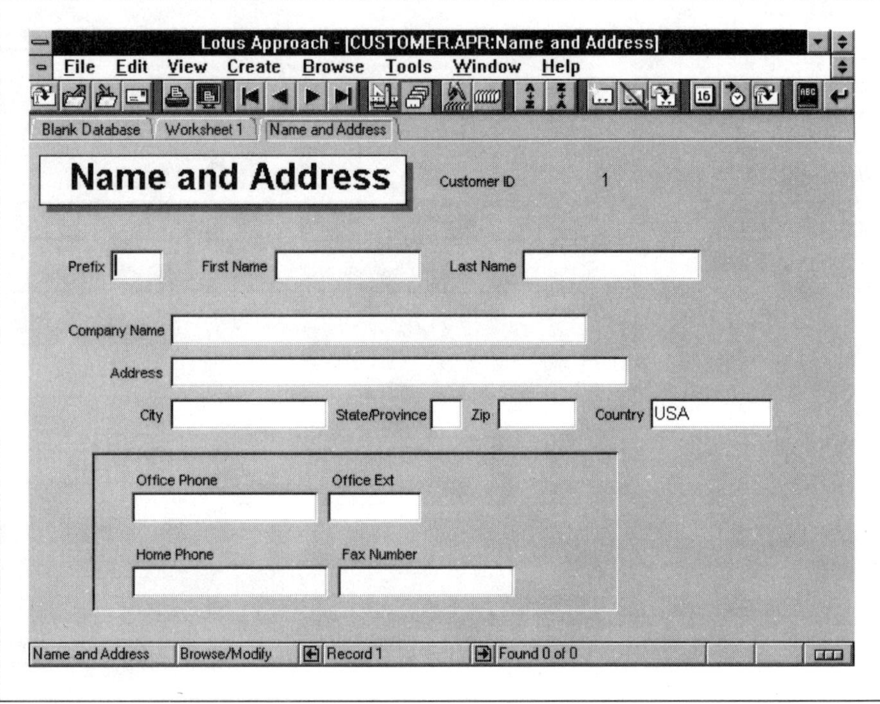

We've also enclosed the telephone numbers in a rectangle, which gives a visual clue that the fields are somehow related. By using fewer fields, placing them in a logical order, and adding graphics clues (such as rectangles), we've improved the usability of the form.

We've placed the fields containing contact data on the form shown in Figure 23.3. This includes the contact data for the next meeting or telephone call as well as the history of previous contacts. The historical data comes from the History database and is presented in a repeating panel. When we use this form in the Browse environment, the repeating panel will display the first three records for the customer. If there are more than three records for the customer, Approach adds scroll bars to the panel, so we can move up and down the list as we like. These scroll bars are added automatically. There is nothing we have to do.

Notice, too, that we've selected alternating colors for the repeating panel. In Figure 23.3 this panel appears with cross-hatching, but when viewed on a color monitor, every other panel uses an alternating color. For example, the first panel might have a light blue background, the

FIGURE 23.3

On the Contact Dates form we'll display all data related to future and past meetings and telephone calls.

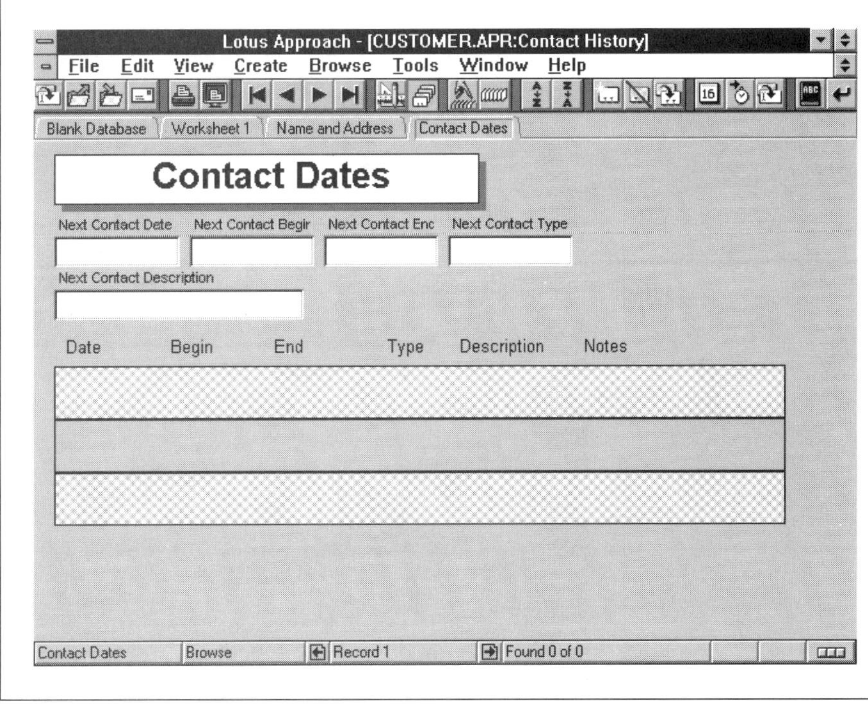

next panel might be gray, the third panel might be light blue again, and so on. We can also control the number of lines (sections) in the repeating panel. We selected three since that provides us with enough room for a two-line Notes field and provides room at the bottom of the screen should we wish to add more fields in the future.

Figure 23.4 shows the miscellaneous fields—those that don't really "fit" anywhere else but fit nicely together under a category we could call "Other."

Approach makes it easy to move between these views. Our original design specified that we were creating this application for your own use, and since you know how to navigate using tabs, the menu at the top of the screen, and the menus in the Status bar, we can quickly jump between the three screens we create. However, we can also place buttons on the form to move us between the different forms more quickly. We'll do just that in Chapter 25 when we explore adding macros to the application.

FIGURE 23.4

On the Miscellaneous form we'll display all the "other" data that doesn't fit on the other forms.

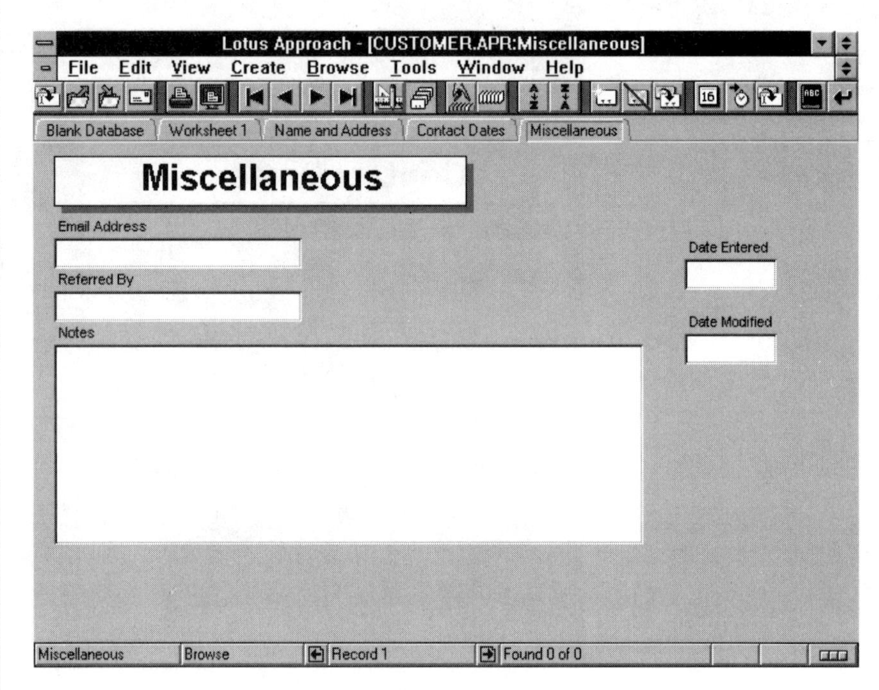

Let's get started. First, we'll create the main Customer view called Name and Address (Figure 23.2). We'll then look at how to create the Contact Dates view (which shows our next appointment and all previous meetings, as shown in Figure 23.3), and finally we'll create the Miscellaneous view (shown in Figure 23.4).

▸▸ Creating the Main Data Entry Form

To create the form shown in Figure 23.2 earlier in this chapter, switch to the Design environment and select Create ➤ Form. (Switch to the Design environment by selecting the Design icon from the SmartIcons toolbar, select View ➤ Design, or press Ctrl+D.)

Approach presents the Form Assistant. Enter **Name and Address** in the "View name & title" text box. Select the Default Style for the SmartMaster style, and choose Standard for the SmartMaster layout. Choose Next or click on the Step 2:Fields tab to move to the next step.

TIP

Whatever SmartMaster style you select for forms, use it consistently on all your forms. It is confusing to users to see screens with different styles. Although variety gives a visual clue to the user about where he or she is, differing formats can be visually jarring and lend a sense of discontinuity to the application.

Select the Customer database, then select the Customer ID field and choose Add (or double-click on Customer ID). This places the Customer ID on the form. Select Done. Approach displays the form with the single field Customer ID on it. This looks quite sparse. We could have used the Form Assistant to place more fields on the form, but it usually turns out that it's easier to place the fields on the form from scratch than to use the Form Assistant and move the fields to the desired position.

Before adding each field, let's make some minor changes to the form as it now stands. Click on the text box containing the form title, Name and Address, and resize it so it is only half as wide as the original, and move the text box to the left side of the screen, as shown in Figure 23.2. Then move the Customer ID field to the right of the Title text box. Change the position of the label of the Customer ID field and change the field color to gray (from white). Your form should now look like Figure 23.5.

Remember that Approach will automatically serialize the Customer ID field. Therefore, while it is useful to display the field on the form, we don't want to be able to change it. Let's change its property to read-only, meaning that Approach can read the value from the database record but will not permit you to change it. Double-click on the field to open the InfoBox. Select the Basics tab. Check the Read-only box.

You'll also want to change some of the field properties to distinguish the Customer ID field from the other fields in which you can enter data. Select the Color tab and choose a green Fill color. Also, change the frame and border colors. Choose the Label tab and choose Left from the "Label position" drop-down list. You may need to change the dimensions of the field to match the dimensions shown in Figure 23.5.

FIGURE 23.5 ▶

So far we've created a form with a text box (Name and Address) and a field (Customer ID).

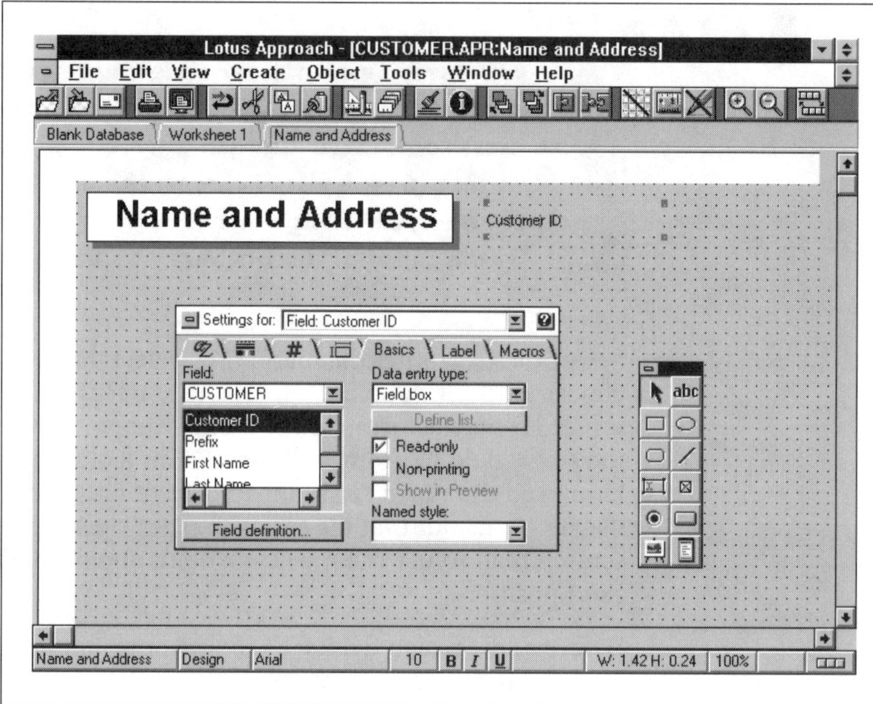

▸▸ Adding Fields

Now let's start adding the rest of the fields, beginning with the company data. To place fields on a form quickly, you can use the Add Fields window. If the window is not already displayed, click on the Add Fields icon in the Drawing Tools palette (display the palette by selecting View ➤ Show Drawing Tools or press Ctrl+L), or select Object ➤ Add Field.

We want to drag the desired field from the Add Field window to the form. It's also helpful to have the grids turned on (select View ➤ Show Grid) and select the Snap to Grid feature to align objects along the grid lines (select View ➤ Snap to Grid or press Ctrl+Y). You can change the grid width by selecting Tools ➤ Preferences and setting the grid units and grid width in the Display options.

Drag the Prefix, First Name, and Last Name fields to one line. Drag the Company name to another line, the Address field to the next line, and the City, State/Province, Postal Code, and Country fields to the next line. Double-click on the Postal Code field to open the InfoBox for the field. Select the Label tab and enter Zip in the Label text field. This is one way to change how labels are displayed. The next section describes other alternatives.

►► Changing Label Positions

By default, Approach has placed the labels above each field's text box. While this is fine for high resolution monitors, it tends to use more space than if we placed the labels to the left of each field. You don't have to change each field via the InfoBox, however. We'll change one field, then copy the formatting to the other fields.

Double-click on the Prefix field and choose the Label tab. Select Left from the Label position drop-down list. Approach changes the field to be twice as high. Change the height by dragging either of the lower square boxes up (or either of the upper square boxes down) to resize the field. Now select the fast format icon from the SmartIcons toolbar (the one that looks like a paintbrush), then click on all fields on the form (from First Name through Country). Notice that, unfortunately, the field heights are also doubled, but you can probably individually change the field more quickly than you can change the location of the field label. You may also take this opportunity to change the field width as appropriate.

You can also align the fields at this time. Notice that in our finished version the Company Name and Address field text boxes are aligned. Sometimes this isn't always as easy as it seems, since Approach aligns a field based on the label as well as the text box. If your text boxes are not precisely aligned, you can enter one or more spaces in the label text (from the InfoBox select label and adjust the Label text field). This "stretches" the label and makes the desired alignment more likely. To get absolute precision, turn off Snap to Grid and use a larger zoom ratio (200%, for example) and drag the field to its precise location. Working with grids is so much easier, however, you may be tempted to leave the Snap to Grid option on and just add spaces to the label text.

It's a good idea to save your design throughout the development process. Now would be a good time to select File ➤ Save Approach File, or press Ctrl+S.

▸▸ Adding GUI Elements

So far our application has several text fields. We need to add some variety, and we'll use well-chosen GUI elements to achieve both variety and enhance data entry accuracy and speed.

Recall that we decided we would use a drop-down list that also allows us to enter new values for the Prefix field. Double-click on the field to open the InfoBox and select the Basics tab. Select "Field box & list" from the drop-down Data entry type list. Choose the "Create list automatically from field data" option. Approach will automatically look through all existing records and add values to the drop-down list as they are added in new records. Once we enter the first record with Mr. in the prefix field, the drop-down menu will automatically show Mr. in the list when we add the second record. If we type Ms. in the Prefix field of the second record, both Mr. and Ms. will appear in the drop-down list when we add the third record. We can pick from the values displayed in this drop-down list, or add yet another value.

Be sure to check the "Show drop-down arrow" box, which adds a down-pointing arrow to the field when we are in the Browse environment, then choose OK. The Prefix field has now been changed to display existing field values and yet permits us to enter new ones as needed.

▸▸ Adding Formatting

Next, it's time to add the telephone number fields. From the Drawing Tools palette select the rectangle and draw a large rectangle underneath the last set of fields (City, State, and so forth). By default the rectangle has a white background and has a 3D look. The latter feature is desirable, but we'll want to make the rectangle gray so the individual telephone number fields stand out. Double-click anywhere in the rectangle, then choose the Color tab and choose the gray square from the Fill color palette. Now drag the four telephone number fields to the rectangle.

If you drag the four telephone number fields (or any other objects, for that matter) to the form and decide you want a surrounding rectangle (or other drawing element, such as a square or circle) added after the fields are already on the form, just add the rectangle in the appropriate area. The rectangle will cover up the fields on the form. Just select the rectangle and choose Object ➤ Arrange ➤ Send to Back. The "hidden" objects will now appear on top of the rectangle.

The telephone number fields (excluding the office extension field) are stored as 10-digit numbers. Unless we change the format string, the numbers will look like 1234567890 when what we want is (123) 456-7890.

To change the format, double-click on any of the telephone number fields. Choose the Format tab, then choose Numeric as the Format type. Choose Telephone for the Current format. Make the same changes for the other two telephone number fields.

Your finished form should look like Figure 23.2 earlier in this chapter, which shows the form in action when adding a new record. Note that your design is slightly different at this point, since it has a drop-down arrow for Prefix. If you want to make changes to this design, do so now. When you're satisfied with the form, select File ➤ Save Approach File or press Ctrl+S.

►► Creating the Contact Dates Form

The Contact Dates view, shown in Figure 23.3 earlier in this chapter, uses a repeating panel to display the historical data. In this case we're going to make use of the Form Assistant, which does a good job of building forms with repeating panels. There will be little we'll do to change the form it creates. Generally, we'll be augmenting the form rather than radically changing it.

To create the form, switch to the Design environment and select Create ➤ Form. (Switch to the Design environment by selecting the Design icon from the SmartIcons toolbar, select View ➤ Design, or press Ctrl+D.)

Approach presents the Form Assistant. Enter **Contact Dates** in the "View name & title" text box. Select the Default Style for the SmartMaster style, and choose Standard with Repeating Panel for the SmartMaster layout. Choose Next.

In the Step 2:Fields tab section we'll select the five Next Contact fields from the Customer database: Next Contact Date, Next Contact Begin, Next Contact End, Next Contact Type, and Next Contact Description. Notice that Approach adds the fields to the "Fields to place on view" list using the database name, a period, and the field name (CUSTOMER.Next Contact Date).

Choose Next to go to the Step 3:Panel tab and define the repeating panel.

Choose the History database name. Include every field except the Customer ID field, then choose Done. If Approach warns you that it could not fit all the fields into the repeating panel, don't panic. Select OK and we'll add the last field in a moment.

Approach puts us in the Design environment. The first thing we have to do is adjust the size of the Text field, the one that contains the words Contact Dates. Make it approximately the same size as the text field on the Name and Address view. See Figure 23.3 earlier in this chapter.

Next let's make it easier to work with the repeating panel by adding some real data to it. Otherwise working with the panel is difficult, if not impossible. We could use the View ➤ Show Data command (to turn this option off) to see just the field names, but with many narrow fields, all we'd see is part of the word History, which wouldn't tell us much.

Switch to the Browse environment. Click at the left side of the first row in the repeating panel. The field displays __/__/__, indicating that a date is required. Enter a date, such as 1/1/95. Press the Tab key.

You'll see __:__:__ __, indicating that a time is desired. This corresponds to the Event Begin time field. Enter a value, such as **13:00:00** (for 1:00 PM). Press the Tab key. You'll see another field with __:__:__.__ for the Event End time. Enter a value, such as **15:00:00** (which is **3:00** PM).

Press Tab again. A small (one character field) is highlighted, corresponding to the event type. Enter M (for meeting). Press Tab and enter **Dummy description** in this field, which corresponds to the Event Description field. Press Tab. If the Notes field was added, enter a dummy note there, too. Otherwise sit tight—we'll add the notes field in a moment.

During the validation set up of the Next fields (in Chapter 22), we specified that the Next Contact Type must contain an M or a T. Therefore, you must enter one of these values in the Next Contact Type field on the form. Notice that because we specified that the value was from a list, Approach has used a drop-down list box for entering the value. This is done for us automatically.

▶ Adjusting the Repeating Panel

Now switch back to the Design environment. We want to change the position of the repeating panel and add the Notes field if necessary.

Click anywhere in the top row of the repeating panel—anywhere a field is not defined. This may take several clicks until you find the right spot. If Approach places small black squares around any field, you have not selected the repeating panel. When Approach places a dark gray border around the first (top) entry in the panel, you've selected the entire repeating panel. The mouse arrow turns into a hand. Grab the mouse and reposition the panel up and a little to the right of its current location.

Now drag the right border of the repeating panel to the right to stretch out the panel (so that the panel fills the entire width of the form), then drag the bottom border to widen each strip of the panel to about double it's original size. Don't worry if it looks as though Approach is only working with the top row. As soon as you release the mouse, the entire panel will be redrawn.

Let's fix two of the fields in the repeating panel. We'll fix the Event Type field first. Click on the M (the Event Type). Approach places square boxes at the corners. On our computer monitor, only the left half of the M shows clearly. Make the field slightly bigger—enough to display the single-character value and a down-pointing arrow for the drop-down list. If the down-pointing arrow is not displayed when you are working in the Browse environment, go back to the Design environment and double-click on the Event Type field to open the InfoBox and from the Basics tab be sure the Data entry type is "Drop-down list." Click on Define list and check the "Show drop-down arrow" box and choose OK. This example shows that even though you've placed a field in a repeating panel you can still use GUI elements (such as drop-down lists, radio buttons, and check boxes) to represent data from a record.

Next, we'll adjust the Description field. Click on the dummy description and drag either of the bottom squares down so that the description occupies both lines within the panel.

Finally, if you need to add the Notes field, select the Event Notes field from the Add Field dialog box and drag it into the top row of the repeating panel. (If the Add Field dialog box is not displayed, select Object ➤ Add Field, or click on the Add Fields tool in the Drawing Tools palette.) Drag the squares so the Notes field occupies the area to the right of Description and uses both lines in the panel area.

▸▸ Adding Titles to the Repeating Panel

As you'll notice, it's easier to understand what's what when you work with actual data, rather than field names. However, Approach does not add text fields as headings for each field in the repeating panel. We'll do that now.

Select the Text icon from the Drawing Tools box and add a text field labeled "Date" over the Event Date column. Enter **Date** in the editing area provided. When you are done, click outside the box to exit text edit mode. Double-click on the text box to open the InfoBox and set the background color to gray (use the Color tab in the InfoBox), choose the first frame style in the Frame drop-down list (a solid black frame), and choose a gray border color. With this field still selected, choose Edit ➤ Copy, then Edit ➤ Paste and drag the copy (which is placed directly over the original) to the right. Click two or three times on the new text box until you switch to edit mode, then change the text in this new text box to **Begin**. Click outside of the box, then click the object again. Repeat the Edit ➤ Paste command until you have headings for all columns, as shown in Figure 23.3 earlier in this chapter.

Since it's a good idea to save your work every few minutes, now is a good time to save what you've done. Select File ➤ Save Approach File or press Ctrl+S.

Switch to the Browse environment. Click anywhere on the description field and enter a new, longer description. Press Tab and enter a note about the appointment. You'll see that both fields use word wrap. Although you can enter only 30 characters for the description, you can enter more text in the Notes field.

►► Setting Properties for the Repeating Panel

Switch back to the Design environment and double-click anywhere in the repeating panel to open the InfoBox, and choose "Repeating Panel" from the "Settings for" drop-down list. Enter the number of lines (on the Basics tab) you want on the form. Depending on your monitor resolution, you may wish to have a large number. We've selected three so that there is still room at the bottom of the form for several buttons, which we will add in Chapter 25 to improve navigation.

From the Basics tab in the InfoBox, choose the Define sort button. Choose the fields from the History database that you want to sort on: Create a sort order with Event Date first, followed by Event Begin. (Use the Ascending option for both fields.) Select OK to return to the InfoBox.

Finally, choose the Color tab and check Alternate fill color. Choose a different fill color (we chose a light blue).

▸▸ Covering Our Tracks—Eliminating the Phony Data

It's time to delete the phony history record, since we've finished using it to successfully design our repeating panel. It doesn't represent "real" data, so we should remove it.

In the Browse environment, select any field and choose Browse ➤ Delete Record, or press Ctrl+Del. Answer Yes when Approach asks you to confirm your deletion. Switch back to the main view (the Name and Address view) and be sure that no record has been created. (One probably has, since creating a new History record forces Approach to add a customer ID number.) Delete this record, too.

▸ The Last Detail: Resetting the Serial Number

We have one more task to complete. Because we added a record and deleted it, we have to reset the next serial number. This is simple, and because we have not entered any actual data, it's harmless. However, if we had already entered data, we would have to use the reserialization macro described in Chapter 16.

To fix the serial number, switch to the Design environment and choose Create ➤ Field Definition. Select the Customer ID field, select the Options button, and enter the new value (that is, 1) in the "Serial number starting at" field. Select OK.

Select File ➤ Save Approach File, or select Ctrl+S.

Whew! Now we've set up two forms: one for name and address and the other for history. Our last task is to create a form for the miscellaneous fields. This is rather simple by comparison.

▸▸ Creating the Miscellaneous Form

The Miscellaneous view, shown in Figure 23.4 earlier in this chapter, displays the fields in our database that haven't been placed on a form already. As with the Contact Dates form, we're going to make use of the Form Assistant, which does a good job of building forms with just a few fields. There will be little we'll do to change the form it creates.

To create the form, switch to the Design environment and select Create ➤ Form. (Switch to the Design environment by selecting the Design icon from the SmartIcons toolbar, select View ➤ Design, or press Ctrl+D.)

Approach presents the Form Assistant. Enter Miscellaneous in the "View name & title" text box. Select the Default style for the SmartMaster style, and choose Columnar for the SmartMaster layout. Choose Next.

Select the fields from the Customer database we haven't put on any form so far: E-mail address, Referred by, and Notes. Also include the Date Entered and Date Modified fields. Select Done.

Approach creates the form. In the Design environment, change the size of the Miscellaneous text box (at the top of the form) to match the size and position of the other forms. Move the two date fields to the right and enlarge the Notes field so there's plenty of room for entering data. Select File ➤ Save Approach File, or select Ctrl+S.

▸▸ Entering Data

In order to bring this design to life, let's enter some data. Switch to the Browse environment and switch to the Name and Address tab. We'll use the Name and Address form to enter data.

Enter the following data in the fields:

Prefix	**Mr.**
First Name	**Adam**
Last Name	**Anderson**
Company	**Anderson Auto Works**
Address	**111 First Avenue**
City	**Seattle**
State	**WA**

Zip	**98000**
Country	This is automatically filled with USA, so no entry is required.
Office Phone	**2065551111**
Office Extension	**123**
Home Phone	**2065551112**
Fax Phone	**2065551113**

Now switch to the Contact Dates form and enter the following:

Next Contact Date	**5/1/95**
Next Contact Begin	**10:00 am**
Next Contact End	**11:00 am**
Next Contact Type	**M**
Next Contact Description	**Check on Auto Part inventory**

Leave the history repeating panel alone, since we don't have any history to record.

We'll leave the Miscellaneous form blank for now.

Notice one thing about the Contact Dates field. Although we know that we're working with Adam Anderson, we don't really have any way to see that fact on this form. We need to add a field that provides the customer name on this form, as well as on the Miscellaneous form.

▸▸ Improving Our Design: Adding a Calculated Field

Switch to the Design environment for the Contact Dates form. Approach saves the data about Adam Anderson automatically. Rather than add two fields (showing first name and last name), let's add a single field that shows both names in one. (We'll ignore the Prefix.) We'll create a calculated field, then place it on the Contact Dates and Miscellaneous forms.

Select Create ➤ Field Definition. Move to the bottom of the Customer database field list. In the first empty line enter **Full Name** and choose the field type "Calculated." Approach automatically expands the Field Definition dialog box with room to enter the formula. Enter the following in the Formula box:

```
Combine(CUSTOMER."First Name", ' ', CUSTOMER."Last Name")
```

You can use the mouse to click on the function name (Combine) and the field names. Be sure to include a space between the two single quotes. When the formula is syntactically correct, the formula flag will be black and the red X through it will be removed.

Select OK to return to the form. Notice that Approach now displays the Add Field dialog box and shows the new field we just defined. Approach assumes that because we have just added a field that we want to place it on the form—which is exactly what we want to do! Drag the field to the right of the Contact Dates text box. Double-click on the field to open the InfoBox. Select the Color tab and turn off all border options. Select gray as a fill color. Note that the Read-only box is checked, since calculated fields can't be changed. Select the Label tab and choose "No label" for the label position.

Click on the field and choose Edit ➤ Copy. Switch to the Miscellaneous form, choose Edit ➤ Paste, and place the same field in approximately the same position on this form.

Switch to the Browse environment and you'll see that Approach automatically calculated the value for our first customer and is displaying it in the new Full Name field. Be sure the Show Data option (from the View menu) is selected.

►► Adding More Data

You can continue to add more records to the database. We added three additional records as noted in the following list. We chose dates for Betsy Blair that are in the past so we can test our Overdue report.

Here are the additional records we added:

Field Name	**Record 2**	**Record 3**	**Record 4**
Prefix	Ms.	Mr.	Mrs.
First Name	Betsy	Clarence	Danielle
Last Name	Blair	Cardman	Davis
Company	Blair Industries	Acme Widgets	Packard Motors
Address	222 Second Avenue	333 Dexter Avenue S.	444 Packard Lane
City	Seattle	Minneapolis	Oakland
State	WA	MN	CA
Zip	98000	55555	94555
Country	USA	USA	USA
Office Phone	2065552221	6125553331	5105554441
Office Extension	123	234	345
Home Phone	2065552222	6125553332	5105554442
Fax Phone	2065552223	6125553333	5105554443
Next Contact Date	2/1/94	3/1/95	4/1/95
Next Contact Begin	10:00	10:00	10:00
Next Contact End	11:00	12:00	14:00
Next Contact Type	M	M	T
Next Contact Description	Discuss new prices	Confirm new ad campaign	Discounts—conference call

►► What About the To-Do List Database Forms?

We haven't forgotten about the to-do list database! The to-do list database is quite simple, so we'll leave the forms as they are for now. We will add new views to this database in Chapter 24. In Chapter 25, we'll also change the forms when we explore how to use macros with the application.

►► Summary and a Look Ahead

In this chapter you've seen how to create the forms needed for the Customer database. You've seen how to create GUI elements on a form, how to build a repeating panel, and how to set up and display a calculated field using a formula.

In Chapter 24 we'll use the data we've just entered to create and test a variety of other views, including a worksheet, a form letter, mailing labels, a crosstab, and a chart.

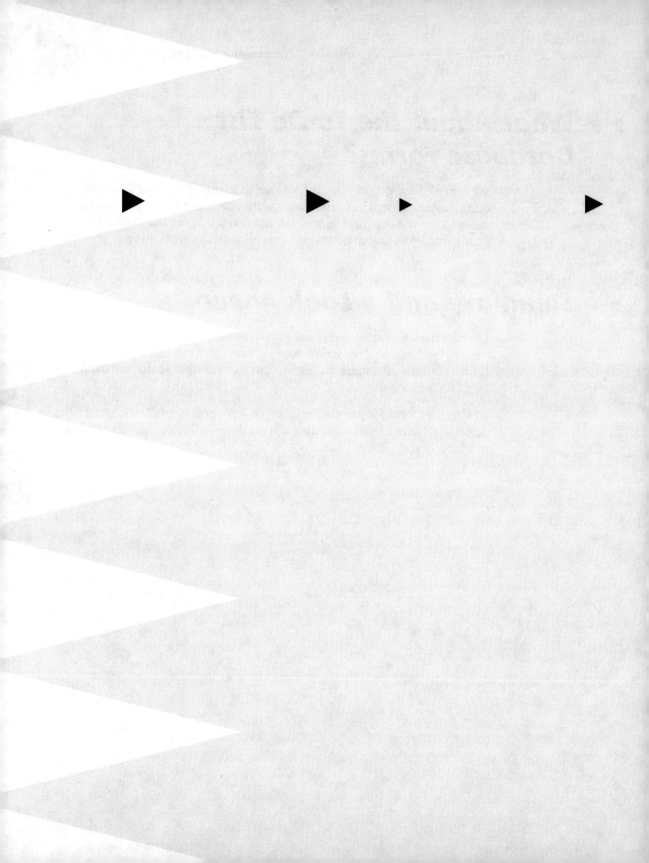

CHAPTER 24

Building Reports

▸▸ FAST TRACK

► *To create form letters* 726

select Create ➤ Form Letter. Using the Form Letter Assistant, enter the form letter name **Special Prices,** choose the Default style for the SmartMaster style, and choose the Modified Block SmartMaster layout. Enter your return address in the Step 2 tab. In the Step 3 tab select the 4-Line address. As each field is selected for a box in the label, Approach fills in the label with the field name. In the Step 4 tab fill in the Salutation, and in the Step 5 tab enter the closing statement. Select Done.

► *To create matching mailing labels* 727

select Create ➤ Mailing Label. Enter **Pricing Labels** in the Mailing label name text field at the top of the dialog box. Choose the 4-Line address layout, and choose the label type (an Avery predefined layout) that matches the labels you have. (If no Avery label format is correct, click on the Options tab and create your own.) Select the same fields you did for the inside address for the form letter and choose OK.

► *To create the To Do worksheet* 728

switch to Design and double-click on the tab and change the name from Worksheet 2 to "List of To Do Items." The worksheet will list all to-do items in the database, completed or not. To select the open items, switch to Browse and select Worksheet ➤ Find and choose Find. In the Complete Date field, enter ~= (a single equal sign) and click on OK to show the records for which there is no entry in the Complete Date field. To find the completed items, open the Find environment and enter **<>** (a less than sign followed by a greater than sign without any spaces between these two characters) and select OK.

▶▶ **In** Chapter 23 you saw how to create several data entry forms. In this chapter we'll examine other types of views. We will create a crosstab and chart to analyze our task list, create a crosstab to see if a mass mailing will be cost effective, and create form letters and mailing labels for our customers.

We'll start by looking at the Customer database. We'll build the following reports:

- A simple report listing our customer's names and addresses.
- A report listing upcoming events.
- A crosstab by zip code to answer the question: Which zip codes give us a postage discount based on volume?
- A form letter announcing new pricing on our products.
- Mailing labels for the form letters.

▶▶ *Creating a Name and Address Report*

The Form Assistant in Approach is particularly helpful in designing reports. In fact, with only minor modifications we'll accept the layout it produces for our next example. Our only job is to select the fields we want on the report. The report we will create is shown in Figure 24.1.

To begin, select Create ➤ Report. Approach displays the Report Assistant. Type **All Customer List** in the "View name & title" text box. Choose the Default style for the SmartMaster style, and choose Standard for the SmartMaster layout. Select Next or the Step 2: Fields tab.

FIGURE 24.1

This report lists our customers' first and last names. We can use this report to look up telephone numbers.

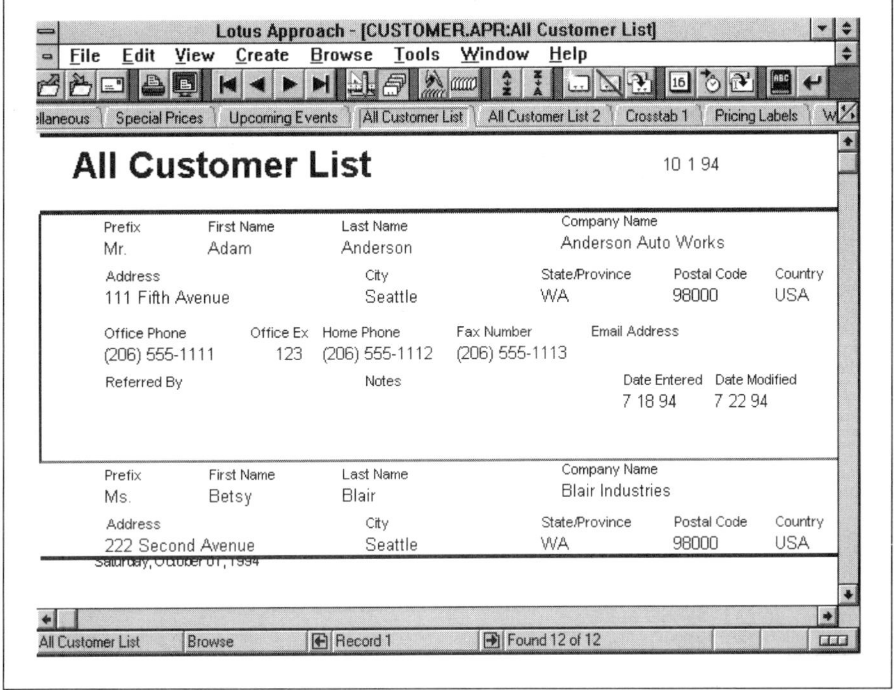

Choose all fields from the Customer database except: Customer ID, the next contact data, and the Full Name field.

Approach goes to work building the report. The resulting layout is shown in Figure 24.2. Approach adds a tab for the report to the existing tabs and uses the report name "All Customer List" as the tab label. You can increase the area each record takes by clicking anywhere within the record (but not on an object, such as a field) so that Approach places a thick border around the record. Drag the bottom border down to increase the area. With a larger area you can begin to rearrange the fields so they are in the desired order. For example, you can move the E-mail address to a separate line and place the City, State/Province, Postal Code, and Country fields on the same line.

You'll certainly want to make one more change: adding a sort order to the report. Because we did not select a summary-style report, the report will list the records in their natural order. The list will be of more use in alphabetical order by the customer's last name. Click on any Last Name field and click on the Sort A-Z icon from the SmartIcons toolbar. (In our database, we already entered the data in last name order, so performing the sort does not change our display. As you add records to the database, however, you'll want to sort your data, so we've included the directions here.)

▸▸ TIP

As an alternative to sorting the report each time it is run, create a report with a leading or trailing summary. Summary reports automatically sort the data. However, when creating summary reports, do not select all the fields you want on the report. Select only one or two for the body of the report, then add the other fields later. If you select all the fields, Approach creates a report that spans screens. You may end up with two or three screens (pages) of data, and you'll spend considerable time dragging fields between screens. It is far easier to use the Report Assistant to create a smaller report and add the fields manually.

You can make some small changes to the report if you like. For example, you can add the report date to the header. Select Report ➤ Insert, then choose Date, or click inside the Header panel, then select Panel ➤ Insert. Drag the field to the desired position within the header area. You'll want to delete the date field from the report footer, which is added by the Report Assistant.

When you switch to the Browse environment for this report, you'll notice that Approach surrounds each record with a blue border. You can edit any record in the Browse environment. To see what the report will look like when it is printed, including any calculated totals (although this report contains none), select the Preview environment. Although you can't edit records in Preview, you will be able to see if records are split between pages. If they are and you wish to prevent this, switch to the Design environment and double-click anywhere on the background of the report to open the InfoBox. Choose the Basics tab and be sure the "Keep records together" box is checked.

FIGURE 24.2

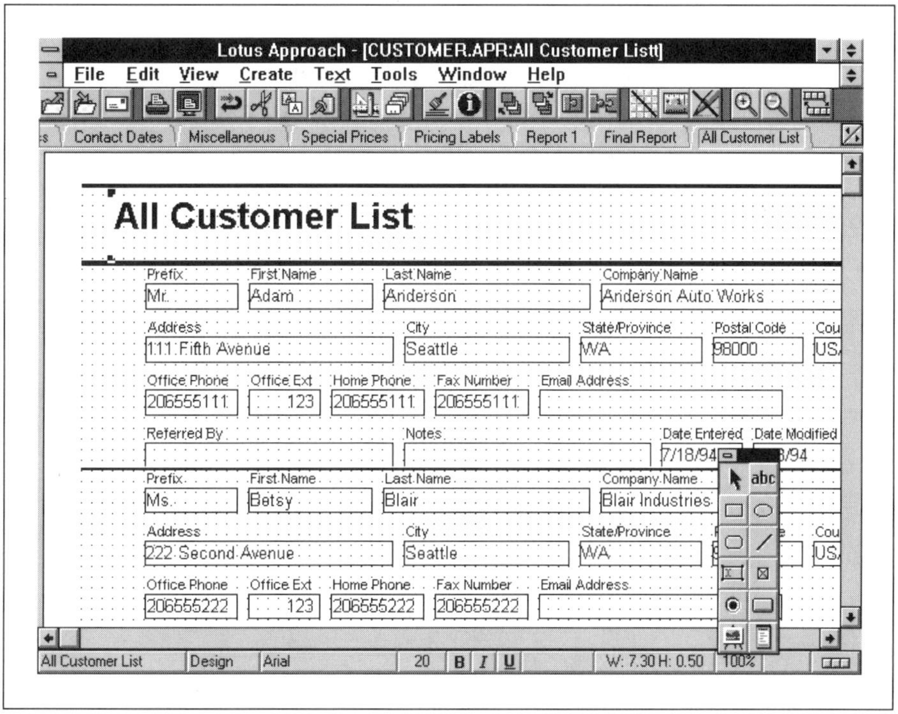

The Name and Address report, as created by the Report Assistant, shown in the Design environment.

Modifying the Name and Address Report

Some field formats should probably be changed to make them easier to read. For example, the telephone number fields show only a numeric value. In the Design environment, double-click on the field to open the InfoBox, choose the format tab, select Numeric from the Format type drop-down list, then choose Telephone from the Current format drop-down list. You can use the Fast Format feature to copy the formatting from one telephone number field to the next, or, with the InfoBox open, select each telephone field and make the identical formatting change. You might need to resize these fields after formatting. Approach also provides a shortcut: Shift+click (hold the Shift key down as you left-click the mouse) on all three telephone number fields and make the change in the InfoBox; the change will apply to all selected objects.

You can also remove the boxes around all the fields on the report quickly. Double-click on any object to open the InfoBox if it is not already open. Select Edit ➤ Select All. The "Settings for" in the InfoBox changes to "Multiple objects." Choose the Color tab and remove the checks from the Border options.

There are, of course, dozens of ways to change this report. You may also want to use the report with a found set. For example, to use the same report—without modification—to list all customers in California, switch to the Browse environment. Perform a Find (click on either of the Find icons from the SmartIcons toolbar, choose Browse ➤ Find, or press Ctrl+F) and enter CA in the State/Province field. Select OK. Approach sifts through the records and displays only those customers in California in the report. You can also perform a Find in another view (such as in a worksheet or a data entry form), and when you switch to the report, Approach uses the found set it already has and builds the report on the records in that set. Found sets are more fully described in Chapter 12.

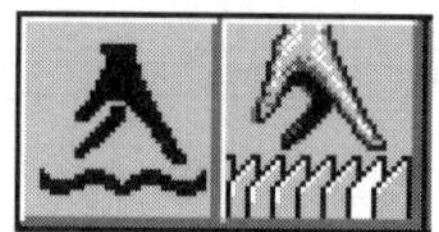

▸▸ Creating a List of Upcoming Events

It's important to know what's coming up, so in this section we'll build a report that lists our upcoming meetings and telephone calls. The report is shown in Figure 24.3.

The key here is to recognize that we'll have to use the Find command before we run the report. That's because we can't "build in" a way to create a found set when we run a report. In Chapter 25 you'll learn how to use a macro to create the found set and run the report, but for now we're only going to build the report.

Start the Report Assistant by selecting Create ➤ Report. Enter the name **Upcoming Events** in the "View name & title" text box, and choose the Default style. Choose the Standard SmartMaster layout.

FIGURE 24.3

The List of Upcoming Events shows us which calls and meetings are in the future.

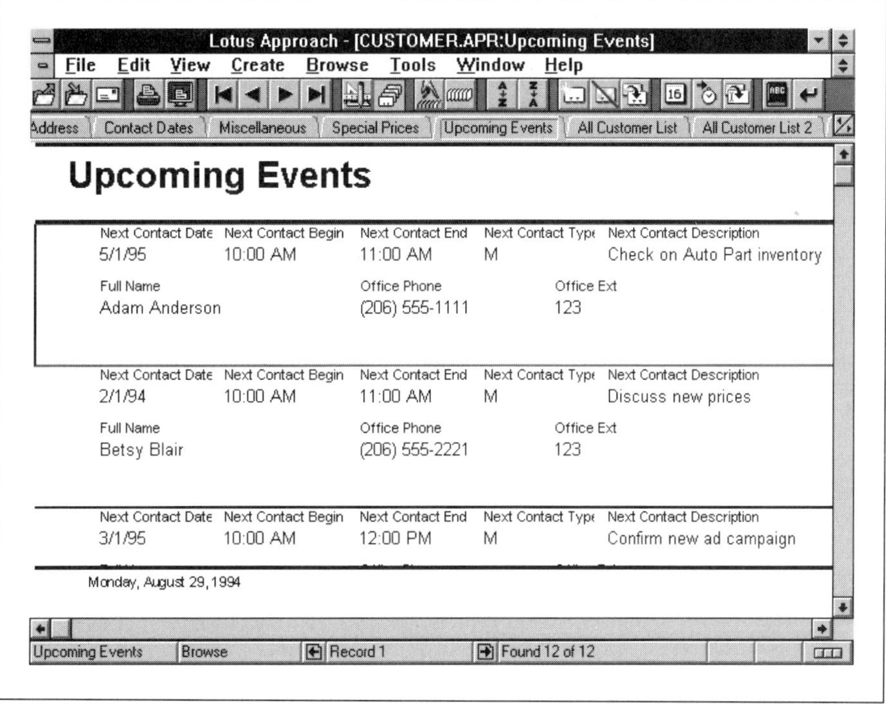

TIP

Whatever SmartMaster style you use for reports, use it consistently on all your reports. As with a consistent style for forms, it is confusing to users to see different styles of reports throughout an application.

Click on the Step 2: Fields tab or choose the Next button. Select the Full Name field, and, if you wish, one or more telephone number fields from the Customer database (Full Name is listed at the bottom of the field list and is in italics, indicating that it is a calculated field). Choose the Next Contact fields from the Customer database: Next Contact Date, Next Contact Begin, Next Contact End, Next Contact Type, and Next Contact Description from the Database fields list. Select Done.

You'll probably want to make some changes to this report. For example, just as when we added the telephone number fields to the Name and Address report, the telephone numbers are shown only as numeric values. In the Design environment, double-click on the field to open the InfoBox, choose the format tab, select Numeric from the Format type drop-down list, then choose Telephone from the Current format drop-down list.

When it's time to run the report, you'll want to list only the events that are in the future, so you'll need to perform a Find on the database. You can click on the Find icon from most views, or switch to the report itself and in the Browse environment choose Browse ➤ Find (or press Ctrl+F). In the Next Contact Date field enter **>= @Today()** and press OK. The Today() function returns the current system date. If you want to know the upcoming events for a different date, such as 7/1/95, enter your find criteria as >= 7/1/95.

Since you did not use a leading or trailing summary layout, you must add a sort to put these records in order by event date and time. Select any Next Contact Date field and click on the Sort A-Z icon from the SmartIcons toolbar. Approach sorts the report instantly.

▸▸ Building a Crosstab

Let's assume for the moment that our customer database has grown to 10,000 records. Our customers are spread across the country. We want to do a mass mailing to all our customers announcing that we are having special pricing on one of our products. In a moment you'll see how to create the form letter and the mailing labels. We know we can obtain special pricing on postage if we mail more than 200 brochures or letters to the same zip code. The question is, will we be able to take advantage of a quantity discount? There are hundreds of zip codes, so we need to know which and how many customers have the same zip code. To answer these questions, we'll build a simple crosstab. We could also build a report to answer the same question, but a crosstab lets us do some further analysis simply and easily. The crosstab we'll build is shown in Figure 24.4.

To begin, select Create ➤ Crosstab. The Crosstab Assistant appears. Step 1 asks for the field we want to place down the left side of the crosstab. In this case, we'll select the Customer database and the Postal

FIGURE 24.4 

A crosstab can tell us which zip codes will qualify for postage discounts.

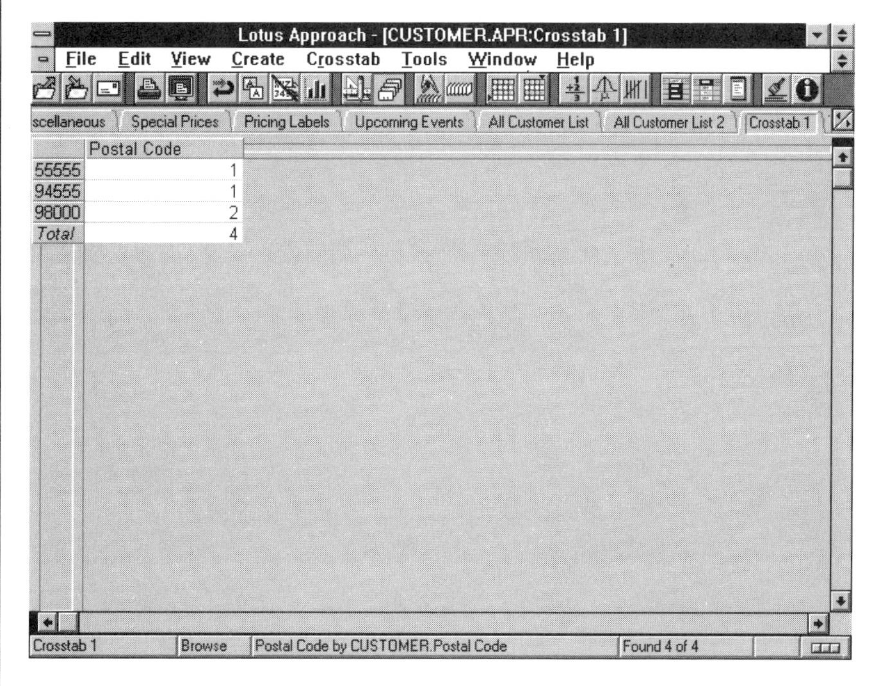

Code field in that database. Double-click on Postal Code, or single-click or highlight it with the arrow key and choose Add. The field name is moved to the "Fields to place on view" list. Click on the Step 2 tab or choose Next.

Unlike most crosstabs, we don't care about the column value. We will only have one value—the number of customers in each zip code, so skip over Step 2 by selecting the Step 3 tab or by clicking Next.

The Step 3 tab asks us to define what we want to summarize. We want to calculate the count (number of items). The field we want to select (to be counted) is from the Customer database. Choose the Postal Code field. When these options have been selected, choose Done.

As you can see from Figure 24.4, we don't have a sufficient number of records to make this report meaningful, at least not yet. However, as our database grows we can use this crosstab to see which zip codes qualify for postage discounts.

▸▸ Creating Form Letters

Let's create the form letter we want to send to our customers. The letter we are going to create is shown in Figure 24.5.

FIGURE 24.5 ▶

Approach's Form Letter Assistant helps create a form letter that is customized to your specific communication needs.

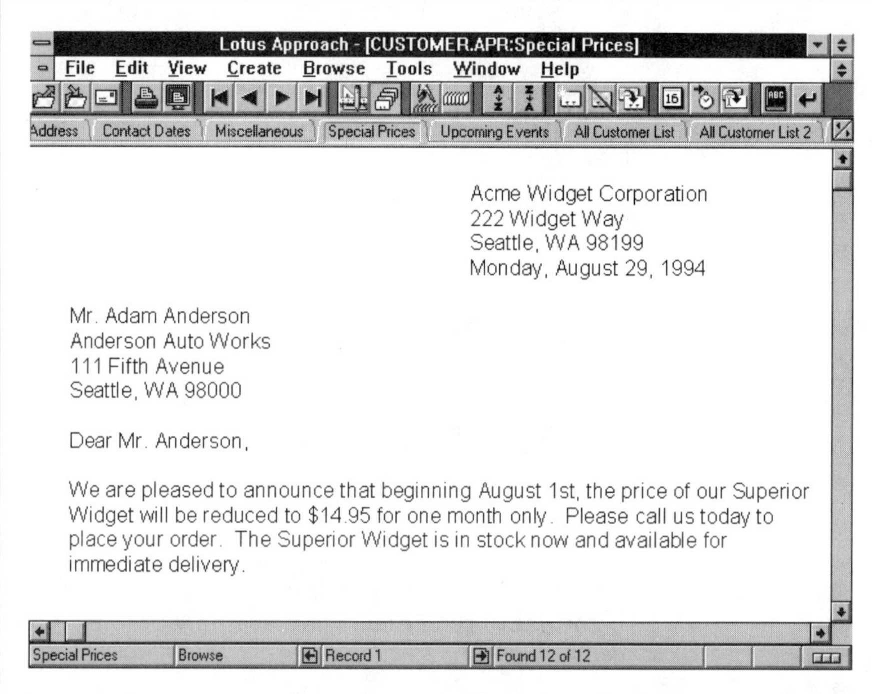

To begin the process, select Create ➤ Form Letter. Approach displays the Form Letter Assistant. From the Step 1 tab enter the form letter name, **Special Prices**. Choose the Default style for the SmartMaster style, and choose the Modified Block SmartMaster layout. Move on to Step 2.

Enter your return address, then move to Step 3. Select the 4-Line address, since we have both a company name and a customer name to include. Move the Prefix field to the first box and the Full Name field to the second box of the first line. (Click the destination [the appropriate square in the label on the right], then either click the database field and choose Add or double-click the database field.) In the second line choose the Company field, and in the third use the Address field. In the last three lines choose the City, State/Province, and Postal Code fields. As each field is selected, Approach fills in the label with the field name.

Move to Step 4. Fill in the Salutation (choose Prefix from the first drop-down list and Last Name from the second drop-down list as the two names you'll use in the salutation, which will read, for example, Dear Ms. Blair,). In Step 5 enter the closing statement. Select Done.

Approach displays the form letter in the Design environment. You can click anywhere within the body of the letter and type the text you want in the body of the letter, such as

```
We are pleased to announce that beginning August
1st, the price of our Superior Widget will be re-
duced to $14.95 for one month only. Please call us
today to place your order. The Superior Widget is
in stock now and available for immediate delivery.
```

You can preview the letter in the Preview environment or print the letter using the File ➤ Print command.

Form letters are more fully discussed in Chapter 13.

►► Create Matching Labels

If you aren't using see-through envelopes (so the address from the form letter appears through a small window in the envelope), you need to create mailing labels. The process for creating labels is similar to that of creating the inside address with form letters.

Select Create ➤ Mailing Label. Enter Pricing Labels in the Mailing label name text field at the top of the dialog box. Choose the 4-Line address layout, and choose the label type (an Avery predefined layout) that matches the labels you have. (If no Avery label format is correct, click on the Options tab and create your own.) Select the same fields you did for the inside address for the form letter and choose OK.

To view the labels with data from each record, select View ➤ Show Data. To print the labels, select File ➤ Print. Mailing labels are more fully discussed in Chapter 13.

▸▸ Making the Most of Form Letters and Mailing Labels

Like reports, we can create a Find and send letters to a selected group of customers. For instance, we can slightly modify the body of the text and then use a Find to choose only the customers in Minnesota, the customers in zip code 98199, or the customers we know we are going to call on (based on our Next Contact Date) next month. You can then switch to the Pricing Labels tab and print the labels for the same set of customers.

▸▸ The To-Do Database

Up to this point, we've focused our attention on the Customer database. For the remainder of this chapter we'll look at the to-do database.

As you'll recall, the to-do database is quite simple: It has only four fields:

Priority	1 (high) to 10 (low)
Description	A 30-character text field for storing a short description
Due Date	The date the to-do task is due
Complete Date	The date the to-do task was finished

We will create four views for the to-do database:

- A worksheet showing all tasks.
- A list of all overdue tasks.
- A crosstab showing all tasks by due date.
- A chart illustrating the results of the crosstab.

In order to make the reports meaningful, let's add some data. Switch to the Browse environment and use the default form or worksheet to enter the following data for three records:

Field	Record 1	Record 2	Record 3
Priority	1	2	3
Description	Mail tax return	Pick up laundry	Plant new shrubs in front yard
Due Date	4/15/95	4/15/95	9/1/95
Complete Date	(Leave blank)	4/12/95	(Leave blank)

►► Creating the To-Do Worksheet

We'll want to list all items in the to-do database. Since there are only four fields, we'll use a worksheet. Fortunately, the default worksheet, created when we created the database, will work just fine. Switch to Design and double-click on the tab and change the name from Worksheet 2 to "List of To Do Items."

The worksheet will list all to-do items in the database, completed or not. To select the open items, switch to Browse and do one of the following:

- Select Worksheet ➤ Find and choose Find.
- Click on the Find icon from the SmartIcons Toolbar.
- Click on the second box in the Status bar and choose Find from the menu that appears.
- Press Ctrl+F.

In the Complete Date field, enter **=** (a single equal sign) and click on OK. We are asking Approach to show the records for which there is no entry in the Complete Date field. To find the completed items, open the Find environment and enter **<>** (a less than sign followed by a greater than sign without any spaces between these two characters) and select OK.

▸▸ Creating the Overdue Task Report

We'd also like to know which of our tasks is overdue—that is, which has a due date in the past and for which the record has no completion date. The report we'll create is shown in Figure 24.6 in the Preview environment. We could easily use the worksheet to do this by switching to the Find environment and entering **<@Today()** in the Due Date field and a criteria (the equal sign) in the Complete Date field (to find "missing" dates) and stop there. As it turns out, we'll use this Find criteria to create a found set, but use a report to print out the results. We prefer to view the found set using the report because of its attractive appearance.

To create the Find, switch to the List of To Do Items worksheet in Browse, select Worksheet ➤ Find ➤ Find, press Ctrl+F, or click on the Find icon in the SmartIcons toolbar. Enter **<@Today()** in the Due Date field and enter = (a single equal sign) in the Complete Date field. Click on OK. Now we have the found set, and we're ready to view this set using a report.

FIGURE 24.6 ▸

The Overdue Task Report shows which tasks have not been completed by the due date. We're running the report against the found set, which includes those records in which the Complete Date is blank.

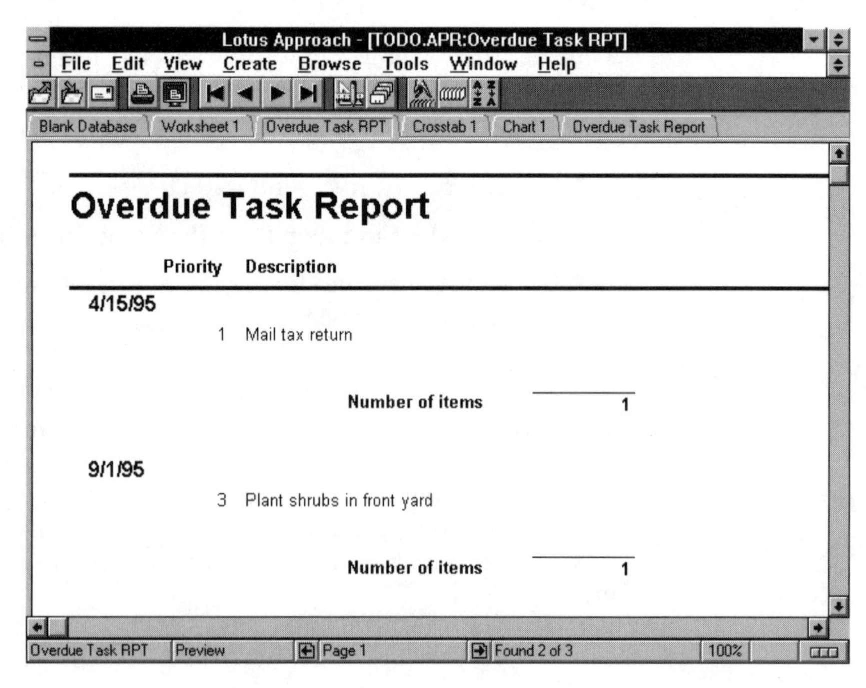

To create the report, select Create ➤ Report. Enter **Overdue Task Report** in the "View name & title" text box. Choose the Default style in the SmartMaster style drop-down list. Choose the Leading Grouped Summary for the SmartMaster layout option. We'll use the trailing summary to total the number of overdue items by date.

Select the Step 2 tab or click on Next to move to the field selection section. Select the Priority and Description fields only, then click Next or choose the Step 3 tab. Check the "Select a field that groups the records" box and click on Due Date.

We want to calculate the count (number of items) per Due Date. Therefore, check the "Calculate the" box and select "count" from the drop-down list that follows. Select the Due Date field in the "of field" list. If you don't select the Due Date field, Approach will not create the summary section, even though you've checked the Calculate option.

Click on Done. Approach creates the report and puts you in the Design environment, shown in Figure 24.7. Remember that since we're working with the found set, not all records from the database are shown in the report, which is what we'd expect.

FIGURE 24.7

The Overdue Task Report in the Design environment.

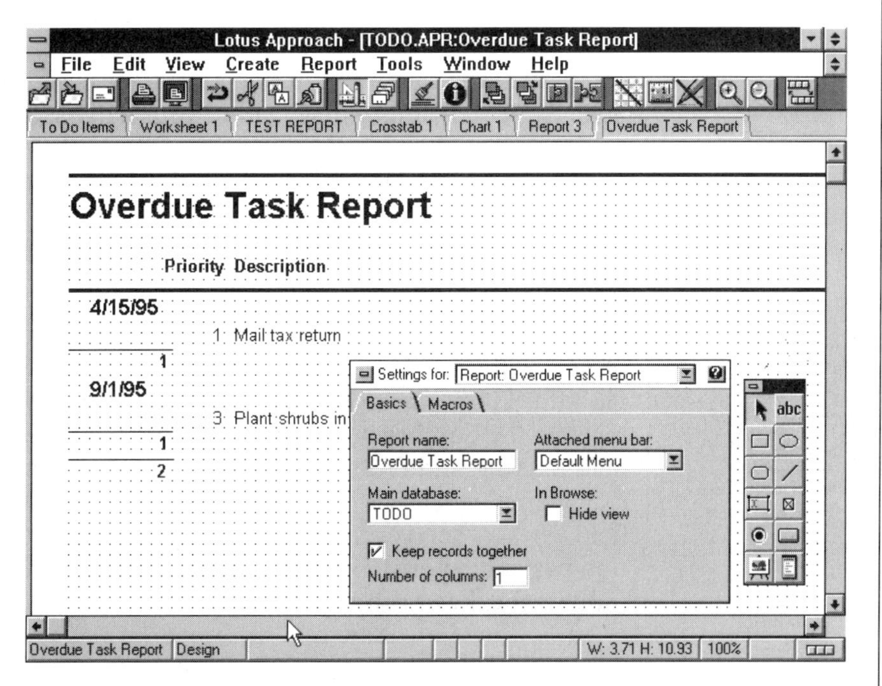

Building Reports ch. 24

Notice that there are two fields with a "1." These are the results of the "number of items" calculation we requested. The "2" is the grand total for the entire report. You can click anywhere to the right of these fields to select the summary panel and change its dimensions. Usually the summary panels are quite narrow, so you can drag the bottom border down to increase the panel's height. To see more clearly what your report areas present, choose View ➤ Show Panel Labels, and Approach places small yellow panel labels on your report. Don't worry, they don't print! Ironically, however, they may cover up fields you'll want to move (such as the calculated fields), so move these fields to the right before turning on the panel labels.

Since we aren't creating a columnar report, turn off the Columns setting. (The Columns setting is used when you need to quickly create subtotals or reposition all other columns on a form when you change the size or position of any column.) Select Report. If the Turn on Columns option has a check mark to its left, the Columns setting is on. If so, select the Turn on Columns option to toggle it off.

▸ New Calculated Fields

When you create a summary panel, Approach will create new summary fields to perform the calculation(s) you requested. For example, because you have asked the program to count items based on the Due Date field, Approach adds a new field to your database, called Auto_Count_of_Due_Date. To examine this field, select View ➤ Field Definition or click on the Field Definition box in the Add Field window.

The formula for the field is SCount("Due Date"). Approach uses the summary function SCount to count the number of items based on the field that is used as a parameter to the function—in this case, the Due Date field. Click on the Define Summary tab and you'll see that Approach will summarize the field on "Summary panels where this field is placed." Thus, placing this field in a summary panel by Due Date summarizes the number of items by the date. You can also include the same field in the grand total panel of the report. Because the summary field is now in a panel that calculates totals for all records and the summary field works wherever it is placed, Approach knows we want the calculation performed on all records. Indeed, that's what we get: a grand total (count) for the entire report.

▶▶ Adding Text to a Report

You can add text to the report. For example, you can add the text "Number of items" to each summary panel (as shown in Figure 24.6 earlier in this chapter). If the drawing tools palette (shown in the lower-right corner of the work area in Figure 24.7 earlier in this chapter) is not displayed, select View ➤ Show Drawing Tools or press Ctrl+L. Next, let's enlarge the trailing summary area (the yellow panel display reads "Trailing summary by Due Date") so we can easily create a new text field in this area. After the field has been created, we can resize the panel to a more reasonable size. Click anywhere there is no object within the trailing summary area to display a border around the area, then drag the bottom border down to enlarge it. Next, select the text tool (the icon with the "ABC" on it) and click and drag an area on the screen in the Trailing Summary By Due Date area. You can create the text field anywhere and drag it to the summary panel area, but it's just as easy to add the field where it's needed.

Inside the text area, type **Number of items:**, then click outside of the box. Click on the arrow tool in the Drawing tools palette and drag the text box to an appropriate position to the left of the subtotal field.

To add the same text to the grand summary panel, click on the text box, select Edit ➤ Copy (or press Ctrl+C), then move the cursor to the grand summary area and select Edit ➤ Paste (or press Ctrl+V). You may wish to eliminate the borders placed around these text fields.

That's all there is to creating the report! However, it must be run on the found set, not on the entire database. There is no way to build in this requirement, but with the use of a macro you can combine the Find command with generating the report. You'll see how to do that in Chapter 25.

You can test your design by switching to the Browse environment. Perform the Find, then examine your report. If no records show as overdue, no records in your database have a date earlier than the current date. Change any (or all) of the Due Dates to dates in the past to see values in the report.

▸▸ Creating the Crosstab

We'll use a crosstab to answer the question: How are the upcoming meetings distributed by priority and date? Which upcoming date has the greatest number of top-priority tasks?

We'd like to know how many tasks we have by priority and date so we can plan our work more efficiently. This calls for a crosstab, and it's simple to create. The crosstab we'll create is shown in Figure 24.8.

First, let's turn off the Find criteria and show all the records. This will make the crosstab results more interesting, since we have such a small sample of data. Select either of the Show All icons from the Smart-Icons toolbar, switch to the Browse environment and select Browse ➤ Show All, or press Ctrl+A. No matter what view we're looking at, we'll have access to all three records, not just the two records that are not complete.

FIGURE 24.8 ▸

This crosstab helps us see how the highest priority tasks are distributed across the calendar.

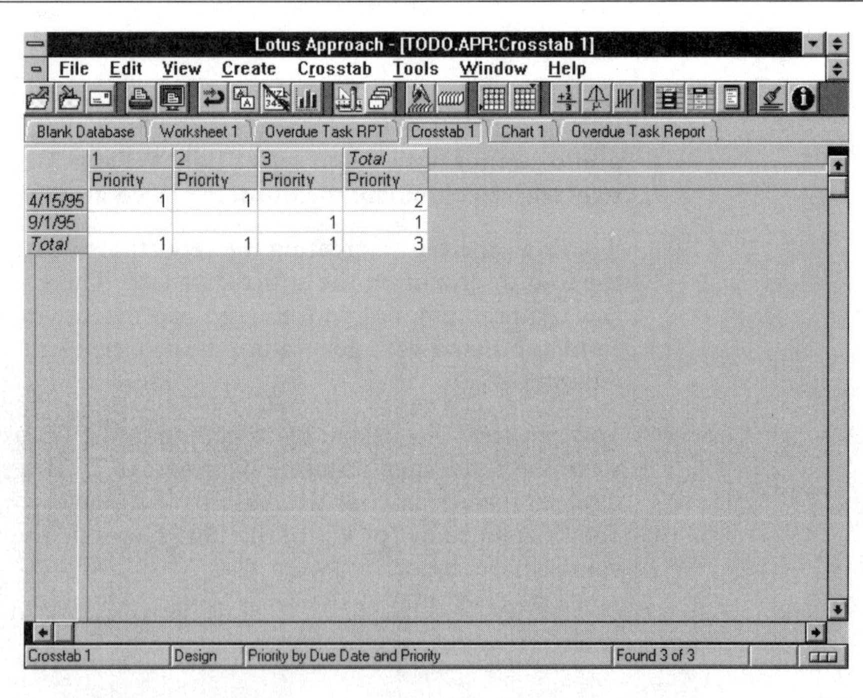

	1 Priority	2 Priority	3 Priority	*Total* Priority
4/15/95	1	1		2
9/1/95			1	1
Total	1	1	1	3

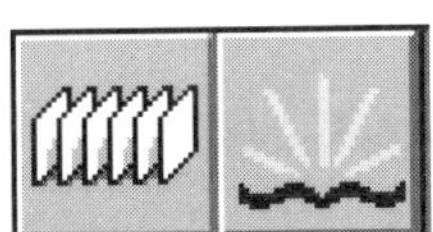

To create the crosstab, select Create ➤ Crosstab, and Approach presents the Crosstab Assistant. In the Step 1 tab we'll select the field whose values we want along the left side of the crosstab. Choose Due Date, then choose the Step 2 tab or select Next. In this section Approach wants to know which field values we want to display across the top of the crosstab. Select Priority, then choose Next or click on the Step 3 tab.

Finally, Approach wants to know what we want in the center of the crosstab. What we need is a count of the number of items for each Due Date/Priority combination. Therefore, select count and choose the Priority field. (In fact, because we are counting items, we could select any of the four fields in the database. Do not, however, select the Auto_Count_of_Due_Date field, which is a calculated field created when we built the Overdue Task report.)

Select Done. Approach creates the crosstab, as shown in Figure 24.8 earlier in this chapter.

To interpret the results, look at the square in the upper-left corner of the crosstab. The 1 there means that there is one Priority #1 task with a due date of 4/15/95. The 1 in the cell to its right means there is one Priority #2 task due on 4/15. The 2 in the far-right column of the first row says there are 2 tasks due 4/15/95.

Likewise, the 1 in the third column of the second row indicates one task with a priority of 3 due on 9/1/95. The 3 in the bottom-right corner of the crosstab says there are 3 records in the entire database, which we know is correct. Blanks in any column mean there are no tasks with the corresponding priority and due date.

►► Charting the Crosstab

The crosstab is helpful, but a chart might make the point more dramatically. Well, OK, with only three records, the chart won't be *that* dramatic.

Charts are, however, sometimes easier to read and interpret than when the same data is presented in a report, crosstab, or worksheet.

It's amazingly easy to create a chart. Click on the Chart Crosstab button from the SmartIcons toolbar or select Crosstab ➤ Chart Crosstab. Approach creates the chart, shown in Figure 24.9, and places you in the Design environment. You may wish to modify the chart at this time, such as changing the y-axis increments to a whole number.

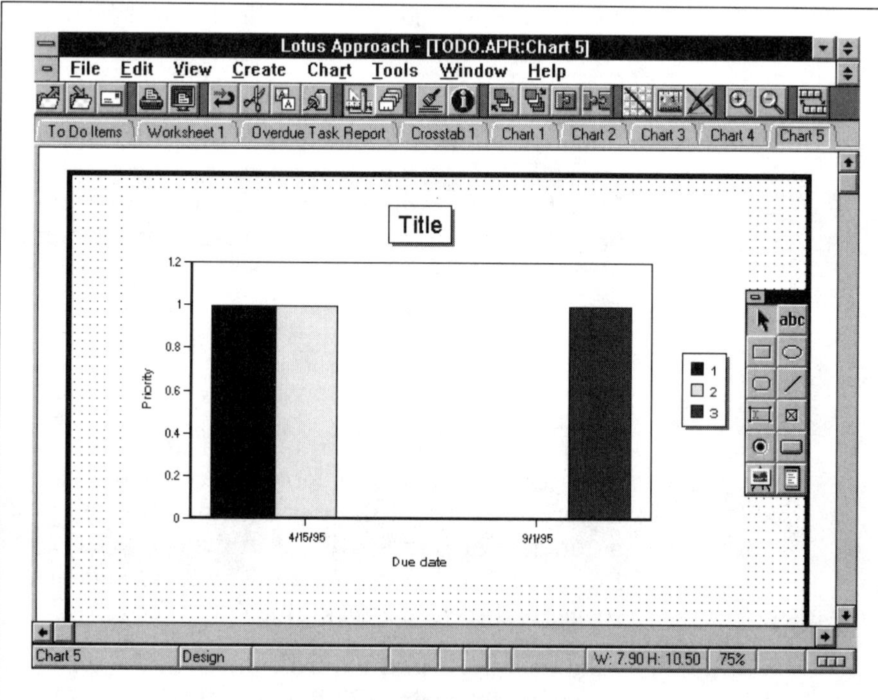

FIGURE 24.9 ▶ *Charts help you quickly understand and evaluate data. This chart was created from the crosstab shown in Figure 24.8.*

▸▸ Summary and a Look Ahead

In this chapter you've seen how to create reports, form letters, mailing labels, crosstabs, and charts. You've seen how to add text and calculated fields to reports.

Chapter 25 takes a look at how to use macros to add a professional touch to your application.

▶ ▶ CHAPTER 25

Adding that Professional Touch with Macros

▸▸ FAST TRACK

To create a button on the Name and Address form and assign it a new macro **743**

switch to the form in the Design environment. Click on the button icon (in the fifth row and the second column) of the Drawing Tools palette, then move the cursor to the form and drag out an area for the button. Double-click the button to open the InfoBox if it does not appear automatically. Click on the Define Macro button and in the Macros dialog box click on New. In the Macro Name text box enter **Switch to Contact Dates**. Choose F4 for the function key shortcut. Enter the macro commands, then click on OK to return to the Macros dialog box, and choose Done to return to the form. At the InfoBox click on the down-pointing arrow in the "On clicked" option and choose the macro just created. Switch to the Basics tab of the InfoBox and enter **F4: Dates in the "Button text" box to change the text on the face of the button.**

To create a macro that opens another Approach file **747**

create a button on the form. Select Define Macro and create a new macro and select a shortcut key if desired. The first command of this new macro should be Open. Select the "Define the file to automatically open when the macro is run" option, then enter the fully qualified (drive and directory) Approach file name, such as C:\APPROACH\TODO.APR, or click on Files and select the file. Select OK, then choose Done. Assign the macro to the button and enter appropriate text for the button's face.

To create a macro that runs a Find before running a report in the To Do Approach file ***749***

switch to the To Do Items view in the Design environment. Display the Drawing Tools palette and drag a button to the form. In the InfoBox click on Define Macro, then choose New. Name the macro, then select Clear All. In the first line of the macro, select the Find command, click on the New Find button, and enter the find criteria. Select OK to return to the Define Macro dialog box and select OK. In the next line select the View command and choose the "Switch the current view to" option. Select the Overdue Task Report from the scrolling list at the bottom of the dialog box. Choose Done. Assign this macro (named Run Overdue Report) to the button placed on the To Do Items form (use the "On clicked" option in the InfoBox), and label the button Run Overdue Report.

To update the historical contact data with a macro ***754***

create a macro that switches to the History fields only view. Save all values from the Next Contact fields in the current Customer record, including the Customer ID number. Issue the Add New Record command. In the new record, store the saved values to the corresponding History fields. Switch back to the original view (the Contact Dates form), then reset the values in the "next contact" fields.

▶▶ **In** building this application, we've encountered some limitations. For example, while we'd like to use the report to show overdue tasks, we have to create a found set first. Our overdue task report, created in Chapter 24, had a leading group summary, which automatically sorts it, but other reports may simply list data and will need to be sorted. That's a lot to remember when we just want to create a seemingly simple report! The answer, as we'll see in this chapter, is to use macros.

We've also seen that navigation is not a problem if the end-user (you, in this case) is working with Approach. However, we can add another GUI element—a button—on many forms to simplify navigation for novice users. Once again, the answer is macros.

In fact, in this chapter we'll add buttons to perform repetitive tasks and navigational duties and create the macros the buttons will run when clicked. We'll add buttons to do the following:

- Jump between the Name and Address, Contact Date, Miscellaneous, and To Do forms
- Automate the creation of the Overdue Tasks report in the To Do Approach file
- Update the next contact data into the History database

Along the way we changed the look of the Name and Address form, opting for a single line for the telephone numbers. That's one of the great things about Approach—it makes prototyping and design changes easy!

▸▸ Creating and Using Macros

As you'll recall from Chapter 16, macros let us specify individual steps to be taken to perform repetitive tasks, such as reserializing a field or performing a find, then a sort, then switching to another view. In a macro you'll need to specify each command to be executed. Each command can be selected from a drop-down menu, and each command has individual options.

Several of the macros we're going to create here are similar. For example, macros to switch between different forms are among the simplest to create, and there are several places where using such macros will benefit the novice user. More complicated macros will be created to perform several tasks. Along the way we'll point out subtle idiosyncrasies of building Approach macros.

There are two ways to build macros: from the Macro dialog box (select Tools ➤ Macros) or from the InfoBox (click on the Macros tab). We will use the second technique throughout this chapter.

Let's start by adding the navigation buttons to the Name and Address form. The final result is shown in Figure 25.1. Open the Customer Approach file, switch to the Name and Address form, and switch to the Design environment. If the Drawing Tools palette is not displayed, select View ➤ Show Drawing Tools or press Ctrl+L. Click on the button icon (in the fifth row and the second column), then move the cursor to the area below the telephone numbers and drag out an area for the button. Approach displays a button labeled "Button." Double-click the button to open the InfoBox if it does not appear automatically. The Macros button is selected.

Click on the Define Macro button and Approach displays the Macros dialog box. We want to create a new macro, so click on New. In the Macro Name text box enter **Switch to Contact Dates**. We can select a function key shortcut at this time. Choose F4.

Since we're already in a view, Approach fills the first command line of our macro with View. This is just what we want to do, but the view we want to switch to is the Contact Dates form. Choose Contact Dates. The completed macro is shown in Figure 25.2.

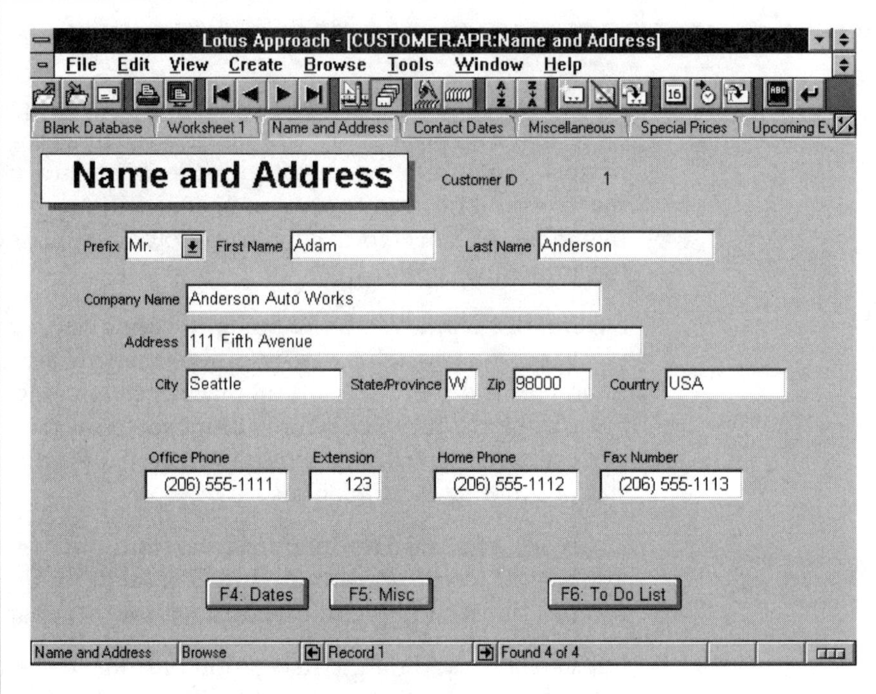

FIGURE 25.1 ►

The Name and Address form with navigation buttons added

Click on OK to return to the Macros dialog box, and choose Done to return to the form. We're back to the InfoBox. Now click on the down-pointing arrow in the "On clicked" option and choose the macro we just created: Switch to Contact Dates.

The button still reads Button, so switch to the Basics tab of the Info-Box and enter **F4: Dates** in the "Button text" box.

Notice that the Non-printing option is checked. This is just what we want. If we choose File ➤ Print to print the form on paper, we don't want the buttons on our output, but we do want to see them when in the Browse environment.

Click anywhere on the form. You may need to change the dimension of the button so that all the text appears.

To test your work, switch to the Browse environment and click on the new button. Approach should move you to the Contact Dates view. If not, select Tools ➤ Macros and select the macro and choose the Edit button and make the changes as needed.

FIGURE 25.2

The completed macro will switch the user to the Contact Dates form when it is assigned to a button. The user can also switch to the Contact Dates form by pressing F4, the shortcut key we defined.

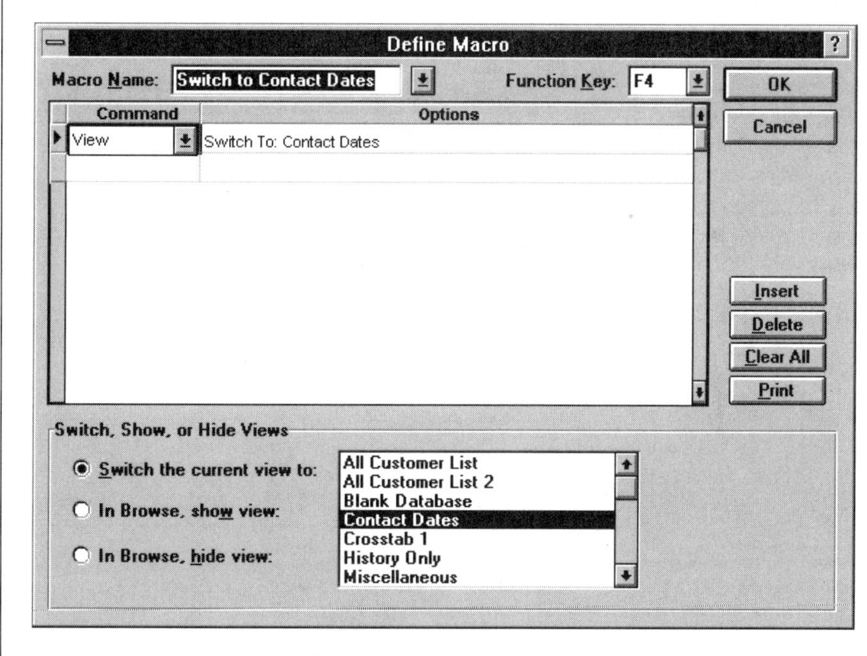

▶▶ Adding Buttons to the Other Forms

In the same fashion, create another button to perform a macro called Switch to Miscellaneous. Place the button to the right of the F4: Dates button. The Switch to Miscellaneous macro should be assigned the shortcut key F5, and your button face should read F5: Misc.

We're going to add buttons to the Contact Dates screen, the end result of which is shown in Figure 25.3. Before you switch to this form, however, select the second button from the Name and Address form and select Edit ➤ Copy, or press Ctrl+C. Switch to the Contact Dates view and select Edit ➤ Paste or press Ctrl+V. This places the button on the Contact Dates form. Drag the button below the repeating panel but don't make it the first button in the row. We're going to put the next button we create as the first button along the bottom of the screen. Create a new button. The button should activate a macro called "Switch to Names" that uses the F3 shortcut key. The button face should read F3: Names.

FIGURE 25.3

The revised Contact Dates screen has several buttons along the bottom of the screen. We've used the bottom of the screen for consistency with the other forms.

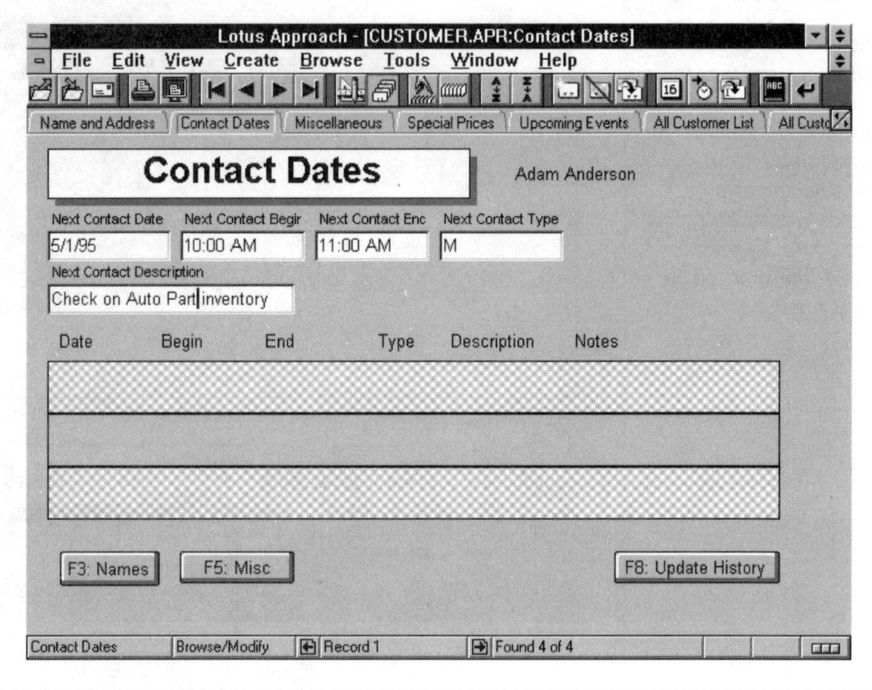

Now we need to create two buttons on the Miscellaneous form. The end result is shown in Figure 25.4.

Here's a shortcut for creating the button: From the Contact Dates form, click on the first button (F3: Names). Press and hold the shift key and click on the F5: Misc button. Now select Edit ➤ Copy or press Ctrl+C. Switch to the Miscellaneous form and select Edit ➤ Paste or press Ctrl+V. The first button, for switching to the Names form, is just fine as is, but we'll have to change the destination of the F5 button. We already have the macro defined to jump to the Contact Dates form. Therefore, click on the F5 button (or double-click on it if the InfoBox is not already displayed). Click on the Macros tab and choose the Switch to Contact for the "On clicked" option. Then select the Basics tab and change the button-face text to **F4: Dates**.

Now all three forms have two buttons to navigate to the other forms.

FIGURE 25.4

The Miscellaneous screen after we added two buttons to the form.

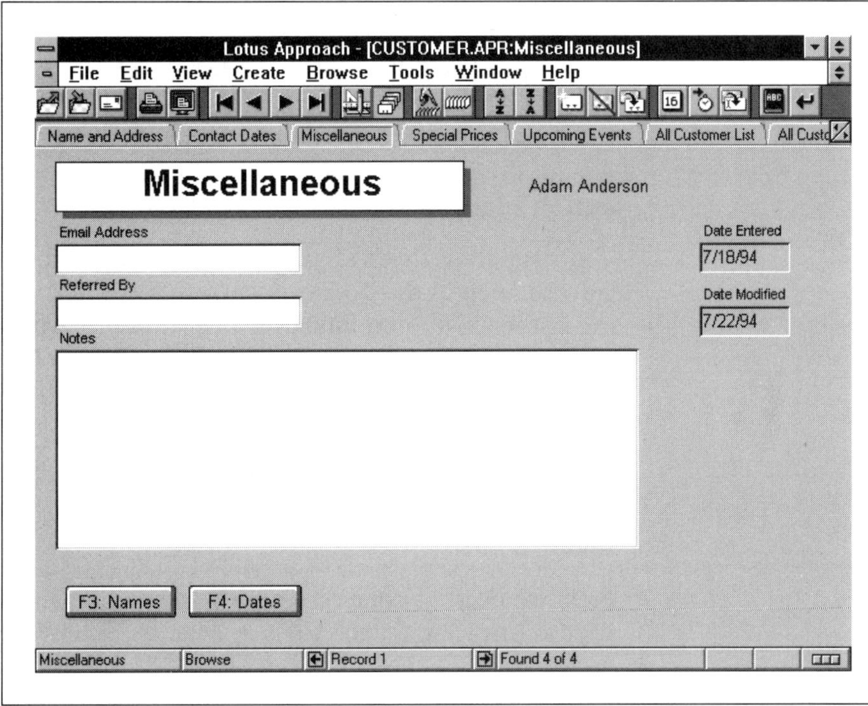

▶▶ Navigating to Other Approach Files

The buttons so far have switched between forms within the same Approach file. However, we also need to add a button to switch to the To Do form. Remember from previous chapters that because the to-do list database does not have any field joined to any of the databases in the Customer Approach file, we used a separate Approach file, called TODO.APR, to store the task data.

Fortunately, macros can open other Approach files. We'll assume, however, that we know the drive and directory of the TODO.APR file, and for convenience we'll assume that both the CUSTOMER.APR and TODO.APR files are in C:\APPROACH. If you used a separate drive or directory for these files, you will need to substitute them in the directions that follow.

Move back to the Name and Address form and drag another blank button to the right of the F5: Misc button. Select Define Macro and create a new macro called Open To Do. Use the shortcut key F6.

The first command of this macro should be Open. Select the "Define the file to automatically open when the macro is run" option, then enter the fully qualified (drive and directory) file name of the TODO.APR file, such as C:\APPROACH\TODO.APR, or click on Files and select the TODO.APR file. Select OK, then choose Done. Assign the macro to the button and enter appropriate text for the button's face, such as **F6: To Do List**.

Unfortunately, that's all this macro can do. You can't specify which view to open in the To Do Approach file, since you are currently working in the Customer database. The solution? We'll have to decide on a view to switch to whenever we open the To Do file. Since the default form, called Blank Database, is suitable, we'll use that.

Open the TODO.APR file, switch to the first tab, and switch to the Design environment. Change the name of the tab to **To Do Items**, and change the text in the heading to **To Do Items**. The form is shown in Figure 25.5.

Next we need to create a simple macro that will always position the user at this view. Select Tools ➤ Macros. Where are the macros we

FIGURE 25.5 ►

Figure 25.5: We've changed the first view (the default view created when we defined the to-do list database). The tab is now called To Do Items, and we've changed the heading on the form. Next we'll define a macro that will force Approach to display this view whenever the TODO.APR file is opened.

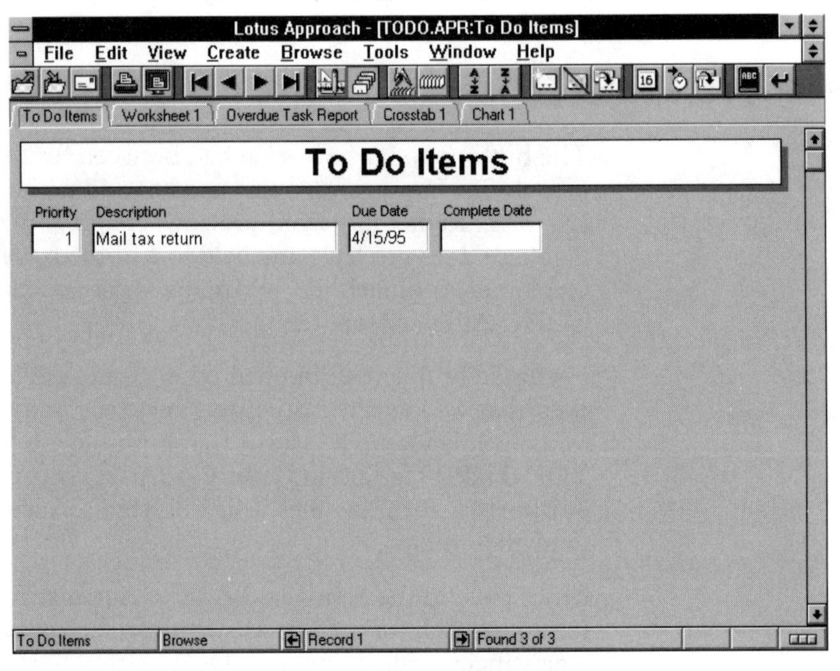

previously defined? Those macros were defined for the CUSTOMER.-APR file. We're currently working with the TODO.APR file. The macros we define here will only be available when we're working with the TODO.APR file.

The name of our special macro is Open. This reserved word is used so that Approach will always run it when TODO.APR is opened. (There is an equivalent reserved macro name, Close, that Approach will run whenever you exit the Approach file.) The first line of the macro should switch the current view to the To Do Items tab, so select the View command and choose the "Switch the current view to" option. Then choose the To Do Items view from the scrollable list at the bottom of the dialog box.

This is not enough, however, because the To Do file may already be open and in the Preview environment. Therefore, add a second line that forces the To Do Items view into Browse. On the second command line select the View command, then choose the "In Browse, show view" option and choose, once again, the To Do Items form. Now we're assured that the form will open to the To Do Items form and be in Browse.

We'll use this macro on other forms within TODO.APR, so use the shortcut key F3. Select OK, then choose Done. Select File ➤ Save Approach File (or press Ctrl+S) to save your work.

To test this macro, switch to another view, then select File ➤ Close. (If the Open macro doesn't work and we select File ➤ Open, we'll be returned to this view, not the To Do List view.) Select File ➤ Open and choose TODO.APR (or choose File ➤ 1, since the first file listed in this drop-down menu should be the name of the file you last used, which is TODO.APR).

If you've defined the macro properly, Approach will open the TODO.APR file and switch to the To Do Items view.

►► Running the Overdue Tasks Report with a Macro

As long as we're working with the To Do Approach file and views, let's update some of the forms here. You've seen how to add buttons to switch to other views, and you can easily add buttons to switch to the Crosstab or the Chart view, so we won't include those directions. As you'll recall, a more complex task is running the Overdue Task Report. We can easily run the report by clicking on the report's tab, but the problem is that we have to remember to create a found set, since we only want the report to show the overdue items, not all items. Of special interest, then, is a macro that can create a found set containing all tasks that are overdue, then switch to the Overdue Task Report to show the results. We'll create that macro now.

Switch to the To Do Items view (if you've moved away from it), then switch to the Design environment. Display the Drawing Tools palette and drag a button to the form. In the InfoBox click on Define Macro, then choose New. Give the new macro the name Run Overdue Report. Approach has filled in the first line in the macro, switching us to the To Do Items view (which is the current view). If there are other lines in the macro, don't worry—we're going to start fresh. We'll get rid of the line and start with a clean slate by pressing Clear All.

Before we proceed, a word about finds and macros is in order. Whenever you begin to define a macro, Approach assumes that the Find command currently in use is desired as part of the macro. If you are defining a macro and wish to use a different Find criteria, switch to the form in which you wish to perform the Find. Select show all records (to start a Find from scratch), then begin to build your macro.

When you create the macro, choose the Find command, select "Perform stored find when macro is run," and click on New Find or Edit Find. Approach will open the current form and is ready for your Find criteria (if you selected Show All Records). If you're working with a found set, Approach will display the current Find criteria (just click on the Edit Find button in the lower portion of the Define Macros dialog box) and Approach will incorporate these criteria in the macro so you don't have to enter them again!

Problems arise if your current form doesn't have the necessary fields for specifying the find criteria: You will have to specify a find using the If( ) function. The If( ) function works, of course, but it isn't as easy to use as filling in the find criteria in the proper form.

In the first line, select the Find command. As just noted, Approach opens the current form in the Find environment when you select "Perform stored find when macro is run" and then click on New Find or

Edit Find. Fortunately, this form has the field(s) we want to use in the Find specification. However, if the form were missing either the Due Date or the Complete Date fields, we'd have to select another form or be prepared to write an If( ) statement in any field on the current form.

Since what we want to find is easy to enter in the Find environment, choose the "Perform stored find when macro is run" option. Since all records were shown before we started to build the macro, we must build the Find from scratch. (If we'd used the form to define a find before defining the macro, Approach would have remembered the Find criteria and let us edit them.)

Click on the New Find button and we're ready to enter the criteria. Remember that the overdue report needs to list the tasks with a due date that is earlier than today (the system date) and the task record must not have a value in the field where we store the date the task was completed. Therefore, enter **<@Today()** in the Due Date field (to find all values earlier than the current system date) and enter = (a single equal sign) in the Complete Date field to find all records in which this field is blank. Because we have specified two conditions in the Find environment, Approach will find records that meet both criteria—that is, the Due Date has passed and the task is not complete.

You may need to use a different date as the criteria in the Due Date field (such as 9/5/95) so that records are found. The due dates used in our original data were in April and September 1995, and if you are running this application earlier than September 1995 (the latest date in our database), your Find will not locate any records.

Select OK to return to the Define Macro dialog box and select OK. In the next line select the View command and choose the "Switch the current view to" option. Select the Overdue Task Report from the scrolling list at the bottom of the dialog box. Then choose Done. Assign this macro (which we named Run Overdue Report) to the button you placed on the To Do Items form (use the "on clicked" option in the InfoBox), and label the button Run Overdue Report.

Test your work by switching to the Browse environment and clicking on the button. (If you did not switch to the Browse environment but were in the Preview environment, the macro leaves you in Preview when viewing the report.)

Notice that Approach leaves you in the report. That's a good start, but what we really want to do is provide our users with a way to get back to where they started. We've got more work to do.

Remember the Open macro we used to move to the To Do Items form when we opened the Approach file? We needed the Open macro because when we switch from the Customer Approach file, we want to always view the To Do Items form. We can use the Open macro, with a slight modification, and place it on a button on the Overdue Task Report.

While you are still viewing the report, switch to the Design environment and add a button to the report view. Yes, you can actually add a button to a report! We'll make sure it doesn't print when we print the report, but it is available to help us navigate through the To Do forms. Place the button in the header, and be sure the Non-printing option is selected in the Basics tab of the InfoBox. Assign the Open macro to this button (click on the Macros tab in the InfoBox and assign Open to the "on clicked" option). Change the text on the button face to **To Do Items**.

Test the design by clicking on the button. As we noted in Chapter 24, if there are no records showing as overdue, it's because no records in the database have a date earlier than the current date. Change any (or all) of the Due Dates to dates in the past to see values in the report.

Click on the Run Overdue Report button in the To Do Items view and you'll jump to the report. Click the To Do Items button on the report and you'll jump back to the To Do Items view. There's a problem, however, with this work. Notice now that when you return to the To Do Items view, the Status bar shows you are working with a found set. (The words "Found x of 3" will appear, where "x" will be 1 or 2, depending on your data.) Therefore, the Open macro as it stands is not what we need. We really want a way to remove the found set (that is, show all records).

In order to do this, we could create a rather complex macro and place it on a button on the report. That macro could first run the Open macro, then run a macro that removes the found set (that is, shows all records). That's not only a lot of work, but a lot of macros to keep track of. Instead, we'll modify the Open macro to show all records once it displays the form.

Remember that the Open macro runs whenever we open the TODO.APR file, so any commands we add to the Open macro to accommodate jumping from the Overdue Task Report back to the To Do Items screen will also be run when we open the TODO.APR file. Fortunately, there is no problem adding a Show All command to the Open command. When we open an Approach file, all records are shown by default. Adding the Show All command when we open TODO.APR may slow the system down slightly, but it's simply a redundant command and does no harm.

By adding the Show All command to the Open macro, we can use the Open macro in two places within our application: when opening the file (by jumping from the Customer Approach file) and when jumping to the To Do Items list from the Overdue Tasks report. This is more efficient than creating separate macros for each task.

To edit the Open macro, select Tools ➤ Macros, select the Open macro and choose Edit. On the second line, add the command Find, and choose the "Show All records" option at the bottom of the dialog box. Choose OK to save the macro, and choose Done to return to the work area.

Now our Open macro does just what we want. Our work with the To Do Approach file is almost complete.

►► Jumping Back

We placed a macro on the Name and Address view to jump to the To Do Approach file, so now we need a way to jump back to the Name and Address view of the Customer Approach file. That's easy! It's just like what we did to create the Jump button in the Name and Address form in the Customer Approach file: Just add a macro that opens the CUSTOMER.APR file. In the To Do List form, add a button, define a macro called Open Customer, and assign a shortcut key if you wish. The first (and only) command of this macro will be Open. Select the "Define the file to automatically open when the macro is run" option, then enter the fully qualified (drive and directory) file name of the CUSTOMER.APR file, such as C:\APPROACH\CUSTOMER.APR. Click OK, then choose Done to return to the InfoBox. Assign the new macro to the button and change the text on the button's face.

Now the To Do List screen has two buttons: one to run the Overdue Report (including running the proper Find), and another to return (jump) to the Customer file. Approach knows that if the CUSTOMER.APR file is already open, it does not need to open another copy. Instead, Approach will return to the open copy and place you at the exact spot where you were before switching to the TODO file.

▸▸ Updating Contact History

The final macro we'll write in this chapter will transfer the Next Contact data into the History database. At some point we'll have attended the meeting or had the telephone conversation noted in the Next Contact fields: the next contact date, begin and end times, and so on. At the point at which this contact has been made, we want to add the data from the Next Contact fields to the History database by clicking on a button and updating the Next Contact fields with new values. In this example we'll assume that we want to keep in contact with our customers by telephone every 30 days.

While the concept is simple, we run into several problems and limitations with Approach. Therefore, the macro we're going to create in this section is more complicated than those created earlier. The limitation has to do with how Approach can add a new record.

In order to add a record to the History database, we'll have to have a form that includes only the fields from the History database. We cannot use the Contact Dates view because it is driven (controlled) by the Customer database. To confirm this, switch to Design, double-click on the form, and select the Form: Contact Dates option from the "Settings for" drop-down list if it is not shown. Notice the Main database setting is CUSTOMER. (For more information about how main and detail databases work, see Chapter 6.)

Why can't we use a form that uses Customer as the main database? Because when we issue the Add New Record command in a macro, Approach will look at which database is the main database and assume we want to add the record to that database. In that case, if we were to use the Contact Dates form and issue an Add New Record command, Approach would think we wanted to add a new record to the Customer database (the main database for the Contact Dates form), when in fact, we want to add a record to the History database. The way to ensure that we add a record to the right database (in our example, the History database) is to create a screen that is driven by the History database. Thus, we need a new form whose main database option points to History.

Why not change the Contact Dates screen to use History as its main database? Although the Customer ID field drives both databases, we know we'll always have a record in the Customer database, but the History database may contain no records for that customer. (Recall that in a one-to-many relationship the "many" side—History in this case—may contain no records for the "one" side record.)

An example will help illustrate the point. Suppose Customer #2 has no history records associated with it. If we display the record for Customer #2 in the Name and Address view, we'll see Customer #2's name, address, and other data. However, when we move to the Contact Dates screen that we've modified to be driven by the History database, Approach comes up empty-handed. Here's why: Since History is the *detail* database for the Contact Dates screen, Approach looks for records in the History database that match the joined value of the current record. The current record's value in the joined field (the Customer ID number) is 2, so Approach looks for records in the History database with a value of 2 in its Customer ID field. However, there are no records in the History database for Customer #2. Approach wants to display something, so it looks for a customer that *does* have historical data. This may, unfortunately, be Customer #1, or Customer #879. Whatever the customer number, it's not Customer #2, so we've jumped from Customer #2 on the Name and Address screen to viewing historical data for a *different* customer on the Contact Dates screen. Talk about confusing!

The solution: Instead of changing the Contact Dates screen, we'll create a screen with only History fields on it. We'll hide the view, too, since its only use is in the macro.

►► The Catch-22 of Adding History Records

Here's an outline of what we want to do in the macro:

1. Switch to the History-fields-only view.
2. Add a new record.
3. Switch back to the original view.
4. Reset the values in the Next Contact fields.

That's the high-level or conceptual view of what we want to do. However, there's yet another challenge! Suppose in Step 1 we're working with Customer ID 4. In Step 2 we want to add a new record, and we must tell Approach the values for each field in the new History record. What value shall we place in the Customer ID field of the new History record? Why, the number 4 of course, since that's the value of the current Customer and is the value in the Customer ID field of the current Customer record. We want to add a History record for the same customer, naturally.

Unfortunately, once we tell Approach to add a new record to the History database, Approach erases from its memory the Customer ID number, because it expects you to enter a new one for the new record. (It has no way of knowing that we want to add a *new* record for the *same* customer.) Since the Customer ID number is the joined field, and by issuing the Add New Record command Approach has wiped out that Customer ID number from its memory (it's waiting for you to tell it the new number), Approach loses track of the current record it was looking at in the Customer database. (Approach ought to remember where it was, but that's just not how things work.)

This is the Catch-22: We want to enter a new record for the current Customer ID, but after we tell Approach to add a record, Approach no longer has the current Customer ID number!

The way to solve this problem is to save the values we need before we issue the Add New Record command, then fill in the History fields with the values saved. We'll save the values in a field type called a *variable* (see Chapter 5). Variables are added in the same way any other field is: Use the View ➤ Field Definitions command and add the variable to the list of fields, using the Field type Variable. Remember that variables are not changed except by us. Unlike fields such as First Name and Zip Code, whose values vary record by record in the database, a variable is given a value with the Set command and that value doesn't change until we issue another Set command for the variable. Thus, if we set the Save Date variable to 1/2/95, that variable retains that value, no matter what customer record we look at, no matter what found set we create, no matter what form we use, until we change the Save Date variable ourselves. Changing variables is done in a macro using the Set command.

Here's the new outline of what we want to do in our macro:

1. Switch to the History-fields-only view.
2. Save all values from the Next Contact fields in the current Customer record. This includes the Customer ID number, too, since once we issue the Add New Record command Approach erases the current Customer ID number from its memory.
3. Issue the Add New Record command.
4. In the new record, store the values from Step 2 in the corresponding History fields.
5. Switch back to the original view (the Contact Dates form).
6. Reset the values in the Next Contact fields.

Before we can create this Update History macro and use a button on the Contact Dates form, we'll have to create a new form with just the History fields. Select Create ➤ Form, enter History Only in the "View name & title" text box, choose the Default style, and choose the Columnar SmartMaster layout. In fact, the layout and style won't really matter, because we're going to hide this form later. Although we could use the form for editing History records, it's only use for now will be for updating the History database using the Update History macro.

Select Next or the Step 2 tab and choose the History database. Add all the fields from this database, including the Full Name field. (If we have to use the form, we'll want to make sure the customer name is correct. Therefore, adding the Full Name field is helpful should a problem arise.) Click on Done.

With the form built (and we won't bother to modify it), we can create the macro. Remember that when you build a macro, Approach assumes you want to work with the form that is currently displayed. That's why we're working with the History Only form and not the Contact Dates form, even though it's the Contact Dates form where the button will be placed to run this macro!

There's one more task we'll have to complete before we get to write the macro. Remember that we need to save the values in the Customer record's Next Contact fields in variable fields. We must define these fields. Select Create ➤ Field Definitions, and choose the CUSTOMER database. Move to the first blank line at the end of the list and click on the Options button to expand the dialog box. Add the following fields, defining each as a data type of Variable. As you add each field you will also need to select the proper field type, as noted in the following list.

Field Name	Variable Options (Field type)
save cust id	numeric
save date	date
save begin	time
save end	time
save type	text
save desc	text

►► **NOTE**

Variables are defined in the database, but are actually only used by Approach. When you export the database, the variable fields are not included.

To build the macro, select Tools ➤ Macros, then click on New. Enter the macro name Update History. Assign the function key F8 to this macro.

Here's what the macro must do:

1. Since the macro is going to be run from the Contact Dates form, we must first switch to the History Only form.
2. Save the Next Contact fields and the Customer ID value from the current Customer record into the variable fields.
3. Tell Approach to add a record.
4. Fill each field from the History record with the values stored in the variables.
5. Switch back to the Contact Dates form.
6. Update the "next contact" fields. Change the Next Contact Type to "T" (for telephone call) and use the date 30 days from today's date in the Next Contact Date field. All other fields should be blank.

To accomplish these steps, fill in the macro as follows. If Line 1 is already filled in, select the Delete or Clear All button to remove it. In the following list we've specified the command and the parameters (which are set at the bottom of the dialog box). Macro lines are numbered here for convenience; there is no numbering in the Define Macro dialog box.

Macro Line	Command	Command Parameters
1	Set	Set save cust id field in Customer database to Customer ID field in Customer database.
2	Set	Set save date field in Customer database to Next Contact Date field in Customer database.
3	Set	Set save begin field in Customer database to Next Contact Begin field in Customer database.
4	Set	Set save end field in Customer database to Next Contact End field in Customer database.
5	Set	Set save type field in Customer database to Next Contact Type field in Customer database.

Macro Line	Command	Command Parameters
6	Set	Set save desc in Customer database to Next Contact Description field in Customer database.
7	View	Switch to History Only form.
8	Records	Create a New Record.
9	Set	Set Customer ID field in History database to save cust id field in Customer database.
10	Set	Set Event Date field in History database to save date field in Customer database.
11	Set	Set Event Begin field in History database to save begin field in Customer database.
12	Set	Set Event End field in History database to save end field in Customer database.
13	Set	Set Event Type field in History database to save type field in Customer database.
14	Set	Set Event Description field in History database to save desc field in Customer database.
15	Set	Set Event Notes field in History database to the value 'ENTER NOTES HERE' (include the single quote marks); since there are no notes in the "next contact" set of fields, we'll use this to highlight the need for notes.
16	Set	Next Contact Date in Customer database to Today()+30
17	Set	Next Contact Begin in Customer database to '' (two single quotes together, no space between, to indicate a blank value).
18	Set	Next Contact End in Customer database to '' (two single quotes together, no space between, to indicate a blank value).
19	Set	Next Contact Type in Customer database to 'T' (including the single quote marks).

Macro Line	Command	Command Parameters
20	Set	Next Contact Description in Customer database to '' (two single quotes together, no space between, to indicate a blank value).
21	View	Switch to Contact Dates view.
22	Sort	Define a sort based on Event Date (ascending) and Event Begin (ascending). Both fields are in the History database.

The first lines of the macro are shown in Figure 25.6.

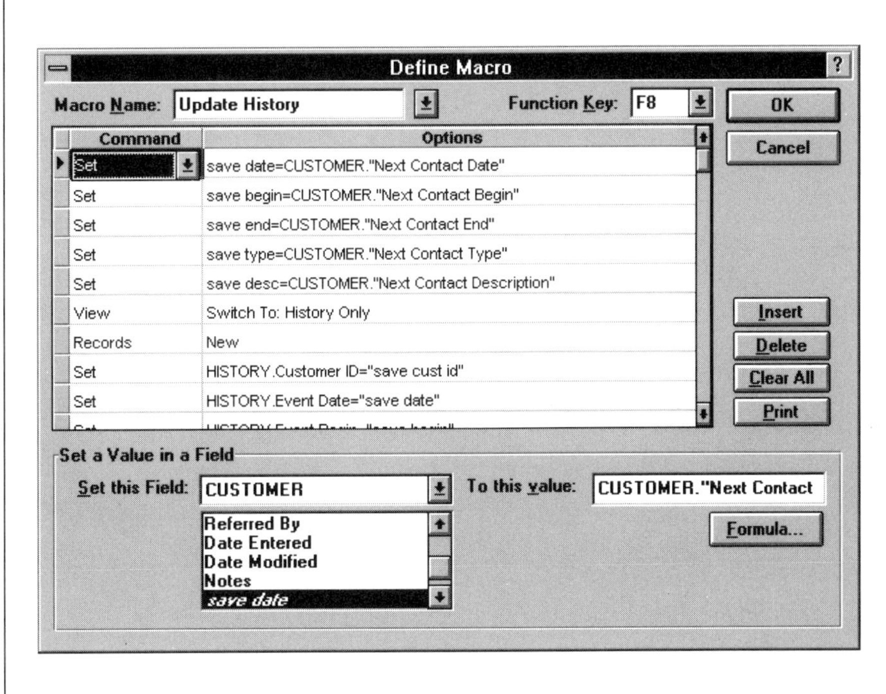

FIGURE 25.6

The first lines of the Update History macro

The rest of the instructions are, by now, routine: Create a button on the Contact Dates form, assign the Update History macro to the button, change the text on the button face to something meaningful (such as Update History), and test the button.

One last task: Hide the History Only form. Select the form, open the InfoBox, choose the form itself (not an object on the form), and choose the Basics tab. Check the Hide view box. Now Approach will not display a tab for the form, but you can jump to it by clicking on the first box in the Status bar and choosing the History Only form from the pull-up form list when you are in Design.

▸▸ Summary and a Look Ahead

In this chapter you've seen how to define macros to perform repetitive tasks. You've also seen that you can use macros to combine tasks, such as performing a Find before running a report.

There are, of course, dozens of additional things you can do with this application. In the next chapter we'll focus on just a few of them—a potpourri of ideas that can give your Approach file the look and feel of a full-fledged application.

▶ ▶ CHAPTER 26

Additional Ideas for the Customer Application

▸▸ FAST TRACK

▶ *To delete past contacts* **770**

use the Find command to locate older records, then delete the found set. Use the Show All command to display all remaining records.

▶ *To dial a customer's telephone number* **771**

add a new field to the Customer database called PickPhone. Make it a text field, one character long, then use it to select the default telephone number that should be dialed. Use the Dial command in a macro to perform the actual communications.

▶▶ **In** Chapters 21 through 25 we've been building an application with a variety of features. By no means have we examined everything that Approach can do within the application. As it stands at the end of Chapter 25, we've built an application that uses two different .APR files, and joined databases, GUI elements, macros and buttons, and a host of other features. We've saved some ideas for this chapter. We'll explore some features you might want to add to fully exploit everything Approach can do. Of course, not even the ideas in this chapter will cover all the possibilities, but you'll get a good idea of some other areas—from the user interface to user features—you might want to incorporate over time.

▶▶ Exit

Believe it or not, one of the biggest complaints from users is their inability to figure out how to get out of an application. The File ➤ Exit command is not intuitive, and some users believe this will close down Windows as well as the current application. Therefore, one simple feature you can add is an Exit button on the Name and Address form in the Customer Approach file to exit the application. The single-command macro can use the Exit command. Not rocket science, to be sure, but a feature your users will appreciate.

▶▶ Multiple Users

As designed, we've created a single-user application. We assume that any contact recorded in the system is done by you and for you as an individual. However, you can easily share the application with several sales agents. The key is to add a field or fields, one called Agent (or Salesperson or other meaningful name), and the other called something like "Next Contact Agent" field. The field can be a text field, perhaps only three characters long to store the agent's initials. You'll want to identify who has the next contact with a customer, so you can add a Next Contact Agent field and choose the Filled in validation option from the Field Definition dialog box to ensure that the field is selected. You'll also want to add the agent's initials (or name) to each item in the History database. (This means you'll have to change the Update History macro, too.)

You may also want to add the agent information in two additional fields: Added by and Modified by. Just as we keep track of two dates within each customer record, you may want to track which agent created the record and which agent last updated the record, using new fields called CreatedBy and ModifiedBy.

Of course, you don't want to hassle with entering the agent name for each record. The key is to create an Open macro for the Customer Approach file. The macro will prompt for a variable, called AgentVar, using a form called GetAgent. Then every time you want to use the agent's initials, you can use the value in the AgentVar field.

For example, add a variable field to the CUSTOMER.DBF file, called AgentVar. Create a new form that prompts you for the AgentVar value. Create the Open macro that switches to the form and uses the Browse environment, then switches to some other view, such as the Name and Address view. When the user starts the Customer application, he or she will see the GetAgent screen. After entering his or her initials, the agent presses Enter and is taken to the Name and Address form. The CreatedBy value can be modified to be a formula, using the Creation Formula =AgentVar in the Field Definition dialog box. The ModifiedBy field can be defined using the Modification Formula =AgentVar.

Unfortunately you can't add validation criteria to the AgentVar field because it is a variable. You don't want to use a full field because then the Agent identifier would be carried in each record, which is wasted space. So there are some limitations. However, you *can* validate the values on the form. Although the CreatedBy and ModifiedBy fields on the form use a Creation Formula and Modification Formula (respectively), you can add the validation logic to either (or both) of these fields. For example, you can specify that the value entered in the field must be "One of" or you can use a "lookup" into another table (one that contains just agent initials and perhaps their full name).

If tracking information about agents is important, you may wish to go an extra step and separate agent data for each customer into a joined database. The agent database could contain the customer ID number (you must have a joined field to join the Agent database to the Customer database), the CreatedBy field, and the ModifiedBy field. You can validate the last two fields as mentioned in the previous paragraph.

▸▸ Referring to the Same Database

If customers in your database are the source of referrals, you can use a drop-down list for the "Referred by" field on the Miscellaneous form. This way your user need only click a down-pointing arrow and select from a list of existing customers. On the Miscellaneous form, in the Design environment, choose the Referred by field and double-click on it. From the InfoBox select the Basics tab (if it isn't already selected). Choose the "Data entry type" of Drop-down list, then choose the Define List button (if the Drop-Down List dialog box does not automatically appear).

Check the Options button. Then check the Create list automatically from field data button. The field you want to use is the Full Name field. This selection means that when using the form and clicking on the down-pointing arrow, Approach will fill the drop-down list with the values from the Full Name field in the found set. (You may wish to add another field, such as LastFirst that combines the Last Name field, a comma, and the First Name field, instead, to place the drop-down list in alphabetical order by last name.) As records (customers) are added, the Referred by drop-down list will be updated.

Be sure to check the "Show drop-down arrow" box before you select OK.

▸▸ Purging the Past

The past is history, but at some point you may wish to delete the oldest records. You can use the History Only form that we hid in Chapter 25 in a macro to find all records where the completion date is earlier than Today()–60 (everything that was completed 60 days or more ago), then use the Delete Found Set command in the macro, followed by the Find/Show All records command.

►► Dialing for Customers

Approach can dial any telephone number as long as you have properly defined the communication setup parameters. Refer to Chapter 20 for details. (Select Tools ➤ Preferences, then choose the Dialer tab.)

Here's what you need to do.

1. Add a new field to the Customer database called PickPhone. Make it a text field, one character long. (If you will only choose from two telephone numbers in the future, you could define this field as Boolean instead. Using a text field allows for growth.)
2. Create a new form called Call Customer. Place both telephone numbers (Office Phone and Home Phone) on the form. Add the PickPhone field and choose the "Display field type" as radio button. In the Define Radio Buttons dialog box enter two options: Clicked Value A with a Button Label of *Office*, and Clicked Value B with a Button Label of *Home*.
3. Define two macros; each dials a telephone number. The first, PhoneOffice, has a single command: Dial, with the option of "Dial the number in this field" pointing to the Office Phone field of the Customer database. The PhoneHome macro has a single command, Dial, with the option of "Dial the number in this field" pointing to the Home Phone field of the Customer database.
4. Create a third macro, called DialCustomer, with two commands. The first switches to the Call Customer view (defined in Step 2). The next line of the macro uses the Run command, with the second option (If) selected. In the text box to the right of If, enter

   ```
   PickPhone = 'A'
   ```

   On the next line, to the right of "is true," choose "run macro" and choose PhoneOffice from the drop-down list that follows. Then check the "else" box, choose "run macro," and choose PhoneHome from the drop-down list that follows.
5. Assign the macro to a button on a form.

If you get an "Error Dialing" error message, it is likely that either your modem settings are incorrect or that Approach is competing with a communications program currently in use. Approach is not particularly smart about your communications ports, so you may wish to exit Windows, then start only Approach, for the dialing feature to work.

▸▸ Summary

In this chapter you've learned how to add more features to the Customer application. This is by no means an exhaustive list, but it gives you a flavor for the kinds of things you can do with Approach.

Experiment with the application. There's still lots of things you can do—from adding a custom menu to exporting your data to another format. Work with new forms and reports, and practice working with the features you've read about in Chapters 1 through 20. You'll soon see that Approach offers a rich development environment while keeping many difficult tasks simple.

Have fun with Approach!

Index

Note: Page numbers in *italics* refer to figures; page numbers in **bold** refer to primary discussions of topic

Symbols & Numbers

A

➤ C

➤ D

▶ E

▶ F

▶ G

▶ H

► I

J

K

▶ L

▶ M

▶ N

▶ O

▶ Q

▶ R

▶ S

▶ T

▶ U

▶ V

➤ W

X

Y

► Z

[1306] Mastering Approach 3 for Windows

GET A FREE CATALOG JUST FOR EXPRESSING YOUR OPINION.

Help us improve our books and get a ***FREE*** full-color catalog in the bargain. Please complete this form, pull out this page and send it in today. The address is on the reverse side.

Name ____________________ **Company** ____________________

Address ____________________ **City** __________ **State** ___ **Zip** _______

Phone ( ) ____________________

1. How would you rate the overall quality of this book?

- ❑ Excellent
- ❑ Very Good
- ❑ Good
- ❑ Fair
- ❑ Below Average
- ❑ Poor

2. What were the things you liked most about the book? (Check all that apply)

- ❑ Pace
- ❑ Format
- ❑ Writing Style
- ❑ Examples
- ❑ Table of Contents
- ❑ Index
- ❑ Price
- ❑ Illustrations
- ❑ Type Style
- ❑ Cover
- ❑ Depth of Coverage
- ❑ Fast Track Notes

3. What were the things you liked *least* about the book? (Check all that apply)

- ❑ Pace
- ❑ Format
- ❑ Writing Style
- ❑ Examples
- ❑ Table of Contents
- ❑ Index
- ❑ Price
- ❑ Illustrations
- ❑ Type Style
- ❑ Cover
- ❑ Depth of Coverage
- ❑ Fast Track Notes

4. Where did you buy this book?

- ❑ Bookstore chain
- ❑ Small independent bookstore
- ❑ Computer store
- ❑ Wholesale club
- ❑ College bookstore
- ❑ Technical bookstore
- ❑ Other ____________

5. How did you decide to buy this particular book?

- ❑ Recommended by friend
- ❑ Recommended by store personnel
- ❑ Author's reputation
- ❑ Sybex's reputation
- ❑ Read book review in ________
- ❑ Other ____________

6. How did you pay for this book?

- ❑ Used own funds
- ❑ Reimbursed by company
- ❑ Received book as a gift

7. What is your level of experience with the subject covered in this book?

- ❑ Beginner
- ❑ Intermediate
- ❑ Advanced

8. How long have you been using a computer?

years ____________

months ____________

9. Where do you most often use your computer?

- ❑ Home
- ❑ Work
- ❑ Both
- ❑ Other ____________

10. What kind of computer equipment do you have? (Check all that apply)

- ❑ PC Compatible Desktop Computer
- ❑ PC Compatible Laptop Computer
- ❑ Apple/Mac Computer
- ❑ Apple/Mac Laptop Computer
- ❑ CD ROM
- ❑ Fax Modem
- ❑ Data Modem
- ❑ Scanner
- ❑ Sound Card
- ❑ Other ____________

11. What other kinds of software packages do you ordinarily use?

- ❑ Accounting
- ❑ Databases
- ❑ Networks
- ❑ Apple/Mac
- ❑ Desktop Publishing
- ❑ Spreadsheets
- ❑ CAD
- ❑ Games
- ❑ Word Processing
- ❑ Communications
- ❑ Money Management
- ❑ Other ____________

12. What operating systems do you ordinarily use?

- ❑ DOS
- ❑ OS/2
- ❑ Windows
- ❑ Apple/Mac
- ❑ Windows NT
- ❑ Other ____________

13. **On what computer-related subject(s) would you like to see more books?**

---

14. **Do you have any other comments about this book? (Please feel free to use a separate piece of paper if you need more room)**

PLEASE FOLD, SEAL, AND MAIL TO SYBEX

SYBEX INC.
Department M
2021 Challenger Drive
Alameda, CA
94501

Default Report SmartIcons Toolbar

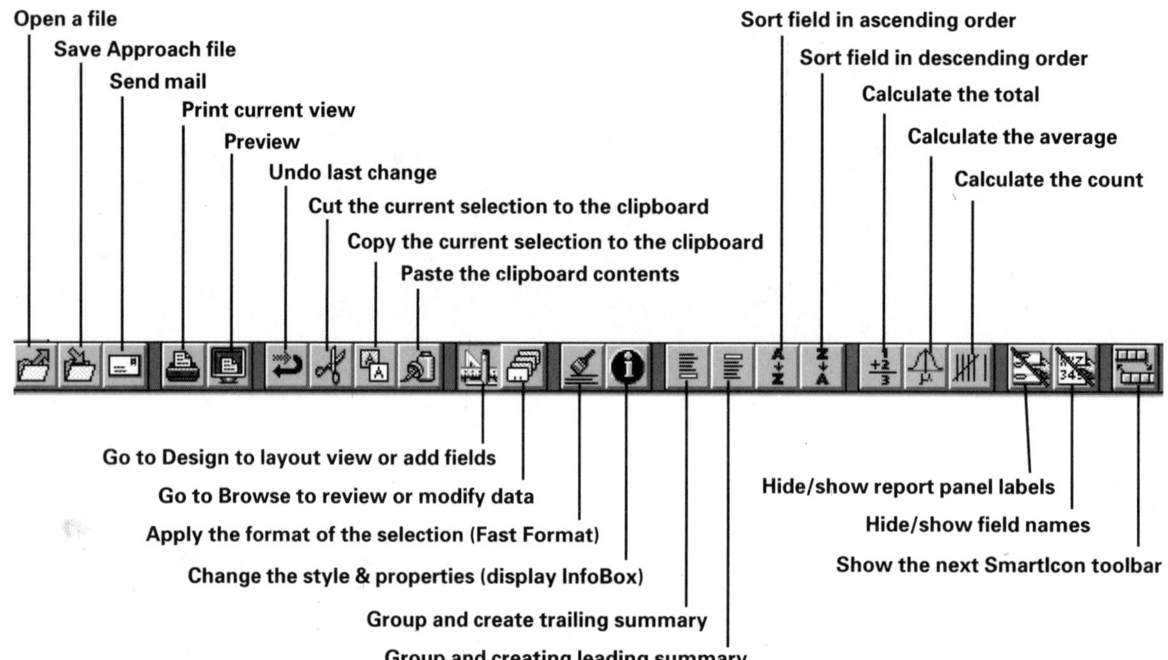

Open a file
Save Approach file
Send mail
Print current view
Preview
Undo last change
Cut the current selection to the clipboard
Copy the current selection to the clipboard
Paste the clipboard contents
Sort field in ascending order
Sort field in descending order
Calculate the total
Calculate the average
Calculate the count
Go to Design to layout view or add fields
Go to Browse to review or modify data
Apply the format of the selection (Fast Format)
Change the style & properties (display InfoBox)
Group and create trailing summary
Group and creating leading summary
Hide/show report panel labels
Hide/show field names
Show the next SmartIcon toolbar

Default Preview Toolbar

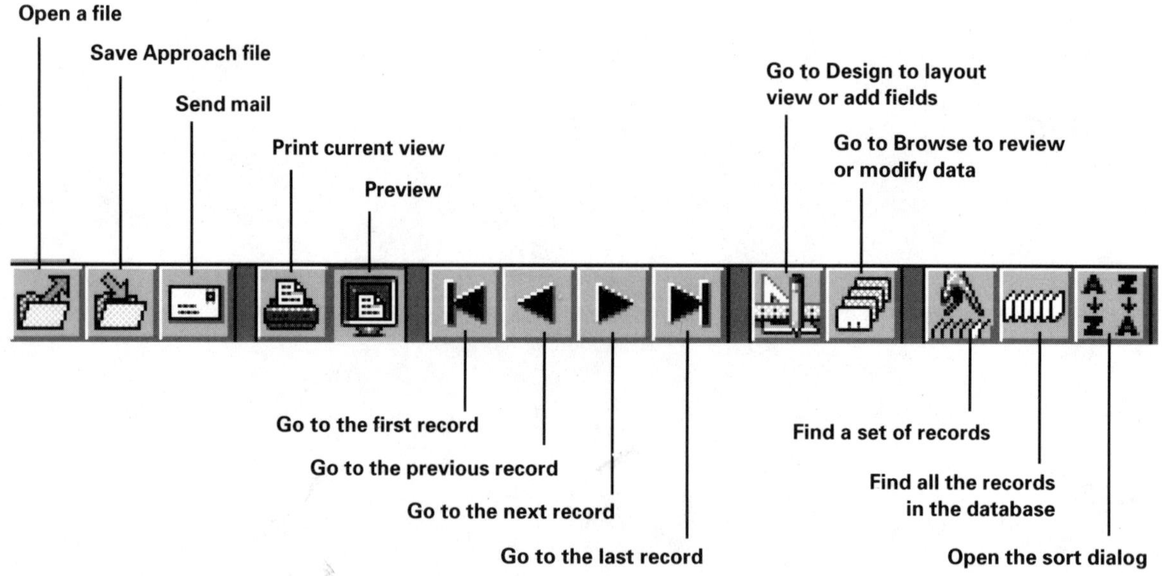

Open a file
Save Approach file
Send mail
Print current view
Preview
Go to Design to layout view or add fields
Go to Browse to review or modify data
Go to the first record
Go to the previous record
Go to the next record
Go to the last record
Find a set of records
Find all the records in the database
Open the sort dialog

A COOKBOOK PUBLISHED BY DAIRY DIARY

FOUR SEASONS

Enjoy British seasonal food

Savour this collection of delicious recipes that champions British ingredients and reflects the influence of the seasons

This collection of delicious recipes celebrates British ingredients, and reflects how the seasons influence the way we cook and what we eat.

We are fortunate to live in a country with four distinct seasons, providing us with a superb variety of foods.

When ingredients are in season they taste better and are generally more nutritious. Eating local seasonal food can be less expensive than buying foods flown in from around the globe and is certainly more environmentally friendly and better for the planet. By making a conscious effort to look out for fresh, tasty, British seasonal food we can rejoice in the wonderful fare grown on our doorstep and support those who work to produce it.

Because of the British weather and its seasonal variations, what we fancy eating changes throughout the year. For example, long summer days are perfect for fresh salads or alfresco evenings with friends sharing crudités and dips. In contrast, autumn brings with it dark evenings, cold winds and a hankering for warm, comforting foods. And in winter, of course, there is fabulous festive food to enjoy.

This cookbook is split into four seasonal chapters, crammed full of imaginative recipes to help you make use of the ingredients you have and cook delicious food to match the mood of each season.

There are helpful suggestions for sourcing, planning, storing and preparing seasonal ingredients and a list of foods available during each season; this can vary by region and is also dependent on the weather.

RECIPE FINDER

RECIPE TESTING

Every recipe in this book has been tested three times: first by the recipe writer, then by an everyday home-cook and finally by the food stylist at the photo shoot.

You can rest assured that each recipe will work perfectly every time and those wonderful fresh ingredients won't go to waste. We ensure that all ingredients are readily available, the method makes perfect sense, and that each one is delicious.

RECIPE NOTES

Each recipe is written in a style that's easy to follow. There are preparation and cooking times, nutritional information, serving suggestions, cook's tips and space for your own notes too.

F Suitable for freezing

V Suitable for vegetarians
(provided that suitable cheeses, yogurts etc. are used)

(V) Suitable for vegans (check labels)

Nutritional information has been calculated by portion or item. Where there are portion variations, e.g. serves 6–8, the analysis given is based on the larger number.

Sugar is 'free sugars' (added sugars, including those naturally present in fruit juice and syrups).

Spoon measures are level unless otherwise stated.

Eggs are large unless otherwise stated in the ingredients.

SAFETY NOTES

Recipes using nuts or nut products are not suitable for young children or those with a nut allergy. Certain at-risk groups, such as pregnant women, babies and sick or elderly people, should not eat raw or lightly cooked eggs.

WHERE TO FIND FOOD IN SEASON

BUYING LOCAL/BRITISH

SUPERMARKETS

There's no denying the convenience of the supermarket, and most offer a range of British produce; look out for UK-grown on the label and, if you can, opt for 'imperfect' or 'wonky' vegetables and fruit, which are often cheaper and saves them from going to waste. Take a look at the seasonal ingredients lists on pages 10–13 then watch out for the produce as it becomes available, such as UK-grown new potatoes or British asparagus. Snap up a couple of punnets of those price-reduced berries and make one of the delicious puds in this book or the conserve on page 90. Seek out jars of British honey, and English rapeseed oil as an alternative to olive oil.

FARM SHOPS, INDEPENDENT SHOPS AND MARKETS

Independent and farm shops often celebrate British food and they will often buy from local growers. At markets you may find bargains as it gets towards closing time, but take a minute to think about how you'll cook or store the produce. Greengrocers, butchers and fishmongers will be experts in their field and should be able to give you advice about cooking and the provenance of their produce. Cheese shop staff can introduce you to a wealth of locally produced cheese. Some cheeses, such as feta, have a Protected Designation of Origin (PDO), which means they can only be made in a specified region or country, but enterprising British cheesemakers have come up with their own versions of these cheeses, which taste very similar (or better!)

VEG BOXES

Enjoy the convenience of home delivery whilst also buying local fruit and vegetables. There are many farms and greengrocers that have a veg box delivery scheme. Your local milkman may also offer the service and there are national box schemes too, with some specialising in imperfect produce.

PICK YOUR OWN

On a warm summer's day, spend a couple of glorious hours choosing your own strawberries, raspberries or gooseberries. Or in autumn there are fresh apples and pears straight from the tree, and pumpkin-picking for Halloween. Look at pickyourownfarms.org.uk to find a location near you.

FORAGING

Oh, the joy of discovering a hedgerow laden with damsons or blackberries! Carry a bag with you on countryside walks in the hope you might collect some of nature's bounty.

PLOT TO PLATE

You can't get more local than picking from your own patch. Growing your own may mean a pot of herbs on a window ledge, an allotment crammed full of edibles, and everything in between! Nurturing however many plants that you have the time and space for can be incredibly rewarding, and will save money too. Grow what you love and you'll be sure to look after the plants and make full use of them come harvest time. And if you're not particularly green-fingered you may be lucky enough to receive edible donations from neighbours, particularly if you reward them with something home-baked in return!

USEFUL TIPS

PLANNING

With the help of the recipe finder on pages 4–5 and the seasonal recipe lists overleaf, you can plan to a certain extent, but when eating seasonal foods, it's often easier to plan meals after you have picked/collected/received your ingredients. If you have plenty of one or two foods, choose a couple of meals and/or desserts and store the rest.

STORING

However you obtain your ingredients, they are precious. Make sure nothing goes to waste by storing or cooking seasonal gluts of fruit or vegetables appropriately.

Freezing: open freeze chopped vegetables or fruits on trays before transferring to freezer-proof containers and labelling. Batch-cook and freeze prepared meals; look out for the Ⓕ symbol on appropriate recipes.

Preserving: brilliant for a glut of one particular fruit or vegetable. Sterilise jam jars by putting through the dishwasher then place on a tray in the oven preheated to 120°C/100° fan/Gas ½. Leave for 10 minutes and then turn off the oven but leave the jars in while you prepare your pickles or jams. Take a look at the recipes on pages 25, 89, 90, 101 and 110.

QUICK IDEAS

This book is a treasure trove of delicious, seasonal recipes, but if you want to make something really quick, celebrating the taste of your ingredients, keep it simple…

Salads: spring and summer vegetables lend themselves to an array of colourful fresh salads, but autumn and winter salads can be joyful combinations of griddled or roasted veg or fruit, and possibly some local cheese. In a jam jar, shake oil, vinegar and honey to drizzle over the top.

Soups: chop any veg you like and simmer in stock, maybe with some herbs. Serve as a chunky soup or purée to make it smooth.

On bread/pizza/tart: fresh salad ingredients with a little mayo and egg or meat on a sandwich; roasted veg or sautéed mushrooms on a toastie or pizza; or ribbons of veg or fruit on a puff pastry tart. You could make your own bread, pizza base or pastry, or buy them ready made for speed.

Roast veg: for deliciously soft yet browned veggies, parboil for 5 minutes and then roast in hot oil, or add a little liquid to the roasting tin and cover for half of the cooking time.

Stewed fruit: gently cook fruit with a splash of water and a sprinkle of sugar or a drizzle of honey and perhaps a sprinkle of ginger or cinnamon. Serve with a swirl of cream, on top of porridge, such as the recipe on page 118, or with a homemade rice pudding.

Pies: add cooked vegetables and meat to a white sauce, maybe with a spoonful of mustard, top with pastry or mash and bake until browned.

SPRING INGREDIENTS

Vegetables
Asparagus
Aubergine
Beetroot
Carrot
Cauliflower
Celeriac
Chicory
Chilli
Cucumber
Kale
Lettuce
Mushrooms
New potatoes
Purple sprouting broccoli
Radish
Rocket
Samphire
Spring cabbage
Spinach
Spring greens
Spring onion
Pak choi
Watercress
Wild garlic

Fruit
Elderflower
Gooseberries
Rhubarb

Fish
Cockles
Crab
John Dory
Mackerel
Monkfish
Prawns
Sea bass
Wild salmon
Trout

Meat
Beef, chicken and pork plus spring lamb

SUMMER INGREDIENTS

Vegetables
Artichoke
Aubergine
Beans – broad, green, runner
Beetroot
Broccoli
Carrot
Cauliflower
Chicory
Chilli
Courgette
Cucumber
Fennel
Garlic
Lettuce & salad leaves
Marrow
Onion
Pak choi
Peas
Peppers
Potatoes
Radish
Samphire
Salad onion
Summer squash
Swiss chard
Tomatoes
Turnip
Watercress
White cabbage

Fruit
Blackberries
Blueberries
Cherries
Currants – black, red, white
Elderberries
Gooseberries
Loganberries
Plums, greengages
Raspberries
Rhubarb
Strawberries

Fish
Crab, lobster
Flounder
Mackerel
Monkfish
Pilchards/sardines
Sea bass
Wild salmon
Trout

Meat
Beef, chicken and pork plus new season lamb

AUTUMN INGREDIENTS

Vegetables
Artichoke
Aubergine
Beetroot
Broccoli
Brussels sprouts
Cabbage – red, Savoy, white
Carrot
Cauliflower
Celeriac
Celery
Chestnuts
Courgette
Chicory
Chilli
Cucumber
Jerusalem artichoke
Kale
Leek
Lettuce
Mangetout
Marrow
Mushrooms
Onion
Parsnip
Peppers
Potatoes
Pumpkin, squash
Radish
Rocket
Spinach
Swede
Sweetcorn
Swiss chard
Tomatoes
Turnip
Watercress

Fruit
Apples
Blackberries
Damsons, sloes
Elderberries
Pears
Plums
Quince
Raspberries
Rhubarb

Fish
Brill
Clams, cockles
Dover sole, lemon sole
Flounder
Mussels
Oysters
Pilchards/sardines
Pollock
Turbot

Meat
Beef, chicken and pork plus duck, guinea fowl, pheasant, venison

WINTER INGREDIENTS

Vegetables
Beetroot
Brussels sprouts
Cabbage – red, Savoy, white
Carrot
Cauliflower
Celeriac
Celery
Chestnuts
Chicory
Fennel
Jerusalem artichoke
Kale
Leek
Mushrooms
Onion
Parsnip
Potatoes
Purple sprouting broccoli
Spring greens
Spring onion
Squash
Swede
Swiss chard
Turnip
Watercress

Fruit
Apples
Pears
Quince
Forced rhubarb

Fish
Brill
Dabs
Grey mullet
John Dory
Mussels
Oysters
Pollock
Scallops

Meat
Beef, chicken and pork plus duck, goose, guinea fowl, pheasant, turkey, venison

SPRING

SALMON, NEW POTATO & ASPARAGUS SALAD

The British asparagus season runs from April through to mid-June and this main course salad combines the fine green spears with other spring favourites such as Jersey Royals, samphire and watercress, topped with fresh salmon.

Serves 2 Preparation 20 minutes Cooking 20 minutes

Baby new potatoes, such as Jersey Royals 250g (9oz), scrubbed

Salt and freshly ground black pepper

Salmon fillet 250g (9oz)

Bay leaf 1

Cold-pressed rapeseed oil 2 tbsp

Asparagus tips 125g (4½oz), trimmed

Samphire 50g (2oz), well rinsed

White wine vinegar 1 tbsp

Fresh tarragon few sprigs, leaves chopped

Fresh dill few sprigs, chopped

Clear honey 2 tsp

Watercress handful

Pickled cucumber 25g (1oz), chopped

Put the potatoes in a saucepan and cover with water. Add a pinch of salt, bring to the boil and cook for 8–10 minutes until tender. Drain and set aside.

Meanwhile, lightly season the salmon and place in a small pan with the bay leaf. Half fill the pan with water, bring to a gentle simmer, cover and cook very gently for 10–12 minutes until cooked through. Set aside.

Brush a frying pan with a little of the oil and heat until hot. Add the asparagus and stir-fry for 4 minutes. Add the samphire and continue to stir-fry for 2 minutes until tender. Cover and keep warm.

Mix the remaining oil with the vinegar, herbs, honey and a little salt and pepper until well combined; set aside.

Line two serving plates with watercress. Using a fork, crush the potatoes lightly and divide between the plates. Top with the asparagus and samphire.

Drain the salmon, discarding the bay leaf, and flake away from the skin into large chunks. Add to the salad and sprinkle with the pickled cucumber. Serve slightly warm, drizzled with the herb vinaigrette dressing.

Tips

As a starter, this will serve 4.

If you prefer, prepare all the vegetables and salmon in advance, leave to cool, then chill and serve as a cold salad.

Samphire is quite salty, so you shouldn't need any other seasoning on the salad.

Prawns, cooked chicken or goat's cheese make great alternatives to salmon if you prefer.

Calories	Fibre	Salt	Sugar	Fat
489	3g	2g	6g	30g of which 4g is saturated

ASPARAGUS CARBONARA

A creamy meat-free version of carbonara that celebrates the taste of fresh green asparagus. Traditionally the start of the British asparagus season is 23 April, St George's Day, finishing on Midsummer's Day in June.

Serves 2 Preparation 15 minutes Cooking 15 minutes 

Asparagus 250g (9oz), trimmed

Salt and freshly ground black pepper

Spaghetti 150g (5oz)

Eggs 2, beaten

Italian-style hard cheese 50g (2oz), finely grated, plus extra to serve

Butter 25g (1oz)

Garlic 1 clove, peeled and finely chopped

Rocket leaves 25g (1oz)

Lay the asparagus on a board, slice off the tips and set aside. Using a vegetable peeler, shave the asparagus stalks into long, thick ribbons. When you can shave no more, thinly slice the remaining part of the stalks.

Bring a large pan of salted water to the boil. Add the spaghetti and cook for 10 minutes until just tender.

Meanwhile, in a bowl mix together the beaten eggs, grated cheese and plenty of black pepper.

Heat the butter in a large frying pan and fry the garlic for 1 minute until softened. Add all the asparagus and stir through for 1 minute.

Using tongs, lift the spaghetti straight from its cooking water into the pan of asparagus.

Remove the pan from the heat, add the egg and cheese mixture and toss through the pasta and asparagus, adding 2–3 tablespoons hot water to help make a sauce.

Immediately transfer to warmed shallow serving bowls. Scatter over some rocket and extra grated cheese.

Tips

If cooking for vegetarians, make sure you use a suitable cheese.

Use asparagus as soon as possible after buying it. Snap off the woody ends, rinse the spears and they are ready to use. Steam, boil or griddle and enjoy with hollandaise sauce or homemade herb butter, in salads or added to pasta dishes like this carbonara.

Instead of plain butter, you could use 25g (1oz) of rosemary and garlic butter (see page 69).

Calories	Fibre	Salt	Sugar	Fat
555	7g	1.5g	0g	24g of which 13g is saturated

ROASTED GNOCCHI WITH PURPLE SPROUTING & MUSHROOMS

Leafier and deeper in colour than regular broccoli, purple sprouting is at its best between February and April. Enjoy it in this quick and scrumptious vegan supper dish.

Serves 2 Preparation 10 minutes Cooking 30 minutes 

Potato gnocchi 400g pack

Chestnut mushrooms 300g (11oz), halved if large

Garlic 2 cloves, peeled and cut into slivers

Sage leaves 6, torn in half

Pine nuts 2 tbsp

Light olive oil 3 tbsp

Purple sprouting broccoli 250g (9oz), trimmed

For the dressing

Lemon 1, juice only

Olive oil 3 tbsp

Garlic 1 clove, peeled and finely chopped

Salt 1 tsp

Fresh chives or parsley 2 tbsp chopped

Preheat the oven to 220°C/200°fan/Gas 7. Place the gnocchi in a large bowl and pour on just enough boiling water to cover. Leave to stand for 2 minutes then drain thoroughly.

Spread the gnocchi and mushrooms in a large roasting tin and scatter on the garlic, sage and pine nuts. Drizzle with the oil and season with salt. Gently mix all together.

Roast for 10 minutes then gently turn the ingredients to mix and add the purple sprouting. Roast for a further 15–20 minutes or until the gnocchi are golden brown and the purple sprouting is tender and crisping around the edges.

Meanwhile, pop the dressing ingredients into a lidded jar and shake thoroughly to blend.

Pile the gnocchi and vegetables onto two plates and drizzle over the dressing. Serve immediately.

Tips

If cooking for vegans, make sure the gnocchi are suitable.

Sprinkle some grated Cheddar cheese or nuggets of soft goat's cheese over the gnocchi just before serving as a vegetarian supper.

Sneak in an extra serving of greens – spoon the gnocchi and vegetables onto a small bed of raw baby spinach leaves.

Calories	Fibre	Salt	Sugar	Fat
773	14g	3g	0g	49g of which 7g is saturated

HERBY EGG ROLLS WITH VEGETABLES & PRAWNS

Full of fresh flavours, these rolled omelettes make a delicious light lunch or supper. Alternatively, serve them cold instead of a sandwich in your packed lunch box.

Serves 2 Preparation 15 minutes Cooking 10 minutes

Reduced calorie mayonnaise 2 tbsp

Garlic 1 clove, peeled and crushed

Vegetable oil 1 tbsp

Spring onions 3, trimmed and halved lengthways

Pak choi 1 small head, trimmed, leaves separated

Eggs 3 medium

Chives small bunch, chopped

Coriander small bunch, chopped

Light soy sauce 2 tsp

Cooked peeled prawns 100g (3½oz)

Red chilli 1 small, deseeded and finely chopped (optional)

Sweet chilli sauce to serve (optional)

Mix the mayonnaise and garlic together and set aside.

Heat half the oil in a wok or frying pan until hot. Add the spring onions and pak choi and stir-fry for 3–4 minutes until wilted. Cover and keep warm.

Line a heatproof dish with non-stick baking paper.

Beat the eggs in a jug with the herbs, soy sauce and 1 tablespoon water. Brush a small (18cm/7in) non-stick frying pan with a little of the remaining oil and place over a medium heat until hot. Pour in half of the egg mixture and cook gently for about 2 minutes until set, tilting the pan to make sure the egg cooks evenly.

Turn over and cook for a further minute until just cooked. Transfer to the lined dish, cover and keep warm. Repeat with the remaining egg mixture, brushing the pan with a little more oil and stirring the egg mixture before pouring.

Spread each omelette with the garlic mayonnaise then top with the cooked vegetables, prawns and chilli, if using. Roll up and serve while still warm. Cut in half for easy eating. Serve with sweet chilli sauce, if you like.

Tips

If the pak choi leaves have wide stems, cut them into thinner strips for even cooking.

Swap the cooked vegetables for salad leaves, baby spinach or sprouting seeds if you prefer.

These are great for a picnic or packed lunch. Leave the omelettes and vegetables to go cold, then assemble as above, wrap in non-stick baking paper or foil and chill until ready to serve.

Calories	Fibre	Salt	Sugar	Fat
275	3g	2g	0g	18g of which 3g is saturated

PINK PICKLED RADISHES

Radishes are a quick and easy crop to grow. When raw, their peppery flavour and crunchy texture are a great addition to any salad, or make this vibrant pink pickle and add to burgers, wraps and salads or serve as a side dish.

Fills a 1 litre Kilner jar   Preparation 35 minutes   Cooking 10 minutes 

Radishes 600g (1lb 5oz)
Mixed peppercorns 2 tsp
Fennel seeds 2 tsp
Yellow mustard seeds 2 tsp
White wine vinegar 200ml (7fl oz)
Caster sugar 3 tbsp
Sea salt flakes 1 tsp
Garlic 4 cloves, peeled and kept whole
Bay leaves 2
Red chilli 1, sliced

Thoroughly wash the radishes. Using a sharp knife, top and tail each one then carefully slice each radish into 2–3mm (approx. ⅛in) thick rounds. Place in a large clean bowl.

Place a saucepan over a medium heat, add the peppercorns, fennel and mustard seeds and toast for 1–2 minutes until fragrant. Carefully pour in the vinegar and 200ml (7fl oz) water, the sugar and salt. Add the garlic cloves, bay leaves and red chilli and slowly bring up to the boil, stirring constantly until the sugar has dissolved. Remove from the heat. Using a slotted spoon, remove all the spices, bay leaves, garlic and chilli and mix these with the radishes.

Spoon the radish mix into a sterilised Kilner jar. Pour over the pickling liquid, making sure the radishes are completely covered.

Seal the lid and leave to cool then place in the fridge and leave overnight. Once opened they will keep well for 2–3 weeks.

Tips

As well as enjoying them raw or pickled, radishes are also lovely roasted, which brings out their sweetness.

Don't waste any part of the radish: the green leafy tops can be sliced and stir-fried in a little oil and garlic until just wilted.

Calories	Fibre	Salt	Sugar	Fat	Based on a 25g (1oz) serving
27	0.5g	0.3g	4g	0.4g of which 0g is saturated	

CRAB, SPRING VEGETABLE & STICKY RICE BOWL

Hawaiian-style poke bowls are popular in trendy cafés. Why not try making one at home, as they are an easy way to use fresh, healthy, seasonal ingredients. Traditionally they are made with slices of raw, sushi grade fish, but we have used fresh cooked crab meat which you can buy from your local fishmonger or the chilled counter of a supermarket.

Serves 2 Preparation 20 minutes plus cooling Cooking 25 minutes

Sushi rice 100g (3½oz), rinsed in cold water
Rice wine vinegar 1 tsp
Caster sugar ½ tsp
Salt and freshly ground black pepper
Mayonnaise 3 tbsp
Sriracha sauce 2 tbsp
Spring onion 1, trimmed and finely chopped
Fresh white and brown crab meat 100g (3½oz)
Spring greens 75g (3oz), finely shredded
Baby spinach leaves 50g (2oz)
Pickled radishes 2 tbsp, drained (see page 25)
Carrots 2, peeled and sliced
Cucumber ¼, sliced
Salad cress ½ box, snipped

Put the rinsed rice into a saucepan and add enough cold water to cover the rice by 1cm (½in). Bring to the boil, stirring occasionally, then cover and cook over a low heat for 10 minutes. Remove from the heat, keep the lid on and leave to steam for 15 minutes. Remove the lid and leave to cool completely.

In a bowl, mix the rice wine vinegar, sugar and a pinch of salt then stir through the rice.

Stir together the mayonnaise, Sriracha sauce and spring onion. Take 1 heaped tablespoon and mix this through the crab meat. Season to taste.

Divide the rice between two bowls. Arrange the vegetables on top of the rice in sections and add the dressed crab. Drizzle with the remaining spicy mayo and add a scattering of salad cress.

Tips

Sriracha sauce is a hot chilli sauce popular in Asian dishes.

Try using other types of rice or grain, vegetables, pickles or tofu.

NOTES

Calories	Fibre	Salt	Sugar	Fat
612	7g	2.5g	5g	39g of which 3g is saturated

BACON-WRAPPED MONKFISH WITH CAULIFLOWER & TARRAGON RISOTTO

Monkfish is common around the deep waters of the British Isles, making it an easy fish to source. Ask your fishmonger to remove the outer skin and membrane to leave you with the lovely white meaty flesh. It is quite an expensive piece of fish but delicious and here it is served alongside an economical cauliflower risotto.

Serves 4 Preparation 35 minutes Cooking 25 minutes

Monkfish tails 2 (approx. 225g/8oz each), trimmed

Tarragon and lemon butter 75g (3oz) (see page 69), softened

Salt and freshly ground black pepper

Dry cured streaky bacon 8 rashers

Olive oil 4 tbsp

Cauliflower 1 small (approx. 650g/1lb 7oz), cut into florets

Fennel seeds 1 tsp

Cumin seeds 1 tsp

Shallots 2, finely chopped

Celery 2 sticks, finely chopped

Risotto rice 175g (6oz)

Dry white wine 150ml (¼ pint) (optional)

Vegetable stock approx. 800ml (28fl oz), hot

Fresh tarragon 2 tbsp chopped leaves, plus extra to garnish (optional)

Preheat the oven to 200°C/180°fan/Gas 6.

Cut the monkfish tails in half so you have four fillets. Spread them all over with half the flavoured butter. Season with salt and pepper. Put the bacon on a board and use the flat side of a knife to stretch the rashers to make them slightly thinner. Wrap two slices of bacon around each fish fillet. Place on a baking tray, making sure the bacon ends are underneath. Drizzle with 2 tablespoons olive oil.

In a roasting tin, toss together the cauliflower, fennel and cumin seeds, 2 tablespoons olive oil and plenty of salt and pepper.

Roast the cauliflower for 15–20 minutes until lightly golden and the monkfish for 18–20 minutes until cooked.

Meanwhile, melt the remaining flavoured butter in a wide pan and fry the shallots and celery for 2–3 minutes until softened. Stir in the rice, coating the grains in the butter. Add the wine, if using, and allow to evaporate for 2–3 minutes. Add the hot stock, a ladleful at a time, stirring frequently, for 20–25 minutes until the rice is al dente and soupy.

Add the roasted cauliflower and chopped tarragon to the risotto and season to taste.

Spoon the risotto into shallow bowls or onto plates, slice the monkfish and place on top. Scatter with extra tarragon, if liked.

Calories	Fibre	Salt	Sugar	Fat
662	4g	3.5g	0g	38g of which 15g is saturated

CHICKEN, NOODLE & SPRING VEGETABLE TRAYBAKE

An all-in-one satisfying supper dish. And when you've finished, there is only one tray to wash up, so you can relax and savour every mouthful.

Serves 2 Preparation 15 minutes Cooking 45 minutes

Boneless chicken thighs 4 (approx. 150g/5oz each)

Salt and freshly ground black pepper

Leek 1, trimmed and thickly sliced

Spring greens 100g (3½oz)

Purple sprouting broccoli 100g (3½oz)

Vegetable oil 1 tbsp

Light soy sauce 2 tbsp

Sweet chilli sauce 2 tbsp, plus extra to serve

Chinese 5 spice powder 1 tsp

Straight to Wok/cooked egg noodles 250g (9oz)

Sesame oil 2 tsp (optional)

Red chilli 1 small, deseeded and chopped (optional)

Preheat the oven to 200°C/180°fan/Gas 6. Season the chicken all over and arrange in a roasting tin. Bake for 20 minutes.

Meanwhile, put the leek, greens and broccoli in a bowl and toss with the vegetable oil, half the soy sauce, half the sweet chilli sauce and the 5 spice powder.

Remove the chicken from the tin and mix the vegetables into the cooking juices. Sit the chicken back on top and bake for a further 15 minutes, stirring the vegetables halfway through.

Mix the remaining soy sauce and chilli sauce into the noodles. Remove the chicken from the roasting tin once again and mix the noodles with the vegetables until well combined. Sit the chicken back on top and bake for a further 10 minutes until everything is cooked through and hot – cover with foil if the noodles or vegetables start to dry out.

To serve, drizzle the chicken with sesame oil and sprinkle with chopped chilli, if using. Serve immediately.

Tips

For even cooking, choose broccoli stems of an even size, preferably quite thin. If the stems are particularly thick, slice them down the middle.

For a veggie version, omit the chicken and cook the vegetables as above, adding pieces of tofu along with the noodles. Serve sprinkled with toasted seeds and nuts. Use egg-free noodles for a vegan version.

If using dry noodles, cook 2 'nests' according to the packet's instructions before adding to the roasting tin.

Calories	Fibre	Salt	Sugar	Fat
685	12g	5g	6g	17g of which 3g is saturated

WILD GARLIC CHICKEN KIEV WITH WILTED SPRING GREENS

Wild garlic is a wonderful spring ingredient to forage for in shady woodland areas. You will no doubt smell it before you see it. Both the leaves and flowers are edible. March is the best time to pick the young leaves. The flowers appear a little later in spring and can look really pretty scattered over soups and savoury dishes.

Serves 4 Preparation 35 minutes Cooking 20 minutes

Unsalted butter 75g (3oz), softened

Wild garlic leaves 50g (2oz), finely chopped

Salt and freshly ground black pepper

Skinless, boneless chicken breasts 4

Plain flour 2 tbsp, seasoned with salt and pepper

Eggs 2, beaten

Panko breadcrumbs 100g (3½oz)

Olive oil 2 tbsp

Spring greens 250g (9oz), finely sliced

New potatoes to serve (optional)

In a small bowl mix together the butter, wild garlic, salt and pepper.

Using a sharp knife, cut a 3cm (1¼in) slit into each chicken breast at its thickest part to make a small pocket without slicing all the way through. Tuck a tablespoon of the wild garlic butter into each chicken pocket then pull the flesh back over the butter to cover it.

Place the flour, eggs and breadcrumbs onto three separate plates. Dip the chicken in the flour to coat it completely, then coat it with the egg and then the breadcrumbs.

Heat the olive oil in a large frying pan over a medium heat. When it is hot, fry the chicken for 6–7 minutes on each side until golden and cooked through. Remove from the pan and leave to rest on a warmed plate.

Add the remaining garlic butter to the pan and lightly fry the spring greens for 3–4 minutes until just wilted. Season well.

Serve the chicken alongside the wilted greens and boiled new potatoes.

Tips

When collecting wild garlic, make sure you pick from an area with plenty of the plants and take just enough for your own use.

If you can't find wild garlic, use a mixture of spinach and chopped garlic instead: wilt 75g (3oz) spinach in the microwave for 30 seconds. Cool then squeeze out any excess liquid. Mix with the butter and 2 cloves of chopped garlic.

Calories	Fibre	Salt	Sugar	Fat
527	3g	1.5g	0g	26g of which 12g is saturated

CHICKEN & ASPARAGUS PIE

The British asparagus season only lasts a couple of months, so make the most of this delicious vegetable while it's fresh. Here it's combined with chicken, carrots, mushrooms and onions in a silky sauce and topped with a crisp pastry. The homely pie is perfect for those spring days when it's still feeling chilly and you're in need of comfort food.

Serves 4–6 Preparation 20 minutes Cooking 35 minutes

Butter 25g (1oz)

Carrots 2, peeled and diced

Baby onions or shallots 8, peeled

Button mushrooms 110g (4oz)

Plain flour 3 tbsp

Wholegrain mustard 1 tsp

Chicken stock cube 1, crumbled

Milk 450ml (¾ pint)

Cooked chicken 450g (1lb), cut into strips

Asparagus 110g (4oz), trimmed and halved if large

Salt and freshly ground black pepper

Single cream 4 tbsp

Puff pastry 225g (8oz)

Egg 1, beaten

Preheat the oven to 200°C/180°fan/Gas 6.

Melt the butter in a saucepan and fry the carrots, onions or shallots and mushrooms for 5 minutes.

Stir in the flour, mustard and crumbled stock cube and gradually add the milk, stirring until the sauce thickens, boils and is smooth.

Remove from the heat and add the chicken, asparagus, seasoning and cream. Pour the mixture into a 1.2 litre (2 pint) pie dish.

Roll out the pastry to the same size as the dish, dampen the rim of the dish and cover with the pastry. Lightly score the top of the pie or use any pastry trimmings to make decorations. Brush all over with beaten egg. Bake for 25 minutes until the pastry is golden brown.

Tips

If some pieces of asparagus are particularly thick, cut in half lengthways to ensure that they cook through.

If you have standard onions instead of baby or shallots, slice before adding to the pan.

Serve with new potatoes if you like.

NOTES

Calories	Fibre	Salt	Sugar	Fat
414	4g	1.5g	0g	21g of which 10g is saturated

PAN-FRIED STEAK WITH CELERIAC FRIES

Cook up a juicy steak and serve with a creamy mushroom sauce with a tangy mustard kick and moreish celeriac fries.

Serves 2 Preparation 15 minutes plus standing Cooking 25 minutes

Sirloin steak 1 (approx. 300g/11oz), trimmed
Salt and freshly ground black pepper
Celeriac 450g (1lb)
Lemon juice 2 tbsp
Vegetable oil for deep frying
Garlic 1 clove, peeled and crushed
Button mushrooms 100g (3½oz), sliced
Wholegrain mustard 2 tsp
Double cream 4 tbsp
Horseradish sauce 1 tsp
Parsley small bunch, chopped
Watercress or cooked spring vegetables

Season the steak on both sides then leave to stand at room temperature for 15 minutes.

Meanwhile, peel the knobbly skin from the celeriac then cut the flesh into strips, approx. 5mm (¼in) thick, like French fries. Place in a bowl and toss in the lemon juice. Put to one side.

Heat 2 teaspoons of the oil in a small frying pan and gently fry the garlic for 30 seconds. Add the mushrooms and fry, stirring, for about 5 minutes until tender. Turn off the heat, stir in the mustard and cream and season to taste. Set aside until ready to serve.

Heat the oil for deep frying to 180°C (350°F). Drain the celeriac and pat dry with kitchen paper. Deep-fry the celeriac for about 8–10 minutes until cooked through and lightly golden. Drain well on kitchen paper and season with salt and pepper. Cover and keep warm.

While the fries are cooking, heat 2 teaspoons of oil in a heavy frying pan until hot. Add the steak and cook over a high heat for 1 minute on each side. Reduce the heat to medium and cook for about 2½ minutes on each side – depending on thickness – for medium done steak. For rare steak, cook for 1½ minutes on each side; for well done, cook for about 4 minutes on each side.

Remove the steak from the pan, reserving the cooking juices, put on a plate and spread with horseradish; cover lightly and leave to stand for a few minutes.

To serve, gently reheat the mushroom sauce, adding the steak pan juices, for 1–2 minutes until hot. Stir in the parsley. Slice the steak, serve on warmed plates and spoon over the sauce. Serve with the celeriac fries and watercress or freshly cooked spring vegetables.

Tips

Any beef steak will work in this recipe; adjust the cooking time according to the cut. Alternatively, pork steaks or grilled chicken would also go well with these flavours.

For a special occasion add 2 tablespoons sherry or whisky to the sauce when adding the mustard and cream.

For extra flavour, season the celeriac fries with celery salt.

Calories	Fibre	Salt	Sugar	Fat
618	12.5g	2.5g	0g	47g of which 21g is saturated

SLOW COOKED ROGAN JOSH LAMB SHANK & AUBERGINE CURRY

The best way to cook lamb shanks is slow and low, resulting in tender meat falling off the bone, with a delicious deep flavour. If you have a large slow cooker, this red curry will be waiting for you at the end of the day.

Serves 4 Preparation 30 minutes Cooking 8¼ hours 

Roasted red peppers in brine 3, drained

Tomato purée 3 tbsp

Garlic 2 cloves, peeled

Root ginger 5cm (2in) piece, peeled

Hot smoked paprika 2 tsp

Ground cumin 2 tsp

Ground coriander 2 tsp

Garam masala 1 tbsp

Lamb shanks 4

Plain flour 4 tbsp, seasoned with salt and pepper

Vegetable oil 2 tbsp

Onion 1 large, peeled and sliced

Bay leaf 1

Chopped tomatoes 400g can

Salt and freshly ground black pepper

Aubergine 1 large, cubed

Fresh spinach leaves 150g (5oz)

Coriander leaves 4 tbsp chopped, plus extra to serve

Naan breads warmed, to serve (optional)

In a food processor, whizz together the peppers, tomato purée, garlic, ginger and spices to make a thick, smooth paste.

Dust the lamb shanks with the seasoned flour. Heat the oil in a large frying pan over a medium–high heat and fry the lamb shanks for 8–10 minutes, turning occasionally, until lightly browned; set aside on a plate. Add the onion to the pan and fry for 3–4 minutes. Transfer to a large slow cooker pot.

Add the bay leaf, chopped tomatoes, spice paste, salt and pepper to the pot, stir well then pour in 600ml (1 pint) water. Add the shanks, making sure they are tucked well into the liquid. Put the lid on and cook on the low setting for 7 hours.

Add the aubergine and continue to cook for another 1 hour or until the meat is very tender. Remove the lamb shanks to a warmed plate and stir the spinach leaves and chopped coriander into the sauce. Place the lamb shanks in shallow serving bowls and spoon over the sauce. Sprinkle with extra coriander leaves and serve with warmed naan breads.

Tips

If you don't want to use lamb shanks, replace with 750g (1lb 10oz) cubed neck fillet.

To bake in a casserole dish in the oven, preheat to 180°C/160°fan/Gas 4 and cook for 2½ hours, adding the aubergine for the last half an hour, or until the lamb is cooked.

Calories	Fibre	Salt	Sugar	Fat
570	9g	1.5g	2g	31g of which 11g is saturated

ROAST LAMB, CAULIFLOWER & JERSEY ROYALS WITH WATERCRESS & MINT SALSA

There's nothing like a delicious roast for a gathering. New season spring lamb is served with a simple to make, robust minty green salsa.

Serves 4 Preparation 15 minutes plus resting Cooking 1½ hours

Leg of lamb 2kg (4½lb)

Garlic 2 cloves, peeled and cut into slivers

Rosemary 2 sprigs

Onions 2 large, peeled and cut into thick slices

Salt and freshly ground black pepper

Jersey Royal potatoes 750g (1lb 10oz), lightly scrubbed

Cauliflower 1, quartered

Light olive oil 3 tbsp

For the salsa

Mint leaves 25g (1oz) or 2 good handfuls

Parsley 25g (1oz), woody stems discarded

Lemon 1, juice only

Anchovies 4–6 fillets, drained

Garlic 1 large clove, peeled

Capers 2 tbsp

Dijon mustard 2 tsp

Extra virgin olive oil 150ml (¼ pint)

Watercress 50g (2oz), woody stems discarded

Preheat the oven to 200°C/180°fan/Gas 6. Using the tip of a sharp knife, make small incisions into the lamb skin and spike with slivers of garlic and rosemary leaves.

Arrange the onions in a large roasting tin, sit the lamb on top, season and roast on the bottom shelf of the oven for 1¼ hours if you like it pink, or 1½ hours if you prefer it more well done.

Meanwhile, make the salsa: place all the ingredients except the watercress into a food processor or blender. Blitz until smooth then add the watercress and blitz in short bursts to coarsely chop the watercress. Transfer to a small serving bowl.

When the lamb has 45 minutes left to cook, tip the potatoes and cauliflower into a roasting tin. Brush the oil onto the cauliflower florets and drizzle over the potatoes. Season with salt and place on the top oven shelf to roast.

Remove the lamb from the oven, transfer to a platter, cover with foil and leave to rest for 10–15 minutes. Check the potatoes and cauliflower: if just tender, turn the oven off, otherwise cook for a further 10–15 minutes while the lamb is resting.

Carve the lamb and serve with the potatoes, cauliflower and a generous spoonful of salsa.

Tips

Make a note of the lamb weight and calculate the roasting time. Roast for 20 minutes, then for 15–20 minutes per 500g (1lb 2oz) depending on how pink you like it. If you have a temperature probe, an internal temperature of 55°C is medium (pink) and 70°C is well done.

If you fancy extra vegetables, toss some chunky cut carrots in alongside the lamb at the same time as the potatoes and cauliflower go in.

Calories	Fibre	Salt	Sugar	Fat
838	9g	2g	0g	49g of which 16g is saturated

ELDERFLOWER CORDIAL

The taste of springtime! Collect clouds of elderflowers from the hedgerows to make this versatile cordial. It's well worth a try as it's so simple to make.

Makes 1.5 litres (2½ pints) Preparation 10 minutes plus infusing 

Elderflower heads 20
Caster sugar 1kg (2¼lb)
Citric acid 50g (2oz)
Lemon 1, thinly sliced
Limes 4, thinly sliced

Gently rinse the elderflowers in a bowl of cold water to remove any insects.

Place the sugar in a bowl, pour in 900ml (1½ pints) boiling water and stir until dissolved.

Add the citric acid, elderflowers and citrus slices, then stir. Cover and store in a cool dry place for 6 days.

Place a sieve lined with muslin or a clean J-cloth over a large clean bowl or wide jug. Strain the cordial through the sieve and discard the fruit and flowers.

Pour into sterilised bottles, seal and store in the fridge for up to a year.

Tip

Elderflower cordial is delicious with ice, sparkling water and a few mint leaves. It also makes a fabulous simple cocktail when mixed with prosecco. Or you could add it to double cream then whip and use to top poached fruits or a sponge cake. It's also used in the recipes on pages 45 and 46.

NOTES

Calories	Fibre	Salt	Sugar	Fat
54	0g	0g	14g	0g of which 0g is saturated

ELDERFLOWER CREAM SANDWICH BISCUITS

Elderflowers can be found throughout the UK from late May to mid-June. The lacy white scented flowers are a forager's delight to pick on a warm dry day. In this twist on a biscuit 'jammy dodger', elderflower cordial flavours the buttercream that sandwiches the biscuits.

Makes 28 Preparation 30 minutes plus chilling Cooking 30 minutes 

Unsalted butter 225g (8oz)

Golden caster sugar 125g (4½oz)

Plain flour 300g (11oz), plus extra for dusting

Salt pinch

Vanilla extract 1½ tsp

Egg 1, yolk only

For the elderflower cream

Unsalted butter 125g (4½oz)

Icing sugar 175g (6oz)

Elderflower cordial 2–3 tbsp (see page 42)

Yellow food colouring (optional)

Place the butter, sugar, flour and salt in a food processor and whizz to crumbs. Add the vanilla extract and egg yolk and whizz again to bring to a smooth dough. Wrap and chill in the fridge for 1 hour.

Meanwhile, make the elderflower cream. Using a hand-held electric mixer, beat the butter until softened. Add the icing sugar, elderflower cordial and a few drops of yellow food colouring, if using, and whisk until smooth.

Preheat the oven to 180°C/160°fan/Gas 4. Line two baking sheets with non-stick baking paper.

Divide the dough in half. Knead half the dough on a lightly floured surface and roll out to 3–4mm (approx. ⅛in) thick. Stamp out 28 flowers, approx. 5cm (2in) diameter. Transfer to the lined baking sheets, spacing them slightly apart, and bake for 12–15 minutes or until lightly golden. Carefully transfer to a wire rack and leave to cool completely.

While the flowers are in the oven, knead and roll out the remaining dough and stamp out 28 more flowers. If you like, stamp out a 1.5cm (⅝in) circle from the middles. Bake and cool as above.

Use the elderflower cream to sandwich the flower biscuits.

Tip

You can freeze half the dough to make more biscuits at a later date.

Calories	Fibre	Salt	Sugar	Fat
178	0.5g	0.1g	12g	11g of which 7g is saturated

GOOSEBERRY PAVLOVA

This dessert is a real crowd-pleaser. The crisp meringue with a marshmallowy centre has a creamy topping with the tangy sharpness of fresh gooseberries.

Serves 6–8 Preparation 25 minutes plus cooling Cooking 1½ hours 

Eggs 5, whites only

Caster sugar 300g (11oz)

White wine vinegar 1 tsp

Cornflour 1 tsp

Vanilla extract 1 tsp

Green gooseberries 450g (1lb)

Double cream 200ml (7fl oz)

Ready-made vanilla custard 150g (5oz)

Elderflower cordial 2 tbsp (see page 42)

Mint leaves and edible flowers such as fresh elderflowers, rose petals and violas to decorate

Line the base and sides of an ungreased 22 x 32cm (8½ x 12½in) baking tin with non-stick baking paper.

Put the egg whites in a large, grease-free bowl and whisk until stiff. Gradually whisk in 250g (9oz) of the sugar, about 2 tablespoons at a time, until the mixture is thick and glossy. Whisk in the vinegar, cornflour and vanilla. Pile into the prepared tin and gently spread the mixture right to the edge of the tin to cover it evenly, but keeping within the paper for easier removal.

Place in the oven and set the temperature to 140°C/120°fan/Gas 1. Bake for 1½ hours: the meringue will be lightly golden and crisp on the outside but still soft and marshmallowy in the centre. Turn off the oven, leaving the meringue to cool in the oven.

Meanwhile, top and tail the gooseberries and put them in a saucepan with the remaining sugar and 2 tablespoons water. Bring to the boil, then cover and cook over a low heat for 8–10 minutes until soft. Leave to cool completely. Push the gooseberries through a nylon sieve to make a purée, cover and chill.

To serve, carefully lift the meringue from the tin and peel the lining paper from the edges. Slide a palette knife underneath to separate the meringue from the paper and carefully transfer the meringue to a serving board or platter.

Just before serving, whip the cream to soft peaks, add the custard and continue whisking until thick. Mix the elderflower cordial into the gooseberry purée and gently fold into the creamy custard to give a marbled effect. Pile on top of the meringue. Serve immediately, sprinkled with mint leaves and edible flowers.

Tips

This dessert should be eaten as soon as possible after serving so the meringue stays crisp. All the separate components can be prepared in advance and then put together at the last minute.

If you have fresh elderflowers, add a head or two to the gooseberries as they cook for an extra floral flavour (remove before serving). Always wash edible flowers before using.

Calories	Fibre	Salt	Sugar	Fat
318	2g	0.1g	44g	13g of which 8g is saturated

ROSY RHUBARB FOOL WITH STEM GINGER BISCUITS

The forced rhubarb season runs from late December through to the end of March; the early rhubarb is starved of light to produce tender, sweet, rosy pink stalks. Matched with a delicate rose flavour it makes a classic English dessert. Ginger is another classic partner for rhubarb, and these ginger biscuits make a perfect accompaniment to the creamy fool.

Serves 4–6 Preparation 35 minutes plus chilling Cooking 20 minutes 

Rhubarb 400g (14oz), cut into 2cm (¾in) pieces

Caster sugar 3 tbsp

Double cream 300ml (½ pint)

Icing sugar 3 tbsp

Rosewater 1 tsp

Half fat crème fraîche 100ml (3½fl oz)

Edible rose petals to decorate

For the stem ginger biscuits

Butter 50g (2oz)

Soft brown sugar 25g (1oz)

Golden syrup 50g (2oz)

Self-raising flour 125g (4½oz)

Bicarbonate of soda ¼ tsp

Ground ginger ½ tsp

Stem ginger in syrup 2 pieces, finely chopped

Place the rhubarb in a pan with the caster sugar and 2 tablespoons water. Bring to the boil, cover and simmer for 6–7 minutes until softened. Remove from the heat and leave to cool completely.

In a large bowl whisk together the double cream, icing sugar and rosewater to soft peaks. Gently fold in the crème fraîche and cooled stewed rhubarb.

Spoon into glass dishes and place in the fridge until ready to serve.

To make the biscuits, melt the butter, sugar and golden syrup together in a pan. Sift the flour, bicarbonate of soda and ground ginger into a bowl then stir in the stem ginger. Pour in the butter mixture and mix to a dough. Leave in the fridge for 1 hour.

Preheat the oven to 190°C/170°fan/Gas 5. Line a baking sheet with non-stick baking paper.

When ready to bake, divide the biscuit dough into 12 balls. Place on the lined baking sheet, spacing them about 5cm (2in) apart and flattening them slightly. Bake for 10–12 minutes or until lightly golden.

Leave on the tray to cool and firm up for a few minutes then transfer to a wire rack to cool completely.

To serve, decorate the fool with a few rose petals and serve with the stem ginger biscuits.

Calories	Fibre	Salt	Sugar	Fat
482	2g	0.5g	22g	33g of which 21g is saturated

RHUBARB & CUSTARD CAKE

The fine pink stalks of spring rhubarb look so pretty in any recipe. In this moist bake rhubarb and white chocolate custard combine to make a truly irresistible treat.

Serves 12 Preparation 20 minutes plus cooling and overnight storing Cooking 55 minutes

White chocolate 225g (8oz), chopped

Lightly salted butter 75g (3oz), plus extra for greasing

Caster sugar 75g (3oz)

Eggs 2 medium

Vanilla extract 1 tsp

Plain flour 100g (3½oz)

Baking powder 1 tsp

Custard powder 50g (2oz)

Rhubarb 125g (4½oz), trimmed and chopped

Preheat the oven to 170°C/150°fan/Gas 3. Grease and line an 18cm (7in) square cake tin.

Put 100g (3½oz) white chocolate and the butter in a bowl over a saucepan of barely simmering water until melted. Remove from the heat and leave to cool for 10 minutes.

Beat the sugar, eggs and vanilla into the chocolate mixture. Sift the flour, baking powder and custard powder over the top and mix until smooth then stir in all but a few pieces of rhubarb along with another 100g (3½oz) white chocolate.

Transfer to the prepared tin and smooth the top. Scatter the remaining rhubarb over the mixture. Bake for 45–50 minutes until risen and just firm to the touch – a skewer inserted into the centre of the cake should have a few crumbs clinging to it. Leave to cool completely in the tin, then remove from the tin, wrap and store until the next day to allow the flavours and texture to develop.

To serve, slice into 12 pieces. Melt the remaining chocolate and drizzle over the top. Leave to set before serving. Keep in an airtight container for up to a week or freeze for up to 6 months.

Tips

Serve cold as a tea-time treat, or pop a slice in the microwave for a few seconds to warm through then serve with custard as a tasty pudding.

If using summer rhubarb, which has thicker, greener stalks, slice the stalks thinly and then halve or quarter the slices before mixing into the cake batter.

Calories	Fibre	Salt	Sugar	Fat
227	0.5g	0.3g	18g	12g of which 7g is saturated

SPICED EASTER CAKE

This gently spiced sponge cake is quite a show-stopper and perfect for serving a crowd. It's lighter than the traditional simnel cake and includes layers of marzipan and lemon curd.

Serves 12 Preparation 20 minutes plus cooling Cooking 20 minutes  

Butter 175g (6oz), softened, plus extra for greasing
Caster sugar 175g (6oz)
Eggs 2, beaten
Baking powder 1 tsp
Ground cinnamon 1 tsp
Ground allspice 1 tsp
Self-raising flour 300g (11oz)
Vanilla extract 1 tsp
Milk 225ml (8fl oz)
Marzipan 250g (9oz)
Lemon curd 75g (3oz)
Mini eggs to decorate

Preheat the oven to 190°C/170°fan/Gas 5. Grease and line three 18cm (7in) sandwich tins.

Cream the butter and sugar together until pale and fluffy. Gradually beat in the eggs. Sift over the baking powder, cinnamon, allspice and half of the flour then fold into the mixture. Fold in the vanilla extract and half of the milk. Repeat with the remaining flour and milk.

Divide the mixture between the prepared tins and bake for 20 minutes or until just firm to the touch. Leave to cool in the tins.

Cut the marzipan into three pieces and roll out into 18cm (7in) circles. Sandwich the cakes together with the marzipan and lemon curd. Use a little lemon curd to fix marzipan and chocolate eggs to the top.

Tips

Derived from the dried, unripe berries of the pimento tree, allspice delivers the flavours of many different spices. If you don't have allspice, add an extra ½ teaspoon cinnamon, ¼ teaspoon ground cloves and ¼ teaspoon ground nutmeg.

If you prefer lime curd, use that instead of lemon.

Instead of the mini eggs you could top the cake with 11 marzipan balls (said to represent 11 of Jesus's disciples, except Judas), like a simnel cake.

Calories	Fibre	Salt	Sugar	Fat
349	1.5g	0.4g	29g	16g of which 8g is saturated

SUMMER

GRIDDLED COURGETTE, HERB & YOGURT DIP

Home-grown courgettes are at their best between June and September. They're a useful vegetable that can be eaten raw or cooked. In this recipe they're griddled to give them a roasted flavour.

Serves 6 Preparation 15 minutes Cooking 10 minutes 

Courgette 1 large (400g/14oz), trimmed
Olive oil 2 tbsp, plus extra for drizzling
Fresh dill 2 tbsp chopped
Mint leaves 2 tbsp chopped
Garlic 1 clove, peeled and crushed
Lemon 1 small, juice only
Greek-style yogurt 250g (9oz)
Salt and freshly ground black pepper

To serve (optional)
Pitta bread toasted
Raw vegetables such as radishes, chicory leaves, sliced cucumber and peppers

Heat a griddle pan until just smoking. Chop the courgette in half then cut each half lengthways. Brush the cut sides with olive oil and place, cut sides down, on the hot griddle. Leave for 3–4 minutes until scorched marks appear. Brush the skin side with more olive oil, turn over and cook for another 3–4 minutes.

Transfer the courgettes to a chopping board and leave to cool completely, then finely dice.

In a bowl mix together the herbs, garlic, lemon juice and yogurt. Stir in the courgettes and season to taste.

Transfer the dip to a serving dish, drizzle with a little olive oil and serve with toasted pitta bread and a selection of raw summer vegetables.

NOTES

Calories	Fibre	Salt	Sugar	Fat
87	1g	0.5g	0g	6g of which 3g is saturated

SUMMER SQUASH & PEPPER HOUMOUS

It's well worth making your own houmous; here's a simple take on the recipe that uses small courgettes or summer squash and peppers. Delicious served with flatbreads and crisp raw vegetables, or spoon a dollop alongside barbecued lamb, fish or chicken.

Serves 6 Preparation 15 minutes plus chilling Cooking 30 minutes 

Summer squash or small courgettes 400g (14oz), halved lengthways
Red or yellow peppers 2, halved and deseeded
Garlic 2 large cloves, skin on
Tahini 3 tbsp
Olive oil 2 tbsp, plus extra to serve
Lemon 1 small, grated zest and juice
Salt 1 tsp
Paprika ½ tsp, plus extra to garnish
Mint leaves or parsley 2 tbsp roughly chopped, plus extra to garnish

Preheat the oven to 220°C/200°fan/Gas 7. Arrange the squash or courgettes and peppers, cut sides up, in a single layer on a baking sheet. Tuck in the garlic cloves. Cook for 30 minutes or until the peppers are slightly charred and blistered.

Remove the skins from the garlic then put the cloves in a food processor with the squash and peppers. Add the tahini, olive oil, half the lemon juice, the salt and paprika. Blitz until smooth. Taste and add more lemon juice or salt if needed. Add the chopped herbs and blitz.

Transfer to a serving dish and place in the fridge to firm up for 30 minutes. Best served at room temperature. To serve, drizzle with olive oil and sprinkle with lemon zest, parsley and paprika.

Tips

Tahini is a paste made from ground sesame seeds; it's vegan, gluten-free, and has a rich, nutty taste that goes well in dressings and dips, such as houmous.

Use young and tender courgettes or soft-skinned summer squash. In older veg the skins can be bitter, in which case scoop out the cooked flesh and discard the shells.

For a coarser texture, use a combination of drained canned chickpeas and courgettes or squash. Use more garlic, or less, or add a small green chilli according to taste.

In autumn, use butternut squash to make this houmous. Wrap the whole squash in foil and bake at 190°C/170°fan/Gas 5 for an hour or until softened. Halve and scoop out the seeds and fibre, transfer the flesh to a food processor and proceed as above.

Calories	Fibre	Salt	Sugar	Fat
137	3g	1g	0g	12g of which 2g is saturated

ROASTED SUMAC TOMATO SALAD WITH BURRATA & LEMON BALM DRESSING

You don't need much space to grow tomatoes, just a sunny spot, and they are relatively easy to care for. If you are buying them look for firm tomatoes on their vine, as they tend to be sweeter. Pop under-ripe tomatoes on the windowsill for a few days and they will happily ripen up. Roasting intensifies their flavour, which goes beautifully with the mild, creamy burrata.

Serves 2 Preparation 15 minutes Cooking 40 minutes 

Ripe tomatoes 750g (1lb 10oz), halved

Rosemary 3 sprigs

Garlic 5 cloves, skin on

Olive oil 5 tbsp

Sumac 1 tsp, plus extra for dusting

Salt and freshly ground black pepper

Sherry vinegar 1 tbsp

Lemon balm leaves 2 tbsp chopped, plus extra leaves to serve

Burrata 150g (5oz), drained

Crusty bread to serve

Preheat the oven to 200°C/180°fan/Gas 6. Put the tomatoes in a large roasting tin, tucking in the rosemary sprigs and garlic cloves. Drizzle with 2 tablespoons olive oil, 1 teaspoon sumac, salt and pepper. Give the tin a good shake to toss together, then roast for 35–40 minutes until the tomatoes are slightly blistered and softened but still holding their shape. Discard the rosemary.

To make the dressing, squeeze two of the roasted garlic cloves out of their skins into a bowl. Add one of the larger roasted tomato halves, first discarding the skin and core. Add the remaining olive oil, the sherry vinegar, chopped lemon balm and plenty of salt and pepper and whisk well.

Spoon the tomatoes onto a large serving plate. Place the whole burrata in the middle and drizzle over the dressing. Scatter over a few lemon balm leaves and a light dusting of sumac.

Serve immediately with some crusty bread to mop up the dressing.

Tips

If you don't have lemon balm, use mint or basil leaves instead.

Burrata is a deliciously smooth, soft cheese made from mozzarella and cream. Mozzarella would also work well in this recipe.

Sumac is a ground spice, often used in Middle-Eastern dishes, which has a tart citrussy flavour.

Calories	Fibre	Salt	Sugar	Fat
381	6g	2g	0g	29g of which 12g is saturated

PEA FALAFELS

These gluten-free Lebanese-style fritters are traditionally made with chickpeas. Here, green peas replace some of the usual pulses to make a colourful lunch or supper.

Serves 2 Preparation 25 minutes plus chilling Cooking 8 minutes  

Freshly shelled (or frozen) peas 200g (7oz)

Cooked (or canned) chickpeas 200g (7oz)

Tahini or other nut butter 1 tbsp (see tip)

Gram flour 2 tbsp, plus extra for dusting

Garlic 2 cloves, peeled and crushed

Ground cumin 1 tsp

Salt and freshly ground black pepper

Coriander small bunch, chopped

Vegetable oil 2 tbsp

For the tomato salsa

Tomatoes 125g (4½oz), chopped

Red chilli 1 small, deseeded and finely chopped

Coriander seeds ½ tsp, toasted and crushed

Cider vinegar 1 tbsp

Caster sugar 1 tsp

To serve (optional)

Flatbreads

Extra herbs or salad

Bring a small saucepan of water to the boil and cook the fresh peas for 1 minute. Drain well. If using frozen peas, place in a bowl, pour over boiling water to defrost, and drain well.

Put the peas in a blender or food processor and add the chickpeas, tahini, gram flour, half the garlic, the cumin, salt and pepper, and some of the coriander. Blitz until well blended and clumpy. If the mixture looks dry, add a little water until it binds together.

Using wet hands, shape into six patties, 8cm (3in) in diameter. Dust with a little gram flour and place on a plate. Chill for 30 minutes or until ready to cook.

Meanwhile, make the tomato salsa. Mix all the ingredients together, along with some more of the fresh coriander. Season to taste. Cover and leave at room temperature to allow the flavours to develop. Chill if planning to serve more than 30 minutes ahead.

To cook, heat the oil in a large frying pan until hot, then cook the falafels for about 4 minutes on each side until crisp and golden. Drain on kitchen paper. Serve with the tomato salsa and accompany with flatbreads and extra herbs or salad.

Tips

Tahini is a paste made from ground sesame seeds. It is rich and nutty and is the predominant flavour of houmous. Any smooth nut butter will work in this recipe.

Gram flour is made from ground dried chickpeas. It is also called besan or garbanzo bean flour and is naturally gluten-free. Use another gluten-free flour or ordinary wheat flour if you prefer.

Calories	Fibre	Salt	Sugar	Fat
508	16g	1.5g	2g	27g of which 3g is saturated

TEMPURA-STYLE SUMMER VEGETABLES

A selection of your favourite summer vegetables encased in a simple crisp batter, which captures all the natural flavours and textures in every bite.

Serves 2 Preparation 25 minutes Cooking 10 minutes 

Prepared seasonal vegetables (see tip) 350g (12oz)

Plain flour 75g (3oz)

Salt pinch

Baking powder ¼ tsp

Egg 1 medium, yolk only

Vegetable oil for deep frying

Sticky rice or noodles to serve (optional)

For the cucumber relish

Small cucumber 1, grated

Mirin or sweet sherry 2 tbsp

White rice or wine vinegar 1 tbsp

Dark soy sauce 1 tbsp

Clear honey 1 tsp

Bring a saucepan of water to the boil and blanch the vegetables as suggested below, then drain and cool under cold running water. Drain well and pat dry with kitchen paper. Place in a bowl and toss with a heaped tablespoon of the flour.

Put the remaining flour in a bowl with the salt and baking powder. Make a well in the centre and add the egg yolk and 100ml (3½fl oz) cold water. Gradually combine the ingredients together until blended and thick – this batter doesn't need to be silky smooth.

Heat the oil for deep frying to 190°C (375°F). Dip individual vegetables in the batter and deep-fry in two batches for about 5 minutes per batch until golden and crisp. Drain on kitchen paper and keep warm while cooking the remaining vegetables.

To make the cucumber relish, mix all the ingredients together in a bowl.

Serve the vegetables as soon after they are cooked as possible. Accompany with the cucumber relish and sticky rice or noodles.

Tip

Just about any vegetable will work in this recipe. Prepare them as follows:

Peppers: halve, deseed and cut into chunky pieces – blanch for 5 minutes.

Courgette, marrow: trim and slice into 1cm (½in) thick pieces – blanch for 2 minutes.

Broccoli, cauliflower: remove thick stalks; cut into small florets – blanch for 3 minutes.

Runner beans: string large, thick beans and slice thickly – blanch for 2 minutes.

Baby sweetcorn, spring onions, baby leek: trim then cut spring onions or baby leeks in half (leave baby corn whole) – blanch for 1 minute.

Carrot, celeriac, potato: cut into slices or batons – blanch for 5 minutes.

Artichoke hearts, aubergine: cut hearts in half and aubergine into slices – blanch for 1 minute.

Calories	Fibre	Salt	Sugar	Fat
377	6g	2g	4g	19g of which 2g is saturated

SUMMER SOUP

This soup will have everyone guessing – what is in it? It's a wonderful way to use up a glut of summer courgettes and tender herbs, simple to make and velvety rich.

Serves 4 Preparation 15 minutes Cooking 30 minutes  

Courgettes 450g (1lb), sliced

Onion or leek 1 large, peeled and chopped

Vegetable or chicken stock 450ml (¾ pint)

Watercress 75g (3oz), woody stems discarded

Parsley or dill large bunch, approx. 50g (2oz), woody stems discarded

Soft cheese with garlic and herbs 150g pack

Double cream 150ml (¼ pint)

Salt and freshly ground black pepper

Extra virgin olive oil and dried chilli flakes to garnish (optional)

Put the courgettes and onion or leek in a large saucepan and add the stock. Cover and bring to the boil, then reduce the heat and simmer for 15 minutes or until the vegetables are very soft.

Add the watercress and most of the parsley or dill, reserving a few leaves to garnish. Simmer for a few minutes, just long enough to wilt the leaves.

Using a stick blender, whizz the soup in the pan. Bring to a very gentle simmer, add the cheese and stir until it has melted into the soup. Do not let the soup boil.

Stir in most of the cream and heat through. Taste and adjust the seasoning. Ladle into warmed bowls and garnish with a swirl of cream and a sprinkling of chopped herbs, olive oil and chilli flakes if you like.

Tips

Freeze the soup at the stage before adding the cheese. Defrost, bring to a simmer, then continue as above.

It's easy to adapt this soup according to the season: instead of courgettes, try any combination of celery, leeks, cauliflower or parsnip – you will need to simmer them for longer until they are very soft.

NOTES

Calories	Fibre	Salt	Sugar	Fat
310	4g	2g	0g	28g of which 17g is saturated

SUMMER HERB BUTTERS

Fresh herbs are abundant in the summer: it is a good time to capture their flavours so you can enjoy them into the next season. Herb-flavoured butters are a great way to enrich soups and sauces, or add a slice to freshly cooked vegetables, fish, chicken or meat. Here are a few flavour combinations to try.

Makes 100g (3½oz) flavoured butter Preparation 15 minutes Cooking none  

Unsalted butter 100g (3½oz), softened

Sea salt flakes and freshly ground black pepper

For tarragon & lemon butter

Fresh tarragon 3 tbsp chopped leaves

Lemon 1, finely grated zest

For sun-dried tomato, black olive & basil butter

Sun-dried tomatoes in oil 4, finely chopped

Pitted black olives 8, finely chopped

Basil leaves 15g (½oz), finely shredded

For rosemary & garlic butter

Fresh rosemary 2 tsp finely chopped

Garlic 2 cloves, peeled and crushed

For coriander, lime & chilli butter

Fresh coriander 3 tbsp, finely chopped

Lime 1, finely grated zest

Red chilli 1, deseeded and finely chopped

Put the softened butter into a bowl and beat using a hand-held electric mixer for 1–2 minutes until pale and creamy. Stir in the flavouring of your choice along with a pinch of sea salt flakes and black pepper.

Either spoon into a small bowl and smooth over the surface, or spoon onto a piece of greaseproof paper and roll into a log. Chill for at least 1 hour before serving.

Tip

To freeze, slice the log into discs so you can grab individual discs when you need them. Freeze for up to 3 months.

NOTES

Calories	Fibre	Salt	Sugar	Fat	Based on a 15g (½oz) serving
81	0g	0.5g	0g	9g of which 5g is saturated	

FISH WITH OREGANO BUTTER & CAULIFLOWER

The creamy crushed cauliflower in this recipe is perfect with fish and such a delicious way to serve it. It's a versatile dish: choose whichever white fish is at its best and change the herbs according to what you have.

Serves 2 Preparation 10 minutes Cooking 15 minutes

Green beans 175g (6oz), trimmed
Cauliflower ½, cut into florets
Double cream 4 tbsp
Freshly grated nutmeg
Salt and freshly ground black pepper
Hake (or other white fish) fillets, skin on, about 450g (1lb)
Olive oil for brushing
Butter 25g (1oz)
Oregano leaves 2 tbsp, plus extra to garnish
White wine vinegar 1–2 tsp

Half fill the base of a steamer with water and bring to the boil. Add the green beans to the water and the cauliflower to the steamer basket. Cover and cook for 5 minutes. Drain and keep the beans warm.

Add the cream to the steamer base with the cauliflower, nutmeg, salt and pepper. Bring to the boil and roughly crush the cauliflower with a fork.

Meanwhile, put a non-stick frying pan over a high heat. Brush the fish with olive oil and cook, skin-side down, for 4 minutes. Turn and cook for about 2 minutes more until cooked through. Remove the fish from the pan and keep warm.

Add the butter and oregano to the pan and let it brown. Remove from the heat and add the vinegar, to taste.

Place the crushed cauliflower on two plates, top with the fish then drizzle with the butter. Garnish with oregano leaves and serve with the green beans.

Tips

Use any white fish that your fishmonger or supermarket has on offer; you may have to adjust the cooking times slightly, so watch until the fish turns opaque.

Instead of green beans, serve with runner or broad beans if you prefer. Replace the oregano butter with one of the herb butters on page 69.

Calories	Fibre	Salt	Sugar	Fat
631	6g	2g	0g	48g of which 25g is saturated

HOMEMADE HERB CHEESE

Herbs need regular trimming to keep them in good shape and encourage healthy new growth, so cut them often. This recipe uses parsley, chives and tarragon but you could use other herbs from your garden.

Serves 8 Time 30 minutes plus 2 days draining and chilling  

Full-fat Greek-style yogurt 500g (1lb 2oz)

Salt 1 tsp

Fresh parsley 3 tbsp chopped

Fresh chives 3 tbsp chopped

Fresh tarragon 3 tbsp chopped leaves

Freshly ground black pepper

Toasted bread, crackers or vegetable batons to serve (optional)

Line a large nylon sieve with clean muslin or a clean, fine tea towel and place over a large bowl.

Mix the yogurt and salt together and pour into the sieve. Leave to drain for at least 12 hours, or overnight, in the fridge.

Gather up the muslin around the cheese and tie with string to make a ball. Suspend over the bowl in the fridge for a further 24 hours until the mixture has stopped dripping and has the texture of soft cheese.

Unwrap the cheese and divide into 8. Mix the chopped herbs with a little freshly ground black pepper and roll each portion of cheese in the herb mixture. Put on a lined plate, cover and chill until ready to serve. Serve with toasted bread, crackers or vegetable batons, if you like.

Tip

For a punchier cheese, mix 2 finely chopped spring onions with the herbs in place of the tarragon. You could use your homemade cheese to stuff the chicken in the recipe overleaf.

NOTES

Calories	Fibre	Salt	Sugar	Fat
89	0.5g	0.5g	0g	6g of which 4g is saturated

CHICKEN STUFFED WITH HERBS

This recipe makes the most of the abundance of the summer's crop of young leaves and fragrant garden herbs. Tarragon or basil's gutsy flavours can lead the way, or use dill and parsley for a milder flavour. It's equally good hot or cold, and you can double or treble the quantities for a larger gathering.

Serves 2 Preparation 10 minutes Cooking 20–25 minutes 

Skinless chicken breast fillets 2, approx. 150g (5oz) each

Streaky bacon 4–6 rindless rashers

Mixed summer leaves such as baby spinach, watercress, rocket, flat-leaf parsley 25g (1oz)

Fresh basil or tarragon 2 tbsp chopped leaves, plus extra to garnish

Soft cheese with garlic and herbs 100g (3½oz)

Lemon ½, grated zest

Salt and freshly ground black pepper

Small tomatoes on the vine to serve (optional)

Preheat the oven to 200°C/180°fan/Gas 6. Slice the chicken breasts in half horizontally through the thickest part without cutting all the way through, and open like a book. Lay between two sheets of non-stick baking paper then gently bash with a rolling pin to flatten to an even thickness of approx. 2cm (¾in).

Lay the bacon on a board and use the flat side of a knife to stretch out the rashers.

Put the leaves and herbs in a food processor with the soft cheese and lemon zest. Blitz until smooth. Season with a little salt and pepper.

Spread the herby cheese mixture evenly over the chicken and roll up, starting from the narrow end. Wrap each breast with two rashers of bacon, not too tightly, and secure each roll with a cocktail stick.

Place in a baking tray and cook for 20–25 minutes. Ten minutes before the end, pop some bunches of tomatoes on the vine alongside to cook.

Slice the chicken and serve with the roasted tomatoes and a sprinkle of extra herbs.

Tips

If you have a summer glut of herbs, you can freeze them in bags: either leave whole to crumble from frozen or chop finely.

Finely chop mint and freeze with a drop of water in ice cube trays – pop out the frozen cubes to add to homemade mint sauce or dressings.

Common garden herbs, such as rosemary, oregano and thyme, are perfect for making simple herb oils to use in salad dressings and drizzling over vegetables and pasta.

Calories	Fibre	Salt	Sugar	Fat
415	0.1g	3.5g	0g	25g of which 12g is saturated

CORONATION CHICKEN PIE

A fine-looking pie, rich, buttery, crisp and lightly flaky, perfect for summer entertaining. Serve with our sweet-sharp instant peach chutney.

Serves 6 Preparation 40 minutes plus cooling Cooking 1 hour 20 minutes

Lightly salted butter 100g (3½oz)

Onion 1, peeled and sliced

Garlic 2 cloves, peeled and crushed

Mild curry powder 1 tbsp

Soft dried peaches or apricots 100g (3½oz), finely chopped

Eggs 2 medium, beaten

Coriander small bunch, chopped

Salt and freshly ground black pepper

Filo pastry sheets 5 large

Cooked skinless, boneless chicken 450g (1lb)

For the peach chutney

Ripe peaches 2, stoned and chopped

White wine vinegar 2 tbsp

Clear honey 1 tbsp

Root ginger small piece, peeled and grated

Nigella (black onion) seeds 1 tsp (optional)

Melt 25g (1oz) of the butter in a pan until bubbling and fry the onion and garlic for 2–3 minutes, stirring. Reduce the heat, sprinkle over the curry powder, cover and cook gently for 15 minutes until soft.

Add 150ml (¼ pint) water and the dried fruit, bring to the boil and simmer for 5 minutes until reduced and slightly syrupy. Remove from the heat and whisk in the eggs. Return to a very low heat and cook, stirring, for 6–7 minutes until lightly thickened, taking care not to scramble the eggs. Stir in the coriander, season and set aside.

Preheat the oven to 200°C/180°fan/Gas 6. Melt the remaining butter and brush some around the inside of a 20cm (8in) springform cake tin. Brush 1 sheet of pastry with butter and push into the tin to line it, leaving an overhang. Repeat with another pastry sheet, laying it at a slightly different angle. Continue with the remaining sheets so that the tin is well lined.

Mix the chicken into the sauce and spoon into the pastry case. Fold over the overhanging pastry to cover the filling. Brush with any remaining butter and stand the tin on a baking tray. Bake for about 50 minutes until the pastry is golden and the chicken is hot. Leave to stand in the tin for 20 minutes.

To make the peach chutney, mix all the ingredients together and season to taste. Leave to stand at room temperature until ready to serve.

Carefully remove the pie from the tin and transfer to a serving plate. Best served warm, accompanied with the peach chutney.

Tips

Use cooked lamb or beef instead of chicken. Try fresh apricots, plums or nectarines instead of peaches in the chutney.

Calories	Fibre	Salt	Sugar	Fat
408	4g	1.5g	6g	19g of which 10g is saturated

HERBY LAMB BURGERS WITH BEETROOT & MINT RELISH

It's that time of year to light the barbecue and enjoy some fine weather alfresco dining. Homemade burgers are simply the best, piled onto soft rolls or flatbreads, topped with pickles, salads and relishes. Herb gardens are now at their best, and this recipe uses herbs generously, both in the burgers and the relish.

Makes 4 Preparation 15 minutes Cooking 10 minutes 

Lamb mince (10% fat) 500g (1lb 2oz)
Onion 1 small, peeled and finely chopped
Garlic 1 clove, peeled and finely chopped
Fresh mint 2 tbsp finely chopped
Fresh parsley 2 tbsp finely chopped
Ground coriander or ground mace ½–1 tsp
Salt and freshly ground black pepper
Olive oil 2 tsp

For the beetroot & mint relish

Beetroot 2 small, cooked, peeled, and diced
Fresh mint 2 tbsp finely chopped
Fresh chives 1 tbsp finely snipped
Greek-style natural yogurt 4 tbsp

To serve (optional)

Burger buns, flatbreads or wraps warmed
Salad leaves, or watercress and cucumber

In a large bowl, knead together the lamb, onion, garlic, mint, parsley, ground coriander or mace, and plenty of salt and pepper. Divide the mix into four and shape each into a patty approx. 2cm (¾in) thick. Cover and chill until required, but let them come back to room temperature before grilling.

To make the beetroot relish, fold together the beetroot, mint, chives and yogurt. Cover and leave in a cool place for the flavours to develop.

Preheat the grill to medium, or place a griddle pan over a medium–high heat, or prepare the barbecue until the embers are glowing. Brush the burgers with a little oil and grill for 4–5 minutes on each side until cooked through and slightly charred.

Serve each burger in a split bun or a flatbread or warmed wrap, with fresh salad leaves or watercress and cucumber. Top with the beetroot and mint relish.

Tips

Pork mince or a mix of pork and lamb work well too.

If buying fresh mince, you can make these burgers well in advance, open freeze them and then pack and freeze for up to 3 months – handy for that impromptu BBQ when the sun comes out! Defrost thoroughly before cooking.

Calories	Fibre	Salt	Sugar	Fat
334	2g	1.5g	0g	22g of which 11g is saturated

STEAK WITH TARRAGON BUTTER SAUCE

Herbs are one of the easiest things to cultivate in the garden, or even on a window ledge. All you need is a pot and a plant or two of your choice, a little sunshine and regular water. Grow a few of your favourites and you'll always have a fresh supply to add to salads, pastas and sauces.

Serves 2 Preparation 5 minutes plus resting Cooking 5 minutes

Ribeye steaks 2, at room temperature
Salt and freshly ground black pepper
Vegetable oil 1 tbsp
Butter 75g (3oz)
White wine vinegar 2 tsp
Egg 1 medium, yolk only
Tarragon 4 sprigs, leaves finely chopped
Chips and salad to serve (optional)

Season the steaks on both sides. Heat a heavy frying pan over a high heat until smoking. Add the oil and 25g (1oz) butter. Fry the steaks for 2 minutes on each side. Put on two warmed plates, cover lightly and leave to rest for 2 minutes.

Whisk the vinegar, egg yolk, salt and pepper in a small bowl. Melt the remaining butter in a microwave on high for about 1 minute until bubbling. Pour onto the egg mixture, whisking well until smooth. Put the sauce back in the microwave and cook for 10 seconds, whisk well, then cook for another 10 seconds to make a thick sauce. Stir in the chopped tarragon.

Serve the steaks and sauce with chips and salad, if you like.

Tips

Use rump or sirloin steaks if you prefer.

Instead of tarragon, you could use chives or fennel fronds. Or some finely chopped home-grown chillies.

NOTES

Calories	Fibre	Salt	Sugar	Fat
567	0g	2g	0g	46g of which 24g is saturated

NO-CHURN BLACKCURRANT ICE CREAM

Blackcurrants are rich in colour, bursting with vitamin C and packed with antioxidants that help protect the immune system. June and July are the best months to harvest these little jewels. They freeze well (see below) so are ideal to make cordials, muffins or crumbles for a tasty dose of vitamin C over the winter months. But as this is summer, try this no-churn ice cream. Later in the year it's delicious served with hot apple crumble!

Serves 8 Preparation 30 minutes plus freezing Cooking 10 minutes  

Blackcurrants 500g (1lb 2oz), fresh or frozen

Double cream 600ml (1 pint)

Condensed milk 397g can

Ice cream wafers or fresh blackcurrant or mint leaves to serve (optional)

Place the blackcurrants in a saucepan with 4 tablespoons water. Bring to the boil then simmer for 5–6 minutes or until the fruit has broken down and the juices have thickened slightly. Remove from the heat and leave to cool a little.

Using the back of a wooden spoon, press the blackcurrants through a metal sieve set over a mixing bowl to extract all the juice. Discard the pulp and stalks.

In another bowl, whisk the double cream until it forms soft peaks. Add the condensed milk and whisk again to soft peaks. Using a rubber spatula, fold in the fruit purée. (Use a figure of eight folding motion to create a lightly marbled effect.)

Pour into a 900g (2lb) loaf tin lined with non-stick baking paper or a shallow freezerproof container. Cover and freeze for at least 4 hours. Transfer to the fridge for about 45 minutes before serving.

Slice the ice cream and sandwich between wafers. Alternatively, scoop and serve with fresh blackcurrant or mint leaves.

Tips

Crumble cookies, meringue or honeycomb and fold in with the fruit purée.

To freeze blackcurrants, tip them onto a tray, discard unripe or damaged berries and leaves and remove stalks. Rinse in cold water and dry completely. Line a baking tray with baking paper then spread with a single layer of blackcurrants and freeze until solid. Transfer to freezer bags or lidded containers, label and return to the freezer. Aim to use within 9 months.

NOTES

Calories	Fibre	Salt	Sugar	Fat
522	3g	0.1g	29g	42g of which 26g is saturated

BRAMBLE MOUSSE

In late summer, the sight of these plump berries growing along the hedgerows conjures up winter warmers like pies and crumbles, jams, and sauces – and they freeze well (see below) – but how about this deliciously light mousse? It's best to gather blackberries in the morning when they are still full of moisture – and, unlike raspberries, gently tug blackberries when picking, to include their centre plug.

Serves 4 Preparation 45 minutes plus setting Cooking 5 minutes

Fresh blackberries 500g (1lb 2oz)

Lemon juice 2 tbsp

Caster sugar 125g (4½oz)

Gelatine leaves 5

Eggs 3

Double or whipping cream 150ml (¼ pint)

Whole blackberries, fresh thyme sprigs, icing sugar to decorate (optional)

Pick over the berries. Tip into a saucepan with the lemon juice and 2 tablespoons of the caster sugar. Simmer until soft and pulpy.

Meanwhile, soak the gelatine leaves in a bowl of cold water for 5 minutes.

Purée the cooked blackberries then, using the back of a spoon, press the berries through a metal sieve back into a clean pan. Bring back to a gentle simmer, tasting and adding a little extra sugar if needed.

Squeeze out the water from the gelatine then stir the gelatine into the hot berry purée until dissolved. Remove from the heat and set aside until completely cold and starting to thicken.

Meanwhile, place the eggs and remaining sugar in a large heatproof bowl set over a pan of gently simmering water. Whisk until the mixture is foamy and leaves a trail. Remove the bowl from the heat.

Lightly whip the cream until almost the same consistency as the egg and sugar mixture.

Gently fold 2 tablespoons of the cream into the cold blackberry purée, then fold in the remaining cream and the egg mixture. When beginning to set, pour into a 1.5 litre (2½ pint) shallow glass serving bowl or 6 individual glasses. Cover and chill until set.

Decorate with whole blackberries and thyme sprigs, if using, and dust with icing sugar.

Tips

To freeze blackberries, wash and then pat thoroughly dry. Line a baking tray with baking paper then spread with a single layer of blackberries and freeze until solid. Transfer to freezer bags or lidded containers, label and return to the freezer. Aim to use within 9 months.

If your recipe calls for gelatine leaves or sheets but you only have powder (or vice versa), don't worry. One packet (1 tablespoon) of powdered gelatine is equivalent to 4 gelatine sheets. This is enough to soft-set approx. 500ml (18fl oz) of liquid.

Calories	Fibre	Salt	Sugar	Fat
379	5g	0.2g	33g	23g of which 13g is saturated

CHERRY CHEESECAKE SQUARES

These cheesecake squares are perfect for using up a glut of soft fruits – cherries work particularly well. Cherries have been grown in the UK for more than 2,000 years, with many orchards in Kent.

Makes 9 squares Preparation 15 minutes plus chilling Cooking 30 minutes 

Digestive biscuits 8, crushed to fine crumbs
Butter 25g (1oz), melted
Full fat soft cheese 280g tub
Natural yogurt 150g (5oz)
Eggs 2 medium, whites only
Caster sugar 3 tbsp
Plain flour 2 tbsp
Vanilla extract 1 tsp
Fresh cherries 150g (5oz), stoned and chopped

Preheat the oven to 190°C/170°fan/Gas 5. Line a 20cm (8in) square tin with non-stick baking paper. Mix the biscuit crumbs with the butter and press the mixture into the prepared tin.

Bake for 6 minutes. Leave to cool while you prepare the filling and fruit.

Using a hand-held electric mixer, soften the cheese in a bowl then add the yogurt, egg whites, sugar, flour and vanilla extract. Whisk well.

Pour the mixture into the tin and place pieces of cherry on top. Bake for 25 minutes. Leave to cool in the tin, then chill. Cut into 9 squares.

Tips

Crush the biscuits in a polythene bag with a rolling pin, or in a food processor.

If you don't have a cherry stoner, remove the stalk and insert a chopstick in the top to push the stone out, then cut in half.

Use blueberries, raspberries or apricots instead of cherries if you like.

NOTES

Calories	Fibre	Salt	Sugar	Fat
219	1g	0.5g	11g	13g of which 8g is saturated

ELDERBERRY SYRUP AND JELLY

The elderberry season runs from August through to the end of October, depending on where you live. Enjoy foraging but do leave some berries for the wildlife to enjoy too. Elderberries make a delicious syrup, which you can drink (diluted with hot or cold water), drizzle over ice cream or desserts, or add to sauces for game and venison. Cook the syrup a little longer to make a jelly to serve with game, venison and turkey.

Makes approx. 1 litre (1¾ pints) Preparation 30 minutes Cooking 30 minutes 

Elderberries 500g (1lb 2oz) prepared weight
Cloves 4 whole
Cinnamon stick 1
Star anise 1
Caster sugar 500g (1lb 2oz)
Lemon 1, juice only

Using a fork, strip the berries from their stalks into a saucepan and pour in just enough water to cover the base of the pan. Add the spices. Bring to a steady boil, then turn down the heat, cover and simmer gently for 15–20 minutes or until the berries have collapsed. Leave to cool slightly.

Strain through a fine sieve into a large jug and measure the juice. Tip the juice back into the cleaned pan and for every 500ml (18fl oz) of juice, add 400g (14oz) of caster sugar. Add the lemon juice, bring up to a simmer and bubble for 10 minutes or until all the sugar has dissolved.

Leave to cool completely before bottling or freezing. It will keep for 3 months in the fridge and up to 1 year in the freezer.

To make 2–3 jam jars of elderberry jelly

If you don't have a sugar thermometer, put a saucer in the freezer at least 15 minutes before you start making the syrup.

Once all the sugar has dissolved in the syrup, increase the heat to a rapid boil until setting point is reached: the syrup should reach 105°C on a sugar thermometer.

Alternatively, to test for setting point, take the saucer out of the freezer and take the saucepan off the heat. Put a teaspoonful of hot jelly onto the saucer. Push your finger through the jelly – it should wrinkle and not flood back in to fill the gap. If the jelly is not quite ready, simmer for a further 5 minutes and test again.

Leave to stand for 10 minutes then carefully pour into warm, sterilised jars and leave to cool completely before sealing tightly, labelling and storing.

Tips

A carrier bag filled with elderberries on stalks will yield approx. 500g (1lb 2oz) prepared weight of berries.

If you have a glut of cooking apples, use the recipe above to make jelly. Begin with 500g (1lb 2oz) chopped apples (no need to peel or core, as the pulp will be strained).

Calories	Fibre	Salt	Sugar	Fat	Based on a 25g (1oz) serving
40	0.7g	0g	10g	0g	

QUICK STRAWBERRY CONSERVE

If you have your own strawberry patch or you've had a fruitful(!) day at a 'pick your own' farm, make this wonderfully fresh strawberry conserve. It's perfect to fill a couple of Victoria sponge cakes or spread onto scones for a summery afternoon tea.

Makes 350g (12oz) Preparation 10 minutes Cooking 15 minutes 

Strawberries 750g (1lb 10oz), hulled and chopped
Caster sugar 150g (5oz)
Vanilla extract 1 tsp
Lemon juice or cider vinegar 1 tbsp
Butter small knob

Heat a large non-stick pan over a medium heat. Add the strawberries, sugar and vanilla extract. Stir until the fruit starts to soften and release juices and the sugar has completely dissolved.

Bring to the boil and cook, stirring occasionally, for about 10 minutes or until slightly thickened. Stir in the lemon juice or vinegar and butter. Remove from the heat.

Pour the conserve into a warm, sterilised jar. Cool and cover with a lid.

Tips

Store the jar in the fridge.

Cover the lid with a pretty fabric top, add a label and give a jar as a gift.

Try with blueberries or rhubarb instead of strawberries.

NOTES

Calories	Fibre	Salt	Sugar	Fat	Based on a 25g (1oz) serving
24	0.8g	0g	4g	0.3g of which 0.1g is saturated	

RASPBERRY & ALMOND CAKE

This impressive cake is perfect for a special occasion. As it uses fresh raspberries, it's best eaten within a couple of days, but that shouldn't be a problem!

Serves 10–12 Preparation 40 minutes plus cooling Cooking 35 minutes 

Butter 350g (12oz), softened, plus extra for greasing
Caster sugar 350g (12oz)
Eggs 6
Vanilla extract 2 tsp
Almond extract 1 tsp
Self-raising flour 175g (6oz)
Ground almonds 175g (6oz)
Ready-made vanilla butter icing 2 x 400g tubs
Raspberries 200g (7oz), plus extra to decorate
Sugar shimmer and sugar flowers to decorate

Preheat the oven to 180°C/160°fan/Gas 4. Grease and line three 18cm (7in) sandwich tins.

Cream the butter and sugar together until pale and fluffy. Add the eggs one at a time, beating well after each addition. Mix in the vanilla and almond extracts, then fold in the flour and ground almonds.

Divide the mixture between the prepared tins. Bake for 35 minutes or until a skewer inserted into the centre comes out clean. Turn out and leave to cool on a wire rack.

Fix the bottom layer to a board or plate with a pat of icing. Spread the top with some of the icing and scatter over half the raspberries. Add the second layer and repeat with the icing and remaining raspberries. Add the third layer (inverted to give a flat top). Using a palette knife, spread the remaining icing over the top, spreading to the edges. Continue to push the icing down the sides, turning, until the cake is covered. Decorate with extra raspberries, sugar shimmer and sugar flowers.

Tips

If you prefer, use one tub of butter icing and spread just between the layers. Leave the top plain or add sifted icing sugar.

To make your own butter icing, mix twice the quantity of icing sugar to butter, add a couple of drops of vanilla extract and beat well, adding a small splash of milk to achieve a spreadable consistency.

Calories	Fibre	Salt	Sugar	Fat
800	1.5g	0.7g	78g	47g of which 23g is saturated

AUTUMN

CAULIFLOWER CHEESE SOUP

When the nights draw in and the temperature begins to drop, we crave cosy, comforting foods. Soup and crusty bread is perfect autumn fare and this recipe is as comforting as you can get.

Serves 2 Preparation 10 minutes Cooking 15 minutes 

Sunflower oil 1 tbsp
Onion 1, peeled and chopped
Cauliflower 1, cut into florets
Vegetable stock 450ml (¾ pint)
Milk 150ml (¼ pint)
Low fat soft cheese 110g (4oz)
Cheddar cheese 75g (3oz), grated
Dijon mustard 1 tsp
Salt and freshly ground black pepper
Snipped chives to garnish (optional)
Walnut or olive bread, warmed, to serve (optional)

Heat the oil in a large saucepan and fry the onion for about 4 minutes until softened.

Add the cauliflower, stock and milk to the pan and bring to the boil. Cover and simmer for 8–10 minutes until the cauliflower is cooked.

Stir in the cheeses and mustard then use a stick blender to whizz until the soup is smooth.

Season to taste and reheat gently until hot. Serve scattered with chives and with warm walnut or olive bread, if you like.

Tips

If you have a leek, use that instead of the onion. Use a head of broccoli instead of the cauliflower, if you prefer.

You could use chicken stock (made from a leftover roast chicken carcass).

NOTES

Calories	Fibre	Salt	Sugar	Fat
404	5.5g	3.5g	0g	23g of which 11g is saturated

SLOW-COOKED MINESTRONE SOUP

Minestrone is a great way to use up a glut of vegetables and can be made over any of the seasons, using whatever is available. It's low in fat and full of protein and fibre. The beauty of this recipe is that the vegetables don't need to be fried – just load up the slow cooker pot, switch on and leave it to do its magic.

Serves 6 Preparation 15 minutes Cooking 5½ hours  

Onion 1 large, peeled and finely chopped

Celery 3 sticks, finely chopped

Green beans 100g (3½oz), trimmed and chopped into 1cm (½in) pieces

Courgettes 1–2 (depending on size), chopped into small cubes

Garlic 2 cloves, peeled and crushed

Bay leaf 1

Oregano 4 sprigs

Chopped tomatoes 400g can

Vegetable stock 800ml (28fl oz)

Salt and freshly ground black pepper

Cannellini beans 400g can, drained

Spaghetti 50g (2oz), broken into small pieces

Kale or Savoy cabbage 100g (3½oz), finely shredded

Basil leaves handful, shredded if large, to serve

Olive oil to serve

Place the onion, celery, green beans, courgettes, garlic and herbs into a large slow cooker pot. Add the tomatoes, vegetable stock, salt and pepper and stir well. Put the lid on and cook on the low setting for 5 hours or until the vegetables are tender.

Add the cannellini beans, spaghetti and shredded kale or cabbage and cook for a further 30–45 minutes or until the pasta is cooked.

Ladle into warmed bowls, scatter with shredded basil leaves and add a drizzle of olive oil.

Tips

For non-vegetarians, why not add a spoonful of Sweet Chilli & Tomato Jam (see page 101) to stir in and add a sweet kick?

To make this without a slow cooker, put all the vegetables, garlic, herbs, tomatoes and stock in a large pan. Bring to the boil, then cover with a lid and leave to simmer for 45 minutes. Add the cannellini beans, spaghetti and kale and cook, uncovered, for a further 15 minutes or until the pasta is cooked. Season to taste.

NOTES

Calories	Fibre	Salt	Sugar	Fat
115	6g	1.5g	1g	1g of which 0.3g is saturated

SWEET CHILLI & TOMATO JAM

Here's a great idea for that tomato glut. A handy jar of spicy sweetness that can be stirred into soups and casseroles or served alongside a cheeseboard. The recipe can be easily doubled or tripled etc, as long as you have enough empty jars!

Fills a 500ml Kilner jar Preparation 10 minutes Cooking 55 minutes

Tomatoes 750g (1lb 10oz), roughly chopped

Garlic 6 cloves, peeled

Long red chillies 4 large, stalks removed

Root ginger 5–6cm (approx. 2in) piece, peeled

Golden caster sugar 500g (1lb 2oz)

Thai fish sauce (nam pla) 3 tbsp

Red wine vinegar 125ml (4fl oz)

Put the tomatoes, garlic, chillies and ginger in a food processor and whizz until finely chopped. Pour into a large saucepan and add the sugar, fish sauce and red wine vinegar. Stir together and slowly bring up to the boil, skimming off any scum that rises to the top. Leave to simmer for 45–55 minutes, stirring occasionally, until thickened and sticky.

Leave to cool slightly before pouring into a sterilised Kilner jar. Seal and leave to cool completely before transferring to the fridge. Once opened use within a month.

Tips

Use 2 or 3 smaller jars if you don't think you'll use a full large jar within a month.

It's delicious with prawn crackers, as in our photograph.

NOTES

Calories	Fibre	Salt	Sugar	Fat	Based on a 25g (1oz) serving
31	0.2g	0.2g	7g	0g	

SMOKY SEAFOOD RICE

A sumptuous meal-in-one that can be served straight from the pan. Use any firm, chunky white fish or seafood, or replace the fish with cooked chicken.

Serves 2 Preparation 20 minutes plus standing Cooking 30 minutes

Vegetable oil 1 tbsp

Onion 1, peeled and sliced

Cooking chorizo 50g (2oz), sliced

Red or yellow pepper 1 small, deseeded and sliced

Paella rice 110g (4oz)

Dry white wine 200ml (7floz)

Fish or chicken stock 350ml (12fl oz)

Smoked paprika 1½ tsp

Salt and freshly ground black pepper

Sugar snap peas 100g (3½oz), strings removed, halved

Skinless hake fillet 225g (8oz), cut into chunks

Cooked seafood such as prawns, mussels, scallops, squid 125g (4½oz)

Parsley small bunch, chopped

Heat the oil in a large frying pan and fry the onion, chorizo and pepper for 5 minutes. Stir in the rice and cook for 1 minute, stirring, until the rice is coated in the cooking juices.

Stir in the wine, stock, paprika, salt and pepper. Bring to the boil and simmer gently for 15 minutes, stirring occasionally.

Stir in the sugar snaps and hake, cover and cook gently for a further 5 minutes. Stir in the seafood, cover and cook gently for a further 5 minutes until the rice is tender and all the liquid has been absorbed. Turn off the heat and leave to stand for 10 minutes with the lid on.

To serve, stir the rice and sprinkle over the parsley. Serve straight from the pan.

Tip

Paella rice is a traditional ingredient for the famous paella dish originating from Valencia in Spain. The grains are short, plump and rounded so that they absorb liquid and flavours quickly. You can use risotto rice instead but you may need to adjust the amount of liquid and cooking times slightly.

NOTES

Calories	Fibre	Salt	Sugar	Fat
658	8g	4.5g	1g	18g of which 4g is saturated

CHICKEN, SQUASH & COURGETTE FRITTATA

If you have leftovers from cooking a whole chicken or roasting joint, this is a great way to use up a few pieces of any cooked meat. This light eggy dish makes a tasty lunch, and you can eat up the leftovers cold the next day.

Serves 2 Preparation 10 minutes plus cooling Cooking 35–40 minutes

Cold-pressed rapeseed oil 1 tbsp

Leek 1, trimmed and sliced

Prepared butternut squash 150g (5oz), thinly sliced

Courgette 1 small, trimmed and sliced

Salt and freshly ground black pepper

Fresh thyme leaves 1 tbsp (or 1 tsp dried thyme)

Skinless cooked chicken 110g (4oz), cut into small pieces

Eggs 5 medium, beaten

Salad, bread and pickles to serve

Heat the oil in a non-stick frying pan (approx. 22cm/8½in diameter) and fry the leek and squash, stirring, for 2–3 minutes. Reduce the heat, cover with a lid and cook gently for 15 minutes.

Add the courgette, salt and pepper, thyme and chicken and cook, stirring, for 5 minutes until everything is heated through.

Pour over the eggs and cook gently for about 15 minutes until the mixture is set and cooked through. To cook the last bit of egg on top, cover the pan with a lid for a minute or two. Alternatively, place under a preheated grill for 1–2 minutes.

To serve, turn out onto a board or plate and cut into wedges. Serve warm or leave to cool. Accompany with salad, bread and pickles.

Tip

For a veggie version, leave out the chicken; once the frittata is cooked, sprinkle the top with grated cheese and flash under the grill if you like. Alternatively, add sliced cooked veggie sausages instead of the chicken.

NOTES

Calories	Fibre	Salt	Sugar	Fat
359	5g	2g	0g	20g of which 4g is saturated

PORK, PEAR & PARSNIP TRAYBAKE

Traybakes are hassle free, quick to prepare and easy to scale quantities up or down. For this quick midweek supper, you could use chicken breast instead of pork, and swap the pears for apples or other orchard fruits such as plums and quinces.

Serves 2 Preparation 10 minutes Cooking 45 minutes

Pork shoulder steaks 2 (approx. 175g/6oz each)

Light olive oil 2 tbsp

Salt and freshly ground black pepper

Potatoes 2 (approx. 300g/11oz total weight), each cut into 6 wedges

Parsnips 2 medium, peeled and cut into wedges

Pears 2, quartered and cored

Thyme 4 sprigs

Sage leaves 6, torn

Medium-dry cider 6 tbsp

Dijon mustard 2 tsp

English cheese such as Stilton or Lancashire 50g (2oz), crumbled

Preheat the oven to 220°C/200°fan/Gas 7.

Place a large shallow flameproof dish or roasting tin on the hob to heat up. Rub the pork steaks with a little oil and season with salt and pepper. Sear the pork on both sides, then remove from the dish and set aside.

Toss the potatoes, parsnips and pears into the hot dish, adding the remaining oil to coat. Season with salt and pepper, cover the dish with foil and bake for 20 minutes.

Mix in the thyme sprigs, sage leaves and cider. Smear the steaks with the mustard and tuck in alongside the vegetables, then sprinkle the cheese over the pork.

Return to the oven, uncovered, for 20 minutes or until the pork is cooked through and the vegetables roasted. Serve on warmed plates and spoon the pan juices over.

Tips

Freeze odd end pieces of hard cheese – they're handy to add to soups and sauces, and frozen cheese crumbles very easily.

Stir a spoonful or two of crème fraîche into the pan juices for an extra treat.

If tarragon is still abundant in the herb garden, it is a delicious alternative to sage.

NOTES

Calories	Fibre	Salt	Sugar	Fat
712	14g	2.5g	1g	30g of which 10g is saturated

SAUSAGE, MUSHROOM & JERUSALEM ARTICHOKE HOTPOT

Jerusalem artichokes are knobbly tubers with a sweet, nutty taste. They are available to buy from November through to March. This comforting combination of flavours is perfect for a chilly autumn evening.

Serves 4 Preparation 25 minutes Cooking 1 hour 40 minutes

Olive oil 2 tbsp

Chipolata sausages such as Cumberland or Toulouse 12

Chestnut mushrooms 150g (5oz), halved

Leeks 2, trimmed and thickly sliced

Carrots 250g (9oz), peeled and sliced

Plain flour 2 tbsp

Medium-dry cider 440ml can

Fresh thyme 2 tbsp chopped

Wholegrain mustard 1 tbsp

Salt and freshly ground black pepper

Jerusalem artichokes 500g (1lb 2oz), peeled and covered in water with lemon juice (see tip)

Rosemary and garlic butter 15g (½oz) (see page 69)

Preheat the oven to 180°C/160°fan/Gas 4.

In a large frying pan, heat 1 tablespoon of the oil and fry the sausages for 4–5 minutes until lightly golden all over. Remove from the pan and set aside. Add the mushrooms to the pan and fry for 3–4 minutes until softened. Set aside with the sausages.

Add the remaining oil to the pan and fry the leeks and carrots for 4–5 minutes, stirring frequently, until lightly golden. Sprinkle over the flour and stir through. Pour in the cider, scraping all the bits from the bottom of the pan and mixing well. Add the thyme, mustard and plenty of salt and pepper.

Transfer the mixture to a 2 litre (3½ pint) lidded casserole and add the sausages and mushrooms. Level the top so everything is submerged in the liquid. Drain the Jerusalem artichokes and slice into 2–3mm (approx. ⅛in) slices. Arrange over the casserole to cover the sausages and vegetables. Dot with the flavoured butter then cover and bake for 1¼ hours.

Preheat the grill to medium. Remove the lid and pop the casserole under the grill for 8–10 minutes or until the topping is lightly golden. Serve immediately.

Tips

Jerusalem artichokes are cooked in similar ways to other root vegetables, but once peeled they should immediately be placed into a bowl of cold water with lemon juice or vinegar to prevent discoloration.

This would be delicious with a dollop of Sweet Chilli & Tomato Jam on the side (see page 101).

Calories	Fibre	Salt	Sugar	Fat
535	14g	2g	3g	33g of which 12g is saturated

RED CABBAGE, BEETROOT & APPLE SAUERKRAUT

Probiotics are good bacteria that help to maintain the balance of bacteria in our gut, keeping us healthy and boosting our immune systems. They're found in yogurts, kombucha, kimchi and other fermented foods and drinks, including sauerkraut. Homemade sauerkraut is an easy recipe to try, using seasonal vegetables. Delicious with cheeses, cured meats, sausages and smoked fish.

Makes 2 x 1 litre (1¾ pint) jars Preparation 2½ hours plus 5–7 days fermenting 

Red cabbage approx. 1.25kg (2lb 12oz), base removed

Beetroot 4, scrubbed, topped and tailed

Eating apples 2, peeled and cored

Red onions 2, peeled and finely sliced

Sea salt flakes 3 tbsp

Black mustard seeds 2 tbsp

Begin by removing a couple of leaves from the red cabbage; set aside. Cut the cabbage into quarters and finely shred, either by hand or in a food processor. Place in a large clean bowl. Coarsely grate the beetroot and apples and add to the bowl with the red onion slices and salt.

Mix all the vegetables together for 1–2 minutes; you will begin to see the juices being drawn out by the salt. Cover the bowl with a clean cloth and leave to stand for 2 hours, mixing occasionally. There will now be liquid in the bottom of the bowl.

Stir in the mustard seeds.

Divide the vegetable mixture and all of the juices between the sterilised jars, pressing it in so it sits in its juices. Top with the reserved cabbage leaves and then weigh down with a ramekin or small jar to hold the mix down in its juices. This is important: if the mix is in contact with the air it will turn mouldy.

Place the jars in a shallow dish to catch any excess liquid that may drip over. Pop on the lids loosely and leave in a cool (18–22°C) place out of direct sunlight for 5–7 days. If the fermentation process is working you will see little bubbles occasionally rising up through the liquid.

Remove the weights, give the sauerkraut a stir then reseal tightly and transfer to the fridge until ready to serve. It will keep unopened for 2–3 months. Once opened eat within 3 weeks.

NOTES

Calories	Fibre	Salt	Sugar	Fat	Based on a 40g (1¾oz) serving
11	1g	1g	0g	0.3g of which 0g is saturated	

GAMMON & APPLE COBBLER

The perfect meal to follow a walk appreciating the autumnal colours. This gorgeous bake, with a cheesy scone topping, celebrates classic British flavours.

Serves 4 Preparation 20 minutes Cooking 50 minutes

Butter 75g (3oz)

Onion 1, peeled and chopped

Eating apples 2, peeled and thickly sliced

Lean unsmoked gammon 500g (1lb 2oz), cut into 2cm (¾in) pieces

Chicken stock 200ml (7fl oz), hot

Dry cider or fresh apple juice 150ml (¼ pint)

Dried sage 1 tsp

Cornflour 2 tbsp

Double cream 6 tbsp

Salt and freshly ground black pepper

Self-raising flour 250g (9oz), plus extra for dusting

Mature Cheddar 100g (3½oz), grated

Melt 25g (1oz) butter in a pan and fry the onion and apples for 5 minutes. Add the gammon and continue to cook, stirring, for a further 5 minutes.

Pour over the hot chicken stock and cider or apple juice, add the sage, bring to the boil, then simmer for 10 minutes.

Mix the cornflour and half the cream to a paste, then stir into the gammon mixture. Cook, stirring, for 2 minutes until thickened, then season to taste. Transfer to a 1.5 litre (2½ pint) gratin dish and cover with foil.

Preheat the oven to 200°C/180°fan/Gas 6. Sift the flour into a bowl, rub in the remaining butter and stir in most of the cheese. Mix 2 tablespoons of the cream with 7 tablespoons water, then mix into the flour.

Turn the dough out onto a floured surface and knead lightly until smooth. Roll out to 1cm (½in) thick and cut out 12 rounds with a 5cm (2in) round cutter.

Remove the foil from the dish. Arrange the dough circles around the edge of the dish, brush with the remaining cream and sprinkle with the remaining cheese. Place the dish on a baking tray and bake for 25–30 minutes until piping hot, golden and bubbling.

Tips

If using windfall apples, you may need 3 or 4 after removing any bruised parts.

Parboil chunks of root vegetables, such as parsnip and carrot, or cubes of squash, sprinkle with a little chilli oil and roast on the baking tray alongside the cobbler.

NOTES

Calories	Fibre	Salt	Sugar	Fat
825	4g	4.5g	1g	46g of which 26g is saturated

SLOW COOKER SPICED BEEF & AUTUMN VEG

Meltingly tender, slow-cooked beef with chunks of golden vegetables and warming spices make this an ideal dish to serve up when the nights are drawing in.

Serves 6 Preparation 15 minutes plus cooling Cooking 10 hours 10 minutes 

Vegetable oil 2 tbsp

Onions 2, peeled and sliced

Carrots 2 large, peeled and sliced

Garlic 2 cloves, peeled and crushed

Ground coriander 2 tsp

Ground cumin 2 tsp

Ground ginger 2 tsp

Salt and freshly ground black pepper

Beef shin 900g (2lb), cut into 2cm (¾in) thick pieces

Cinnamon stick 1

Beef stock 1 litre (1¾ pints), hot

Prepared pumpkin or squash 500g (1lb 2oz), cut into 2cm (¾in) thick pieces

Dried ready-to-eat apricots 250g (9oz)

Clear honey 1 tbsp

Couscous and chopped fresh coriander or mint to serve (optional)

Heat the oil in a frying pan and fry the onions, carrots and garlic for 5 minutes until lightly browned. Use a slotted spoon to transfer the vegetables to a slow cooker pot. Put the lid on and switch the cooker on to the low setting.

Mix the ground spices together with salt and pepper and mix into the beef. Reheat the frying pan juices and cook the beef, stirring, for 4–5 minutes until browned all over.

Transfer the beef to the slow cooker, add the cinnamon stick and pour over the stock. Put the lid back on and cook on the low setting for 7 hours.

Stir in the pumpkin or squash, cover and cook for a further 2 hours. Stir in the apricots and honey, cover and cook for a further hour until everything is tender.

To serve, ladle over steamed couscous and sprinkle with chopped coriander or mint.

Tips

Make this dish with cubes of any stewing beef or lamb shoulder if you prefer. Use soft pitted prunes instead of the apricots.

To cook conventionally, cook everything in a large saucepan, with a tight-fitting lid, on the hob over a gentle heat for about 2½ hours, adding the pumpkin, apricots and honey after an hour of cooking.

NOTES

Calories	Fibre	Salt	Sugar	Fat
383	10g	2g	3g	14g of which 4g is saturated

SPICY PUMPKIN SEEDS

Halloween is becoming more of an event each year. Love it or loathe it, you can still 'treat' yourself to something scrummy. Have fun pumpkin carving then enjoy these crunchy seeds and the pumpkin flesh in the recipe on the previous page.

Serves 4 Preparation 8 minutes Cooking 2 minutes (V)

Pumpkin seeds 50g (2oz), washed and dried
Vegetable oil ½ tsp
Sweet smoked paprika ½ tsp
Ground cumin ½ tsp
Coarse salt ¼–½ tsp

Put the seeds in a frying pan and cook over a medium heat for about 2 minutes until they start to jump but not brown.

Take the frying pan off the heat. Add the oil and stir to coat the seeds then sprinkle in the paprika, cumin and salt and stir well.

Tip onto a plate and leave to cool for a few minutes. Serve as a snack with drinks.

Tip

Flavour with cayenne pepper and chilli powder, or other spices if you prefer.

NOTES

Calories	Fibre	Salt	Sugar	Fat
75	1g	0.5g	0g	6g of which 1g is saturated

CHOCOLATE PORRIDGE WITH FORAGER'S COMPOTE

A real treat for breakfast or brunch. Chocolate porridge is a simple yet indulgent way to start the day and can be served with fresh fruit or this simple compote.

Serves 2 Preparation 10 minutes plus cooling Cooking 15 minutes 

Prepared seasonal fruit such as blackberries, plums, damsons, apples or pears 300g (11oz) (see tip)

Clear honey 2–3 tbsp

Jumbo rolled oats 75g (3oz)

Salt pinch

Cocoa powder 1 tbsp

Semi-skimmed milk 350ml (12fl oz)

Vanilla extract 1 tsp

Double cream 2 tbsp (optional)

Put the fruit in a saucepan along with 2 tablespoons water. Heat until the fruit starts to steam, then cover and cook gently for about 10 minutes, depending on the ripeness of the fruit, until tender. Set aside or leave to cool completely, then sweeten to taste with honey; cover and chill until required.

To make the porridge, put the oats, salt and cocoa in a saucepan and stir in the milk and 1 tablespoon of honey. Bring to the boil, then simmer, stirring, for 5 minutes until cooked. Turn off the heat and stir in the vanilla and cream if using.

Serve the porridge in warmed bowls, topped with the warm or cold fruit compote.

Tips

Always wash foraged fruit well. Remove the stones of plums and damsons before cooking for safer eating. Apples and pears are best peeled, cored and chopped into small pieces so that they cook in the same time as the other fruits.

Jumbo rolled oats make a hearty, more textured porridge, but you can use regular rolled oats if you prefer.

For a vegan version, replace the dairy milk and cream with plant-based alternatives, and sweeten with agave or maple syrup.

NOTES

Calories	Fibre	Salt	Sugar	Fat
314	8g	1g	10g	7g of which 3g is saturated

BLACKBERRY & WHITE CHOCOLATE MACAROONS

Blackberries are found in hedgerows all over the UK in late summer. They are a great way to introduce children to foraging, as they are easy to identify – though beware of the thorns – and can be eaten immediately or taken home to freeze, or to bake in these chewy macaroons.

Makes 12 Preparation 15 minutes Cooking 15 minutes 

Butter for greasing
Caster sugar 125g (4½oz)
Eggs 2, whites only
Vanilla extract ½ tsp
Desiccated coconut 100g (3½oz)
Plain flour 1 tbsp, sifted
Blackberries 12 (approx. 150g/5oz)
White chocolate 50g (2oz), chopped

Preheat the oven to 180°C/160°fan/Gas 4. Lightly grease a 12-hole fairy cake tin.

In a large bowl, using a hand-held electric mixer, whisk the sugar and egg whites together for 3–4 minutes to soft peaks. Fold in the vanilla extract, coconut and sifted flour.

Divide the mixture between the prepared tins and pop a blackberry into the centre of each one. Bake for 12–15 minutes until lightly golden. Leave to cool slightly in the tins then transfer to a wire rack to cool completely.

Melt the white chocolate in the microwave or in a bowl over a pan of barely simmering water. Drizzle over each cake and leave to set.

NOTES

Calories	Fibre	Salt	Sugar	Fat
123	2g	0g	11g	6g of which 5g is saturated

PEARS & PRUNES IN RED WINE

The scent of warming spices will fill the kitchen as the pears cook. Brighten up a dark evening with this rich, warm dessert.

Serves 4 Preparation 10 minutes Cooking 1¼–1½ hours 

Firm pears 4

Soft pitted prunes 200g (7oz)

Vanilla pod 1, split and halved lengthways

Cinnamon sticks or cassia bark 4 pieces

Caster sugar 150g (5oz)

Red wine 600ml (1 pint)

Arrowroot 3 tsp (1 x 8g sachet)

Pouring cream or plant-based alternative to serve (optional)

Preheat the oven to 180°C/160°fan/Gas 4.

Using a sharp knife, cut each pear in half, slicing through the stalk, if possible. Peel the halves and scoop out the cores.

Lay the pear halves in a large shallow baking dish, cut side up. Scatter the prunes around the pears, tucking in the vanilla pod and cinnamon or cassia bark. Sprinkle on the sugar and pour in the red wine.

Lightly cover with foil and bake for 40 minutes. Baste the pears well then cook for a further 30–40 minutes or until the pears are tender all the way through when tested with a cocktail stick. Using a slotted spoon, carefully lift the pears and prunes onto a large shallow serving dish, along with the vanilla pod and cinnamon or cassia bark.

Pour the cooking wine into a saucepan. Mix the arrowroot with just enough water to make a paste. Bring the wine to a steady simmer then whisk in the arrowroot. Continue whisking until the wine becomes slightly syrupy. Pour over the pears and prunes.

Serve warm or at room temperature with lashings of pouring cream.

Tips

It is important to use hard pears for this recipe but bear in mind the cooking time might vary depending on their size and ripeness. Use pears of a similar size and shape if possible.

If you prefer, replace the red wine with cider or apple juice.

Check the wine is suitable for vegans, if necessary.

NOTES

Calories	Fibre	Salt	Sugar	Fat
413	8g	0g	39g	0.4g of which 0g is saturated

CHOCOLATE & PEAR BROWNIES

The British pear season extends from late August right through to May, with several varieties to choose from. Long, conical Conference and Concorde pears and the shorter, chubbier Comice and Williams pears are all equally tasty. If cooking with pears it is better to choose slightly under-ripe ones so they don't go too mushy. Pears and dark chocolate are a classic match: here they meet in a gooey brownie.

Makes 16 pieces Preparation 15 minutes Cooking 25 minutes 

Unsalted butter 200g (7oz), cut into cubes, plus extra for greasing
Dark chocolate (70%) 200g (7oz), broken into chunks
Eggs 3
Golden caster sugar 275g (10oz)
Plain flour 100g (3½oz)
Cocoa powder 2 tbsp
Pears 2, chopped into 2cm (¾in) cubes

Preheat the oven to 180°C/160°fan/Gas 4. Grease a 20 x 30cm (8 x 12in) baking tin and fully line with non-stick baking paper.

Put the butter and chocolate into a bowl then set over a pan of gently simmering water, stirring occasionally, until completely melted. Remove from the heat.

In a large bowl, using a hand-held electric mixer, whisk the eggs and sugar together for 4–5 minutes until pale and doubled in volume. Carefully but thoroughly fold the melted chocolate through the egg mixture. Sift over the flour and cocoa powder and fold through the mixture.

Pour the mixture into the prepared tin and level with a spatula. Scatter the chopped pears evenly over the top. Bake for 20–25 minutes until the top is papery and shiny and the sides are just coming away from the edge of the tin.

Leave to cool completely in the tin then cut into pieces.

NOTES

Calories	Fibre	Salt	Sugar	Fat
269	1.5g	0g	26g	15g of which 9g is saturated

TOFFEE APPLE CRUMBLE

It's difficult to improve on a classic apple crumble but this recipe – reminiscent of toffee apples from childhood – does so. The oats and almonds provide a wonderful nutty flavour and texture, and the fudge, which melts to toffee in the oven, adds a sweetness in contrast to the sharpness of the fruit.

Serves 8 Preparation 30 minutes plus standing Cooking 40 minutes 

Butter 150g (5oz), cut into small cubes

Rolled oats 150g (5oz)

Ground almonds 150g (5oz)

Demerara sugar 110g (4oz)

Cooking apples 2 large, peeled, cored and thinly sliced

Dessert apples 2, peeled, cored and thinly sliced

Orange or lemon juice 1 tbsp

Golden syrup 3 tbsp

Fudge 50g (2oz), cut into thin slivers

Cream, custard or ice cream to serve (optional)

Preheat the oven to 200°C/180°fan/Gas 6. In a bowl, rub together the butter, oats and almonds to an even crumb. Add the sugar and mix through.

Put all the apples in a 2 litre (3½ pint) ovenproof dish. Sprinkle with orange or lemon juice, drizzle with golden syrup and stir to coat the apple slices.

Spoon the crumble mixture evenly over the apples and scatter with slivers of fudge. Bake for 40 minutes until piping hot and lightly golden. Leave to stand for 10 minutes before serving with cream, custard or ice cream, if you like.

Tips

Use light muscovado sugar instead of demerara for an even richer taste. Opt for ready-chopped mini fudge chunks if short on time.

NOTES

Calories	Fibre	Salt	Sugar	Fat
461	2.5g	0.1g	22g	28g of which 11g is saturated

APPLE FLAPJACK TART

Two classic bakes rolled into one. Apple tart meets everyone's favourite oaty bake in this delicious sweet treat. Serve it hot with custard as a pudding or cold as a slice with a coffee.

Serves 15 Preparation 25 minutes plus chilling and standing Cooking 1 hour 25 minutes

Lightly salted butter 200g (7oz), softened, plus extra for greasing

Demerara sugar 165g (5½oz)

Vanilla extract 1 tsp

Plain flour 225g (8oz)

Baking powder 1 tsp

Cooking apples 500g (1lb 2oz)

Lemon juice 3 tbsp

Ground cinnamon 1½ tsp

Sultanas 50g (2oz)

Golden syrup 50g (2oz)

Rolled oats 225g (8oz)

Custard to serve (optional)

Grease and line an 18 x 28cm (7 x 11in) cake tin. Put 110g (4oz) butter in a bowl with 75g (3oz) sugar and beat until smooth. Stir in the vanilla and gradually mix in the flour and baking powder to make a crumbly mixture. Press the mixture over the bottom of the tin to cover it evenly. Prick with a fork then chill for 30 minutes.

Preheat the oven to 180°C/160°fan/Gas 4. Bake the base for 25 minutes until set and lightly golden.

Meanwhile, peel, core and thinly slice the apples and mix with the lemon juice, cinnamon and sultanas; put to one side.

In a saucepan, melt the remaining butter and sugar together with the syrup. Stir in the oats and mix well.

Drain the apple slices and spread out evenly over the cooked base. Spoon over the oaty topping to cover the apples and gently press down with the back of the spoon. Stand the tin on a baking tray and bake for about 1 hour until the apple filling is cooked through and the top is golden and crisp. If the top browns too quickly, cover the tin with foil.

Leave to stand for 15 minutes to firm up before slicing into 15 pieces; serve warm, with custard if liked. To serve cold, leave to cool completely before removing from the tin.

Tips

To make this recipe gluten-free, use gluten-free plain flour, gluten-free baking powder and gluten-free oats.

As a variation, replace the apples with sliced pears and flavour with ginger instead of cinnamon.

Calories	Fibre	Salt	Sugar	Fat
281	2.5g	0.4g	14g	13g of which 7g is saturated

BOBBING APPLES CAKE

Who remembers autumn apple bobbing as a child? This clever and scrumptious cake uses balls of apple in a soft sponge. Perfect served with the flavoured cream, curled up in front of the fire.

Serves 10–12 Preparation 20 minutes plus cooling Cooking 50 minutes 

Butter 150g (5oz), softened, plus extra for greasing

Dessert apples 3 or 4 large

Lemon 1, finely grated zest and 2 tbsp juice

Golden caster sugar 150g (5oz), plus 4 tsp

Egg 1

Vanilla extract ½ tsp

Soured cream 300ml (½ pint)

Plain flour 225g (8oz)

Baking powder 2 tsp

Salt pinch

Double cream 150ml (¼ pint)

Calvados 2 tbsp

Preheat the oven to 180°C/160°fan/Gas 4. Butter a 23cm (9in) springform cake tin.

Use a melon baller to make rounds of apple (keep the skin on). Aim for about 36 balls. Mix the lemon juice with 3 teaspoons of caster sugar and stir through the apple balls. Set aside.

Cream the butter and 150g (5oz) sugar together until pale and fluffy. Beat in the egg, then beat in the vanilla extract and 200ml (7fl oz) of the soured cream.

Fold in the flour, baking powder, salt and lemon zest. Spoon the mixture into the prepared tin. Push the apple balls into the cake mix, skin side up. Bake for 50 minutes until firm to the touch.

As soon as the cake is out of the oven sprinkle over 1 teaspoon of caster sugar. Leave to cool for 15 minutes then remove from the tin and cool on a wire rack.

Whip the double cream to soft peaks, then whisk in the remaining soured cream and Calvados. Serve with slices of cool or warmed cake.

Tips

If you don't have a melon baller, you can cut the apple into chunks.

Add a little ground cinnamon to the cake mixture if you like.

Instead of Calvados, you could mix the cream with elderflower cordial (see page 42).

NOTES

Calories	Fibre	Salt	Sugar	Fat
350	1g	0.4g	13g	22g of which 14g is saturated

HEDGEROW FRUITS GIN

Scour your local hedgerows for wild fruits or find locally grown plums in your nearest farm shop. Flavoured gin is a simple and delicious way to preserve the fruit. A store cupboard treat to offer unexpected guests, it's particularly good topped up with prosecco or champagne.

Makes 34 servings Preparation 45 minutes plus infusing 

Good quality gin 600ml (1 pint)

Light brown muscovado sugar 150g (5oz) (see tip)

Plums or damsons about 450g (1lb), halved, stoned and sliced

or

Sloes approx. 500g (1lb 2oz), each pricked with a fork

Pour the gin into a large sterilised jar and add the sugar. Stir well until the sugar has dissolved.

Add the fruit to the jar then cover with a tight-fitting lid.

Store in a cool, dark place for about 3 months, stirring weekly.

When the gin has developed a good, fruity flavour, strain it through muslin, discard the fruit and pour into sterilised bottles. Store for at least 1 month before drinking.

Serve the gin chilled, over ice. For a long drink, top up a shot of the fruity gin with apple juice or elderflower tonic, or add a dash of cherry brandy and pour in champagne for a truly decadent cocktail.

Tips

Wash the fruit before preparation.

Sloes are more tart than plums and damsons, so you may want to increase the quantity of sugar to 225g (8oz). If you don't want to prick the sloes, you can freeze them overnight to split the skins instead.

Use in the recipe on page 145.

NOTES

Calories	Fibre	Salt	Sugar	Fat
56	0g	0g	4.5g	0g

WINTER

CHRISTMAS

ROAST SAVOY CABBAGE WITH CHEESE SAUCE

This delicious dish celebrates the flavour of Savoy cabbage, which roasts so well. You could serve as a meat-free meal with mashed carrot and swede and perhaps some butterbeans.

Serves 4 Preparation 10 minutes Cooking 30 minutes 

Savoy cabbage 1 small or 350g (12oz), cut into 4 wedges
Olive oil 2 tbsp
Salt and freshly ground black pepper
Butter small chunk
Coarse fresh breadcrumbs (white or brown) 4 tbsp
Fresh parsley or mint leaves 1–2 tbsp chopped
Full fat soft cheese 110g (4oz)
Milk 4 tbsp
Grated mature Cheddar 4 tbsp

Preheat the oven to 220°C/200°fan/Gas 7. Remove the core then brush the cabbage wedges all over with oil. Put in a roasting tin, season well and roast for 30 minutes, turning halfway through, until crisp on the outside and tender in the middle.

Meanwhile, melt the butter in a small saucepan. Add the breadcrumbs and fry until crisp and golden. Remove from the heat and stir in the parsley or mint, to taste. Sprinkle the breadcrumbs over the cabbage.

In a small saucepan warm the soft cheese with the milk until just hot then stir in the Cheddar and season to taste. Serve in a bowl to spoon over the cabbage.

Tips

You could try using a flavoured soft cheese. Or serve the sauce and breadcrumbs with roasted cauliflower or butternut squash.

If you want to serve with meat, it works really well with shredded ham hock.

NOTES

Calories	Fibre	Salt	Sugar	Fat
332	4g	2g	1g	23g of which 12g is saturated

VEG BOX MAC 'N' CHEESE

A veg box isn't essential for this dish: its aim is to use up any veg that may need eating and provide a comforting meal to warm you up on a frosty day.

Serves 4–6 Preparation 15 minutes Cooking 25 minutes 

Macaroni 200g (7oz)

Vegetables such as squash, broccoli, cauliflower, carrots 500g (1lb 2oz), peeled if necessary and cut into bite-sized pieces

Butter 75g (3oz)

Plain flour 75g (3oz)

Whole milk 900ml (1½ pints)

Wholegrain mustard 1–2 tbsp

Mature Cheddar 300g (11oz), grated

Dry breadcrumbs 25g (1oz)

Salad to serve (optional)

Preheat the oven to 200°C/180°fan/Gas 6.

Cook the macaroni according to the packet's instructions, adding the vegetables for the last 5–10 minutes of cooking, depending on the type of veg. Drain well.

Meanwhile, put the butter, flour and milk in a saucepan and whisk continuously until the mixture bubbles. Simmer for 2 minutes, stirring. Remove from the heat, stir in the mustard to taste and 200g (7oz) of the cheese. Fold into the macaroni and vegetables.

Transfer the mixture to a 2 litre (3½ pint) baking dish and sprinkle with the breadcrumbs and the remaining cheese. Place the dish on a baking tray and bake for about 15 minutes until the topping is golden and the cheese has melted. Serve with salad, if liked.

Tips

If you have any leftover plain crisps or tortilla chips, crush and use instead of breadcrumbs (children will love this!) Or you could top with torn pieces of kale, which will crisp in the oven.

NOTES

Calories	Fibre	Salt	Sugar	Fat
599	5g	1.3g	0.2g	34g of which 21g is saturated

BLACK PUDDING POTATOES

Many regions produce their own version of black pudding, with Lancashire producing a particularly prized variety. Though traditionally served with an English breakfast, it pairs beautifully with potatoes. A great way to use up spuds!

Serves 6   Preparation 20 minutes   Cooking 2 hours

Goose or duck fat 2 tbsp

Garlic 1 clove, peeled and quartered

Thyme 4 sprigs

Potatoes 4 large, scrubbed and thinly sliced

Salt and freshly ground black pepper

Black pudding 110g (4oz)

Chicken stock 400ml (14fl oz), hot

Preheat the oven to 170°C/150°fan/Gas 3. In a small saucepan, warm the goose or duck fat with the garlic and thyme until sizzling, then remove from the heat and leave to infuse.

Layer half the potato slices in a 1.5 litre (2½ pint) ovenproof dish, spooning over a little of the fat and seasoning as you go.

Crumble the black pudding over the potato slices, then layer over the remaining potatoes. Pour over the hot chicken stock, then spoon over the remaining fat and season again.

Cover the dish with foil, place on a baking tray and bake for 1½ hours. Remove the foil and increase the oven temperature to 220°C/200°fan/Gas 7. Bake for 20–30 minutes until crisp and golden; serve hot.

Tips

Serve alongside roast chicken, turkey or pork and steamed green vegetables.

King Edward or Maris Piper potatoes work well, but any 'floury' variety can be used.

NOTES

Calories	Fibre	Salt	Sugar	Fat
174	2.5g	1.4g	0g	7g of which 2g is saturated

PAN-FRIED DUCK BREAST WITH A SWEDE, TURNIP & CARROT CRUMBLE

Duck is a real treat and here is a simple way to prepare it while the root vegetable crumble slowly bakes in the oven. Duck breast portions are readily available in most supermarkets.

Serves 4   Preparation 35 minutes   Cooking 1 hour

Olive oil 1 tbsp

Bacon lardons 100g (3½oz)

Leek 1 large, trimmed and sliced

Dry white wine 150ml (¼ pint)

Vegetable stock 800ml (28fl oz)

Swede 300g (11oz), peeled, chopped into 3cm (1¼in) cubes

Turnips 300g (11oz), peeled, chopped into 3cm (1¼in) cubes

Carrots 300g (11oz), peeled, chopped into 3cm (1¼in) cubes

Crème fraîche 100ml (3½fl oz)

Dijon mustard 2 tsp

Plain flour 2 tbsp, plus 175g (6oz) for crumble

Flat-leaf parsley 3 tbsp chopped

Salt and freshly ground black pepper

Butter 100g (3½oz), cut into small cubes

Parmesan 50g (2oz), grated

Walnuts 75g (3oz), chopped

Duck breast portions 4

Steamed kale or Savoy cabbage to serve (optional)

Preheat the oven to 200°C/180°fan/Gas 6.

Heat a large saucepan, add the olive oil and fry the bacon for 2–3 minutes until golden. Add the leek and fry for a further 2–3 minutes until softened. Pour in the wine and allow about half to evaporate off then pour in the stock.

Add the swede, turnips and carrots and bring the liquid up to the boil. Cover and simmer for 8–10 minutes until just softened.

In a small bowl stir together the crème fraîche, mustard and 2 tablespoons plain flour. Stir this through the vegetables and leave for 2–3 minutes to thicken. Stir in the chopped parsley and season to taste. Spoon into a 1.5 litre (2½ pint) ovenproof dish.

To make the crumble, put 175g (6oz) flour in a bowl with the butter and rub together until the mix resembles chunky breadcrumbs. Stir in the Parmesan and walnuts and scatter this evenly over the vegetable mix. Place the dish on a baking tray and bake for 35–40 minutes until golden.

Meanwhile, place the duck breasts on a board, score the skin with a sharp knife and season well. Heat a large frying pan and place the duck skin side down in the pan. Leave over a low heat for about 8–10 minutes until golden. Turn over and cook for another 5 minutes. Transfer to a warmed plate, cover with foil and leave to rest.

To serve, carve each duck portion into five pieces and serve alongside the savoury crumble and some freshly steamed kale or Savoy cabbage.

Calories	Fibre	Salt	Sugar	Fat
1079	13g	4g	0.3g	68g of which 30g is saturated

BRAISED VENISON WITH SLOE GIN

A warming, wintery casserole. Venison benefits from long, slow cooking, with time to soak up bold flavours, spices and herbs – this is an easy introduction if you are 'new to the game'! Much of the venison produced in the UK is from deer that roam freely or in parkland, rather than being intensively farmed – a delicious, rich meat at a reasonable price.

Serves 6 Preparation 30 minutes Cooking 2¾ hours 

Olive oil 2 tbsp

Venison shoulder 1kg (2¼lb), cut into chunks

Onions 2, peeled and chopped

Celery 2 sticks, thickly sliced

Carrot 1 large, peeled and thickly sliced

Bay leaves 2, torn in half

Thyme few sprigs, plus extra to garnish

Rosemary few sprigs

Juniper berries 1 tsp, bruised

Mixed (or black) peppercorns 1 tsp, crushed

Salt pinch

Tomato purée 2 tbsp

Sloe gin or Hedgerow fruits gin (see page 133) 300ml (½ pint)

Passata 200ml (7fl oz)

Potato mashed with parsnip or celeriac, and steamed kale to serve (optional)

Heat the oil in a large flameproof lidded casserole over a medium–high heat and brown the meat, in batches, until well coloured. Using a slotted spoon, transfer the meat to a plate.

Add the vegetables, herbs and spices to the pan, together with a large pinch of salt, cover and cook gently for 15 minutes or until the vegetables have softened slightly.

Stir in the tomato purée, gin, passata and 150ml (¼ pint) hot water. Return the meat to the pan, cover and simmer gently for 2 hours, stirring from time to time. Remove the lid and simmer for a further 30 minutes or until the venison is very tender and the sauce has reduced slightly.

Taste and adjust the seasoning and serve, garnished with sprigs of thyme, accompanied with mash and steamed kale.

Tips

Choose park (free-range) or wild venison over farmed.

Venison is one of the leanest, heart-healthiest meats available – it has less fat than skinned chicken breast and contains healthy omega 3 fats. High in protein and packed with zinc, it has higher levels of iron than any other red meat.

As a variation, replace the sloe gin and passata with red wine and beef stock, adding a teaspoon or two of Elderberry jelly (see page 89) for a hint of sweetness.

Calories	Fibre	Salt	Sugar	Fat
376	3g	0.8g	1.5g	7g of which 2g is saturated

HAGGIS WITH SCALLOPS, APPLES & WHISKY SAUCE

Whether you celebrate Burns' Night or not, this is a must! Everyone at the photo shoot adored it and the photographer now cooks this recipe regularly. The combination of classic Scottish flavours makes a tremendous dish.

Serves 4 Preparation 20 minutes Cooking 20 minutes

Celeriac 1, peeled and cut into small chunks

Double cream 4 tbsp

Salt and freshly ground black pepper

Haggis 2 x 227g 'sausage-shaped' packs

Olive oil 1 tbsp

Butter 25g (1oz)

Queen scallops 12

Dessert apple 1, cored, quartered and each wedge cut into 5 slices

Clear honey 1 tbsp

Cider vinegar 2 tbsp

Whisky 4 tbsp

Dijon mustard 2 tsp

Put the celeriac in a saucepan, cover with cold water, bring to the boil and simmer for 20 minutes or until tender. Drain and return to the pan to dry off then transfer to a food processor and whizz until smooth, gradually adding the double cream. Season to taste.

Meanwhile, cut each haggis into slices. Heat the oil in a frying pan, add the haggis and cook over a low heat for 3 minutes, then flip the slices and cook for 2 minutes until crispy. Remove from the pan and place on a plate in a warm oven.

Wipe the frying pan with kitchen paper. Add the butter and increase the heat, add the scallops and cook for 1½ minutes on each side or until cooked. Remove from the pan with a slotted spoon and keep warm in the oven.

Add the apple slices to the pan and cook until just browned. Add the honey and cook until caramelised. Stir in the vinegar, whisky and mustard and heat through to make a glossy sauce.

Spoon the celeriac purée onto warmed plates. Add the haggis slices, top with the scallops and apples, and spoon the whisky sauce over.

Tips

Dijon mustard is easy to obtain throughout the UK. You can buy Scottish mustard if you're lucky enough to be visiting a Scottish farm shop or deli. Haggis is readily available in most supermarkets.

NOTES

Calories	Fibre	Salt	Sugar	Fat
544	8g	3g	5g	35g of which 15g is saturated

CURRIED BEEF PIE WITH ROOT MASH

This makes good use of all those odds and ends in the veg box at the end of the week. You can use this recipe as a template to incorporate your favourite winter vegetables and create a 'waste not want not' comforting pie.

Serves 2   Preparation 15 minutes   Cooking 40 minutes 

Vegetable oil 1 tbsp

Onion 1 large, peeled and chopped

Celery 1 stick, sliced

Grated root ginger 1 tsp

Beef mince 300g (11oz)

Leek 1 small, trimmed, halved lengthways and shredded

Garlic 1 clove, peeled and finely chopped

Curry powder 1 tbsp

Cumin seeds ¼ tsp

Chicken or vegetable stock 150ml (¼ pint)

Field mushrooms 2 large, chopped

Kale 50g (2oz), shredded

Carrots 2, peeled and cut into 2cm (¾in) chunks

Potato 1 large, peeled and cut into 2cm (¾in) chunks

Swede ½ small, peeled and cut into 2cm (¾in) chunks

Butter 25g (1oz)

Nigella (black onion) seeds 1 tsp

Salt and freshly ground black pepper

Heat the oil in a saucepan and gently fry the onion and celery for 5 minutes, stirring occasionally, until softened and golden.

Add the ginger and minced beef, increase the heat a little and stir-fry for 5 minutes or until the beef has lost its pink colour and is crumbly. Add the leek, garlic, curry powder and cumin seeds and cook, stirring occasionally, for a further 2–3 minutes.

Add the stock, mushrooms and kale to the pan. Bring to a simmer, partly cover and cook for 15 minutes or until the liquid has reduced and thickened slightly.

Meanwhile, boil the carrots, potato and swede in a large pan of water for 10–15 minutes until tender. Drain thoroughly, add the butter and black onion seeds and crush to a coarse mash.

When the beef is cooked, season to taste and spoon into a baking dish or two individual heatproof dishes.

Preheat the grill to medium. Spoon the mash over the beef mixture, smoothing it over to cover. Grill until the top has crisped up a little and serve hot.

Tips

Use your favourite winter root veg in the mash: try celeriac, parsnip or turnip.

Root through your spice cupboard and rediscover some flavours. Fennel, caraway and cumin bring earthy warmth and aniseed flavours to meat and vegetables. Dried herbs are rarely out of place in savoury meat dishes – try thyme, rosemary, chives or parsley.

Calories	Fibre	Salt	Sugar	Fat
730	18g	1g	0g	42g of which 17g is saturated

SCOTCH PANCAKES WITH RHUBARB COMPOTE

Pancakes with lemon and sugar are scrumptious, but why not try something a little different this Shrove Tuesday? Make the most of the bright pink forced rhubarb now appearing in the shops and cook this moreish compote. The drop pancakes are really simple to make.

Makes 10–12 small pancakes Preparation 10 minutes Cooking 30 minutes  

Rhubarb 400g (14oz), sliced

Stem ginger in syrup 1 piece, drained and finely chopped

Caster sugar 75g (3oz), plus 1 tbsp

Self-raising flour 125g (4½oz)

Egg 1, beaten

Milk 150ml (¼ pint)

Sunflower oil 1 tbsp

Double cream whipped, to serve (optional)

Put the rhubarb into a saucepan with the stem ginger and 75g (3oz) of the caster sugar. Add 1 tablespoon water and stir well. Slowly bring to a simmer over a low heat. Cook gently for 8–10 minutes, stirring often, until the rhubarb is soft. Taste and check the sweetness, adding a little more sugar if necessary. Leave to cool.

Sift the flour into a bowl and stir in the remaining 1 tablespoon sugar. Make a well in the centre and add the egg. Starting in the centre, gradually whisk in the milk until the batter is smooth and has the consistency of thick cream.

Wipe a non-stick frying pan with a little oil and heat until hot. Turn down the heat to medium. Cook the pancakes in batches: drop tablespoons of mixture into the frying pan, spaced well apart, and fry for 1– 2 minutes on each side until the surface puffs and bubbles. Keep warm.

Serve the pancakes with the rhubarb compote and whipped cream, if using.

Tips

You could serve the compote with ordinary pancakes, or spoon over your morning porridge.

Instead of compote, serve the pancakes with pear slices, gently fried in butter and drizzled with maple syrup.

NOTES

Calories	Fibre	Salt	Sugar	Fat
85	1g	0.2g	7g	1.5g of which 0.4g is saturated

CARROT & NUTMEG PUDDINGS

Carrots add moisture and natural sweetness to cakes and puddings. These fruity puddings make a lighter alternative to traditional Christmas pudding.

Makes 2 Preparation 15 minutes Cooking 50 minutes by steam; 1½ hours in a slow cooker

Baking margarine 50g (2oz), plus extra for greasing
Soft light brown sugar 50g (2oz)
Egg 1 medium
Wholemeal self-raising flour 65g (2¼oz)
Ground nutmeg ¼ tsp
Grated carrot 40g (1½oz)
Sultanas 40g (1½oz)
Custard or pouring cream to serve (optional)

Lightly grease and flour two 150ml (¼ pint) pudding moulds.

Put the margarine, sugar, egg, flour and nutmeg in a bowl and whisk together until well blended. Stir in the carrot and sultanas. Spoon into the prepared moulds and smooth the tops. Place a circle of non-stick baking paper directly on top of the mixture and cover the moulds completely with foil, pleated to allow space for the mixture to rise.

To cook in a slow cooker, put the moulds side by side in the slow cooker pot. Pour in enough hot water to come halfway up the sides of the dishes, put the lid on and cook on the high setting for about 1½ hours until risen and firm to the touch.

To steam, either put the moulds on a trivet in a saucepan and pour in enough hot water to come just above the trivet, or place the moulds in a steamer basket above a pan of simmering water. Cover and steam for about 50 minutes. They are cooked when a skewer inserted into the centre of the puddings comes out clean.

To serve, unwrap the puddings and invert onto serving plates. Serve immediately with custard or pouring cream.

Tips

For a more traditional flavour, replace the nutmeg with ground mixed spice or cinnamon to taste.

Instead of sultanas, use an assortment of luxury dried fruits if you prefer.

NOTES

Calories	Fibre	Salt	Sugar	Fat
480	5g	0.1g	25g	24g of which 5g is saturated

QUINCE BROWN BETTY WITH TOFFEE SAUCE

This under-used orchard fruit cooks much like apples and pears. When ripe, the skins turn golden yellow and the fruit is very fragrant.

Serves 6   Preparation 35 minutes   Cooking 55 minutes  

Fresh breadcrumbs (white or wholemeal) 200g (7oz)

Lightly salted butter 150g (5oz)

Soft light brown sugar 215g (7½oz)

Ripe quince 675g (1½lb)

Lemon juice 4 tbsp

Ground cinnamon 2 tsp

Double cream 125ml (4fl oz)

Vanilla extract 1 tsp

Preheat the oven to 180°C/160°fan/Gas 4. Put the breadcrumbs in a bowl. Melt 100g (3½oz) butter and stir into the crumbs along with 50g (2oz) sugar. Spoon half of the mixture into a 1.5 litre (2½ pint) ovenproof dish.

Peel and core the quince. Cut into thin slices and place in a bowl. Toss in the lemon juice, and mix in the cinnamon and 50g (2oz) sugar. Spoon evenly into the dish over the crumbs. Spoon over 4 tablespoons water and top with the remaining breadcrumb mixture.

Stand the dish on a baking tray and bake for about 50 minutes until the quince is tender – test with a skewer. Cover with foil if the topping browns too quickly.

While the pudding is in the oven, make the toffee sauce. Put the remaining sugar, butter and half the cream in a saucepan and heat gently, stirring until dissolved. Increase the heat and boil for 4–5 minutes, stirring to prevent burning, until thick and syrupy. Remove from the heat and stir in the remaining cream and vanilla. Cover and keep warm – it will thicken as it cools.

Serve the pudding hot or warm, drizzled with the toffee sauce.

Tips

Quince browns very quickly once it is peeled, but mixing with lemon juice helps keep this to a minimum. You can use thinly sliced cooking apples for this dish if you prefer. If you have pears, under-ripe pears work better; adjust the sugar to sweeten the filling accordingly.

To freeze, bake in a freezerproof dish, leave to cool completely then freeze for up to 3 months. To reheat from frozen, cover with foil and bake in a preheated oven at 200°C/180°fan/Gas 6 for about 30 minutes until piping hot. Make the toffee sauce while the pudding is in the oven.

Calories	Fibre	Salt	Sugar	Fat
567	0.5g	0.8g	36g	32g of which 20g is saturated

FROSTED PARSNIP & SULTANA CAKE

Parsnips are closely related to carrots, so why not try this variation of the classic carrot cake? Parsnips are in season from September to March but are available to buy most of the year.

Serves 10–12 Preparation 15 minutes Cooking 50 minutes 

Eggs 2, beaten

Groundnut oil 175ml (6fl oz), plus extra for greasing

Light brown muscovado sugar 200g (7oz)

Parsnips 150g (5oz) (1 large), peeled and grated

Sultanas 100g (3½oz)

Pecans 75g (3oz), chopped

Self-raising flour 200g (7oz)

Baking powder 1 tsp

Mixed spice 2 tsp

Salt pinch

Full fat soft cheese 200g (7oz)

Icing sugar 50g (2oz)

Orange 1, finely grated zest

Mini white chocolate stars to decorate

Preheat the oven to 190°C/170°fan/Gas 5. Grease and base line a 1.2 litre (2 pint) loaf tin (approx. 22 x 12 x 6cm/8½ x 4½ x 2½in).

Put the eggs, oil and sugar into a large bowl and lightly whisk together. Stir in the grated parsnip, sultanas and pecans.

Sift in the flour, baking powder, mixed spice and salt and fold together. Spoon into the prepared tin, level the top and bake for 45–50 minutes or until a skewer inserted into the centre comes out clean.

Remove from the tin and leave on a wire rack to cool completely.

Using a hand-held electric mixer, whisk together the soft cheese, icing sugar and orange zest until smooth. Spread over the top of the cake and sprinkle over some mini chocolate stars.

NOTES

Calories	Fibre	Salt	Sugar	Fat
397	2g	0.6g	21g	24g of which 6g is saturated

CHRISTMAS

PEAR & GINGER FIZZ

A festive recipe to use up a few ripe pears you have hanging around. Perfect served with the Sweet & Salty Spiced Chestnuts overleaf.

Serves 2 Preparation 15 minutes 

Ripe pears 3, peeled and cored
Lemon ½, juice only
Ice 2 handfuls
Traditional ginger beer 300ml (½ pint), chilled
Spiced rum 75ml (3fl oz)

Chop 2½ pears into cubes and place in a blender with the lemon juice and a handful of ice. Whizz until smooth. Set a sieve over a large measuring jug and push the mixture through the sieve, discarding the pulp.

Stir in the ginger beer and rum, then taste, adding more rum or ginger beer if you like.

Thinly slice the remaining ½ pear and pop into two gin glasses along with some ice. Pour in the pear cocktail and serve immediately.

Tips

If you like, peel a couple of thin strips of rind off the remaining lemon half and use to decorate.

If you would rather not make this cocktail alcoholic, try adding a dash of elderflower cordial to liven it up instead of the rum.

NOTES

Calories	Fibre	Salt	Sugar	Fat
234	6g	0.5g	12g	0.2g of which 0g is saturated

SWEET & SALTY SPICED CHESTNUTS

Chestnuts are available to buy in farm shops and supermarkets from October to December. This recipe makes a tasty festive snack – far healthier than the tub of chocolates!

Serves 4–6 Preparation 15 minutes Cooking 25 minutes 

Fresh chestnuts in their shells 450g (1lb), washed and dried

Sea salt flakes 2 tsp

Light brown muscovado sugar 2 tbsp

Ground cinnamon ½ tsp

Ground ginger ½ tsp

Ground nutmeg pinch

Ground cloves pinch

Brandy or rum 3 tbsp

Preheat the oven to 200°C/180°fan/Gas 6.

Place the chestnuts on a board, flat side down. Using a small sharp knife, score a cross on each shell, making sure you don't cut too deep.

Place in a roasting tin, cut side up, and roast for 20–25 minutes or until the skins are just beginning to burst open. Leave to cool slightly until cool enough to handle.

Mix together the salt, sugar and spices in a small bowl.

Serve the chestnuts while still hot, and let everyone remove the shells and husks. Once peeled, dip into the brandy or rum and then into the sugar spice mix.

Tips

If you prefer, use ready-cooked chestnuts, warmed though.

Use apple juice or ginger beer instead of the brandy if you like.

If you're not keen on one of the spices, just leave it out.

NOTES

Calories	Fibre	Salt	Sugar	Fat
170	4g	1.3g	7g	2g of which 0.4g is saturated

PARSNIP, CELERIAC & CHESTNUT DIP

This lovely creamy dip is ideal for serving with drinks during the festive period. It's also a great way to use up a few of those veg box or allotment veggies and leftover chestnuts.

Serves 8–10 Preparation 20 minutes Cooking 30–35 minutes 

Olive oil 2 tbsp
Parsnips 300g (11oz), peeled and cut into small chunks
Celeriac 300g (11oz), peeled and cut into small chunks
Cooked chestnuts 175g (6oz)
Garlic 1 clove, peeled and crushed
Vegetable stock 200–250ml (7–9fl oz)
Bay leaves 2
Celery salt ½ tsp
Freshly ground black pepper
Red chicory 4 heads, leaves separated
Smoked paprika (optional)

Heat the oil in a large saucepan over a medium heat, add the parsnips and fry for 3 minutes. Add the celeriac, chestnuts and garlic and cook for 3 minutes, stirring occasionally.

Pour in just enough stock to cover the vegetables and add the bay leaves. Cover the pan and cook over a low heat for about 25 minutes until all the vegetables are very tender.

Remove the bay leaves and use a stick blender to whizz to a purée. Season with celery salt and black pepper.

Arrange the chicory leaves on a serving dish, spoon a teaspoon of dip onto each and dust with paprika, if you like.

Tips

Serve with breadsticks and seeded crackers, or carrot sticks if you prefer.

Or instead of serving as a dip, this purée makes a great accompaniment to roast chicken, instead of potatoes; the quantity will serve 4.

NOTES

Calories	Fibre	Salt	Sugar	Fat
62	4g	0.4g	0g	1g of which 0.2g is saturated

BRUSSELS SPROUTS, STUFFING & BACON SOUP

There are plenty of Christmassy flavours in this moreish hearty soup. If you have leftover cooked sprouts or greens you can use them instead – see the tip below.

Serves 2 Preparation 20 minutes plus cooling Cooking 25 minutes 

Vegetable oil 2 tsp
Onion 1 small, peeled and chopped
Lean smoked streaky bacon 3 rashers, finely chopped
Brussels sprouts 250g (9oz), trimmed and thinly sliced
Chicken or vegetable stock 550ml (19fl oz)
Fresh sage a few leaves (or 1 tsp dried sage)
Salt and freshly ground black pepper
Sage and onion stuffing mix 15g (½oz)
Butter 15g (½oz)
Double cream 2 tbsp

Heat the oil in a saucepan and gently fry the onion for 5 minutes without browning. Add half the bacon and cook, stirring, for a minute until the bacon is lightly cooked but not brown.

Add the sprouts, stock, sage, salt and pepper. Bring to the boil, then reduce the heat, cover and simmer for 10 minutes until the sprouts are tender. Leave to cool slightly then use a stick blender to whizz until smooth.

Meanwhile, mix the stuffing with 2 tablespoons boiling water and leave to stand for 5 minutes until soft. Melt the butter in a frying pan until foaming. Break off pieces of stuffing into the butter and fry, stirring, for about 2 minutes. Add the remaining bacon and continue to fry and stir for about 3 minutes until cooked and crisp. Drain on kitchen paper and keep warm.

To serve, stir the cream into the soup and heat through for 2–3 minutes until piping hot. Ladle into bowls and sprinkle with the stuffing pieces and crispy bacon.

Tips

To use up leftover greens, follow the recipe above but don't simmer the greens in the stock – just add them to the hot stock and blend, then finish the recipe in the same way.

For a veggie version, leave out the bacon and serve the soup sprinkled with a little crumbled blue cheese.

You can freeze the puréed soup before adding the cream and toppings. Defrost and reheat gently until piping hot, adding the cream and toppings shortly before serving.

Calories	Fibre	Salt	Sugar	Fat
439	9g	4g	0g	35g of which 13g is saturated

SLOW-COOKED RED CABBAGE WITH TREACLE

Originally in an old *Dairy Diary*, our Managing Editor cooks this for every Christmas dinner and so we felt it should make a comeback. The slow, gentle cooking brings out the flavour of the cabbage, with added sweetness and richness from demerara sugar and treacle.

Serves 4–6 Preparation 10 minutes Cooking 1 hour 10 minutes 

Red cabbage 700g (1lb 9oz), cored and shredded

Red wine vinegar 4 tbsp

Demerara sugar 6 tbsp

Salt 1 tsp

Butter 25g (1oz)

Black treacle 1 tbsp

Fresh parsley 1–2 tbsp chopped, to garnish (optional)

Place the cabbage, vinegar, sugar and salt in a large saucepan. Pour in 225ml (8fl oz) water and bring to the boil. Reduce the heat to low, cover and cook gently for about 1 hour or until the cabbage is very tender.

Drain well then stir in the butter and treacle. Serve immediately, sprinkled with parsley, if using.

Tips

Don't use an aluminium or copper saucepan, as the vinegar will react with the pan. Cook in a slow cooker on the low setting, if you prefer.

Serve with roast poultry, game, ham or gammon. You could add cooked chestnuts just before serving, if you like.

Calories	Fibre	Salt	Sugar	Fat
84	3g	1g	7g	4g of which 2g is saturated

ROAST TURKEY CROWN WITH CHESTNUT, PEAR & BACON STUFFING

For smaller gatherings, a turkey crown is easier and quicker to cook than a whole bird. Latticed bacon keeps the breast moist during cooking. Use your autumn preserves to jazz up the turkey gravy and add sparkle to your Brussels sprouts.

Serves 6–8 Preparation 30 minutes plus resting Cooking 2 hours

For the stuffing

Shallots 6 small, peeled and quartered

Pears 2 large, peeled, cored and cut into chunks

Bacon lardons or thick rashers, snipped 75g (3oz)

Fresh parsley 30g pack, woody stems discarded

Thyme leaves 2 tsp finely chopped

Rosemary 1 tsp finely chopped

Butter 75g (3oz), plus extra if greasing a dish

Fresh breadcrumbs (brown or white) 225g (8oz)

Cooked chestnuts 225g (8oz), roughly chopped

Salt and freshly ground black pepper

Egg 1, beaten

For the turkey crown

Free-range turkey crown approx. 2kg (4½lb)

Thyme leaves 1 tbsp chopped

Butter 75g (3oz), softened

Lemon 1, grated zest and juice (reserve the lemon halves)

Unsmoked streaky bacon 14 rashers

For the gravy

Plain flour 3 tbsp

Port or red wine 3 tbsp

Turkey or chicken stock 450ml (¾ pint), hot

Light soy sauce 2 tbsp

Elderberry jelly 1 tbsp (see page 89)

To serve

Roast potatoes, glazed sprouts and red onion

Make the stuffing in advance, cover and chill for up to 48 hours, or bake and freeze (see tips).

Place the shallots, pears, bacon, parsley, thyme and rosemary in a food processor or blender and blitz briefly until finely chopped but not mushy.

Melt the butter in a saucepan, add the shallot and pear mixture and cook for 4–5 minutes to soften slightly. Add the breadcrumbs and chestnuts and mix thoroughly. Season with salt and pepper, then mix in just enough beaten egg to bind the ingredients together.

Spoon into lightly greased muffin tins, or into a shallow ovenproof dish, or roll into 20–24 balls to cook alongside the turkey or on a shallow baking tray. Bake for 25–35 minutes or until crisp and hot right through.

For the turkey, preheat the oven to 200°C/180°fan/Gas 6.

Mix the thyme with the softened butter, lemon zest and juice. Starting from the narrow end of the turkey crown, work your fingers under the skin of the breast to open up a pocket on each side of the breastbone, being careful not to tear the skin. Divide the flavoured butter between the two pockets, spreading it evenly under the skin.

Tuck the lemon halves in around the neck cavity.

Sit the turkey crown in a small roasting tin and season with freshly ground black pepper. Put the bacon on a board and use the flat side of a knife to stretch the rashers a little. Lay the rashers across the breast to create a lattice (or overlap), covering the whole crown.

Roast for about 1½–2 hours: check every 30 minutes, baste occasionally and cover with foil if the bacon is crisping too quickly. To test that the turkey is cooked through, pierce the thickest part with a skewer: the juices should run clear with no traces of pink.

Transfer the turkey to a serving platter, cover loosely with foil and set aside to rest for 30 minutes.

To make the gravy, pour the juices from the roasting tin into a jug and leave to settle. Skim all but 4 tablespoons of the fat from the top, then tip the remaining juices into a saucepan and place over a medium heat until just simmering.

Whisk in the flour until the mixture is smooth, then pour in the port or wine and stock and whisk again until smooth. Simmer until the gravy starts to thicken, then add the soy sauce and elderberry jelly. Bring the gravy to a steady boil, adding any additional turkey juices released while the meat was resting. Season to taste then pour into a warmed jug ready to serve with the turkey.

Glazed sprouts

Boil the Brussels sprouts (as many as you like) until just tender, then drain thoroughly in a colander. Melt 50g (2oz) butter in the hot pan and fry thin wedges of red onion for 5 minutes or until softened and slightly caramelised. Tip the sprouts back into the pan, add 1 tablespoon elderberry jelly (see page 89) and toss well to glaze the sprouts with the jelly. Season with black pepper and serve hot.

Tips

The stuffing can be cooked, cooled and frozen. Defrost overnight in the fridge. Crisp in a hot oven for 10–15 minutes.

To check the seasoning for the stuffing, fry a teaspoonful in a little hot oil then taste and adjust the seasoning as required.

For a vegetarian stuffing, replace the bacon with button chestnut mushrooms. Some fresh sage leaves would be a nice addition.

For a meatier stuffing, skin your favourite sausages then mix the sausage meat into the chopped stuffing mix.

Use redcurrant jelly instead of elderberry jelly if you like.

Calories	Fibre	Salt	Sugar	Fat
600	4g	2g	3g	21g of which 12g is saturated

TURKEY MEATBALL BROTH

A great start to the New Year! This wholesome midweek supper uses leftover cooked turkey to make delicious meatballs in a light vegetable broth.

Serves 2–3 Preparation 10 minutes Cooking 35 minutes

For the meatballs

Fresh breadcrumbs (white or wholemeal) 50g (2oz)

Milk 2 tbsp

Cooked turkey 250g (9oz), finely chopped or minced

Fennel seeds 1 tsp (optional)

Fresh sage leaves 1 tbsp chopped

Fresh parsley 1 tbsp chopped

Dried thyme ½ tsp

Worcestershire sauce 1 tsp

Salt and freshly ground black pepper

Egg 1, beaten

Light olive oil for frying

For the broth

Onion 1 large, peeled and finely chopped

Carrot 1 large, peeled and diced

Celery 1 stick, finely sliced

Garlic 1 clove, peeled and finely sliced

Chicken or turkey stock 1 litre (1¾ pints), hot

Green cabbage, such as January King or Savoy 250g (9oz), shredded

Crusty bread, warmed, to serve

In a large bowl, sprinkle the breadcrumbs over the milk and leave to soak for a minute. Add the turkey, fennel seeds, if using, herbs and Worcestershire sauce. Mix well and season with salt and pepper.

Add just enough beaten egg to bind all the ingredients together. Form into 12 small, walnut-sized meatballs. Heat a little oil in a saucepan and cook the meatballs until lightly browned all over. Transfer to a plate.

Add the onion, carrot, celery and garlic to the pan, cover and cook over a low heat for 10–15 minutes or until softened but not coloured. Add a splash of the stock if the vegetables are sticking.

Return the meatballs to the pan, pour in the stock and bring to a gentle simmer. Add the cabbage and cook for 5 minutes. Check that the meatballs are piping hot. Taste and adjust the seasoning. Ladle into large shallow bowls and serve with warm crusty bread.

Tip

Strip all the meat from the Christmas turkey, separating the dark from the white meat, and freeze for up to 3 months. The white meat is ideal to add to cheese sauces or to serve with pasta and the more succulent, darker meat is perfect for meatballs, soups and curries.

Calories	Fibre	Salt	Sugar	Fat
346	8g	3g	1g	8g of which 2g is saturated

INDEX

THANKS TO

Commissioning/Managing Editor	Emily Davenport
Marketing Executive	Katy Hackforth
Designer	Graham Meigh
Editor	Maggie Ramsay
Recipe Writers	Kathryn Hawkins, Clare Lewis, Wendy Veale
Photographer	Steve Lee
Food Stylist	Sian Davies
Props Stylist	Olivia Axson
Recipe Testers	Katy Hackforth, Jean Johnson, Joanna Leese, Laura Pickering
Nutritional Consultant	Paul McArdle
Proof Reader	Aune Butt
Indexer	Ruth Ellis
Market Research	Penny Meigh, Step Beyond
Production	Siobhan Hennessey

Published by Trek Logistics Ltd
Dairy Diary, PO Box 482, Crewe, CW1 9FG
www.dairydiary.co.uk

Printed May 2023

ISBN 9781911388470